JOSEPH E. PERSICO

NUREMBERG

INFAMY ON TRIAL

PENGUIN BOOKS

PENGUIN BOOKS
Published by the Penguin Group
Penguin Books USA Inc., 375 Hudson Street,
New York, New York 10014, U.S.A.
Penguin Books Ltd, 27 Wrights Lane, London W8 5TZ, England
Penguin Books Australia Ltd, Ringwood, Victoria, Australia
Penguin Books Canada Ltd, 10 Alcorn Avenue,
Toronto, Ontario, Canada M4V 3B2
Penguin Books (N.Z.) Ltd, 182–190 Wairau Road, Auckland 10, New Zealand

Penguin Books Ltd, Registered Offices: Harmondsworth, Middlesex, England

First published in the United States of America by Viking Penguin,
a division of Penguin Books USA Inc., 1994
Published in Penguin Books 1995

3   5   7   9   10   8   6   4   2

THE LIBRARY OF CONGRESS HAS CATALOGUED THE HARDCOVER AS FOLLOWS:
Persico, Joseph E.
Nuremberg: infamy on trial/Joseph Persico.
p.   cm.
Includes bibliographical references and index.
ISBN 0-670-84276-1 (hc.)
ISBN 0 14 01.6622 X (pbk.)
1. Nuremberg Trial of Major German War Criminals,
Nuremberg, Germany, 1945–1946.   I. Title.
JX5437.8.P37   1994
341.6´9—dc20   94–2879

Printed in the United States of America
Set in Adobe Janson Text
Designed by Francesca Belanger

To brother Richard and sister Annabelle

CONTENTS

INTRODUCTION

AFTER A HIATUS of nearly half a century, Nuremberg is again on people's lips. After over one hundred wars, insurrections, civil conflicts, and revolutions that have racked the world over the past forty-five years and claimed more than 21 million lives, after hardly a breath of outrage over atrocities committed in the name of ideology, liberation, independence, and religion, people at last have begun to cry out for justice that can penetrate national borders, for a Nuremberg-style prosecution of war criminals. The cry arose in 1990 after Saddam Hussein seized Kuwait, then bloodily supressed Iraq's Shiite and Kurd minorities. The cry for justice, for a new Nuremberg, became full-throated with the black-and-white images of Auschwitz and Buchenwald updated in color in Serbian concentration camps in the former Yugoslavia, with accounts of mass deportation, calculated extermination, and organized rape, with the campaign of "ethnic cleansing" of Bosnian Muslims, an echo of Adolf Hitler's call to "cleanse the world of Jewish poison."

Finally, the family of nations acted. On February 22, 1993, the United Nations Security Council voted to create an international tribunal to prosecute war crimes committed in the crumbling lands that once formed Yugoslavia. In May, the court was established. Another Nuremberg.

But what was Nuremberg? What happened in that shattered city between 1945 and 1946? Were lessons learned or lost after the trials of Nazi leaders? Why did its hope blaze so brightly and then burn out, the flame of its example reduced thereafter virtually to historic ash?

It would be convenient to say that this book was written in response to the current interest in Nuremberg, to invoke history's guidance in dealing with war criminals in our time. Actually, the book has older, more personal roots. Its impetus has been an image lodged in my memory for nearly fifty years, a photograph that appeared in news-papers in October 1946: Hermann Göring, his face contorted in death, just after he committed suicide on the eve of his scheduled execution as the leading surviving Nazi war criminal. To one too young to have fought in World War II, but old enough to have been shaped by that cataclysm, the trial and execution of the major Nazi leaders has a riveting fascination. The trial seemed to say that good must triumph over evil, a perception perhaps stronger in a boy then sixteen than in a man now in his sixties.

Through the years I dipped casually into the story. What I en-countered was a considerable literature dealing with the legal dust kicked up by the trial of the Nazis before the International Military Tribunal of Nuremberg. Most of these books made a contribution to understanding. Some were outstanding in dissecting the juridical con-troversies. What they whetted the appetite for, but failed to satisfy, was my curiosity about the human drama that must have been un-folding in Nuremberg during 1945 and 1946. As I was to discover when I began my research, beneath the legal battle pitting prosecution against defense lay several simultaneous conflicts. Nuremberg set de-fendants against defendants. Hermann Göring, for example, wanted his fellow Nazis to go down with the swastika flying; Albert Speer preached confession and contrition. Speer, in turn, vied against Fritz Sauckel to see which one would have to bear the heaviest guilt for the Nazi slave labor program. Robert Jackson, the American prosecutor, on leave from the U.S. Supreme Court, battled professionally and personally with Francis Biddle, the American Nuremberg judge. Bid-dle, disappointed at being deprived of the chief judgeship (Jackson's doing), maneuvered the other judges to try to make himself de facto head of the IMT. The representatives of the four nations—the United States, the Soviet Union, Great Britain, and France—that made up the court fought to see whose system of jurisprudence would prevail, the Anglo-Saxon or the Continental. The prison commandant was determined to maintain an escape-proof jail, only to lose three pris-oners to suicide. The prison psychiatrist and psychologist, who had unlimited access to the defendants, turned this unprecedented oppor-tunity into a race to see who could publish the first insider book on the psyche of war criminals. In the testy relations between the staffs representing the Western Allies and the Soviet Union, we see intimations of the coming Cold War in microcosm in a Nuremberg courthouse. And outside the courthouse, while American prosecutors inside were trying defendants for the murderous consequences of Nazi racism, white GIs brawled with segregated black GIs, importing America's own brand of racism.

Overarching all these subdramas was the major theater, the Nuremberg trial itself. Was it victors' vengeance or the authentic pursuit of justice? Indeed, can a just court be created to try acts which have not been defined as crimes until after the fact? The charge of ex post facto law was to haunt the IMT from its first day to its last. How valid is the jurisdiction of a court that permits a British prosecutor to try a German national before a Soviet judge for crimes committed in Poland? If aggression was on trial at Nuremberg, then what were Soviet judges doing on the bench? Their nation had invaded Finland and conspired with Germany to divide up Poland. And, granted that Nazi atrocities dwarfed the misdeeds of other belligerents, had not war crimes been committed on all sides? Why were only those on the losing side tried?

These anomalies raise the age-old distinction between law and justice. They are not the same. If the law at Nuremberg was flawed, does it follow that the justice meted out was flawed as well? Before, during, and after the trial, respected voices argued that honest vengeance was purer and preferable to rickety legality. Winston Churchill was but one of many who wanted the top Nazis shot out of hand with minimal legal fuss.

This work is an attempt to reveal these intersecting dramas. That I was able to proceed was largely the result of serendipity. In Washington, D.C., in March 1991, alumni of the Nuremberg International Military Tribunal held a forty-fifth-anniversary reunion. The reunion answered a question I had posed to myself. What fresh perspectives could be brought to a trial that ended in 1946 and has since been written on voluminously? To my good fortune, the reunion organizers had published a directory of persons still living who had been involved in the trial. But for a few protagonists, Nuremberg turned out to have been largely a young person's game. Many participants were still available to provide firsthand accounts of their experiences. I was able to interview people who had never before talked about Nuremberg: prosecutors, interpreters, researchers, journalists, jailers, secretaries, drivers, and bodyguards, whose individual contributions are recognized in the acknowledgments section.

The most moving part of the research was an odyssey to the sites where the story took place: to work in the same courtroom where Hermann Göring displayed his perverse brilliance (a longhaired, slack-jawed drug dealer was on trial during my visit); to stand on the podium from which Hitler whipped the Nazi faithful to a frenzy during *Parteitagen* (Party Days) at Nuremberg's Zeppelin Field; to pore over letters the defendants wrote to their families on the last days of their lives and to see unpublished photographs of their executions at the Berlin Documents Center; to go through Auschwitz, the scene of events so exhaustively exposed at the trial, with a party of Austrian Jews, all of whom had family ties to the Holocaust and some of whom were survivors.

One question I pondered was how to deal with the massive and sickening evidence of atrocities introduced during the trial. Though it may not seem so to the reader, I have chosen to keep such material to a minimum, just enough to communicate the nature and magnitude of these depredations. To include more would risk numbing rather than quickening the reader's sensitivities.

Nuremberg stands as a powerful drama in its own right in its own time. But what does it say to our time? Beyond punishing the guilty, the dream of those who championed this historic experiment was to set precedents, to give would-be aggressors pause, and to hold future aggressors accountable. Until virtually this moment, that dream has failed abysmally. Does Nuremberg offer lessons, a usable matrix that can be salvaged from the bin of history and put to good service to deal with war crimes in our era? Given the UN's recent actions, we may be about to find out.

My treatment of the trial is intended for the lay reader and general student of history more than for the academic or legal historian. For that reason, I have chosen a strongly narrative style, hoping to interest a new generation in an old but important story. The style does not influence the factual foundations of the book. In light of recent controversies and court actions, there has arisen in publishing a heightened sensitivity to the authenticity of words and thoughts attributed to figures in works professedly of nonfiction. When I have described subjects of the present work as thinking, saying, or doing something, I have drawn from their own writings, letters, oral and written histories, and from other books, archival documents, contemporary press accounts, the above-mentioned interviews, and the forty-two-volume transcript of the trial itself. The account is narrative supported by historic fact.

THE TRIAL CAST

AMEN, John Harlan: U.S. colonel, associate trial counsel, head of interrogations.

ANDRUS, Burton: U.S. colonel in charge of the Nuremberg prison.

BALDWIN, William: assistant U.S. prosecutor.

BARRETT, Roger: lawyer who ran the documents room.

BERNAYS, Murray: War Department lawyer, drafter of the initial proposal for prosecuting international war criminals.

BIDDLE, Francis: former U.S. attorney general, American justice on the court.

BIRKETT, Sir Norman: alternate British justice on the court.

BORMANN, Martin: secretary to Hitler; missing, tried in absentia.

BRUDNO, Walter: assistant U.S. prosecutor.

BURSON, Harold "Hal": Armed Forces Network correspondent covering the trial.

CONTI, Leonardo: SS "mercy killing" doctor; first suicide in the prison.

D'ADDARIO, Ray: U.S. Army Signal Corps photographer.

DIPALMA, Emilio: U.S. Army cell guard.

DIX, Rudolf: defense counsel for Hjalmar Schacht.

DODD, Thomas J.: associate and later deputy U.S. prosecutor.

DÖNITZ, Karl: grand admiral, commander of the German U-boat fleet, successor to Raeder as commander in chief of the German navy.

DONNEDIEU DE VABRES, Henri: French justice on the court.

DONOVAN, William J.: U.S. general, founder and chief of the Office of Strategic Services, briefly a prosecutor at Nuremberg.

DOSTERT, Leon: first head of the Language Division and initiator of simultaneous interpretation at Nuremberg.

DOUGLAS, Elsie: secretary to Robert Jackson.

EXNER, Franz: German law professor and General Jodl's defense counsel.

FABER-CASTELL, Roland and Nina: members of German pencil-manufacturing family, owners of the castle in Stein where the Nuremberg press was housed.

FALCO, Robert: alternate French justice on the court.

FISHER, Adrian "Butch": legal advisor to the American justice, Biddle.

FLÄCHSNER, Hans: Speer's defense counsel.

FLANNER, Janet: correspondent for *The New Yorker*.

FRANK, Hans: governor general of Nazi-occupied Poland.

FRICK, Wilhelm: Nazi minister of the interior, later Protector of Bohemia and Moravia.

FRITZSCHE, Hans: chief of radio operations in the Nazi propaganda ministry.

FUCHS, Moritz: U.S. sergeant, bodyguard of Robert Jackson.

FUNK, Walther: president of the Reichsbank.

GAU, Lilli: mistress of Hans Frank.

GERECKE, Henry F.: U.S. major, chaplain for the Protestant defendants.

GILBERT, Gustav M.: prison psychologist.

GILIAREVSKAYA, Tania: interpreter for General Nikitchenko.

GILL, Robert J.: U.S. general, administrative officer for the prosecution staff.

GLENNY, William: U.S. Army cell guard.

GÖRING, Carin: Hermann Göring's first wife.

GÖRING, Emmy: Hermann Göring's second wife.

GÖRING, Edda: Hermann Göring's eight-year-old daughter.

GÖRING, Hermann: *Reichsmarschall*, chief of the Luftwaffe, Hitler's designated successor until supplanted by Dönitz.

HARRIS, Whitney: assistant U.S. prosecutor.

HAUSHOFER, Karl: professor of geopolitics, mentor of Rudolf Hess.

HESS, Rudolf: deputy führer, third-ranking Nazi until his flight to Scotland in 1941.

HIMMLER, Heinrich: *Reichsführer*, head of the SS; a suicide by the time of the trial.

HOESS, Rudolf Franz Ferdinand: commandant of Auschwitz, a witness at Nuremberg.

HOFFMANN, Heinrich: Hitler's personal photographer, a prison trusty and photograph expert for the prosecution.

HORN, Martin: Ribbentrop's second defense counsel.

HORSKY, Charles: lawyer, Washington liaison aide to Robert Jackson.

HOSSBACH, Friedrich: German general who took notes at what came to be called the "Hossbach Conference."

JACKSON, Robert H.: chief U.S. prosecutor, on leave from the U.S. Supreme Court.

JACKSON, William E.: lawyer; assistant to his father, Robert Jackson.

JODL, Alfred: colonel general, operations chief of the German armed forces.

JODL, Luise: wife of General Jodl, employed by her husband's attorney during the trial.

KALNOKY, Ingeborg: German-born countess who ran the Witness House during the trial.

KALTENBRUNNER, Ernst: head of the RSHA, the Nazi security apparatus, second to Himmler in the SS.

KAUFFMANN, Kurt: defense counsel for Kaltenbrunner.

KEITEL, Wilhelm: field marshal, chief of staff of the German armed forces.

KELLEY, Douglas: U.S. major, prison psychiatrist.

KEMPNER, Robert: German-born former official of the Prussian Interior Ministry, later an American citizen and head of the Defense Rebuttal Section at Nuremberg.

KILEY, Daniel: OSS officer, architect who restored the Palace of Justice.

KORB, Rose: secretary to the prison commandant, Colonel Andrus.

KRANZBUEHLER, Otto: German navy judge, Dönitz's defense counsel.

KRUG, Willi: German POW employed in cellblock C.

LAMBERT, Thomas F.: assistant U.S. prosecutor.

LAWRENCE, Sir Geoffrey: British justice and president of the court.

LEY, Robert: head of the German Labor Front.

MARGOLIES, Daniel: assistant U.S. prosecutor, husband of Harriet Zetterberg.

MAXWELL-FYFE, Sir David: de facto head of the British prosecution, nominally under Sir Hartley Shawcross.

MITCHELL, William: U.S. general, administrative officer for the justices.

NEAVE, Airey: British major, lawyer, aide to the justices.

NELTE, Otto: defense counsel for Keitel.

NEURATH, Konstantin von: Germany's foreign minister before Ribbentrop; Protector of Bohemia and Moravia, 1939–41.

NIKITCHENKO, Ion Timofeevich: major general of jurisprudence; Soviet justice on the court.

O'CONNOR, Sixtus: Catholic priest, chaplain for the Catholic defendants.

OHLENDORF, Otto: SS general, commander of Einsatzgruppe D; a witness.

OWENS, Dorothy: secretary to Francis Biddle.

PAPEN, Franz von: German chancellor before Hitler, vice chancellor under Hitler, ambassador to Turkey.

PARKER, John J.: alternate U.S. justice on the court.

PFLUECKER, Ludwig: German POW employed as physician for the defendants.

POKROVSKY, Y. V.: deputy Soviet prosecutor.

POLEVOI, Boris: *Pravda* correspondent at the trial.

POLTORAK, Arkady: documents officer for the Soviet staff.

RAEDER, Erich: grand admiral; until 1943 commander in chief of the German navy.

RIBBENTROP, Joachim von: Nazi foreign minister.

ROBERTS, Geoffrey Dorling "Khaki": leading counsel under Maxwell-Fyfe for the British prosecution.

ROHRSCHEIDT, Gunther von: Hess's first defense counsel.

ROSENBERG, Alfred: Nazi minister for the Occupied Eastern Territories and head of Einstab Rosenberg.

ROWE, James: former Roosevelt aide and naval officer, legal advisor to Biddle.

RUDENKO, Roman A.: lieutenant general, chief Soviet prosecutor.

SADEL, Gunther: U.S. counterintelligence agent on the staff of General Watson.

SAUCKEL, Fritz: head of the German conscript labor organization.

SAUTER, Fritz: Ribbentrop's first defense counsel; also Funk's and Schirach's counsel.

SCHACHT, Hjalmar Horace Greeley: president of the Reichsbank prior to Funk, and former minister of the economy.

SCHIRACH, Baldur von: head of the Hitler Youth, later governor and *Gauleiter* of Vienna.

SCHMIDT, Paul: Hitler's personal interpreter, held as a material witness.

SEIDL, Alfred: Hess's second defense counsel, also Frank's defense counsel.

SERVATIUS, Robert: Sauckel's defense counsel.

SEYSS-INQUART, Arthur: Nazi commissioner of occupied Holland.

SHAWCROSS, Sir Hartley: formally chief British prosecutor, who delegated the day-to-day task to Maxwell-Fyfe.

SHIRER, William L.: CBS correspondent covering the trial.

SMITH, Howard K.: CBS correspondent covering the trial.

SPEER, Albert: Reich minister for armaments and war production.

SPRECHER, Drexel: assistant U.S. prosecutor, later prosecutor at subsequent war-crimes trials.

STAHMER, Otto: Göring's defense counsel.

STEER, Alfred: U.S. Navy officer and linguist, succeeded Leon Dostert as chief of the Language Division.

STEWART, Robert: U.S. major, legal advisor to alternate justice Parker.

STOREY, Robert: U.S. colonel, head of U.S. prosecution team under Jackson.

STREICHER, Julius: publisher of the anti-Semitic newspaper *Der Stürmer*.

STRENG, Otto: German POW employed as prison librarian, mailman.

TAYLOR, Telford: U.S. general, prosecutor of the High Command case, later chief prosecutor at subsequent trials.

TEICH, F. C.: U.S. major, deputy commander of the prison under Colonel Andrus.

TROYANOVSKY, Oleg: son of the first Soviet ambassador to the United States, interpreter for the Soviet justices.

UIBERALL, Peter: official in the Language Division.

VOLCHKOV, Alexander: alternate Soviet justice.

VONETES, John: U.S. housing officer for the trial staff.

WALCH, Katherine: British researcher in the Defense Rebuttal Section.

WATSON, Leroy H.: U.S. brigadier general, commandant of the Nuremberg-Furth Enclave; Colonel Andrus's superior.

WECHSLER, Herbert: chief legal advisor to the American justice, Biddle.

WHEELIS, Jack G. "Tex": U.S. officer on the prison staff, responsible for the baggage room.

WOODS, John: U.S. master sergeant, Third Army hangman.

ZETTERBERG, Harriet: lawyer on the U.S. prosecution staff, wife of Daniel Margolies.

ABBREVIATIONS

ACC: Allied Control Council. Body representing the four nations (United States, Great Britain, France, Soviet Union) that governed occupied Germany.

IMT: International Military Tribunal. The court established by the Allies to try German war criminals.

ISD: 6850th Internal Security Detachment. The military force that operated the Nuremberg prison.

NKVD: Soviet secret police at the time of the trial; forerunner of the KGB.

OKW: Oberkommando der Wehrmacht, High Command of the German armed forces.

OSS: Office of Strategic Services. U.S. intelligence service during World War II.

RSHA: Reich Central Security Office. Component of the SS that controlled the Gestapo, the secret political police, the criminal police, and the SD, or security service.

SA: Sturmabteilung. The Nazi storm troopers, or Brownshirts.

SD: Nazi security service, essentially engaged in political intelligence, counterintelligence, and clandestine operations.

SS: *Schutzstaffel.* Literally "guard detachment"; became the umbrella organization for Heinrich Himmler's empire, including SS military forces (the Waffen SS), the RSHA, and the operation of concentration camps.

CHAPTER I

PRELUDE TO JUDGMENT

1

WILLI KRUG COCKED AN EYE at the battered alarm clock he kept within arm's reach on the floor. Five-thirty, still dark out, with only the pewter light of the moon angling down from the barred window and spilling through the open doorway of his cell. The rare sound of a truck revving and pulling out of the prison yard had awakened him. Earlier his sleep had been broken by the noise of hammers banging and the muffled shouts of GIs. He had fallen back to sleep until the truck woke him again.

Willi swung his legs out of the cot and planted his feet on the cold stone floor. He started pulling on his clothes, cast-off U.S. Army fatigues dyed black for prison staffers like himself. He left his cell and paused on the catwalk. An uneasiness swept over him. The hammering in the night, the sound of the departing vehicle. This could be the day. Ever since the sentences had been handed down, two weeks before, on October 1, the unknown had hung over the prison like a cloud.

He began making his way down a stairwell strung with chicken wire to prevent suicide leaps. He had made this dawn descent every day for nearly fourteen months, ever since the defendants had been sent here for trial. Krug was not a reflective man, or he might have pondered the odd existence he led—confined to prison yet not a prisoner, something more than a trusty, but still something less than the well-fed American jailers for whom he worked.

In the last days of the war, he had been a corporal attached to a field kitchen in General Wenk's Twelfth Army, which had been deployed to halt the Russian advance on Berlin. Willi's immediate concern had not been whether they could stop the Red Army. That hope was forlorn. His aim had been to keep himself out of Russian hands. He had eventually succeeded, along with hundreds of thousands of his comrades, thanks to a man now caged in this prison, Grand Admiral

Karl Dönitz. Dönitz had succeeded Adolf Hitler at the end, and with all lost, had determined to drag out the surrender negotiations the few precious days that allowed Germans like Willi to flee West and entrust their fate to the expectedly more tender mercies of American and British captors. Willi had once tried to express his gratitude to the old man, but something stiff and forbidding in Dönitz's manner had held him back.

After his surrender to the American Ninth Army, Willi had been herded into a cage at Bad Kreuznach near the Rhine, one of two hundred American pens holding over four million defeated Germans. They had been left out in the open, rain or shine, fed half rations and one cup of water a day. In those POW cages, Willi's comrades, who had survived the heat of North Africa and the winters of Russia, died by the thousands. And they call Germans war criminals, he and his comrades had complained.

He had survived through the cunning of the desperate. Willi had picked up a smattering of English while working as a waiter before the war, and managed to have himself selected to serve as a trusty at an improvised prison in Bad Mondorf, Luxembourg. There he was astonished to find himself among German leaders whom he would have once considered as remote as the stars. When over a dozen of them were shipped to Nuremberg to be tried as war criminals, Willi was given a choice. He could be released and go home, or else work for the Americans in the Nuremberg prison. For Willi Krug home was the bombed-out shell of what had been an apartment building in Schweinfurt, rubble that had entombed his wife and child. He had been offered what amounted to a roof over his head and regular meals—more than millions of his countrymen could now hope for. But he would have to live in the Nuremberg prison. Willi gratefully seized the offer.

On the main floor of the cellblock he looked out on a familiar scene. On each side of the corridor stood the GI guards, one to a cell, condemned to stare through a square porthole, never taking their eyes off their charges, two hours on and four hours off, for twenty-four-hour stretches. Usually they greeted him, "Hey Willi, *wie geht's*, you old Kraut," and other fractured German gibes as he passed by. His morning arrival was the signal for the guards to turn off the spotlights that they directed through the portholes onto the sleeping prisoners' faces. But this morning's air of anxiety had tempered even these brash young Americans, and they let him pass with bare nods.

He headed for the basement to fill the tin washbasins that he brought to each cell every morning. En route, he passed cell 5 and glanced in. He briefly caught sight of the *Reichsmarschall*'s square face, defiant chin, long sharp nose, and thin lips. Hermann Göring lay there, hands resting outside the blankets, regulation style, so the guard could see them. Willi hurried by. He was required only to dispense cold water for washing up. But whenever he had time, he liked to heat the water for the *Reichsmarschall*, particularly this morning when he wondered if he might ever perform this small kindness again. The corporal posted at the end of the cellblock waved him down the basement stairway to the kitchen. Willi smiled. He always smiled, even at their taunts. The truth was that he did not much like the guards. They were like badly brought-up children. Their behavior toward the prisoners, addressing once-powerful leaders of the Reich by first names, even nicknames, shocked him.

He checked the stairwell carefully as he descended. It was the GIs' habit to grab an unauthorized smoke on the stairs, and it was a rare morning on which he did not find a treasured butt or two.

Hermann Göring had not been asleep when Willi Krug passed by. He had slept fitfully that night. The Amytal and Seconal pills that Doctor Pfluecker always gave him had failed. He too felt the foreboding, and with far more reason than Krug had. The guard snapped off the hated light and Göring allowed his eyes to open. His exposed hands felt cold. He felt scant desire to rouse himself, and closed his eyes again.

He might well have been recalling the last days of the other war, the war of his early manhood. One memory always stood out as crisply as the sun on that July morning in 1918. Three months before, their squadron commander, the living legend Baron Manfred von Richthofen, creator of the Flying Circus, single-handed destroyer of eighty enemy planes, had himself been shot down and killed over France. Göring, with twenty-one kills to his credit, holder of the Pour le Mérite, the coveted "Blue Max" presented personally by the Kaiser, and with enough panache to rival the Red Baron, fully expected to be his successor. Instead, the squadron went to a by-the-book flying bureaucrat, Wilhelm Reinhardt. Göring, impatient and impetuous, had been judged lacking in the steadiness required of a commanding officer.

That July morning, he and Reinhardt had been sent to Adlershof field to meet Anthony Fokker, the Dutch-born builder of German warplanes. On the way out of the officers' mess, Göring spotted an awkward-looking biplane in a corner of the airfield. What was that? he asked Fokker. Just an experimental craft, Fokker said. He wanted to fly it, Göring announced. It had been insufficiently tested, Fokker warned. Göring insisted. After a quick explanation of the controls, he found himself bumping along a grassy runway and nursing the aircraft aloft. He beat up the field, flying at times almost at zero altitude. He looped and spinned and yawed and finally, after a breathtaking pass down the runway on canted wings, brought her in and jumped out of the cockpit before an astonished crowd.

Reinhardt's pride demanded that he too take up the plane. He was, after all, commander of the Richthofen Flying Circus. The spectators watched Reinhardt streak toward the sun. And then it happened: a resounding crack, audible from the ground. The left wing simply drifted away from the fuselage. That was how Hermann Göring, at the age of twenty-five, became commander of the Flying Circus.

Two weeks later, he stole from behind a cloud, locked his guns on a British Spad, and shot down his twenty-second plane. It was the last time he would experience the pure adrenaline joy of the kill. After that, it all fell apart. The Kaiser fled to Holland. The despised Communists paraded down Berlin's Unter den Linden. On November 11, a courier handed Göring a dispatch. Germany had surrendered. He was to turn over his squadron at a French airfield near Strasbourg. They could go to hell, he answered. His commanding officer threatened a court-martial. Göring sent a few token aircraft to the French and led the rest of the squadron back to a field at Darmstadt. As he neared the end of the field, he slewed the plane around until the wingtip struck the ground. He kept churning until the Fokker was ground to junk. The other pilots followed his lead.

A polite tapping on the cell door broke Göring's reverie and he sat up with a start. Framed in the porthole was the sad, smiling face of Willi Krug, announcing that he had brought the *Reichsmarschall* his water. Göring reluctantly threw off the covers and took the washbasin. He set it on the table opposite his cot. Despite all the power and glory that had followed, those days in the van of the Flying Circus had been the acme of his life. This day was certainly the lowest and possibly the last of the mad adventure he had lived. He had managed to cheat the victors of his planes at the end of the last war. All he wanted now was to cheat them of the vengeance they expected to exact from him. He began to unbutton his blue silk pajamas, bent over, and splashed the water over his face. It was, he noted, agreeably warm.

2

WASHINGTON, APRIL 1945

THE TRAIN OF EVENTS that put Hermann Göring into a Nuremberg jail cell had been set in motion a year and a half before, by a phone call from the White House to the Supreme Court. Samuel Rosenman, speechwriter and confidant of President Franklin D. Roosevelt, was calling Associate Justice Robert H. Jackson. Rosenman asked if he might stop by; what he had to say, he explained, was best discussed confidentially in Jackson's chambers. Rosenman's call came barely two weeks after America had been staggered by the sudden death of FDR, whose successor was an as yet unknowable quantity, Harry S Truman.

On his arrival, Rosenman, an old-fashioned man, gave Jackson's secretary, Elsie Douglas, a courtly nod and smile. Mrs. Douglas was attractive, blond, a slightly plump widow of early middle age who managed to combine a good nature with brisk efficiency. She ushered Rosenman into a wood-paneled chamber.

Jackson rose and greeted his visitor warmly. The justice's solid appearance, the banker's blue suit, the gold chain stretched across the faintest suggestion of a paunch, suited the august quarters he occupied. The two men embraced almost as members of a family still feeling a grievous loss. Jackson motioned his guest to a leather-upholstered armchair, and asked his secretary to bring in coffee and hold all calls.

They talked for a time about the death of the president. Then Rosenman, speaking in the rolling cadences that evoked the speeches he had written for Roosevelt, came to the point. He had been in England with Churchill, he said, just three days before FDR died. He had gone there to discuss what was to be done with the Nazi leaders when the war in Europe ended, as it soon must. Rosenman's eyes crinkled as he repeated a story that Churchill had told him. In his last meeting with Stalin, Churchill had remarked that whenever they captured one of the Nazi bigwigs, he ought to be summarily shot. With that, Stalin announced sanctimoniously, "In the Soviet Union, we never execute anyone without a trial." Churchill responded, "Of course, of course. We should give them a trial first." Rosenman and Jackson roared. The butcher of the Soviet show trials of the thirties insisting on due process, while a champion of Western civilization called for drumhead justice.

Rosenman was not sure what the president had really wanted—when he said "president," he still meant Roosevelt. At times, Rosenman recalled, FDR had also leaned toward shooting the Nazi leaders out of hand. But, Rosenman had argued, if it was a crime for Germans to shoot people without a trial while at war, why was it less a crime for the Allies to do so when the war was over? Finally, last February at Yalta, FDR, Churchill, and Stalin had all gone on record as favoring the law. There would be war-crimes trials soon, Rosenman announced, and Harry Truman wanted Bob Jackson to prosecute for the United States. Rosenman explained that Truman had not forgotten Jackson's earlier reputation as a formidable prosecutor.

Jackson was an old Washington hand, and he accepted that whenever a president did something, there was a good reason and then there was the real reason. Sam Rosenman was giving him a good reason. He asked if Rosenman knew of his recent speech on war criminals before the American Society of Law. He opened the door and called to Elsie Douglas to bring in a copy. Jackson had told the society, "If we want to shoot Germans as a matter of policy, let it be done as such. But don't hide the deed behind a court. The world yields no respect to courts that are merely organized to convict."

Mrs. Douglas handed the speech to Rosenman. He flipped quickly through the pages with a lawyer's practiced eye. He saw no problem, he said. What Truman wanted was a fair trial with all the protections due a defendant, not a legal lynching.

Jackson's mind was racing. This was a minefield that had to be trodden with exquisite care. Was one of his Supreme Court rivals trying to get him off the bench? Would this assignment mean leaving the court? he asked. Of course not, Rosenman replied. Jackson wanted the weekend to think the matter over. Fair enough, Rosenman answered, and rose to take his leave.

Jackson expected to put the time to good use. He was going to a dinner party Saturday evening with Senator Alben Barkley. Barkley had just returned from a trip to a recently liberated concentration camp. Just the man for Jackson to talk to about war crimes.

The man Truman wanted to prosecute war criminals was unique on the twentieth-century Supreme Court. Robert Jackson did not possess a law degree. He had been born on a farm fifty-three years before in rural Pennsylvania. His father, William, was a self-taught, self-made entrepreneur who always had his hand in something—a sawmill, a hotel, a stable of harness-racing horses. Jackson's mother, Angelina Houghwout, was descended from an old Dutch family that had been in America since 1660. When young Bob was five, the Jacksons moved to the Jamestown area of western New York State, and there he was raised in a world long since vanished, reading the Bible, singing hymns, and learning his letters from *McGuffey's Reader*. He was also absorbing, from his profane, hard-drinking father, an independent streak. The elder Jackson was a lone, outspoken Democrat in a community of rock-ribbed Republicans.

Young Bob was drawn to the law in part because his father opposed it. He spent a year at Albany Law School on money borrowed from an uncle, and received a certificate of completion, but not a degree. Thereafter, he settled in Jamestown, population 31,000, and, over the next twenty years, became a success in his small corner of the world, representing banks, railroads, industries, and wealthy estates. But a populist streak in him also propelled Jackson to defend the tiny local telephone company against the giant Bell system. He defended, without a fee, a poor black accused of stabbing a white farmer to death; his client went free. By 1932, Bob Jackson was prosperous, a Jamestown pillar, married to his law school sweetheart, Irene Gerhardt, and the doting father of a son, William Eldred, and a daughter, Mary Margaret.

In a single evening, fate conspired to remake his life. Jackson had gone to a Jamestown Democratic fund-raising dinner. In that spring of 1932, the burning issue for Democrats was the massive corruption recently revealed in the administration of New York City's bon vivant mayor, Jimmy Walker. To Jackson's dismay, not a single speaker made any reference to the Walker scandals. When it was his turn to speak, Jackson said that this omission was a disgrace: "It comes perilously close to putting the state Democratic party in Walker's back pocket," he warned.

Months later, New York's governor, Franklin Delano Roosevelt, was elected president and Bob Jackson was invited to Washington by Henry Morgenthau, a man he scarcely knew. Morgenthau, a confidant of the president, had been appointed Roosevelt's secretary of the treasury. "I didn't like your Jamestown speech," he told Jackson, "but I did admire your intentions. It took courage to say what you said. That's what the president is looking for down here."

Thus it was that Bob Jackson warily gave up the good life as "just a country lawyer" and entered the New Deal. He started in the White House, drafting tax legislation, and soon was receiving appreciative "Dear Bob" notes from an admiring FDR. His rise was swift. Roosevelt named him head of the antitrust division in the Department of Justice, then solicitor general, in which capacity he argued the government's cases before the Supreme Court. At age forty-seven, Bob Jackson became U.S. attorney general.

There was about him an almost innocent integrity. At one point, Roosevelt invited the Jacksons for a Potomac River cruise on the presidential yacht. Jackson declined, saying he had to attend his son's graduation from Saint Alban's school. His secretary was horrified. "You don't say no to the president," she advised. But he had, and a half hour later the White House secretary was back on the line saying the president wanted to congratulate young Bill on his graduation, and was delaying the yacht's departure until the Jacksons could make it aboard.

In 1940, FDR, running for an unprecedented third term, was shopping for a new vice-presidential running mate, and Bob Jackson figured on the short list. There was speculation about his succeeding FDR in the future. But, the president noted, "The trouble with Bob is that he's too much of a gentleman." That crusty and perceptive Roosevelt aide, Harold Ickes, made another judgment of Jackson that was to haunt him in prosecuting war criminals: "He has not yet learned to stand up to fire directed at him personally."

Roosevelt was nevertheless still high on Bob Jackson. In July 1941, when the Supreme Court's chief justice, Charles Evans Hughes, resigned, Jackson was a strong candidate to become Hughes's successor. Roosevelt was pressured instead to name a sitting associate justice, Harlan F. Stone, as chief. But the country lawyer from Jamestown, lacking a law degree, was named an associate justice when Stone moved up to the top spot. Jackson hoped that Roosevelt would name him chief justice when Stone left.

On Sunday afternoon, three days after Rosenman's proposal, Jackson sat alone in the study at Hickory Hill, his rambling home in the Virginia hunt country. He had seen Senator Barkley at the dinner party the night before and had pulled him aside at an appropriate moment. He confided to Barkley that he regarded these tales of Nazi horrors with skepticism. Barkley's usually amiable air vanished. Believe them, he said. He was just back from Buchenwald.

Now in the seclusion of his study, Jackson turned over the Truman offer. He recalled the attempt to punish war criminals after the First World War—a fiasco. The victorious Allies had drawn up a list of over 4,900 potential defendants, and quickly trimmed it to 901 names. Of these, twelve men were ordered to trial by a German court in Leipzig in 1922. Three of the twelve simply failed to appear. Charges were dropped against three more. The remaining six got off with laughably light sentences.

Now the president was asking Jackson to become part of an effort to try again, this time through an international tribunal. There were no precedents, no existing body of law, not even a court. The legal instruments for prosecuting a drunk driver in any county in America were better than those for prosecuting the murderers of millions during a war. The risks to Jackson's career were high, the rewards uncertain. The course of prudence was to turn Truman down. Yet the truth was that Jackson had become bored on the Supreme Court. The titanic legal battles of the thirties over FDR's New Deal legislation were over. The main arena now was abroad, in a world turned upside-down by war. Jackson had also made a formidable enemy on the court, Associate Justice Hugo Black. Black resented Jackson's assumption that he was Stone's heir apparent. Black, a former Ku Klux Klansman from the deep South, a man whose integrity Jackson suspected, was an alien figure to the upright Yankee. Their constant clashes had drained much of the pleasure out of Jackson's service on the bench. He had been thinking about resigning even before Truman's offer dropped from the blue. He remembered what his father had once told him after a horse-swapping deal. "How do you dare trade that way, Pop," the boy had asked, "when you don't know what you're getting?" The old man answered, "Bob, it's sometimes enough just to know what you're getting rid of."

Jackson picked up the phone and dialed his son, Bill, recently graduated from Harvard Law School and now a navy ensign assigned to a Washington desk job. He told Bill that he was inclined to take Truman's offer, and as his first staff appointment he wanted to hire Ensign Jackson. "Not bad for your first case," the father added. Bill hesitated briefly. It meant leaving his recent bride for an uncertain period, since the trial would be held in Europe, and wives, his father made clear, were not coming. Jackson went on, "You'll be defending me on this one long after I'm gone. That's one reason I want you there. Anyway," he added, "I expect we'll be home before Christmas."

On May 2, President Truman issued Executive Order 9547 appointing Robert Jackson as U.S. representative and chief counsel for the prosecution of Axis war criminals. Jackson planned to leave soon for London to meet with his Allied counterparts. But before he left, he made two more appointments. He named quiet, loyal Charles Horsky, a lawyer and former subordinate in the Department of Justice, as his Washington special assistant. In the treacherous Washington terrain, Jackson needed someone to watch his back, to serve as his eyes and ears with the press, the White House, and the Pentagon, and especially at the Supreme Court. He trusted Horsky implicitly. And there was one more person whom he had no intention of leaving in Washington: his secretary, Elsie Douglas.

3

TWO DAYS BEFORE Robert Jackson was named the American war-crimes prosecutor, his greatest prey escaped him. On April 30, in a bunker twenty feet below the Berlin sewer system, Adolf Hitler took his own life. That left the man expected to succeed Hitler, Reichs-marschall Hermann Göring, as the ranking Nazi. Göring had last seen Hitler in the bunker at a maudlin birthday party held for the Führer ten days before his suicide. At that point, the Russians were one mile away, yet Hitler refused to leave the doomed capital. Göring felt no such compulsion and explained to Hitler that he had to head south to organize the defense of what was left of Germany. Hitler gave Göring a cool handshake and a look that suggested he smelled treachery and cowardice.

Göring flew from Berlin to Berchtesgaden and there made a fate-ful decision. Hitler, by remaining in Berlin, would soon be dead or captured. Göring retrieved from his safe his copy of the Führer Decree dated June 29, 1941. Its meaning was unmistakable. In the event of Hitler's death or incapacity, Göring was to become leader of the Reich. He fired off a telegram to the bunker saying that unless he heard otherwise, he was taking over the nation's leadership. It was a rash gamble, and Hermann Göring lost. An enraged Hitler read the message as absolute proof of treachery. Göring's keenest enemy, Mar-tin Bormann, secretary to the Führer, seized the moment to try to finish off his old adversary. He issued orders to the political police in Berchtesgaden to have Göring shot.

Göring, his wife, Emmy, and their eight-year-old daughter, Edda, were riding in a Mercedes touring car inching along an icy Bavarian road clogged with retreating troops when they learned of the broad-cast out of Radio Hamburg. Reichsmarschall Göring, the report an-nounced, was suffering from acute heart disease and had asked to be relieved of his posts. Upon discovering Bormann's execution order as well, Göring did what Willi Krug and hordes of other ordinary Ger-mans were doing in those waning hours of the war. He headed for the American lines.

On May 6, U.S. Army Lieutenant Rolf Wartenberg, earlier a refugee from Nazi Germany, found himself stripping medals from the fleshy, heaving chest of Hermann Göring. Göring took it all with good hu-mor. So far his captivity had been lovely, reminding him of the chivalry that had prevailed among enemy aviators on the Western front in the Great War. He recalled the time an English flier's guns had jammed. He had simply given his foe a salute and flown off.

General Carl "Tooey" Spaatz, commander of the Eighth Air Force, which, with the RAF, had virtually blown Göring's Luftwaffe out of the sky and reduced German cities to rubble, came to greet the *Reichsmarschall*. Spaatz broke out the champagne for his fellow airman. They toasted bravery and daring in the heavens. That night Göring was invited to dine in the officers' mess, where his hosts vied to buy him drinks. An American major sat down at a piano and began banging out "Deep in the Heart of Texas." Göring joined in the circle around the piano and quickly caught on to the song's clapping refrain. Sweat coursed down his puffy face. He told Lieutenant Wartenberg, remover of his medals, that in the mountain of luggage he had brought with him was an accordion. The accordion was promptly produced and soon the *Reichsmarschall*'s pudgy fingers were picking out the melody to "Ich weiss nicht was soll es bedeuten," which Göring rendered in a clear baritone. At two a.m., a tipsy, happy prisoner toddled off to bed.

But wire service photos of the famous Nazi being feted by American officers produced a howl back in the United States. An embarrassed and angry General Dwight Eisenhower, the Supreme Allied Commander, reprimanded the offending officers. Hermann Göring, Ike ordered, was henceforth to be treated no differently from any other prisoner of war.

Actually, he was to be treated much differently. He was to be transferred to a place called Bad Mondorf in Luxembourg. At first, the place presented a pleasant prospect to Göring; it was a spa, a watering hole of some repute. But why necessarily Bad Mondorf, he asked his captors? That, he was told, was where the Americans were rounding up war criminals.

4

Justice Jackson eagerly read the document before him, only six pages plus a cover memo, bound in a blue folder with "Top Secret" stamped across the cover and on every page. A week had passed since his appointment as American prosecutor, and saying yes to the job now seemed to have been the easiest part. He was beginning with virtually nothing. Yet here, condensed in a few pages entitled "Trial of European War Criminals," he detected a brilliant start, a simple concept from which all else might flow. He flipped back to the cover memo to note again the author's name: Colonel Murray Bernays, Special Projects Branch, Department of War.

If prosecuting war criminals was new to Bob Jackson, Murray Bernays had been living with the issue for the previous nine months. The assignment had fallen to the fifty-one-year-old Bernays virtually by default.

Upon getting his new assignment, Bernays had given himself a crash course in the subject. In 1944, President Roosevelt had handed the War Department responsibility for figuring out how to bring war criminals to justice. But the president's old friend Treasury Secretary Henry Morgenthau, the man who had brought Bob Jackson to Washington, rushed a plan to Roosevelt's desk before the War Department could act. Morgenthau belonged to one of New York's old Jewish families, and had clear ideas about what Germany deserved.

On a sweltering Washington day in August 1944, Secretary of War Henry Stimson received a copy of Morgenthau's plan bucked over from the White House for his comments. Stimson was an old man, already in his seventies, a Republican of unbending rectitude in a New Deal cabinet. He read the proposal in the backseat of his government limousine, dabbing a handkerchief across his brow to absorb the sweat caused either by the heat or the words he was reading. Morgenthau proposed stripping Germany of all its industry and turning it into an agricultural society. He wanted to use German POWs as forced labor to rebuild a ravaged Europe, to exile Nazi party members to remote places, and to give advancing Allied armies a list of Nazis to shoot on capture. Morgenthau's plan even provided for dealing with children of members of the SS, the umbrella organization of Nazi elites. Stimson stuffed the memorandum back into his briefcase as though he wanted to forget its existence. Morgenthau's plan was virtually an eye for an eye.

When Stimson reached his office, he summoned Assistant Secretary of War John McCloy and directed him to come up with something more reasonable. But the war was still far from won, and more urgent problems than war criminals occupied McCloy's thoughts. The order was bumped down to a lower level, where, in turn, it was bumped still lower, until it finally landed in the office of a three-man catch-all unit called the Special Projects Branch, headed by Colonel Murray Bernays.

Bernays's life had been a model immigrant success story. His Lithuanian Jewish parents had brought him to America in 1900, when he was six years old. Bernays was a brilliant student, graduated from Harvard and then Columbia Law School, and eventually was associated with the prestigious New York firm of Morris Ernst. He had married Hertha Bernays, a niece of Sigmund Freud, and found it advantageous to take her name. He had left a prosperous practice to join the army.

The idea of branding Nazi atrocities as war crimes, Bernays's research revealed, had arisen even before America came into the war. President Roosevelt had been outraged to learn that the Germans had executed French hostages en masse soon after they defeated France in 1940. In 1942, the whole world learned of the obliteration of the Czech village of Lidice and the murder of 1,331 inhabitants to avenge the assassination of Reinhard Heydrich, deputy chief of the Gestapo. By 1942, the evidence was irrefutable that the Third Reich was embarked on a calculated policy of exterminating the Jews.

On September 15, 1944, a Saturday afternoon, just a week after Bernays received the war-crimes assignment, he sat in his small office on the third floor of the War Department building on Pennsylvania Avenue, a gothic stone pile next to the White House, and tore open his second pack of Camels. The chain-smoking lawyer had been working nonstop. Now he slumped back in his chair, the job done. The freshly typed draft that his secretary had just brought in, he believed, outlined what could become the single most important step in the history of international law.

He had expected the task of inventing legal machinery for bringing mass murderers, plunderers, and aggressors to justice to be monumental. Two traps especially had to be avoided. He did not want an approach that bogged down in an attempt to deal individually with hundreds of thousands of SS flunkies who had beaten a prisoner to death or loaded the gas chambers; nor did he want legal machinery that would allow the top leaders to escape simply because there was no blood directly on their hands.

The idea had struck him like a burst of light, beautiful in its simplicity. The Nazi regime was a criminal conspiracy, a gigantic plot. The whole movement had been a deliberate, concerted effort to arm for war, forcibly seize the lands of other nations, steal their wealth, enslave and exploit their populations, and exterminate the people from whom Bernays himself sprang, the Jews of Europe. If the whole Nazi movement was a criminal conspiracy, then those who created it were, ipso facto, criminals. This part of Bernays's net caught the ringleaders, the masterminds who did not themselves blow up the safe, shoot the bank guard, or drive the getaway car. Bernays's second inspiration had been to declare the organizations that made up the Nazi apparatus— such as the party, the SS, the Gestapo—criminal as well. This approach would catch the lower-level war criminals. If you could prove that the SS was a criminal organization, then you did not have to go through the near-impossible task of proving that individual members were criminals. You need only demonstrate that the man belonged to the SS and hand down appropriate punishment.

Bernays reworked a few phrases and called his secretary back. He told her to cut a stencil, run off multiple copies, and classify the document top secret. He was by now practiced in the ways of the bureaucracy and knew that just as the problem had bumped its way down to his cubicle, his solution would now have to climb its way back up to the top of the Roosevelt administration.

Secretary Stimson had a trusted friend, his former law partner William C. Chanler, who was just back from Europe, where he had been serving as a colonel in military government. Chanler had sent Stimson an idea to mix into the Bernays brew: make the waging of aggressive war a crime itself, Chanler urged. He had worked up a lawyerly rationale. Germany was a signatory of the 1928 Kellogg-Briand Pact for "the Renunciation of War as an Instrument of National Policy." Germany, by breaking the treaty, was not waging legitimate war when invading its neighbors; it was committing murder, assault, and destruction of property.

President Roosevelt liked Bernays's thesis: Nazism as a criminal conspiracy. He also liked Chanler's contribution: aggression as a crime. He wanted the combined plan circulated to a few key administration officials for their reaction.

Herbert Wechsler frowned at the folder, stamped "Top Secret," resting on his desk. Bernays's plan had come over to Wechsler's office in the Justice Department preceded by considerable fanfare. Wechsler's boss, Attorney General Francis Biddle, had passed it along to the subordinate whose judgment he trusted most. Before entering the wartime government, Wechsler had been a distinguished legal scholar at the same Columbia Law School that had produced Murray Bernays, and he found Bernays's scholarship slapdash and superficial. What was this conspiracy nonsense? Any international court was obviously going to have to include the major allies, America, Britain, Russia, and France, in a war-crimes court. Yes, Anglo-Saxon law recognized criminal conspiracy. But the concept did not even exist in the courts of France, Germany, or the Soviet Union.

And defining acts as criminal after they had been committed? That was ex post facto law, bastard law. And declaring that whole organizations—some of whose members numbered in the hundreds of thousands, some in the millions—were criminal? This meat-ax approach was fraught with potential for injustices. Bernays was ignorant of the law, his plan was full of holes, and Wechsler intended to tell the attorney general so. He felt like an art expert who had exposed a fake.

At this point, Wechsler's quarrels with the Bernays plan were largely theoretical. Neither Wechsler or Biddle yet knew that both were fated to play out roles at the future trial; nor that the flaws Wechsler believed he detected in Bernays's grand design would haunt them to the very end.

Bob Jackson still found the Bernays plan inspired. He savored the imagery of a single net flung wide and snaring all his prey. He invited Bernays to his Supreme Court chambers so that he could meet the author of this imaginative idea. Bernays sat before him, smoke rising from his ever-present cigarette and swirling around his large, handsome head. Murray Bernays was an impressive-looking man, but for his sallow complexion and tired, cavernous eyes. He spoke in cultivated tones, his speech marked by well-turned phrases that Jackson savored. After half an hour, they concluded their talk and Bernays departed.

It was Jackson's habit, before he left the office at night, to dictate into his diary the high points of the day. The final entry this afternoon was that he intended to hire Murray Bernays as his executive officer, his right arm.

5

ON THE OTHER SIDE of the world, another lawyer, Hans Frank, contemplated the irony of his existence. When Frank was a young man, his single driving obsession had been to make himself a respected figure in his profession. Instead, at age forty-five, he was sitting in a prison cell, running his thumb along the edge of a gardener's knife and hoping it was sharp enough to slit his wrist.

His body ached. Before dumping him here in the Miesbach jail in Bavaria, American GIs had formed a double line seventy feet long and forced Frank to run the gauntlet. He had staggered between their ranks, stumbling under a hail of kicks and punches, only to be hauled to his feet and shoved ahead for more blows. His tormentors were combat veterans of the Seventh Army's Thirty-sixth Regiment who, days before, had passed through the concentration camp at Dachau. Hans Frank, they had learned, was "the Jew butcher of Cracow," a man said to be engaged in a line of work similar to what they had just witnessed.

Lilli Gau, it seemed to Frank, had been the motive force behind the decisions that had led him to this fate, his body beaten to a pulp, his life forfeit of meaning. She was the beautiful, elegant, dark-haired daughter of a rich and much-respected Munich industrialist, the girl Frank had loved from boyhood. Frank's roots were not remotely similar to hers. His middle-class father was a weak, womanizing lawyer of suspect ethics. His mother came of peasant stock. While Hans was in his teens, she deserted her husband and three children to run off with another man. That scandal had soon been eclipsed by another.

Hans had just taken his law degree at the University of Munich and had joined his father's practice. Forever seared into his memory was the day when the police came and arrested Frank senior for embezzlement—for which, soon thereafter, he was disbarred and imprisoned. All this had gone on while Hans was courting Lilli. Even before the disaster, the Gau family had disapproved of the shyster lawyer's son. Now, the thought of their daughter marrying the son of a jailbird horrified them. The engagement was broken and a marriage quickly arranged between Lilli and a suitable magnate. Hans rebounded into a marriage with Brigitte Herbst, a typist for the Bavarian parliament and the daughter of a factory worker. She was five years his senior and worldly beyond her humble origins. Unknown to Hans, Brigitte managed to bring along her lover on their honeymoon.

After his marriage, Frank vowed he would expunge the stain of his father's disgrace. He would achieve recognition and respectability as a professor of law. In the meantime, with one child and another on the way, Frank had to earn a living. In October 1927, he read a classified ad in the Nazi party organ, the *Volkischer Beobachter*. A dozen storm troopers had broken into a Berlin restaurant where a party of Jews was having dinner. They proceeded to tear the place apart. The police were called and the storm troopers arrested. The *Volkischer Beobachter* was looking for a lawyer to defend these "poor party members without means." Strapped though he was financially, Frank made a rash gamble. He wrote to the paper saying that he would take the case without a fee. His offer was snapped up. He then traveled by train, third class, to Berlin and got the rowdies off with a light sentence.

After the trial, he stopped by the Nazi party office on Schillingstrasse, where Adolf Hitler himself appeared to meet this youthful prodigy of the law. "You must come and work for the party," he told Frank. "But," Frank demurred, "I'm planning an academic career." Hitler waved aside the objection, and Frank soon found himself defending hundreds of Nazis against charges of slander, libel, assault, attempted murder, and destruction of property. By the age of twenty-eight, he was the Nazis' chief counsel. His party work won headlines and soon other clients flocked to his Munich office. Hans Frank never traveled third class again.

In 1930, Hitler summoned him and thrust a list of Reichstag candidates into his hand. He had placed the name of Hans Frank on the Nazi slate. Frank was elected and, at thirty years of age, became one of the Reichstag's youngest members. The Nazis came to power in 1933, and Frank continued to prosper. By 1939 he was Germany's minister of justice, founder and president of the Academy of German Law, the highest-ranking jurist in the land, a man of undeniable respectability, all before his fortieth birthday.

But he never forgot Lilli Gau. As the nanny readied his children for school, as he sprang down the steps of his villa, as his chauffeur opened the door to his Daimler-Benz limousine, he often wondered, what would Lilli think of Hans Frank now?

When the war broke out, Frank joined his Bavarian regiment as a lieutenant. Within weeks after Poland's defeat, an orderly delivered a personal telegram from the Führer. Frank was to come to Hitler's private railway car in Silesia to discuss an assignment more suitable to his talents. After the meeting, Frank raced back home and burst into his wife's dressing room. "Brigitte," he exclaimed, "you are going to be the queen of Poland!" As Frank explained, a huge chunk of western Poland had been absorbed into the Third Reich for German settlers. The Soviet Union had taken a slice of eastern Poland. What remained in the middle, some forty percent of the original country, was to be ruled by Frank as "governor-general," exercising "supreme powers"; or almost supreme powers, since the Führer had explained that Frank would have to share some of his authority with Reichsführer Heinrich Himmler, head of the SS. Himmler's repressive apparatus was needed to run the concentration camps that would keep the unruly Poles in line. Where would they live? Brigitte wanted to know. In Cracow, he told her, in a palace.

At his first sight of Wawel Castle, the ancient seat of Polish kings, Frank behaved like a child given a huge toy. His open touring car roared through the gateway and into the courtyard of a structure dating from the tenth century. Resplendent in a personally designed uniform with flaring breeches and black boots, he bounded up the steps to the main entrance, trailed by adjutants. He entered the throne room, its walls cloaked with medieval tapestries depicting Noah's ark. Here, he decided, he would hold official receptions. Nearby he found an only slightly smaller room, its twenty-foot walls sheathed in tooled red leather. This would be his private office. In another wing he came upon the royal bedchamber, the bed raised up on a platform approached by marble steps. Over the bed a canopy of gilded brocade hung suspended on four marble pillars. He spied a jewel-like chapel off the bedroom. This would please Brigitte, who had never abandoned their Catholic faith as Frank had done in order to advance his career under atheistic Nazism.

As Hans Frank began to rule over this remaining rump of Poland, he felt uneasy only at the arrival of the intimidating Himmler. Frank well knew Himmler's priority, and was eager to please. Thus, his first official act as governor-general was to order all Polish Jews to report for assignment to German labor offices.

Nazi Jewish policy was ticklish for Frank. As an intelligent, cultivated man who could recite the verses of Heine by heart, he did not believe the Nazi party's crude anti-Semitic claptrap. More troublesome, Frank had a dark secret thus far kept from the party's arbiters of purity. Though he had been raised as a Catholic, he was part Jewish. The family name was believed to have been Frankfurter originally. Frank overcompensated with zeal. On his first anniversary at Wawel Castle, he invited his staff and their families to the throne room for a celebration. Beneath the ancient tapestries long tables were set up, burdened with Polish hams, cheeses, and bottles of vodka. Frank took the center of the floor and reviewed the year's progress, achieved in great part, he said, because so many "lice and Jews had been eliminated." "I am telling you quite candidly," he went on, "there must be a stop to them one way or another." As he spoke, a young, bespectacled officer scribbled furiously. Frank had ordered that everything he said, in public or in his office, was to be recorded for posterity. They had met their quota, Frank boasted, by deporting 1.3 million Poles for forced labor in Germany. And, "At the current level of permitted rations, some 1.2 million Jews could be expected to die of hunger." That was not enough, he went on. "We must obliterate the Jews. We cannot kill them with poison. But somehow or other we will achieve their extermination."

Afterward, Brigadeführer Strechenback came up and thanked the governor-general for a letter of commendation he had recently received. "What you and your people have done, *Brigadeführer*," Frank had written, "must not be forgotten and you need not be ashamed of it." What Strechenback had done was to round up 3,500 prominent Poles and have them shot.

Cracow was to have been their Camelot, and in the beginning, Brigitte Frank reveled in the glittering social life her husband inaugurated, with its stream of Nazi luminaries to whom she played hostess. She relished her trips to the city's Jewish section and up to the Warsaw ghetto. She loved the craftsmanship of the hand-sewn camisoles the Jews made, the furs, gold, and carpets that, in their desperation, they would sell for practically nothing. Frau Frank was greedy, but not insensitive. The reports sent back to Germany about the improved lot of the Poles under her husband's leadership were contradicted in the wizened face of every child she saw, and by the Jewish corpses littering ghetto streets. The undisguised hatred that greeted her every appearance in Poland began to depress her. And so she retreated to her country home in Schliersee in Bavaria and had the Polish loot shipped to her.

Hans Frank became lonely. He sent for his thirteen-year-old son, Norman, and gave him the bedroom once occupied by the Polish queen Jadwiga. Norman was enrolled in a school for the children of Nazi officials. On a day in May 1941, while he and his classmates were playing soccer, they heard men singing the Polish anthem outside the school walls. The boys stopped to listen when the song was cut short by the crack of rifle fire. What was that? Norman asked the teacher. "Oh that," he said. "They're shooting Poles." After school Norman came into his father's office and asked why the Poles had been shot. The smile with which Frank had greeted his son vanished. "This is war," he said. "Don't ever ask such foolish questions again."

Later, a classmate of Norman's drew a picture of a factory with Jews entering a chute at the top and bars of soap emerging at the bottom. The teacher found the drawing amusing and passed it around the class. That night when his father came to say good night to him in the cold, damp Queen Jadwiga bedroom, Norman wanted to ask about the picture but decided not to.

Hans Frank, whatever the surface glitter of his life, was close to a nervous breakdown. On Himmler's most recent visit, the *Reichsführer* had confronted Frank with proof of massive corruption in his administration, including a fur-smuggling operation carried on by his wife. Himmler told Frank he was willing to drop the investigation on one condition: Frank was to turn over to the SS all police functions in Poland. Frank knew that this meant unfettered exploitation of the Poles and accelerated extermination of the Jews. He wrote a letter to the chief of the Wehrmacht, Field Marshal Wilhelm Keitel, asking to be returned to military duty. The lackey Keitel immediately showed the letter to Hitler, who read it and said, "Out of the question." Frank thereafter accepted Himmler's conditions. The flow of Jews to the concentration camps quickened.

Then, when all seemed hollowest, her letter arrived in a pale blue envelope. The familiar handwriting jolted him. It was from Lilli, whom he had not seen for over twenty years. It began, "My Dearest Hans," and in it she appealed to him, as a powerful figure in the Reich, to help a heartbroken mother. Her son had been killed on the Russian front and she begged him to find out the details. Frank immediately set his staff to work on the case. He flew to Germany and personally delivered his finding to Lilli at her country home in Bavaria. The electricity between them still crackled, and he found her husband surprisingly tolerant. Lilli took an apartment in Munich for their love nest and Frank flew from Cracow almost every month to be with her.

He felt as if he had been reborn. In Poland he may have signed a pact with the devil in order to maintain his station and to keep Himmler at bay—but these acts only affected backward Poles and wretched Jews. In Germany he could again be the man he had started out to be, a champion of the law. Lilli had inspired him. He was going to ask Brigitte for a divorce and marry Lilli. He was going to remake his life.

In June 1942, he went home to address the Academy of German Law. He made a speech the likes of which had not been heard since Hitler had taken power, a speech certainly that no other member of the Führer's inner circle would have dared. Germany, Frank said, must return to the rule of law. No civilized nation could permit the arbitrary arrests, the imprisonment without due process, carried out by the Gestapo and the SS. "Law either exists or it does not," Frank warned. "Where there is no system of justice, the state sinks into a pit of darkness and horror." He made three similar speeches, one at his

Munich University alma mater, to the wild cheering of the law students.

Frank was summoned before the Führer, expecting the worst. Hitler told him that he could excuse an occasional lapse of judgment, and that he intended to regard Frank's bizarre behavior as such. In the future, however, Frank was to confine his speeches to Poland and to the party line. And as for Frank's divorcing his wife, that was impossible.

Hans Frank returned to Poland and dutifully delivered up the conscript workers to the labor czar, Fritz Sauckel, and the Jews to Himmler. Most of the latter, he knew, were sent to a camp some thirty miles from Cracow called Auschwitz. He resumed his chant of hate. One month after he gave the speeches on restoring law to Germany, he pulled together a group of Polish collaborators and told them, "Jews? Yes, we still have a few of them around, but we'll soon take care of that."

In January 1943, Frank summoned his closest associates to his private office. "All of us gathered here are now duty-bound to stick together," he said. "We are on Mr. Roosevelt's list of war criminals." And, he added cockily, "I have the honor of being number one." As he spoke, the bespectacled aide took down every word, which he would later type up for the governor-general's diary, just as he had done for the past three years.

The mad round at Wawel Castle went on. An endless parade of Nazi *Bonzen*—propaganda minister Joseph Goebbels, the party's chief theorist, Alfred Rosenberg, as well as a stream of movie stars, musicians, and opera singers—continued to arrive for Frank's fabled parties, traveling in Frank's private railway car. But when he was alone, the inner torment became agonizing. He would retreat to the piano in his bedroom, where he played Chopin and Beethoven. He also began writing a novel, called *Cabin Boy of Columbus*. These distractions helped him to forget what Hans Frank had become.

In early 1945, as the Red Army thrust deep into Poland, Frank fled Cracow. He took with him, among other art treasures, Leonardo da Vinci's masterpiece *Lady with an Ermine*, stolen from a Polish museum. He also brought along his diary, now bound in forty-two red-and-gray volumes totaling 11,367 pages.

He returned to his home in Schliersee and set up a "branch office" of the Polish governor-general. He was fooling no one, least of all himself. He was simply waiting for the war to end. When the Americans found him in May, he put up no resistance, since he was convinced he had a strong hand to play. First, he led Seventh Army officers to a cellar and told them he was turning over twenty-two priceless works of art, including the Leonardo, works he said he had been protecting from the Russian barbarians. He also gave the Americans his diary. It was all there, the words that would save him, his improvement of the lives of the Poles, his fights with Himmler, his brave law speeches in Germany, his attempts to resign the governor-general's job. Certainly, the Americans would see through the pro forma anti-Semitic rabble-rousing. It was simply the lip service any Nazi official was expected to spout in order to keep his job.

Instead of receiving gratitude from the American officers, Frank had been beaten, kicked, and spat upon by their troops. They had thrown him into the back of a truck for the trip to Miesbach prison. As the truck bumped along the shell-pocked road, he had taken out an army knife and slashed at his throat. An alert GI had pried the knife from his hand. The cut was superficial. A military doctor bandaged his neck and the trip continued.

Now, he sat in Miesbach prison, a pasty, soft-looking man with thick lips, thinning dark hair, and dark-rimmed sad eyes, the gardening knife clutched in his right hand. As he drew it across his left wrist, a GI burst into the cell and flung him to the ground, thwarting his second suicide attempt. Hans Frank had been saved for eventual transport to Nuremberg, where he would face trial for war crimes and crimes against humanity.

6

ROBERT JACKSON HAD staffing problems. The Democratic national chairman wanted him to hire hack lawyers as political payoffs. A Jewish delegation from New York tried to tell Jackson which witnesses to call and which Jewish lawyers to hire. He pointed out the damage they would do if they let this become a "Jewish trial." They had to get away from the racial aspects. They were prosecuting these Nazis not because they had killed Jews but because they had killed people. The trial must not be seen simply as an exercise in vengeance.

Jackson's resources at this point were undeniably thin: a six-page master plan, a secretary, his son and a friend as aides, and a potential executive officer in Murray Bernays. Bernays impressed him, but Jackson was disappointed by the rest of the War Department. The department staff had collected only sketchy data on scattered atrocities thus far, hardly the quality of evidence that forms the life's blood of any successful prosecution.

And then Senator Alben Barkley tipped him off to where the gold lay. The key was a proud man, a power in his own right, and wooing him could be tricky, Barkley warned. Jackson was prepared to chance it. He buzzed Elsie Douglas and told her to ring up the Office of Strategic Services on Q Street and arrange a lunch date for him with General Wild Bill Donovan.

They had much in common. Both were upstate New Yorkers, boys of humble birth who had made good; both were Justice Department alumni who loved the law; and both were members of the club of influence, Jackson on the Democratic and Donovan on the Republican side.

Jackson came to Donovan like a man hungry for a crust of bread. Fifteen minutes into their meeting, Donovan seemed to have spread a banquet before him. Until now, Jackson had known little of Donovan or of his creation, the hush-hush OSS. The pudgy, modest-looking general had been the most heavily decorated American officer to come out of the First World War. He had gotten rich between the wars in a gilt-edged New York law practice. In this war, he had fought the naysayers and bureaucratic rivals in the FBI and the armed forces to build the OSS from nothing into America's first intelligence service.

The OSS, Donovan explained, had field operations throughout Europe. His people had been tracking potential war criminals since 1942, and had accumulated substantial dossiers. Furthermore, he had every imaginable specialist within his ranks: scientists, linguists, even architects who could build Jackson a courthouse if need be. Best of all, he had attracted some of America's brightest young lawyers into the OSS. Depending on the demands of the war in the Pacific, he could make many of these people available to Jackson.

As Donovan talked, Jackson considered a bold gamble. Wild Bill not only had an organization in place, but knew how to open doors throughout Washington and the military. If Jackson had Donovan at his side, the battle of preparation, recruitment, and organization would be half won. He took the plunge. He did not know how, he said, to make his offer attractive to a man of Donovan's stature—but would the general possibly consider becoming his lead prosecutor? The general's pale blue eyes gazed off briefly and then he said, "I'll think about it."

7

THE WAR IN EUROPE ended in the ancient cathedral city of Rheims in a sterile red brick building, the Boys' Technical and Professional School. On May 6, 1945, its windows were jammed with Allied military personnel eager to catch a glimpse of history. On the second floor, in what had once been a drafting classroom, General Eisenhower gazed out as a dun-colored U.S. Army command car pulled up bearing an eagerly awaited party.

Colonel General Alfred Jodl, small, trim, erect, with the pinched expression of someone weaned on a lemon, stepped from the car. Jodl began to raise his hand in a salute that was barely acknowledged by Allied officers who regarded him with cold curiosity. Jodl was escorted into a room where, before the war, French schoolboys had played Ping-Pong and crammed for exams. Jodl sat down with Eisenhower's deputies, since the supreme commander had refused to negotiate with a Nazi general. Jodl proceeded to carry out the orders given him by Grand Admiral Karl Dönitz. His instructions were simply to stall as long as possible before surrendering. Every day, every hour gained would mean more German units could escape the clutches of the Russians and surrender instead to the British and Americans.

As Jodl dragged his feet through the deliberations, Eisenhower lost all patience. He directed his aides to inform Jodl that either he signed the instrument of surrender or he would seal the Western front. Fleeing Germans would then march into gunfire instead of POW cages. The game was over. At 2:38 a.m., May 7, Jodl affixed his signature to the terms of surrender to take effect in forty-eight hours. Six years of world war in Europe were about to end. The next day another ceremony took place in Berlin to satisfy the Russians.

After the surrender, Jodl returned to Flensburg, near the Danish-German border, where Dönitz was headquartered. There he learned that the stalling strategies had allowed over 900,000 German soldiers originally facing the Russians to reach the American and British lines.

Grand Admiral Dönitz had set up his government in Flensburg just days after succeeding Adolf Hitler as führer. He had placed a plaster bust of Hitler on his dresser in the captain's stateroom of the Hamburg-American line's steamship *Patria*, where he established his living quarters. Every morning the admiral was driven in one of Hitler's Mercedes autos five hundred feet from the *Patria* to his head-quarters, where the flag of the German military still flew. There he met with the government he had formed: a minister of education to deal with schools in the postwar era, a minister of war who was determining what salutes, flags, and medals would be used in the new Germany. Dönitz had named Albert Speer, Hitler's armaments chief, as minister of economics and production in this Potemkin village government. After the surrender, with the official photographer present, Dönitz had presented the Knight's Cross to General Jodl for his performance at Rheims.

Dönitz, a slight, gray man, might well have passed for a small-town pharmacist. This unprepossessing figure had, however, been the terror of the Atlantic. Karl Dönitz invented the "wolf pack" submarine strategy that had sunk 2,472 Allied ships. Hitler had called him "the Rommel of the Seas," and eventually gave Dönitz command of the entire German navy. Since he had few political convictions, other than a distaste for messy democracy and a hatred of Bolshevism, Dönitz had let Hitler become his political compass. The usually cool technocrat became mesmerized in the Führer's presence. After a few days, Dönitz admitted he had to flee the Führer's headquarters to regain his independence of mind. Why Adolf Hitler had chosen him, a simple sailor, to succeed as führer still mystified Dönitz. He was an outsider, hardly one of the old party fighters. He had accepted the appointment with the same spirit that had governed his entire naval career: obeying an order was an officer's highest duty.

On May 23, fifteen days after the surrender, British tanks rolled into the Flensburg town square. A British officer arrived at Dönitz's office and asked the admiral if he would be good enough to gather his ministers in the lounge of the *Patria*. On their arrival, General Eisenhower's personal representative, Lowell W. Rooks, announced, "Gentlemen, I am empowered by the supreme allied commander to inform you that as of this moment, the Flensburg government is dissolved. You have one half hour to pack one bag before you are taken to your respective places of detention." Rooks then drew a list from his pocket and said that the following men would be taken to Bad Mondorf as defendants in future war-crimes trials.

When his name was called, Dönitz summoned the discipline of a lifetime to mask his shock and outrage. He caught sight of an equally stunned Jodl as the general's name was called. The Flensburg net also swept up as war-crimes suspects Field Marshal Wilhelm Keitel, chief of staff of the armed forces, Alfred Rosenberg, the philosopher of Nazism, and Albert Speer.

Dönitz went to his room and began packing a black leather bag. He looked briefly at the Hitler bust and decided it was now excess baggage. In the passageway on his return to the lounge, he encountered Jodl. What did the admiral suppose all this war-criminal talk meant? Jodl asked. Were they not soldiers doing what a soldier does —Eisenhower, Montgomery, Zhukov, the whole lot of them? Dönitz gave him a mirthless smile. In his case, the admiral observed, Hitler was dead, so his successor evidently would have to do.

8

The sun at Washington's National Airport was blazing the morning of June 26. The air shimmered off the tarmac, enveloping the silvery hull of an Army Air Forces C54C transport fitted out for VIP service. Justice Robert Jackson, in a dark, three-piece suit, felt his shirt collar form a damp noose around his neck. He motioned to Elsie Douglas to mount the portable staircase to the plane's hatchway. As she started up, he gave her hand a squeeze. He knew that she was uneasy. It was her first flight. The rest of the party—seventeen lawyers, secretaries, and assorted staff—fell in behind Jackson for the trip to London.

Inside the plane, an Army Air Forces sergeant suggested that Jackson take a first-row seat next to the window. Jackson turned and signaled for U.S. Army Colonel Robert Storey to sit next to him. As the transport became airborne, Jackson looked out and caught a last glimpse of the Supreme Court building below.

Colonel Storey, a Texas lawyer before the war, had paid a courtesy call soon after Jackson was appointed chief American prosecutor. A mild-mannered, balding man in his fifties, Storey fit Jackson like an old shoe. The colonel also had a useful background. Jackson was off to meet his foreign counterparts to organize an international court, including representatives of the Soviet Union. Everything he had learned thus far persuaded him that the Russians were going to be trouble. In the final months of the war, Storey had carried out an OSS mission with the Red Army, and as the Soviets advanced into Germany, he had witnessed war-crimes trials, Communist-style. Jackson valued this experience, and he liked Storey. Thus he had enlisted the man for his staff.

As the plane leveled off, Jackson began questioning Storey about his Soviet adventure. The Russians, Storey explained, would put the accused on the witness stand, convict him by confession, and execute him, usually before the sun went down. Often, the condemned were not war criminals at all, Storey had concluded, but simply opponents of Communism. Jackson should know, he warned, that the Russians understood only one language: power.

The trial of war criminals, Jackson had become convinced, must signal not simply the triumph of superior might, but the triumph of superior morality. He was in a position to fashion a future in which aggressive warfare would no longer be resignedly accepted as the extreme edge of political activity, but dealt with as a crime, with aggressors treated as criminals. That could be the greatest leap forward in the history of civilization. Surely, it surpassed anything he had yet done, including his service on the Supreme Court.

On arriving in London, the Jackson party checked into Claridge's Hotel. To one who had never witnessed war, the scene from Jackson's window was sobering. Skeletons of buildings stood silhouetted against the night, their blasted windows gaping like empty eye sockets. He watched Londoners weave around craters and along paths cut through the rubble. This brave city, pockmarked and bleeding, with thousands of innocent dead, confirmed his sense of mission. War-crimes trials were a splendid idea, Jackson thought.

Robert Jackson and Britain's attorney general, Sir David Maxwell-Fyfe, were entering Church House on Great Smith Street, which the British government had provided for the Allied war-crimes negotiations. Jackson found himself chatting with a dark-skinned man in his mid-forties, thickset, heavily jowled, with full lips, thinning hair, eyes set in deep recesses, and the self-effacing manner of a secure personality. He resembled a Syrian diplomat or an Egyptian merchant far more than the Scot that he was. "Swarthy and ugly," was how Sir David described himself, "and my waistline has launched a career of its own."

The delegations from the Big Four powers seated themselves at a table of India teak in the conference room. The others seemed to expect Jackson to take the place at the head of the table. The Americans had pressed hardest for trying war criminals; they held most of the expected defendants in custody. More to the point, in a Europe enfeebled by war, they were in the best position to pick up the tab for whatever this enterprise cost. Jackson presented the agenda. What the delegates faced was the legal equivalent of drafting the Ten Commandments, he began. Every nation had its criminal statutes. But for the world at large, none existed. They had to invent a court and give it authority. They had to agree on procedures. They had to write a statute that would describe the crimes the defendants had perpetrated and the penalties for conviction.

Jackson looked around, judging the colleagues from whom he would have to extract a consensus: Maxwell-Fyfe and his fellow Britishers—probably reasonable; the French delegation—inscrutable; the Russians—likely obstructive. General Donovan's OSS had provided Jackson with a profile of the principal Russian negotiator, Major General of Jurisprudence Ion Timofeevich Nikitchenko. Jackson had read the report at Claridge's the night before. Nikitchenko, fifty years old, had gone to work in a coal mine in the Donbass at age thirteen. The Communist revolution provided his escape. He became a Red Army soldier and fought in the Russian civil war. Afterward, he took a law degree at Moscow University and rose to his present position as vice president of the Soviet Supreme Court. Jackson knew the facts, but could read nothing beyond them in that broad Slavic face with its steel-gray, unblinking eyes.

For ten days the delegates wrangled. Jackson was looking forward to escaping, at least temporarily, to check out possible trial sites on the Continent. This evening, he was stretched out in his suspenders and stocking feet in his sitting room in Claridge's, dictating to Elsie Douglas. He wanted to get down on paper where the negotiations stood before he left London. She flipped open her steno pad as Jackson began the resonant phrase-making that always pleased and impressed her.

The greatest problem they faced, he said, was to overcome criticism that they were creating ex post facto law. *Nullum crimen et nulla poena sine lege*, the ancient Romans had said: No crime and no punishment without law. Obviously, the Nazis had committed naked aggression and unspeakable acts. But what *laws* had they broken? What statute, what chapter of what code could a prosecutor cite? Yes, Germany, along with sixty-three other countries, had signed the Kellogg-Briand Pact outlawing war. Germany had also signed peace pacts with Poland and the Soviet Union. Germany had signed the Treaty of Versailles, and the Locarno Pact. Germany was a signatory of the Hague Rules of Land Warfare of 1907 and the Geneva Conventions of 1929. Jackson read off Germany's violations of these solemn agreements with biblical righteousness: 1939, Poland invaded; 1940, Norway, Belgium, Luxembourg, and the Netherlands invaded; 1941, Greece, Yugoslavia, and the Soviet Union invaded. Four days after Pearl Harbor, the Germans had declared war on the United States. As for the accepted norms of warfare, Germany had left the Geneva and Hague agreements in tatters.

Jackson began to craft his rationale as to why the Allies were not engaged in ex post facto law, dictating it to Elsie Douglas. By creating a court and defining procedures and punishment, they were merely adding the missing element of enforcement. If no punishment followed violation, what was the point of august figures gathering in world capitals and signing all these treaties? Jackson warmed to his argument. "Let's not be derailed by legal hair-splitters. Aren't murder, torture, and enslavement crimes recognized by all civilized people?

What we propose is to punish acts which have been regarded as criminal since the time of Cain and have been so written in every civilized code."

Colonel Storey had warned Jackson about the Russians, and General Nikitchenko proved Storey a prophet. Still, the man puzzled Jackson. Nikitchenko could sit motionless as a Buddha for hours, though Jackson thought he detected in those cool eyes the fleeting bemusement of a man performing a part. Some of Nikitchenko's argumentativeness, however, was understandable. The French displayed it too, though less belligerently. To the Continental Europeans it seemed that the Anglo-Saxons were trying to ram an alien court system down their throats. Nikitchenko listened as Jackson and Maxwell-Fyfe explained adversarial law, with its opposing attorneys, direct examination, and cross-examination, before a judge who acted as umpire. That was not how it was done in his country, he said. The French agreed. Their judges did not demean themselves by prying battling lawyers apart like a referee at a prizefight. Judges took evidence from witnesses, from the accused, from the police, from the victims, sifted it, weighed it, and arrived at their decisions. Lawyers were merely to help the accused prepare a defense. They had little role in the court itself. Lawyers are not so important, Nikitchenko concluded with a lecturing tone; judges are important. And this matter of pleading guilty or not guilty: Were they really going to allow a man like Ernst Kaltenbrunner, responsible for the Gestapo and for concentration camps, to stand up in a court of law and declare himself not guilty?

When at last they adjourned for lunch, Maxwell-Fyfe invited Jackson to his club.

Jackson, whose capacity for outrage occasionally left him drained, envied Maxwell-Fyfe's self-containment. They might as well accept it, Sir David said over lunch, they were going to wind up with a hybrid, given the national differences that had to be conciliated. At least they had reached agreement on the number of judges, four principals representing each country, and four alternates. Multiple judges provided the Continental touch. Sir David regarded it as a major victory that they had finally been able to persuade the Russians and French to accept the adversarial system of opposing lawyers. Jackson mentioned

Nikitchenko's fight for easy convictions. They had won that point too, Sir David pointed out. They had agreed on three of four votes to convict, causing Nikitchenko to howl. And they had a name for the court, the International Military Tribunal—rather grand, Sir David observed.

Jackson asked what he thought they should do when the accused raised the defense that they were simply carrying out superior orders. That, Sir David said, could not be permitted; the whole prosecution case would collapse. The Germans under Hitler had operated on the *Führerprinzip*, the concept that the leader has absolute authority. What the Führer ordered, his subordinates carried out. What those below him ordered, their subordinates carried out in turn, and so on, down the pyramid of power. If they allowed the defense of "superior orders," they would be able to convict only Adolf Hitler, and he was dead.

Jackson remained uneasy. In the final months of the Italian campaign, an American GI had gunned down defenseless German prisoners and escaped punishment through a "superior orders" defense. Sir David countered with the statement printed in the paybook of every German soldier: he was not required to obey an illegal order. If that was true for a corporal in the Wehrmacht, why would it not apply to those immediately under Hitler? Jackson suggested that they at least consider superior orders in mitigation of sentence.

What surely would give them the devil of a time, Maxwell-Fyfe went on, was tu quoque, the "so-did-you" defense. If the crimes they were defining applied only to the Germans, how would they escape history's verdict that the trial was not justice but merely victor's vengeance? Atrocities had been committed on all sides. Further, they were planning to prosecute aggression as a war crime. Yet sitting in judgment would be Russians whose nation had invaded Finland in 1940 and grabbed a chunk of Poland under its 1939 pact with the Nazis.

Tu quoque, Jackson said, had to be another unacceptable defense. It implied that because some murderers went free, then all murderers must go free—a mockery of justice. The Nazi murders had been committed on an unimaginable scale. How could the world simply walk away from the deaths of from six million to ten million people? It would be hypocritical to deny that there was no element of vengeance in a war-crimes trial. Germans were going to be in the dock because

Germany had lost the war. But, Jackson pointed out, a thief or embezzler is only in the dock because he gets caught. All well and good, Maxwell-Fyfe persisted. But how did Jackson suggest that they get around tu quoque? They would simply state in the statute that tu quoque was inadmissible, Jackson suggested. Sir David looked at his guest with renewed respect. He had not anticipated Yankee pragmatism.

9

ERNST KALTENBRUNNER, whose very name incensed General Nikitchenko, was what people expected in a Nazi. So many of these oncefearsome figures were a disappointment up close—like Dönitz, with his clerklike mien. A man like Jodl would have escaped notice in a group of five people. Kaltenbrunner, chief of the RSHA, the Reich Central Security Office, however, was out of central casting. His neck rose directly from his shoulders to his head without tapering. Huge hands dangled at his sides. His horse face was seamed by a thin, cruel mouth and a scar that cut a purple swath across his left cheek. At six feet six inches tall, he managed somehow to look fleshy and gangling at the same time.

At the war's end, Kaltenbrunner had been hiding out in a chalet in the Austrian Alps near Alt Aussee, where a patrol from the U.S. Third Army stumbled onto him. The lumbering giant, just another kraut officer to General Patton's GIs, surrendered meekly. Twelve days after his capture, Frau Rosel Plutz heard on the radio that the Americans had arrested a high-ranking SS officer. The unemployed thirty-three-year-old mother, with a missing soldier husband, was desperate. Here was a chance to ingratiate herself with the victors. She immediately went to the American military government office at Nordhausen. She had been a typist, Frau Plutz told the captain in charge, at a concentration camp called Dora-Gestapo. One of her duties had been to type death sentences. She remembered the signature that appeared on all of them: that of Ernst Kaltenbrunner.

After his denunciation, Kaltenbrunner was placed in the military prison near Nordhausen. A few days after his arrival, he approached a GI guard and tried to bum a cigarette from him. The American was reading a U.S. tabloid, and flashed the paper under the prisoner's nose. Kaltenbrunner saw his photograph and a bold headline. What did it say? he asked. It said, the soldier explained, "Gas Chamber Expert Captured." Kaltenbrunner went deathly pale. Soon afterward, he was bundled into the back of an Army six-by-six truck and taken to Bad Mondorf.

10

NOT UNTIL EARLY JULY did Justice Jackson manage to disentangle himself from the London negotiations long enough to look for a trial site. He traveled in a Dakota transport with his son, Bill, and Wild Bill Donovan, whose OSS personnel always met them with useful information wherever they landed. By July 7, they had checked out Wiesbaden, Frankfurt, and Munich, where they met with Ike's deputy, General Lucius Clay. Clay had suggested the merits of Luxembourg as an appropriately neutral site. Jackson, however, insisted that the place to drive home German criminality was Germany. The Russians, Donovan noted, would insist on Berlin for the trial. Clay frowned. The army could not find housing for the trial staff in that shattered city. He had a better alternative, he said as they reboarded the Dakota.

Jackson dozed off briefly, only to be wakened by Clay pointing earthward. That was it, the general said. Jackson gazed out the starboard window. He had seen the bomb damage in London, the ruins of Frankfurt and Munich. But nothing had prepared him for the urban corpse below. Where were they? he asked. Where Jackson would likely find his courthouse, Clay said. That was Nuremberg.

Until the war, Nuremberg had preserved its medieval aspect. Tourists, particularly well-to-do Britishers, loved scaling its eleventh-century watchtowers and walking along the banks of the gently winding Pegnitz River, spanned by bridges built four hundred years before. Some might find the gingerbread charm of the city cloying, but most delighted in Nuremberg's houses with their high-pitched, red-tiled roofs and carved dormers jutting out overhead, their gables crowned with painted wooden statuettes.

Nuremberg had given Germany its first railroad line and the

world its first pocketwatch and clarinet. It was a toy-making center
famed for exquisite miniatures, perfectly replicated trains, the engine
no bigger than a man's thumb, and tiny cannons that actually fired.
Nuremberg had also given Germany her greatest artist, Albrecht
Dürer, whose birthplace still stood on the square that bore his name.
Emperor Charles IV had christened Nuremberg his *Schatzkästlein*, the
treasure chest of his kingdom.

It was also in Nuremberg that the Nazis had found their spiritual
home. The medieval aura suited the movement's mystical streak. And
the local police could be counted on to be sympathetic. By 1933, with
Hitler in power, the annual Nuremberg rallies had become the chief
celebration of Nazi life, weeklong extravaganzas choreographed by
Hitler's brilliant young architect, Albert Speer. The *Parteitagen* began
in September with church bells tolling Hitler's arrival at the railroad
station. The city's streets rumbled with the pounding of hobnailed
boots. The night sky lit up like a giant bonfire as party faithful from
every corner of the Reich bore their torches through the ancient
streets. Their destination was Zeppelin Field on the edge of town, a
massive stadium that held a quarter of a million people arrayed in
ranks of hypnotizing precision, shouting themselves into an orgiastic
frenzy at the words of Adolf Hitler.

This was also the city where the Nuremberg Laws had been proclaimed, statutes that deprived German Jews of their rights, their
property, and eventually their status as human beings.

The treasure chest of the kingdom had been transformed into the sight
that chilled Justice Jackson by men like Lieutenant Colonel Chester
Cox, 388th Bomber Group, U.S. Eighth Air Force. At 7:28 a.m. on
February 19, 1945, Cox and his B-17 crew had taken off from a field
in England's East Anglia. Cox rendezvoused with 1,249 other Flying
Fortresses and set a course for Nuremberg. At 11:11 a.m. they were
over the target. Captain Hanlen, the bombardier, hunched over his
bombsight, looking for the pretargeted marshaling yards, locomotive
shops, and a tank factory. The bomb-bay doors swung open and the
plane disgorged five 500-pounders and five incendiaries. The aircraft,
suddenly lighter, shot upward as Cox banked her hard to get away
from the flak bursts exploding around them, and headed home.

The day before, another 900 B-17s had struck Nuremberg, dropping 11,042 bombs. Today's raid rained 6,693 high explosives and 4,624 incendiaries on the city. From the time the RAF had first struck in October 1943 until the war's final raid, Nuremberg was bombed eleven times. In the final siege, the American Third and Forty-fifth infantry divisions pounded the city with an artillery barrage followed by five days of house-to-house fighting.

After the surrender, an American military government team surveyed Nuremberg and declared it ninety-one-percent destroyed. Of 130,000 original dwellings, only 17,000 had survived intact. Of a population of 450,000 people, 160,000 remained. The city gave off a stench from an estimated 30,000 bodies trapped beneath the rubble. Nuremberg was a city without electricity, public water, public transportation, telephone, mail, or telegraph service, and without a government. Until the occupation authorities took over, the streets belonged to looters, thieves, and rapists. The Americans declared Nuremberg "among the dead cities of the European continent." Yet there survived on its western edge a huge, frowning structure, the *Justizgebaude*, the Palace of Justice: the courthouse of the government of Bavaria.

The Jackson party landed at an airfield outside of Nuremberg designated by the military as Y28. As the Dakota taxied to a halt, a motorcade of staff cars and jeeps snaked out to the runway. Young Bill Jackson noticed an angle iron welded perpendicular to every jeep's front bumper and rising well above the hood. What were they for? he asked. A driver explained that the angle iron served as a knife to cut wires the Germans strung across the road at night. Several GIs had already been decapitated by them.

The ride into town proved a grim confirmation of what Jackson had glimpsed from the air. Shabbily dressed people wound their way through trenches of rubble, heads bent, faces vacant, movements listless. The few standing walls along the route were plastered with signs warning GIs against fraternizing with German nationals. A girl in a tight dress pointed to one such sign as Jackson's party rolled by. She slapped a shapely behind and shouted, *"Verboten!"*

The motorcade slowed and turned through a gateway in a wrought-iron fence surrounding a fortresslike structure. Their arrival put a halt to games of pitch-and-catch that GIs were playing in the yard. Jackson stared up at a three-story stone building capped by a steeply pitched roof. Most of the windows were blasted out. The yard was littered with spent cartridge cases, and the façade of the court-house pitted with bullet holes. A U.S. Army colonel approached and introduced himself as their escort. The colonel informed the party that the Palace of Justice had taken five hits, with one bomb plunging from the roof to the basement. The building seemed simply to have shrugged off the blows and gone on dominating what was left of Nu-remberg's skyline.

Inside, they entered a maze of corridors, the walls blackened by fire and the floors wet with leakage from burst water mains. Army quartermasters had strung Lister bags along the walls to provide pure drinking water. The colonel led them up a stairwell littered with scorched books. General Donovan picked one up. "Law text," he said and tossed it aside. They arrived at room 600 on the third floor, the main courtroom. Over the entry was a sculptured tablet representing the Ten Commandments.

As they entered, a group of GIs came to desultory attention. A keg of beer sat on what had been the judge's bench. Behind the bench a red-lettered sign proclaiming TEXAS BAR was flanked by several pin-ups and another sign announcing BEER TONIGHT, ½ MARK. The room was strewn with broken chairs, Coke cases, beer bottles, and candy wrappers. Wedged between two desks stood an upright piano. Only the ornate chandeliers, a huge baroque clock, and bas-relief figures of Adam and Eve carved in marble over the doorway reminded the vis-itors of the Texas Bar's previous incarnation.

There was something else they must see, the colonel said, and led the party across a driveway to a twenty-foot brick wall. Behind that wall, he explained, were four wings of cellblocks fanning out from a center core, enough cells to accommodate twelve hundred prisoners. The prison was currently full of ordinary criminal defendants. One wing, however, could quickly be cleared for war criminals. The best hotel in Nuremberg, the Grand, was also standing, miraculously in-tact, the colonel explained. In this virtually dead city, General Clay pointed out, were a courthouse with plenty of office space, a jail, and first-class hotel accommodations for top staff. That, Jackson observed, was precision bombing.

As the motorcade began its crawl back through the defiles of destruction, Jackson wondered how they could ever hope to operate amid this chaos. How would he sell Nuremberg to the British and French, and talk the Russians out of Berlin? Clay said he would make a start. He could have General Patton move in fifteen thousand German POWs in the next forty-eight hours to clear the streets.

11

LIEUTENANT ROGER BARRETT was a thirty-year-old Chicago lawyer with a knack for spotting significant documents—a trait acquired from his father, a noted collector of Lincolniana. Barrett had before him a complaint filed by a German construction official attached to a plant in the Nazi-occupied Ukraine. In it, Hermann Graebe described in detail how, out of curiosity, he had followed a German SS unit that he saw herding thousands of Jews out of the town of Dubno to an earth embankment outside the city. "Without screaming or weeping," Graebe had written, "these people undressed, stood around in family groups, kissed each other, said farewells. . . . An old woman with snow-white hair was holding a one-year-old child in her arms and singing to it and tickling it. The child was cooing with delight. . . . A father was holding the hand of a boy about ten years old and speaking to him softly; the boy was fighting his tears." An SS man standing at a pit concealed behind the embankment shouted to one of his comrades guarding the now naked Jews. The latter counted off about twenty persons and instructed them to go behind the earth mound. Graebe's report went on: "I well remember a girl, slim, with black hair, who, as she passed close to me pointed to herself and said, 'Twenty-three years old.' "

Barrett forced himself to keep on reading. The German next described how he went behind the earth mound and saw the pit "already two-thirds full. . . . I looked for the man who did the shooting. He was an SS man, who sat at the narrow end of the pit, his feet dangling into it. He had a tommy-gun on his knees and was smoking a cigarette." Thus the five thousand Jews of Dubno perished in a single afternoon. What struck Barrett most forcefully was that this report was no confession coerced by Allied interrogators from a reluctant

Nazi. It was one of thousands of ordinary documents found in the Nazis' own files.

Earlier, when he had been dependent on the War Department, Justice Jackson had worried about a dearth of evidence. Now, thanks to his partnership with Wild Bill Donovan's OSS, a river of documents was pouring in. In June, Jackson had named Colonel Robert Storey as chief of a new documents division. Storey had set up shop in Paris at 7 rue de Presbourg, near the Arc de Triomphe, while a trial site was being decided. Barrett worked for Storey.

In mid-July, Storey received an urgent phone call from an OSS ensign named English. The naval officer, in the unfathomable ways of the OSS, had been sent to scour Eastern Europe for documents. He was calling, he said, because he had come across something that might interest Storey. A German nobleman, Baron Kurt von Behr, chief aide to Nazi party philosopher Alfred Rosenberg, had offered to reveal the hiding place of all of Rosenberg's files if the Americans would reserve a part of the baron's sixteenth-century castle for his exclusive use. Baron von Behr thereupon conducted the Americans to a cellar five stories below the castle and to forty-seven crates of green ring binders. The next day, the nobleman and his baroness retreated to their bedchamber and took poison washed down with a bottle of 1918 Champagne.

Storey ordered Ensign English to fly the crates to Paris, and four days later a C-47 touched down at Orly field bearing three thousand pounds of the Nazi party's meticulously recorded past, dating back to 1922.

It was as if a dam had burst. The Rosenberg find was followed by a tip from a German Foreign Office archivist who led Storey's people to the Harz Mountains and 485 tons of diplomatic papers. Hitler's personal interpreter, Paul Schmidt, turned over twelve volumes of his notes of the most secret foreign policy conferences. In a salt mine in Obersalzburg, GIs discovered the Luftwaffe's records along with art that Hermann Göring had looted from all over Europe.

Late in July, another bombshell burst. Storey immediately put through a call to Jackson in London. The keystone of the Bernays thesis was that the Third Reich had carried out a deliberate conspiracy to commit aggression. But how to prove it? As Storey explained to Jackson, one of his researchers had found the notes of a General Friedrich Hossbach, Hitler's adjutant, recording a meeting at the Reich Chancellery in Berlin on November 5, 1937. The meeting involved Hitler, Göring, Foreign Minister von Neurath, Grand Admiral Raeder, and a handful of other top leaders. According to Hossbach's notes, Hitler told his subordinates that he was about to reveal "my last will and testament." Germany's 85 million people, he said, represented Europe's purest racial entity. The country's present boundaries were inadequate to serve this population, a condition that "justified the demand for more living space." "The German future," Hitler went on, "is therefore dependent exclusively on the solution of the need for living space, no later than 1943–45." In short, since her neighbors were unlikely to give up their soil to Germany, and since Germany's expansion was justified, the country was left with no recourse but acquisition by aggression. There it was, from the Führer's lips to General Hossbach's notes and now in Storey's hands.

The Hossbach coup, along with files containing Nazi invasion plans and material like the Graebe report that Roger Barrett had unearthed, had brought Jackson to a major decision. The Allies could convict the Nazis simply by introducing German documents in evidence. Witnesses would be far less necessary and less convincing than anything the Nazis themselves admitted.

12

HIS GREATEST ENEMY thoughout the war, Albert Speer explained to a Frankfurt symposium on "The Organization of German War Production," had been bureaucratic inertia and stupidity. The American and British officers nodded knowingly as the former armaments minister of the Third Reich described how, at one point, he could not get gasoline to the front because 180,000 desperately needed gas cans had been reclassified as water cans for use by the Afrika Korps. By then, he said, the Germans had been driven out of North Africa for two years.

Speer's participation was the high point of the two-week symposium. The forty-year-old architect was a legend to insiders on both sides of the war, the wunderkind who had increased German production of weapons seven times, ammunition six times, and tanks and other armored vehicles over five times in only three years. He had reached his peak output just ten months before the war ended, despite crippling shortages and incessant day and night bombing. The Allies wanted to know how he had done it.

Since the war's end, all had gone well for Albert Speer. Though he had initially been arrested along with the rest of the Dönitz government, he sensed early on that he held a special interest for the Allies. Soon after his arrest, he was interviewed by three members of the U.S. Strategic Bombing Survey who wanted to know how effective Allied air raids on Germany had been. His interrogators (visitors would be a better word, given their respectful behavior), were an economist, John Kenneth Galbraith, and two Pentagon war planners, George Ball and Paul Nitze.

Speer was aware that Wernher von Braun and other German rocket scientists were already saving their skins through knowledge they possessed and that the West wanted. Maybe his freedom too could be bought by what he held in his head. The fatal effect of the bombing, he had explained to the three Americans, had not been to his armament plants but to fuel production. It made scant difference that he was turning out the world's first operational jet fighters if they could not fly. Allied air attacks had cut fuel production by ninety percent. That, Speer said, had been catastrophic for Germany.

Along with intellectual brilliance and limitless energy, Albert Speer possessed charm. People were drawn to this handsome, cultivated man. His *Gauleiter* liked him; Adolf Hitler liked him; even the Twentieth of July plotters, who tried to kill Hitler, had wanted Speer in their government. The famed German filmmaker Leni Riefenstahl had once clipped Speer's photograph from a newspaper, hoping to cast him in a movie. Now the Allies seemed to be succumbing to this combination of usefulness and attractiveness. After his meetings with Nitze, Galbraith, and Bell, Speer had been transferred to a comfortable incarceration near Versailles. From Versailles he had been sent to Frankfurt to lecture his former enemies.

The first thing he had done, when Hitler appointed him armaments czar in 1942, Speer told his Frankfurt audience, was to throw out the military chiefs and put arms manufacture in the hands of professionals—industrialists, engineers, and administrators. Next, he borrowed the strategies of Walther Rathenau, the great Jewish chief of the German economy in World War I: parts standardization, division of labor, maximum use of the assembly line, dispersal of plants to reduce bombing disruptions, and total control of raw materials kept in his own hands. He had been lucky, Speer said, when his arms ministry was destroyed in a raid on November 22, 1943. The bombing had rid him of useless paperwork and paper pushers. The only factor he left out of this account of his production feats was the role of slave laborers.

The session ended on a note that left his listeners stunned. Nazi Germany, Speer claimed, had been only a year or two from producing an atomic bomb when the war ended. The delay, he added, with disarming contrition, served Germany right, since she had driven out so many of her most brilliant scientists, particularly Jewish physicists. When his talk ended, the audience gave Speer a standing ovation.

Outside the meeting room, a British lieutenant was waiting. Speer was to report to the commandant's office before returning to house custody. He felt no alarm. They were probably going to ask him to repeat his lecture somewhere else, perhaps in England, maybe even America. On Speer's arrival at the office, the commandant informed him that he was under arrest as a major war criminal.

13

LESS THAN THREE WEEKS had passed since Justice Jackson's visit to Nuremberg. The challenge now was to persuade the other countries' delegations to accept the city. He returned there on July 21, this time with Sir David Maxwell-Fyfe, French representative Robert Falco, Wild Bill Donovan, Bill Jackson, Elsie Douglas, Murray Bernays, and others who formed the latest Jackson coterie. Nikitchenko, under orders from Moscow, had refused to come. The Soviets were still holding out for Berlin in their zone of occupation.

Bernays was relieved at being included. Jackson had become a magnet for ambitious people who wanted to be part of a historic moment. Donovan would play a key role just under Jackson. Storey, who seemed to Bernays to be an amiable plodder, had sewn up the vital documents operation. Jackson had also taken on John Harlan Amen, a tough New York racket-busting prosecutor in the Thomas E. Dewey mold, to head up an interrogations unit. The operation was getting crowded at the top. Still, it was Bernays's concept that guided them all. There had to be a meaningful place for him.

Jackson was particularly relieved to have Maxwell-Fyfe along. He had recently come close to losing his strongest ally. In July, Sir David's Conservatives had lost power in the first British general election since the end of the war in Europe. Churchill was out. Maxwell-Fyfe had managed to hold on to his seat in Parliament, but was no longer attorney general. His Labour party successor, Sir Hartley Shawcross, had been named Britain's chief war-crimes prosecutor. But, with the European war over, Shawcross was more interested in the anticipated social revolution at home than in war-crimes trials, and had asked Maxwell-Fyfe to stay on as Britain's de facto chief prosecutor.

Nuremberg looked as stricken as before, though General Clay had made good on his offer to clear the streets of rubble. Donovan's OSS had come up with Captain John Vonetes, a twenty-nine-year-old graduate of the Cornell University school of hotel management, to scout for housing and dining facilities in the battered city. Vonetes, a fast-talking Greek American from Binghamton, New York, was of the breed that every army produces, the soldier who can turn up Scotch for the party, nylons for the ladies, gasoline for the junket. Just don't ask too many questions. At Jackson's request, Vonetes arranged a luncheon at the scarred but still elegant Grand Hotel. The British and French, who had not dined so well in years, were suitably impressed. Vonetes also told Jackson that he had located nearly one hundred relatively undamaged homes on the outer ring of the city for the trial staff. For Jackson he had found a castle, the manorial seat of the Faber-Castell family, Europe's pencil magnates. Jackson took a quick tour through its rococo interior, replete with cherubs clutching pencils, and bathrooms with tubs, as Jackson put it, "not quite big enough for swimming pools." The press would be all over him for living in such splendor, Jackson concluded. They ought to use the castle to billet reporters. "They're the only ones who can live here without being ridiculed because they control the laughs," he said.

On the last night, the Jackson party attended a concert at the Nuremberg Opera House. Most of the roof had been blown off; the top of the piano was missing. The musicians, in ragtag clothes and army castoffs, performed a spiritless Beethoven's Fifth Symphony.

Nuremberg had a courthouse, a luxury hotel, housing, a prison, even remnants of culture. The British and French delegates agreed that the trial of the Nazi war criminals should be held here. As for the Russians and Berlin, they were out of luck. Jackson had a three-to-one vote.

On August 8, roughly six weeks after the Allied representatives had first assembled in Church House, they were ready to sign an agreement to try war criminals in an international court. The document defined the crimes, the structure of the court, the procedures and punishments. But what to name this new instrument? Nomenclature had been tricky. To call it a law, a statute, a code, would brand it, at the outset, as ex post facto. And so a neutral term, *charter*, was settled on: the Charter of the International Military Tribunal.

Murray Bernays took his copy of the charter back to his office on London's Mount Street. It was only nine pages, scarcely longer than his original memo. He read the document with a suffusion of pride. The heart of the charter was Article 6, three short paragraphs essentially expressing the idea born in his imagination eleven months before, that Nazism had constituted a criminal conspiracy. The charter defined four crimes: conspiracy to carry out aggressive war; the actual launching of aggression; killing, destroying, and plundering during a war not justified by "military necessity"; and "crimes against humanity," including atrocities against civilians, most flagrantly the attempt to exterminate the Jews.

At the time the Allies signed the charter, they finally agreed on who was to be tried. The Americans, British, French, and Russians had horse-traded, compromised, placated national pride and pet hates, and come up with a list of twenty-three major war criminals. Hermann Göring topped it, followed by Hitler's foreign minister, Joachim von Ribbentrop, who had managed to escape the Allied dragnet until June 13, when the son of a business partner turned him in. The last führer, Admiral Dönitz, also made the final list, along with General Jodl, signer of Germany's surrender. Others included Rosenberg, Speer, Kaltenbrunner, and Hans Frank.

The Americans held most of these men, but the Russians insisted on producing their own defendants. Two men in Soviet hands, Grand Admiral Erich Raeder and Hans Fritzsche, were thus added. Raeder had been Dönitz's predecessor as head of the German navy, but had been out of the war since 1943. Fritzsche was a third-string operative in Josef Goebbels's propaganda apparatus. They were the best the Russians could produce.

Murray Bernays walked down the hall to his office the day after the agreement was signed. Coming toward him from the opposite direction were Colonels Storey and Amen and three other recent Jackson appointees. They moved past him with a bare nod. He turned and watched them disappear into Jackson's conference room. Increasingly, he was being brushed aside.

Bernays had become a pain to the Jackson staff. He was seen as a zealot who resisted any changes in his original idea. The men now around Jackson were compromisers, adroit legal politicians. Even Jackson, with his own streak of righteousness, found Bernays's purist posture discomfiting.

Bernays stopped by Jackson's office and told Elsie Douglas that he had to see the boss, privately, as soon as possible. At the tag end of a hard day, a tired Jackson braced himself for the encounter with Bernays. A man who reveled in legal combat, Jackson dreaded personal confrontations. Bernays told Jackson that his health was bad. He hoped he might be relieved of his duties and return home to the States. Jackson was all solicitousness and understanding. He agreed instantly.

That night Bernays wrote to his wife, "I'm not to blame if these glory thieves made away with my property. They're practical men. I'm only a dreamer." He settled up his affairs and was soon on his way home. Murray Bernays was to have no further involvement in the Nuremberg war-crimes trial.

14

THE ONLY INSTRUCTION First Lieutenant Robert G. Denson had been given this Sunday, August 12, 1945, was to fly his C-47, *Jinx*, to an airstrip near Bad Mondorf to take on "classified cargo." Denson jumped from the hatch to the ground just as several ambulances emerged from a side road. The first ambulance pulled alongside his plane and an army colonel leaped out. Something in the officer's appearance and bearing brought Denson to immediate attention. The colonel wore a green, brilliantly shellacked helmet, rows of ribbons, and kept a riding crop tucked under his arm. His round face possessed a severity heightened by steel-rimmed glasses and a thin mouth under a pencil-line mustache. His posture was rigid. The colonel asked Denson if he was prepared to load. His voice was high-pitched yet authoritative, the voice of a man accustomed to being obeyed. By now, the drivers had hopped out and began opening the rear doors of the ambulances.

Denson looked on in puzzlement as several middle-aged, unshaven, haggard-looking men in disparate dress emerged and shuffled listlessly toward his plane. Only one had any bounce in his step. The stout, smiling figure gestured toward *Jinx* and said in heavily accented English, "Good machine." Denson's eyes popped. He recognized Hermann Göring. His classified cargo was obviously the Nazi war criminals he had been reading about.

The officer who had addressed Denson was Colonel Burton Andrus, recently commandant of Bad Mondorf prison. Burt Andrus liked to say that he had first gone under hostile fire at age two months while his West Point father was serving on the Indian frontier in the 1890s. Unlike his father, Burt Andrus had not managed to make the military academy, but he did earn a regular army commission during World War I. Instead of France, however, Andrus had found himself assigned to the army stockade in Fort Oglethorpe, Georgia. The jail housed the army's worst cases—murderers, armed robbers, and drug addicts.

The Fort Oglethorpe stockade, young Lieutenant Andrus quickly discovered, was a disgrace, run by a kangaroo court of incorrigibles and subject to frequent escapes. As Andrus told the story in later years, he spotted the leaders "by the defiance in their eyes," and immediately clapped them into solitary. He then clamped an iron discipline over the prison. Soon there were no further escapes from Fort Oglethorpe. In his subsequent twenty-seven years in the army, however, Andrus had had nothing further to do with prisons.

The end of World War II found him serving as a combat observer with General George Patton's Third Army in Bavaria. Andrus idolized Patton, and proudly identified himself as a fellow cavalryman.

He wrote a friend, "I will go anywhere with Georgie, anytime, for any purpose." It was on Patton that he had modeled his shellacked green helmet, the riding crop, and a penchant for the theatrical. Andrus had been on leave in London after V-E Day when his Fort Oglethorpe service caught up with him. He received orders to take command of the detention and interrogation center at Bad Mondorf, which the GIs had christened "Ashcan."

Andrus had clear opinions about his Nazi charges. He wrote a friend, "I hate these Krauts and they know it and respect me for it. I guess that's why I got this job. It's too bad we could not have exterminated them and given that beautiful country to someone who was worthy." Just before the London charter was signed, Andrus received secret orders to bring the leading Nazis from Bad Mondorf to Nuremberg and to assume command of the prison there.

The colonel provoked mixed feelings. One officer who had visited Ashcan wrote afterward that he was astonished to find "an old acquaintance, Burt Andrus, as commandant," adding that "he was generally noted for his lack of judgment, pettiness, and naïveté." Andrus was, admittedly, a spit-and-polish stickler. Some took his addiction to smart appearance as the sign of a martinet, his devotion to rules and regulations as the mark of a closed military mind, his peacock strut and the riding crop as the affectations of an insecure man. He was, at bottom, simply an old-fashioned soldier who loved his profession. Another colleague may have summed him up best: "A great guy. Maybe not the brightest, but a great guy."

Colonel Andrus surveyed his charges sitting on the canvas pulldown seats that lined both sides of the fuselage. He studied the broad back of Hermann Göring standing in the rear of the plane using the portable urinal. As Göring came back, buttoning his fly, he peered out a window. "Well, my friends, take a good look at the Rhine," he said. "It's probably the last time we'll ever see it." The gray, impassive faces laughed weakly at the *Reichsmarschall*'s joke. Sitting down, Göring caught the eye of Colonel Andrus and mutual contempt flared between them.

The antipathy had begun the moment Göring arrived at Bad Mondorf. Andrus had stared at the puffed, sweating, smiling face of his prisoner in near disbelief. Göring, at 264 pounds packed over a five-foot-six-inch frame, came accompanied by a valet and sixteen pieces of matching luggage. Andrus muttered to one of his subordinates that here was one prisoner he intended to whip into line. The luggage contained, along with a trove of jewelry, over twenty thousand paracodeine pills, of which Göring took twenty a day.

Andrus put Göring on a diet, and gradually started withdrawing the paracodeine. By the time they left Bad Mondorf, the *Reichsmarschall* was sixty-five pounds thinner and drug-free. As Göring regained his health, he regained his latent powers. He was no longer a sluggish voluptuary. His restored wit and intelligence made him a formidable adversary for his jailers. During an early strip inspection at Bad Mondorf, Göring had deliberately left a cyanide capsule in his clothes to be found and to distract the Americans from other capsules he had secreted elsewhere.

Next to Göring on the plane sat General Jodl, and next to Jodl, Field Marshal Wilhelm Keitel, Hitler's chief of staff for the armed forces. Just before they left Bad Mondorf, Andrus had stood Keitel and Jodl before the others and torn off their emblems of rank. "You are no longer soldiers," he said. "You are war criminals."

Opposite the military men on the plane sat the former foreign minister, Joachim von Ribbentrop. As Ribbentrop rose to use the urinal, Andrus watched him clutching his baggy, beltless trousers, flopping about in shoes without shoelaces. A small humpty-dumpty figure in the forward part of the plane leaned out and gave Andrus a hopeful smile. Weeks before, Walther Funk, former president of the Reichsbank, had come to Andrus, eyes brimming with tears. There was something he had to get off his chest, he told the colonel. Jews had been murdered for their gold teeth. The camp guards had tried at first to yank out the teeth while the Jews were alive. But that had proved too difficult. So they killed them and then pulled their teeth. The gold, Funk confessed, had been deposited in his Reichsbank.

Next to Funk sat Arthur Seyss-Inquart, Reich commissioner for conquered Holland. When Seyss-Inquart first took up his duties in 1940, Holland had 140,000 Jews. By the end of the war, eight thousand remained. Among the dead was a girl three months short of her sixteenth birthday, Anne Frank, who died at the Bergen-Belsen concentration camp.

The presence aboard the plane of the old man with the corded neck and imperious manner puzzled Andrus. Hjalmar Horace Greeley

Schacht had been reared in America by German immigrant parents. The family eventually returned to Germany, where the brilliant Schacht became president of the Reichsbank, Funk's predecessor. Here was a man, Andrus reflected, who had been found by the Americans in Dachau, where he had been sent for his alleged role in the Twentieth of July plot to assassinate Hitler. Why was Schacht being flown to Nuremberg to face trial as a war criminal?

One German aboard the plane enjoyed Colonel Andrus's total confidence. Dr. Ludwig Pfluecker was in his seventies, a neurologist, drafted into the German army medical service. Pfluecker had initially been brought to Bad Mondorf because he spoke English, and because the younger POW doctors had been unable to cope with their high-ranking Nazi patients. Dr. Pfluecker had agreed to come to Nuremberg under the same conditions as Willi Krug and the other POW prison workers. He was to live in the Nuremberg prison, and be available twenty-four hours a day. It was a way, for the time being, to survive. Pfluecker's presence comforted Andrus, since, above all, the colonel had one objective, to keep these men healthy and alive until judgment day.

Lieutenant Denson cut the engine speed and the plane began to descend. The prisoners twisted around to look out the windows. As the C-47 broke through the cloud cover, the carcass of Nuremberg spread beneath them. Colonel Andrus remembered the famous boast Göring had made as Luftwaffe chief: "If any enemy bombers ever make it across the German border," he had said, using an old German expression, "then my name is Meir." He studied Göring, who was calmly peering out the window.

By four p.m. on a gray, drizzly afternoon, the aircraft was on the ground at Y28. Another cavalcade of ambulances appeared. The prisoners disembarked from the plane and walked to the vehicles. The first leg of a long journey had been completed.

15

CHARLES HORSKY WENT into the men's room of the law firm of Covington and Burling, took off his civilian clothes, and put on the uniform of a Coast Guard lieutenant commander. Horsky, a Harvard lawyer who had once worked for Jackson at the Department of Justice, carried out this routine several times a week, ever since he had become the justice's man on the scene in Washington. Jackson had pulled strings to get Horsky the quickest military commission possible—in the Temporary Reserve of the Coast Guard—plus an office in the Pentagon to facilitate his work. Today, Horsky was meeting Jackson's son, who was back briefly from Nuremberg, to try to unravel a vexing challenge.

The language problem had surfaced as soon as the first talks began in London. These negotiations had been confusing enough, with English-, French-, and Russian-speaking principals trying to hammer out the charter. But what were they going to do in the courtroom when an American prosecutor's questions had to be understood by a German-speaking defendant and the German's response had to be understood by one judge who spoke Russian, another who spoke French, and a third who spoke English? Jackson had sent his son, Bill, to Geneva to find out how the League of Nations handled the situation. Bill's report was discouraging. What they did at the League, he found out, was consecutive translation from written documents. A translator read in French, then another in English, another in Spanish, and on and on. At that rate, Jackson realized, the trial would drag on forever. But while in Geneva, Bill had learned about something promising that IBM was working on in the States. How would he like a chance to get back to Washington and see his wife and check up on this system? his father had asked. Bill leaped at the opportunity.

In an auditorium at the Pentagon, Horsky and young Jackson were met by a short, dapper army colonel with a pronounced French accent. Leon Dostert was a naturalized American citizen, former head of the French department at Georgetown University, more recently an interpreter for General Eisenhower. Dostert asked Horsky and Ensign Jackson to have a seat midway back in the auditorium and proceeded to place earphones on their heads. On the stage were three men and a woman, each with a separate microphone. Off to one side, an IBM engineer stood before a control panel.

Dostert called out to the woman on the stage, who began to speak extemporaneously in English about some of the tourist attractions of

Washington. The three men began speaking into their microphones in a babel of tongues. Dostert smiled triumphantly toward Horsky and Jackson. But the smile faded instantly when he saw their puzzled expressions. "Nothing?" he asked. Dostert cursed in French and went up to the stage and conferred with the engineer. He signaled the woman to start speaking again. A piercing feedback shot through the earphones. The engineer fiddled with the terminals and dials, and Dostert gave another signal to the woman. What did they hear now? he asked his visitors. English, Bill Jackson answered. Dostert shouted an instruction to the engineer. What now? Dostert asked. French, Horsky answered. A triumphant Dostert called out again. What were they hearing now? Russian. And now? German.

What they were getting, Dostert explained, was everything the young woman had been saying in English translated, almost as she spoke, into the three other languages that would be used in the trial. Obviously, the gremlins still had to be worked out, Dostert admitted. But IBM was eager to pioneer the world's first system of simultaneous interpretation. The company believed it could perfect the technology by the time the trial began.

Horsky cabled Robert Jackson that afternoon. If IBM could make the system work, a trial in four languages could proceed almost as rapidly as a trial in one.

16

CAPTAIN DANIEL KILEY HAD one thing in common with his new boss, Robert Jackson. Neither man held a degree in the profession he practiced. Kiley had studied architecture at Harvard just long enough to know that he needed no formal education to pursue his visions. What he did best was devise the optimal use of space. This was what he had been doing in Washington as the thirty-year-old head of his own firm, developing wartime housing. Later, he was recruited into Bill Donovan's OSS. Kiley became chief of the Presentations Branch, which, among other tasks, built mockups of clandestine targets.

Kiley's appearance belied his character. He was delicate, almost elfin-looking, and had never weighed more than 130 pounds. The slight frame, however, pulsated with energy and contained a will of steel. "I never take no for an answer," he liked to say.

Late in August, Kiley arrived at Nuremberg's Grand Hotel and was assigned room 412, the Adolf Hitler suite. The army had been instructed that this mild-looking, low-ranking officer enjoyed carte blanche, for Kiley's assignment was to restore the Palace of Justice for the war-crimes trials.

The next morning, an army car and driver were waiting outside the hotel for Kiley. He had come to Nuremberg earlier, on the last Jackson trip, and now he noted that the smell of buried bodies was slowly being overcome by disinfectant. Still, he found disconcerting the sight of German women performing heavy labor, loading rubble into small cars and hauling it away on movable rails.

When Kiley arrived at the Palace of Justice, a broad-chested army colonel eyed him uncertainly, as though this were not the man he expected. The officer came forward and asked if he might be Captain Kiley. Kiley nodded curtly. The colonel introduced himself as John F. Corley, commander of the First Division's battalion of engineers, and added that whatever Kiley wanted, he would get. Kiley headed wordlessly for the courthouse.

After two silent hours of scouring the building, Kiley and Corley reemerged into the sunlight of the courtyard. Kiley turned to the colonel. He wanted carpenters, plasterers, electricians, plumbers, even chimney sweeps, recruited locally or flown in, if necessary. They would need 250 German POWs as laborers. They were going to double the size of the courtroom, vertically and horizontally. He wanted the rear wall taken out and the attic over the courtroom cut into for a visitors' gallery. Throw out all those fancy chandeliers and that gingerbread molding, he ordered, and install fluorescent lighting. He wanted office space for six hundred personnel. And they would need cabinetmakers to build office furniture. He preferred white oak. He would design the furniture himself.

Colonel Corley scribbled on a notepad. They would also need glass, tiles, brick, and plywood, Kiley went on. Corley, a man used to getting things done, nevertheless, interrupted to ask where in this ravaged city they would find these materials. There were factories around Nuremberg, Kiley said. Just put them back into operation. The glass they could fly in from Belgium. He started to head for the waiting car. When would he be back? Corley asked. In a day or so, Kiley answered. He was going to Ansbach, where he had seen some seats in a theater. They would be just right for the visitors' gallery.

17

THEY LOOKED SO FORLORN, these onetime goliaths of the Reich, Hans Frank thought. Here was Field Marshal Keitel, once the very model of a Prussian Junker officer, the discolorations visible where the insignia had been ripped off his uniform, still clicking his heels every time Göring passed by. And Wilhelm Frick, a lawyer like himself, promulgator of the Nuremberg Laws, wearing an incongruous plaid sport jacket with all the buttons done up the front. Most pathetic were Robert Ley and Julius Streicher, who had arrived at Nuremberg with only the clothes on their backs. The U.S. Army had issued them dyed black fatigues, class X, which meant "unfit for further use." One thing could be said for Ley, Frank thought. Here in prison was the only place he had ever seen the former head of the German Labor Front sober. Their belts, suspenders, and shoelaces had been taken away. On August 12, they had been marched into C wing, one of four cellblocks that radiated from a central core in the prison behind the courthouse. Cells lined both sides of the wing and ran up three tiers served by a spiral stairwell at each end.

"I have been here before, several times," said Streicher, a short, bald, powerfully built man of sixty who spoke with an air of foolish pride. Before the Nazis took power, he had indeed been jailed for slandering Jews. Of all the prisoners, it was Streicher whom Hans Frank loathed most. This vulgar little man robbed Nazism of even the pretense of respectability. Streicher was founder and editor of *Der Stürmer*, the anti-Semitic newspaper that read on a comic-book level. Frank would not have been caught dead reading Streicher's rag. "There is a plaque," Streicher said wistfully. "It used to be over my cell, number 258, in another wing." Cell 258 had been a tourist stop for faithful Nazis visiting Nuremberg in palmier days. The plaque had since been torn off by a GI souvenir hunter.

A German-speaking U.S. sergeant told Streicher to shut up. He called off their names and assigned each prisoner a cell. Frank entered number 14. What struck him instantly was the stale air, as though it too had been imprisoned. The walls were stained and unclean. The only fresh patches were where hooks, protrusions, and electrical connections had been pulled out and plastered over. Immediately to the right, Frank spotted a toilet in an alcove, with no door, no toilet seat. An iron cot with a filthy mattress occupied the left wall. Opposite it, on the other side of the cell, was a table. Frank tapped the top. It was made of flimsy cardboard. A steam pipe ran along the back of the cell and above it a small barred window exposed a patch of gray sky.

Frank was startled by the metallic slamming of an iron bolt. He walked to the door and looked out of a square porthole. A pair of GI eyes stared back. This was not going to be Wawel Castle.

Colonel Andrus tried to dictate over the cacophony of banging hammers, shouting voices, and the rumble of wheelbarrows outside his office door. Captain Kiley's restoration was in full sway. The blazon was to be on a field of azure, the colonel repeated to a GI serving as his secretary, one who was clearly unfamiliar with the language of heraldry. "The bordure is sable, charged in chief with a key argent. . . ." Andrus was determined to make of his prison staff an elite unit, and nothing, he believed, added more to unit pride than distinctive insignia and uniforms. He was personally designing a coat of arms for the 6850th Internal Security Detachment, the ISD, as his prison command had been designated. He had sketched a shield with a key at the top to symbolize prison security, the scales of justice in the middle, and, at the bottom, a broken Nazi eagle. He could envision numerous uses for the coat of arms: the ISD shoulder patch, a letterhead, a pin for female staffers. His keenest hope was to have Justice Jackson adopt his design as the official symbol of the IMT.

Andrus heard a tapping over the din. His visitor was Major Douglas Kelley, an army psychiatrist. The army had recognized that sound minds had to be produced before the IMT, along with sound bodies; and so Kelley had been assigned to the prison. Headshrinkers, as the colonel called them, were an alien species to this career soldier. He had been relieved, however, to find Kelley a genial, witty man and not some brooding behavioral mystic.

Kelley saluted casually and asked for a few minutes of the colonel's time. Once they had the prisoners settled in, Kelley said, he believed they should set up a small library for them. They were going to have a great deal of time on their hands. It was the kind of request that rankled Andrus, and he reminded Kelley of his principal mission, to keep him advised of suicidal tendencies among his charges. That was precisely the problem, Kelley explained. They had to keep the prisoners' minds occupied. Andrus relented. "All right, I don't want them to go stir-crazy. A guy could go nuts in a little cell with what some of those boys have on their minds." As Kelley started to leave, Andrus asked him to stick around. He was going to give the guard detachment its first briefing in a few minutes, and it might be useful to have the psychiatrist watch.

Corporal Emilio DiPalma, a combat veteran of the First Division— the "Big Red One"—lacked enough points to be shipped home yet. He had been assigned, with other GIs at loose ends, to report to the ISD. On a late August afternoon, DiPalma found himself with a dozen other soldiers standing in the exercise yard, a plot of hard earth and straggling weeds between C wing and a building the GIs used as a gym. A sergeant's bellow brought them to attention. A party of officers emerged from cellblock C into the yard. In the lead strode a colonel whom DiPalma studied closely. The character of his new commanding officer would determine the quality of his life from now until he got out of the army. The officer's uniform was pressed to razor-edged sharpness. The shellacked green helmet was something new to Di-Palma, and that riding crop tucked under the arm did not suggest an easygoing civilian in uniform.

Colonel Andrus ordered the men at ease, though there was nothing easy in his voice or manner. Andrus began speaking softly but firmly in the faint drawl adopted so often by career officers. They were, as of now, he informed them, part of the ISD, and it was going to be a proud unit, charged with a historic task: guarding the worst criminals mankind had ever known. The first thing that they as "sentinels" had to understand was that these men were prisoners of war. Their rank did not matter. There was to be no exchange of salutes or other military courtesies. When a sentinel entered a cell, the prisoners were to stand. When an American came down a corridor, prisoners were to stand aside.

The colonel's continual reference to them as sentinels, not guards, made DiPalma uneasy. The word had an unwelcome spit-and-polish ring to a combat veteran. Sentinels, Andrus went on, would pull twenty-four hours on and twenty-four hours off. When they were on duty, they would spend two hours on the cellblock and four hours off. A dayroom had been provided on the third floor of cellblock C. Cards, Ping-Pong, bunks, and books would be available there. Each guard was responsible for four cells, Andrus went on. No more than thirty seconds were ever to elapse before a sentinel peered through the porthole directly into the cells to observe his four prisoners. A sentinel's chief responsibility was to keep these men alive. At no time were the prisoners ever to be allowed to talk to one another or to the sentinels. Nor were the sentinels to talk to each other. DiPalma began to imagine two-hour stints lasting an eternity.

The rest of Andrus's talk was a drone of daily routines. Breakfast at seven a.m. Afterward, defendants mop and clean their cells. Lunch at twelve, supper at six. Cold showers once a week. Library privileges in the afternoon. Lights out at nine p.m., at which time prisoners were to turn in their glasses, pens, and watches, anything that could cut or stab. Cells were to be inspected whenever prisoners were out of them; and that included the sentinel putting his head down low for a good look inside the toilet bowl. Virtually all of Andrus's pronouncements were followed by, "Failure to obey will be considered a court-martial offense."

Sentinels would be unarmed on the cellblock, the colonel said. However, a leather blackjack packed with cotton and lead pellets would hang beside each cell door. The sentinels were to carry this club only when accompanying prisoners outside the cell. If they had to use the blackjack, they were to apply it only to the elbows and shoulders. A blackjack, Andrus explained, was the ideal jailer's weapon. It hurt like hell but did not break the skin.

The voice became almost paternal. "Just about all of you men have seen combat," the colonel said. "You've seen the bodies of your buddies on the roadsides, in the woods, hanging out of burned-out tanks. You've seen the cemeteries where your friends will never earn enough points to get home. These prisoners are the men who put them there. Your job is to see that they survive long enough to be brought to justice. That is all." As Andrus turned to leave, Emilio DiPalma did not know if he liked or disliked the colonel under whom he was now to serve.

The next day, the corporal of the guard came bursting into Colonel Andrus's office in the Palace of Justice. "Dr. Pfluecker says you got to come right away," he said breathlessly.

As Andrus entered the cellblock, the old German physician explained that, after breakfast, a guard had handed Göring a mop and pail and ordered the *Reichsmarschall* to clean his cell. Göring had raged and then collapsed on his bed, breathing unnaturally. Dr. Pfluecker was called and found him in tachycardia—a rapid heartbeat, the doctor explained—two hundred to three hundred beats a minute. It could lead to heart failure. He had given Göring a shot and he was resting comfortably.

Andrus was enraged. Less than twenty-four hours had elapsed since he had issued his first regulations and already the worst of the prisoners was presenting him with an impossible choice. He went to Göring's cell and stared through the port. The bulky figure was stretched on his cot. No matter what his personal feelings, his mission was to keep the prisoners alive. Andrus accepted that he would have to make a medical exception. In the future, one of the POW prison staff was to be assigned to clean Göring's cell. Mastery of the prison was going to be a contest of wills, Andrus recognized, and round one, it seemed, had gone to Hermann Göring.

18

ON SEPTEMBER 5, 1945, Justice Jackson was back briefly in Washington for consultations with the president. Jackson was impressed by Harry Truman. Not that the man possessed a shred of the grandeur of his predecessor—quite the contrary. It was the quiet confidence with which this common man filled the shoes of a giant that had won Jackson's admiration.

What rank did he want for the Nuremberg job? Truman asked with a knowing smile. No rank, Jackson replied. Nor did he have the slightest desire at this point in his life to start wearing gold braid and epaulettes. That was not what he meant, Truman explained. Simulated rank was what he had in mind. He knew all about the military from his days as an artilleryman in the last war. Without rank, Truman said, Jackson would have trouble getting a haircut from the army, much less proper support for a major trial. How about lieutenant general? Truman asked. Jackson admitted that it had a pleasant ring.

Truman mentioned that he needed to appoint an American judge and an alternate to the court. What did Jackson think of Francis Biddle, the recently dismissed attorney general, as the principal judge? Jackson was caught off guard. He was temporarily leaving the Supreme Court to associate himself with what he expected to be a historic event in law. The appointment of less than a great jurist to sit on the Nuremberg bench would diminish the occasion. Francis Biddle had served a few unhappy months as a judge on a federal circuit court, where he had not distinguished himself, and he had gladly left to succeed Jackson as attorney general. Biddle, in Jackson's estimate, did not qualify for the IMT. Instead of responding to Truman's suggestion, Jackson raised the name of Owen J. Roberts, recently retired as associate justice of the Supreme Court. Roberts would not take the job, Truman answered; he had already asked. What about John Parker, Jackson suggested, naming a distinguished judge on the Fourth Circuit Court of Appeals. Jackson knew that Parker had missed going on the Supreme Court in 1930 by a heartbreaking single vote. The Senate had tied on his appointment, and Vice President Charles Curtis could not be found in time to break the tie. Truman said that he would happily name Parker, but as the alternate.

The next day, Jackson got a call from Francis Biddle, who asked if he could come out to Hickory Hill. The Jacksons and the Biddles had been part of a tight Washington social set. They were often in each other's homes and had gone to the Chicago Democratic Convention together in 1936 to see Roosevelt nominated for a second term. Still, Jackson did not want Biddle at Nuremberg. He had talked the matter over with Bill Donovan, and Donovan agreed. Jackson also thought that his lukewarm reaction to Biddle had dissuaded the president from naming him. He wondered what Biddle wanted.

The man who came to Hickory Hill was a lean, tanned Philadelphia aristocrat, aloof in appearance, but unaccustomedly humble this day. Jackson was obviously in the throes of preparing to move to

Nuremberg, and Biddle apologized for taking up his time. Neverthe-less, he said, he thought they ought to have a chat in light of their probable close professional relationship in the future. He had been vacationing in Quebec province, Biddle said, when the White House switchboard tracked him down. He had simply been killing time since being dropped as attorney general, and the prospect of returning to private practice in Philadelphia, after the adrenaline charge of the New Deal, appalled him. Truman's offer had arrived like a life ring thrown to a drowning man.

The way that Truman had fired him as attorney general had been clumsy and painful, Biddle went on. Of course, he had worked against Truman's nomination for vice president in 1944, and he supposed that was the reason why Truman resented him. But to fire him by a phone call from a White House staffer? That was poor form. After being asked to resign, he had asked for an appointment with the president. With the two of them alone in the Oval Office, Biddle continued, he told Harry Truman that he had expected his dismissal; but shouldn't Truman have called him in personally and asked for his resignation? That was how these things were done. After that, Biddle said, he got up to leave, and as he did so, he put his hand on the president's shoulder and said, "You see. It's not so hard."

Jackson accepted the story, including the final touch. It was just the sort of Main Line condescension that would have made Tru-man dislike Biddle. But now, at least, Jackson understood why Biddle had been given the Nuremberg judgeship. It was Truman's bad conscience.

Since Biddle was going to take the job, Jackson said, he hoped that he would fly to Germany as soon as possible. Organizing a four-power bench from scratch was going to take time. Was Irene coming? Biddle asked. No, Jackson answered, his wife was not coming. Biddle said that he hoped he would be able to bring his Katherine along. Jackson rose and jammed his hands into his pockets—his favored courtroom stance. Europe was full of GIs, he said, who had been separated from their families for years. It would be the worst possible blow to the morale of these men to allow VIPs to bring their wives. General Patton had already ruled that since his GIs could not have their spouses in the American Zone of occupation, no one else could. He fully supported Patton's position, Jackson said. Biddle had no idea what a sinkhole Nuremberg was. The smell of death, the plague of rats, the mood of gloom. It was no place for an American woman. Yes, Biddle said, he understood perfectly. As soon as he could put together some sort of staff, he would make arrangements to get to Germany quickly.

Soon after his conversation with Jackson, Francis Biddle called on President Truman in order to accept formally his appointment to the IMT. He took the occasion to ask if he might have the president's permission to bring his wife to Nuremberg eventually. Yes, Truman said, still wanting placate a man he had wronged. Biddle also arranged for passage to Europe, not by air, but by sea.

19

Major Douglas Kelley had another request of Colonel Andrus. The prisoners desperately needed exercise, he warned. Andrus looked skeptical. He had earlier allowed women prisoners from another wing into the exercise yard, including the notorious Ilse Koch, wife of the commandant at Buchenwald concentration camp. As the women came out, the guards had lined up and urinated in their direction. He wanted no more such spectacles, Andrus said.

Kelley pressed on. "Exercise is important to relieve psychological stress," he explained. "The tension these men are under causes an endocrine imbalance which produces psychological debilitation and . . ." Kelley sensed that he was boring Andrus. What he meant was that exercise let off destructive steam. He would think about it, Andrus said.

On September 11, a memo to the staff crossed Kelley's desk, entitled "Exercise Yard, Regulations Governing." Kelley scanned it. No talking, no sitting down, no picking up anything, thirty feet between prisoners, twenty minutes per day. But, at least, Kelley had persuaded the colonel.

On the first day in the exercise yard, Göring, disregarding the colonel's rule, delivered a pep talk to his fellow inmates. They were in prison, he said, for one reason only. They had lost the war. But someday a grateful nation would honor them with marble sarcophagi. He himself, Göring said merrily, expected a special place in Valhalla. "Shut up and spread out!" a guard barked.

The military men walked in single file, Dönitz, Keitel, and Jodl, purposeful and silent. In another corner the untouchables milled uncertainly, like lost molecules trying to attach themselves to a larger organism: Streicher, founder of the Jew-baiting *Der Stürmer*, running in place, working up a sweat that glistened on his bald, neckless head; the towering Kaltenbrunner, lurching from group to group; runty Fritz Sauckel, labor "plenipotentiary" of the Reich, the man who had herded millions of workers from their homelands and delivered them to the Nazi war machine. The loner by choice was Hjalmar Schacht, whose haughty air made clear that he had no business among such people. The prisoner who most concerned Major Kelley these days was Robert Ley, destroyer of German labor unions and creator of the ersatz Nazi Labor Front. Ley looked disoriented, stumbling about the yard with the halting steps and furtive glances of a cornered animal.

"Time's up!" a sergeant shouted, and the ragtag collection formed into a single line to return to the cellblock that was now their home.

20

THE FIRST THING Robert Jackson observed on his return to Nuremberg on September 13 was that the nonfraternization rule was being torn to shreds. On the way in from Y28 his party drove along a street that had become a flesh market, with knots of GIs and German women engaged in intimate negotiations. They were heading for the suburbs—Jackson and his son, Bill, Elsie Douglas, housing officer John Vonetes, and Colonel Robert J. Gill, a handsome, wealthy Baltimore lawyer who was expected to relieve Jackson of the administrative duties he loathed. The party also included a bodyguard and driver. Vonetes had commandeered for Jackson a sixteen-cylinder Mercedes-Benz touring car with six forward speeds that had formerly belonged to Joachim von Ribbentrop. He would keep this car for ceremonial occasions, Jackson said, but for everyday use he wanted something less ostentatious.

And a bodyguard? Jackson protested. He had no desire to have some plug-ugly following him day and night. Still, the clean-cut young sergeant assigned to protect him, Moritz Fuchs, hardly seemed cast to type. How much did his protector weigh? Jackson asked. About 155 pounds, the five-foot-nine-inch Fuchs answered. It did not seem like much protection, Jackson observed with amusement.

They entered Dambach, a village of solid homes on the western edge of Nuremberg barely brushed by the war. The huge car slid to a stop before a buff-colored stucco home at 33 Lindenstrasse. The door was opened by a stout woman who introduced herself in English as Mrs. Hassel. "I am your housekeeper," she said. "I have lived five years in America." Her attitude was servile, except when she addressed the rest of the staff, which included a maid, a cook, a cook's helper, a waiter, and three gardeners.

Vonetes conducted them to the justice's bedroom on the second floor, then to Mrs. Douglas's room.

Each of three bedrooms had its own bath. The tub in the master bedroom was four feet deep and six feet long. Jackson noted the shower, sitz bath, tub, and bidet, which, he observed, would allow him to bathe standing, sitting, lying, or squatting, according to his mood. What did Jackson think of his billet? Vonetes asked. The house, Jackson said, combined all that was godawful in Teutonic taste; everything was heavy and gloomy. But it would do fine. That evening, he and Elsie Douglas stood looking out the picture window of the room he had chosen as his study. What did Bob guess all those sullen faces they saw in the streets thought about the forthcoming trial? she asked. People without a roof over their head and empty bellies did not much care what happened to Hermann Göring, Jackson believed.

21

JOHN HARLAN AMEN, "the Tom Dewey of Brooklyn," now head of the interrogation division, had brought a formidable reputation to Nuremberg. In civilian life, Amen had successfully prosecuted the notorious Louis "Lepke" Buchalter of Murder Incorporated, the outfit that killed for a fee. But his specialty had been nailing crooked politicians in over a hundred corruption cases. He was hard-driving, hard-living, hard-drinking, and a womanizer with a penchant for the dramatic, his favorite role being that of Mr. District Attorney. His first drink went down while he was shaving in the morning, and there was little letup all day. The alcohol appeared to have remarkably little effect on Amen. One colleague had dubbed him "the sterling knight of the bed, the bottle, and the ego." Amen was also engaged in a rivalry with the more placid Bob Storey for Jackson's favor.

Amen had gone out to 33 Lindenstrasse to discuss a sticky ethical question. To interrogate these prisoners would be the equivalent of a district attorney's going into a cell and questioning a defendant for evidence that could be used against him in a trial. To meet the legal niceties of this situation, they concluded that, since none of these men had been formally indicted yet, they were still technically prisoners of war—and POWs could be interrogated. As they parted, Jackson asked Amen if he would take his son, Bill, along the next time an interesting interrogation came up. The experience would do a young lawyer good.

On a late September morning, with Bill Jackson in tow, Amen headed for room 55, the interrogation room in the Palace of Justice, to question an obscure but promising figure. As they entered, Amen ordered the American guards to clear out a POW work party that was still putting the finishing touches of plaster on the ceiling. Amen tilted his chair against the wall and lit a cigarette. A guard appeared with one of the least appetizing prisoners the two Americans had yet seen. Albert Göring was an engineer by profession; he was a year younger than his brother, Hermann, and bore not the slightest resemblance to him. GI fatigues hung on his skeletal frame like clothes on a coat hanger. He was bald and his skin was sallow. That morning a prison doctor had counted over seventy carbuncles on his back and neck; some of them poked above his collar.

Albert Göring immediately began complaining about the injustice of his plight. He had always been anti-Nazi. He had voluntarily approached the Americans the day after the war ended, and they had rewarded him by throwing him into jail. That was no way to treat a man who had been arrested by the Gestapo four times for helping Jews and for calling Hitler a criminal. Never mind Albert's attitude toward the Jews, Amen said through the interpreter, he wanted to know about brother Hermann's attitudes.

That, the younger Göring said, was not so simple. His brother was not a deep or consistent thinker. Hermann was motivated by the whim of the moment. Was the colonel aware, for example, that Hermann had saved the lives of two old Jews after Kristallnacht? He had been badly wounded during the failed Munich beer-hall putsch of 1923—Hitler's attempt to overthrow the Bavarian government. A policeman's bullet had ricocheted off the Odeonplatz and struck Hermann in the groin. Storm troopers had carried him into the nearby house of Ilse Ballin, the Jewish wife of a furniture dealer. Frau Ballin and her sister had tenderly cared for the young Nazi, who would otherwise have bled to death. Fifteen years later, in 1938, after storm troopers had gone on their window-smashing rampage against Jewish store owners, Hermann sent a Luftwaffe aide to find the two sisters. Exit visas were arranged for them, and they got out of Germany with all their money, Albert explained, thanks to Hermann.

Amen's tilted chair came crashing to the floor. Wasn't this the same Hermann Göring, he said, who also proposed that the Jews be assessed a billion marks to save the insurance companies who would have to pay for all that broken glass? That was Hermann, Albert conceded, a bundle of contradictions.

Amen nodded to Bill Jackson to take over the questioning. Had he ever discussed the plight of the Jews directly with Hermann? young Jackson asked. A friend of his, Albert said, had come back from Poland and told him that Jews were being herded aboard trains like cattle, taken somewhere and machine-gunned, even women and children. Albert had written to Hermann reporting this matter. What happened then? Jackson wanted to know. When he got no answer, Albert said, he made an inquiry and was told that his report had been referred to the "appropriate department." Which meant? Jackson asked. Himmler's SS, Albert answered.

Albert noted that he probably could do himself good by denouncing his brother. But he just could not bring himself to do it. Hermann had bailed him out every time the Gestapo had arrested him. Hermann had gotten him a good job at the Hungarian office of the Skoda works. Though Hermann considered this brother the black sheep of the family, he had been good to him.

22

J<small>OHN</small> H<small>ARLAN</small> A<small>MEN</small> <small>RUSHED</small> to Jackson's unfinished offices and told Elsie Douglas that he had to see the chief right away. Mrs. Douglas sat amid a chaos of overspilling cardboard boxes, typing at an Underwood set on a crate. She herself, however, looked crisp in the uniform without rank or insignia that most of the civilian trial staff had adopted. Amen apologized to Jackson for the interruption, but said he was sure Jackson would want to see immediately the letter he had brought.

The handwriting was cramped, the English stilted, yet Jackson found the message electrifying. Joachim von Ribbentrop had written that he was ready to take full responsibility for the actions of the leaders jailed with him. If Ribbentrop was ready to take responsibility for the crimes of the regime, then they would be acknowledged, per se, as crimes, and the prosecution was halfway home. Ribbentrop had set a condition, however. He would take responsibility, he wrote, only if the Allies dropped the trial. They would cross that bridge when they came to it, Jackson told Amen. In the meantime, he intended to interrogate this prisoner himself.

As they threaded their way through an obstacle course of scaffolding and carpenter's horses on the way to the interrogation room, Amen briefed Jackson. Ever since his arrest, Ribbentrop had been acting bizarrely, writing letters to Winston Churchill and Anthony Eden, offering to come to England to explain why war between the British and German peoples had been a tragic error. He babbled incessantly about the titled Britons he expected to call in as witnesses in his defense, including King George VI and Lady Astor. Amen reminded Jackson that Hitler, in his last will and testament, had dumped Ribbentrop as foreign minister for Arthur Seyss-Inquart. Between that shock and the subsequent blow of being cited as a war criminal, Amen said, Ribbentrop's mental stability was questionable. Jackson stopped before room 55 and braced himself for his first face-to-face encounter with a Nazi.

Ribbentrop jumped to his feet as Jackson entered. The former foreign minister wore a shapeless gray suit, a frayed shirt with no tie, and laceless shoes. His manner suggested that of a whipped dog. The two Americans sat down behind the interrogators' table, facing Ribbentrop. When one of Amen's cigarettes rolled off the table, the German started to dive for it, but caught himself at the last second. Amen picked up the cigarette and handed it to Ribbentrop, who stuffed it into his jacket pocket as Jackson posed his first question.

Jackson's annoyance was visible, his face flushed and his voice harsh. He was only in this room, he said, because Ribbentrop had written that he was ready to take responsibility for the acts of his fellow prisoners. Specifically, what was he taking responsibility for? Could Jackson finally get a straight answer? Ribbentrop continued to emit a verbal fog, as he had done for the past fifteen minutes. "Let's try again," Jackson said. "Do you take responsibility for the war of aggression?" Of course not, an injured Ribbentrop answered. What about the violation of treaties? Ribbentrop's answer was unintelligible. "Are you responsible for the shooting of American airmen?" No, he could not have done that, Ribbentrop replied. What about the deportation of slave labor? Another muddled answer. The mistreatment of Russian prisoners of war? The shooting of hostages? The destruction of Lidice? The Warsaw Ghetto? The concentration camps? No. No. No. No, Ribbentrop replied plaintively.

"Do you at least take responsibility for the foreign policy of the Third Reich?" Jackson asked. Again, Ribbentrop demurred, saying that he did not know the foreign policy. Jackson's eyes rolled in disbelief. "Do you really want me to go to my associates and tell them that the foreign minister of the Reich didn't know what the foreign policy was?" "I am sorry," Ribbentrop said. "I must tell you that the Führer never revealed his aims to anybody."

Striding angrily toward his office, Jackson told Amen this was the last time he expected to set foot in the interrogation center. The waste of time with Ribbentrop had convinced him that the documentary route was the best way to convict these people. Certainly, nothing coming out of the prisoners' mouths would help. Jackson's words troubled Amen. He had hoped this firsthand experience would hook Jackson on the importance of calling witnesses. Instead, documents, the domain of Amen's archrival Robert Storey, were winning the day.

23

THE GUARDS PREFERRED duty on the second tier of cellblock C, where the less important Nazis were held. Here, as they put it, they caught less of Colonel Andrus's chickenshit. The corporal responsible for the last four cells on the floor this Friday morning, October 5, was leaning sleepily against the stairwell when Willi Krug appeared at 6:30 a.m. with his washbasins. Willi smiled mechanically and nodded as he passed by. Seconds later, Krug let out a cry. The startled soldier came running.

Colonel Andrus was shaving when he received the call from the duty officer. Within twenty minutes he was entering cell 110. Andrus studied the bloated, purple face of Dr. Leonardo Conti, chief of health in Heinrich Himmler's SS. Conti was known as the "mercy killing doctor," specializing in quick, painless injections that eliminated inmates of asylums, jails, and homes for the aged. He was not a major defendant, but was being held for later trial. Conti had fashioned a noose from a towel, tied one end to the middle bar of his window, and jumped off his chair. "Cut him down," Andrus ordered.

The point was not to panic, to think through how this disaster had happened and to make sure it could not happen again, Andrus told himself. But first there was the galling necessity of informing his superior, the commanding officer of the Nuremberg-Furth Enclave, that Burton Andrus had lost his first prisoner.

They had not even had their breakfast yet, Kaltenbrunner complained as the prisoners filed down the stairwell to the basement shower room. The corporal of the guard ordered them to strip and face the wall. An army doctor arrived and told the prisoners to "bend over and spread your cheeks." Ribbentrop translated the order for the others. As the doctor went by, peering up their rectums, other GIs searched their clothing, producing a nail from one pocket, a broken razor from another, a tiny file from a third. After the search, the prisoners were marched into the exercise yard and told to sit on the ground, no closer than thirty feet apart. Hours went by as a crew of Dan Kiley's POW workmen ripped the bars out of the cell windows in cellblock C, plastered over the holes, and covered the windows with something the army called "cello-glass," which admitted only a blurred patch of sky. When the prisoners returned to the block, they found that they had been assigned new cells. The guards warned them that their chairs were never to be placed within four feet of any wall. Colonel's orders.

The plan agreed upon at headquarters command was that Conti would be taken to the base hospital, where he would be pronounced dead of unknown causes *after* his arrival. A report of the actual manner of his death, classified top secret, was spirited back to Third Army Headquarters in Heidelberg. As the days slipped by and no inquiries were made by the press, the prison staff began to relax.

24

TURBULENCE OVER the English Channel tossed the RAF Anson about like a kite. Dr. Ellis Jones noticed his patient's stricken expression and shoved a pail under his chin, into which Rudolf Hess vomited. Hess felt embarrassed at getting sick in a plane. He was a skilled pilot who, just five years before, had carried out one of the most sensational flights of the war.

In 1940, Hess had been deputy führer, the third-ranking Nazi in Germany, one of a handful of old party fighters whom Hitler addressed by the familiar *du*. That August, Hess had been visited by his old professor from the University of Munich, Dr. Karl Haushofer, the seminal influence on young Rudolf's thinking. The professor taught geopolitics and believed that the Anglo-Saxons and Germans, possessing superior blood, were destined to rule the world. As a student, Hess had drunk deeply of the professor's wisdom. They had remained close, and Hess usually refered to Haushofer as "Uncle Karl."

One Sunday afternoon, after a vegetarian dinner that Hess had inflicted on his mentor, Haushofer suggested that they go for a walk in the Grünwald. He was unhappy, the professor said, that Germany was at war with England. War between these racial cousins made no sense. When Germany went to war against Russia, as she inevitably must, she would face a geopolitical disaster. England would bring in the might of the United States from the West. Germany would face the Bolshevik hordes in the East. The fatherland would be crushed between two jaws. Somehow, Germany had to make peace with the British. Haushofer had an idea. His son, Albrecht, also a professor at Berlin's Hochschule für Politik, was a personal friend of the duke of Hamilton, and the duke was in contact with Churchill and King George. Haushofer proposed that his son write to the duke through a woman he knew in neutral Portugal, and suggest that Albrecht and Hamilton get together in Lisbon. What did Hess think of the idea? the professor asked. Hess explained that he too had a passing acquaintance with the duke, whom he had met at the 1936 Berlin Olympics. He had invited the Briton to his home for lunch in view of their common interest in aviation. Uncle Karl's idea, he concluded, was splendid.

The letter was sent on September 23, 1940. Its contents were made known to the duke, but not as Haushofer and Hess had hoped. The letter had been intercepted by British censors. Such correspondence to an English nobleman, now on active duty with the RAF, aroused the suspicions of British intelligence. Hamilton was closely questioned about the letter and his relationship with Albrecht Haushofer.

As weeks went by and the younger Haushofer received no response, an obsession began to take root in the mind of Rudolf Hess. Hess recognized that he was being elbowed out of the Führer's inner circle by craftier players. Once, cooling his heels in the Führer's anteroom, he had complained to Felix Kersten, an aide to Heinrich Himmler, of his neglect. He was determined, he told Kersten, to do something spectacular, to make of his life "one great deed."

Flying was Hess's passion. In 1934 he had won a race around the Zugspitze; but Hitler, furious that one of his chief lieutenants had risked his life for a ridiculous trophy, had ordered Hess grounded. Secretly, however, Hess persuaded Willi Messerschmitt, the aeronautical engineer, to let him fly Messerschmitt's ME-108 and ME-109 fighter planes out of the company's Augsburg works. He then persuaded Messerschmitt to let him try the still secret ME-110. Over a cup of coffee one morning, Hess bet the engineer that he could not add two more fuel tanks to the plane without losing maneuverability. Messerschmitt took up the challenge. An ME-110 was refitted, and Hess was ready to attempt his "one great deed."

In December 1940, he went to the Augsburg field determined to embark on his solitary crusade. In order not to let even his secretary know what he was up to, Hess carried a peace proposal that he had written in longhand. The weather, however, proved unflyable. He actually got into the air in January 1941, but turned back because of a faulty aileron. Later, he made a third attempt, and again the weather defeated him.

On April 27, 1941, Hitler announced to his inner circle his intention to invade the Soviet Union in eight weeks. Hess heard the words in a confusion of fear and exhilaration. Here was Uncle Karl's nightmare come true, Germany entangled in a two-front war. Hess determined that he must reach the duke of Hamilton and talk England out of the war before Germany attacked Russia. On May 10, a quiet Saturday afternoon, he drove out to the Augsburg field, wearing a Luftwaffe uniform so that he would not be treated in Britain as a spy. He dared not confide his intention to anyone except his aide, Karlheinz Pintsch, and Professor Haushofer. Yet Hess was sure Hitler would approve of his mission. The Führer shared Haushofer's view that enmity between Germany and England made no sense. Hitler was only unhappy that England refused to see the light.

Hess had the mechanics at the Messerschmitt works roll out the ME-110 with the extra fuel tanks. He handed Pintsch a letter to deliver personally to the Führer. In it he described his intention to seek out an Anglo-German peace. Hess added that if his enterprise failed, "it will always be possible for you to deny all responsibility. Simply say that I was out of my mind." By 5:45 p.m., Hess was airborne with nine hundred miles of night flying and devilish navigation ahead of him, much of it over the North Sea. His destination was Dungavel Hill, thirty miles south of Glasgow, ancestral seat of the duke of Hamilton.

Five hours later he approached his objective. Hess doubted that he could land the plane without being shot out of the sky first. And so, from an altitude of twenty thousand feet, he made his first parachute jump. David McLean, a Scottish plowman, discovered Hess in a field of barley, trying to slip out of his chute. As the Scot approached, Hess smiled his bucktoothed grin and announced in English, "I have an important message for the duke of Hamilton." He later liked to boast that he had landed thirteen feet from his destination. It was more like thirty miles from Dungavel Hill. Still, it had been extraordinary flying.

After reading Hess's letter, a stunned Hitler was uncertain how to handle the affair. Yes, peace with England. But the number-three Nazi dropping unannounced out of the sky into the enemy camp? No one was going to take this lunatic seriously. After waiting two days, still not knowing if Hess had arrived in Britain, Hitler decided to take the man's advice. He issued a statement on May 12 that read: "Party member Rudolf Hess has set out on an unauthorized flight from Augsburg and has not yet returned. A letter he left behind unfortunately shows by its distraction, traces of a mental disorder, and it is feared that he was a victim of hallucinations."

Thus far, Hess's wild gamble appeared to be succeeding. The morning after the flight, he actually had a conversation with the duke of Hamilton, not at Dungavel Hill, but in a British army barracks. Germany's victory was inevitable, Hess said, and he hoped that the duke would persuade leading members of his party to discuss peace with Germany.

Hamilton subsequently received instructions to brief the prime minister. Churchill was staying at a favored hideaway near Oxford, Ditchley Park, an eighteenth-century mansion owned by Churchill's wealthy friend Ronald Tree. On his arrival, the duke was put off until after the prime minister had watched a movie, *The Marx Brothers Go West*. Thereafter, Churchill grilled Hamilton until two a.m., trying mostly to establish that their aerial visitor was in fact Rudolf Hess.

Hess was subsequently interrogated by British officials of escalating rank, up to Home Secretary Lord Simon. And then his fortunes began to decline. His proposal that Germany would leave the British Empire unmolested in exchange for German domination of Europe struck the British as laughable. His premise that England was soon to be defeated and therefore could ignore these generous terms only at her peril infuriated a pugnacious Churchill. Most damaging, those who met him soon came to believe that Rudolf Hess had a disturbed mind. Churchill thereafter ordered him treated no differently from any other high-ranking POW. For the next five years, Hess sat out the war. While Hitler invaded country after country, while millions were herded into Germany as forced laborers, while the gas chambers did their work, Hess occupied a succession of British jails and military hospitals, a figure judged somewhere between eccentric and mad.

Yet, on October 9, 1945, he was being flown to Nuremberg to stand trial as a major war criminal. True, he could be tried on the conspiracy count since he was an early, high-ranking member of what the Allied prosecutors considered a criminal cabal. Hess's real crime, however, had been to antagonize the Soviet Union. Through its spy in Britain, Kim Philby, then working for the BBC, the Russian NKVD had learned within four days of Hess's arrival in Scotland of the details of his mission. When, six weeks later, Germany invaded the Soviet Union, the Russians had no doubts. Hess was no crackpot acting out of quixotic impulse, they believed. He was clearly Hitler's agent in a scheme to get England out of the conflict so that the Germans could fight the Russians in a one-front war. When the Allies began negotiating the list of major war criminals, the Russians insisted that they wanted Hess in the dock. The British, in order to dispel any suspicion that they had ever considered pulling out on their Russian allies, willingly delivered him up to the IMT.

Later, accounts would circulate that British intelligence had lured Hess to England. After intercepting the first Albrecht Haushofer letter to Hamilton, MI5 was supposed to have initiated a faked correspondence between Hamilton and Hess. Yet Hess had made three unsuccessful attempts to fly to England *before* the false correspondence was supposedly initiated. There had been no necessity to lure Hess to Scotland. He was eager to get there.

Since learning that he would be tried, Hess had had plenty of time to rehearse the stance he would assume in his latest captivity. In England, after accepting the failure of his mission, he had decided that he had to protect the Führer. If Adolf Hitler had said that Rudolf Hess was crazy, then Hess would make the lie credible. Furthermore, he had to behave in a way that would reveal no Reich state secrets useful to the enemy. Finally, he wanted to enhance his chances of being repatriated in a prisoner-of-war exchange. His best strategy, he had reasoned, was to claim amnesia. The pose had served him well in England. How could the Allies try, much less convict, a man in Nuremberg who did not remember anything?

25

JUSTICE JACKSON and General Donovan dined in early October at the Grand Hotel, where the OSS chief had taken a room upon his return to Nuremberg. Jackson was furious, he told Donovan. First he had urged Francis Biddle to come to Europe as soon as possible. Instead, Biddle had chosen to take his sweet time, coming over on the *Queen Elizabeth* on one of the liner's first civilian crossings since the war. Now it looked as if Biddle had maneuvered himself to become president of the court. That, Donovan said, would never do. The Americans already dominated the show. They had picked a trial site in their zone and had provided most of the defendants—and Jackson would clearly be the principal prosecutor. They had to give the court a more international flavor. Biddle had to be derailed, the two men agreed.

The converted Lancaster bomber could scarcely have carried two less similar passengers than the judge the British government had selected for the war-crimes trial and his alternate. The unhappier of the two was the alternate, Sir Norman Birkett. Before his elevation to the bench, Birkett had been the most famous trial lawyer in England. When Radclyffe Hall was charged with obscenity for writing the lesbian story *The Well of Loneliness*, Birkett defended her. When Wallis Simpson wanted to divorce her husband so that she could marry King Edward VIII, she went to Birkett. One of Birkett's clients was found with the decomposed body of a murder victim in his room, where it had been kept for weeks; Birkett won an acquittal. A colleague described Sir Norman, now sixty-two years old, as "one of the ungainliest men ever to have been miscreated." At six feet three inches tall, with undisciplined red hair, hatchet features, and teeth like "a misaligned picket fence," he looked as if the various parts of his anatomy had been assembled from different persons. He also possessed a lively wit and effervescent charm.

Initially, the lord chancellor of England had asked Birkett to be Britain's chief judge at Nuremberg. Three days later, the lord chancellor had called with most distressing news. The Foreign Office insisted on a law lord for the post. Would Birkett be willing to take the alternate position? the lord chancellor asked. Birkett was trapped. To say no to the one post after saying yes to the other would appear unpatriotic. He accepted, but wrote in his diary that night, "I cannot record the secret anguish this has been to me: To have been selected as a member, then asked to become an alternate, merely because of the absurd snobbishness of the Foreign Office!"

The man who had supplanted him was sitting across the aisle of the Lancaster. After minimally correct English amenities, neither man had spoken another word. The twitchy energy of Norman Birkett was nowhere present in Sir Geoffrey Lawrence. He sat placidly leafing through the cattle breeders' quarterly. An unruffled calm emanated from this rotund, glowingly bald, Pickwickian figure. With his wing collar and black suit, Sir Geoffrey might have stepped from another age. He was currently lord justice of appeals, a position he came by almost as a hereditary right. His father had been lord chief justice of England.

Birkett had scant respect for Lawrence's legal talents. Yet, at Nuremberg, Lawrence would occupy a place of substance, and Birkett would serve only as his shadow.

The judges from the four nations met for the first time on October 13 in Berlin, as a sop to the Russians. As soon as they could pick a chief judge, however, they would be on their way to Nuremberg. To Francis Biddle, his expected election as president of the IMT fed a hungry ego. He had been fired as attorney general. He was nearing sixty. Nuremberg was likely his last chance. If he presided over this trial, his name would surely achieve a certain immortality. Biddles were not accustomed to being cast aside as cavalierly as Harry Truman had dismissed Francis. He was the product of two blue-blooded lines, the Randolphs of Virginia and the Biddles of Philadelphia. He had been born in Paris while his parents were making the grand tour. He spoke fluent French from childhood. As a new boy at Groton, he had looked on the sixth-former Franklin Delano Roosevelt as "a magnificent but distant deity, whose splendor added to my shyness." In later years, President Roosevelt had recruited his fellow Grotonian into the service of the common man's New Deal. Eventually, Roosevelt had appointed Biddle to succeed Jackson as attorney general.

On the transatlantic crossing aboard the *Queen Elizabeth*, Biddle had brought his chief aide, Herb Wechsler, the Columbia Law School professor, who still harbored doubts about the Bernays plan and the legitimacy of the trial itself. Biddle expected his wife to follow later. As the ship plied the ocean, Biddle and his staff wrestled endlessly with the most nettlesome issue that would face the judges, just as it had bedeviled the drafters of the charter: the cry of ex post facto law. The procedures and punishments decided on in London had undeniably been devised after the alleged crimes. The last night aboard, Biddle simply announced that the charter made no provision for challenging its authority. He must either support it, or resign before he started. And Francis Biddle had no intention of losing his main chance.

The four-power Allied Control Council that ran occupied Germany threw a cocktail party for the judges and alternates in Berlin. Robert Jackson flew up from Nuremberg, but not for the sociability. Midway into the party, he took Francis Biddle to a quiet corner. Why, he asked, had Biddle taken so long to get to Germany? Biddle admitted that he had deliberately chosen to sail rather than fly. But, he explained, he and his staff had worked hard aboard the *Queen Elizabeth*. The time spent had not been wasted.

Jackson understood, he said, that the British were prepared to support Biddle as president of the court. That would not do. The French role in the war had been too minor to merit the presidency, Jackson said; the Soviets' right to judge aggressors was already shaky; and the Americans were too dominant. Surely Biddle must recognize that. What Biddle must do, Jackson continued, was to persuade the French to throw their support to a Briton. Jackson went on to say that he had already spoken to Maxwell-Fyfe and that Sir David was working on Sir Geoffrey Lawrence to accept the presidency. Right there were the necessary three votes—British, American, and French. Biddle's disappointment was deep, but he accepted Jackson's logic. The next day, Sir Geoffrey Lawrence was elected president of the IMT. His selection rubbed more salt into the wound of his alternate, Sir Norman Birkett.

26

JOHN HARLAN AMEN DID NOT KNOW what to make of the new prisoner. Rudolf Hess, sitting opposite Amen in the interrogation room, certainly looked like a mental case. Amen studied the lipless line of the mouth, the angular head with the skin stretched taut over every hollow and cleft. It would have been a weak face, given the receding chin and sloping forehead; but the protruding brow and deeply sunken eyes gave Hess's gaze a disturbing intensity. Amen had seized the opportunity to interrogate Hess the moment the prison psychiatrist, Major Kelley, had told him that Hess was claiming amnesia. Amen had stared down hundreds of lying, forgetful, crooked local officials in his racket-busting days. He leaned so close that Hess could smell the morning liquor on the man's breath. "When did you get the idea of losing your memory? When did you think it would be a smart thing?" The American fired the question in his best break-the-witness style.

"You imagine I think it would be a good idea to lose my memory to deceive you," Hess answered.

"If you didn't remember your crimes, that would make it tougher for us, wouldn't it?" Amen said. "When you directed the murders of various people."

"I never did that," Hess objected.

"So the witnesses say," Amen added.

Hess gave him a bucktoothed smile. "Am I supposed to think because I can't remember something, that makes your witnesses more credible?"

"You say you can't remember your wife's name," Amen went on, "yet the British told us you wrote to her all the time. What kind of amnesia do you call that?"

"Ah yes, I received letters from her, so I copied the name from the envelope. In my trial, I will be fighting for my skin," Hess added, "and the only weapons I will have are my brain and my memory. Do you think I would deliberately give them away?"

The man had the cunning of a trapped rat, Amen concluded. Still, he planned a surprise for this afternoon, and it ought to prove whether or not Hess was faking.

Hess was marched back into room 55 after lunch to face his mentor, Dr. Karl Haushofer, and Hermann Göring. Göring beamed as though he had found a long-lost brother. "Rudolf, you know me," Göring said, springing forward to take Hess's hand, until a guard shoved him back into his seat. Hess's eyes were unfathomable. "Who are you?" he said dully. "But," Göring said, "we were together for years! Listen, Hess, I was supreme commander of the Luftwaffe. You flew to England in one of my planes, behind my back. Don't you remember?" "No," Hess answered. Göring reminded him of a memorable day in the Reichstag when Hitler announced Göring as his successor and Hess as Göring's successor. Surely he could not have forgotten that.

"I have lost my memory," Hess said. "It is terrible."

Amen motioned to Dr. Haushofer. The old man looked at Hess with tears in his eyes. He spoke, using the familiar *du*. He had news of Hess's family, he said. "I have seen your wife and your little boy. He is seven now, you know." Hess muttered only, "I don't remember." "The little boy is now a big boy," Haushofer went on, "a wonderful little man." Hess's eyes were fixed on the floor. His own son Albrecht, Haushofer continued, who initially wrote to the duke of Hamilton, was dead. "Albrecht was arrested because he knew some of the Twentieth of July plotters," Haushofer explained. Hess shook his head. He did not remember any Albrecht, nor did he remember the mentor of twenty-two years now standing before him.

As Amen ended the session, Göring rose and grumbled, "He's crazy."

While the Hess interrogation was going on, Colonel Andrus summoned Dr. Kelley to his office. The doctor found Andrus sketching the outfit he planned for the guards who would serve in the courtroom: white helmet, white web belt, white gloves, white leggings, and a white billy club setting off the olive drab of their uniforms. Kelley told Andrus that it looked sharp. What did the psychiatrist make of Hess? Andrus wanted to know. The Polish invasion had come as a shock to Hess, Kelley said. "His father substitute proved not to be a god, but a cruel and . . ." Andrus interrupted him. He did not want to hear any psycho-lingo. What did Kelley think of Hess's current mental state? Was he crazy? He was, Kelley said, probably borderline insane.

Hess was a fake, Andrus announced bluntly, a sham, a phony. If this fellow's memory was gone, the colonel wanted to know, how was it that he remembered how to speak English? He wanted Kelley to make a deal with Hess. If Hess would agree to testify against the others, Kelley would agree not to reveal him as a fraud, and Hess would get off lightly as an amnesiac and a crackpot. "Otherwise, tell him you'll expose him," the colonel said. Kelley gave a vague response. It was so hard to discuss these matters with a layman.

27

CAPTAIN DREXEL SPRECHER PASSED Göring coming out of Hess's interrogation. Colonel Amen was still in room 55, chatting with two aides. What did Sprecher want? Amen asked gruffly. He had come to take part in the interrogation of Dr. Ley, Sprecher said. Justice Jackson had assigned him to prosecute the former Nazi trade union chief. The short, combative Amen looked up at the six-foot-three-inch Sprecher with gleeful malice. That was exactly why Sprecher had no business here, Amen said. Sprecher was part of Storey's operation, not Amen's interrogations division.

Drexel Sprecher was an affable, energetic young officer. An OSS veteran, he had impressed Jackson by his ability to condense the essence of a prosecution case into a single page. Jackson sent his memos around as models to the other lawyers. Sprecher recognized the roots of Amen's present belligerence. Initially, Amen had assumed that because his people conducted interrogations, they would serve as prosecutors in court, and Storey's people would merely provide documentary evidence. But, as Jackson leaned increasingly toward a trial conducted via documents, Storey had risen in Jackson's stock. The justice had recently placed him in charge of the prosecutors who would go into court. Amen's people had largely been reduced to showing documents to the prisoners, having them confirm that a particular record was authentic, that the facts were correct, that Keitel's or Jodl's or Sauckel's signature was genuine. Amen had been forced into the hateful role of servicing his rival, and Sprecher was part of that team.

28

UNTIL NOW THEIR STATUS had been ambiguous. Technically, they were prisoners of war. For the military men, this state made sense. But for Funk, a banker? Or Franz von Papen, briefly Germany's chancellor? Julius Streicher, a publisher of anti-Semitic trash? On October 19, 1945, their status would become all too clear.

The instrument of change was a twenty-nine-year-old Englishman who sought to overcome a boyish countenance by deadly earnestness. Major Airey Neave was already a British legend. He had been captured in France in 1940, escaped, was recaptured and thereafter subjected to the mercies of the Gestapo. Later, Neave had led the most spectacular break of the war, out of the supposedly escape-proof Colditz Castle, from which he made his way back to England in 1942.

Neave was by profession a lawyer and had been picked by the president of the court, Sir Geoffrey Lawrence, to assist the bench at Nuremberg. He had barely settled into a room in the Grand Hotel when he received a message to report at once to the American judge, Francis Biddle, in the dining room. He found Biddle lunching with a portly, kindly-looking man, the American alternate, Judge John J. Parker, who greeted Neave in a warm North Carolina accent. Biddle was brusque: "Major Neave, is it? You look remarkably young." The voice had an aristocratic nasality, rare in Americans Neave had met. Biddle wore a chocolate-brown suit, a paisley bow tie, and a blue shirt; the flashiness of his dress contrasted sharply with his patrician manner. Biddle informed Neave that the following day he was to deliver the indictments to the prisoners and help them find lawyers.

On Friday morning, a party consisting of Neave, Colonel Andrus, Dr. Kelley, an interpreter, and two GIs loaded down with bulky copies of the indictments entered the cellblock. Andrus wanted Kelley along to note whether delivery of the charges seemed to affect any of the prisoners emotionally. The door of the cellblock clanged shut behind them and Neave felt a shiver of memory. That morning, he had put on his best dress uniform with a Sam Browne belt and polished brass. He had memorized a little speech: "I am Major Neave, the officer appointed by the International Military Tribunal to serve upon you a copy of the indictment in which you are named as defendant. I am also here to advise you as to your rights to counsel."

"I hope I shan't make a balls of it," Neave confided to Colonel Andrus as their heels clicked hollowly down the corridor. They stopped before the first cell, and Neave braced himself to meet Hermann Göring.

The public image of jolly Hermann, the fat favorite of the German masses, had led Neave to expect an evil buffoon, a malignant clown. Instead, he found a man with quick, ferret-like eyes, a body still too heavy for his short frame, but far lighter than the overstuffed voluptuary captured five months before. Neave sensed something indefinably feminine and feline about the man, not homosexual, but more like a sybaritic ancient Roman. Göring began to tell Neave that his father had been Chancellor Bismarck's commissioner for the German Empire in South-West Africa, as if appealing to Neave as a fellow imperialist. When the gambit met with dead silence, Göring looked suddenly deflated. He shrugged and began to glance through the indictment.

Neave explained Göring's right to have a lawyer. "I have nothing to do with lawyers," Göring said. He had lived as a law unto himself for years. "You find one for me," he instructed Neave. As they were about to leave, Dr. Kelley suggested that Göring might want to write on the indictment his reaction to it. He handed Göring a pen. Göring wrote in quick, bold strokes, "The victor will always be the judge and the vanquished the accused."

The party moved to the next cell. "We've had this bird a little over a week," Andrus observed. "He's a charmer, you'll see." On their entering the cell, Rudolf Hess jerked himself to attention like a robot. Neave was astonished at the gauntness of the face, the spidery wrists, as he handed Hess the indictment. Hess tossed it on the table. His eyes rolled. He began to groan and fell to the bed, clutching his stomach. "Cramps," Andrus said wearily, "that's the latest." After making his set speech, Neave started to leave. Kelley handed the moaning Hess a pen and asked him to write something on the indictment. "I can't remember," Hess wrote in a surprisingly neat hand.

They continued down the corridor to the cell of Wilhelm Frick, drafter of the Nuremberg Laws, who, in his incongruous checked jacket, struck Neave as an aging actor with a worn-out wardrobe. "The most colorless man in the place," Kelley observed. Then to Julius Streicher, who met them with hands poised arrogantly on his hips. Streicher looked at Neave's list of possible lawyers and said, "Jews, these are all Jew names, and I know the judges are Jews too."

Neave braced himself before cell 25. The brutal figure of Ernst Kaltenbrunner loomed in the doorway. Neave had long wondered what impulses drove men like Kaltenbrunner, the executive-suite officials of the factories of extermination. After his first escape from a prison camp at Torun in Poland, Neave had been questioned by a young, coldly handsome, blond, blue-eyed Gestapo officer. The grilling had been tough and conducted without a trace of recognition that Neave was a fellow human being. Then, at one point, the young officer's voice softened, and he offered Neave a cigarette. Neave was emboldened to ask, "Please tell me what you were doing before all this began." The man looked almost wistful. "I was taking my doctorate in philosophy at the university," he said. Then, as though suddenly embarrassed, he barked for a guard to take Neave away.

Neave left Kaltenbrunner's cell in disgust. The giant had flopped onto his cot, sobbing inconsolably, "I want my family!"

Dumpy Walther Funk also cried on reading the indictment. "Be a man, Funk," Andrus said, "and listen to the major." To Neave, the Hitler Youth leader Baldur von Schirach suggested a bisexual with "dansant eyes," the sort that molests little boys. Ribbentrop's untidy cell actually stank. After hearing Neave out, the onetime foreign minister handed him a scribbled list of British aristocrats. "They can give evidence of my desire for peace," he said. Dr. Ley, head of the Nazi labor unions, screeched, "Why don't you just line us up against a wall and shoot us?"

Neave found it taxing to be civil to Seyss-Inquart. The Britisher had spent the final months of the war in Holland on the banks of the River Waal. Every night, Dutch resistance fighters had crossed the river bearing tales of mass death by starvation, and of atrocities in the part of Holland still under Seyss-Inquart's control.

The military men, Dönitz, Keitel, and Jodl, behaved stoically. The admiral said that he wanted a certain German naval lawyer, Otto Kranzbuehler, to defend him. Failing that, he wanted an American or English U-boat captain. They would know that he had fought an honorable war, Dönitz said. Neave noticed that Field Marshal Keitel wore carpet slippers. He remembered standing barefoot for hours on a cold stone floor in the Gestapo prison in Plotsk, after his recapture, until his feet went numb. Neave had responded to the soldier's duty to try to escape. A fellow officer like Keitel must have understood that duty. Yet, this man, who looked every inch the soldier, had signed orders that sent brave British POWs to their deaths for doing exactly what Neave had done. Keitel had issued orders that meant death to thousands of Russian POWs as well, and mass shootings of innocent civilians as hostages. The man, in Neave's judgment, had disgraced his profession.

Cell 13 meant another emotional jolt for Neave. He had been imprisoned in Nazi jails in Poland, where Hans Frank ruled. Frank, this day, was wearing a woolen glove over his left hand to conceal the scar inflicted when he had tried to slit his wrist. Neave could see the fresh pink wound where Frank had also tried to cut his throat. Frank began speaking breathlessly: "It's as though I am two people," he began, "the Frank you see here, and Frank, the Nazi leader. I wonder how that other Frank could do those things. This Frank looks at the other and says, 'Hans, what a louse you are.'" Andrus told Frank to save his soul-baring for Dr. Kelley and to listen to Major Neave.

The prison had turned a monochrome gray with the failing of the afternoon light. Neave felt drained. There remained one more cell to visit, in the far corner: number 11, housing Albert Speer. Speer, who had only recently arrived in Nuremberg, had been distressed to discover Fritz Sauckel in cell 9. Sauckel, the conscript labor czar, represented Speer's greatest danger. Which of them would be found most responsible for what the Allies were calling the slave labor program— Sauckel, who had recruited the workers, or Speer, who had used them? Speer had to play it carefully. If he tried to dump all the blame on Sauckel, he would come across as a manipulative schemer. If he took the blame himself, it could be his neck instead of Sauckel's. Earlier, Fritz Sauckel had made a dreadful impression on Neave. The little man with the Hitler mustache had stood in his cell, sweat pouring off his bald head, whining, "I know nothing of crimes against humanity. And who will defend me? I know none of these lawyers." His mouth had trembled and tears rolled down his cheeks.

Speer, by contrast, was cool, dignified, and spoke fluent English in a cultivated voice. He read the indictment and started to speak. The first move of his survival strategy must strike just the right note. "This trial is necessary," he said. "There is a common responsibility for such crimes, even in an authoritarian state." Dr. Kelley asked politely if Speer would mind writing that sentiment on his indictment.

They were no longer a disparate collection of captives. They were now criminal defendants whose trial was scheduled to begin November 20, Neave had informed them. They would still be interrogated, but were no longer required to respond. What surprised him was how eager most of them were to keep talking.

29

Major Kelley went directly from cellblock C, after delivery of the indictments, to his office down the hall from Colonel Andrus. He felt frustrated as prison psychiatrist by his inability to speak German. Before the day was out, he believed he might have a solution to that problem. Kelley almost missed the officer waiting for him in a corner, thumbing through one of the psychiatrist's professional journals. The man rose gravely and introduced himself as Captain Gustav Gilbert.

Gustav Mahler Gilbert spoke fluent German, learned from his Austrian immigrant parents. Though a psychologist, Gilbert had spent the latter part of the war in intelligence, interrogating POWs. After the European fighting ended, he had been quartered in a private home where he engaged in conversations with ordinary Germans about the war. He quickly grew weary of their teary rationalizations. None of them had ever wanted war. None of them had favored persecution of the Jews. Their familiar, rhyming refrain became burned into his memory: *"Man hat uns belogen und betrogen* [We were lied to and betrayed]."

Gilbert had learned that an interpreter with a background in psychology was needed at Nuremberg, and seized the chance for a transfer. The assignment was not wholly satisfactory. Interpreting meant an underuse of his talents. Still, Gilbert sensed an unprecedented opportunity. Nuremberg offered access, as he was later to write, "to history's most perfectly controlled experiment in social pathology."

What made civilized human beings join the Nazi movement and do what they did? If he could get into those cells, he might find the answers. If the only way was as an interpreter, so be it.

Kelley found Gus Gilbert's gravity a trifle much. Still, here was someone who could interpret for him and who was a professional colleague to boot. He invited Gilbert to come with him down the hall to the CO's office. Before he could take Gilbert on board, he said, he would have to win the approval of Colonel Burton Andrus.

30

KEITEL AND JODL HAD WORKED together for so long, the former passing along Hitler's orders, the latter drafting operations, that they were closely attuned to each other's moods. As they walked the exercise yard this morning, Jodl detected a heaviness in the field marshal's step. Keitel had been interrogated the day before, and Jodl asked, in a whisper, what he had been questioned about. "The Commando Order," Keitel said out of the side of his mouth. Jodl nodded. That was bad.

When Colonel Amen had grilled him about the Commando Order, Keitel thought that his explanations must satisfy any soldier. Clearly, the colonel could understand an officer's duty to obey orders. Amen's response had stunned him. Under the London charter, obedience to orders was not an acceptable defense. How, Keitel wondered, as Amen dismissed answer after answer, could he ever make these people understand the force of Adolf Hitler's will? That August morning in 1942 was typical. They were in the Wolf's Lair, the Führer's headquarters in an East Prussian pine forest, near the Russian front. On the agenda was a recent Canadian commando raid on the Nazi-occupied French coast at Dieppe. Hitler, in a rage, fumed that these commandos were not soldiers. He had evidence that they had been recruited from the ranks of criminals. He flung a report at Keitel. Look at what these barbarians did, he pointed out. The report described German prisoners bound in "death slings," with a noose tied around the neck and the other end tied behind the back to their legs, so that with every movement, they strangled themselves. The Germans also found a British *Handbook of Irregular Warfare* on one of the commandos. Hitler read from it: "Never give the enemy a chance, the days when we could practice the rules of sportsmanship are over. For the time being, every soldier must be a potential gangster. . . . Remember, you are out to kill." With all the strategic decisions before them, Keitel was amazed at how much time Hitler spent ranting over the commandos. They were thugs. They violated the Hague Convention on Land Warfare. Gangsters, he noted, did not enjoy the protections of the Geneva Convention.

A month after Dieppe, twelve British commandos were captured in Norway on a mission to blow up a power station. Henceforth, Hitler announced, all commandos were to be shot, even if they were in uniform and surrendered willingly. "They are to be slaughtered to the last man," he said, and without a trial. Hitler directed Keitel and Jodl to get the word out to the armed forces in a formal order. Both professional soldiers understood the rashness of this act. But they had also witnessed the futility of resisting Hitler. Two fine fellow officers, Generals von Fritsch and von Leeb, had been sacked for opposing the Führer. The Commando Order was issued, over Keitel's signature, on October 18, 1942.

This order had not been the first corruption of Keitel's soldierly ethic. Earlier, in October 1941, soon after the invasion of Russia, Hitler told the senior staff that Russian guerrilla operations had to be stopped. Fifty to one, one hundred to one, that was a proper price for every German soldier the guerrillas killed. The Slavs, he said, were simply brutes, "and neither Bolshevism nor Czarism can change that." Furthermore, political commissars assigned to Russian units were unregenerate Communists who would always make trouble, even as prisoners. They were to be liquidated upon capture. Keitel was to issue orders to that effect.

Keitel had gone back to his quarters and drafted the Reprisal Order and Commissar Order. One month afterward, twenty-three hundred Russian civilians were herded together and executed in retribution for ten German soldiers killed and twenty-six wounded in a guerrilla attack. The original Reprisal Order, Commissar Order, and Commando Order, with Keitel's signature penned in purple ink, were now in the Palace of Justice documents room.

Since his arrest, Keitel thought often of how he had sunk into this pit. Martial appearance apart, he had never wanted to be a career soldier. He once hoped to be a gentleman farmer in his native Helmscherode. His fellow officers had been stunned when Hitler, in 1938, named him chief of staff of the Armed Forces. The reason soon became apparent. Hitler had taken personal command of the military, and, as he pushed the generals around like so many toy soldiers, he would mock Keitel. "I could never get away with this with Blomberg," he liked to say. Field Marshal Werner von Blomberg had been Keitel's esteemed predecessor.

Keitel, on occasion, tried to stand up to Hitler. He remembered the time he had flung his briefcase on the table and stormed out after Hitler again demeaned him in front of his colleagues. After issuing the infamous execution orders, he offered his resignation, and when that failed, he considered suicide. But he always came back, held in thrall by Hitler's hypnotic powers. He had learned to endure the taunts that he knew were made behind his back. "Lakeitel," his colleagues called him, a pun on the German word *Lakai*, a lackey; or "Nichgeselle," a toy donkey that constantly nods its head. The stenographers liked to joke that they never had to write down the first words Keitel said at a meeting: they would always be the last spoken by Hitler.

He complained once to a fellow officer about the things Hitler made him do. The colleague reminded him of the old Prussian maxim "Opt for disobedience if obedience brings no honor." Other officers had dared to disregard improper orders and had survived, his friend reminded him. They believed in the words contained in a German soldier's paybook: "No enemy can be killed who gives up, not even a partisan or a spy." Those officers, Keitel replied, had never worked directly under Adolf Hitler.

He had also paid a crushing personal price to this regime. His youngest son had been killed in action, another was missing, and the third was held prisoner, all on the Russian front, where his Reprisal and Commissar orders had taken so many innocent lives. Yet his doglike devotion to Hitler never really flagged. Keitel had been in the room on the twentieth of July when the plotters' bomb miraculously failed to kill Hitler. It was Keitel who carried him from the shattered building, crying, "My Führer, my Führer. Thank God you're alive."

"Time's up," a guard shouted to the shuffling men in the exercise yard. Back in his cell Keitel took out his copy of the indictment and reread it. Was it possible, he wondered, that a soldier could be punished simply for following orders?

31

AFTER MEETING CAPTAIN GILBERT, Colonel Andrus had to make a decision. The whole lot, psychiatrists, psychologists, left Andrus uncomfortable. Kelley, at least, with his voluble charm, did not look or act the part. But this Gilbert fellow came across as just what bothered him most, one of those deep Jewish thinkers who always looked as if he were X-raying your mind. In the end, however, the colonel went along with Kelley's wishes and approved of Gilbert as the psychiatrists' interpreter.

Soon afterward, Kelley took Gilbert on his first round of cell visits. As they entered cell 5, Hermann Göring, speaking serviceable English, asked, "Do you know what you have if you have one German? You have a fine man. If you have two Germans, you have a bund. Three Germans? You have a war!" Göring slapped his thigh and roared with laughter. Kelley mentioned that they had seen Hess earlier, and that the man was demanding that his food be tested for poison. "Ah, Hess." Göring shook his head. "When the Führer announced that he would be next in line after me, I was furious. I told Hitler, how could he give that nincompoop such a position? The Führer said to me, 'Hermann, be sensible. When you become führer, *poof!* You throw Hess out and name your own successor.' The Führer had a genius for handling men, you know," Göring said. Kelley asked what Göring thought about Hitler's committing suicide. Was that not the act of a coward? Not at all, Göring responded. It was unthinkable to imagine the head of the German state sitting in a cell like this awaiting trial as a war criminal.

Gilbert hazarded a question. What about his own death? Was he concerned? "What is there to be afraid of," Göring said grimly. "I have given orders to hundreds of thousands of men to go into battle knowing full well many would not come back. Why should I, their leader, cringe when called on to face the enemy?" He gave out a joyless laugh. "I know that I'm going to hang. But let me tell you something. Fifty years from now they will erect statues of me all over Germany. Big statues in the parks and little statues in every German home." He paused for a moment and then started laughing again. "One Englishman? You have an idiot. Two, a club. Three, an empire!"

Kelley invited Gilbert to dinner with him that night at the Grand Hotel. Through the dining-room windows, they watched sullen Nurembergers passing by; children's faces pressed to the windows as the two Americans waded into their steaks. Kelley asked Gilbert if he knew what psychological treasure was at their fingertips. Of course, Gilbert answered. He himself had been thinking of a study of the Nazis based on visits to their cells. Kelley noted that their minds were running along the same track. But there was more than an academic monograph here. They had the raw material for a book, a major book, a collaborative effort, Kelley said. He wanted Gilbert to start taking notes after the cell visits, getting down everything that was said. Gilbert did not mention that he had already recorded every word of Göring's that he could remember.

32

GENERAL DONOVAN HAD BEEN in the Far East for weeks, out of touch with Nuremberg. Nevertheless, Jackson was alarmed by the way Donovan had moved in since his return. It was not a raw power grab; rather, it was the magnetic loyalty the man generated. The OSS veterans still seemed to think that Donovan's wishes amounted to orders.

Later in October, Jackson called a meeting of the top prosecution staff. Donovan immediately suggested the priority order of business, to choose the first witness and who would examine him. That suggestion, Jackson said, started on precisely the wrong foot. He realized that Donovan had not yet had time to learn the advantages of the documents approach over the witness approach. Jackson asked one of his aides to summarize a document recently found, written by a German doctor in Kiev. The young lawyer began quoting Dr. Wilhelm Schueppe, of the "Reich medical department," telling of his work in a Kiev hospital. His assignment, Schueppe had written, was to liquidate through morphine injections one hundred people daily who were "unworthy, mentally defective, terminally ill or from inferior races, such as Jews and gypsies." This, Jackson said, was an example of the evidence available in documentary form to prove, for example, count four, crimes against humanity. Donovan ought to see the other incriminating material coming out of Hans Frank's diaries, Rosenberg's papers, and a dozen other written sources.

Donovan remained unpersuaded. He had been talking to reporters, he said, and documents struck them as deadly dull. If the people in this room wanted the world to listen, they had better put some flesh-and-blood witnesses on the stand. Jackson was not eager to have his authority challenged in a staff fracas. He brought the meeting to an early close. On the way out, he suggested that Donovan come to his place for dinner that night. He had an excellent cook.

The dinner went well as long as they stuck to small talk. Donovan ate with zest, particularly Frau Hassel's *Apfelstrudel*, but only nursed a white wine. After dinner, they retired to the music room. "This trial is going to be far more than a lawsuit," Donovan remarked. Nuremberg could provide the stage for the greatest morality tale ever enacted. And they needed live actors, witnesses. Jackson had to understand the public-relations dimension of the trial. Jackson was unpersuaded. His experience had convinced him of the preferability of documents over witnesses. Documents, unlike witnesses, did not have faulty memories or commit perjury. He intended, he claimed, to write a record that would outlive the hammer of the critics. Of course they would call a few witnesses. But by relying essentially on documents, they could convict these people with their own words. Donovan abruptly announced that it was time for him to leave.

As Jackson watched Donovan's car pull away, he accepted that he had probably alienated the general. Still, he was certain he was on the right track. What he did not admit was that it had been a long time since he had examined a witness in court. The documentary approach, along with its intrinsic superiority, seemed far less daunting.

33

IN LATE OCTOBER, with less than a month until the November 20 trial-opening date, the court members gathered in what had been designated the Judges' Room. They sat around a conference table covered with an army blanket, the room illuminated by a portable electric lamp. Alternate justice Norman Birkett was complaining about living conditions, his hawkish nose sniffing. Since Major Airey Neave was the court's liaison man, the heat of Birkett's ire fell on him. Neave sat against the wall, as one of his colleagues described him, "looking twenty, being thirty, acting forty." Birkett's voice grew more shrill as he tried to speak over the hammering, sawing, and shouting of the workmen outside. He had arrived in Nuremberg, he said, to find his house at 16 Steilenstrasse unprepared. The pillows were made of cast iron. Not a thought had been given to the most ordinary comforts. Sir Geoffrey Lawrence, sitting at the head of the table as president of the court, listened with infinite patience. He turned to Neave and asked if the major would please report Sir Norman's unhappiness to that American housing gentleman, Captain Vonetes.

Birkett said that he was not yet finished. Couldn't something be done about the dining arrangements? It might be admirably democratic to stand in line with all ranks and have one's food dumped into a tin tray by a GI, but it was hardly befitting the justices of an international tribunal. Francis Biddle, by now a friend of Birkett's, tuned out this outburst by the ordinarily charming Englishman. Instead, his attention was focused on Nikitchenko's interpreter, Tania Giliarevskaya, a small, exquisitely proportioned beauty. Though he was nearly sixty, Biddle's eye for a handsome woman was undimmed.

As Birkett went on, a flicker of annoyance flashed across Sir Geoffrey's face. They would soon be dining privately in this very room on bone china which this Kiley chap had somehow managed to unearth, Sir Geoffrey explained. Birkett slumped back in his seat, knowing that his tirades made him look petty, and that they were born of thwarted ambition.

Perhaps they could turn to more pressing matters, Sir Geoffrey suggested, particularly the need to provide lawyers for the defendants. He turned to Neave. Many of the defendants, Neave said, were asking for lawyers who had been Nazis. He needed the court's guidance on this matter. The usually impassive face of General Nikitchenko tightened. The beautiful interpreter rendered his cold anger into a colloquial American English that charmed Biddle. Nazis as officers of the court? Nikitchenko asked, disbelieving. Men who should be in the dock themselves? Surely this was some sort of a bad joke.

Biddle broke in, extracting some papers from his briefcase. Göring had requested a lawyer from Kiel named Otto Stahmer. Biddle read from a letter that a Frau Noak had written to the American occupation authorities on Stahmer. Just five months before the war ended, he had complained to his landlady that a fellow tenant, Frau Noak, was a Jew, protected only by the fact that she was married to a Gentile. If the landlady did not throw the Noak woman out, Stahmer said, he intended to denounce her under the Nuremberg Laws. Thus, Frau Noak had wound up in the Theresienstadt concentration camp. As Biddle read, Nikitchenko nodded sagely. Clearly this Stahmer was an unregenerate Nazi. Was he to be allowed to defend war criminals? Precisely, Biddle said. The London charter stated unequivocally that defendants were to be allowed the counsel of their choice. It said nothing about excluding Nazi, Communist, or vegetarian lawyers, for that matter. The point, Biddle said, was that these men must not be given the slightest excuse to protest afterward that they had been denied a fair trial. Nuremberg must not become a legal Versailles, planting a smoldering resentment in the breasts of Germans. Sir Geoffrey supported Biddle. It was agreed that Nazi defense lawyers could be appointed.

34

HERB WECHSLER, Judge Biddle's chief assistant, sat poring over an appeal from one of the defendants. General Jodl was demanding documents relating to Allied war crimes. Jodl had sent his appeal to Biddle, who bucked it to Wechsler to draft a reply. Jodl's request was just what Wechsler had feared from the first moment he had read Murray Bernays's plan. Jodl was saying, If we committed war crimes, so did you. If we are being tried for them, why aren't you? Emotionally, Wechsler wanted to see these people punished. As a Jew, he found that his sleep, since coming to Germany, had been tormented by nightmares. But he was a distinguished legal scholar to whom the law was sacred and immutable. In a world of pure justice, Jodl had a point. Yet, the charter drafters had already decided that tu quoque would not be accepted as a defense.

Wechsler was wrestling with this issue when he got a phone call from Biddle. Luise Jodl, the general's wife, had just turned up at the Palace of Justice. Would Herb please see what it was all about? Biddle asked.

The cool detachment Wechsler felt when faced with a legal riddle deserted him at the prospect of confronting the wife of an accused Nazi. He entered a small office to find a GI guard and a woman wearing a fedora of the kind favored by German women in the thirties, a mannish overcoat, and flat shoes that had seen hard use. She was not stylish or beautiful, but her unaffected dignity struck him. She rose and introduced herself in fluent English. He guessed her to be in her mid-thirties, a good twenty years Jodl's junior.

Luise Jodl had been married for only a year and a half. She had previously worked as a secretary in the German High Command and had been a friend of Jodl's first wife, Anneliese. She had nursed Anneliese through a terminal illness, until the woman's death in the spring of 1944. Dr. Kelley found Jodl the coldest man in cellblock C. To Luise, however, the general had revealed an impetuous romantic streak. He told her bluntly that the war was lost well before he dared tell anyone else. They should, therefore, marry as soon as possible and wring from life whatever brief happiness it offered.

Wechsler asked Frau Jodl to sit down, while he occupied the desk opposite her. She had walked, she told him with a self-conscious glance at her battered shoes, virtually all the way from Berchtesgaden to Nuremberg to be near her husband. She had found a room in a half-destroyed house that she was sharing with the wife of Field Marshal Keitel. She had come here to do everything in her power to save her husband. She wanted Wechsler to tell her what that might be.

Wechsler found himself responding to Luise Jodl's sincerity. He asked how she came by her command of English. Through a British grandfather, she answered. An English-speaking secretary would be a tremendous advantage to her husband's lawyer, he told her. Did Jodl have a lawyer yet? That was another matter, she said, where she asked for his help. Professor Franz Exner of the University of Munich was an old friend of the Jodl family. Could Mr. Wechsler engage him for her husband? Wechsler knew Exner; they had met when the German came to Columbia University before the war. Wechsler knew him to be a master of criminal law. He would ask Major Neave to try to track down Exner, Wechsler said. And he would try to arrange a job for Frau Jodl with her husband's lawyer. She thanked him, and they parted with a handshake.

Back in his office, Wechsler wondered why he had been so sympathetic, until he reflected on Jodl's plight. He knew the charges the man faced, particularly for his role, along with Keitel, in transforming Hitler's manias into military orders. He also knew that he would have to recommend to Biddle that Jodl's request for documents on Allied war crimes be denied because of the IMT's position on tu quoque. No, he was not doing too much for an admirable woman whose husband, he suspected, would end up on the gallows anyway.

Airey Neave spent ten hectic days locating lawyers in a country split into four occupation zones, where telephones rarely worked, mail delivery was erratic, public transportation was disrupted, and his quarry were often living in bombed-out ruins. In the end, counsel was found for all the defendants. Nearly half had been Nazi party members.

35

Hans Frank awoke with a shudder, felt the eruption and sticky dampness. He had just had another wet dream. It was embarrassing to have this happen in his forty-fifth year. In some dreams, his daughter appeared, making him feel, when he awoke, depraved. He explained these nocturnal arousals to himself as the result of the passion he had been experiencing ever since he started rereading the Bible and meditating on his Catholic boyhood.

That afternoon he told Dr. Kelley and the new man, Dr. Gilbert, that he believed he was undergoing a moral regeneration. "I tell you," he said, "the scornful laughter of God is more terrible than any vengeance of man. Here we are, the would-be rulers of Germany, in tiny

cells with four walls and a toilet, waiting to be tried as common criminals. Is that not proof of God's amusement with men who lust for
power?"

What did he think of Hitler now? Gilbert asked. "If only one of
us had had the courage to shoot him," Frank said, "what misery the
world would have been spared." Hitler's mesmerizing gaze, Frank now
believed, had been nothing but the stare of a psychopath. The man
was a primitive, an egoist, contemptuous of conventional human standards. "That's why," Frank went on, "he hated all legal, diplomatic,
and religious institutions, any social values that restricted his own im-
pulsive ego." Outside, the two Americans agreed that Frank's dissec-
tion of the Hitlerian psyche was worthy of their own professions.

Saturday afternoon, October 20, Frank made up his mind. He begged
the guard to summon Father Sixtus O'Connor. Tough luck, the soldier answered, the American chaplain was out at Soldiers Field, watching his football team, the undefeated Big Red One, take on the
Eightieth Division.

Father Sixtus had indeed gone to watch his old division play. The
Catholic priest from Oxford, New York, had been an outstanding student before the war at the University of Munich, which he left just
two days before the invasion of Poland. He had also been mad about
sports since his youth—a fact that endeared him to Colonel Andrus's
sentinels. Father Sixtus was currently serving his smallest congregation
ever, the six defendants who had been born Catholic. The half-crazed
Streicher, he feared, was hopeless. Every time O'Connor went into
his cell, Streicher would tell him he was no "last-minute Christian,"
and launch into a jeremiad against the Jews. Streicher, however, never
failed to hit up the chaplain for chewing gum, which had become his
latest obsession.

When he returned from the ball game, O'Connor found a message from Hans Frank.

Colonel Andrus had barely hung up his shellacked helmet that Monday morning when Father O'Connor burst into his office. "Colonel!"
O'Connor cried, "Hans Frank has been saved! He has returned to the
faith!" Frank had asked the priest to baptize him again in the Catholic

church. What did that mean as far as the man's mental stability was concerned? the colonel asked. O'Connor was puzzled. Did this mean, Andrus wanted to know, that he was more or less likely to commit suicide? The priest laughed. The Catholic church condemned suicide, he assured the colonel. Suicide meant a quick trip to perdition.

Days afterward, with Frank kneeling on the stone floor of cell 15, and with Willi Krug holding a tin washbasin of holy water, Father O'Connor rebaptized Hans Frank. The priest also urged the prisoner to start writing his memoirs.

36

ON OCTOBER 23, Gilbert and Kelley visited the cell of Dr. Robert Ley, the puffy, red-faced, alcoholic former chief of the German Labor Front. When first arrested, Ley had entertained hopes of salvation. He had written to Henry Ford, offering to share with Ford his experience in manufacturing Volkswagens. But now he appeared to live in a permanent state of distress.

Gilbert strove for a professional objectivity toward all the prisoners. But one of Ley's earlier demands had nearly shattered his composure. Ley had told him that he wanted a Jewish lawyer to defend him. He had in mind a respected man from Cologne. What, Gilbert wondered, was the likelihood of finding any Jews left in Cologne, much less an eminent attorney? This afternoon, he and Kelley found Ley unusually agitated. Flinging his indictment to the floor, Ley cried, "Am I supposed to defend myself against crimes which I knew nothing about?" He plastered himself against the cell wall and spread his arms out. "Stand us against a wall and shoot us," he said. "But why should I be brought before a tribunal like a cuh——, cuh——, cuh——" "A criminal?" Gilbert offered. "Yes," Ley said, dropping his arms. "I can't even say the word."

Afterward, Gilbert went to the prison office, an empty cell fitted out with a desk, to record the conversation. He believed that note-taking in front of the prisoners would inhibit their frankness. He always provided a copy of his notes to Kelley, who assured him that this material was pure gold for their book.

37

"JESUS CHRIST!" the guard passing in front of cell 25 groaned. "Will you look at him." He was peering through the port at Julius Streicher. Earlier, the guard had watched in disgust as Streicher carried out his customary morning routine, vigorous calisthenics in the nude, with all parts flopping about freely. Now, sweating profusely, Streicher was washing his face in the toilet bowl. The man had become a pariah, reviled by his captors and shunned by his fellow defendants. Streicher was convinced that the source of his ostracism lay across the corridor, with Hermann Göring, in cell 5.

Before the war, Streicher had prospered with his tabloid newspaper, *Der Stürmer*, filled with stories of Aryan maidens defiled by debauched Jews and pseudoscientific disquisitions on the quality of Jewish sperm. He had also possessed political power as the much feared *Gauleiter*, the Nazi party leader of Franconia. One oft-told tale concerned a Nuremberg schoolteacher jailed for insulting Streicher. The *Gauleiter* had horse-whipped the teacher senseless. Afterward, Streicher left the prison sighing—"I needed that. Now I feel relaxed."

He became notorious, even by Nazi standards, for abusing his office. Streicher forced Jews to sell him their property for ten percent of its value, then resold it at the market price. He had once ordered his subordinates to turn in their gold wedding rings so that they could buy a suitable birthday present for the Führer. Instead, Streicher used the gold to have an elaborate brooch made for his current girlfriend.

Streicher had been outraged to learn that Göring's actress wife, Emmy, consorted with Jews, and so he printed in *Der Stürmer* a photograph of her shopping at Jewish stores. Finally, he went too far. In 1940, he printed a story that Göring was impotent and that his daughter, Edda, had been conceived through artificial insemination. Göring thereafter engineered the appointment of a six-man tribunal of fellow *Gauleiter*s to investigate the cesspool of corruption that Streicher presided over. The tribunal found Streicher "unfit for human leadership." He was stripped of all party posts and banished to his farm at Pleikershof, outside Nuremberg. He continued to publish *Der Stürmer*, but otherwise, Julius Streicher sat out the war.

As defeat became inevitable, Streicher grew a beard, assumed the name Seiler, retreated to a tiny village near Berchtesgaden, and passed himself off as an artist. On May 23, 1945, he was sitting on his terrace painting a watercolor, when two American officers appeared, brandishing revolvers. Streicher's cover quickly collapsed. He later described what happened. "Two niggers," he said, stripped him, burned his nipples with lit cigarettes, and beat his genitals. They pried his mouth open and spat into it. He was forced to march around with a placard reading JULIUS STREICHER, KING OF THE JEWS.

At Nuremberg, Streicher's lawyer, Dr. Hans Marx, listened to his client ranting and asked that Streicher be given a psychiatric examination. A crackpot, Marx said, should not have to stand trial. During the course of the examination, Streicher was asked to strip. A female Russian interpreter turned her back to him, and Streicher said, leering, "What's the matter, don't you want to see something nice?" The psychiatrists concluded that Julius Streicher had a monomania, his obsession with the Jews. "But, his ideas, while false and odd," Major Kelley wrote, "cannot be classed as true delusions. He is sane."

38

ON THE EVENING of October 25, Colonel Andrus was at his living quarters writing to an old army friend. Shortly after 8:30 p.m., his phone rang. His deputy, Major Fred Teich, was calling. Something terrible had happened, Teich said. The colonel must come to the prison at once.

Second Lieutenant Paul Graven, twenty-one years old, had taken over as duty officer on cellblock C at eight p.m. A long night stretched ahead of Graven, and so he had gone to the prison office and started reading a paperback novel. Barely ten minutes passed before the corporal of the guard burst in on him. The lieutenant had better take a look at Robert Ley. Something looked fishy. Graven tossed aside the book and hurried to cell 9. He peeped through the porthole. Because the toilet was in a tiny alcove to the right, only Ley's feet were visible, with his pants around his ankles. Graven called to the prisoner, but there was no answer. He flung open the bolt of the door and went in. Ley was seated on the toilet, bent forward, his face swollen and blue-

black, his eyes bulging. Around his neck he had looped a noose improvised from a strip of towel and tied it to a water pipe against the
wall. Ley had stuffed a rag into his mouth to stifle any cry, and had
apparently leaned forward until he choked himself to death. Burton
Andrus had lost his second prisoner in less than three weeks, this time
a major defendant.

The Leonardo Conti suicide had been successfully hushed up,
but the nature of Ley's death would be impossible to keep from others
in the cellblock. The next day, Andrus ordered Major Teich to assem-
ble the prisoners in the corridor. "When unpleasant news needs to be
published, as in this case, I myself will do it," the colonel said. "Ley
has killed himself. He gained time to do this by giving the appearance
of making a call of nature."

Hermann Göring whispered to Hess from the side of his mouth.
"It's just as well. I had my doubts about how Ley would stand up to
a trial." Colonel Andrus cut Göring short, and sent the prisoners back
to their cells. He directed his staff to meet with him immediately in
his office.

Andrus looked drawn and tired. Losing a prisoner was rather like
a captain losing his ship, and proud Burton Andrus had lost two.
Security was obviously not tight enough, he began. From now on,
instead of one guard for four cells, they would post one on each
cell. Two hours on, four hours off. And never during those two hours
was the guard to take his eyes off the prisoner. This system would require more men, an officer noted. Andrus recognized that, he said
testily, and he would take up the matter with the commandant of the
Nuremberg-Furth enclave.

The next morning, Andrus was having coffee in the courthouse
cafeteria when Boris Polevoi, a Russian journalist for *Pravda*, came up
and asked him about the Ley suicide. That sort of thing was over now,
Andrus answered. He explained to Polevoi the new measures he had
taken. His jail, he said, was now suicide-proof.

39

ROBERT JACKSON SAT in his office in the Palace of Justice amid a clutter of mimeographed documents. He was speaking on the phone in a controlled rage. The officer who handled all his administrative headaches, Colonel Robert Gill, was calling to tell him that Gill's counterpart, the judges' administrative officer, had just bounced some of Jackson's people from their housing. There was nothing Gill could do about it, because the court's man, General William Mitchell, outranked him. He would see about that, Jackson said, ending the conversation. As far as Jackson was concerned, this was Francis Biddle's doing. Biddle might resent being deprived of the presidency of the court, but Jackson was damned if he was going to lose control over this show to him. He called to Elsie Douglas and dictated a cable to President Truman.

It was shocking, Francis Biddle told General Mitchell, the empire that Bob Jackson was building. "Do you know what my driver told me this morning?" Biddle said. "He was amazed that the prosecution needed six hundred people just to hang twenty-one." Jackson's people, he went on, "are overrunning this city. They're either monopolizing transportation and communications or else sitting around drinking in the Grand Hotel." Mitchell agreed. He had just dealt with Jackson's administrator and had taken over some of the prosecution's housing, he explained.

What Jackson understood more clearly than ever, he told Elsie Douglas, was the fundamental difference between himself and Francis Biddle. Biddle was Main Line, and Jackson was Main Street. And Main Street had just outsmarted Main Line. He wanted her to summon Colonel Gill. Jackson intended to read him personally the response he had just received from the White House. Gill had been promoted by direct presidential action. Now Jackson and Biddle each had his own general. There would be no more rank-pulling by the Main Line.

40

Gustav Gilbert found the letter painful to write. He had not seen his wife, Matilda, since the fall of 1943. He had a fifteen-month-old son, Robert, whom he had never seen. He now had enough discharge points to go home, and he was writing to tell her that, instead, he was staying on in Nuremberg.

Gilbert's character had been forged early in poverty, work, and striving. His Austrian immigrant father had died when the boy was nine. His mother, overwhelmed by the responsibility of raising him and two younger brothers, turned the children over to a Jewish welfare agency. They were sent to an orphanage in Westchester County. Quiet, studious Gustav eventually won a scholarship to the Ethical Culture School in Manhattan, and went on to the Harvard of poor but bright students, City College of New York. He earned a doctorate in psychology from Columbia University in 1939.

At Nuremberg, he had been chagrined at first to be regarded simply as an interpreter, but thanks to Major Kelley, his future looked promising. The idea of a book on the psychopathology of the Nazis, with the subjects as available to him as laboratory mice, had proved irresistible. How could he turn his back on this chance? He hoped Mattie would understand. He dropped off the letter at the army post office in the Palace of Justice and returned to his office, where he learned that the colonel was looking for him.

Gilbert, who had never been summoned to Andrus's office before without Kelley, felt apprehensive. Colonel Andrus greeted Gilbert with forced bonhomie and asked the captain to have a seat. After chitchat about the suitability of Gilbert's quarters, the colonel rose, closed the door, and resumed his place behind the desk. He appreciated, he said, that Gilbert spoke German so well. You could never know what these birds were up to if you could not understand their lingo. Yes, Gilbert was doing fine interpreting, Andrus went on. But, that was only half the job. What he also needed was "an observer," Andrus said. He wanted Gilbert to hang around with these fellows in the exercise yard, even when they took their weekly showers. Win their confidence, become a friend. Pick up whatever they said. And, if it proved interesting, Gilbert should report back to the prison commandant immediately.

Andrus wanted him to be a spy, Gilbert realized. At one time, he might have found the idea repugnant. Now, instead, his mind was racing. Of course, he would be happy to report on the defendants in the prison and the yard for the colonel, he said. But imagine what they could learn once the trial began, if Gilbert could also have access to the courtroom. Surely, a good case could be made to the bench for having a trained psychologist there to watch how the proceedings affected the defendants' psychological well-being. If, at the same time, Gilbert could gather useful intelligence for the colonel, so much the better. Andrus liked the idea and said that he would try to obtain permission from Sir Geoffrey Lawrence, the president of the court.

One more point, Gilbert said, as he rose to leave. Would not all this have a better chance of succeeding if instead of being simply an interpreter, Gilbert could be designated as prison psychologist? Andrus reached for his helmet and riding crop. He was about to conduct a white-glove inspection of the sentinels' quarters, he said. Gilbert's request was all right with him if it was okay with Major Kelley.

When the day's work was done, Gilbert suggested that he and Kelley have a drink at the Grand. It was not the kind of invitation the taciturn Gilbert ever extended, and Kelley was delighted to accept. After they had settled into a quiet corner of the hotel bar, Gilbert described his conversation with the colonel. Kelley did not instantly embrace the idea of Gilbert alone getting access to the courtroom and the new title. But, if they were going to do a book, Gilbert's observation of the defendants' behavior in court would obviously be valuable. Of course Gilbert could consider himself the prison psychologist, Kelley said.

41

ON NOVEMBER 6, Hermann Göring was delivered to the interrogation room and surprised to find there an older man, a civilian of quiet, dignified bearing, who introduced himself as Dewitt Poole of the U.S. State Department. Poole took Göring's hand, before the guard could stop him. He told Göring that he was not there to interrogate him. His interest, Poole said, was strictly in diplomatic history.

"Our studies lead us to the conclusion," Poole went on, "that among those close to Hitler, only you showed independence of thought and action in foreign relations." Göring listened warily. "Let me read from a cable our ambassador in Berlin sent on you in 1938," Poole continued, taking a paper from his breast pocket: "He is boyish, likable, and still carries with him something of the air ace out on a spree. . . . The painters and sculptors who are his friends are legion. In this respect, Göring is like an Italian prince of the Renaissance." Göring was now beaming. Here was an American gentleman among so many barbarians. Of course, Göring said, he virtually conducted his own foreign policy in the Third Reich. What about Ribbentrop? Poole asked. Göring laughed. Ribbentrop had convinced Hitler that he knew all the people worth knowing in France and England, Göring said. "We didn't fully grasp at the time that he knew the French only through champagne and the English only through whiskey." Poole laughed appreciatively.

Hitler's decision to break his nonaggression pact with Russia, Poole asked—would Göring tell him about that? He had talked to the Führer for three hours privately before the invasion. There was no end to that country, Göring had explained. Once you got to the Volga there were the Urals. Once you got past the Urals, there was Siberia. Germany was already at war with Britain; with America likely to come in, it would be madness to take on the Soviet Union too. He had left Hitler that day believing he had dissuaded him from a catastrophe.

As Poole continued his gentle probing, Göring recalled his past. On an evening in 1922, the unemployed air ace went to the Café Neumann in Munich to hear the leader of the tiny National Socialist German Workers Party. Adolf Hitler's subject was the peace treaty of Versailles. Göring could still remember that voice, shy at first, almost inaudible, building to a crescendo. "Only bayonets can back up our threats to the French," Hitler had roared. "Down with Versailles!" The next day Göring joined the party. He had provided just the ornament that Hitler was looking for—an authentic, respectable, colorful war hero.

Years of struggle followed in which Göring sank to unimaginable depths, which he was not about to describe to Dewitt Poole. In 1928, his fortunes finally began to change when he became one of a handful of Nazis elected to the Reichstag. In 1932, the party won the largest bloc of seats, and Göring became president of the Reichstag. It was he who delivered the news to Hitler on January 30, 1933, that the Führer would be named chancellor of Germany.

Hitler appointed him minister of the interior for Prussia. In this post, Göring created the Secret State Police—Geheime Staatspolizei —to eliminate political opponents. The agency's name was soon abbreviated to "Gestapo." Göring also established places of confinement for political enemies, soon called concentration camps. Both enterprises gained such notoriety worldwide that Göring feared for his reputation. He gladly let the Gestapo and the concentration camps slip into the ever-expanding orbit of the ambitious SS chief, Heinrich Himmler.

Göring's appetite for power found other outlets. The old flier became chief of the Luftwaffe in 1935. In 1937, despite a near-total ignorance of economics, he persuaded Hitler to name him head of the Four Year Plan. He was going to make the country self-sufficient, build synthetic-gas and -rubber plants, do whatever was required so that in the event of war, Germany could withstand a blockade. He had the iron and coal mines and the steel mills of the Ruhr named the "Hermann Göring Werke," and raked off millions through payoffs and kickbacks.

During the Polish campaign, Göring's shrieking Stuka dive-bombers knocked the Polish air force out of the war. Hitler was much impressed by the strategic potential of airpower and, in 1940, he elevated Göring to *Reichsmarschall*, the highest military rank in Germany. A year later, he formally designated Göring as his successor in the event of his death.

Göring was enjoying the session with Poole, telling him how he had befriended Charles Lindbergh in the thirties, and that Lindbergh had sent a gift of a silver dish when Göring's daughter, Edda, was born. He had presented Lindbergh, in turn, with a Nazi medal, the Service Cross of the German Eagle with Star.

Was it true, Poole wanted to know, that Göring had willingly supported German rearmament? Of course, Göring said, but not to oppress other people, only to ensure Germany's freedom after the evils of Versailles. He had told the German people, he explained, "What is the point of being in the concert of nations if Germany is only allowed to play the kazoo? I told them, would you rather have butter or guns? Shall we produce lard or iron ore?" He laughed and slapped at his still ample belly. "I told the people, butter only makes you fat!"

Poole questioned Göring about the widespread conviction that he had arranged the burning of the Reichstag shortly after Hitler came to power. The fire had been used by Hitler to justify the suspension of civil liberties in Germany and to launch the mass roundup of political opponents. This was an old chestnut, Göring said. If he had burned down the Reichstag, it would not have been for political reasons, but because the place was an architectural offense. The next thing they would be saying was that he had stood around watching the blaze wearing a Roman toga and playing the violin.

The interview went on into the night, finally ending at 10:30 p.m. Dewitt Poole was exhausted when he left. Göring had proved a fascinating combination, a quick mind, a ready wit, a student of history —and clearly an amoral man.

Göring returned to his cell exhilarated. At last he had been treated with the respect he deserved. He felt important again, a world figure to be reckoned with.

42

WITH THE TRIAL only two weeks off, the world press began descending on Nuremberg. Howard K. Smith, CBS's man, arrived in late October. Despite a boyish demeanor, Smith was already an old European hand. He had been reporting from Berlin when America entered the war and had managed to get out of Germany one hour before the border was sealed. After the war, he had succeeded the legendary Edward R. Murrow as the network's European chief. He had been delighted to get the Nuremberg assignment, until the CBS news director informed him that, once the trial got under way, Murrow would also be coming, along with William L. Shirer and maybe Eric Sevareid. What, Smith began to wonder, would be left for him?

Smith arrived at a press camp unlike any he had ever known. The U.S. Army had taken Justice Jackson's offhand remark literally. It had turned the castle of the Faber-Castell family, in the Nuremberg suburb of Stein, into a press billet. As the jeep carrying him came to a halt, Smith got out and gazed at a heavy-handed version of a fairy-tale castle, gray, massive, with stout round towers and turrets. The castle rose like a stone island in a sea of devastation. Not only had it been spared the bombing, but the source of the family fortune, the Faber-Castell pencil factory next door, was still humming, unscathed.

The GI house manager led Smith upstairs, where the pleasant prospect of palatial living collapsed. Correspondents were jammed twenty to a room and sleeping on army cots. The bathrooms were ornate, but there were only four of them to serve what would eventually swell to over three hundred correspondents. Already, Smith could detect the sour odor of overused toilets. He stretched out on an unoccupied cot, feeling lonely. After a courtship plagued by the intrusions of war, he had finally managed to marry his Danish sweetheart, Benedicte Traberg, a fellow journalist. He and his wife were scheming to get her accredited to the Nuremberg trial. In the meantime, this crowded castle was to be his home.

With the trial not yet under way, Smith was eager to get out into the city to experience the ground truth. On a Sunday morning, he started on foot from the courthouse. Outside the main entrance he watched an honor guard of forty-five Frenchmen parade by, men with the spirit gone out of their step. You could read national character, he thought, in these units. The Russian honor guard used a belligerent stomp just short of a goose step. The most colorful were the Scots, with flashing bayonets accompanied by the spine-tingling wail of bagpipes. His own Americans marched with a slouching nonchalance, some chewing gum. Smith was unperturbed. He had seen enough of what strutting militarism could do to a country.

Away from the courthouse, it was as if a curtain had descended on civilization. The first street he turned into was a trench between mounds of debris; the houses on both sides vanished. He spotted smoke from a pipe peeping above the rubble. People were living under there, he knew. Nuremberg was an upside-down city, its inhabitants occupying cellars, air-raid shelters, the basements of destroyed apartment houses and hotels. The music of Haydn issued from the ruins of the Frauenkirche, a splendid thirteenth-century Gothic structure, now looking like a tattered, windblown piece of theatrical scenery. Out of the church stepped a bride in white, clutching a bouquet, walking daintily through the debris with her groom at her side.

Some German women wore shabby coats, out at the elbows. Others sported chichi frocks, stylish shoes, and silk stockings brought back from Paris by a Wehrmacht husband or Gestapo boyfriend. Inside the Grand Hotel, guests dined on chicken and ice cream, while in the street old women ransacked garbage cans and cooked what they found on open fires. Smith passed a cart pulled by two young boys and a woman. They were hauling a piano, headed, no doubt, to the only remaining prosperous part of Germany—the farmlands. Nurembergers would gladly swap a piano for a sack of potatoes.

The last leg of Smith's tour took him past the destroyed railroad station. Here, on the few standing walls, scraps of paper hung from a nail or were held in place by a stone. "Any word of Franz Fuschl, last seen at Cassino? Inform Red Cross," one read. "Klaus Werner, father is missing. Mother at Aunt Helga's," another read. Nurembergers stood before them, faces upturned in hope. As the light began to fade, a mood of menace settled over the ruins. Smith headed back toward the Palace of Justice. Still, little violence was reported nowadays. No more GIs were decapitated by wire strung across roads. For the Germans, apathy had become stronger than anger.

43

WHAT HAD STARTED as a teapot tempest was getting more serious. Robert Jackson's administrator, General Gill, had directed Captain Kiley to have chairs made for the judges, high-backed, thronelike seats for the four principals, and modest armchairs for the alternates. Judge Parker, the American alternate, had been outraged. The ordinarily placid North Carolinian complained that the "little seat" was an insult. Furthermore, the distinction in chairs pointed up the ambiguous state of the alternates. Just why were they in Nuremberg? What were they supposed to do beyond waiting for someone to take sick or die? Not only did Parker expect an equivalent chair, he wanted an equivalent vote. Otherwise, he was going home.

That afternoon, Jackson was summoned to a meeting in the Judges' Room at which he tried to explain that the London Charter gave the alternates no vote. They became active only when their principal was absent. To Jackson's annoyance, Francis Biddle sprang to Parker's defense. Biddle insinuated that General Gill's chair policy had been deliberately designed to sow dissension among the judges. At that, Jackson stormed out. The court could do whatever it pleased about chairs and votes. He was particularly upset by Biddle's lack of support and wondered what it boded for a more serious test coming up in a few days.

One of the defendants was not on cellblock C. Though indicted, he was still living at home, an old man suffering from hardening of the arteries, incipient senility, partial paralysis, incontinence, and impaired speech. His name was Gustav Krupp, of the arms dynasty. German industrialists, Robert Jackson knew, had connived in bringing Hitler to power because they knew he would break the Communists. Without the businessmen's complicity, there could have been no Third Reich. When the war came, they willingly powered the German war machine. The very name Krupp summoned visions of huge guns rolling off assembly lines. Gustav Krupp was on the list of major war criminals because Jackson wanted the German industrialist class represented in the dock.

The problem with having Krupp personify the guilt of his class was his incapacity, already verified by a team of doctors. Jackson was undaunted. Gustav Krupp had a son, Alfried, who throughout the war had served as president of the Krupp works. Jackson had petitioned the court to indict Alfried if it could not try his father. On November 14, the issue brought the court into its first formal sitting in Nuremberg. The Krupp family lawyer argued the injustice of indicting a man because his father could not stand trial, while Jackson argued that the German industrial class bore criminal guilt for the war and must be tried.

After the hearing, the members retired to the Judges' Room to debate their decision. Sir Norman Birkett shuddered in disbelief. Jackson's argument, he said, was abhorrent. "This is not a football match. You don't simply field a reserve because one of the other players is sick." Jackson's petition was denied.

After the session, Judge Biddle asked Herb Wechsler to join him in his chamber. He had not enjoyed opposing Bob in front of the others, he said. But Jackson had behaved outrageously, Biddle believed, even foolishly. He was starting to detect, he said, a self-righteousness in the man, a fanaticism. Had Wechsler noticed this behavior? Biddle asked. "I thought," Wechsler answered, "that when the judges rejected Jackson's motion, he was going to have a nervous breakdown."

Francis Biddle himself was enjoying Nuremberg. No, he was not the de jure president of the court. That amiable plodder, Sir Geoffrey Lawrence, held that honor. Still, it was almost embarrassing, Biddle believed, the way the other judges went along with virtually everything he wanted, on the Krupp case, on the issue of the chairs, even on what they should wear in court. On the latter point, Biddle had suggested they wear whatever they pleased, within the bounds of propriety. That idea too had been accepted. It was late in the day.

Jackson was putting in a crushing day. His young assistant prosecutors, researchers, document specialists, and translators were also working sixty and seventy hours a week, preparing for the trial now only days off. What enraged Jackson about the petty power struggles, the housekeeping crises, the squabbling with Biddle, was that it detracted from the matter uppermost in his mind. It was his responsibility to deliver the prosecution's opening speech. This lover of words, this gifted phrasemaker, wanted all the time available to polish his address to an incandescent glow. Yet they were grinding him down with inconsequentials, deciding who would bunk in what house, and in what type of seat a North Carolina judge would plant his derrière.

44

"*Plus vite! Plus vite!*" Colonel Dostert shouted. The colonel, former interpreter for General Eisenhower, champion of the still unproven IBM simultaneous-translation system, had set up a mock courtroom in the attic of the Palace of Justice. One person was playing the prosecutor, another the defendant, another a judge. Dostert was testing a job applicant to see if she could keep up with the "witness." Speed was the acid test. An interpreter could not delay more than eight seconds before starting to translate. Otherwise, too many words backed up. Academics might be able to interpret written passages of Nietzsche or Schopenhauer, but often fell apart when the subject was toilet arrangements in a concentration camp. One of Dostert's assistants, Lieutenant Peter Uiberall, a Viennese-born American, had developed a practical test. Uiberall would ask candidates to reel off in two languages the names of ten trees, ten birds, ten medical terms, ten automobile parts. They were looking for breadth of experience, people with curious minds as much as language mastery. Uiberall was always surprised by the number of city people who could not name ten farm implements in any language.

Dostert had made one basic decision. The best work was done when the interpreter listened in his native tongue and translated into the second language. They found that the interpreter first had to understand perfectly what was being said and then could usually find suitable words in the second language to express the thought.

Their greatest headache was German. Because the verb usually appeared at the end of the sentence, the interpreters never knew which way a thought was headed. Yet they dared not wait too long to start interpreting. The sentence in English might be, "I deny all knowledge of the existence of the death camps." But what the interpreter heard in German was "Of the existence of the death camps all knowledge I deny."

Dostert had dispatched his deputy, Alfred Steer, a navy lieutenant commander and a gifted linguist himself, to scour Europe for the talent they needed. Steer raided the League of Nations in Geneva. But he found that many interpreters there were older, accustomed to translating from written documents, and unable to adapt readily to the pressure of interpreting on the spot. Steer had better luck at the Paris international telephone exchange. The operators were used to everyday foreign conversation under time pressure. In the end, whatever the candidate's background, Steer found that only one prospect in twenty had the mental agility to listen and talk at the same time.

With the latest candidate dismissed, Dostert went searching for Captain Dan Kiley, restorer of the Palace of Justice. Robert Jackson was hounding him. Everything depended on having the interpreting system in place on opening day. Dostert found Kiley downstairs in the courtroom supervising the installation of the witness box. Had the IBM equipment arrived yet? he asked frantically. Kiley answered with an unflustered no.

45

ON A MORNING in November, the call had gone to the documents researchers from Robert Jackson's office. The chief prosecutor wanted the most compelling items for his opening speech. Jackson's request came on top of demands from other prosecutors, as well as defense counsels, all of which had turned Lieutenant Roger Barrett's documents room in recent days into organized bedlam. Steel shelves rose dizzily from floor to ceiling to house the ceaseless delivery of paper. Document clerks clambered up and down rolling ladders in quest of the one key statement a prosecutor wanted that could doom a defendant. Recently, Admiral Dönitz's staff had relinquished an additional sixty thousand German navy documents which would have to be processed and added to the already bulging inventory. Barrett had put through a call to his superior, Colonel Storey, for more space and more help. He had scant faith in the colonel's executive followthrough. He regarded Storey as pleasant enough, but in over his head. The staff liked to mimic Storey's folksy manner and colloquial locutions, particularly his referring to the papers they worked with as "dockaments."

Barbara Pinion showed up, an attractive, brisk British war widow, just back from a documents run to Berlin. These Germans were unbelievable, she told Barrett. One report she had brought back described how an enterprising SS team had filled a van with inmates of an asylum, had run the exhaust pipe into the back of the van, and then had driven to a graveyard. By the time the vehicle reached its destination, the passengers were asphyxiated and ready for burial. That had not shocked Pinion so much. By now she had read of virtually every combination and permutation of barbarism. What astonished her most were the postscripts to these reports: "Give my best to Frau Himmler and all the little Himmlers." How could they have kept this stuff? she wondered. They must never have considered the possibility of losing the war.

They faced an occupational hazard, Barrett knew. As chief of the documents room, he felt particularly susceptible to it. A report substantiating the shooting of thirty innocent hostages was not even worth translating, so much worse was available. It had taken the recent delivery of the *Todesbücher*, the "death books" retrieved from the Mauthausen extermination camp, to jolt Barrett anew. The Teutonic passion for recordkeeping required that every life dispatched there be recorded. Obviously, the truth would not do. And so SS clerks painstakingly entered into the books each victim's name and the time and cause of death; according to this record, people, during a given hour, died in alphabetical order, one minute apart, all from heart attacks, the next hour all from strokes, the next hour from another imaginary cause.

But most of the time repeated exposure to horror developed a callus on the conscience, Barrett found. The first time you read of the murder of children it was with disbelief, the tenth time with sadness, the fiftieth time with one part of the brain wondering what would be on the menu that night at the Grand Hotel. That, Barrett believed, was the worst part of the job.

46

November 15, five days before the trial was to begin, a team of IBM engineers landed at Y28 in a C-47 with a cargo of six crates. The simultaneous-interpreting equipment, including 550 headsets for court officials and visitors, had gone wildly astray, some of it to Peru. With the gear finally arrived, Colonel Dostert badgered Dan Kiley to get it installed. Kiley was already juggling a dozen crises. Most recently, a section of the courtroom floor had fallen through to the basement. The architect was getting by on four hours' sleep a night, usually on his office couch. He assured Dostert that his interpreting system would be in place on opening day.

47

COULDN'T THAT WOMAN leave anything alone! Robert Jackson bellowed. He was in the glass-enclosed conservatory upstairs at the house on Lindenstrasse. Elsie Douglas came running in and gasped when she saw the mess. Jackson had organized the documents he was drawing from for his opening speech in piles. Their busybody housekeeper, Frau Hassel, Jackson said, had insisted on opening the windows to air out the room. A storm had come up and now all his carefully ordered papers were in disarray. Mrs. Douglas was already on her hands and knees reassembling the scattered sheets. Jackson slumped into a chair and watched her deftly retrieve order from chaos. It was Sunday night, and evenings were virtually the only time he could piece together a few uninterrupted hours to work on the speech.

"Melancholy grandeur," Jackson said. That was the tone he wanted in the opener. That was the mood he envisioned for the trial. He considered this speech, he said, the most important act of his life. He wanted it to proclaim to the world "the why of Nuremberg." They retreated to his study. He took an armchair while Elsie sat at a desk. Their work patterns were so synchronized that few words were needed. Jackson drew a yellow legal pad from his briefcase and she went for her steno pad. "Germany became one vast torture chamber," he began. "The cries of its victims were heard round the world and brought shudders to civilized people." She was always surprised at how his words, inspired by a few scribbled notes, took on a finished quality as soon as he started to dictate.

He shifted from the resonant tone. He had a problem, he said. The London Charter provided for the death penalty. And when a crime was heinous enough, it was customary for a prosecutor to ask for the ultimate penalty. Yet, all his life he had opposed capital punishment. "A completely civilized society," he noted, "would never impose the death sentence." All that capital punishment did was to sanction violence. Yet, he could understand how Nazi butchery had ignited a cry for blood retribution. Did he have the right to reject the sternest and largely justified punishment that the charter allowed, because of his personal morality? What penalty did he intend to ask for?

Elsie queried. He would simply say nothing on that point, he concluded. Punishment was for the judges to decide. His role was to
convict.

48

"CHAPLAIN," Colonel Andrus said, eyeing his latest staff arrival, "just
remember, you are here to fulfill the requirements of the Geneva
Convention. You are to provide spiritual counseling. You are not here
to convert anybody." The man standing before Andrus, Major Henry
F. Gerecke, was a portly fifty-four-year-old Lutheran army chaplain
from St. Louis just assigned to the ISD. Raised on a farm in a German-
speaking family in Missouri, Gerecke spoke an unsophisticated version
of the language. He had joined the army at an age when most men
would have been content to stay home and hear about the war on the
radio. Two of his sons had been badly wounded fighting against the
men Colonel Andrus was about to take him to meet in the cellblock.

The Protestant prisoners found the new chaplain, with his modest
demeanor and everyman looks, the kind of simple clergyman that the
Nazi regime would have crushed. Field Marshal Keitel, however, immediately took to Chaplain Gerecke. Keitel had a sense that Gerecke,
unlike his captors and his fellow prisoners, did not despise him.

After the cell visits, Andrus asked Gerecke what he thought of
the prisoners. Gerecke answered that the question of their earthly guilt
was not his concern. His duty was only to look after their souls. They
passed by the cell used as the prison office. Andrus stopped to introduce Gerecke to his Catholic counterpart, Father Sixtus O'Connor.
O'Connor took Gerecke's hand. "At least we Catholics are only responsible for six of these sinners," he said with a grin. "Your side has
fifteen chalked up against you." Gerecke laughed. He suspected that
he and the priest were going to get along.

Gustav Gilbert was recording the answers of the defendants to an IQ
test he and Kelley had scheduled. With the trial only days off, the two
Americans realized that any distraction would help reduce the prisoners' anxiety. The test results would also make a fascinating contribution to their book.

The men were given a German version of the Wechsler-Bellevue Adult Intelligence Test, designed to measure memory, ability to think in words and figures, problem-solving, speed of mind, and power of observation. Hermann Göring attacked the test like a brash, bright schoolboy. On the memory portion, repeating increasing strings of numbers, Göring could remember up to eight numbers forward and six backward. "Oh come on, doctor," he begged, "give me one more chance." He had already done the best of all, Gilbert told him. Sixty-nine-year-old Hjalmar Schacht was worried that his years might hurt his score. Gilbert assured them that the results were adjusted for age. Schacht, ordinarily so arrogant, confessed to Gilbert that he was weak on simple arithmetic. The genius who financed the remilitarization of Germany? Gilbert asked. Schacht answered, "Any financial wizard who is good at arithmetic is most likely a swindler."

Julius Streicher confirmed Gilbert's suspicions of his intelligence. It took the old rabble-rouser a minute to figure out how much change he would get from fifty pfennigs if he bought seven two-pfennig stamps. "Don't bother me with these childish sums," Streicher said. "Try me on calculus."

On a scale in which 100 indicated average intelligence and 120 to 140 was to be expected of university graduates, Streicher scored lowest, 106. The highest raw score, 141, was achieved by quiet, scholarly Arthur Seyss-Inquart, the Reich commissioner of the Netherlands. But with the age premium, Schacht came out on top with 143. Precisely, Schacht said, what he had expected. Gilbert was surprised that the extraordinarily able Albert Speer scored only a modest 128. The test, Gilbert knew, was a limited tool, unable to plumb the myriad factors that made up ability. Hans Frank, at 130, scored considerably lower than the third-ranking Göring at 138. Still, Gilbert had dealt with both men, and Frank was clearly Göring's superior in his grasp of philosophical abstractions, social issues, and aesthetic nuance.

49

A SURPRISED ELSIE DOUGLAS poked her head into Robert Jackson's office and announced that General Rudenko was demanding to see him at once. Of course, Jackson said, he should come right over. Roman A. Rudenko, of the Soviet Judicial Service, was Jackson's counterpart, the chief Russian prosecutor, a thirty-eight-year-old Ukrainian of peasant stock with a broad, handsome face. Jackson hoped that Rudenko's visit was in response to his repeated requests for more documents from the Russians. Too much of the evidence was being provided by the American side. Thus far, the Russians' idea of documentation was a confession wrung from some Nazi by a Soviet political commissar, which hardly met Jackson's standard of objective, self-incriminating evidence. Rudenko had assured Jackson a few days before that a truckload of files fitting Jackson's request was on the way from Leipzig in the Soviet Zone; it was supposed to arrive in Nuremberg this very day.

Rudenko took a seat and glared belligerently. The documents would not be coming, he said. American soldiers had broken into the truck and deliberately burned the Soviet files. Jackson tried to suppress his annoyance. The Russians, he knew, had suffered far more at the hands of the Nazis than any other people. Their military and civilian dead totaled over twenty million. He was sympathetic, but could not fathom their self-defeating contrariness. Was this another stall? Had American GIs really burned precious Soviet evidence? Of course, Jackson told Rudenko, he would track down what had happened to the Soviet documents. But in the meantime, he said, he looked forward to seeing the general at the banquet he was giving on Saturday, November 17, in honor of the visiting Soviet deputy foreign minister Andrei Vyshinsky. Jackson's cordiality seemed to mollify Rudenko.

Justice Jackson received a report from the army on the fate of the truckload of Soviet records. A group of GIs had indeed burned the files. They had been cold and the load of paper provided the nearest available fuel. Jackson hoped that the bash he was throwing for Vyshinsky would soothe relations with the Russians. He had directed Captain Vonetes to stint on nothing. In the meantime, he had to deliver the implausible explanation to Roman Rudenko.

50

NUREMBERG HAD BECOME an emotional life raft for General Donovan. True, Donovan had returned from his long stay in the Far East to find most positions of power at the trials already staked out. And after the uncomfortable dinner at Jackson's home, he was well aware that his honeymoon with the chief prosecutor was over. Still, he was grateful to have a place to land. Harry Truman viewed a postwar OSS as an incipient American Gestapo, and had virtually killed off the intelligence agency that was Donovan's reason for being. The general's restless energies now sought a new outlet at the Palace of Justice.

Donovan, nevertheless, had little to do and spent time roving the halls making small talk with secretaries. Then his break came—a letter from Hjalmar Schacht. The wily Schacht buttered up Donovan, calling him "an officer of high standing" and a "well-deserved international reputation." The old financier went on to ask if Donovan would be interested in looking at "a brief summary of the underlying reasons and conditions of the dreadful Nazi regime, as I experienced them." Donovan, a seasoned courtroom lawyer, could smell a defendant ready to turn state's evidence a mile off. If he could get Schacht on the stand testifying against the others, that would be a major breakthrough.

When Göring learned that Donovan appeared open to offers, he too seized the opportunity. He sent Donovan word that, for a price, he was willing to testify against Ribbentrop, Kaltenbrunner, Schacht, and Speer, all of whom had crossed him through the years, and against that swine Streicher, who had maligned his manhood. Göring's price was that he be given an honorable death before a firing squad instead of a shameful death at the end of a rope. Donovan could envision it all: Schacht testifying against Göring, Göring against Speer, Speer against Sauckel. What a spectacle: the Nazi leaders consuming each other before the world. Donovan began interrogating Schacht and Göring personally.

Justice Jackson first got wind of what was happening when John Harlan Amen came complaining about Donovan's horning in on his territory. Was he or was he not the head of the interrogations operation? Amen wanted to know. Why was Wild Bill usurping his role? Jackson faced a painful dilemma. He knew all too well his debt to

Donovan. Yet he resented the general's interference and disapproved of the direction in which Donovan wanted to take the trial. Jackson sent Colonel Storey to find out from Donovan what role, precisely, he had in mind for himself. Donovan was insulted, especially since Jackson had used Storey, an OSS veteran, to run this errand. Men of their stature, Donovan believed, did not deal through intermediaries.

Jackson thereafter invited Donovan to his office. It was still "Bob" and "Bill," but the tension in the room was palpable. Jackson did not immediately raise the sharpest point of contention. He had a preliminary complaint, information that Donovan opposed indicting the High Command of the German armed forces as a criminal organization. Not entirely true, Donovan said. He favored prosecuting individuals in the military. And he certainly favored prosecuting organizations like the SS and the Gestapo. Membership alone should be sufficient to convict those people of war crimes. But to convict top-ranking generals and admirals simply because they were top-ranking? He had led troops in combat himself as commander of the famed Fighting Sixty-ninth regiment in the First World War. He knew that his "Micks," in the heat of battle, had shot surrendering Germans. If Germany had won that war, would that have made Bill Donovan a war criminal? Hang a general because he committed a crime, Donovan said, not because he was a general. Jackson replied that he was going ahead with the prosecution of the High Command anyway.

Jackson next raised the issue of Donovan's dealings with Schacht and Göring. "I don't want any deals," Jackson said. A prosecutor might plea-bargain and turn one accomplice against another to crack an ordinary criminal case. But such courtroom shenanigans had no place in an international tribunal involving profound moral issues. Whenever a defendant was convicted on the testimony of an accomplice turning state's evidence, the conviction had a bad odor, Jackson said.

Get up in that courtroom and tell the Germans that their leaders are guilty because we say so, and they won't believe it, Donovan countered. But put the most popular man in the Third Reich on the stand and get a public confession from him, and that will convince everybody. "Bill, you may be right," Jackson said. Time alone would tell. "But it so happens that I have the responsibility. And I'm going to try this case by indisputable documentary proof."

The next day Donovan received a note from Jackson saying that he saw no further use for him in any position of prominence in the trial, "because of our different viewpoints." Wild Bill had been fired. He did not go quietly. He called on Francis Biddle and told him that the trial would be flat as Kansas with all that paper evidence. Furthermore, he had discovered that Jackson was a poor manager and that the prosecution office was a shambles. He did not want to be part of this fiasco anyway. Nor was he talking behind Jackson's back, he made clear. He had said the same things in a letter to Jackson.

51

THE STRATEGY THAT Albert Speer had settled on was to take manly responsibility for his acts and express genuine contrition for Germany's aggressions and barbarous conduct of the war. But from what he had been able to gather about the conniving between Göring, Schacht, and the Americans, he concluded it might be time to play another card. Had he not given the U.S. Strategic Bombing Survey team invaluable information after his capture? Had he not persuaded other German scientists to cooperate with the Americans? He was sure this collaboration had proved useful in the defeat of Japan. While they were in no position to admit it openly, the Americans were clearly preparing for an inevitable confrontation with the Russians, and when it came, Speer's knowledge could be priceless. He had to act quickly. It was November 17; the trial would be under way in three days. Speer asked his cell guard for a pencil and paper and began writing in neat block letters, "I am in possession of certain information as to military and technical questions that should be made known to the right persons." He was the only one, he went on, who knew what mistakes had been made in the air war against Germany, mistakes the Americans would not want to repeat. He knew how any industry could be put out of action for good. In the event of a jail sentence, he wrote, "I should not fall into Russian hands. My knowledge should stay on this side of the fence." In the event of a death sentence, he pointed out, all that he knew would be lost. He folded the paper, and wrote on the outside, "For transmission to Justice Jackson."

Jackson, his son, Bill, and Elsie Douglas left the house on Lindenstrasse and entered the army Chevrolet staff car that had replaced the
grand Ribbentrop vehicle. Jackson had hoped to spend the drive in
polishing the latest draft of the opening speech. But Wild Bill Donovan's meddling had evidently spread the word through cellblock C
that deals could be cut with the prosecution. How else to explain the
letter he drew from his briefcase? Jackson finished reading Speer's
proposition much annoyed. Speer had ended it by advising that nothing he knew should be heard by "third parties," meaning the Russians.
The only way that the Russians could be cut out was if Speer never
had to go to court. Apparently, the defendants did not yet know of
the fall of Bill Donovan and his prosecutorial machinations. Albert
Speer was going to stand trial along with the lot of them.

52

THE MONTH BEFORE, the Russians had made a social splash with an
October Revolution party. The guests had been happily stunned to
discover bowls of caviar, rivers of vodka, and delicacies flown in from
the Caucasus. Andrei Vyshinsky, the Soviet deputy foreign minister,
had just arrived in town for the opening of the trial, and now it was
Jackson's turn to repay the Russians' hospitality at the Grand Hotel.
Vyshinsky had a fearsome reputation as the chief prosecutor in the
Soviet show trials of the thirties. He supposedly had engineered the
trial and execution of a comrade named Serebrevkov in order to get
the man's pretty little dacha outside Moscow. Here in Nuremberg,
Jackson found Vyshinsky a fascinating contradiction, one minute a
dogmatist denouncing the West with all the standard Communist clichés, and the next minute an exuberant, witty companion. Vyshinsky,
Jackson concluded, was as much actor as party stalwart. When Jackson
extended his invitation to the Russian, he thought it prudent to mention that the IMT judges would also be present, and that Vyshinsky
should say nothing bearing on the trial.

During the cocktail reception, tongues wagged over what looked
like a budding and likely perilous romance. Judge Parker's chief aide
was a handsome veteran of the Battle of the Bulge, Major Robert
Stewart. Bob Stewart, like his boss a Southerner, had served as Par-

ker's law clerk in civilian life and was performing the same function at Nuremberg. This night, Stewart seemed unable to tear himself from the most attractive woman in the room, General Nikitchenko's interpreter, Tania Giliarevskaya. The petite, blond, blue-eyed beauty had made her Nuremberg social debut at the October Revolution party. She had proved charming and vivacious, talking about *Gone with the Wind*, the writings of Mark Twain, and the latest Hit Parade songs, all in slangy American English. Stewart had become the first to breach an unspoken barrier between East and West. He had asked Tania Giliarevskaya to lunch at the Grand. There, they felt the hard-eyed stare of the Russian alternate judge, Lieutenant Colonel A. F. Volchkov, rumored to be the NKVD's man in Nuremberg, the Soviet secret police watchdog. The next day, Stewart had asked Judge Biddle's advice about the propriety of what he had done, to which Biddle replied, "*Toujours l'audace*"—"Be bold, always." Now, at the banquet for Vyshinsky, Stewart was monopolizing the young woman's attention, and she seemed a willing accomplice.

Lights were dimmed, signaling that the dinner was about to begin. Between dessert and coffee, Jackson rose and made a gracious toast to the guest of honor. He closed by introducing "Mr. A. I. Vyshinsky of the Foreign Office, who I trust will say a few words." Vyshinsky rose, vodka glass in hand. Standing off to his right was a shy-looking young man who could have passed for an American college student. He was, in fact, a graduate of Dartmouth College named Oleg Troyanovsky, son of the first Soviet ambassador to the United States. Troyanovsky had been dispatched to Nuremberg as a translator for the bench.

Vyshinsky emptied his glass and said, "Vodka is the enemy of man, and therefore it must be consumed!" The guests cheered and followed his example. He then made a little speech about the brotherhood of the law and how lucky they all were to be in a profession where they could speak their minds, not like diplomats who had to behave "like a dog on a leash." More laughter followed. Vyshinsky raised a refilled glass and said, "I now propose a toast to the defendants." A stillness fell over the room. Vyshinsky went on. "Here's to the conviction of all the men who will go on trial next Tuesday." Oleg Troyanovsky looked uncomfortable, but rendered the words into English. Vyshinsky spoke again. "May their paths lead directly from the courthouse to the grave," Troyanovsky translated, and a few nervous titters were heard. Judge Parker whispered loudly to Colonel Storey, "I will not drink a toast to the conviction of any man, regardless of his guilt, before I hear the evidence."

Riding back to Lindenstrasse, Robert Jackson slumped in the backseat of his car, deep in thought. After the fiasco at the Grand, he was trying to fathom the behavior of Vyshinsky and Rudenko, indeed of most of the Soviets—by turns bombastic, self-conscious, boorish, charming, oversensitive, or thoughtless. The British and American staffs constantly joshed each other and traded good-natured barbs. The Russians could never be kidded. They immediately became defensive. All that boozing, the over twenty toasts that had been drunk this night, what was it about? Some Americans thought it was a trick to loosen their tongues for the benefit of Soviet intelligence. Jackson thought not. The Russians, with their revolution, had eradicated their aristocratic class. They had crushed the middle class and its values. What was left was a proletarian leadership. The heavy drinking was designed to lower the socializing to a level where they were comfortable, down to the trite masculine rite of seeing who could drink whom under the table. Their conduct led Jackson to one inescapable conclusion: The Russians suffered a national inferiority complex.

53

KALTENBRUNNER WAS COMPLAINING of terrible headaches, and Streicher had spat at a new prisoner in the exercise yard, Major Teich reported to Colonel Andrus on returning from a tour of the cellblock. Had a doctor been notified of Kaltenbrunner's condition? Andrus asked. Yes, Teich answered. Which prisoner had Streicher spat on? Andrus wanted to know. Hans Fritzsche, Teich said, just turned over by the Russians. Suspend Streicher's exercise privileges for a week, the colonel ordered.

Streicher had tried to cozy up to Fritzsche. After all, he said, they were fellow journalists. Streicher's *Der Stürmer*, Fritzsche replied, was a detestable rag that cheapened the Nazi movement. "Whenever I saw that muck quoted in the foreign press," Fritzsche told Streicher, "I winced." It was at that point that Streicher had spat in his face. Streicher's ensuing scuffle with the guards had distracted everyone from Kaltenbrunner's odd behavior. He had been moving about the yard unsteadily. Later, back in his cell, he collapsed. The doctors found that he had suffered a subarachnoid hemorrhage and sent him to the hospital. A blood vessel located in the membrane covering his brain had ruptured. The condition could be fatal.

Colonel Andrus was upset. Kaltenbrunner's sickness was not his fault. Still, he was going to fail to deliver another defendant to the dock on opening day. What happened? he asked Kelley and Gilbert. Fear and stress had probably raised the man's blood pressure to the bursting point, they explained. Andrus sighed. Fear and stress. These were the very conditions that a prison psychiatrist and psychologist were supposed to prevent.

54

THE DAY BEFORE the trial was to open, the Palace of Justice was a hive of crises. Dan Kiley was supervising the last-minute laying of the courtroom carpet, purchased on the Paris black market. He left the installation crew long enough to check on the press arrangements. He looked over the fluorescent lighting installed in place of the junked chandeliers. These lights would allow photographers to shoot without using distracting flashbulbs. He had built positions behind heavy, non-glare glass from which movie cameras could shoot soundlessly. He popped down to check out the pressroom he had installed on the floor below, large enough to accommodate over one hundred reporters at a time.

In the pressroom, William L. Shirer, who, with Howard K. Smith, was reporting for CBS, sat at a typewriter pounding out a story. Germany had been Shirer's beat throughout much of the rise of Nazism, and in returning for its burial he felt a satisfying symmetry. He was now reporting his impressions after touring the ruins of the city. "Nuremberg is gone," Shirer wrote, "a vast heap of rubble beyond description and beyond hope of rebuilding." He had tried to find his favorite beer garden, the Bratwurstglöcklein. It had vanished. He had hitched a ride out to Zeppelin Field and stood before the grandstand where he had heard Hitler speak in 1937. He remembered watching throngs of Germans shouting themselves hoarse as Hitler proclaimed, "The German form of life is definitely determined for the next thousand years."

Shirer was depressed by the way even the best Germans he met interpreted their present misfortune. He had asked an anti-Nazi engineer about the morality of Germany's military buildup during the thirties. If Göring had done a better job of building up the Luftwaffe, the engineer said, their cities would not now be in ruins. As Shirer wrapped up his story, he turned to a German journalist working next to him and asked how much interest his people had in the trial. "Oh, they think it's all propaganda," the German replied.

The defendants with nothing presentable to wear to court the next day were gathered in the cellblock corridor to be fitted with suits of an unappetizing blue-brown color. A conscripted German tailor measured Streicher's cuffs. Sauckel was trying on a pair of new shoes and Frank a white shirt. In the stiff, cheap, ill-cut outfits, they looked like a bunch of hicks on their first visit to the big city.

Colonel Y. V. Pokrovsky, General Rudenko's deputy, was calling Justice Jackson, insisting on seeing the prosecutor. Pokrovsky came into the office bearing the usual shield of belligerence carried by Soviet bearers of bad tidings. The trial would have to be postponed, Pokrovsky announced. Jackson eyed him in disbelief. Postponed? How long? Jackson asked. Indefinitely, the Russian answered. General Rudenko was in Berlin and ill. He had come down with malaria. Jackson experienced simultaneous incredulity and rage. This trial was not going to be derailed at the eleventh hour, he said. To start without the chief Soviet prosecutor, Pokrovsky warned, would be viewed by the Soviet Union as an affront. With that, he withdrew.

General Nikitchenko delivered a similar message to his fellow judges. Jackson got word to come to a meeting in the Judges' Room that afternoon to resolve the crisis. In the meantime, he instructed Elsie Douglas to call the army medical office and find out what the likelihood was of anyone coming down with malaria in Berlin.

Jackson's press relations man, Gordon Dean, soon learned of the latest Russian monkeywrench. He explained to Jackson that he was supposed to brief the press within minutes on trial arrangements. Should he cancel? he asked. Jackson told him that everything was to proceed as though the trial would start on time.

The crush of reporters stepped back to make way for Dean and Colonel Andrus. For most of the press it was a first look at the prison commandant, who, in appearance and bearing, seemed born to the role. What they did not know was how much Andrus hated dealing with them. Until this inescapable appearance, he had fobbed off most press contacts to his deputy, Major Teich.

Dean began describing the technical support available to the journalists. He gestured to a soldier who pressed a button. A buzzer sounded once. One buzz, Dean said, signaled something useful coming up in the courtroom. Two buzzes meant something important. Three buzzes meant something sensational. They would be able to hear the buzzer virtually anywhere in the building. Loudspeakers had also been positioned around the courthouse so that they could hear the proceedings even if they were not in the courtroom.

A cacophony of voices erupted as soon as Dean finished. Was it true, a reporter asked, that Ernst Kaltenbrunner had tried to commit suicide? Dean turned the floor over to Colonel Andrus, who explained that Kaltenbrunner had suffered a mild stroke, and that the doctors expected that the man should be able to stand trial. When could they interview the defendants? a reporter asked. No interviews would be permitted, Andrus answered. He was, however, arranging tours for small groups of the press corps to pass through the prison, where they could briefly observe the lions in their cages.

Jackson arrived at the Judges' Room, where he met Sir Hartley Shawcross, just arrived from England. Though Shawcross intended to allow Maxwell-Fyfe to conduct day-to-day prosecution business, he had, as England's chief prosecutor, decided to handle the opening. Also present was General Rudenko's deputy, Colonel Pokrovsky. Jackson informed the judges that he had it on good medical authority that contracting malaria in Berlin was near impossible, and that he wanted the trial to proceed. They need do nothing that involved the Russian prosecution, Jackson noted, until Rudenko arrived. In the meantime, could not Pokrovsky stand in for Rudenko?

Shawcross rose. Nothing in his perfectly groomed appearance or languid speech suggested his membership in Britain's Labour party. If a delay was what the Russians wanted, Sir Hartley observed, perhaps the court should grant it. Jackson looked dismayed. But, Shawcross added, Colonel Pokrovsky would have to convey to his government that the Russians must take full responsibility before the world for delaying the trial of Nazi war criminals.

Just before this meeting, Pokrovsky said, he had received good news. Because of recent medical advances, General Rudenko was making a remarkable recovery. He could be in Nuremberg in days. Pokrovsky sat down, wearing a sickly smile. In that case, Sir Geoffrey said, he was going to rule that the trial commence on schedule the following morning.

Jackson left, as baffled as ever by the Russians' behavior. Why had they tried to delay the trial? He did not understand this any more than he did their sudden decision to have Rudenko miraculously recover.

The first rays of daylight knifed between the heavy drapes of the courtroom windows. At six a.m., November 20, Dan Kiley collapsed into the chair behind his desk and began scribbling on a pad. He wanted to get it all down while it was still fresh in his mind. The restoration of the Palace of Justice was complete. It had involved an average 875 workers daily, 5,200 gallons of paint, 250,000 bricks, 100,000 board feet of lumber, a million feet of wire and cable. His pencil dropped as his head rested on his desk, and he dozed off.

CHAPTER II

THE PROSECUTION CASE

1

THE DEFENDANTS WERE AWAKENED, as on every other day, not by any call of reveille, but by the crashing of washbasins and raucous GI repartee during the changing of the guard. By nine a.m., they were milling about the corridor between the cells, some in their prison-made suits, the military men in uniforms with discolored patches where their insignia had been stripped away. For the first time in their captivity they were allowed belts, ties, and shoelaces. Göring wore one of three dove-gray Luftwaffe uniforms he had brought to Nuremberg. The tunic, tailored for a much heavier man, sagged at the neck.

As Colonel Andrus arrived, the duty officer assembled the prisoners and brought them to attention. "Hitch 'em up," the colonel ordered. Eventually, they might be allowed to go to the courthouse without handcuffs, but on the first day, he was taking no chances. The escorts handcuffed the prisoners, guard's left wrist to defendant's right wrist. The party marched out of the cellblock and entered a covered wooden walkway connecting to the courthouse. As the last man filed out, Andrus shouted to the remaining guards, "Search the cells."

The defendants waited by an elevator in the courthouse basement. The guards were to take off the cuffs, Andrus ordered, and bring the prisoners up three at a time.

Buses, jeeps, and command cars jammed the courthouse yard. The honor guards of four nations stood at attention as Sir Geoffrey Lawrence's black limousine arrived, glistening in the sunlight. The chief judge of the Nuremberg trials stepped out wearing a long blue broadcloth coat, a bowler, and a prim smile for the photographers. He passed by sentries checking passes and rifling through the handbags of women visitors. His short, rotund figure disappeared into the throng.

———————

POWs were still sweeping up shavings and sawdust and the hallways gave off a bracing smell of fresh paint as the correspondents filed into the press gallery. They had a choice position, just behind the prosecutors' tables, with the dock to their left and the judges to their right. Among them were Janet Flanner and Rebecca West, covering for *The New Yorker*, the novelist John Dos Passos for *Life* magazine, Marguerite Higgins for the New York *Herald Tribune*, and Smith and Shirer for CBS. Correspondents from twenty-three nations crowded into 250 plush maroon tip-up seats that Dan Kiley had confiscated from a German theater. In a balcony above them, visitors filed into 150 similar seats.

The courtroom had achieved the "melancholy grandeur" that Justice Jackson sought. Heavy sage-green drapes, dark paneling, and thick carpeting that silenced footsteps contributed to the solemn aura. The muted effect was broken only by the harsh fluorescent lighting and a few bright touches of color provided by the flags of four nations, which a GI was smoothing out behind the bench.

A small sliding door opened in the rear of the dock and the rumble of conversation halted. Out stepped Göring, Ribbentrop, and Hess. They blinked under the bright lights and made their way uncertainly toward the dock. Behind them, against the wall, stood six American sentries, arms folded behind their backs like a basketball team being photographed for the yearbook.

Howard Smith found his attention riveted on Ribbentrop. He remembered his telephone ringing in Berlin in the middle of a July night in 1941 and a voice ordering him to come at once to the Foreign Office. After the foreign press had been left cooling its heels for an hour, Ribbentrop appeared, deeply tanned from a sun lamp, announcing imperiously, "Gentlemen, we have just invaded Bolshevik Russia." Could this dishrag in the dock be the same man? Smith wondered.

Janet Flanner started taking notes: "You look at Nuremberg, and you are looking at the result of the war. You look at the twenty men in the dock, and you are seeing the cause. . . ." She was interrupted by a voice out of the Old Bailey, that of the marshal, Colonel Charles W. Mayes, shouting, "Atten-shun! All rise. The tribunal will now enter!" The British and American judges, wearing black robes, came through a small door. The two French judges, Henri Donnedieu de Vabres and Robert Falco, wore robes adorned with white bibs, ruffles

at the wrist, and a touch of ermine, as if they had stepped from a Daumier sketch. Nikitchenko and his alternate, Volchkov, were resplendent in chocolate uniforms with green trim and gold shoulderboards.

At ten a.m. sharp, Sir Geoffrey rapped his gavel, a handsome piece of oak that Francis Biddle had brought, thinking he would preside over the court. Biddle had generously given the gavel to Lawrence. "This trial, which is now to begin," Sir Geoffrey began in a precise, metallic voice, "is unique in the annals of jurisprudence." The first order of business, he announced, would be the reading of the indictment.

The voices of the prosecutors, with each nation taking turns reciting the catalogue of Nazi duplicity and barbarism, occupied the entire morning. A young French lawyer, just months out of a concentration camp, began his turn tremulously: "Out of a convoy of 230 French women deported from Compiègne to Auschwitz in January 1943, 180 were worked to death within four months," he recited. "Over 780 French priests were executed at Mauthausen. . . ." Keitel bowed his head. Ribbentrop dabbed at a sweating brow. Funk sobbed softly. Göring sat with a bored expression, occasionally writing on a piece of paper. He was keeping track of the number of times his name was mentioned in the indictment. So far, he was the clear leader, with forty-two citations.

After two and a half hours, Sir Geoffrey temporarily adjourned the court. Colonel Andrus realized that he had made no plans for the defendants' lunch. He hastily summoned his aides and ordered that the prisoners be fed in the courtroom. For the next hour, they enjoyed a treasured taste of freedom, chatting freely among themselves for the first time since their captivity. Some of them had never met before. Göring discovered a small gate in the front of the dock and soon the defendants were spilling down into the lawyers' area, luxuriating in their attorneys' comfortable seats.

What was all this fuss about breaking treaties? Ribbentrop asked Captain Gilbert. Was that not how the British had built their empire, through broken treaties, aggressive warfare, and the mass murder of subjugated peoples? Did they notice that the food was better today? Hans Fritzsche remarked. "Yes," Schirach, the Hitler Youth leader, commented, "I suppose we'll get steak the day before they hang us."

The afternoon session continued with the reading of the indictment. The room became hot and airless. Robert Jackson itched to get
back to editing his address, which he would deliver the next day. As
a young Russian prosecutor droned on, Jackson threaded his way
through the press gallery and headed for the exit. He smiled at the
sentry at the door and started to walk out. The sentry blocked his
way. Did the soldier know who he was? Jackson asked. Yes, the sentry
answered, but he had his orders. No one was to be allowed out until
the court adjourned. By whose orders? Jackson asked. General Mitchell's, the guard replied. Jackson reddened. Were Biddle and his coterie
to hound him everywhere? He heard a firm, quiet voice over his shoulder. "I outrank General Mitchell and I say open that door." Jackson
turned to see Wild Bill Donovan. The guard quickly complied, and
the two men stepped out. They greeted each other awkwardly. After
this purely ceremonial appearance, Donovan would be flying home.
Jackson wished that it had all worked out better between them.

After the court adjourned, Ray D'Addario, an army pictorial service
photographer, brought his four-by-five-inch Speed Graphic down to
the courtroom floor to take shots of the now-empty chamber. As he
focused on the bench, another army photographer appeared in his
viewfinder. The GI was stealing Sir Geoffrey's oak gavel. "Are you
crazy?" D'Addario shouted. "Put that thing back. You'll get us all
court-martialed." "Like hell," the man responded, shoving the gavel
into his pocket. "This is history!"

2

ELSIE DOUGLAS TUCKED a snowy handkerchief into Robert Jackson's
breast pocket and stepped back to examine her handiwork. Bob certainly looked splendid.

In front of the house, the touring car waited, waxed to a fine
sheen and brought out for the occasion. Moritz Fuchs, the bodyguard,
opened the back door for Jackson, Mrs. Douglas, and young Bill. As
the car began rolling down Lindenstrasse, Jackson turned to his son
with a wry smile. "This is the first case I've ever tried," he said, "where
I had to persuade others that a court should be established, then help

establish it, then find myself a courthouse to try the case in." Mrs. Douglas handed him a freshly typed copy of his speech with the latest corrections. She had clipped a slip of paper to the first page on which she had written in red ink, "Slowly!"

The reading of the indictment ended by midmorning. Sir Geoffrey announced that the defendants were now to enter their pleas, and called first upon Hermann Göring. Göring made his way to the center of the dock. He held a typed statement, which he began to read. He was cut off by a sharp rapping. In the absence of a gavel, Sir Geoffrey was tapping a pencil on the bench, the sound resonating through a microphone. "I have already explained," Lawrence remarked tartly, "the defendants are not to make a speech." Göring angrily snapped, "I declare myself, in the sense of the indictment, not guilty." He returned to his seat. Hess was called on next. He moved like a tin man to the microphone and uttered a single word: "*Nein*." "That will be entered as a plea of not guilty," Sir Geoffrey said as quiet laughter rippled through the courtroom. Hans Frank, his eyes bothered the day before by the lighting, stepped forward wearing sunglasses. The unfortunate effect was to increase the resemblance of this jowly, full-lipped man to a gangster. Frank pleaded not guilty. The other defendants, in various forms, made the same plea, "*Nicht schuldig*."

Fritzsche, the last defendant, had finished his plea, when, unbidden, Göring again headed for the microphone. Again, Lawrence cut him off. "You are not allowed to address the tribunal except through your counsel, at the present time," he said with icy courtesy. The staff, which had previously judged Sir Geoffrey as a pleasant cipher, began seeing a different man.

All eyes turned to a distinguished figure in a morning coat and striped trousers making his way to the prosecutor's stand. Robert Jackson gazed around the room with imperturbable calm. He squared the pages of his text and set them on the lectern. "May it please your honors, the privilege of opening the first trial in history for crimes against the peace of the world imposes a grave responsibility," he began. "The wrongs which we seek to condemn and punish have been so calculated, so malignant, and so devastating that civilization cannot tolerate their being ignored because it cannot survive their being repeated. That four great nations, flushed with victory and stung with injury, stay the hand of vengeance and voluntarily submit their captive enemies to the judgment of the law is one of the most significant tributes that power has ever paid to reason." Jackson's style was by turns Elizabethan, Spenserian, and Gladstonian—the oratory of a passing age, soon destined to disappear.

He wanted the legitimacy of the court recognized. "The world-wide scope of the trial has left few neutrals," he said. "Either the victors must judge the vanquished, or we must leave the defeated to judge themselves. After the first world war, we saw the futility of the latter course." He signaled the prosecution's strategy. "We will not ask you to convict these men on the testimony of their foes," he said. "There is no count in the indictment that cannot be proved by books and records." The accused, he noted with a brief smile, "shared the Teutonic passion for thoroughness in putting things on paper." He rejected criticisms that it had taken too long to launch the IMT. Courts in America dealing with comparatively limited events, he noted, seldom began a trial in less than a year. "Yet, less than eight months ago, the courtroom in which we sit was an enemy fortress in the hands of SS troops."

After he had spoken for two hours, Sir Geoffrey declared a recess for lunch.

Colonel Andrus was not about to repeat the lunchtime mistake of the day before, when the defendants had run all over the courtroom. He had arranged a dining room for them in the attic of the courthouse. Göring dominated the room, rather like a coach bucking up a losing team at halftime. He told fat little Walther Funk not to worry about any crimes the prosecution might charge him with in the financial area. He, Hermann Göring, as head of the Four Year Plan, would assume all responsibility. Funk's baggy eyes brimmed with gratitude. The defendants bolted their lunch and crowded the attic windows. They had seen virtually nothing but prison walls for too long. Today, they could look beyond the shambles of Nuremberg and see the Peg-nitz River leave the city behind and wind through forests and fields toward the mountains. Their eyes drank in the view.

Elsie Douglas had set two large chairs together to form an impromptu couch for Bob in his office. His eyes were closed and she hoped he was asleep. She waited until the last minute to shake him. As they headed back toward the courtroom, she warned him that the interpreters' red and yellow warning lights had flashed often during the morning. He was still speaking too fast when he became carried away, she warned.

Jackson took a document from Elsie Douglas's outstretched hand. He wanted to read the court, he said, a few excerpts from the diary of the defendant Hans Frank. "The Jews must be eliminated. Whenever we catch one, it is his end." Jackson turned a page and the rustle could be heard in the silent room as he continued to read, "Of course I cannot eliminate all the Jews in one year's time . . ." Frank's head lowered as his words from Wawel Castle echoed in the mouth of an American prosecutor.

Mrs. Douglas next handed Jackson a large leather-bound book. He was quoting from the report of the German general Jürgen Stroop entitled "The Destruction of the Warsaw Ghetto," Jackson explained. He read of German troops turning flamethrowers on apartment buildings, and of Jews jumping to their deaths from smoking upper stories or gunned down as they poured from doorways. The yellow light on the prosecutor's stand flashed, signaling Jackson to slow down. He paused. "You will say I have robbed you of your sleep," he went on, "but these are things which have turned the stomach of the world." The defendants, all but Hess, listened in rapt attention, eyes open wide.

Jackson turned to the bench. "And let me make clear that while the law is first applied against German aggressors, the law includes, and if it is to serve a useful purpose, it must condemn, aggression by any other nation, including those which sit here now in judgment." Jackson picked up his text and returned to his seat.

The defendants filed out of the dock and into the elevator. The force of Jackson's words was not wholly responsible for their subdued state. Frank's lawyer, Alfred Seidl, had just passed a note to his client, which Frank shared with the others. A week before, an American military court had hanged five German civilians for murdering the crewmen of a downed B-17. Just four days before, a British court had sentenced eleven concentration camp officials to death, including the commandant of Bergen-Belsen. If minor Nazis fared thus, what must be their own fate?

3

JACKSON WAS MOBBED. Howard Smith told him that, while he had covered Germany for years, he had never understood until now what had been the fate of his disappearing Jewish friends. Shirer said Jackson's words had sent shivers down his spine. Possibly the most erudite man on Jackson's staff, Colonel Telford Taylor, concluded that Jackson's opener marked the pinnacle of legal writing thus far in the century and was not to be easily surpassed. The next day, the word from Charlie Horsky, Jackson's man in Washington, was music to the prosecutor's ear. The speech had made the front page of *The New York Times* and *The Washington Post*—in long stories that quoted generously from Jackson's text.

Shortly afterward, Sir Hartley Shawcross, Great Britain's chief prosecutor, delivered an opening address that nearly equaled Jackson's in eloquence. Shawcross, handsome as a matinee idol, read from the Hermann Graebe report on the fate of the Jews of Dubno. "The people put down their clothes in fixed places, sorted according to shoes, outer clothing, and underwear . . . they stood around in family groups, kissed each other and said farewells . . . they went down into the pit, lined themselves up against the previous victims and were shot . . ." As Shawcross spoke, Fritzsche buried his face in his hands. Göring yanked off his earphones. "I looked at the man who did the shooting," Shawcross went on reading; "he was an SS man, who sat with his feet dangling into the pit. He had a tommy gun on his knees and was smoking a cigarette."

Later, Shawcross confronted the ex post facto argument. "I suppose the first person ever charged with murder," he observed, "might well have said, 'See here, you can't do that. Murder hasn't been made a crime yet.'"

General Rudenko arrived in time to deliver the opening argument for the Soviet Union. The Russians had counted the pages in Jackson's speech, and made Rudenko's speech one page longer. The moment

Rudenko took the stand, Göring and Hess tore off their earphones, as if members of one gang had suddenly found a member of a rival gang daring to accuse them.

4

ROSE KORB, Colonel Andrus's new secretary, loved her job. Just turned twenty-three, out of Hammond, Indiana, Korb suddenly had a ringside seat at history. She found Andrus, by turns, stern or fatherly, but thoughtful on the whole, and she liked him. One exception had been the time that Captain Gilbert left the office and the colonel made an anti-Semitic remark. It always hurt more, this young Jewish woman thought, when nice people did those things.

Another advantage of her job was that Rose got to meet the new men assigned to the ISD first and could report on them to her roommates in the apartment building known as "Girls' Town." She particularly liked the second lieutenant who had joined the ISD two months before, Jack G. Wheelis; he was strapping and ruggedly handsome. Wheelis had told Rose at the time, with a drawl and a grin, to call him Tex.

Colonel Andrus had plans for Wheelis. The colonel was having a deuce of a time with personnel. In his judgment, the security mission required superior people; yet the army kept sending him green second-raters. And the minute his experienced personnel reached the requisite discharge points, they went home. This brawny Texan had a commanding presence and certainly looked like a leader. Andrus was going to appoint him assistant operations officer.

On the way back from Chaplain Gerecke's Protestant service, Göring saw Father Sixtus O'Connor. What was this baseball that the priest was always talking about? he wanted to know. Was there money in it? Branch Rickey, general manager of the Dodgers, earned ninety thousand dollars a year, nearly a million reichsmarks, Father Sixtus informed him. Göring clapped the priest on the back and said, "You see, Father, you and I went into the wrong business!"

Göring was fast becoming the guards' favorite. He would ask them where they came from and whether their rations were adequate, as though he could do something about it. Privately, the young Americans' lack of decorum disgusted him, as when they addressed him bluntly as "Göring." Still, it served his purposes to win them over. This day, November 27, Göring was expecting to meet his lawyer, Dr. Otto Stahmer, in preparation for the next session of the court. The prosecution was expected to deal with Germany's annexation of Austria, in which Göring had figured prominently. He had barely returned to his cell from the chapel when one of the guards shouted, "Bring Fatso to the visitors' room."

The room was split down the middle by a mesh screen with chairs along each side. Sliding plastic slots allowed defendants and lawyers to pass documents back and forth through the screen, after a guard examined them. Tex Wheelis was on duty this morning in the room, and Göring went after him like a politician after a voter. So the lieutenant was from Texas? Good hunting there, he had heard. Did the lieutenant like to hunt? It was the *Reichsmarschall*'s passion. In fact, he had been Germany's chief gamekeeper. There was wonderful shooting around his estate at Carinhall. Too bad he could not show the lieutenant around it.

Wheelis asked Göring how the trial was going. He had the best seat in the house, Göring explained cheerily. Right in the corner of the dock. Göring looked around at the audience of guards and asked, Did they know the difference between a German and an Englishman? A German has a soft heart but a hard hand, Göring said. And an Englishman has a soft hand but a hard heart. The Americans laughed, especially Tex Wheelis, who directed the guard to remove the *Reichsmarschall*'s handcuffs.

The lawyer, Stahmer, arrived, a large man in his seventies whose appearance suggested an aging, belligerent stag. He let the guard frisk him and check his briefcase, then took his place opposite Hermann Göring. Göring told Stahmer in German that he believed Wheelis was a friend.

5

A WEARY HOWARD SMITH came out of the Stein castle into the chilly night and stumbled aboard the army bus for the trip to the Palace of

Justice. Smith felt grimy. Only on weekends could he get into the bathroom long enough to shave, and a five-day stubble spiked his chin. One week had passed since the trial opened, and he intended in tonight's broadcast to deliver a state-of-the-court report. He was having trouble, however, staying awake. Bill Shirer was down with the flu, and Smith was covering the trial alone for CBS, writing stories and broadcasting a half dozen times a day.

He fell asleep on the bus, and the driver had to wake him up as they pulled into the gate of the courthouse. Smith made his way to the third floor and the ladder leading to the attic broadcast booths. Facing a microphone that carried his voice through a chain of land lines and shortwave feeds into American living rooms, he began. Three trials were under way in Nuremberg, he said. The first was the American trial, its purpose to warn aggressors and to give the world a body of law for trying future war criminals. Second was the Europeans' trial, particularly the Russians and the French, "an enterprise of passion, a tribunal of vengeance." Finally, there was the defendants' Nuremberg, marked by the Nazis' growing awareness that the trial was fair and that "it may still be possible to squeeze out of this pinch with a prison term instead of death, maybe even with a shred of dignity." Two stars thus far had emerged at Nuremberg, Smith noted. The surprise winner was the IMT's president, Sir Geoffrey Lawrence, the sort of man who let people underrate him, and then capitalized on their mistake. The other was Hermann Göring, who was becoming something of a bellwether. Every time the prosecution sought to score a point, all eyes turned to Göring to measure the reaction of that mobile, expressive face. By the time Smith finished his broadcast and made his way back to the castle, it was nearly 1:30 a.m. He would be back at the courthouse by seven in the morning.

6

WHAT SMITH AND THE REST of the press corps did not publicly admit, since no salesman wants to disparage his product, was that the trial was bogging down. As a legal strategy, Jackson's documentary approach was unassailable. As drama, it had become stultifying. Colonel Storey had his assistant prosecutors introducing documents wholesale, often without even having them read in court. Charlie Horsky reported from Washington that U.S. press play of the trial was dwindling. Jackson grudgingly recognized that the prosecution had to come alive.

On Thursday morning, November 29, the defendants filed through the sliding door into the dock five minutes before the ten a.m. opening time. Göring took his seat in the front-row corner and looked up to meet the gaze of a short, thickset man with close-cropped gray hair. "*Guten Morgen, Herr Reichsmarschall,*" the man said in perfect German. Göring looked at him blankly and asked, "Do I know you?" Of course, the man explained; he had worked for Göring at the Prussian Ministry of the Interior years before. His name, he said, was Robert Kempner. Göring searched the face skeptically. Kempner offered to refresh his memory. In 1933, he had been general counsel to the Prussian police, and Göring, as minister of the interior, had fired him. Why? Göring asked warily. Because, Kempner said, he had successfully prosecuted storm troopers before the Nazis took over. He had also urged dissolution of the Nazi party and the arrest of Adolf Hitler for treason. And, Kempner added, he probably had been fired because he was part Jewish. Göring glared belligerently. Kempner went on. He remembered what Göring had said after dismissing him. His words had been, "Get out of my sight. I never want to see you again." Well, here he was again, Kempner said, moving down the dock.

He stopped at the eighth position. "*Guten Morgen, Herr Doktor Frick,*" Kempner said. The usually phlegmatic Wilhelm Frick looked up, startled. He remembered Kempner all too well. Frick, after succeeding Göring as minister of the interior, had deprived Kempner of his German citizenship and had him thrown into a concentration camp. Frick avoided Kempner's eyes. Kempner left and resumed his seat at the prosecution table. He had fled Germany long ago and was now an American citizen attached to Jackson's staff. He was in charge of the Defense Rebuttal Section, charged with anticipating the arguments of these men in the dock and preparing counterevidence to crush them. Kempner sat back to enjoy the morning's proceedings.

The afternoon session continued with the annexation of Austria. The prosecution introduced verbatim transcripts of Göring's virtually directing the takeover by telephone. A tale of bullying and deceit unfolded, and Göring winked, nodded, and smiled at his codefendants as it was told. During a brief recess, he turned and asked, What was the point of calling the *Anschluss* "aggression"? Didn't the Austrians pave the Führer's way from the German border to Vienna with flowers? Who had ever seen such joy?

7

DURING THE RECESS, the spectators saw a new face approach the prosecutors' stand. Navy Commander James Donovan was about to provide Jackson's answer to the complaint that his paperwork prosecution was too dry. "May it please the tribunal," Donovan began, "I refer to document number 2430 PS, a motion picture entitled 'Nazi Concentration Camps,' which the United States now offers into evidence. It was compiled from motion pictures taken by Allied military photographers as the armies in the West liberated areas in which these camps were located." The film had been ordered, Donovan explained, by General Eisenhower, and produced by one of Hollywood's leading directors, then on army duty, Lieutenant Colonel George Stevens. The courtroom went dark, except for the dock where the defendants were kept illuminated for security purposes. At one end of the dock stood Captain Gilbert.

A projector began whirring and cut a cone of light through the room, delivering images to a screen on the back wall behind the witness stand. Later generations might become hardened by repeated exposure to these sights, but scenes of bulldozers shoving moon-white corpses into mass graves were being seen for the first time by this audience. On the screen, GIs, wearing gas masks, pointed out bodies stacked like cord wood. Jack Taylor, an American navy lieutenant captured on an OSS mission behind the lines, appeared in the film and described the Mauthausen extermination camp. Prisoners were compelled to carry huge stones out of a quarry on their backs until they died of exhaustion, Taylor explained. Occasionally, bored guards amused themselves by dropping a prisoner back to the bottom of the quarry. This was called "parachuting." Quiet weeping sounded in the courtroom. A woman fainted and had to be carried out.

Film taken by the Germans themselves was shown next, most of it unearthed from hiding places by an OSS team. One reel had been shot at a camp near Leipzig. Some two hundred prisoners were shown being herded into a barn. SS men then doused the building with gasoline and set it afire. The few prisoners who escaped were mowed down by machine guns. Gilbert jotted down the defendants' reactions: Keitel wipes brow, takes off headphones; Frank trying to stifle tears; Funk blows nose, wipes eyes; Speer swallows hard; Dönitz bows head; Göring leans on elbows, yawns.

The films went on for over two hours, a phantasmagoria of broken, charred, gray bodies, ribs protruding, legs like sticks, hollow eyes gaping. When it was over, the lights went on. Silence hung like a pall over the room. Sir Geoffrey rose and left almost at a run, without adjourning the court. The defendants headed toward the elevator. Hans Frank remained seated, incapable of movement. A guard took him by the arm and led him away.

On their return to the prison, Göring noted that white enamel name plates had been placed over each cell. He was annoyed that the Americans, as usual, had neglected any civility. His plate read simply, "H. Göring," no rank, no title, as if he were a shopkeeper. He could always tell by the rearrangement of the photographs and his few personal articles that his cell had been searched during his absence. He feared most that the Americans might also have gone through his luggage stowed in the prison baggage room, two doors down from him. Two cyanide capsules were concealed there, one in a jar of face cream, another in his ultimate hiding place. He could only hope that they were still there. In order to go to the baggage room himself, he would have to be accompanied by a guard, and he did not want to draw attention to his cache.

Gilbert and Kelley waited until after supper before going to the cells to get the defendants' reaction to the films. Hans Fritzsche sat, head hung low, on the edge of his cot. For years his voice over the radio had stirred Germans to a hatred of the Jews. "No power on heaven or earth will erase this shame from my country," he said quietly. "Not in generations, not in centuries." Wilhelm Frick, who had promulgated the Nuremberg Laws, which had foreshadowed the atrocities shown, said he didn't understand how such things could have happened, then asked, Would there be time for an evening walk in the exercise yard? Göring was morose. They had all been having such a good time over the Austrian case, he said, before that wretched film spoiled everything.

General Alfred Jodl refused to talk to his visitors. But before lights out, he wrote a note for Dr. Exner, his lawyer, to pass to his wife, Luise. "These facts are the most fearful heritage which the National Socialist regime has left the German people," he told her. "It is far worse than the destruction of German cities. Their ruins could be regarded as honorable wounds suffered during a people's battle for its existence. This disgrace, however, besmirches everything, the enthusiasm of our youth, the entire German Wehrmacht and its leaders." He assured Luise that he knew nothing of such matters. He would, he said, "not have tolerated it for a single day."

While Kelley and Gilbert visited the cells, Robert Jackson was at home preparing a second surprise.

8

THE WITNESS HOUSE, a square, solid, two-story structure, stood at the end of a dead-end street in the Nuremberg suburbs. The house was run by a smokily beautiful aristocrat, the Countess Ingeborg Kalnoky. Nothing in her earlier life would have foretold the countess's present fate. Ingeborg Kalnoky, the daughter of a Prussian officer, had married into the Hungarian nobility. In the spring of 1945, Kalnoky was living in Budapest with her three young children and was pregnant with a fourth. As a German and a noblewoman, she feared for her safety as the Red Army approached. Leaving her husband behind, she had fled with the children to Germany. Her fears had had nothing to do with pro-Nazi sentiments. Once while summering in a Hungarian village, she had watched freight cars filled with Jews, packed like cattle, pass through for an entire week. She had heard their cries, glimpsed their tortured faces, and felt ashamed to be German.

The countess had found herself in a Nuremberg military hospital the night before she was to give birth to her child. She had been wondering what would befall her next when an American occupation

officer asked if she would like to manage a house that had been commandeered to lodge witnesses for the war-crimes trial. She seized the
opportunity.

On a night toward the end of November, Kalnoky answered the
door at the Witness House to find two MPs delivering a tall, gaunt,
palely poetic figure, unshaven and dressed in filthy clothes. The man
introduced himself as General Erwin Lahousen, in better times an
intelligence officer attached to the German High Command. Countess
Kalnoky found Lahousen a room, gave him soap and a razor, and left
him some GI rations.

That evening the fifty-eight-year-old Lahousen sat by the radio,
listening to classical music, his face buried in his hands, sobbing.
He was obviously a broken man, which the countess duly reported
to her American superiors. To her surprise and embarrassment, an
MP showed up the next day with a dark-haired, good-looking girl,
whom Kalnoky was directed to put up in Lahousen's room. Who she
was the countess never knew, but she visibly improved Lahousen's
spirits.

On Thursday, November 29, Hermann Göring's face displayed min-
gled shock and contempt as General Lahousen marched to the witness
stand. Field Marshal Keitel's face expressed terror. Documents had
already been introduced that established Germany's aggressive intentions against Poland. In one, Hitler was quoted saying, "Further suc-
cesses cannot be obtained without shedding blood. . . . Poland must
be attacked at the next suitable opportunity. . . . It is a question of
expanding our living space in the east." Thus, the charge of aggression
seemed amply proved out of Hitler's mouth. Still, Jackson had become
sensitive to criticism that the trial lacked fire. Erwin Lahousen's appearance, Jackson believed, could lend a human dimension to the
charge. He had assigned the old gangbuster, John Harlan Amen, the
direct examination of Lahousen. Lahousen testified that, in mid-
August 1939, he received an odd order from his superior, the chief of
Abwehr intelligence, Admiral Wilhelm Canaris, to provide Polish uniforms, weapons, and false papers for a secret operation planned by
Heinrich Himmler. The Canaris order smelled fishy to Lahousen. He
nevertheless complied.

As soon as he heard the communiqué reporting that Polish troops had attacked a German radio installation at Gleiwitz, Lahousen became suspicious. The next day, Admiral Canaris revealed to him the full story. An SS team had forced concentration camp prisoners to don Polish uniforms and then shot the men in front of the radio station, making it appear that Poles had attacked it. Hitler had his provocation for invading Poland.

Amen introduced document 1795 PS, dated August 17, 1939, the transcript of a meeting between Keitel and Canaris. The document made it clear that the Gleiwitz scheme had originated with the SS. But it was Keitel who had approved the army's participation and who ordered Canaris to come up with the uniforms for the synthetic attack that launched World War II.

The next day, Amen questioned Lahousen about orders Keitel had given for the recapture and execution of two fugitive French generals, Maxime Weygand and Henri Giraud, before they could slip back to France. "The order to liquidate, that is, to murder Weygand and Giraud was given to me by Canaris, who received it from Keitel," Lahousen testified. But he and Canaris had connived so that the odious order was never carried out. As Lahousen spoke, Keitel's posture slackened visibly.

9

ERWIN LAHOUSEN CONTINUED on the stand, implicating Göring, Keitel, and Jodl in the destruction of Warsaw, the Reprisal Order, and the extermination of the Polish intelligentsia, nobility, and clergy. Cross-examination of him by the defense attorneys revealed their clumsiness with the unfamiliar technique. They merely elicited further testimony so damaging that they stopped questioning the general.

When Lahousen had finished, Sir Geoffrey declared a recess. The court was to be cleared of all visitors, he announced. A delicate issue was about to be decided in closed session: the competency of Rudolf Hess to stand trial. His behavior raised reasonable doubt—eating while lying on the floor, goose-stepping in the exercise yard, refusing to wear earphones, making obscene asides, and reading novels in court. Three weeks before, at the court's request, Hess had undergone examination by a ten-man panel of psychiatrists from America, Great

Britain, and the Soviet Union. The panel concluded that Hess's amnesia would "interfere with his ability to conduct his defense and to understand the details of the past." The final decision on his competence to stand trial, however, rested with the justices.

Shortly after the experts had examined Hess, Major Kelley had gone to see Jackson with an idea for restoring Hess's memory. Hess's condition was what psychiatrists called "hysterical amnesia," Kelley explained. The man might be snapped out of it by "truth drugs," Amytal or Pentothal. Kelley was familiar with the use of them in over a thousand cases with no ill effect, he said. Still, Jackson turned him down. If Hess was struck by lightning a month later, he feared, the drug would be blamed. They could not take the chance. Jackson was, nevertheless, curious to know what Kelley thought of Hess. "If one considers the road as sanity and the sidewalk as insanity," Kelley said, "then Hess spends the greater part of his time on the curb." Maybe so, Jackson replied, but he was going to urge the judges that Hess be tried.

During the recess before the competency hearing, Captain Gilbert approached Hess in the dock. Gilbert was convinced of the authenticity of the man's amnesia, but thought he ought to warn him of the likely consequences. If the judges found Hess incompetent to stand trial, "You probably won't be coming to court anymore," Gilbert advised, and he would soon be separated from the other defendants.

Hess looked stunned. In the few minutes before the court would resume, he had to make a decision. He had already spent five years in an alien, unsympathetic land. For the past two months, however confined, he had lived again among his compatriots, speaking his native tongue. Even coming into court daily represented more sociability than he had known in all those years.

The bailiff shouted, "Attention." The judges returned, and Sir Geoffrey declared the court back in session. He gestured toward Hess's lawyer, Gunther von Rohrscheidt, an older man whose previous practice had been in automobile accident liability cases. The diminutive Rohrscheidt adjusted his robe and began to explain why his client should not stand trial, quoting extensively from the psychiatric panel's report. Because of his memory loss, Hess could not follow the court proceedings, could not testify, could not challenge witnesses, in short, could not defend himself.

As the lawyer spoke, Hess ripped a sheet from a notebook and scribbled on it. He signaled to a guard to take the note to Rohrscheidt. The lawyer glanced at it but kept on talking. Hess began gesturing wildly for Rohrscheidt to stop. Justice Lawrence, unable to ignore the defendant's behavior, asked Rohrscheidt if Herr Hess might speak for himself. Hess rose and a microphone was brought to him. The court observed a Rudolf Hess not seen before at Nuremberg. His manner was calm, the voice steady. "Mr. President," he said, "henceforth, my memory will again respond to the outside world. The reasons for sim- ulating loss of memory were of a tactical nature. . . . My capacity to follow the trial, to defend myself, to put questions to witnesses, to answer questions myself is not affected." Dr. Rohrscheidt was not a part of this deception, Hess went on. He had fooled the lawyer too. He rejected the authority of the IMT, Hess maintained. However, he was competent to stand trial. A stunned Lawrence quickly adjourned the court.

As reporters rushed to the pressroom phones to file the news, Douglas Kelley and Gustav Gilbert hurried to Hess's cell. They had believed in the man's mental impairment. Their professional reputations were on the line. They found Hess smiling calmly, the mad stare absent from his eyes. He spoke easily, answering in detail their questions about his youth, his conversations with Hitler, his flight to Scotland. Gilbert asked if Hess remembered his saying he might not be coming to court anymore. "Yes," Hess said, "that's when I decided to stop playing the game."

The two men left, subdued. Could they have been wrong and a layman like Burton Andrus right? Kelley ventured that Hess's amnesia was still real. It was this sudden cure that was the hoax. He was aware of numerous cases, he said, where amnesia patients, in order to pre- serve their ego, claimed that they had only pretended loss of memory.

Gilbert excused himself to duck into the prison office and write out his notes. After recording their conversation with Hess, he wrote his assessment: "Rejected as insane by the Führer, Hess seeks refuge in amnesia, then snaps out of it to avoid the same reaction by his friends." Hess's amnesia was therefore real, Gilbert concluded, but controllable at his discretion.

Gilbert next stopped by Keitel's cell. He knew that the field marshal, after General Lahousen's testimony, had been much distraught. "I don't know what to say," Keitel began, speaking of the plot to murder the two escaped French generals. "I know that an officer and a gentleman like yourself must be wondering about me. These charges attack my honor as an officer. I don't care if they accuse me of starting a war. I was only doing my duty and following orders. But these assassination stories, I don't know how I ever got mixed up in this." He had violated a sacred tenet of the Prussian officer corps: the inviolability of another general's person, whether friend or enemy. During the lunch break today, he said, the other military men, Dönitz, Raeder, even his longtime associate Alfred Jodl, had cut him dead.

The Saturday morning after Hess's turnabout, the judges announced their decision on the man's competence. Hess would stand trial. The legal definition of sanity that had guided them was a defendant's capacity to distinguish between right and wrong. In the judgment of the IMT, Rudolf Hess had moved off the curb and into the road.

10

THE GUARD ON Julius Streicher's cell motioned to the GI on Wilhelm Frick's cell to come over. What he wanted to show would only take a second. Frick's guard made sure his prisoner was asleep in the proper position, back to the wall, hands outside the covers, and came over to Streicher's cell. Streicher's guard had fashioned a tiny hangman's noose from a piece of string. He was dangling the string in front of the spotlight directed into the cell. The light projected the shadow of the noose, full size, against the back wall. Streicher's guard banged on the door. Streicher awoke, sighted the shadow of the swinging noose, and let out a bloodcurdling scream. The guards laughed uproariously.

To Colonel Andrus it seemed that not a day went by without a defendant's filing a complaint. At the top of the pile this December morning was Streicher's grievance about the noose trick. Ribbentrop was complaining that he got no sleep because the guards sang "Don't Fence Me In" all night. Rosenberg protested at having to keep his hands outside the blanket. They got cold, he said, and every time he slipped them under the covers, the guard jabbed him with a pole. Göring objected to eating in the same room with a toilet bowl. Schacht disliked having VIPs parading through the cellblock, staring at the defendants like animals in a zoo. A defense lawyer wrote complaining that the colonel addressed the defendants by their last names only. In Germany that was considered rude. At least he might refer to them as "Herr so-and-so." Andrus called in his secretary, Rose Korb, and dictated his response to the lawyer: "*Herr* is a German term. It is not my practice to speak German."

These people were a mystery to him, he told her. The United States government provided them with the pencils and paper necessary to write their complaints and fed them eighteen hundred calories a day, more than other Germans were allowed. They had a six-hundred-book library, a pound-a-month tobacco ration, and a little machine for rolling their own. Dr. Pfluecker and an American physician tended to their health needs daily. They received free dental care, as long as they did not ask for anything long-term like bridges or dentures. Yet these men who complained to him about cramped quarters represented a regime that had shipped human beings to their deaths in cattle cars. Men who complained about delays in getting mail from their wives had led a regime that snatched people from their beds in the middle of the night, people who were never to be heard from again. Andrus had an idea, one form letter for answering all complaints. He started dictating to Korb: "You are hereby informed that your protest against the treatment given you is wholly unwarranted and improper. You are entitled to nothing under the Geneva Convention, which your country repudiated. . . . Your treatment here is superior to any treatment ever accorded by Germany to any of its prisoners, foreign or domestic. . . . The kind and considerate treatment you receive in this jail is accorded to you not because you deserve it, but because less would be unbecoming to us, your conquerors."

11

THE DEFENSE COUNSELS were up in arms, Sir Geoffrey Lawrence told his fellow judges. They were objecting to the flood of prosecution documents introduced in court in English with no German translations available. The Germans were further convinced that, when they requested documents, the prosecution dragged its feet in complying. An obstructed defense would make a mockery of justice, and the trial would be seen as an extravagant exercise in revenge, Lawrence feared. He asked Sir Norman Birkett to look into the complaints. Though he disliked taking direction from Sir Geoffrey, Birkett welcomed the outlet for his energies. Robert Jackson agreed to have Colonel Storey meet with Birkett and acquaint him with all that was being done to aid the defense.

Storey and Birkett drove to the courthouse together the next day. Storey described the difference between this trial and what he had observed on his OSS mission to Bulgaria six months before. In Sofia, he had watched a war-crimes trial that began in the morning. By four p.m., the verdict had been announced. By eleven p.m., the condemned men rested in a common grave. They had received virtually no defense. Sir Norman took the point, he said, but Nuremberg was not Bulgaria.

At the courthouse, the two men entered a doorway marked DEFENSE INFORMATION CENTER. Storey pointed out the library. Every law book the prosecution had been able to lay its hands on was here and available to the defense, he noted. The German lawyers were provided with secretaries, stenographers, and translators at no cost. The center was open until ten p.m. every night, seven days a week. Every day, the prosecution posted in this room a list of documents to be introduced the following day. They were available to the defense in German. As they left the center, Storey remarked, "I wonder what facilities the Germans would provide us if we were the ones being tried?" Birkett said nothing, but that night he wrote in his diary of the Defense Information Center: "More of the vaunted American efficiency, another expression of their superficial-ity." Soon afterward, Sir Geoffrey received another complaint from the defense lawyers. There were not enough coffee cups in their lunchroom.

12

DAVID Low had had a particularly good session this Monday morning, December 10. The artist had been commissioned by *The New York Times* to sketch and write impressions of the defendants. His spidery lines quickly caught the essence of his subjects. Hans Frank may have rediscovered religion, but Low's sketch captured Frank's fixed cynical sneer. Underneath it, the artist wrote, "The nastiest person present." Ribbentrop, with his pursed lips, struck Low as "a fussy family solicitor." The woeful banker, Walther Funk, had "a fat-sick face." Göring "looked jolly, until you noticed the cruel cut of his mouth." After the lunch recess, Low returned to his seat in the press section, and a new subject caught his eye: towering Ernst Kaltenbrunner. Kaltenbrunner, sufficiently recovered from his stroke, was making his first appearance in the dock. Low took out his sketch pad and began to limn a brute.

Kaltenbrunner had been released from the hospital and returned to his cell the previous weekend. While away, he learned from a friendly POW orderly the best news since his arrest. SS Major Franz Ziereis, commandant of the Mauthausen concentration camp, was dead. Quite possibly the most damning witness against Kaltenbrunner had gone to the grave.

Knowing that Kaltenbrunner's return from the hospital was imminent, Captain Gilbert had reviewed the man's dossier in advance of a cell visit. Gilbert found in Kaltenbrunner a classic Nazi success story. He had been born in Austria to a Catholic family in 1903 in Ried on the Inn, virtually next door to Hitler's birthplace, Braunau. Kaltenbrunner was a third-generation lawyer and liked to boast that he had put himself through school working the night shift in a coal mine and thus considered himself a friend of the workingman. Kaltenbrunner joined the Austrian Nazi party in the thirties and soon amassed useful credentials, beating up democratic Austrians, robbing to support Nazi party activities, tapping telephones, and instigating riots. He soon caught the eye of Heinrich Himmler, chief of the SS. Kaltenbrunner came into prominence in 1942, when Czech agents tossed a bomb into the Mercedes sports car of Reinhard Heydrich, head of the RSHA, the Nazi police apparatus. Himmler plucked Kaltenbrunner, then a relatively unknown provincial SS leader, to succeed Heydrich. He had substantial shoes to fill. Heydrich had masterminded the phony Polish attack on the Gleiwitz radio station for Heinrich Himmler. Heydrich had been in charge of the *Einsatzgruppen*, the extermination squads that followed the German armies into Poland and Russia. Heydrich had drafted the protocol for the "Final Solution of the Jewish problem."

Kaltenbrunner may have lacked Heydrich's icy finesse. He may often have been drunk. But he went at his duties—chief of the Gestapo, the concentration camps, the ŠD—with crude energy. Along the way he developed ideas that might have seemed odd to anyone except fellow Nazis. Kaltenbrunner believed that all German women of fertile age must bear children. If their husbands could not do the job, then proven fathers should do it for them. The father of three children himself, Kaltenbrunner had also acquired a titled mistress, the Countess Gisela von Westaupwolf, who gave birth to twins toward the war's end.

Even the inevitability of defeat had not tempered Kaltenbrunner's zeal. As the Allied armies plunged into Germany, he had sent out an order to the concentration camps: "The liberation of prisoners or Jews by the enemy, be it by the Western enemies or the Red Cross, must be avoided. . . . They must not fall into their hands alive." Just eleven days before the war ended, he informed Franz Ziereis, the Mauthausen commandant, that his quota was still 1,000 Jews to be killed daily. When time ran out on that schedule, he ordered Ziereis to herd all remaining prisoners into a tunnel, seal off the entrance, and suffocate them. Even Ziereis, who had supervised the deaths of 65,000 people, blanched at this last order and did not comply. When the desperation of his plight had pierced even Kaltenbrunner's alcoholic fog, he played his last card. He ordered the surrender of Mauthausen and its survivors to General Patton. It was this final order, and not the orders to the dead Ziereis, that he was counting on to save him.

Of all the papers in Kaltenbrunner's dossier, one that impressed Gilbert was a report by a doctor who examined the man after he had been appointed chief of the RSHA. Never, the doctor wrote, had he seen such a lummox, or one so stupid. "The man would have to get drunk to be capable of reasoning," the doctor concluded.

Kaltenbrunner's appearance that afternoon triggered a three-alarm press alert and a correspondents' stampede for the courtroom. The photographers were particularly pleased; Kaltenbrunner was a Nazi out of central casting. He lumbered into the dock with a lopsided smile on his long horse face. He put a hand out to General Jodl, who refused to take it. He greeted Hans Frank, but Frank turned away. He took his place next to Keitel, who suddenly felt a need to talk to Ribbentrop. Kaltenbrunner spied his lawyer, Kurt Kauffmann, a fellow Nazi. He rose, leaned over the rail of the dock, and put out his hand. Kauffmann clasped his hands behind his back and gave Kaltenbrunner a brief nod.

Justice Lawrence called the court to order. The first business this afternoon was to hear the plea of Ernst Kaltenbrunner, he announced. Kaltenbrunner rose, looking like a helpless giant. When the indictment had been served on him nearly two months before, he had written on it, "I do not feel guilty of any war crimes. I have done my duty as an intelligence operative. I refuse to serve as an ersatz Himmler." Throughout his captivity, he had taken the position that he was only nominally responsible for the Gestapo and the concentration camps. His superior, the late Reichsführer Himmler, had his own people who actually ran those operations. Kaltenbrunner merely sat on top of them in an organization chart. His true role, he intended to convince the court, had been to run the SD, essentially an intelligence service. The guard handed him a microphone. Kaltenbrunner ran his fingernail across the face of it to see if it was live. In a voice totally at odds with his brutal appearance, a voice smooth, cultivated, and reasonable, he said, "I am not guilty."

David Low sketched in Kaltenbrunner's long purple "dueling scar." Like so much about the man, the scar was a fraud. It had been earned not in a test of manliness, but against a windshield in an auto accident after a drunken spree.

13

ONE OF THE STREAM of visitors to Nuremberg that December was Major Albert Callan of the army's Counterintelligence Corps, who had come ashore on D-Day and later fought with the French resistance. Before he went home on points, Callan wanted to witness the war-crimes trial. While applying for a visitor's pass at the Palace of Justice, Callan ran into an old CIC buddy now posted to Nuremberg, who invited him to lunch at the Grand Hotel.

Their waiter spoke the lightly accented English of an educated person and seemed unusually attentive, Callan thought. As the waiter left, Callan's friend said quietly, "One of ours." "What?" Callan asked. "He works for CIC. We've got agents spotted all over town to keep an eye on the Commies. They report anything useful to us." CIC people, he explained, were also searching any cargo the Russians trucked in. Feelings were running high between the American and Russian military, Callan's friend added, and matters were getting touchy. Just a few nights before, a Red Army driver, waiting outside the Grand for his superior, had been shot to death in an argument with a GI. As Callan listened to the catalogue of friction and suspicion, he said, "There goes the alliance."

14

COLONEL ANDRUS COULD virtually hear the air crackle between himself and his superior, Brigadier General Leroy Watson, commander of the Nuremberg-Furth Enclave. From their first encounter, Watson had been antagonistic, examining the colonel's shining helmet and riding crop as if they were contaminated objects. Andrus resented the way Watson had summoned him this December afternoon. "You will report personally and immediately to explain . . . ," the memo had begun. Andrus stood in Watson's huge office, just inside the entrance to the courthouse, waiting for Watson to express the elementary courtesy of asking a fellow officer to sit down. The gesture was long in coming. The two men were roughly the same age, with the gray-haired, stocky Watson even tougher-looking than Andrus.

Watson was obsessed with security. Unfortunately for Andrus, this concern did not appear to extend to the safekeeping of the prisoners in the colonel's charge. Andrus had put in a request to Third Army Headquarters for more personnel. Watson had disapproved. Instead, he cut Andrus's roster. He was getting the dregs, Andrus complained. "I can't be held responsible for the court and the prisoners with insufficient manpower." Watson cut him off. That was not why he had summoned him. He wanted to know how two CIC agents had been able to slip into the courthouse past Andrus's guards without passes. What kind of security did he call that? Watson demanded.

Sitting outside in the general's waiting room was a cherub-faced nineteen-year-old private first class, Gunther Sadel, who could hear every word. Sadel sensed the steeliness in Watson's voice and wondered what it boded for him, since he was just reporting for duty in the Watson operation. Sadel was half-Jewish and had escaped Germany in 1939 at the age of thirteen. His Gentile mother had been forced to divorce Sadel's Jewish father and had stayed behind in Berlin. Sadel had never heard from her again. He eventually joined his father in America, and had been drafted late in the war. His command of German had saved him from becoming an infantry replacement during the bloody fighting along the Rhine. He was assigned instead to the CIC, and was now posted to Nuremberg.

Andrus left, and Sadel was summoned into Watson's office. The general spoke almost paternally to Sadel, with far more courtesy than he had shown Andrus, though he quickly got down to business. The nonfraternization policy had failed miserably, Watson explained. One only had to look at the epidemic of venereal diseases to know it. It was just as well that the army had dropped the policy. But a lot of these GIs, and officers too, Watson said, were taking out the wrong kind of girls, probably divulging secrets to them. Who knew what information these women might be passing along to the lawyers for the defense, or to the Communists? From now on, they had to be screened. Once a girl checked out okay, Watson's office would issue her a "social pass" with her picture on it. The pass would allow a girl into the various enlisted men's clubs. The social pass would not apply to the Grand Hotel. There were too many secrets floating around the Marble Room already. No German women were to be allowed there. He was giving the job of implementing the pass system to Sadel.

The day the announcement appeared that German women would need a pass to enter a GI club, Gunther Sadel feared he had unleashed a riot. A surging mob surrounded the Nuremberg Opera House, where applications were to be submitted. Sadel knew that more than a date with a GI was at stake. For a German girl, the social pass meant a decent meal, maybe a little extra food that could be slipped back to a hungry mother or kid brother. And with this winter proving the harshest in a generation, a date at a GI club meant, if nothing else, a warm night. Sadel had drafted rules for obtaining the social pass: no married women, no former Nazi party members, no members of the Bund Deutscher Mädel (the female version of the Hitler Youth), no prostitutes, and no one with a criminal record. He found the recently reactivated Nuremberg police only too willing to curry the favor of the Americans by divulging anything in their files on their women.

15

COMMANDER JIM DONOVAN, who had shown the earlier concentration camp movie, had recently sold Robert Jackson on a film that could make the conspiracy charge something more than a paper abstraction. George Stevens and the writer Budd Schulberg had compiled this film from captured German newsreels and propaganda footage. They called it *The Nazi Plan*. The morning session of December 11, the courtroom lights went out, and a projector threw a test pattern on the screen. The defendants sat resignedly, remembering the disastrous effect of the earlier film. *The Nazi Plan* opened with a familiar voice. The defendants turned to Alfred Rosenberg, who could be heard narrating scenes from the Leni Riefenstahl propaganda masterpiece, *Triumph of the Will*. Nuremberg, as it had once been, appeared on the screen during the Party Day rallies. Albert Speer could not suppress a smile as he watched the spectacle of his invention, ranks of powerful searchlights throwing an ethereal "cathedral of ice" over Zeppelin Field. Under this luminous arch, throngs of torchbearers marched to an insistent drumbeat, platoons of Hitler Youth and phalanxes of goose-stepping troops. Throaty male voices lifted the "Horst Wessel" song into the night air, and a quarter of a million Germans chanted, "*Ein Reich, ein Volk, ein Führer!* [One state, one people, one leader!]" Hitler appeared, his voice tracing its familiar cadence, almost inaudible at first, building slowly, climaxing in calculated hysteria. Gustav Gilbert studied the faces in the dock. The defendants were leaning forward in hypnotic fascination. Ribbentrop cried openly. Göring turned to Hess and said, "Justice Jackson will want to join the party now!"

The film shown in the afternoon was less pleasing to the defendants. In the aftermath of the Twentieth of July assassination attempt on Hitler, suspected conspirators had been tried by the People's Courts, some of them here in room 600. American troops had discovered eleven hours of film taken during these virtual kangaroo proceedings, of which the court was now seeing excerpts. The defendants' rapt attention of the morning gave way to restless fidgeting. Two SS men were seen dragging a defendant before a judge named Roland Freisler. The man was clutching at his beltless, falling trousers. As Freisler browbeat him, the People's Court audience could be heard laughing. Another defendant, an army officer, began describing murders he had witnessed in Poland. "Murders?" Freisler shrieked. "You piece of garbage!" The defendant sagged visibly. "Are you collapsing under the stress of your vulgarity, you filthy rogue?" Freisler went on. After the plot against Hitler, nearly five thousand Germans had lost their lives through People's Court justice.

That evening, Kelley and Gilbert made cell visits to assess the reaction to the films. They found Göring despondent. "You know what hurt me more than even the concentration camp film, bad as it was?" he asked. "It was that loudmouth, Freisler. It actually made me squirm the way he screamed at the defendants. After all, these were German generals, not yet proven guilty. I tell you, I could have died of shame." Gilbert left the cell buoyed. Something was getting through to the defendants. The difference between their trial and what passed for justice under the Nazi regime could not have escaped them.

The visit to Ribbentrop, however, was less satisfying. The man's eyes shone as he spoke of the Riefenstahl film. "Couldn't you just feel the force of the Führer's personality?" he asked. Getting no response, he added, "Well, maybe it doesn't come through on the screen." Then the eyes lit up again. Ribbentrop virtually purred: "Even though I am here in jail on trial for my life, if Hitler were to walk into this room and command anything, I would do it immediately without any thought of the consequences."

16

THE BULLETIN BOARDS POSTED around the courthouse were avidly read. To visitors, they were like a playbill, announcing what dramas would be performed next, and who would enact the featured roles. To the prosecution staff, the announcements were a starting lineup, revealing who would be getting into the game, since the goal of most of Jackson's lawyers was to appear in court. For the defense attorneys, the bulletin board revealed the opponents they would be facing. The December 11 posting indicated that the case against slave labor was scheduled next. The prosecuting attorney listed was Thomas Dodd, a former FBI man who stirred mixed feelings at Nuremberg. Socially, Dodd was a boon companion, a raconteur, enlivening an evening in the Marble Room with well-told stories. Others saw him as a born politician with a talent for maneuvering himself into the limelight. Rumors circulated that the political bosses in his native Connecticut had engineered Dodd's appointment to Nuremberg to prepare him for a run for the U.S. Congress, maybe the Senate. To his more erudite colleagues, those most at home researching law books and drafting briefs, Dodd was a lightweight who used their work to prop up his own thin legal scholarship. All were eager to observe his first performance in the arena.

As he moved to the prosecutor's stand, Dodd cut an impressive figure, his hair steel-gray, his profile classic. He stood out among the sea of uniforms in a well-tailored banker's blue suit. The most uneasy men in the dock, as Dodd spread his notes on the lectern, were Albert Speer and Fritz Sauckel. Their respective guilt for the death and suffering inflicted by the slave labor program had become a topic of hot debate in evening bull sessions at the Grand Hotel. Dodd's performance could resolve the debate.

Ernst Friedrich Christoph Sauckel, known all his life as Fritz, sat in the dock in the same state of emotional befuddlement that had marked his entire confinement. Sauckel was the least imposing figure among the defendants, a little man with a shining dome, sad brown eyes, and a silly mustache patterned after the Führer's. He was as puzzled to find himself on trial as he had been to discover that Germany had lost the war. What pained Sauckel most was that no one at Nuremberg seemed to understand his logic. How could he be guilty of crimes against working people when he himself sprang from the working class? When Airey Neave delivered the indictments in October, Sauckel had written on his, "The abyss between the ideal of a social community which I advocated as a seaman and a worker and the terrible things that happened in the concentration camps has shaken me deeply."

He was fifty-one years old, the son of a mailman and a seamstress, raised in a strict religious home. He had gone to sea as a boy of fifteen, and sat out the First World War in a French prison after his merchant ship was captured. When he came home in 1919, few berths were available for merchant seamen. Germany was convulsed by Communists and right-wingers battling for the souls of unemployed workers like Fritz Sauckel. "I could not be a Communist," he told his Nuremberg interrogators, "because Marxism states that religion is the opiate of the masses. Marxism states that private property is theft. Marxism embraces the concept of class warfare which must lead to civil war." On the other hand, he could not join the conservative political movements, "because they ignored people of my station." Then he had heard Adolf Hitler speak. "I had found a man who could create a union of all German people whatever their level, whatever their calling, workers and intellectuals." He joined the party and became an energetic if unimaginative recruiter. In the meantime, he worked as a toolmaker in a ball-bearing factory. By 1927, Sauckel was *Gauleiter*— district party chief—of Thuringia. He had risen not by flair or connections, but by tireless, plodding effort. He was uncomfortable at party affairs where other men swapped war stories and spoke of heroic deeds and medals won during a conflict which he spent in a French jail. He was uncomfortable with cultivated people. He had never read a book in his adult life. All the intellectual stimulation he needed, he said, was supplied by Adolf Hitler. Fritz Sauckel felt truly at home only within the bosom of his family, with his wife and ten children.

He remained a *Gauleiter* until a fateful day in 1942. Sitting with Sauckel in the second row of the dock, four places to his left, was the man responsible for what happened that day.

In 1942 Albert Speer, then thirty-seven, had just been appointed armaments minister. A principal task he faced was to move labor where it was most needed. But the *Gauleiters* refused to give up workers from their regional fiefdoms to send to other districts. Nominally, solving the problem should have been the responsibility of Hermann Göring, head of the Four Year Plan and presumably chief of the German economy. That, Speer knew, was laughable. Göring had become a self-indulgent sybarite barely capable of directing the Luftwaffe, much less German industry. Speer went to Hitler and persuaded him that the regime needed a labor czar, someone who could break the grip of the *Gauleiters*, preferably someone from their own ranks whom they would heed.

In March 1942, Fritz Sauckel found himself with Speer and Hitler in the Reich Chancellery in Berlin. "This has been a brutal winter," Hitler said, pacing. "We've suffered a heavy drain on our vehicles, trains, fuel. We've taken heavy manpower losses. We can only keep pace if every German enters either the military or the armaments industries." He looked directly at Sauckel. "This is a gigantic job. And you, Sauckel, are going to perform it. You have the ability. You are a party man and a patriot. Now you have a chance to fulfill your obligation as a soldier." Sauckel overcame his speechlessness long enough to ask why this honor had fallen to him. Speer spoke up. "Because," he said, "we think you've got the guts to break through the bureaucracy, to overrule the *Gauleiters* and get the job done."

Sauckel was enough of a bureaucrat to ask what authority he would have to perform this job. He was to be, Hitler said, plenipotentiary general for the allocation of labor. He would have authority to issue orders to commissioners of occupied lands, to heads of civil agencies, even to generals and admirals, to round up the labor needed. His powers in this sphere were unconditional.

Within days, Sauckel was called again before Hitler. This time there was no praise for his energy and patriotism. Hitler had Sauckel's recently proposed manpower plan crumpled in his fist. Where in it, Hitler fumed, was there provision for conscripting foreign workers? The job could not be done with German manpower alone. Sauckel was to raise 1.6 million foreign workers in the next three months, Hitler ordered. Sauckel shifted uneasily. Did not conscription of foreigners violate international law? he asked. That was not Sauckel's concern, Hitler replied. Ask for volunteers in the occupied territories; and if they did not volunteer, conscript them. Besides, the Soviet Union was not even a party to the Hague or Geneva conventions, and there were millions of able bodies there. Sauckel was to stop quibbling and start bringing in workers.

However dilatory a legal scholar, Tom Dodd was proving a dramatic courtroom performer. With well-controlled emotion, he read into the record document 294 PS, which described how a Sauckel manpower directive was carried out in the Soviet Union. The author of this report, Dodd pointed out, was Sauckel's fellow defendant Alfred Rosenberg. "You cannot imagine the bestiality," Rosenberg had written Sauckel. "The order came to supply twenty-five workers, but no one reported. Then the German militia came and began to set fire to the houses of those who had fled. . . . People who hurried to the scene were forbidden to extinguish the flames. Instead, they were beaten and arrested. They fell on their knees to kiss the hands of the policemen, but the policemen beat them again with rubber truncheons and threatened to burn down the whole village. . . . The militia went through the adjoining villages and seized laborers. . . . The imprisoned workers are locked in the schoolhouse. They cannot even go out to perform their natural functions, but have to do it like pigs in the same room. Among them are lame, blind, and aged people. We are now catching humans like dog catchers used to catch dogs."

In the beginning it had been different, Sauckel knew. He had been able to get Frenchmen, Dutchmen, Belgians, and Russians to come voluntarily to work in Germany for good wages. But after the defeat at Stalingrad, all that changed. Workers had to be dragooned, transported in handcuffs.

As Dodd went on, Sauckel waited to hear Speer's role in all this. The way the system had worked, manufacturers would inform Speer of their labor needs. A tank factory might inform him, for example, that it needed a hundred die makers, two hundred welders, and a thousand common laborers. Speer would aggregate such requests from all industries and direct Sauckel to come up with the required number of workers. Speer coordinated this task through a central planning board, of which Sauckel was not even a member. Sauckel merely saw himself as Speer's procurer.

Speer had never let up the pressure; he was forever demanding more and more workers. Sauckel suspected that Speer was hoarding labor far beyond his needs, while the army desperately sought more men. At one point, Sauckel added up all Speer's pending demands, and they totaled more workers than the entire German economy required. Complaining did no good. Sauckel knew where he stood in the pecking order. Speer had once snapped at him in Hitler's presence, "You are my man." During another squabble, Speer sent Hitler a memorandum insisting that Sauckel be treated as his assistant. Hitler himself had made clear that "Herr Speer is my main authority in all economic spheres."

A despondent Sauckel listened to Dodd pour on the incriminating evidence and wondered why nothing was said of his efforts to have foreign workers treated decently. In one directive to recruiters he had written, "Underfed slaves, diseased, resentful, despairing and filled with hate, will never yield that maximum of output which they can achieve under decent conditions." He told the *Gauleiter*s, "Beaten, half-starved or dead Russians do not supply us with coal and are utterly useless for steel production."

Dodd was now describing conditions Russian workers endured in a typical armaments factory: three-quarters of a cup of tea at four a.m. when the workday started, a quart of watery soup and two slices of bread fourteen hours later at the day's end. The workers caught mice to supplement their diet. Sauckel waved to attract the attention of his counsel, Robert Servatius. Servatius must make clear that he, Sauckel, had not been responsible for working conditions. That was Speer's bailiwick. Dodd was already reading into the record further damning evidence, Sauckel's words spoken at a meeting with Speer: "I have even employed and trained French and Italian agents of both sexes to do what was done in the old days, to shanghai, to go hunting for workers and dupe them using liquor to get them to Germany."

The Führer had given him an impossible job, and one defendant in the dock knew how hard Sauckel had tried to get out of it. During the war, Admiral Dönitz had been astonished by a radio message from one of his U-boat skippers, Captain Salmann, reporting that he had found a stowaway among the torpedoes: Fritz Sauckel. Sauckel was begging to be allowed to stay aboard in any capacity. Dönitz had ordered the sub to bring Sauckel back to port.

Sauckel traced his final fall from the Führer's grace to August 4, 1944. With the Allies securely entrenched in France, with the Red Army closing in from the east, Hitler had decided that a plenipotentiary for total war was required to maximize manpower. He called a meeting of Speer, Sauckel, Keitel, and the propaganda minister, Josef Goebbels. Goebbels immediately began attacking Sauckel. Sauckel had allowed millions of Germans to stay in soft civil service jobs, Goebbels charged. He had failed to mobilize Germany's women. Why, he said in disbelief, 500,000 females were still working as charladies!

Ever since he had taken the labor job, Sauckel had known nothing but abuse from Speer and Goebbels. They would never give this little proletarian any credit, no matter how many bodies he delivered to Germany. Behind his back they called him "Saukerl," the equivalent of "jerk." Speer regarded Sauckel as in a class with the trashman— one who served an essential function, but God forbid that he should sit down at the same table with Speer.

Without these charladies, Sauckel said, who would clean all those offices in Goebbels's propaganda ministry? Most of these women did their work before the bureaucrats even arrived, and then went to second jobs to support their families. Goebbels's own bureaucracy was larded with useless people, Sauckel noted. Yet every time the army tried to get at them, Goebbels threw the army recruiting officials out. Sauckel, by contrast, had given the lives of two of his soldier sons to Germany.

Goebbels ignored him, and said that he would be happy to take on the additional burden of plenipotentiary for total war. Keitel saw Hitler start to nod, and quickly added that this was a splendid idea. Dr. Goebbels was going to be in charge of the total war effort, Hitler announced, and Sauckel had better do as he was told. Goebbels was still not through. "History," he warned Sauckel, "will find you weak, guilty of not freeing enough men for service at the front, guilty of losing the war!" Sauckel looked to Hitler, who he thought would certainly defend him from such calumny. The Führer said nothing. Instead, he closed the meeting, expressing perfect confidence in Goebbels. After that day, Sauckel had toiled as hard as ever; but he had been invited to no more high-level meetings. Every time he tried to see Hitler, the watchdog, Bormann, said that the Führer was not feeling well. Sauckel never saw Hitler again.

Dodd returned to document 294 PS. His voice filled with cold anger as he quoted a German officer's report on a labor roundup in Russia: "Recruiting methods were used which probably have their precedent only in the blackest periods of the slave trade. A regular manhunt was inaugurated."

Captain Gilbert went to see Sauckel in his cell. He found him sitting on his cot, head bowed, hands dangling between his legs, yet eager to talk. The captain must understand, Sauckel said: "About the abuse of foreign workers, I am really not responsible. I was like a seaman's agency. If I supply hands for a ship, I am not responsible for any cruelty they may experience on board. I just supplied workers. If they were mistreated, it was not my fault." The ship's captain was to blame, he said, and the captain of the German war industry had been Albert Speer.

17

THE PLACE TO ESCAPE the sullen city when the day's work was done was the Marble Room in the Grand Hotel, where the food was good, the drinks large, and both subsidized by Uncle Sam. Five dollars easily financed an evening of dining and drinking, and the waiter would be happy with a two-cigarette tip. Major Airey Neave threaded his way through the jeeps and command cars that clogged the hotel's entrance as the sounds of Kamil Behoneck's orchestra filtered out into the street. Herr Meyer, the manager, always smiling, greeted Neave, displaying his phenomenal memory for names. Neave entered the Marble Room, where Zarah Leander was singing, "*Der Wind hat mir ein Lied Erzählt*." Leander had been a singer and film star of some prominence. Now her voice had a mechanical quality, like a piano roll played too often. Her gown, once fashionable, was now frayed and faded, like her song. Years before, even months earlier, she would have been singing the same refrain for storm troopers and party stalwarts.

Neave made his way around the dancers to a table where he

joined British friends. Under the festive disorder, the Marble Room had a traceable structure. American men dominated the room, usually sitting together, though they might have with them as many British women as Americans. The American women were easy to spot— smartly dressed, spared the six years of clothes rationing that European women had undergone. At one American table, Tom Dodd, fresh from his presentation of the slave labor case, held court in an ebullient mood.

Neave was struck by the contrast between the horror revealed in the courtroom during the day and the determined merriment of the Marble Room at night. He sat down, and his companions asked what Neave thought of Dodd's performance. Whatever their respective guilt, Neave observed, the contest between Sauckel and Speer was going to be influenced by social class. Look at the men on the bench. Then look at Speer and Sauckel. Whom would they invite to their club? A companion disagreed. The Speer-Sauckel case would revolve around another question: Who had been the motive force in the slave labor operation, Sauckel the slave trader, or Speer the slave driver? If it had been the latter, then it seemed hard to believe that Speer could suffer a lesser fate than Sauckel. Neave hoped the bench could be that objective.

18

DURING THE GLORY DAYS, Heinrich Hoffmann had often stayed at the Grand Hotel with Adolf Hitler. Now Hoffmann occupied a cell in the Nuremberg prison. As Hitler's personal photographer, Hoffmann had been shrewd enough on his arrest to bring with him a cache of photos. Since he was the only one who knew what they portrayed, Hoffmann managed to have himself made a trusty and was given the job of indexing the pictures. Hoffmann had a son-in-law in the dock: Baldur von Schirach, the youth leader, was married to his daughter, Henriette. This relationship, however, did not prevent Hoffmann from happily gathering photographic evidence against Schirach or any of his other former colleagues.

Hoffmann was supervised by lean, athletic Richard Heller, a thirty-year-old navy lieutenant and lawyer who spoke a smattering of

German. The first time Heller saw Hoffmann, the old man was lost in an oversize set of dyed army-reject fatigues. Yet, a twinkle shone in his eye as he introduced himself with a flourish as "Professor Hoffmann, doctor of fine arts."

Hoffmann constantly badgered Heller that there was no reason to keep him locked up. He was not going anywhere, and he could be far handier to the prosecution if he were free. He knew where tons of photographs were hidden, he said. Heller trusted Hoffmann, or at least recognized him as a predictable opportunist with no loyalties except to his own survival, and persuaded his superiors to allow him to take Hoffmann on a photographic hunting expedition.

Their jeep no sooner set out on the bomb-cratered road to Munich than Hoffmann piqued Heller's curiosity by mentioning that it was he who had introduced Eva Braun to Hitler. He had been running a photography shop in Munich at the time, he said, and felt uneasy about Hitler's interest in young girls, particularly in Hoffmann's seventeen-year-old daughter, Henriette. Hitler at the time had been in his forties. Hoffmann deliberately steered the Führer to another seventeen-year-old—his shop assistant Eva Braun. What Hoffmann omitted from this account was that much of his business had been in pornographic postcards and photographs of nude dancers. His models had been girls who worked in second-rate bars—including Braun, who had become both his assistant and his mistress. He had happily handed Eva over to the Führer.

Hoffmann was a shrewd businessman. He had persuaded Hitler to grant him a monopoly on selling photographs of the top Nazi leaders to the German people. He then founded a publishing house, and his turnover for the pictures and albums totaled 58 million marks in the twelve years of Nazi rule. Still, the old pornographer and court jester hungered for respectability, and he had persuaded Hitler to have the degree of doctor of fine arts conferred on him.

When Hoffmann and Heller arrived in Munich, the German indeed unearthed a photographic lode. He also hit up a friend for a feathered hat, a Tyrolean jacket, and a pair of formal striped pants several sizes too big, an outfit that was to become his everyday attire. After Munich, Heller wanted to take a side trip to Dachau. In the camp, which still exuded the odor of death, Hoffmann put on a sober face and professed his shame. His contrition, however, was short-lived.

As they hit the road again, this time for Berchtesgaden, Hoffmann began again entertaining Heller with stories of the Nazi court. The others around Hitler had been spellbound by the man, Hoffmann confided. But he was not. He knew too much about the private Hitler. Eva Braun, for example, was so coarse that Hoffmann's wife had to tell her how to dress. Heller wanted to know if Hitler's affair with Eva had ever been consummated. He was not sure about the Führer's sexuality, Hoffmann said. If he had to guess, he would have said that Hitler was probably asexual.

By the time the expedition ended, they had unearthed enough photos to fill two army trucks. On their return to Nuremberg, Heller concluded that there was no further need to cage Heinrich Hoffmann. He arranged more desirable lodgings for his traveling companion.

Countess Inge Kalnoky opened the door of the Witness House to an older man, his white hair tinted with a blue rinse. Tyrolean hat in hand, he made a sweeping bow and introduced himself as Professor Heinrich Hoffmann. He was, he said, going to be her guest.

Hoffmann quickly established himself as the house jester. Over dinner, he regaled other guests with stories of life in Hitler's entourage. Someone asked if he had known Hess. Of course, Hoffmann said. He had been with Rudolf when somebody hit him in the head with a brick at a rally in Munich. That explained why Hess was so loony, Hoffmann said. Kalnoky had lodged several men like General Erwin Lahousen, broken by their experiences under Nazism. She found Heinrich Hoffmann, however, irrepressible, a man untouched by shame, suffering, or defeat.

19

IT WAS COLONEL ANDRUS'S POLICY that his staff not talk to reporters. So why, he wanted to know, had Captain Gilbert been giving interviews? He had information, the colonel said, that Gilbert had talked to Reuters on December 12 and to the London *Daily Express* on December 13. It was true, Gilbert admitted. Day after day, the reporters saw him in intimate conversation with the men in the dock whom they were not allowed to interview. Consequently, they hounded him for insider stories. For a long time, he had resisted. Avoiding the press had seemed part of an unspoken arrangement with Kelley not to give away anything intended for their book. But Kelley himself had gone on Armed Forces Network, the most listened-to station in Europe. Harold Burson, a twenty-four-year-old tech sergeant heading the Nuremberg AFN bureau, had chosen the congenial Kelley over the deadly earnest Gilbert for an interview about Göring. On the air, Kelley had described Göring as "dominant, aggressive, merciless, yet a jovial extrovert capable of occasional tenderness. The only real leader among them." Kelley had given away other tidbits. He had described how he once told Göring that it seemed Hitler's entourage was composed entirely of yes-men. That was true, Göring had replied: "All the no-men are six feet under." On learning of the Kelley broadcast, Gilbert concluded that if one coauthor could give interviews, why not the other? That was when he had spoken to Reuters and the *Express*.

Gilbert apologized to Andrus, promised to sin no more, and left the office. He had two relationships with the colonel, as if he were two different people. In one role, he became Dr. Gustav Gilbert, practitioner of a suspect profession, to be treated warily and at arm's length. In the other role, he was Captain Gilbert, spy for the prison commandant, to be dealt with confidentially if not necessarily warmly. He had performed the latter role well. Gilbert arranged to have German-speaking soldiers among the white-helmeted GIs guarding the dock. They reported to him daily what they overheard the defendants saying to each other. He had set up a similar arrangement with the escort guards who brought the prisoners from the cellblock to the courtroom. Whatever Gilbert gleaned, he passed on to Andrus. He was also supplying the same information to Justice Jackson.

Gilbert wondered if Kelley fully appreciated him. It was not only that he could speak to the defendants in their own language. Gilbert, with his formal manner, using the old-fashioned forms of respectful address, came across to the defendants as more European than American. The confidence he enjoyed in the cellblock was now near total. All of them, except the clamlike Jodl, had opened their hearts to Gilbert. And these confidences, Kelley should realize, would be the making of their book.

Nuremberg at the time of the trial, and after eleven Allied air raids. *(Walter Sanders/Life magazine © Time-Warner)*

RIGHT: Hermann Göring, the number-two Nazi after Hitler, in the dock and some sixty-five pounds lighter than at the time of his arrest. *(U.S. Army Signal Corps)*

BELOW: Field Marshal Wilhelm Keitel, chief of staff of the German armed forces, derided by the Nazis as "lakeitel," Hitler's "lackey." *(National Archives)*

Fritz Sauckel, organizer of the conscript labor program. A key trial issue: who was guiltier, Sauckel the slave trader or Speer the slave driver? *(National Archives)*

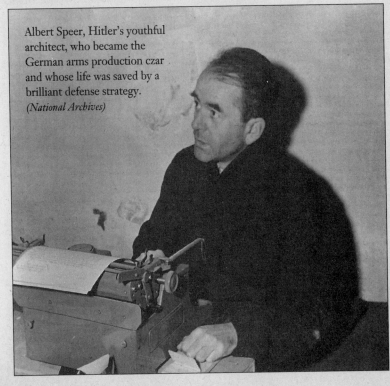

Albert Speer, Hitler's youthful architect, who became the German arms production czar and whose life was saved by a brilliant defense strategy. *(National Archives)*

In the dock: Grand Admiral Karl Dönitz, chief of the German navy and the man Hitler chose as his successor. *(National Archives)*

Baldur von Schirach, creator of the Hitler Youth, later gauleiter of Vienna, who compared his youth movement to the American Boy Scouts. *(National Archives)*

ABOVE: Ernst Kaltenbrunner, scar-faced chief of the RSHA, whose responsibilities included the Gestapo and the death camps. *(National Archives)*

RIGHT: Hans Frank, the "Jew Butcher of Cracow," Nazi governor-general of occupied Poland, who may have shared a secret with Hitler: possible partial Jewish ancestry. *(National Archives)*

LEFT: Julius Streicher, publisher of the tabloid anti-Semitic newspaper *Der Stürmer*, a man so corrupt that even a Nazi tribunal called him "unfit for human leadership." *(National Archives)*

BELOW: Alfred Rosenberg, Nazi party "philosopher," minister of the Eastern Occupied Territories, and art thief for Hitler and Göring. *(National Archives)*

BELOW: Grand Admiral Erich Raeder, earlier chief of the German navy, who heard Hitler declare his intention to make aggressive war, yet stayed on. *(National Archives)*

LEFT: Arthur Seyss-Inquart, an Austrian who helped turn his country over to Hitler and later became Nazi commissioner of Holland. *(National Archives)*

BELOW: Wilhelm Frick, minister of the interior, who prepared some of the earliest anti-Semitic laws, described as the most colorless man in the dock. *(National Archives)*

RIGHT: Colonel General Alfred Jodl, operations chief of the German armed forces, who might have suffered a lesser fate if the Russians had not insisted on including him among the major war criminals. *(National Archives)*

BELOW: Rudolf Hess, third-ranking Nazi, who made the quixotic peace flight to Scotland. Behind him is Gustav Gilbert, psychologist. *(National Archives)*

OPPOSITE: Jewish children held for medical experiments at Auschwitz. Part of the trial's photographic record. *(National Archives)*

ABOVE: Nazi roundup of Jews from the Warsaw Ghetto. Part of the trial's photographic record. *(National Archives)*

BELOW: Jewish women herded past German troops at a concentration camp in Poland. Part of the trial's photographic record. *(Lydia Chagall; courtesy U.S. Holocaust Museum)*

RIGHT: A canister of the gas Zyklon (Cyclone) B, used to exterminate inmates at Auschwitz and other camps. Part of the trial's photographic record. *(National Archives)*

BELOW: Boxes containing gold teeth extracted from murdered concentration camp inmates and later deposited in the Reichsbank. *(National Archives)*

BELOW: Two inmates at the crematorium in the Mauthausen extermination camp. *(U.S. Army Signal Corps; courtesy Air Force Academy)*

The Palace of Justice. Behind it lies the prison, comprising four buildings. The defendants were held in the right-hand wing. The small structure angled to the right of that wing is the gym, where the executions were carried out. *(National Archives)*

Cellblock C, where the defendants were jailed, with a twenty-four-hour guard posted at each cell. The wire fencing in the upper tiers was designed to prevent suicide leaps. *(National Archives)*

RIGHT: Colonel Burton Andrus (left), the prison commandant, in the walkway that joined the prison to the Palace of Justice. *(National Archives)*

LEFT: A cell, looking toward the door. The toilet was concealed from the guard's vision, an arrangement that permitted the defendant Robert Ley to carry out his suicide undetected. *(Charles Alexander)*

RIGHT: Guarding Hermann Göring's cell. A spotlight was beamed on the prisoners during the night while they slept. *(U.S. Army Signal Corps; courtesy U.S. Air Force Academy)*

BELOW: Interior of the courtroom. The prisoners' dock is at the far left, the bench at the far right, and the witness stand at the rear. Seated before the dock are the defense counsels. Seen in the far left corner are the interpreters' booths, and the prosecutors are seated in the foreground. *(National Archives)*

Mementos on the table in Hermann Göring's cell. *(National Archives)*

RIGHT: Hermann Göring in the visitors' room posing with Lieutenant "Tex" Wheelis, who befriended the Nazi and may have played a role in Göring's suicide. *(U.S. Army Signal Corps; courtesy Rose Korb Williams)*

Master Sergeant John Woods, who hanged the condemned men. *(AP/Wide World Photo)*

Captain Drexel Sprecher, who prosecuted Schirach and Fritzsche. *(Ray D'Addario)*

The International Military Tribunal (left to right): Robert Falco, Henri Donnedieu de Vabres, Ion Timofeevich Nikitchenko, Sir Geoffrey Lawrence, Alexander Volchkov, General William L. Mitchell (court administrative officer), Francis Biddle, Sir Norman Birkett. (Missing is John Parker, the American alternate.) *(U.S. Army Signal Corps; courtesy U.S. Air Force Academy)*

LEFT: Chief Soviet prosecutor Lieutenant General Roman Rudenko, who later prosecuted the American U2 spy-plane pilot Gary Powers. *(National Archives)*

BELOW: The American chief prosecutor, Associate Justice of the U.S. Supreme Court Robert Jackson, in court. To his left is Sir David Maxwell-Fyfe, the major British prosecutor on the scene. *(National Archives)*

On a December evening, the two Americans stopped by Göring's cell to find the *Reichsmarschall* in a fury. He had seen a newspaper photograph of Heinrich Hoffmann sorting out pictures for the prosecution. "When I think of the money that bastard made selling my picture!" Göring fumed. "It must have been at least a million marks, at five pfennings apiece. And now he's finding pictures to hang me!"

Kelley turned the conversation to the prosecution's charge of aggression. They did not have to show those films or read all those boring documents to prove that Germany armed for war, Göring said. "I rearmed Germany until we bristled! When they told me I was playing with war by building up the Luftwaffe, I told them I certainly wasn't running a girls' finishing school."

One of the guards had recently passed along to Gilbert a paper found on Ribbentrop's floor. In it, Ribbentrop described a conversation with Hitler one week before the Führer's suicide. According to Ribbentrop's recollection of the conversation, Hitler had said that Göring did not understand aircraft development and that the man was a fount of misinformation. When the Americans started bombing Germany with four-engine planes, Göring told Hitler that this was splendid; these planes were the easiest to shoot down. According to Ribbentrop, Hitler had considered Göring's failure in the air to be the chief cause of Germany's defeat.

Gilbert confronted Göring with this story. Göring gave out a contemptuous laugh. Did the Americans know what Ribbentrop had done when he was presented to the king of England? Göring asked. He gave the Hitler salute. "I told the Führer," Göring went on, "how would you like it if Stalin sent an ambassador to Berlin and he greeted you with 'Long live the Communist revolution'?" After the assassination attempt on Hitler, Ribbentrop had said foolish things, Göring claimed, so "I hit him with my marshal's baton. I said, 'Shut up, Ribbentrop, you champagne peddler.' And he said, 'Remember, I am still foreign minister and my name is *von* Ribbentrop.'" Göring laughed uproariously. The way that Ribbentrop had virtually bought the noble *von* was a standing joke among the Nazis, he said.

Kelley asked if Germany had not behaved criminally by breaking foreign treaties. "Just between us," Göring said, "I considered your treaties so much toilet paper."

Göring stretched Gilbert's professional demeanor to the breaking point. Gilbert was sickened that the man had developed a following among Americans and Britishers at Nuremberg. Many of them openly admired his blunt honesty, his unapologetic admission of his acts, his pungent humor. Howard Smith, the broadcaster, had reported that Göring had become a courtroom barometer. If Göring looked up in surprise at a fact, the prosecution double-checked it for accuracy. If he nodded, the prosecution knew that the defense would not challenge the fact. If Göring shook his head, it meant the prosecution had it wrong. And the court never tried to rein him in.

Gilbert had found ways to inflict his own quiet punishments on Göring. He knew it was important to the *Reichsmarschall* to board the courtroom elevator first, so he arranged with the guards to put him on last. Gilbert also knew that Göring hated to be ogled by the spectators on his way up to the lunchroom during the midday break—Göring tried to make himself less conspicuous by walking among a knot of other prisoners—so Gilbert instructed the guards to push him out front.

20

On December 13, Tom Dodd again demonstrated his talent for the dramatic. Some of his diffident colleagues were scandalized that Justice Jackson had approved Dodd's approach, in what looked this time like a total retreat from the documentary strategy. The evidence that Dodd planned to introduce had been kept in paper bags by Lieutenant Barrett, chief of the documents room. Now concealed by white sheets, the exhibits rested on the prosecutors' table in the courtroom. No trace of flamboyance marked Dodd's manner today; he spoke with grim matter-of-factness. The first exhibit, he explained, was the result of an order that had gone out in 1939 from Standartenführer Karl Koch, commandant of the Buchenwald concentration camp. Koch had ordered all tattooed prisoners to report to the dispensary. Those with the most interesting and artistic tattoos were put to death by lethal injection. Dodd whisked the sheet from USA exhibit 253. The exposed, pale, leathery objects with the designs of ships and hearts still visible, Dodd said, were human skin. The Buchenwald commandant's

wife, Ilse Koch, now confined here in the Nuremberg jail, liked to
have the tattooed flesh tanned and fashioned into household objects
like lampshades.

USA exhibit 254, Dodd explained, originated with the punishment the Nazis reserved for Poles who had sexual relations with
German women. Those caught were hanged, Dodd said, pulling away
the sheet from the next exhibit. From a distance it was not easy to
identify the fist-size, nut-brown object. It was, Dodd explained, the
head of an executed Pole, shrunken and used as a paperweight by
Koch. As Dodd took his seat, the stillness in the courtroom was interrupted only by nervous coughing. To some, Tom Dodd was a
grandstander. One critic described him as a "photogenic phoney,"
another as a "glory hound." But to others, he was a formidable prosecutor and a quick study. Give Tom the right material in court, and
he would make it sing.

Justice Lawrence averted his gaze from the exhibits as he called
upon the defense to cross-examine. Rudolf Dix, a sixty-one-year-old
Berliner, well thought of by the judges because he had defended Germans hauled before the People's Courts in the Nazi era, had been
chosen this day as defense spokesman. Dix looked shaken. He would
put off his cross-examination regarding the exhibits, he said, until the
next day.

Commander Jim Donovan moved to the prosecutors' stand next.
Donovan requested the court's permission to show yet another film,
this one only ninety seconds long, and damaged by fire. It had been
taken with an eight-millimeter movie camera by an amateur SS photographer and found in a barracks near Augsburg. The film was believed to have been shot during the razing of a ghetto. The lights went
out and the film flickered on the screen, its images rough but identi-
fiable: a naked woman running out of a house, her face twisted in
terror; a street strewn with bodies; a soldier dragging an old woman
across the road by her hair; other soldiers standing by, idly watching.
So quickly had the film passed that Donovan asked the court if he
might run it again in slow motion.

That night, Janet Flanner began writing her report for *The New
Yorker*: ". . . naked Jews, male and female, moving with a floating,
unearthly slowness and a nightmare-like dignity among the clubs and

kicks of the laughing German soldiers. . . . One thin, young Jewess
was helped to her feet by an officer, so that she could be knocked
down again."

The next morning, Justice Lawrence asked Rudolf Dix if he was ready
to proceed with the cross-examination. Dix rose gravely, wearing a
dark blue robe trimmed in burgundy, emblematic of his university,
Leipzig. The exhibits seen the day before, Dix began, were undeniably
horrifying. But, here in a court of law, they must confine themselves
to the admissibility of evidence. Mr. Dodd had based his knowledge
of USA exhibit 253, the tattoos, on an affidavit by an alleged Buchenwald inmate named Andreas Pfaffenberger. But where was this Pfaffenberger, so that Dix could cross-examine him and determine the
authenticity of the exhibits? If Pfaffenberger could not be produced,
the evidence should be disregarded by the court.

Kaltenbrunner's counsel, the tall, combative ex-Nazi Karl Kauffmann, sprang to his feet. In a Continental court, Kauffmann argued,
the prosecutor is expected to produce evidence both favorable and
unfavorable to the accused. Yet, on the matter of Standartenführer
Koch, the prosecution conveniently omitted one salient fact. The Buchenwald commandant had been condemned to death by an SS court.

Subsequently, the prosecution introduced evidence demonstrating that Koch had indeed been convicted by an SS court, but not for
torturing, mutilating, and murdering inmates of Buchenwald. Those
acts were not crimes in the SS canon. Koch had been condemned for
embezzlement of SS funds and for killing a fellow Nazi in an argument.

During the lunch break the defendants filed morosely out of the courtroom, avoiding the eyes of the curious who lined the roped-off passageway through which they had to walk. They looked forward to
gazing from the attic windows of the lunchroom out over the Pegnitz
Valley, but today they found that the Americans had sheathed the
windows with corrugated metal. They glumly took their places at five
folding metal camp tables.

Gustav Gilbert circulated among them while they ate. Ribbentrop, sitting next to Frank, asked if Hitler might have known of the
terrible deeds revealed in court. "It would not have been possible

otherwise," Frank answered. "They were done at his orders." Göring leaned back from a neighboring table and gave Frank a murderous look. Frank went on. "Hitler got us into this," he said, and added that the Führer had then abandoned them through suicide. Gilbert observed Göring's mounting anger. Too often, the defendants were guarded in the *Reichsmarschall*'s presence. Frank had broken ranks.

Göring rose, took Gilbert aside, and spoke confidentially. "I don't want to exaggerate my love for the Führer," he said quietly. "You know how he treated me at the end. But I think in the last year or so he just, well, he left things up to Himmler." Heinrich Himmler was indeed the most chilling figure in the Hitler entourage, a remote, self-contained enigma who had accumulated terrifying power. The death camps, the Gestapo, the *Einsatzgruppen*, all the components of terror had been in his grip. Now Himmler was conveniently dead, having taken a cyanide capsule soon after British soldiers captured him, the perfect scapegoat.

"Hitler and Himmler certainly must have had an understanding," Gilbert said. "Otherwise it would have been impossible for such horrors to happen." Göring started to explain how, in the confusion of war, details could easily have escaped Hitler's attention. Gilbert walked away.

Baldur von Schirach, creator of the Hitler Youth and *Gauleiter* of Vienna, spoke to the psychologist. "After today it's all over," he said in flawless English, "I wouldn't blame the court if they just chop off all our heads, even if a couple of us are innocent. What are a few more among the millions already murdered?" Gilbert wondered if Schirach too might be ready to stand up to Göring.

21

FOR A PROSECUTION LAWYER, getting into court was a rite of passage. Many of those at Nuremberg were in their early thirties, some still in their twenties; to be at the prosecutor's stand here was, briefly, to be at the center of the legal universe. Sam Harris's turn came a few days after Tom Dodd's presentation. Harris had come to Nuremberg via the U.S. Securities and Exchange Commission. For his day in court, he had enlisted the help of Roger Barrett from the documents room.

Barrett had found Harris intelligent, thorough, well organized. As the two men had reviewed the documents to be presented, however, Harris had appeared uncertain and ill at ease.

Justice Lawrence called the court to order. Sam Harris approached the prosecutor's stand and said with a nervous grin, "The sound you hear is my knees knocking. They haven't knocked so hard since I asked my wonderful little wife back home to marry me." The awkward silence was broken only by a loud guffaw from Hermann Göring. Justice Lawrence glared over the top of his glasses. Birkett whispered, "Unbelievable." After Harris finished his questioning and the court adjourned, Gordon Dean, the IMT press officer, begged the reporters to forget the young lawyer's gaffe. Reporting it would make a laughingstock of an able lawyer and could ruin his future.

Harris's performance provided further proof of what many of the British had come to believe about their American colleagues—that they lacked the courtroom finesse, classical education, and intellectual polish customary at the British bar. Other frictions grated as well. Justice Jackson's staff, from lawyers down to mimeograph operators, approached 700. The total British delegation at Nuremberg numbered 168. A middle-ranking American civilian lawyer earned $7,000 a year at the IMT. Sir Geoffrey Lawrence, president of the court, was paid by the British government roughly at the level of an American translator, approximately $2,800 a year.

Bizarre inequities crept into the system. A British researcher working for the Americans found herself earning more money than a British judge. The Europeans pressured the Americans to adopt two pay scales, a higher one for their own citizens and a lower scale for non-Americans. This solution created new disparities. Two interpreters would be working side by side, on the American payroll, with an American earning four times the salary of a British or French employee doing identical work. Barbara Pinion, a British researcher caught in that anomaly, liked to joke that Fritz Sauckel was not the only one at Nuremberg guilty of exploiting slave labor.

Sir Norman Birkett expressed his opinions of the Americans in his diary. The Germans may have been guilty of murdering millions, he wrote, but the Americans were guilty of murdering the English tongue. He winced at the U.S. prosecutors' constant use of "privatize, finalize, visualize, argumentation and orientation." After one particularly annoying session, Birkett wrote, "Words I never intend to use again while life lasts: concept, applicable, ideology, and contact (as a verb!)"

22

ON SUNDAY, December 16, Major Henry Gerecke, the Protestant chaplain, stopped by cell 5 to invite Göring to attend church. Of course he would go, said Göring, who never missed any chance to get out of the cell. As the guard opened the door, Göring put his hand out to the chaplain, who took it. Handshakes were against regulations, Gerecke knew, but how could he win somebody's soul if he refused to touch his hand? The chaplain felt optimistic with Göring beside him. He was keeping track, and so far, he believed, he had brought half the defendants in his charge back to Christ. He was sure that he could soon enter Göring in the "saved" column. What he hoped to hear from the defendants was a clear "Yes, I accept Christ." Those exact words were not always forthcoming, and in certain cases Gerecke had been satisfied with nothing more than a promising smile.

The chapel was two cells with the intervening wall knocked down. The cold concrete of the walls had been softened by olive drab army blankets. The altar was a crate, also covered by a blanket, and in one corner stood a wooden crucifix. A former SS colonel, who was turning state's evidence, played a small, battered organ. The men assembled in the chapel were downcast. Baldur von Schirach regularly received newspapers through his American relatives, and the news that had swept the cellblock this morning was that the Japanese general To-moyuki Yamashita, the "Tiger of Malaya," had been sentenced to death for war crimes in a Philippine court. Göring responded to the news by increasing his swagger as he marched to the front pew.

Most of the staff fled the gloom of Nuremberg on weekends; but not Gustav Gilbert. He assuaged his guilt over not returning to his family by working virtually seven days a week. This Sunday afternoon, he spoke briefly to Schacht, Sauckel, and the former foreign minister, Konstantin von Neurath. He saved the best for last, indulging his grudging fascination with Göring. Göring was asleep, as he frequently

was of late—a form of escapism, Gilbert concluded. With the arrival
of the psychologist, he jumped to his feet and became instantly alert.

Gilbert asked Göring to talk about his relationship to Hitler. "I
just can't get it through my head that he really did those things,"
Göring said. Gilbert thought he meant the horrors committed in Hitler's name. Then he realized that Göring was talking about how hateful Hitler had been to *him*. His troubles began, Göring said, with the
famous boast he made while touring the air defenses of the Ruhr and
the Rhineland—that if any enemy plane got through, you could call
him Meir. On the night of May 30, 1942, 150 British bombers ham-
mered Cologne. Göring, off disporting himself at one of his castles,
had been summoned by the Führer. Hitler had pointedly refused Göring's hand on the *Reichmarschall*'s arrival, humiliating him in front of
other Luftwaffe officers. "The Führer would scream about the inef-
ficiency of the Luftwaffe with such contempt and viciousness that I
would actually blush and squirm and would have preferred to go to
the front to avoid these scenes," Göring told the psychologist. The
raids went on. Over 250 British bombers struck Berlin, destroying
twenty thousand homes and killing seven hundred people in a single
raid. Soon the Americans were coming by day and the British by night,
a thousand bombers at once blackening the sky, until an astonishing
portion of urban Germany had turned to rubble.

Enemy aviators who destroyed homes, women, and children were
not soldiers, Hitler had told Göring. They were terrorists. He ordered
that Allied crews bailing out of downed aircraft be shot. Göring tried
to explain that if Germany did that, the Allies would reciprocate. "I
see," Hitler observed. "The Luftwaffe operates on the mutual life
insurance policy. You don't hurt me and I don't hurt you."

But wasn't Göring just as hard and cruel as Hitler? Gilbert asked.
What about the Röhm purge? Ernst Röhm, head of the SA, the storm
troopers, had taken seriously the "socialism" in National Socialism.
Röhm wanted to break the Prussian aristocracy and swallow up its
army into his populist Brownshirts, so called for the mud-colored uniforms they wore. The Junkers, the Prussian militarists, had let Hitler
know that if he would crush these "leftist" Nazis, he could have the
army's support.

Göring hated Röhm, he told Gilbert. Röhm had accused Hitler
of betraying Nazism by tolerating a corrupt reactionary like Göring.

Röhm publicly referred to Göring as "Herr Reaktion." In 1934, Gö-ring, by then heading the Prussian police, retaliated with a vengeance. He persuaded Hitler that Röhm was plotting to overthrow him. He drew up for Hitler a list of the most disloyal Brownshirts. He showed Hitler pictures of Röhm and his SA lovers caught in their homosexual pleasures, disgracing the manly code of Nazism.

On June 30, carrying Göring's list, Hitler flew to Munich and tracked Röhm to a sanitarium where he was reportedly involved in a tryst. While Hitler's gunmen eliminated the suspect Brownshirts, in-cluding Röhm, Göring was in Berlin leading a police team to SA headquarters. He went from room to room saying, "Arrest him, and him . . . no, not him." Thirty-two Brownshirts were taken away and shot on Göring's orders. The leader of the German nation and the chief of the Prussian police had simply rounded up their political op-ponents and killed them. No charges had been made, no trial held, no evidence presented, and no objections raised.

Gilbert asked Göring if the killings of Röhm and the others had not been murder. Göring jumped to his feet. "Now, there was a clique of perverted bloody revolutionists. They are the ones who first made the party look like a pack of hoodlums with their wild orgies and beating Jews on the street and smashing windows. . . . They were bent on wiping out the whole general's corps, the whole party leadership, all the Jews, of course, in one grand bloodbath. . . . It's a damned good thing I wiped them out, or they would have wiped us out."

Wasn't it odd, Gilbert said, that Hitler had had to build his or-ganization out of a bunch of hoodlums like the SA? Göring started to defend Hitler, when there was a tapping at the cell door. The guard said that it was time for supper. Gilbert glanced at his watch. He had been with Göring for two and a half hours. "We'll have plenty of time to talk these things over before the verdict," he said.

"Death sentence, you mean," Göring said glumly. "Death doesn't bother me, but my reputation in history does. That's why I'm glad Dönitz got stuck with signing the surrender . . . a country never thinks well of its leaders who accept defeat. As for death? Hell, I haven't been afraid of death since I was twelve years old."

23

THE MORNING OF DECEMBER 20 was bitter cold. Secretaries and prosecutors, translators and journalists, their breath visible in the air, filed
into the courthouse. They gratefully entered the building, well heated
by the U.S. military government. The more compassionate among
them wondered how the Nurembergers they had passed that morning
on Furtherstrasse, heads bent against the blustering wind, were getting
by in the coldest European winter in living memory. Snow had begun
falling in November and had stayed on the ground as temperatures at
times hovered barely above zero.

Two days before, the prosecution had begun the most novel part
of the original Bernays plan—the attempt to prove that seven organizations were criminal: the Nazi party leadership, the Reich cabinet,
the SS, the Gestapo, the SD (an intelligence and clandestine operations agency), the SA, and the High Command. The Americans alone
held some 200,000 potential war criminals, and individual trials of so
many were impractical. Thus, Jackson had seized on the concept of
group guilt. If the organizations they served could be proved criminal,
then the members would automatically be guilty.

Not until this new phase of the trials did an indifferent German
public wake up to what was happening at Nuremberg. The Allied
Control Council, the four-power body that governed occupied Germany, had issued Edict 10, making clear that any member of an organization found criminal would be subject to penalties ranging up to
death. Four and a half million Germans had belonged to the SA alone.
Membership in the SS numbered in the hundreds of thousands. Potentially, half the families in Germany had members who would be
touched by Edict 10. Letters poured into the Palace of Justice from
POWs, wives, mothers, fathers, and children until by the end of December they averaged two thousand a day. One day, five thousand
letters arrived. The message was virtually unchanging: Franz or Dieter
or Klaus was not a criminal, but merely a guard, or a clerk, or a cook,
doing his duty.

The organization case had an unexpected effect. Robert Kempner, head of the Defense Rebuttal Section, had surveyed Germans of
all classes and found near unanimity. They wanted the defendants

convicted and punished. As Kempner wrote to Jackson, "If the leaders are found guilty then the onus of guilt is removed from those who merely did their bidding."

The issue on the docket this morning, as Justice Lawrence called the court to order, was the role of the SS in conducting "medical" experiments for Göring's Luftwaffe. The Luftwaffe had faced a problem. Pilots shot down over the North Sea had often survived the crash into the frigid waters, only to die later in lifeboats after being rescued. The problem had been brought to the attention of Dr. Sigmund Rascher, a professor of aviation medicine, who worked out of a secret "laboratory" at Dachau.

A British prosecutor read the affidavit of a Dachau inmate named Anton Pachelogg, according to whom Dr. Rascher ordered inmates dropped naked into water tanks. Chunks of ice were then added until the water approached freezing. Thermometers were thrust into the often unconscious subjects' rectums to determine if they were properly chilled. The inmates were then plunged into hot water, warm water, or tepid water, or warmed by the bodies of naked female inmates, to see which method would best revive a freezing human being. The prosecutor read from Dr. Rascher's meticulously kept records: "It was evident that rapid rewarming was in all cases preferable to a slow rewarming because, after removal from the cold water, the body temperature continued to drop rapidly. Therefore rewarming by animal warmth or women would be too slow." Dr. Rascher added that most of the subjects of his research went into convulsions and died.

As the testimony ended, Justice Lawrence announced that court would adjourn and resume twelve days later, on January 2, 1946, after a Christmas holiday.

Justice Jackson threw a Christmas party at the house on Lindenstrasse principally for the judges, lawyers, and a few secretaries. The Russians, however, had pressed hard for an invitation for a man identified as I. V. Rasumov, carried on the Soviet roster as chief of the Russian Translations Division. From the instant the Soviet delegation arrived, his countrymen displayed unusual deference to Comrade Rasumov, who played the piano and told dreadful jokes.

General Nikitchenko stood next to Birkett, by now his good friend, joining in the group singing. The Russian was tipsy, as he usually was at parties. His ordinarily grim-set mouth was upturned in a smile as he kept time with a waving glass. Birkett had long since concluded that Nikitchenko was a decent chap and a covert liberal, but a man imprisoned behind the ideological bars of the regime he served.

Mrs. Douglas took over the piano and started to play "Silent Night." Glasses stopped tinkling and conversation faded as a short, blond Russian officer with a bell-like baritone began singing, "*Stille Nacht, heilige Nacht. Alles schläft, einsam wacht* . . ." Jackson looked out happily over the faces of his guests. The camaraderie with the Russians pleased him. Outside this oasis of harmony, relations between East and West in Nuremberg had become increasingly chilled. The GIs posted here now were youths who had not fought against Nazism. The Nurembergers told them about their sons killed fighting Communists on the Russian front and of the atrocities committed by the Red Army, the mass rape of German women in the Soviet sector. The young GIs were sympathetic. They liked these people. They were so tidy, so hardworking, so honest, just like the folks back home. The Russians, by contrast, were foreign, incomprehensible to boys from Ohio and Tennessee.

As the last notes of "Silent Night" faded, Comrade Rasumov gave an unobtrusive hand signal and the Russian guests left in a body. At least, Jackson thought, now they knew who ran the Soviet secret police in Nuremberg.

Francis Biddle resented that he had not yet been able to arrange to have his wife join him. Bob Jackson refused to buck the army's ban on spouses. Why should the brass and VIPs enjoy a privilege that occupation officials could not provide to thousands of married GIs? the army's reasoning went. Biddle was convinced, however, that personal rather than democratic impulses explained Jackson's acquiescence. Bob obviously did not want his wife there, since he had, in his secretary, all the companionship he desired. Inflaming Biddle's sense of the arbitrariness of it all was the fact that the British and French felt themselves unbound by U.S. Army restrictions. Chief Justice Lawrence's handsome, statuesque wife sat in court every day.

24

HANS FRANK SAT at his table, puffing his pipe and reading a letter. He had taken to wearing a glove while in court. But now the glove lay on the table, revealing a left hand starting to shrivel from nerve damage caused when he had slashed his wrist. In the old days, when confronted with unpleasantness, he had played the piano. Now he conjured the music—chamber pieces, whole oratorios, even symphonies—in the auditorium of his mind. The particular unpleasantness he was seeking to drive off today was news contained in a letter from his wife, Brigitte. All their homes had been confiscated, and she was desperately trying to find a place to live. She had had to send their two youngest children out into the street to beg. Minister of justice at thirty, Frank thought, governor-general of Poland at thirty-nine, jailbird and father of homeless beggars at forty-five.

He heard a tapping at the cell door. It was Gilbert. Frank quickly pulled the glove on. Gilbert came in and Frank stood at attention. Frank told Gilbert how grateful he was that he and the Catholic chaplain, Sixtus O'Connor, came to see him. If you could say "virgin" about a man without being facetious, that man was Father Sixtus, Frank said, "so delicate, so sympathetic, so maidenly, you know what I mean." Though Gilbert found Frank much too glib, he was coming around to believe that his religious reawakening and his remorse were sincere.

Göring had been after him lately, Frank said. "The fat one is sore because I turned in those forty volumes of my diaries. 'Why didn't you burn them?' he scolded me." But, Frank went on, he had heard the voice of Christ telling him, "You cannot hide the truth from God." And so he had given the diaries to the Americans, he told Gilbert—handily ignoring his original motive, his belief that their contents would exonerate him. The fat one had also attacked him for saying at lunch the other day that Hitler must have known of the atrocities. Gilbert nodded sympathetically. Any defendant standing up to Göring had to be encouraged.

It was torture, Frank told Gilbert, to sit through the trial and hear Germany's sins bared before the world. "The shame is devastating," he said. Here in court he saw such admirable figures, Justice

Lawrence and the American prosecutor, Jackson. "They sit on one side, and I sit among repulsive characters like Streicher, Göring, Ribbentrop."

How could he have been part of such an apparatus? Gilbert asked. "I don't know," Frank answered. "I can hardly understand it myself. There must be some basic evil in me. In all men. Mass hypnosis? Hitler cultivated this evil in man. When I saw him in that movie in court, I was swept along again for a moment, in spite of myself. Funny, one sits in court feeling guilt and shame. Then Hitler appears on the screen and you want to stretch out your hand to him. . . . It's not with horns on his head or with a forked tail that the devil comes to us, you know," Frank said. "He comes with a captivating smile, spouting idealistic sentiments, winning one's loyalty. We cannot say that Adolf Hitler violated the German people. He seduced us."

Was he still having troublesome dreams? Gilbert asked, alluding to Frank's earlier confessions of nocturnal emissions involving dreams of his daughter. That had ended, Frank said. In his latest dream he was conducting a Bach violin concerto. As Gilbert rose to leave, Frank added with a bitter smile, "*Mitgegangen, mitgefangen, mitgehangen* [We sinned together, we fell together, we'll hang together]."

With Gilbert gone, Frank picked up the autobiography he had begun writing. His lawyer's mind could fix the exact point at which an ambitious but basically decent man became an ambitious, corrupt man. It had been in 1934, during the Röhm purge—*Nacht der langen Messer*, the night of the long knives. He was then minister of justice for Bavaria and had received a call from the jailer at Stadelheim prison informing him that SS men were filling the cells with storm troopers, including Ernst Röhm, the SA chief. Frank rushed to the prison and went directly to Röhm's cell. Röhm had no need to fear the SS, Frank assured him. "Remember, Ernst, you are in my palace of justice."

Sepp Dietrich, a high-ranking SS officer close to Hitler, arrived at the prison and informed Frank that these men had been denounced personally by the Führer and were to be shot at once. Frank refused to release the prisoners. An angry Dietrich phoned Hitler at the Brown House, the party headquarters in Munich. He handed the phone to Frank. Hitler's voice shattered Frank's ear. "I decide the fate of criminals in the Reich, not you!" he shouted. But these were men who had marched with them in '23, party fighters whom he had defended in court, Frank argued. They had been dragged out of bed and thrown into jail with no charges placed against them. "I am a man of the law," Frank said. "You don't shoot 110 men without a trial." The conversation ended with Frank believing he had won. Then, the phone rang again. It was Rudolf Hess calling this time. The Führer had relented, Hess reported. Of the 110 men, only 19 were to be shot. On what grounds? Frank wanted to know. The Führer was getting impatient with this foot-dragging, Hess warned.

The price of standing by his principles would be exorbitant, Frank recognized—his position, the servants, the limousines, his several homes, the twin narcotics of power and wealth. In the end, he turned over the prisoners, including Ernst Röhm, to their SS executioners. "All revolutions devour their own children," Röhm had warned Frank on the way to his death. When the shots rang out that day, Hans Frank found himself defined. He was more Nazi than jurist. Hitler had known his man.

Frank finished the passage in his autobiography and glanced again at the letter from his wife. He returned the latter to the smoking-tobacco tin which he used as a file box. He needed to lift the pall of despair settling over him. The guard heard him humming Beethoven's "Ode to Joy."

25

COLONEL ANDRUS INFORMED his staff that the defendants were to be treated no differently on Christmas Day than on any other day. There would be no special meals served. Most certainly there was to be no exchange of gifts. However, since it might be their last Christmas, he would allow religious services. That was a damn sight more consideration than they had ever shown their victims, he noted.

On Christmas Eve, in the chapel, thirteen Protestant defendants listened to Chaplain Gerecke read the Gospel According to Saint Luke in his low German. His knowledge of the language had been acquired from uneducated immigrant parents. It was as if a Kentucky mountaineer were reading the Bible to the British cabinet. His lack of sophistication, however, did not matter. Since his arrival, the clergyman had won over his strange flock. Major Gerecke did not judge them; that was what they appreciated. He wanted only to reclaim their souls, an objective most of them increasingly shared. As the organist began playing "*O du Fröhliche, O du Heilige,*" they joined Gerecke in subdued voices, except for Göring, who belted out the song.

Before Major Kelley slipped away for the Christmas break, he and Gus Gilbert talked about their book. They were onto something big, Kelley said. He confided that he had received a request from the U.S. surgeon general, who wanted to study the brains of the defendants after they were executed. That request had been followed by an appeal from a group of New York psychiatrists, who wanted to interview the defendants. On Kelley's recommendation, Justice Jackson had turned down both requests. He and Gilbert had the field to themselves. They were going to produce, Kelley said, a magnum opus. Sometimes the arrangement seemed a bit lopsided to Gilbert. He was monitoring the defendants in the dock and during their lunch break, and making most of the cell visits. Kelley received a copy of every note Gilbert took after his talks with the defendants. Yet it was Kelley who was going away for the holidays while Gilbert continued to work.

Field Marshal Keitel was on Gilbert's Christmas Day rounds. The psychologist had learned from Tom Dodd, the prosecutor, that a remorseful Keitel had recently considered pleading guilty, but Göring had bullied him out of it. The old soldier, Gilbert thought, might need some spine-stiffening.

Keitel stood at rigid attention, as if he were meeting Bismarck rather than a U.S. Army captain. "I thank you from the bottom of my heart for this Christmas visit," Keitel said. "You are the only one I can really talk to." Gilbert noted Keitel's Christmas dinner, the tin mess kit containing remnants of corned beef hash, potatoes, and cabbage, which the prisoners were required to eat with a spoon. The conversation drifted to Hitler's wrongheadedness in attacking the Soviet Union in the summer of 1941. He himself had been convinced that the invasion was a blunder, Keitel said. Had he made this opinion known to Hitler? Gilbert asked. Keitel was silent.

What interested Gilbert most was not Keitel's views on military strategy, but how a member of a caste steeped in a code of honor could have drafted instruments like the Commando and Reprisal orders. In France alone, nearly thirty thousand innocent people had been shot under the latter order. Cruelest of all was *Nacht und Nebel*, the "Night and Fog", decree, intended to terrorize resistance movements. Suspects were arrested in the middle of the night and never heard of again. They were secretly shot and their families never learned their fate. As Hitler liked to put it, "They disappeared into the night and fog." Keitel had issued the *Nacht und Nebel* order.

"I am dying of shame," Keitel told Gilbert. "I only wish I had spent more time in the field. I spent too much time in Hitler's company. Please let me talk to you once in a while, as long as I am not yet a sentenced criminal," Keitel pleaded, as Gilbert rose to leave. Snapping to attention, the old soldier wished Gilbert a happy Christmas. In a sense, Gilbert pitied Keitel. He had behaved criminally, thinking he was behaving correctly. Now, with that illusion stripped away and the true nature of his acts clear to him, his mediocre mind lacked even the solace of rationalization. He stood naked before his sins.

Not so with the next soldier on Gilbert's visiting list. He agreed with Kelley that General Jodl was their most impenetrable case. The guards called Jodl "Happy Hooligan" after the sad-faced comic-strip character of the time. The gibe was on target, Gilbert thought as he entered Jodl's cell. The general was sitting erect at his desk, his face pinched, his nose a veined strawberry, his complexion blotchy, his cold blue eyes peering at nothing. He stood and clicked his heels. Gilbert was reminded again of what a small man Jodl was physically.

Gilbert asked Jodl how men of honor could have signed such brutal orders? Jodl answered that the prosecution's naïveté surprised him. All this documentary evidence with his and Keitel's initials on it meant nothing. When a directive to the armed forces began "The Führer has ordered . . . ," it meant that the command had been given orally by Hitler and that he and Keitel had merely committed it to paper, not invented it. They were little more than errand boys. If a military order is given to a lieutenant, Jodl went on, does he have the right and responsibility to say, "Just a minute, Captain, I have to consult the Hague Convention on Land Warfare to see if I am allowed to carry it out"? Their relationship to Hitler was no different. "And if we had disobeyed, we should have been arrested, and rightly so," Jodl observed.

Gilbert argued that without the acquiescence of the generals, Hitler could never have waged war. That was true, Jodl agreed. Equally true, if the infantryman did not march, if no arms maker supplied weapons, if the cooks did not cook, there would be no war. Is the soldier, the gunsmith, the cook therefore guilty of committing aggression? "I don't know how you people can fail to recognize a simple fact," Jodl concluded. "A soldier's obligation is to obey orders. That's the code I've lived by all my life."

Gilbert asked about what went on in the death camps. He had no idea about ninety percent of it, Jodl said. "It's impossible for me to understand what kind of beasts could have been in charge of the camps and actually have done those things."

Gilbert got up to leave. "Germans, obeying orders, no doubt," he said.

26

THE "WHY" STILL GNAWED at Gus Gilbert after every cell visit. They were not dealing with the denizens of some savage society. Hans Frank could spout yards of Schiller. Speer could move comfortably at any social level. Seyss-Inquart was a man of powerful intellect. Frick was trained in the law. It would be hard to pick out most of these men as war criminals from a gathering of Rotarians or accountants. If he and Kelley could not ultimately explain their behavior, then all they could present to the world in their book would be the riddle, but not the key.

Gilbert had learned that thirty-nine SS men were being held in the former concentration camp at Dachau awaiting execution after having been convicted by an American military court. The Nazi defendants at Nuremberg were able to put a protective layer of distance between themselves and the actual crimes committed. None of them had shoved anyone into a gas chamber, shot a prisoner in the neck, or injected a human guinea pig with a lethal drug. The men at Dachau, by contrast, were the journeymen of the death trade. One of them, whom Gilbert had read about, a former pastry chef named Mussfeld, had killed twenty thousand people—not supervised their killing, but killed them all by his own hand. By studying these men firsthand,

Gilbert thought, he might better understand the murderous impulses of Nazism. And so he arranged to spend part of the Christmas break at Dachau.

On his arrival, he found a sanitized charnel house where the U.S. Army now ran guided tours. Gilbert remembered stories he had heard. When the crematoria were turned on, the gas in nearby homes had gone down. Ashes spewing from Dachau's chimneys settled over the landscape for miles around. People said they had no idea what the source was.

Gilbert interviewed and administered intelligence tests to twenty of the condemned men. Their IQs, he found, averaged 107, in the "dull normal" range. Many, he learned, had been unemployed before Hitler became chancellor. After they had experienced powerlessness, the opportunity to dominate others had enormous appeal to them. What dismayed Gilbert most was their self-pity. They had simply carried out their assignments as ordered, and Heinrich Himmler, escaping via suicide, had left them holding the bag.

Two days later, Gilbert boarded a train back to Nuremberg, feeling emotionally exhausted. As the train rolled north through soft, rolling hills, the flurry of impressions began sorting themselves out. He believed that he now understood at least one piece of the puzzle. Every one of the condemned men at Dachau had confirmed it. Germany was a society where people did what they were told. You obeyed your parents, your teachers, your clergymen, your employer, your superior officer, your government officials. The German was raised from childhood in a world of unquestioning submission to authority. This compulsion to obey explained part of the riddle of "why." To produce a Dachau, an Auschwitz, a Buchenwald, required not a few sadists, but hundreds, even thousands of unquestioning, obedient people.

That explanation would account for the dull-normal minions at Dachau, but what about the sophisticated defendants at Nuremberg? One of the condemned SS men had complained to Gilbert, "We didn't dare oppose the orders of the Führer or Himmler." The excuses of the workaday killers and those of the men on cellblock C were identical.

27

ONE MORNING AFTER CHRISTMAS, Albert Speer lay on his cot staring at cracked walls covered with flowing figures and animals he had sketched with a piece of soft coal given him by a guard. Speer and Streicher had emerged as the two cellblock artists. He rose, went to the square porthole, and asked the guard to inform the colonel's office that defendant Speer would like to meet with Dr. Flächsner, his defense counsel. Speer operated at Nuremberg on a modified version of the old saw that says, "Treat a lady like a whore, and a whore like a lady." He treated everyone with courtesy. It worked. None of the guards called Speer by the derisive nicknames reserved for the others. He was always "Mr. Speer" or "Herr Speer."

Speer faced his current situation precisely as he would have handled a production bottleneck or a steel shortage in the old days. The goal of his survival was to be pursued by rational analysis, by breaking the task down into its component parts. Where was he now? Where did he want to be? And what actions must he take to get there? His last strategy, trying to trade his technical knowledge for preferential treatment, had failed when Jackson turned it down. He had to find an alternative. That was why he wanted Flächsner.

Albert Speer had always found intellectual beauty in the technical, the logical, the mechanical. His most vivid childhood memory was of being allowed to sit behind the wheel of the family's limousine, pretending to drive. Of this moment he later wrote, "I experienced the first sensations of technical intoxication in a world that was still scarcely technical."

The automobile was of a piece with the rest of the world that Albert Speer had been born into in 1905. The Speers were a leading family in Mannheim. Albert's father and grandfather before him had been architects. Speer grew up in a fourteen-room apartment furnished in the French style, attended by butlers, maids, and a chauffeur in purple livery. When he was thirteen, a fortune-teller at a fair predicted that he would win fame and retire early. He had never been entirely able to drive the seer's prediction from his mind.

One day in 1931, while Speer was teaching architecture at the

Institute of Technology in Berlin, his students urged him to come to a lecture. They proceeded to a shabby room over a workingmen's beer hall. Speer expected a roughneck demagogue. Instead, he found himself entranced by Adolf Hitler. The next day, he joined the Nazi party.

He subsequently returned to Mannheim and set up his own architectural practice. Not much business came his way in those depression years. He entered competitions, yet never placed better than third. Then, through party connections, he won a commission to design a Nazi district headquarters. Hitler, by now chancellor, found the work impressive. He chose Speer to stage the Nuremberg party rally of 1933. Speer was next asked to build the Reich Chancellery and Hitler's private residence in Berlin. During work on the Berlin commissions, the Führer invited Speer to join him for dinner one evening with other party leaders. Speer, covered with dust, begged off. Nonsense, Hitler said, and sent his valet to fetch clothes for the architect. That evening, the status-conscious Göring stared curiously. There, next to Hitler, sat an unknown young man, wearing the Führer's blue blazer with the gold party badge.

Speer became Hitler's personal architect, closeted alone for hours with the most powerful man in Europe. He sat next to Hitler at the theater and dined with him in the best restaurants—heady stuff for a man just twenty-eight. To Hitler, Speer reflected what he saw in himself, but in none of the party philistines: the soul of an artist. Hitler once told the architect that he wanted a massive grandstand built at Nuremberg's Zeppelin Field, where an old streetcar depot now stood. As the depot came down, Speer noticed how poorly modern construction lent itself to noble ruins. Ugly, rusted, twisted reinforcement rods protruded from the broken cement. Speer came to Hitler with an idea. He was going to build "ruin value" into the grandstand. He made sketches showing how the structure would look in a thousand years, crumbling but dignified. It was the sort of vision Hitler prized.

As for Speer, he occasionally glimpsed the dark side of his new master; but he was, by his own admission, "intoxicated by the desire to wield pure power, to order people to do this or that, to spend billions." Hitler made it all possible—the Führer as Ludovico Sforza, Speer as his da Vinci.

If Hitler could be described as having a friend, that friend was Albert Speer. After Speer completed the Reich Chancellery, Hitler took him into his office and shyly presented him with a gift, a water-color of a Gothic church that Hitler had painted in Vienna in 1909. Speer was flattered by the gesture, but appalled by the painting. It was, he later wrote, "precise, patient, and pedantic. Not a stroke had any life."

Speer recalled those early years with Hitler as the romantic chapter. The realistic phase began with unexpected suddenness on February 8, 1942. Speer had gone to the Wolf's Lair, the Führer's East Prussian headquarters at Rastenburg, to discuss building plans. Also present was the armaments minister, Dr. Fritz Todt. Speer intended to fly back to Berlin with Todt the next morning, but Hitler kept him up until two a.m. with a rambling monologue on the degeneracy of modern art. Speer decided to skip the flight and sleep in.

He was awakened by a jangling phone. Hitler's physician, Dr. Karl Brandt, informed Speer that Dr. Todt had been killed in a plane crash. Before the day was out, Hitler appointed Speer as Todt's successor. As minister of armaments and chief of construction, he immediately found himself in control of 2.6 million workers. As he later absorbed the naval production program, he directed 3.2 million workers. By the time he wrested aircraft production from Göring and became minister of the economy, 12 million Germans and foreigners worked under Speer. By age thirty-eight, he had fulfilled half of the fortune-teller's prophecy.

To run a country's arsenal was, by itself, no war crime. But at Nuremberg Speer might have to explain actions less easily defended. In December 1943, he had visited a plant carved out of the Harz Mountains, the manufacturing site of Germany's secret rocket weapon, the V-2. The dank limestone caverns held over fifty thousand slave laborers. Once these workers entered the caves, they remained for three months, working seventy-two hours a week, fed a daily diet of eleven hundred calories. Sanitation facilities and housing barely existed. Because of the dampness and air pressure, the workers' muscle and bone tissue deteriorated quickly. Some spaces were so low that the men worked stooped over until they could no longer stand up straight. Deaths in the plant averaged 180 a day.

Speer was appalled. Following the visit, he wrote a report that this kind of work imposed intolerable emotional strains on the SS guards who had to drive these workers. Some of the guards' nerves became so shattered that they had to be sent away from time to time.

Speer also visited the Mauthausen extermination camp, where prisoners hauled stones out of the quarry up 186 steps until they dropped dead of exhaustion. He had already explained to his American interrogators that he had gone there to inspect a site for a new railhead and had seen only a small part of the camp. He had witnessed no atrocities.

Hardest to explain away, he knew, would be his relationship with Heinrich Himmler. As procurement of workers became more difficult, Speer had gone to Himmler, who controlled hundreds of thousands of people in the concentration camps. In October 1943, both men were speakers at a meeting in Posen of Nazi party officials—*Gauleiters* running regions, and *Reichsleiters* with national posts. Speer threw the fear of God into the party functionaries. When it came to producing manpower, he said, he was not going to tolerate any obstructionism. "I have spoken to Reichsführer Himmler," Speer warned, "and from now on I shall deal firmly with districts that do not carry out these measures."

Then it was Himmler's turn to speak. The bespectacled, chinless *Reichsführer* told the *Gauleiters* that he wanted them to understand the crushing burden he and his SS carried. It was easy enough to say "the Jews must be exterminated," he said. But what did that mean to the poor rank and file who had to do the job? "I ask you only never to talk about what I tell you in this circle," he went on. "When the question arose, what should be done with the women and children, I decided to adopt a clear solution. I did not feel justified in exterminating the men, while allowing their children to grow up to avenge themselves on our sons and grandchildren. The hard decision had to be taken. These people must disappear from the face of the earth." Speer told the Allies that he had somehow missed this speech. Whether this was true or not, his interrogators found it inconceivable that its message had not reached his ears.

One of Himmler's lieutenants described Speer's demands for labor as "insatiable." In the spring of 1944, he asked for 400,000 workers from Auschwitz. Speer could hardly disclaim knowledge of the nature of the camp. Earlier, a friend, Karl Hanke, the *Gauleiter* of Lower Silesia, had warned him. He had seen death in battle, Hanke said, but never had he witnessed anything to compare with Auschwitz.

Speer should never accept an invitation to go there. Speer had not pressed for details.

His captivity had given Speer abundant time to examine how a man of his cultivation, of his station and advantages, had slipped into this moral ditch. His conscience, he concluded, had been elbowed aside in the desperate arms race he was running against the Allies. His fixation on production blurred all human feeling. The sight of people suffering affected his emotions but did not influence his conduct. He was, he admitted to himself, fonder of machines than of people.

Defending his behavior as munitions chief was near impossible, he knew. His salvation, he was convinced, lay in his actions during the last months of the war. Toward the end, Hitler had issued an order that stunned Speer. With the Allied armies advancing into Germany, Hitler had directed that everything in their path be destroyed—every factory, bridge, power plant, road, and mine. The Allies were to conquer nothing but ashes. Hitler told Speer, "If the war is lost, the people are lost too. It is not necessary to worry about the fundamentals that the people will need for a primitive future existence. On the contrary, it would be better to destroy these things. The German people have shown themselves weaker and the future belongs to the stronger peoples of the East. Those who survive the war will, in any event, be only the inferior. The best have fallen." In his scorched-earth order, Hitler had finally and fully revealed his maniacal nature to Speer.

The war was indeed lost, and Speer's practical mind was already on postwar Germany. He was a scion of the industrialist class, and he feared a long, dark, primeval night if the country's industrial base were destroyed. Hitler's dictum had to be undone. On his own authority, Speer ordered high explosives, supposed to be used for blowing up iron and coal mines, to be hidden. He had pistols issued to factory workers to defend their plants. He arranged for orders to be sent to the armed forces, directing that rail lines and bridges not be destroyed. In the meantime, he begged Hitler to rescind this policy of national suicide. By late March, he had made some headway. He persuaded Hitler that only military considerations should determine which facilities would be blown up. On April 10, Speer wrote a speech revealing the hard truth to the German people. The war was lost. No fresh armies, no miracle weapons were going to save them. They were to destroy nothing vital to rebuilding the nation. He was waiting only for the right moment, he told himself, to deliver the address over the radio.

Still, for all his disillusionment, Speer had felt an overpowering urge to see the Führer one last time. He braved Allied strafing and Russian artillery to fly into besieged Berlin, landing near the Brandenburg tower in a moth-like reconnaissance plane. He made it to the Führerbunker as Russian shells were slamming into the Reich Chancellery that he had built. Hitler kept him waiting until three a.m. Finally, in the Führer's private quarters, Speer had his farewell visit. He complimented Hitler on his decision to stay in Berlin. History emphasizes the last act, Speer observed, and the Führer's denouement in Berlin would be judged as heroic. Hitler displayed no interest in anything Speer said. The visit ended with Hitler examining Speer with cold, protuberant eyes, then extending a limp hand. He expressed no gratitude for what Speer had done for Germany, no good wishes for his family. All that he said in a barely audible voice was, "So you're leaving. Good. *Auf Wiedersehen.*"

As he fled Berlin, Speer was convinced that Hitler would soon be dead, probably by his own hand. He headed for the next most powerful Nazi, Heinrich Himmler, who was holed up in a hospital in Hohenlychen, about sixty miles north of Berlin. A few days later, Speer learned that the Führer had died, bypassing all likely heirs and naming Dönitz as successor. At the news he wept. Speer then headed for Plön, where Dönitz had temporarily set up his government. There, the admiral named Speer minister of economics and production. The government moved to Flensburg, where Speer found himself a player in the tragicomic death scene of Nazi Germany. While there, he kept a plane standing by to whisk him off to Greenland, if that seemed desirable. Instead, when the Allies came on May 24, he was arrested.

To the very end, he had been unable to turn his back on Hitler. And he had never found the right moment to deliver his brave the-war-is-lost speech to the German people.

At three p.m., the escort guard took Speer to the visitors' room, where Flächsner was waiting behind the wire mesh. Speer spoke quietly, guiding his lawyer through his defense strategy—how, for example, they should play the mistreatment of conscript workers and the visit to the death camp. Understatement and contrition were to be the watchwords. He had one strong, persuasive case that Flächsner must hammer at: Here was a man who stood up to Hitler and his diabolic orders, fully aware that others had been shot for just such disobedience. The judges must see him as a man who risked his life to salvage his nation's future. And he had an even more compelling story to tell. Speer's voice dropped to a whisper. Did Flächsner know that Speer had once tried to assassinate Hitler?

28

To THE MEN ON CELLBLOCK C, New Year's Day was indistinguishable from all others. As Dr. Pfluecker made his daily rounds, Joachim von Ribbentrop pestered the old physician with questions he could not answer. How soon before the prosecution rested its case? When would the defense start? Should he mention the secret protocol he had arranged with the Soviet Union in 1939? Would that risk turning the Russian judges against him? Did Pfluecker think he had a good lawyer? Ribbentrop also asked the doctor why he was always tired. Pfluecker was not surprised. This insomniac never fell asleep before three a.m. and was awake by six. Pfluecker had given him sleeping pills, but Ribbentrop complained that the pills were destroying his mind.

Would the doctor please tell Colonel Andrus that he needed Fräulein Blank again? Ribbentrop said. His former secretary, Margarete Blank, was a prisoner in the women's wing, being held as a material witness. The month before, Ribbentrop had pleaded that he needed her to take dictation. How could he be expected to write out eight years of German foreign policy with a pad and pencil? The colonel had arranged to have Fräulein Blank brought down to Ribbentrop's cluttered cell; but Ribbentrop had abruptly dismissed her without explanation a few hours later. Now he needed her again. Ribbentrop's nickname among the prison staff was "the Mad Hatter."

When Dr. Pfluecker got up to leave, Ribbentrop barely noticed. He was too busy rummaging through the documents that littered his cell, desperate to find something proving the secret protocols he had engineered with Stalin. The pact with the Soviet Union had marked the acme of his career. It was one of the rare times that he had been able to sell Hitler on a foreign policy. The idea had struck Ribbentrop in March 1939, while he was reading a speech by Stalin in which the Soviet dictator maintained that he did not intend to pull the capitalists' chestnuts out of the fire. Ribbentrop read this line as a slap at Great Britain and France. He approached Hitler with the unthinkable—that the Nazis and the Communists might find common ground. Less than five months later, the pact that jolted the world was signed. Germany and the Soviet Union agreed on the spheres where each would dominate, and Stalin, in effect, gave Hitler the green light for the invasion of Poland.

How close Ribbentrop had come to missing his eminent role in the Third Reich. He might as easily have become a concert violinist. He had shown great musical promise as a child. He might have become a Canadian citizen. At age seventeen, he had emigrated to Canada to seek his fortune and only returned home when Germany went to war in 1914. He won a commission, and afterward courted Anneliese Henkell, daughter of a champagne magnate. He went to work as a salesman for his in-laws and benefited from his one genuine talent, a knack for languages, which served him well in foreign markets. When he was thirty-two, he had himself adopted by an aunt whose husband had been knighted. Thus, plain old Joachim Ribbentrop became Joachim von Ribbentrop.

He had not entered Hitler's orbit until 1932, when he managed to get an appointment with the rising political star. His qualifications to be foreign minister of a great nation were slender to invisible. Ribbentrop's formal schooling had ended at age sixteen. Yet, in a dazzling display of name-dropping, he persuaded Hitler that he knew all the best people in Europe. Göring took an instant dislike to the upstart. Hitler insisted that Ribbentrop could be invaluable since he knew Lord so-and-so and Lady so-and-so. Göring replied that it was true. Unfortunately, they all knew Ribbentrop.

Göring had spotted Ribbentrop for what he was, a parvenu whose intelligence was no match for his ambition. When Göring learned that Hitler intended to appoint this "champagne salesman" to a high diplomatic post, he urged Hitler to make it Rome. Any Nazi could get by in that sister fascist state. Instead, Hitler sent Ribbentrop to the Court of Saint James's. At dinner parties, Ribbentrop launched monologues aping Hitler's words and mannerisms, but without the mag-

netism. Soon, the word was out. The German ambassador to Great
Britain was a boor and a bore.

The opinion, however, was not unanimous. Ribbentrop was welcomed in one corner of English society, among the Nazi sympathizers,
Hitler admirers, anti-Semites, and the peace-at-any-price set. Reports
circulated that Ambassador von Ribbentrop sent red roses every day
to Wallis Simpson, the king's mistress and intended wife, who would
cost Edward VIII his throne. Ribbentrop was rumored to be having
an affair with the woman and paying her to influence the king in favor
of Germany.

Down the corridor from Ribbentrop at Nuremberg, cell 10 was
occupied by the man who inadvertently helped elevate him to foreign
minister in 1938. Konstantin von Neurath, at the time, held the post
himself. Neurath had been present at the Hossbach Conference,
where Hitler baldly spelled out his intention to make war. Neurath
was horrified, and said so. Thereafter, Hitler wanted someone more
pliant in the Foreign Office, a diplomatic errand boy to deliver his
foreign policies, not to resist them. Joachim von Ribbentrop fit perfectly.

In his new job, Ribbentrop substituted energy and ambition for
competence and intelligence. During fourteen-hour days, he swelled
the Foreign Office bureaucracy from 2,300 to over 10,000. His single
original triumph had indeed been the Soviet-German pact, and now
he was desperate to produce a copy of its secret clauses so that he
could demonstrate the duplicity of the Russians and their unfitness to
judge him as a war criminal.

He was seeing his lawyer, Dr. Fritz Sauter, today, and he hoped
that Sauter might have found a copy. They met in the visitors' room,
with Sauter, at six feet five inches, towering over his thin, haggard
client. Before the war, Sauter had joined the Nazi party, drawn by its
promises of national unity; but he had been thrown out for defending
Jews and Communists in court. He was a famous advocate in Germany, and Walther Funk and Baldur von Schirach had also hired him.
Sauter possessed an ego to match Ribbentrop's. During the visit, he
treated Ribbentrop as he had on every other occasion, with professional coolness. He informed his client that he had not been able to
unearth the secret passages of the German-Soviet nonaggression pact.

When Ribbentrop returned to his cell, he demanded to see the duty officer. He wanted a message delivered to Colonel Andrus at once. Fritz Sauter was to be fired as his defense counsel. It was New Year's Day, and Sauter had failed to wish him a happy New Year.

29

ON JANUARY 2, the staff returned to the Palace of Justice, flashing ID cards before red-cheeked guards who stood stamping their feet in the nine-degree Fahrenheit cold. At ten a.m., Justice Geoffrey Lawrence reconvened the International Military Tribunal. Sir Geoffrey's pink, cherubic countenance glowed after a vacation spent at his beloved Hill Farm in Wiltshire among his pedigreed cows and horses. Back in November, when the trial had opened, this Dickensian figure of plain speech and plain interests had been judged a mediocrity. Now, his simplicity was seen as the attribute of an uncluttered mind, a secure ego, and a strong if understated will. His evenhanded treatment of prosecution and defense alike had begun to persuade the defendants that room 600 might be a genuine arena for truth seeking and not necessarily the anteroom to the gallows.

Colonel Storey reopened the criminal-organization case, presenting evidence against the Gestapo and making a botch of it. Storey's idea of prosecuting was to introduce documents wholesale, the more the better, as though the sheer weight of the paper would ultimately tip the scales. When he became lost in this swamp of his own making, he might read the same document twice or prove the same point with five different documents. Sir Geoffrey, his patience wearing thin, strove to keep Storey on track. Storey kept piling on evidence the way a stoker shovels coal. As his assistants watched their efforts aborted in a feckless execution, they took to calling Storey "the Butcher of Nuremberg."

To the court's relief, a fresh face took the stand after lunch. Lieutenant Whitney Harris was a thirty-three-year-old navy officer and lawyer whose film-star handsomeness belied a serious character. He was conscientious, driven, and rarely seen among the habitués of the Grand Hotel. Harris had won this courtroom appearance for his work on the Ernst Kaltenbrunner case. As the day's session drew to a close, Harris was describing "the ninth crime for which Kaltenbrunner is responsible": that he had ordered the mass liquidation of prisoners at Dachau and other camps only days before they would have been liberated by the advancing Allies.

The following morning, John Harlan Amen replaced Harris at the stand. Amen had seized the spotlight for the direct examination of the next witness, SS General Otto Ohlendorf—yet Ohlendorf was in this court only because of Harris's initiative. Harris had interrogated him in order to obtain evidence against Kaltenbrunner. Ohlendorf, short, mousy, thirty-eight years old, had been a ranking member of the SD, the Sicherheitsdienst, the SS component that carried out intelligence, covert operations, and liquidations. Harris had begun his interrogation with routine questions, asking Ohlendorf's date of birth, place of birth, and SD assignments. One answer piqued his curiosity. Ohlendorf said that he served with the SD except for one year in 1941 when he headed Einsatzgruppe D in the East. Knowing the murderous reputation of the *Einsatzgruppen*, Harris had fired a question from the blue: "How many people did you kill?" The answer, delivered matter-of-factly, staggered him.

Harris then asked Ohlendorf how he had come to be given the *Einsatzgruppe* assignment? He had been trained in economics and the law at the universities of Göttingen and Leipzig and had a law degree, Ohlendorf explained—suitable background for his first SD assignment, economic intelligence. But he annoyed Heinrich Himmler by complaining about the mass killings of Jews in Poland. Ohlendorf, Himmler concluded, was obviously, "a product of too much education." With exquisite malice, he assigned Ohlendorf to head Einsatzgruppe D. As they talked, Harris concluded that this man should not merely be providing background for the Kaltenbrunner case: he belonged on the stand testifying directly against him. When Colonel Amen saw a copy of Harris's interrogation, he had claimed Ohlendorf for his own.

The witness walked to the stand wearing an unpressed gray suit. Amen's opening questions were calculatedly dull, queries about Kaltenbrunner's place in the RSHA organization chart, how long Ohlendorf had known his chief, what their relationship was. Then, abruptly, Amen asked how many people Einsatzgruppe D had killed. "In the year between June 1941 and June 1942 the *Einsatz* troops reported ninety thousand people liquidated," Ohlendorf answered. Did that include men, women, and children? Amen wanted to know. Yes, Ohlendorf replied. Amen next asked if mass shooting was the only method of execution. No, it was not, Ohlendorf explained. Reichsführer Himmler had noted that shooting women and children placed a terrible strain on the *Einsatz* personnel, especially family men. Therefore, beginning in 1942, women and children were gassed instead in closed vans. How many men did it take to kill ninety thousand people? Amen asked. His *Einsatzgruppe*, Ohlendorf said, had a strength of five hundred men. Walther Funk closed his eyes as Ohlendorf began explaining how the dead victims' gold and jewelry were shipped off the to Reich Ministry of Finance.

During the defense attorneys' turn to cross-examine, Sir David Maxwell-Fyfe listened attentively. He was famous for his own traplike cross-examining and was surprised at how the Germans still failed to get the point of it. Kaltenbrunner's lawyer, Kurt Kauffmann, kept hammering at Ohlendorf, trying to get him to admit that Kaltenbrunner had no authority to issue orders to concentration camps. Didn't such orders go directly from Himmler to the head of the Gestapo, Heinrich Müller, bypassing Kaltenbrunner? Ohlendorf replied that Kaltenbrunner fit directly into the chain of command. He was Müller's superior; hence he could relay orders from Himmler or initiate his own. Kauffmann, Sir David knew, had committed a classic cross-examination blunder: he had asked a question to which he did not know the answer.

The next defense examiner was Egon Kuboschok, substituting this day for Speer's attorney, Fritz Sauter. Since Ohlendorf considered himself primarily an intelligence officer, did he know, Kuboschok asked, that Albert Speer had taken actions to sabotage Hitler's scorched-earth orders? Ohlendorf answered that he did. Did Ohlendorf know, further, that Speer had tried to turn Heinrich Himmler over to the Allies at the end of the war? Ohlendorf's heretofore expressionless face registered amusement. He had never heard of such a thing, he said. Did Ohlendorf know, Kubuschok went on, that the Twentieth of July plotters had wanted Speer in their government? That he did know, Ohlendorf admitted. Finally, Kuboschok asked if the witness knew that Speer had planned an attempt on Hitler's life toward the end of the war. Excited whispers swept the courtroom. Göring turned around and glared at Speer. No, Ohlendorf said skeptically, he had never heard of such a plan.

Albert Speer listened, satisfied. Kuboschok had been less skillful than Sauter would have been. Still, the seeds of Speer's defense strategy had been planted.

Justice Lawrence called a brief adjournment. Instantly Göring was clambering over the chairs, thrusting his face next to Speer's. How dare he break up their united front against the prosecution? Göring shouted. What united front? Speer answered, turning away, as the guards pulled Göring back to his seat.

When the session resumed, an unasked question hung heavily in the air. It was posed, unexpectedly, by a defense counsel, sixty-four-year-old Ludwig Babel, who had the daunting task of defending the SS. Ohlendorf's cool recitation had so astonished Babel that he felt compelled to ask: "But did you have no scruples about the nature of these orders?" "Yes, of course," Ohlendorf answered. Then how was it that he had carried them out? Ohlendorf seemed surprised at the question. "Because it is inconceivable to me that a subordinate would not obey orders given by leaders of the state," he replied. Babel gazed at the witness for some time, then sat down wordlessly.

Francis Biddle had seen a name crop up from time to time, and had written in the margin of the document he now held, "Who is he?" The name was Adolf Eichmann. This afternoon, Biddle's curiosity was satisfied. An American prosecutor, Smith Brookhart, had begun questioning the next witness, an SS colleague of Otto Ohlendorf's named Dieter Wisliceny. Brookhart elicited from Wisliceny that in August 1942 he had gone to see Adolf Eichmann, head of Department IVA4 of the RSHA, the section dealing with Jewish matters. Wisliceny told Eichmann that he was being pressured by Slovakian officials to find out what had happened to seventeen thousand of their Jews deported to Poland. The Slovakians wanted to visit them and see how they were faring. Eichmann finally admitted that such a visit was impossible. The Jews were dead. How could that be? Wisliceny wanted to know. Extermination of the Jews was official policy, passed down from the Führer to Himmler to the RSHA, Eichmann explained. A disbelieving Wisliceny asked to see the order. He testified that Eichmann then took a document from his safe and showed it to him. This, Wisliceny said, was the first time he had heard of the Final Solution.

Smith Brookhart shifted the questioning to Kaltenbrunner. Kaltenbrunner had not been RSHA chief when the Final Solution began, he noted. But, he asked Wisliceny, after Kaltenbrunner took over, was there any change in the extermination policy? "There was no diminution or change of any kind," the witness answered. Did Kaltenbrunner know personally his subordinate who directed the Final Solution? There was no doubt of it, Wisliceny said. Kaltenbrunner and Eichmann were fellow townsmen from Austria. Kaltenbrunner's father had been the lawyer for the electrical firm managed by Eichmann's father. Their sons had gone to school together. Whenever Kaltenbrunner called his RSHA staff to Berlin, Wisliceny remembered, he had greeted Eichmann with special warmth, inquiring about his wife and children.

Late in the afternoon, Brookhart posed his last question. "Did Eichmann say anything at that time as to the number of Jews that had been killed?"

"He said he would leap laughing into the grave," Wisliceny answered, "because the feeling that he had five million people on his conscience would be for him a source of extraordinary satisfaction."

30

THE PRESS BAR WAS CROWDED, noisy, and smoke-filled. Still, the crush of reporters had thinned considerably since the trial's opening. The papers back home were no longer giving heavy daily play to a trial that, no matter how sensational the evidence, had already gone on for six weeks. Reporters had begun scrambling for fresh angles. Hal Burson, twenty-four-year-old bureau chief for the Armed Forces Network, had gone to Colonel Andrus with an idea. Burson wanted to get into cellblock C posing as a member of the guard detachment. "Son," Colonel Andrus told him, "this is serious business," and turned him down. Since he could not get into the cellblock himself, Burson cultivated the guards as sources. His resulting report revealed that the sphinxlike Jodl was the least popular prisoner. Keitel was the neatest. Hess and Ribbentrop ran neck-and-neck for sloppiest. One of the most popular prisoners was Speer. And, hands down, the GI favorite was Göring.

An Australian journalist had asked Andrus if he might query the defendants about their dreams. Andrus had taken up the request with the psychiatrist, Kelley, who put him off. The question would upset the prisoners, Kelley said. What he omitted was that the stuff of dreams was precisely the material he wanted saved for the book he and Gilbert planned to write. The persistent Australian then went to the defense lawyers and asked them if they knew what their clients dreamed about. Eight of the defendants, they reported, confessed to recurrent and frightening dreams about Colonel Andrus.

31

REPORTERS CHECKING the bulletin board Friday, January 4, found the prosecution taking on the German High Command. Of all the organizations indicted, conviction of this group seemed most difficult. Six years of war movies, newsreels, books, and Allied propaganda had made names like the Gestapo and the SS synonymous with fear and horror. But the High Command? These were generals, admirals, the men who direct wars that politicians begin, in Germany as in any nation. The prosecution had to prove not only that these professionals waged war, but that they had played a hand in starting it, and then fought it criminally. The prosecutor of the High Command was to be Colonel Telford Taylor.

The assignment was not one that Taylor would have chosen. He had come to Nuremberg via the Ultra codebreaking operation at Bletchley in England, one of numerous lawyers subsequently stockpiled by Jackson in the Palace of Justice. At Nuremberg, he had thus far occupied himself with an untaxing job as Jackson's liaison to the Russians. Since the High Command case was virtually going begging, Taylor had taken it for lack of anything better. At the same time, he made a compensating arrangement. The prison was full of lesser Nazis to be tried after the big fish. To prosecute at these subsequent trials, Robert Jackson had spotted a capable successor in Telford Taylor. The prospect of following Jackson as chief prosecutor provided Taylor the incentive for staying on and taking over the thankless, if challenging, High Command case.

From the moment Taylor approached the stand his performance attracted attention. He was an arresting presence—slim, wavy-haired, handsome, with the air of a poet in uniform. On the Nuremberg social circuit, Taylor had the reputation of a Renaissance man: tennis player, pianist, clarinetist, composer, writer, bridge expert, dancer. Only his self-protective air of detachment put some people off. He neither possessed nor sought the common touch.

His powers of reason held the court spellbound as he traced the corruption and transformation of an honorable officer corps into an unsoldierly, dishonorable tool of Hitler. He was, as a colleague put it, "smart in the way lawyers judge smartness. He had a keen memory, could recall precedents and marshal his case with a logic that marched." His only peer in court in the mastery of language was Jackson. Taylor had set himself a minimum objective. It might be impossible to prove the entire High Command guilty, but he was determined to convince the tribunal that individual German generals could be war criminals.

Monday morning, January 7, dawned bright and cold. Colonel Taylor resumed the prosecution, asking the court's permission to read a document into the record. As he did so, Otto Nelte, Field Marshal Keitel's lawyer, threw a quick glance at his client. The old soldier sat expressionless, like someone standing on a track who did not hear the train coming. "General Anton Dostler, on or about 24 March 1944, in the vicinity of La Spezia, Italy, contrary to the laws of war," Taylor read, "did order to be shot summarily, a group of United States Army personnel. . . ."

OSS people in the court knew the story. A fifteen-man team had slipped ashore behind the lines in northern Italy to blow up a railroad tunnel. The men were in uniform on a legitimate military mission when they were captured. On Dostler's orders, they had been shot without a trial. Dostler had defended his action by saying that he was carrying out the Commando Order, signed by Field Marshal Keitel. Taylor pointed out that Dostler had been tried by a military court in Italy and executed the month before.

Taylor went to the prosecution table and picked up another document, 551 PS, which he said would disprove the constant defense refrain that even Hitler's vilest wishes had to be obeyed on pain of punishment, including death. As the Allies gained a foothold in France after D-Day, German generals in Supreme Command West asked if the Commando Order still remained effective. The reply came back stating that it was "fully in force." Any Allied troops found operating beyond the battle perimeter, and any captured parachutists, were to be shot. Furthermore, Supreme Command West was to report daily how many of these "saboteurs" had been liquidated. This directive too had been issued by Field Marshal Keitel. Keitel and his ilk, Taylor went on, would have the court believe that failure to carry out the Führer's wishes was not an option: they must shoot or be shot, as it were. That was untrue. The paybook of every German soldier made clear that to carry out, knowingly, an illegal order was a crime. Perhaps the bravest German soldier of all, Field Marshal Erwin Rommel, on receiving the reaffirmed Commando Order, had simply burned it.

As soon as the court adjourned that afternoon, Captain Gilbert sped from the dock to the court reporters' room. He was looking for a statement against the High Command made that day by a witness named Erich von dem Bach-Zelewski, a forty-six-year-old general in the Waffen SS, the military arm of Himmler's empire. The reporter who had taken the testimony flipped through his notes, rolled a sheet of paper into a typewriter, and typed out the passage Gilbert wanted: "I am of the opinion when, for years and for decades, the doctrine is practiced that the Slavic race is an inferior race, and the Jews are not even human, then such an explosion was inevitable." The "explosion" that Bach-Zelewski had referred to was his role in putting down guerrilla resistance in Russia.

On the stand, Bach-Zelewski had been an unlikely-looking villain, tall, thin, blue-eyed, with the genial air of a popular schoolteacher. He nevertheless had won a reputation for ruthlessness in catching guerrilla fighters and executing them, along with thousands of hostages. Hitler had once called Bach-Zelewski "the model partisan fighter." The defense on cross-examination tried to have Bach-Zelewski establish that only outfits like his own SS—not soldiers in the regular army—had slaughtered people en masse. But the witness had spread guilt over the whole German war machine.

When Gilbert had heard Bach-Zelewski say in court that the Jew was not even considered human, something clicked into place. He took the statement the court reporter had typed out for him and went back to his office. There he dug out the notes he had taken the week before on Otto Ohlendorf's testimony and Wisliceny's account of Adolf Eichmann's macabre boast of sending millions of Jews to their deaths.

The search for the "why" of ingeniously organized, routinely administered mass murder carried out by presumably civilized people consumed Gilbert. His visit to the condemned men at Dachau had furnished one piece of the puzzle: a culture that fostered unthinking obedience. Ohlendorf's testimony had confirmed it. Bach-Zelewski's statement today provided a second piece, one that had been much on Gilbert's mind of late. Ordinary Germans would not kill innocent human beings. But what if Germans had been bombarded for years, as Bach-Zelewski pointed out, with propaganda that the Slav or the Jew was not a true human, but a corruption of the race, responsible for Germany's woes? What if this attitude was the official government position? What if the very laws of the land denied to Jews rights available to the lowliest German—the right to work, to own property, to marry freely, even to hold citizenship? Then a personality conditioned to unquestioning obedience, told to rid society of such pestilential vermin, could find the rationale to do it. These two factors explained much of the "why," Gilbert concluded. Still, there had to be more.

32

THE PROSECUTION CASE against the organizations had ended. Their defense would take place later. Next on the court's schedule was the prosecution of individual defendants. On January 8, documents incriminating the first batch—Göring, Hess, Ribbentrop, and Keitel— fell like a blizzard. The following morning, as the defendants were leaving the exercise yard, Keitel clicked his heels and turned aside to let Hermann Göring precede him into the cellblock. He intended to tell his lawyer, Otto Nelte, when they met this evening, how Göring could help him.

Keitel looked forward to Nelte's coming, as much for the break in the monotony as anything else. With the days now so short, it was virtually impossible to read or write a letter after supper. They were left in semidarkness to sit and brood until nine p.m., when it was time to go to bed, and when, perversely, the guards would shine the hated spotlights into their cells. The only time a pair of eyes was not peering at them was when they sat on the toilet in the alcove, when only their feet were visible. Life for them was reduced to the court proceedings on weekdays and solitude during nights and weekends, broken only by meetings with their lawyers, visits from Kelley and Gilbert, and a few minutes in the exercise yard. Keitel even looked forward to the weekly cold shower, in spite of the embarrassing rectal examinations.

Otto Nelte was one of the former Nazis on the defense team, a tax lawyer who had found the party tie useful in his practice. As they met in the visitors' room, Nelte asked Keitel if it was true that during the earlier interrogations he had authenticated his signature on the Commando Order. Keitel nodded. What choice had he had? The Prussian code of honor compelled him to speak the truth. What did Keitel think Göring could do for him? Nelte wanted to know. Keitel explained that he had once begged Göring to get him a frontline command. Even as a field marshal, he would have been content to lead a single division—anything to escape daily humiliation by the Führer. If Göring would testify in court that Keitel had made the request, Keitel reasoned, it would prove that he had not been a willing member of Hitler's court. As they parted, Nelte asked if Keitel had any word to pass along to his wife, who was now in Nuremberg with Jodl's wife. The shame he had brought onto his family was, Keitel said, his heaviest cross. Just ask her to pray for him, he told the lawyer.

Frau Keitel, though her husband was too much the Prussian ever to blame her, was partly responsible for his present fate. In 1934, Keitel had come close to his dream. After his father died, he had wanted nothing so desperately as to leave the army and become lord of the family estate in Helmscherode, Braunschweig. Lisa, a brewer's daughter, had been adamant. Why would she want to be a farmer's wife when she could be a general's lady? Keitel thus stayed in the army, and was as shocked as his fellow officers when Hitler named him chief of staff of the OKW, the high command. When Hitler once described

Keitel as having "the brains of a movie usher," another officer asked why the Führer had made him the highest-ranking figure in the German military. Because the man was "loyal as a dog," Hitler replied.

Keitel, so imposing, so military in bearing, served another purpose. In 1938, at Berchtesgaden, while Hitler was bullying Austrian chancellor Kurt von Schuschnigg to hand over his country, he loudly summoned Keitel from an anteroom. Was the German army in a state of invasion readiness? the Führer demanded. It was, Keitel replied, standing there in full dress uniform, every inch the soldier. The unspoken message had not been lost on Schuschnigg.

Hitler had been only a corporal in World War I, yet Keitel found himself mesmerized by the Führer's military genius. No matter what arguments his generals raised, Hitler could throw back Moltke or Schlieffen or Clausewitz. Keitel readily confessed that, in military matters, "I was the pupil, and the Führer the master."

After the visit with his lawyer, Keitel was marched back to his cell. All was deathly silent but for the bolt slamming behind him. He took off his clothes, folded them neatly, and laid them on the stone floor —they were allowed no hooks or hangers. Keitel asked the guard if he might sit up in bed this night since he had a painful boil on his neck. He had not reported it to Dr. Pfluecker. He never reported his ailments. His stoicism, however, was conditioned rather than natural, and purchased at a high price. His current blood pressure was 180 over 100. He had once confided to Major Kelley that he considered killing himself three times during the war. Kelley had written of Keitel, "At present, he has nothing to live for. Consequently, he is one of the most profound suicide risks."

The defense counsels had found a hangout, a surviving tavern near the courthouse, Gasthaus zum Stern. There, Otto Nelte repaired after his meeting with his client. A failing wood fire was being coaxed to life as he entered. Its meager warmth felt good. Nelte spied only one of his colleagues at this late hour—Ludwig Babel. The tavernkeeper brought a stein to Nelte. German beer was one thing that had survived the war intact, Babel said. Nelte spoke wearily. He wished to God that the Dostler affidavit had never surfaced. How, he wondered, was he to save the man who had issued the Commando Order when a German general had already been shot for obeying it?

33

THE PROSECUTORS HAD GONE AFTER the defendants in the front row, one by one, like ducks in a shooting gallery. January 9 was Alfred Rosenberg's turn. While Streicher worked the anti-Semitic gutter, Rosenberg sought to elevate anti-Semitism to a respectable philosophy. He reveled in Nazi titles that seemed out of comic opera, such as Deputy Führer for the Supervision of the Entire Ideological Training and Education of the Party, and Commissioner for Safeguarding the National Socialist Philosophy for Party and State. He was on trial for his later roles as minister for the Occupied Eastern Territories and chief of Einstab Rosenberg, the art-looting operation.

Major Douglas Kelley sat in the visitors' gallery, from which he could watch his colleague, Gustav Gilbert, hovering around the dock. As Kelley studied Rosenberg, handsome in a lifeless sort of way, his hair parted and combed in a pompadour familiar to any American teenager of that era, he remembered his first visit to the man's cell. Rosenberg had spoken to him of his book *The Myth of the Twentieth Century*. The word *myth* was a poor translation; *legend* would have been better, since Rosenberg propounded a semimystical theory of the blood superiority of the German race. On its publication in 1934, a quarter of a million copies of the book had sold. Its principal feature, however, seemed to be unreadability. The book was written in the dense, tortured style of much German philosophy. Hitler had leafed through it. Göring had never touched it. The propaganda minister, Josef Goebbels, called *Myth of the Twentieth Century* "an ideological belch." Goebbels, however, knew his countrymen. If they could not comprehend Rosenberg, then they would think the man must be profound.

Kelley had taken a young American interpreter with him on that early visit. Rosenberg asked if Kelley knew what a U-boat crewman did as soon as he crawled, filthy and oil-stained, out of the engine room to his bunk? He reached for his copy of *The Myth*, Rosenberg explained. Kelley asked the interpreter to translate a passage from Rosenberg's copy. The Nazi started to hand over the dog-eared book. But first, he asked the soldier's religion. Catholic, the interpreter replied. Rosenberg pulled the book back. "This young man is working for his country," he said. "He is a good soldier and a good Catholic. If he were to read my book, he would renounce the church immediately. I do not want to be responsible for that."

As Kelley had left the cell that day, Rosenberg had handed him a sheaf of papers written in longhand. It was a memorandum, he said, of great potential value to the United States—a plan for "the settlement of American Negroes in Africa." He had done the required calculations, Rosenberg wrote, and if America did not follow his advice, "in 150 years there will be no more Americans, only an unholy mongrelization."

The summation against Rosenberg this day was being delivered by a new face. Walter Brudno's appearance in court represented the triumph of talent over rank. Brudno was a rarity at Nuremberg—a lawyer without a commission, a private first class in a sea of brass. Though impressive in appearance and able, Brudno had been sidetracked by his superiors—and this included practically everyone—until Jackson spotted him. The chief prosecutor solved Brudno's hierarchical problem with a pragmatic stroke: he had had the army discharge Brudno, in effect promoting him to civilian. The fact that this was Brudno's maiden voyage, however, had not spared him Sir Geoffrey Lawrence's sharp tongue. The justice, rimless glasses perched at the tip of his nose, remarked, "Mr. Brudno, you have referred us to *The Myth of the Twentieth Century* on several occasions." "Yes, your honor," Brudno said, nodding. "We don't want to hear about it anymore." It was the voice of an English headmaster, prim yet not to be brooked.

Lawrence's impartiality had at first confused the defendants. Even his entrances into the courtroom signaled his attachment to fair play. Clad in a black robe and striped pants, he would bow first to the prosecution and then to the defense before taking his seat. By now, the attitude toward him of the defendants and their lawyers approached worship. Their respect heightened on learning that

Lawrence had won the Distinguished Service Order as a gunner in the First World War. Hans Fritzsche, the radio propagandist on trial, listened to Sir Geoffrey's precise, economical speech with awe. He particularly admired the man's gift for maintaining total authority without ever raising his voice. Fritzsche remarked to his countrymen that Lawrence was "so English, so un-German."

As Brudno wrapped up his summation, Douglas Kelley's eyes remained on Rosenberg. A foolish man, a pompous man, and, in the philosophical rubbish he had peddled, a muddled mind. But a capital case? Kelley wondered. Granted, the prosecution had proved that Rosenberg oversaw the wholesale theft of art and furnishings from Jewish homes in subjugated countries. But he had never killed anyone. In his role as minister for the Occupied Eastern Territories, he had actually tried to prevent the wholesale butchery carried out in the Soviet Union. His authority, however, had quickly been undermined by more brutal SS figures. As Kelley studied the face in the dock, he asked himself who had helped indoctrinate these butchers to their murderous hatred. He thought of Lord Acton's words: "The greatest crime is homicide. The accomplice is no better than the assassin. The theorist is the worst."

34

HOWARD K. SMITH HAD a fresh idea for a broadcast. Back home, women had filled countless jobs as the men went off to war—the Rosie the Riveter phenomenon. Here at Nuremberg, Smith had observed that easily half of the six hundred American staff members were women, employed not only as secretaries but as researchers, interpreters, and translators. Two lawyers on the American prosecution staff were women. In his report, Smith told America about WAC Major Catherine Falvey, who was going home to run for the Massachusetts state legislature. He described Harriet Zetterberg, a brilliant thirty-year-old law review graduate of the University of Wisconsin, known for preparing masterful briefs. What passed unnoticed, except perhaps by Zetterberg, was that she did not appear before the court. That role was reserved for the men on the staff. She was married to another prosecution lawyer, Daniel Margolies; because of the ban on spouses, the couple posed as unmarried and "living in sin" in a room at the Grand Hotel.

On the morning of January 10, as the defendants were marched from the prison to the courthouse, Captain Gilbert walked alongside Hans Frank to provide moral support. The twenty-one defendants formed four imprecise, sometimes shifting cliques—the unrepentant, dominated by Göring; the indignant, headed by Schacht; the confused, typified by Sauckel; and the penitents, led by Speer and Frank.

In the courtroom, Major William Baldwin, a glider veteran out of the OSS, began the Frank prosecution by introducing entries from the diaries Frank had kept while he was governor-general of Poland. "In September of 1941," Baldwin read from document 233 PS, "defendant Frank's own chief medical officer reported to him the appalling Polish health conditions. I read now from page forty-six of the diary. 'The Poles now have about 600 calories allotted to them, while the normal requirement for a human being is 2,200. . . . The number of Poles with communicable diseases has reached forty percent. . . . This situation presents a serious danger for the soldiers of the Reich coming into the Government-General.' " Yet, Baldwin went on, "In August 1942, Frank approved a new plan which called for a much larger contribution of foodstuffs to Germany at the expense of the Poles. I quote again from the diary, page thirty. 'Before the German people suffer starvation, the occupied territories and their people shall be exposed to starvation. This means a sixfold increase over that of last year's contributions by Poland. The new demand will be fulfilled exclusively at the expense of the foreign population. It must be done cold-bloodedly and without pity.' "

Captain Gilbert, standing to the left side of the dock, studied Frank. Baldwin's arguments were striking like hammer blows. Gilbert could virtually see the man buckle. Gilbert feared that this pounding might cause Frank to recant and seek sympathy and understanding in the camp of the diehards—in the Göring wing.

Friday, January 11, Harriet Zetterberg and her husband, Daniel Margolies, eagerly entered the courtroom. The couple had spent the Christmas break tracking down a physician, Dr. Franz Blaha, in

Czechoslovakia. Blaha's experiences, the prosecution believed, could incriminate several defendants. The doctor was testifying today as Tom Dodd's prosecution witness.

Early in the war, Blaha had been arrested by the Nazis and committed to Dachau, where, as a physician, he was ordered to carry out typhoid experiments on healthy patients. He refused and was banished to the autopsy room. By the end of the war, Blaha had performed twelve thousand autopsies. What struck Margolies and Zetterberg as the doctor took the stand was the innate dignity the man had managed to preserve. His face was deeply creviced, his eyes tired, the voice convincing by its very calmness.

The effect of the *Nacht und Nebel* decree had previously been described only in documentary evidence. Keitel's instructions when he issued the order read, "Intimidation can only be achieved either by capital punishment or through measures by which the relatives of the prisoners and the population cannot learn the fate of the criminals." Dodd asked Blaha to describe firsthand what happened to people spirited from their homes under the decree. The victims he had seen, Blaha testified, were shot in front of the Dachau crematoria to speed up the process of their obliteration. As the Germans liked to put it, this was where "we turn them into fog."

Dodd asked Blaha if he had ever seen any of the defendants in the dock at Dachau. The question was critical. Most of them had denied any knowledge of concentration camp operations. Blaha pointed and intoned the names, "Rosenberg, Frick, Funk, Sauckel." Another face had arrested Blaha's attention from the moment he arrived in court. There in the dock was his shy, studious boyhood chum, Arthur Zajtich. Zajtich had left Czechoslovakia for Austria and become a rising Nazi, Frank's apprentice in ruling Poland and later a power in his own right as Reich commissioner of the Netherlands. Blaha's friend had long since changed his name to Seyss-Inquart.

35

ON JANUARY 12, the prison had taken on its Saturday-afternoon aura, with the drama of the courtroom temporarily suspended and life reduced to the limits of a concrete cube. Weekends produced Gustav

Gilbert's most profitable visits, with the defendants' loneliness deepest and their guard down. As the psychologist entered the cellblock, a POW trusty was coming out, lugging a sack that once held army flour. Gilbert was by now familiar with the undercurrents of prison life. The sack, he knew, contained used coffee grounds salvaged from the kitchen, and was being smuggled out of the prison for sale in Nuremberg. He encountered the prison librarian, Otto Streng, another trusty, rolling a cartload of books from cell to cell. Gilbert asked Streng if he had anything for Speer. Streng handed him a single volume. Gilbert noted the title, *Memoirs of a German Painter*, by Ludwig Richter.

In cell 17, Speer eagerly awaited Gilbert's visit. He was determined to break Göring's hold over his fellow defendants, particularly after the way Göring had attacked him when the lawyer Kuboschok claimed that Speer had planned to assassinate Hitler. Speer understood clearly what the prosecutors and the bench hoped for from the defendants—not Göring's bid for unified defiance, but individual confession and remorse. Speer was trying to bring the more pliable defendants along with him onto that course. He had high hopes for the youth leader, Baldur von Schirach. Schirach was now talking about writing a denunciation of Hitler. This malleable man had to be kept away from Göring, Speer believed. Earlier, Frank too had seemed to be safely in the penitents' corner. But, after the prosecution mauled him, Frank had been wondering aloud why he should forsake his old comrades. Maybe he ought to make his last stand with Göring rather than with people who despised him. Speer marveled at Göring's capacity to intimidate and dominate without possessing a shred of real power. That was what he wanted to talk about to Gilbert.

Speer had long been familiar with Göring's bullying and bluster. Late in the war, he had shown Göring a still experimental jet aircraft. Göring immediately rushed to Hitler with the news. Hitler became ecstatic. How many of these planes could the Luftwaffe have operational, and how soon? Hitler wanted to know. At least five hundred, almost immediately, Göring assured him. He made the claim knowing that Speer was nowhere near ready to begin production. When the jets failed to appear in the sky quickly enough, Hitler raged, and Göring placed the blame on Speer.

The weak Kaltenbrunner might also be enlisted as a penitent,

Speer believed. And Speer would much rather have him as an ally than as an adversary. Only Kaltenbrunner knew what had really happened to Speer in the days after the Twentieth of July plot. Speer was so adroit that, though he served the Nazi regime, he had still managed to retain the respect of the conspirators. After the plot failed, Kaltenbrunner came to see him. He spoke in a tone of cordial menace. In a safe at Bendlerstrasse, the High Command headquarters, Kaltenbrunner said, his people had found a description of the government the plotters intended to install. He took out an organization chart and handed it to Speer. In a box labeled "Armaments," Speer's name appeared in neatly printed letters. Speer quickly pointed out a penciled notation alongside the box that read, "If possible." The plotters might have wanted him, but he had wanted no part of them, he said. Speer denied knowing about the plot. With that, Kaltenbrunner gave him an enigmatic smile and left.

The next day, Speer summoned his senior staff to a "loyalty meeting." In past speeches he had shunned party bombast. This day, however, he ladled it on like a *Gauleiter*. He praised Hitler's leadership to the skies and expressed his undying faith in the "Führer's greatness." He expected the same loyalty to Germany's leader, he said, from anyone who worked for him.

In the wake of the plot, nearly five thousand Germans were executed, many with far less connection to it than Speer. Hitler, of course, knew what Kaltenbrunner knew. That Speer's life was spared could only be explained by the rarest of Hitler's emotions: he felt genuine affection for Albert Speer. Would the whimpering giant in cell 26 keep quiet about Speer's eager display of loyalty after the plot? Speer could only hope so.

On Gilbert's arrival, Speer greeted the psychologist warmly in fluent, though heavily accented, English. Gilbert had observed the effect of Speer's language facility. When interpreters were occasionally stuck for a word, Speer would scribble his suggestion on a piece of paper and pass it along to the glass-enclosed interpreters' booth. His meaning, the interpreters agreed, was invariably the closest. In more than one sense, Gilbert concluded, Speer and his captors spoke the same language.

Gilbert handed Speer the library book. A rapport had grown between the two men. After his previous visit, the psychologist had written, "Speer is apparently sincere in his insistence that he is not trying to save his neck by this stand, since he is the only one who admitted a common guilt in his supporting the regime even *before* the trial started."

Speer thumbed idly through the book, all the while commenting to Gilbert on how cowardly he had been in the past. He hated Göring. Yet, with the others, he had celebrated the man's birthdays. Here in prison, he had finally broken free. Most of the defendants, however, were still in Göring's thrall. Frank was wavering. Speer and Göring were openly wrestling for Schirach's soul. "You know," Speer said, "it is not a good idea to let the defendants eat and work together. That is how Göring keeps whipping them into line."

After Gilbert left the cellblock, he pondered Speer's point and decided to suggest a new arrangement to Colonel Andrus.

36

Captain Drexel Sprecher gave the attractive German cashier in the cafeteria a practiced eye before he paid for his coffee and pastry. He took a seat at a nearby table. Sprecher was thirty-one, a tall, broad-shouldered, open-faced American whose boundless energy fueled a life of hard work and hard play. He had never given the nonfraternization rule the slightest respect, even when it was in force. Just coming out of an unhappy marriage and a divorce, Sprecher had dated German girls from his first week in Nuremberg.

He had brought with him to the cafeteria papers relating to his latest case. Sprecher had been deeply disappointed when Robert Ley's suicide cheated him out of his first major prosecution. Thereafter, he had been assigned Hans Fritzsche, the propagandist, who, Sprecher knew, hardly belonged in the dock with Adolf Hitler's chief lieutenants. As Sprecher's succinct, masterful briefs continued to please Jackson, the lawyer was sent after more challenging game, Baldur von Schirach. Schirach, as the former leader of the Hitler Youth, hoped to pass himself off as little more than the German equivalent of the national director of the Boy Scouts. Sprecher was developing a far darker record.

The letters he reviewed over his coffee both amused and exasperated him. American descendants of the signers of the Declaration of Independence were writing to the court, pleading for clemency for Baldur von Schirach! The accused Nazi war criminal was, in fact, three-quarters American. Schirach's grandfather had emigrated to America, served as a major in the Union army, lost a leg at Bull Run, and was an honorary pallbearer at the funeral of Abraham Lincoln. The grandfather married an American heiress and then returned to Germany. Schirach's father had also married an American woman who traced her forebears to a signer of the Declaration of Independence —hence the DAR support.

Sprecher believed Schirach, like Speer and Frick, to be a traitor to his class. Schirach's father had been director of the National Theater in Weimar, and young Baldur grew up in a world of poetry, theater, and music. The economic disaster that followed World War I, however, cost the senior Schirach his job. As the family's fortunes plunged, Baldur began reading such anti-Semitic tracts as Henry Ford's *The International Jew*, and by age eighteen he had become that rarity, a cultured storm trooper.

Sprecher had studied his quarry in the courtroom. There was a softness about Schirach; the flabby body and smooth face suggested too many cream pastries. Between his position as a youth leader and his appearance, Schirach was inevitably subjected to speculation about homosexuality. Marriage and four children had not insulated him from suspicion. One courtroom observer thought Schirach exuded "a whiff of the kind of scoutmaster who winds up in the Sunday newspapers."

In 1933, Hitler had named Schirach, then twenty-six years old, leader of German youth. From this post, he wove a net that snared nearly every German boy and girl. At age ten, boys were inducted into the Jungvolk and the girls into the Jungmädel. By age fourteen, the boys became full-blown Hitler Jugend and the girls entered the Bund Deutscher Mädel. At eighteen, the boys became party members. By 1939, Schirach's fiefdom numbered nine million young people, presumably pursuing health, beauty, and culture. "Every German boy who dies at the front is dying for Mozart," Schirach liked to say.

Sprecher recognized that heading a movement of robust, marching, singing boys and girls could hardly be viewed as a war crime; he hoped to convict Schirach on the basis of the ultimate purpose of all his efforts. Schirach was charged with conspiracy to commit aggression, and the very songs the Hitler Youth sang on Alpine hikes rang with aggressive intent:

> If all the world lies in ruins,
> What the devil do we care?
> We will still go on marching,
> For today Germany belongs to us,
> And tomorrow the world.

Sprecher's strategy was to add the evidence proving conspiracy to a still blacker count against Schirach: count four, crimes against humanity. In 1940, Hitler had pulled Schirach out of the army, where he had served for six months, and made him *Gauleiter* of Vienna. For the youth leader, now thirty-three, this was at last a grown-up's job, and with enviable perquisites, including a magnificent villa with seventeen servants.

When Reinhard Heydrich, Kaltenbrunner's predecessor as head of the RSHA security organization, was assassinated in Czechoslovakia, Schirach sent a "Dear Martin" letter to Hitler's secretary, Bormann. He had an idea that he wanted Bormann to put before the Führer. Everybody knew the British had masterminded the Heydrich killing. The Czechs were otherwise happy under German occupation and the British were simply trying to stir up trouble, Schirach pointed out. He had a plan: "A sudden violent air attack on a British cultural town would be most effective as 'The Revenge of Heydrich.'" Sprecher intended to introduce this document. It should have considerable effect on the British justices.

Sprecher hoped to convict Schirach not simply for song lyrics and a braggadocio memo. Soon after becoming *Gauleiter* of Vienna, Schirach informed Hitler that there were sixty thousand Jews in Vienna unfit for work. At the same time, the city faced an acute housing shortage. He needed relief. Hitler ordered that Schirach deport his Jews to the government-general of Poland. Schirach later boasted, "If anyone reproaches me with having driven from this city . . . tens of thousands into the ghettos of the East, I will reply, I see this as an act contributing to European culture." Schirach's cultural contribution resulted in the death of these tens of thousands of Jews in Auschwitz.

Thus soft-looking, cultivated Baldur von Schirach had taken an action worthy of an SS brute. That was the case Sprecher hoped to make: that Schirach had helped shape a generation of Germans to carry out barbarities, with himself as a model.

Shortly after concluding the prosecution of Schirach, Drexel Sprecher received a visitor in his office, Wolfe Frank, star of the language division. Given the English he spoke, Frank could have passed himself off as a lord. He was actually a German Jew born in Munich who had fled to England during the thirties. He had acquired his aristocratic enunciation during five years as a British army officer.

Wolfe Frank asked Sprecher if he had ever known a titled old German woman in Switzerland before the war. Sprecher remembered that in his student travels he had visited a distant relative in Zurich. The woman had turned out to be a minor member of the German nobility. What he remembered most was a picture of Hitler hanging on her wall. Though Sprecher came from solid small-town Republican stock, college had turned him into a "semi-Socialist," and he was shocked at the woman's choice of a hero. Why, he had asked, did she keep Hitler's photograph? "This man," she said, "will restore Germany."

Wolfe Frank explained that he had recently been visited by a woman, the Countess Faber-Castell. She had heard on the radio about Sprecher's prosecuting Baldur von Schirach, and his name sounded familiar. Could this be the same young man who had visited her mother in Zurich ten years before? If so, she hoped that Sprecher would call on her and her husband. She had given Wolfe Frank an address in the country some ten miles from Nuremberg.

Like most of the staff, Drexel Sprecher fled the bleak city every free weekend. And his curiosity had been piqued by the Faber-Castell invitation. Still, he was an Allied prosecutor. He knew nothing of the politics of these people, and he remembered the photograph of Hitler in Zurich. He decided it was best not to go alone and took with him Wolfe Frank as well as Bill Baldwin, the prosecutor of Hans Frank. The sky was a bright, hard blue as their canvas-topped jeep took them through rolling hills and great forested stretches of Franconia. They arrived at a rustic-elegant *Jagthaus*, the Faber-Castells' hunting lodge.

They were met by the Countess Nina and her husband, Roland Faber-Castell.

Sprecher's reticence soon began to melt in the bonhomie of the Faber-Castell home. They had no resentment over the U.S. occupation forces taking over their castle in Stein to house the press, Roland Faber-Castell said. The Nazis had done much the same, turning the castle to their purposes. As for his politics, Roland explained that he had barely escaped arrest after the Twentieth of July plot because of his known opposition to the Nazis. He had already been denazified by the American occupation authorities and was now busy rebuilding his business empire.

An attractive, talented thirty-year-old, Nina Faber-Castell entertained her guests by singing and playing her own songs on the piano. She noted, impishly, that Minister Goebbels had once called on her to compliment her on her talent. Roland Faber-Castell invited Sprecher to join him on a walk around the grounds. Tall pines shattered the sun's rays and scattered them over patches of snow and ice. Sprecher was thinking of similar winters in his native Wisconsin, when suddenly they came upon a scene of utter devastation. Hundreds of great trees had been snapped off at the base and splintered into virtual matchwood, their wounds still fresh and white. Allied bombers, Faber-Castell noted wryly, did not always hit their intended targets.

Hours later, after good food, good talk, and good drink, the visitors prepared to leave. On the drive back, an air of well-being settled over the three men. This afternoon's entertainment had not been the catered hospitality of the Grand Hotel or the seized comforts of a confiscated villa. The *Jagthaus* was a real home of sophisticated, amusing, friendly people. Sprecher was also relieved by the enlightened politics of his hosts. But then, one never seemed to meet a Nazi in Germany these days, except for the few in the dock at Nuremberg.

37

THE FIRST TIME Otto Kranzbuehler had shown up at the courthouse gate, the guards had been alarmed. Admiral Dönitz's lawyer was wearing the full naval uniform of the defeated enemy. The dashing thirty-nine-year-old Kranzbuehler was a *Flottenrichter*, a fleet judge, in the German navy. Admiral Dönitz believed that he had fought the war at sea as cleanly as the men of any other nation. A fellow naval officer, he had concluded, could best make that case.

Major Neave had located Kranzbuehler in the legal office of a German minesweeping unit which the British allowed to function to clear ports on the North and Baltic seas. At Nuremberg, Kranzbuehler had insisted on his right to wear the uniform, since it was the Allies who had kept him on active duty. He also hoped by appearing in uniform to register the point that most Germans had simply fought for their country; this was the role in which he intended to cast his client, Dönitz.

The hallways of the courthouse were virtually deserted this Sunday afternoon as Kranzbuehler made his way to the now-familiar mesh cages of the visitors' room. The next day, January 14, the prosecution would begin its case against Dönitz, and Kranzbuehler had come to discuss last-minute strategies. His client was already waiting. Dönitz was not an easy client; the moment the man opened his thin lips, any suggestion of the kindly grandfather vanished. His voice had the whine of a dentist's drill. He retained the habit of command, unbroken by his months of confinement. Kranzbuehler was thoroughly aware of the stories told about Dönitz in the German navy. Dönitz's twenty-one-year-old son, Peter, had been lost aboard one of the submarines in his father's wolf-pack fleet, one of twenty-five thousand German submariners out of forty thousand who perished. In May 1944, another son, Klaus, was killed aboard a reconnaissance ship looking for signs of the Allied invasion buildup along the English coast. When an aide brought him the news, Dönitz said nothing and kept working at his desk. He went home to tell his wife and then informed her that she was to accompany him for a luncheon date with the Japanese ambassador. Not a word was spoken during the lunch about their loss. The moment the lunch was over, Dönitz's wife collapsed.

Kranzbuehler had gone to the document room days before to obtain copies of the evidence the prosecution expected to introduce against Dönitz. Here in the visitors' room, he went over them with the admiral, who snapped out the objections Kranzbuehler should raise in court. The *Laconia* Order was going to be the most troublesome, the lawyer said. The order, issued by Dönitz after one of his subs sank the British transport *Laconia* in 1942, had a particularly harsh ring. It forbade German naval vessels to pick up survivors, even to help them into lifeboats or give them food and water. Dönitz had ended the order: "Be hard. Remember, the enemy has no regard for women and children when he bombs German cities."

The only reason he had issued the order, Dönitz told Kranz-buehler, was that American aircraft had attacked his submarines while the crews were trying to rescue the *Laconia*'s survivors. He knew for a fact that the American navy operated essentially under the same conditions as the *Laconia* Order. Yes, Kranzbuehler said, he of course intended to make this point on cross-examination. But the admiral had to understand, right or wrong, fair or not, this court would not entertain a defense of tu quoque.

The prosecution could also be expected to introduce evidence that Dönitz, beyond being simply a professional sailor, had been a staunch supporter of Hitler and Nazism. The day after the Twentieth of July attempt on Hitler's life, Dönitz had gone on the radio. "An insane clique of generals, which has nothing to do with our brave armed forces," he had said, "instigated this cowardly attempt at mur-der. . . . If these scoundrels think removal of the Führer can free us from our hard but inexorable struggle, they are wrong." That was not the speech he was concerned about, Dönitz said. Did the Americans have the address he had made on the struggle against Jewry? In it he had said, "I would rather eat dirt than have my grandson grow up in the Jewish spirit and faith." Fifty-two copies of the speech had been run off. Fifty-one had been destroyed. Did the prosecution have the last copy? Dönitz asked. They seemed to have everything else. Kranz-buehler said that he did not know.

As they finished, Dönitz asked if his lawyer knew why he was being tried. Before Kranzbuehler could reply, the admiral answered. They could not try Krupp, so they had gone after his son, Alfried. Since they could not try Himmler, they had settled for Kaltenbrunner. They could not try Goebbels, so they had indicted Fritzsche. And they could not try Hitler, so they had settled on him, as the Führer's suc-cessor. His indictment, Dönitz said, was "an example of American humor."

The British had felt all along that the Americans were hogging the stage. They particularly believed that the German navy was their game. They, after all, had fought the real fight against the *Kriegsmarine*. Thus, on Monday, January 14, Barrister-at-Law H. J. Phillimore opened the prosecution case against Grand Admiral Karl Dönitz. Dönitz was charged with complicity in waging aggressive warfare and with crimes committed during the war. As Phillimore introduced the issue of the *Laconia* Order, Major Airey Neave listened with bitter memories. A friend of his, as well as the man's wife and baby, had drowned when the ship went down. The prosecutor next moved to Dönitz's role in passing along Keitel's Commando Order to the German navy. As a result, captured British commandos had been shot without trial.

So far, the evidence against the admiral had dealt only with military actions, and had raised questions of how cruelly or fairly any war could be fought. The next phase of the prosecution, however, moved Dönitz into a less savory realm. He had stoutly maintained to his interrogators that he knew nothing of the horrors of the concentration camps. The British prosecutor introduced documents proving that Dönitz had personally requested twelve thousand camp inmates to work in navy shipyards.

On cross-examination, Kranzbuehler countered the charges as skillfully as the evidence permitted. Still, when the day was over and he retreated to the Nuremberg home where he was boarding, he faced a cross-examination of self. He had been a career legal officer, in the navy since 1934. He sat as a judge at court-martials and had sought to dispense justice within the law. He was mortified by the revelations of room 600. Had he known nothing of what had gone on? In that case, he must be an idiot. Had he been part of it? In that case, he must be a criminal. Had he known, yet done nothing? In that case, he must be a coward. The choices—idiot, criminal, or coward—all left Kranzbuehler depressed.

38

FEW COULD MISS the symmetry. On January 16, Robert Kempner opened the prosecution case against Wilhelm Frick, the man who had turned Hitlerian grudges into German law. Frick had headed the Ministry of the Interior, from which Kempner had been fired. Frick had promulgated the laws that drove Kempner from Germany. But for Frick, Kempner would not be standing in this courtroom this day as an American citizen and as his antagonist. The only things that had pried Kempner from a life he would happily have lived out in Germany were the deeds of the defendants. If anyone in the courtroom fit the German stereotype—ostentatiously learned, brusque, and didactic—it was Robert Kempner. A heavy accent completed the image.

The psychiatrist, Major Kelley, had found the sixty-nine-year-old Frick the most colorless of the defendants. Day after day, Frick sat in the dock looking, with his expressionless face, lifeless eyes, and incongruous checked sport jacket, like a professor whose courses students assiduously avoided. Frick's proudest achievement had been to make Adolf Hitler a German. Hitler had renounced his Austrian citizenship in 1925 to pursue his political star in Germany. His German citizenship application was initially turned down because he had been convicted of treason after the 1923 Munich putsch, his failed attempt to topple the Bavarian government. Frick tried another tack. Anyone named to an official post in Germany was automatically entitled to citizenship. Frick used his influence as a member of the Reichstag to have Hitler appointed constable of a small town called Hildburghausen. Hitler was offended and tore up the appointment. Other gambits failed, but Frick persevered. In February of 1932, he finally managed to have Hitler named a councilor for the state of Braunschweig. Less than a year later, Hitler became Germany's chancellor.

As early as 1924, Frick had introduced two then-shocking bills, one barring Jews from holding public office and another forbidding mixed marriages with Jews. He was merely trying to correct an imbalance, he had argued. The Jew was too powerful. Nearly half of the physicians in Germany were Jews, as were over half of the lawyers and eighty percent of theater directors. To support the proposed ban on intermarriage, Frick read accounts of lurid Jewish sex crimes from a new newspaper, *Der Stürmer*, published by one Julius Streicher.

In those early years, Frick was looked upon simply as another Nazi crank. By 1933, however, Hitler was in power and Frick became minister of the interior. That March, within a month after the Reichstag fire, which Hitler blamed on the Communists, Frick signed the Enabling Law giving Hitler the right to promulgate any measure without the Reichstag's approval. Frick further signed a decree entitled "Securing the Unity of Party and State," which established that the Nazi party controlled the German government and not the other way around. Hitler's authority was now total. Frick had served his Führer well. He had given the patina of legality to despotism.

Still, a Jew might have continued to live in Germany but for Frick's subsequent acts. Kempner began reciting the decrees ratified at the 1935 Congress of the Nazi Party in Nuremberg. Jews were deprived of their citizenship. No matter that twelve thousand of them had died for Germany in World War I and countless others had won Iron Crosses. Their German identity was effaced. Not only marriages, but sexual relations between Jews and Gentiles became a crime. Year by year, the noose tightened. Jews were denied employment, first in journalism, then in medicine, then in dentistry, then in law. They were forbidden to own property. Some decrees seemed a parody. Any Jew with a non-Jewish first name was to assume the name Israel if male and Sara if female. Jews were forbidden to keep canaries. In 1943, Frick signed a decree placing the Jews completely outside the law. You could do what you wanted to a Jew without fear of punishment. The process had begun in Nuremberg; hence this codified persecution became known collectively as the Nuremberg Laws. When the first laws were promulgated, there had been ten thousand Jews in Nuremberg. At the end of the war there were ten.

Kempner's courtroom style was too similar to his adversaries' for some of the Allies—too Teutonic, too dogmatic. Still, prosecutors at the British table whispered their relief that, for once, a lawyer on the American side had displayed a sense of historical perspective. The British prosecutors, in their black coats and striped trousers, formed a small, select corps, skilled in their profession and steeped in the historical context of each case. By contrast, as Howard K. Smith noted in a broadcast: "The weakest feature of the case has been Justice Jackson's staff . . . their briefs are written for them by assistants and many appear not to have read them over before entering the courtroom. They were probably quite skilled at defending railroads or prosecuting gangsters back home. But with a few brilliant exceptions, they have shown absolutely no knowledge of Nazism." Janet Flanner, in her January 5 piece for *The New Yorker*, noted the succinct, reasoned cases the British prosecutors made. But the Americans, she wrote, had managed to make frightful war crimes "dull and incoherent." Katy Walch, a British researcher working for the Americans, confided to a fellow Briton, "You see, they haven't had a classical education."

Jackson's huge staff was suffering from the inefficiencies of scale. For all the prosecutor's other strengths, administration was not among them. He was spending almost no time in the courtroom these days; instead, he willingly delegated the prosecution to assistants, who ran competing duchies. Jackson also recognized, too late, that he had made a fundamental mistake. The small corps of British prosecutors constituted a legal elite. Jackson, instead, had taken on phalanxes of American lawyers of mixed talents from the military. Most were civilians in uniform. They would acquire the requisite points for discharge, and within days would be on their way home, with hardly enough time to show their successors where the PX was, much less the intricacies of cases in progress. Jackson found himself begging people not to leave in the middle of a prosecution. Only 13 of his 150 original lawyers were still with him by January. Jackson complained that his staff was melting away.

Equally aggravating for him were reports from the courtroom of Justice Biddle's behavior on the bench. Biddle could be heard, in stage whispers, denigrating the performance of his countrymen. Poor preparation. Sloppy organization. Amateurish examination. In Jackson's view, Biddle, who months before had been lucky to get a job, had become haughty and full of himself.

At one point during the Frick prosecution, the justices noticed a wave of whispering that swept through the dock. A note was being passed from hand to hand. Hans Fritzsche had written that Major Gerecke was going home: the defendants must do something. The St. Louis chaplain had not seen his wife for more than two years. His soldier sons had made it home, while the aging Gerecke was still abroad eight months after the war had ended. He had indeed decided that it was time to leave.

Back in his cell, later that afternoon, Fritzsche wrote a letter addressed to "Mrs. Reverend Henry Gerecke, St. Louis, Missouri." "Your husband has been taking religious care of the undersigned for more than half a year," Fritzsche began. "We have heard that you wish to see him back home. Because we have wives and children, we understand this wish. Nevertheless, we beg you to put off this desire to have your family once more around you. We cannot lose your husband. No one else can break through the walls that have built up around us, both spiritual and material. We shall be deeply indebted to you. . . ." Fritzsche finished the letter and asked the officer of the day if he might have it circulated among the Protestant defendants.

When Colonel Andrus read Fritzsche's petition, signed by all the Germans, his reaction was instantaneous. The last thing he needed was to break in a new chaplain. He sent a copy of the petition to Gerecke. When the chaplain read it, he fell on his knees and prayed for guidance. If these men facing death needed him, surely his wife must understand.

39

LATE SATURDAY AFTERNOON, January 19, Captain Gilbert sat glassy-eyed, listening to the man who had influenced the political formation of Baldur von Schirach and Wilhelm Frick. He found his visits to Julius Streicher's cell an ordeal. Still, if he was to understand the impulses of the Nazi psyche, he had to understand one of its molders, this squat, coarse, hook-nosed, bullet-headed figure sitting on the cot opposite him. The floor of the cell was littered with Streicher's sketches. He would draw anything—a guard's face, his mess kit, even the toilet bowl. At the end of the day, he threw all the drawings out. The work, Gilbert had to admit, was good, and he wondered at the incongruity of artistic sensibility in so crude a man.

For Gilbert, the worst part of dealing with Streicher was to be patronized. "Circumcision was the most amazing stroke of genius," Streicher was saying. "It wasn't just for sanitary reasons, you can be sure. It was to assure racial consciousness. Do you know what the poet

Heine said about circumcision? You can wipe away baptism, but you cannot wipe away circumcision. Diabolical, isn't it?" As he spoke, Streicher popped a wad of gum. He supported this latest addiction by trading the guards his autograph for the gum. As Streicher talked, Gilbert was reminded of Walther Funk's complaint. He had already been punished enough, the banker said, since every day in court he had to sit next to Julius Streicher.

Fritzsche considered Streicher's *Der Stürmer* an embarrassing rag, and Gilbert, after reading a few issues, understood why. In one article, Streicher had written, "The male sperm in cohabitation is partially or completely absorbed by the female and thus enters her bloodstream. One single cohabitation of a Jew with an Aryan woman is sufficient to poison her blood forever . . . never again will she be able to bear pure Aryan children." Jews, Streicher had written, believed it was morally acceptable to violate a Gentile girl as young as three years old. Jews believed that Christ's mother was a whore. Jews believed that they had the right to take a Christian's money. Streicher had once lectured an audience of professors about a divining rod he had perfected for distinguishing between Jews and Gentiles. He had also amassed an impressive collection of pornography; he had bought it from Jews, he said, and kept it to show the kind of filth they read.

Gilbert marveled that this vulgar man had once been the most powerful figure in Nuremberg, as *Gauleiter* of Franconia, the part of Bavaria within which the city lay. Streicher had begun his professional life as a schoolteacher. He enlisted during the First World War, and by constantly volunteering for the most dangerous missions had won the Iron Cross first class and a battlefield commission. Streicher told Gilbert about the brightest moment in his life. He had formed his own right-wing party after the war. In 1922, he heard Hitler deliver a three-hour oration in Munich. He elbowed his way to the speaker's platform and offered the two thousand members of his group to Adolf Hitler "as a gift."

Streicher had ridden high until his libels against Göring's manhood led to the investigation and condemnation of his seamy business and sexual practices. Göring told the other defendants, "At least we did one good thing. We got that prick Streicher kicked out of office." Streicher indeed had had no power after his 1940 fall. *Der Stürmer* had been not a government organ but a private journal owned by

Streicher, and during the war years the paper's circulation dropped from over a million to fifteen thousand.

Part of Gilbert's problem, as he dealt with inmates like Hess, Rosenberg, and Streicher, was to find the line between true paranoia and culturally conditioned pseudoparanoia. In short, were these people crazy or had they been caught up in a crazy world? As Streicher discoursed on the nature of Jewish sperm, Gilbert had little doubt in this particular case. The larger question was whether the prosecution would be able to slip a noose over this neckless head. Could a fanatic be hanged for publishing racial rubbish?

40

Saturday, January 26, a night of numbing cold, with the temperature at ten degrees Fahrenheit, Maxwell-Fyfe held a soiree. On the drive out to Sir David's house in suburban Zirndorf, the British compound, Justice Jackson's staff car rolled past now-familiar sights: a stack of bathrooms, the tubs exposed, where a bomb had neatly blown off the side of an apartment house; a British plane hanging precariously from the steeple of the church into which it had crashed.

Sir David's party was to celebrate the birthday of Robert Burns. Scottishness ran deep in Sir David's being. He enjoyed the fact that his villa at 7 Goethestrasse was located on land where one of his Scottish ancestors had commanded a regiment during the Thirty Years War. On Sundays he would give his bodyguard the slip and retrace the ebb and flow of that long-ago battle. Though his father had been a poor schoolmaster and he himself a scholarship boy, his attachment to the past had bred in Sir David a deep conservatism. He had been elected to Parliament as a Conservative in 1935, and still held his seat. His celebrity at Nuremberg was burnished by the fact that his wife, Sylvia, was the sister of the actor Rex Harrison.

The party was clearly a roaring success. At a signal from the host, Scottish bagpipers in full Highland regalia marched in, accompanying the haggis Maxwell-Fyfe had ordered flown in from Scotland. After dinner a quartet of British prosecutors singled out the energetic Drexel

Sprecher for one of the parodies that had become a staple of Nuremberg entertaining:

They sang, to the tune of "Old Man River":

> Old man Sprecher, dat old man Sprecher,
> His hands keep wavin',
> He keeps us slavin',
> He keeps on hollerin',
> And we keep follerin'
> . . . along!

Sir Norman Birkett buttonholed Biddle's aide, Herb Wechsler, and violated a cardinal rule of Nuremberg social life by talking shop. The standards of the IMT, Sir Norman informed Wechsler, did not begin to compare with those of the high courts of England. Birkett also explained how much more elevated the Nuremberg bench would be had he been named president. Wechsler was uncomfortable. He tried to steer Birkett off the subject, only to have Sir Norman ask confidentially, Did Wechsler know that Lawrence took young ladies for long rides? And did he know that the British prosecutors referred to the American judges on the bench as Piddle and Barker? Wechsler knew of Birkett's fame in the British courts. Still, his behavior suggested an insecure personality lacking the easy confidence that comes naturally to the wellborn. A minute later, the gangly, wild-thatched jurist excused himself and was off charming a knot of guests with a sonorous recitation of Shakespeare. Wechsler liked that Birkett much better.

41

CAPTAIN GILBERT HAD CONSIDERED escaping for the weekend. The psychologist was emotionally burned out after months of standing in court all day and making nightly and weekend cell visits. He was worried, however, about the stability of Hess and Ribbentrop. Weekend or not, he decided, he would have to see them.

Hess did not stand as required when Gilbert entered the cell that Saturday afternoon. He never stood for anyone, including Colonel

Andrus. On his previous visit, Gilbert had sensed a deterioration in Hess's mental condition. For a time after his electric November 30 announcement that his memory had returned, Hess had stopped reading novels in the courtroom; his performance on the number-memory test had improved. But now he was reading in court again. At first, the guards had yanked the books from his hands, but after a time, Justice Lawrence told them not to bother. He feared that, with no other distraction, Hess might disrupt the proceedings by worse antics.

This day, Gilbert again administered the number-recall test. Hess slipped from a recall of eight digits forward and seven backward the previous time, to five forward and four backward today. He had difficulty remembering witnesses who had testified just days before. Gilbert left the cell and proceeded to the prison office to write his assessment. "The current apathy and beginnings of real and ostensible memory failure," Gilbert wrote, were "part of a negativistic pattern of reaction to the final smashing of the ideology which had supported his ego and now faces him with an intolerable choice between accepting a share of the guilt of Nazism or rejecting his Führer. He'll probably end up by rejecting reality again."

Major Kelley appeared at the door. They needed to talk, he said, leading Gilbert out to the empty exercise yard. As a friend and partner, Kelley went on, he wanted to warn Gilbert that his disdain for the military mind was becoming obvious to the colonel. It was hard, Gilbert replied, to have his work constantly second-guessed by a layman, but he would try to be more respectful. What Kelley left unsaid was that Andrus had suggested getting rid of Gilbert. Kelley had talked him out of it. The psychiatrist expected to be leaving Nuremberg soon, and Gilbert would be his sole pipeline to the data vital to their project.

Shortly after Gilbert left, Hess received another visitor, the court's liaison man, British major Airey Neave. Neave arrived in the midst of a minor tumult. Hess had just flung his mess kit, full of food, at a junior officer who dared peer into his cell. Why, Hess asked Neave, had he been left without a lawyer for a week? The major explained, as he had several times already, that Hess's counsel, Gunther von Rohrscheidt, had slipped on the ice and broken his leg. Very well, Hess said, he would defend himself. This was precisely the outcome

Neave had been sent to forestall. Hess defending himself would turn the trial into a circus, the judges feared. He and Hess could talk the matter over again tomorrow, Neave said, buying time.

As soon as Neave was gone, Hess demanded a pencil and paper from his guard. He was going to write a letter to the members of the court, he said. He had no faith in Rohrscheidt. He wanted him dismissed.

All correspondence from the defendants to the court had to pass through Colonel Andrus's hands. The colonel too had come into his office on Saturday, and he had just read Gilbert's latest evaluation of Hess as "passive suggestible . . . a gullible simpleton. Like the typical hysterical personality, he is incapable of facing reality and avoids frustration by developing a functional disorder, in this case, hysterical amnesia." The colonel was eager to read what this "passive suggestible" personality had written to the IMT. "I draw the attention of the court," Hess's letter read, "to the fact that I have now been a whole week without a defending counsel, while I have not been permitted the right to which the statute entitles me of pleading my own case. In consequence, I was prevented from questioning even a single witness of all those who came forward during this period, although again, I was entitled by the statute to do this." It hardly seemed the letter of a "gullible simpleton," Andrus thought. He forwarded it to Sir Geoffrey Lawrence's chamber.

42

On Sunday, January 27, the day after the Hess visit, Gilbert went to see his other problem patient, Joachim von Ribbentrop. Sauckel and Kaltenbrunner collected stamps. Keitel played solitaire. Göring slept. Ribbentrop fidgeted. Gilbert found the man a windmill of unfocused energy, pacing his cell, scribbling furiously on a sheet of paper, wadding it up and flinging it to the floor, badgering the guards, the doctors, his lawyer, and then forgetting what he wanted of them. He was driving his current counsel, Fritz Sauter, mad. They would adopt a line of defense, and the next day Ribbentrop would deny that he had agreed to it. Ribbentrop would demand a certain witness and then, as soon as Sauter had arranged for the witness's appearance, would reject that person. "The man," Sauter concluded, "is impossible to defend." In Gilbert's view, the erratic behavior reflected a collapsed ego, one that had had the supporting timbers yanked away.

Gilbert tried to associate this Ribbentrop with the man described in an affidavit made by one of the former foreign minister's subordinates: "He would enter a room as though he were descending from a cloud and then suddenly, with a start of surprise, notice that others— mere humans—were also in the room. He would require his entire staff to line up at an airport and wait for five or six hours, even in the rain, until his plane arrived. He would appear and greet us with a frozen smile, raise his hand in the Heil Hitler salute, and be driven off. He was extremely theatrical. We called him the movie actor. He treated us like dogs." This was the same unkempt, ash-gray figure now stretched on his cot, complaining to Gilbert about another insomniac night.

He had a headache, Ribbentrop said. For how long? Gilbert wanted to know. On and off, for five years. Ribbentrop could cite the precise date when the problem began: July 28, 1941, six days after Germany invaded Russia. His diplomatic masterpiece had been the nonaggression pact between Germany and the Soviet Union. Hitler's action had left the treaty in shreds. For once, Ribbentrop had decided that he had to speak his mind. He told the Führer that he had opposed war with the Soviets all along; the outcome of the invasion was now beyond their control. Hitler flew into a rage, shrieking at Ribbentrop, abusing him until the foreign minister was left cowering and trembling. Ribbentrop was going to give him a stroke, Hitler screamed. Never, never must he oppose him on anything. After the tirade, Ribbentrop took to his sickbed for days. His right arm and leg became temporarily paralyzed. He never again stood up to Hitler. That was when the headaches had begun.

Ribbentrop's adjutant, Baron Gustav Steengracht von Moyland, had witnessed the triggering incident. When interrogated at Nuremberg, he had explained that Ribbentrop's uncharacteristic opposition had also made Hitler sick. The event provided Steengracht von Moyland insight into the darker caves of the Führer's personality. "The basic trait of his character," the baron told his interrogator, "was probably lack of confidence. Experts and decent people who tried to influence Hitler were engaged in a vain task. On the other hand, irresponsible creatures who incited him to take violent measures found him extremely accessible. These men were seen as strong, whereas the behavior of anyone halfway normal was condemned as weak or defeatist." Steengracht von Moyland's words resounded in Gilbert's mind as Ribbentrop described the incident of five years before. By sensibly objecting to the invasion of Russia, Ribbentrop had stepped out of the sycophant chorus into the role of sensible counselor. The move apparently had touched a nerve of Hitler's self-doubt and ignited the tantrum.

Gilbert had one more visit. Baldur von Schirach needed propping up to keep him in the penitents' camp. On entering the cell, Gilbert mentioned his visit to Ribbentrop. Schirach sneered and repeated the story of Ribbentrop's shameless acquisition of the aristocratic *von*. "Do you know what Goebbels said about Ribbentrop?" Schirach asked. "He was a husk without a kernel. He bought his name. He married his money. He swindled his way into office." Gilbert looked at this fop and wondered who was more reprehensible, the climber who clawed his way up or the patrician who stooped down to enjoy the fruits of Nazism.

43

The trial had not been under way for more than an hour on Monday morning, January 28, when Sir Geoffrey appeared to be slipping into a coma. Charles Dubost, the deputy French prosecutor, was droning away on the stand. During the war, Dubost had been a judge by day and a Resistance leader by night, adept at blowing up trains and bridges. Now, the man had about him a weariness reflected throughout much of the French delegation. The chief French judge, Henri Donnedieu de Vabres, looked magnificent, with his medieval dress, massive hunched shoulders, long gray hair, and drooping mustache—but he never said anything, never asked a question. Donnedieu de Vabres was driven about town in an ancient black Citroën, and was frequently seen standing disconsolately beside it while his chauffeur repaired a breakdown. Airey Neave, who admired the French, thought perhaps their mood reflected the exhausted state of their country. The French staff had not been paid for almost three months.

The entire bench appeared on the verge of sleep as the next witness recited what appeared to be the entire inventory of goods stolen from France during five years of Nazi occupation. Göring nudged Hess. "I'm glad for every bottle of cognac and every cigar we took from them," he said. Hess answered, "Maybe if you hadn't taken all those things, you wouldn't be sitting here now." "Listen, Rudolf," Göring went on, "you don't smoke and you don't drink. And here you are, stuck with me all the same."

Dubost called on a parade of listless concentration camp victims to testify. Sir Geoffrey roused himself, "Monsieur Dubost," he asked, "are you proposing to call still more witnesses on the camps?" Yes, the prosecutor said sheepishly.

Suddenly, the torpor in the room lifted. Something about the woman in the tailored dark blue suit approaching the stand commanded attention. Marie Claude Vaillant-Couturier, age thirty-three, stood erect, her hair pulled back tightly, her face free of makeup, exuding dignity. She had taken leave of her post as a deputy in the French constituent assembly to testify. Dubost began drawing out her story. When France fell, Vaillant-Couturier had been an antifascist journalist, she testified. In 1942, she was arrested, interrogated, and ordered to sign a false confession. "I refused to sign it," she told the court. "The German officer threatened me. I told him I was not afraid of being shot. He told me, 'We have means at our disposal far worse than being shot.'" Soon afterward, Vaillant-Couturier found herself packed on a train with 230 other Frenchwomen en route to Auschwitz. They were given neither food nor drink throughout the journey.

Vaillant-Couturier was assigned to a sewing block at the camp. "We lived right where the trains stopped," she said. "They ran practically right up to the gas chamber. Consequently, we saw the unsealing of the cars and the soldiers letting men, women, and children out. We saw old couples forced to part from each other, mothers forced to abandon their young children. All these people were unaware of the fate awaiting them. To make their arrival more pleasant, an orchestra composed of pretty girls in white blouses and navy blue skirts played during the selection process, gay tunes from *The Merry Widow* and *The Tales of Hoffmann*. Those selected for the gas chamber, old people, mothers, and small children, were escorted immediately to a red brick building.

"All my life," the witness went on, "I will remember Annette Epaux. I saw her on a truck that was taking people to the gas chamber. She had her arms around another French woman. When the truck started she called to me, 'Think of my little boy, if you ever get back to France.' Then they began singing the 'Marseillaise.'" The courtroom was quiet, but for the simultaneous interpreters echoing Vaillant-Couturier's words behind their glass enclosures.

As Dubost urged her gently on, the woman's head bowed. Her voice became barely audible. "One night, we were awakened by horrible cries," she said. "The next day we learned that the Nazis had run out of gas and the children had been hurled into the furnaces alive." Dubost asked her how many of the 230 Frenchwomen in her train survived Auschwitz. Forty-nine, Vaillant-Couturier answered.

After she was dismissed, the woman walked past the dock and stopped within feet of Hermann Göring. This was a moment that would never come her way again, she knew. As she wrote later, "I wanted to see them up close. I wanted to see the expressions on their faces. I looked at each of them in turn. They looked like ordinary people with a normal, human side, which somehow didn't surprise me. At Auschwitz, one of the SS used to bring sugar to a five-year-old gypsy boy after he gassed the boy's mother and sister."

During the midday break, Otto Kranzbuehler unexpectedly appeared in the doorway of the attic lunchroom, his ashen face contrasting sharply with his navy blue uniform. He looked at his client, Admiral Dönitz. "Didn't anybody know anything about these things?" he asked. Dönitz shrugged and went on eating. Göring looked up. "You know how it is," he said, "even in a battalion, the battalion commander doesn't know what's going on at the front. The higher up you are, the less you see of what's going on below." Kranzbuehler shook his head and left.

44

AFTER THE COURT ADJOURNED that day, Otto Streng, the librarian, brought Albert Speer *The Autobiography of Benvenuto Cellini*, as the prisoner had requested. But Speer had difficulty concentrating. The Vaillant-Couturier testimony had sent the court reeling, and he recognized one thing clearly. Of all the areas of evidence, association with the concentration camps was the most damning. He had done well so far, he believed, threading his way through the minefield of guilt. His lawyer had planted his two most attractive defenses in evidence, the Hitler assassination attempt and Speer's resistance to the Führer's scorched-earth directives. The nature of the relationship with Sauckel, as to who was superior to whom, was still up in the air. But a proven connection to the camps could be fatal. Speer had hard thinking to do.

The witness on the morning of January 29 was François Boix, a tall, lean, intense man. Boix had survived the Mauthausen concentration camp because he was a professional photographer. His testimony had begun the day before, following Marie Vaillant-Couturier's appearance. He had testified about a Mauthausen escapee who had been led to the gallows while a band played a ballad. Boix's reappearance today promised no letup in the grim chronicle of camp life.

Charles Dubost asked if Boix had ever seen any defendant in the dock at Mauthausen. "Speer," the witness replied. During the interrogation phase, Speer had admitted to being at Mauthausen, but only on the periphery, to consider construction of a railhead. Dubost asked Boix when he had seen the munitions chief. In 1943, Boix answered: "I did not see him myself, but the head of the identification department took a roll of film with his Leica, which I developed. I recognized Speer and some SS leaders." Dubost pressed on: "You saw Speer in the pictures you developed?" "Yes," Boix answered. "Afterward, I had to write his name and the date on the print." Some of the pictures, Boix said, had been taken at the Mauthausen quarry, where inmates were worked to death carrying out stones and "parachuted" to the bottom for the guards' amusement. "There are even pictures which show him congratulating Franz Ziereis, the commandant of Mauthausen, with a handshake," Boix added. All told, he said, he had seen Speer in thirty-six shots.

Documents introduced after Boix's appearance established that Speer had worked with Heinrich Himmler to obtain camp inmates for arms production. Minutes read from a meeting of the Central Planning Board recorded Speer's words: "There is nothing to be said against the SS taking drastic steps and putting known slackers into concentration camps. There is no alternative." A memo from the files of the SS was read into the record: "Albert Speer has been enrolled as an SS man on my staff by my order," signed "Heinrich Himmler, *Reichsführer*."

A proud Harriet Zetterberg sat at the prosecution table. The evidence placing Speer at Mauthausen and in contact with Himmler was the fruit of her research.

As the court adjourned, Speer recognized that the day had been a disaster. He had been placed squarely at Mauthausen and in association with the commandant, Ziereis, a sadist known to take pleasure in carrying out executions personally. To be linked as well to Himmler was to be stained ineradicably. For the first time, Albert Speer felt brushed by the wingtip of the angel of death.

45

ROSE KORB WAS SORTING through the mail and came across something she thought the colonel might enjoy. Andrus spread it on his desk, a child's watercolor of snowflakes descending on a field of yellow and blue flowers. "Ah yes," he said, "done by the Himmler brat." To the Allies, Heinrich Himmler, after Hitler, had been the most chilling figure in the Nazi pantheon. It was Himmler who had rendered the Führer's abstract manias into the tangible solutions of Zyklon B gas and the crematoria. After Himmler's suicide, his wife had been arrested and she was now in the colonel's jail, held as a material witness. That left the problem of what to do with Himmler's daughter. Andrus had gone to some pains to find a still-operating school, and had her enrolled there. He had also given the child a watercolor set. She responded with presents addressed to "Dearest Colonel Andrus," one being a cotton snowman which Andrus kept on his desk. Still, it was not wise to be thought too soft, hence the colonel's references to "the brat."

The colonel's main concern this morning was not a Nazi off-spring, but Major Kelley's impending departure. All along, Andrus had felt a better rapport with the gregarious Kelley than with the reserved Gilbert, though both men's contact with the press made him nervous. A few weeks before, *Stars and Stripes* had broken the hushed-up story of Dr. Leonardo Conti's October suicide. Through his intelligence network, Andrus learned that Kelley had been talking to reporters. His sources further informed him that Kelley was "misappropriating" official files. This information had been followed by Kelley's abrupt announcement that he was going home on points.

Andrus had also learned about the Kelley-Gilbert book collaboration from Boris Polevoi, the *Pravda* correspondent. Polevoi had assiduously cultivated Gilbert, who he knew had access to the defendants. Gilbert had put off Polevoi time and again, saying it was against Andrus's regulations for him to talk to reporters. Finally, after Polevoi's endless pressure, Gilbert had blurted out, "I can't. I'm saving all that for a book." Polevoi thereupon began pressing Andrus for inside stories, and inevitably revealed his awareness of the book project.

On learning of Kelley's impending departure, Gilbert cornered the major and expressed his own surprise. Kelley explained that he was going home to pursue a new interest; he was going to write a book on racial prejudice. But what about their project? a stunned Gilbert asked. Kelley put an arm around Gilbert's shoulder. "Look, Gus," he said, "there's been a big fall-off in the public's interest in this trial." Gilbert asked Kelley where he could reach him after his discharge. He did not know, Kelley said; but he would be in touch.

On February 6, Major Douglas Kelley flew from airfield Y28 to the nearest port of embarkation. After he was gone, Gilbert discovered that Kelley had taken all the handwritten originals of the autobiographies they had asked the defendants to write. He had also taken a copy of all of Gilbert's notes on his cell visits. What Gilbert did not yet know was that Kelley had already approached the American publisher Simon and Schuster about a book of his own on the twenty-one men in the cells at Nuremberg.

46

THE DAY KELLEY LEFT, the prosecution opened the case of the stolen art treasures. Janet Flanner, Paris correspondent for *The New Yorker*, had eagerly awaited the moment. She had managed to obtain, on the eve of the case, a document that recorded Hermann Göring's lecture to an audience of *Gauleiter*s on how to treat conquered France. "What happens to the French is of complete indifference to me," Göring had told the party leaders. "Maxim's must have the best food for us but not for the French. . . . I intend to plunder in France, and profitably. There will be such inflation in Paris that everything will go for smash. The franc will not be worth more than a well-known type of paper used for a certain purpose." Göring was, Flanner had to admit, a man of his word. It began on June 21, 1940. Göring, in his sky-blue field marshal's uniform, had accompanied Hitler to the forest of Compiègne. Here the Germans savored the sweet revenge of having the French surrender in the very railway car where the Germans had been forced to capitulate in 1918. Afterward, Göring slipped away to the Jeu de Paume in the Louvre Museum, where he covetously eyed the works of Rubens, Fragonard, Velázquez, and the Cranachs, elder and younger. The *Reichsmarschall* and Hitler, both considering themselves connoisseurs, came up with a scheme through which Germany would become the "protector" of Europe's art treasures. The key was Alfred Rosenberg. Was Rosenberg not party chief for ideological training and education? Three months after the conquest of France, Hitler gave Rosenberg a simple, sweeping power, the right to confiscate art anywhere in occupied Europe.

Alfred Rosenberg was not really a German. He had been born in Reval, Estonia, into a German-speaking family. In gossip-ridden party circles, word spread that Rosenberg was not even an ethnic German. Supposedly, his artisan ancestors had simply taken the Germanic name of the local landowner. Rosenberg had not set foot in Germany until he was twenty-five years old. Though he rose spectacularly in the party, he knew that philistines mocked his intellectual aspirations; they joked behind his back about his *Myth of the Twentieth Century*. The new assignment gave Rosenberg the opportunity to show the Führer a man of action as well as a philosopher. He created Einstab Rosenberg to carry out his new art mission. His operatives followed simple procedures. If a desired painting, sculpture, or carving belonged to foreign Aryans, the owners were compelled to sell it. If it belonged to Jews, it was merely taken. The latter task was facilitated by the fact that thousands of French Jews had fled or been driven from their homes. Their property was declared "ownerless," and Einstab Rosenberg had an obligation to store it in safe places in the Reich. Rosenberg's proudest report to the Führer described 69,619 Jewish apartments in Paris emptied of their contents, filling 29,984 freight cars with art and fine furniture. Every Parisian moving company had to be hired to finish the job.

The prosecution possessed a document written by a Dr. Hermann Bunjes revealing how Göring benefited from Einstab Rosenberg. Dr. Bunjes, an art historian, had been engaged as Göring's personal agent in France. Seven months after the fall of Paris, Göring ordered Bunjes to meet him on his arrival at the Jeu de Paume. As Göring went through, he would tap his baton on the works to be sent to Germany. An uncomfortable Bunjes pointed out that French officials bitterly objected to the Einstab Rosenberg operations. This was Bunjes's first meeting with Göring, and the words came hesitantly. He sensed Göring's annoyance and sought to bolster his argument by pointing out that Rosenberg's activities contravened the Hague Convention on Land Warfare. Göring blew up, his voice echoing throughout the museum. "My orders are final! These art objects in the Jeu de Paume are to be taken to Germany immediately. Those for me are to be loaded into two railroad cars and attached to my private train." Bunjes went on manfully pointing out that even German army lawyers objected to these confiscations. "My dear Bunjes," Göring said, "let me worry about that. Don't you know I outrank any jurist in Germany?"

Göring had always contended that he was merely holding the works of art until a gallery could be erected for the German people; further, he clearly meant to pay for everything. But, as he once put it, "My collector's passion got the better of me." His major collecting rival had been the Führer, who had first crack. But Hitler's taste was much narrower than the *Reichsmarschall*'s. Göring was thus able to keep the works of artists whom Hitler considered degenerate—Chagall, Grosz, Klee, van Gogh, Cézanne, Gauguin, and Picasso. Göring also acquired works of Goya, Van Dyck, Hals, Velázquez, Titian, Raphael, and Fragonard. He once complimented Rosenberg on his performance and told him, "I have now obtained by purchase, presents, bequests, and barter, the greatest private collection in Europe."

It all came out in the prosecution case. And few, even in the dock, accepted Göring's claims that he had paid for much of the art. An assistant prosecutor, Thomas Lambert, listening to the evidence of Göring's looting, told a colleague, "There are now three grades of larceny: petty, grand, and glorious."

47

THE MOMENT WAS SWEET for Burt Andrus. After months of bureaucratic maneuvering, the colonel had finally managed to have his sketches approved as the official symbol of the IMT. The shield with the scales of justice dominating a broken swastika and fallen Nazi eagle now appeared on letterheads, as a shoulder patch on uniforms, as a pin for women's blouses, and in a dozen other uses. And here in his office stood the one Russian who had conquered the Americans, Nikitchenko's enchanting interpreter, Tania Giliarevskaya, seeking more information on the new insignia.

The seductive Tania also begged the colonel to add another name to the guest list for his Saturday soiree. Andrus's opera-dinner parties had become a feature of the social scene. He had established a reputation as an energetic and attentive host. It pleased him to have a U.S. Supreme Court justice, eminent English jurists, and bemedaled generals of four nations at his table. On February 9, he was throwing a party in honor of the Soviets who had arrived for their phase of the prosecution. Both Russian judges had accepted, Sir David and Lady Maxwell-Fyfe were coming, and so were a half dozen attractive women from the IMT staff. It was so convenient to entertain graciously here. The army provided the transportation, the dinner was written off as official entertainment, and Special Services produced the opera tickets.

The man Giliarevskaya wanted the colonel to invite was Major General Alexandrov. The gesture would please General Nikitchenko, she said. Andrus found the woman impossible to deny. Of course, he said, the general was welcome—though in Andrus's opinion, Alexandrov, not Comrade Rasumov, was probably the NKVD man on the scene, and merely wanted to come to keep an eye on his countrymen. Giliarevskaya thanked the colonel profusely and left with sample letterheads, shoulder patches, and a pin for herself, all depicting the colonel's insignia.

Despite the obstacles of politics and nationality, Tania and Major Bob Stewart had been seeing each other. Most of the time, their romance savored of forbidden fruit; but the forbidden nature also produced deep stresses. Jim Rowe, Stewart's colleague on the judges' staff, had taken the handsome major aside and warned him about how the Soviet security apparatus, the NKVD, worked. The woman was likely a plant, spying on the Americans through Stewart. It depressed Stewart to have to imagine himself and Tania as pawns in the games of nations and not simply as two human beings in love. Yet he could not entirely dismiss Rowe's warning. American intelligence was not without its own resources, and Rowe informed Stewart that Tania was married to a Russian general and had a child.

The colonel's party was a success. A performance of Verdi's *Ballo in Maschera* was followed by a night of dancing at the Grand. The young women whom Andrus had invited were especially grateful. Her invitation confirmed Katy Walch's good opinion of the colonel, and while dancing with Nikitchenko, the researcher picked up some intelligence of her own. In the coming days, the Russian prosecution expected to drop a blockbuster on the courtroom.

48

ON MONDAY MORNING, February 11, a Soviet prosecutor, General N. D. Zorya, was attempting to establish that Germany's invasion of the Soviet Union represented criminal aggression in violation of a binding peace pact. He read into the record an affidavit taken in Moscow from German field marshal Friedrich Paulus, who had surrendered at Stalingrad. In the statement, Paulus swore that he had had personal knowledge of Germany's aggressive intent.

The very mention of Paulus stirred bitter memories for the Germans. Jodl, Speer, Dönitz, even Göring—any of the shrewder minds in the dock—had recognized after the defeat at Stalingrad in 1943 that the war could not be won. The Germans had suffered horrific losses. Flags flew at half mast for three days of national mourning. The people were told that Field Marshal Paulus had fallen in battle with his troops. Actually, Paulus had gone over to the Russians after surrendering, and he subsequently broadcast speeches urging German soldiers to give up the hopeless struggle. His name became synonymous with treachery. But from Paulus's standpoint, he was no traitor. His Sixth Army had been surrounded. Hitler promised that Göring's Luftwaffe would come to Paulus's relief, but the planes never came. Still, Hitler had ordered the field marshal to fight on to the last man. In Paulus's judgment, Hitler had condemned 300,000 Germans to starvation, sickness, freezing cold, and ultimately to death or Russian captivity. He could find no reason to remain loyal to such a leader.

Otto Stahmer, Göring's lawyer, objected. Stahmer was a big, formidable man whose manner commanded authority. The Paulus affidavit was merely a piece of paper coerced from a traitor general by the Communists, Stahmer said. It proved nothing. If Paulus was such an important witness, let the prosecution produce him so that the defense could cross-examine him, or else they should withdraw this worthless evidence.

The Soviet chief prosecutor, Roman Rudenko, rose, a barely concealed smile on his face. He would indeed like to call Field Marshal Paulus as a witness, Rudenko told the court. In fact, he could produce him that afternoon. The three-alarm signal rang throughout the building. Reporters came barreling out of the pressroom, the cafeteria, the PX, jamming the entrance to room 600. Sir Geoffrey Lawrence asked if he was hearing correctly. The Soviet prosecutor replied that Paulus had been secretly flown in to Nuremberg and was now waiting in Rudenko's quarters.

As Sir Geoffrey called the court to order, a white-helmeted guard opened the door and a lone figure appeared, lean, dignified, wearing a dark blue suit that could not conceal the bearing of a soldier. In the visitors' gallery, Russian VIP guests leaned forward eagerly, among them Marshal Georgi Zhukov and the novelist Ilya Ehrenburg. Boris

Polevoi, the *Pravda* correspondent, studied Friedrich Paulus with particular interest. Polevoi had been in Stalingrad on the fateful day of
the surrender. He remembered a young Soviet officer, pale and sweating in the midst of the Russian winter, standing before a destroyed
building. The officer had been told that Paulus was trapped in the
basement, and he was to go down and bring the field marshal out.
Suspicious wires protruded from the basement stairway. The Russian
descended warily. Minutes later, a gaunt, stooped figure, his cap and
fur-lined greatcoat frosted with snow, had come up the stairs. He drew
a revolver from his coat while the Russians stood frozen. He flung the
weapon at their feet. Field Marshal Paulus had surrendered.

Hans Fritzsche too had been at Stalingrad. He had gone there to
report to the German people on radio the heroic stand their sons were
making. He had been appalled at the frightful conditions, the lack of
food and medicine, the frozen hillocks of bodies dotting the fields. On
his departure, he had bidden Paulus good-bye and seen defeat written
in the man's eyes.

In the interpreters' booth, Lieutenant Peter Uiberall adjusted his
earphones with a shaking hand. Thus far, Uiberall had been working
in the Dostert operation testing other interpreter candidates, and this
was his first stint behind a microphone. As Paulus began to testify,
Uiberall was much relieved. The field marshal's speech was calm, slow,
deliberate.

Until now, the defendants had expressed their contempt for the
Soviet prosecution by ignoring the proceedings and reading novels
concealed behind official papers. But this day, their attention was riveted. Roman Rudenko conducted the questioning. He first established
that a Russo-German nonaggression pact had been in force between
August 1939 and June 1941. What, he asked, had General Paulus been
doing during that period? In September 1940, Paulus explained, he
had been named a deputy chief of the general staff. What were his
duties? He had been specifically assigned to develop an operation ultimately known as Barbarossa, a surprise attack on the Soviet Union.
"Who of these defendants," Rudenko asked, "was an active participant
in initiating the war of aggression against the Soviet Union?" Paulus
surveyed the dock. "As I observed them," he said, "they were the chief
of the OKW, Keitel, the chief of operations, Jodl, and Göring, as
commander in chief of the air force."

As Justice Lawrence declared a recess, a ruckus broke out in the dock. Göring was shouting to Stahmer, "Ask that dirty pig if he knows he's a traitor. Ask Paulus if he's taken out Russian citizenship papers!" At the other end of the dock, Fritzsche was telling Schacht, "You see, that's the tragedy of the German people, right there. Poor Paulus was caught between the devil and his duty. If a man like that could betray his country, there must have been something wrong with the country."

49

PAULUS RETURNED ON FEBRUARY 12 for cross-examination. Keitel leaned toward Ribbentrop and said, "Just think of it. Paulus was supposed to take Jodl's place. If he had, Paulus would be up here instead of Jodl." Jodl knew it too, and throughout the hours of Paulus's cross-examination, the caprices of fate taunted him.

His American custodians found Alfred Jodl impenetrable, encased in glacial reserve. He made clear to Gilbert during cell visits that the psychologist's attentions were unwelcome. He was emotionally self-sufficient, and his practical mind could project his probable fate in this court as clearly as it had worked out Hitler's military operations.

Like Keitel, Jodl was a member of the militarist caste and inclined to deprecate upstart politicians. Thus, his eventual veneration of Hitler had come as a surprise to himself. In 1939, just before the Polish campaign, Jodl, on Keitel's recommendation, had been named operations chief of the general staff. Thereafter he had stood virtually at the Führer's elbow. As he witnessed Hitler's successful bluff in sending German troops into the presumably demilitarized Rhineland, the bloodless conquest of Austria, the humbling of Chamberlain at Munich, the easy early victories in Poland and France, he had been seduced. "It is all well and good for me as a member of the privileged class to look down my nose on the Austrian corporal," he once wrote. "But that would show not how lowborn he is, but how petty I am."

His analytical mind, however, could not be turned off when Hitler began to fail. As early as 1942, after Hitler had committed Germany to a two-front war, Jodl knew that his country could not win. He came to realize that the blunders of genius could be as colossal as its victories. The exhilaration of the early years vanished. Life under

Hitler's thumb, on the endless round from Berlin to the Wolf's Lair in Rastenburg to Berchtesgaden, became for Jodl a "cross between a monastery and a concentration camp."

In August of 1942, Hitler became infuriated by the lack of progress of Field Marshal Wilhelm List in the Caucasus campaign. He dispatched Jodl to goad the hesitant List onward. On his return from the front, Jodl reported that List's behavior was militarily correct. He himself had seen the snow-clogged mountain passes that List was operating in, and agreed that it was impossible to carry out Hitler's orders. Hitler leaned over the map table, eyes bulging. "I didn't send you, Jodl, to hear you report on all the difficulties," he began. "You were supposed to represent my view! That was your job! Instead you come back completely under the influence of the frontline commanders. You are nothing but their megaphone! I didn't need to send you there for that."

After the List affair, Hitler decided to replace Jodl with Paulus as operations chief, just as soon as Paulus conquered Stalingrad. Jodl too was eager for the change. How preferable that would have been, he thought, as he watched Paulus being cross-examined: Paulus up here, an indicted war criminal, and he, Alfred Jodl, permitted an honorable soldier's death alongside his men.

50

RAY D'ADDARIO, the signal corps photographer, received word to bring his camera to Justice Jackson's office. On his arrival, Mrs. Douglas informed him that today, February 13, was Jackson's birthday. She had planned a little surprise party, quietly putting out the word for the judges and senior staff to stop by the office as soon as court adjourned. First, she wanted D'Addario to take the justice's picture. Jackson protested modestly, but began clearing the debris from his desk while D'Addario set up the camera. The photographer was just about to shoot when Mrs. Douglas started combing Jackson's hair. D'Addario thought this would make an appealing picture, and clicked off several frames before shooting the justice alone.

That evening, Francis Biddle wrote to his wife, Katherine, that he was still the power behind the bench. "This is not an able crowd," he wrote. "Lawrence never has a thought of his own . . . though he does make an admirable presiding officer. The French add almost nothing.

"As Bob's birthday is today," he continued, "they had a cake for him with presents and jokes. But we all thought the affair really stuffy . . . too much spontaneous preparation, little piercing cries of delight by Mrs. Douglas, rouged to the eyes and trying to do a 'grand dame.'" Among the staff, the closeness of Jackson and his secretary was well known. The rumor was that Jackson had an unhappy domestic situation back home. While Biddle was caustic, others who dealt with Elsie Douglas found the woman charming and capable. To Jackson, Elsie was just right, professionally indispensable and his trusted confidante. And she was sensitive to appearances. Ray D'Addario received a call from Mrs. Douglas the day after the party. Any photographs of her combing the justice's hair were to be destroyed, including the negatives, she instructed him.

51

On the morning of February 14 the defendants welcomed the opportunity to walk and chat briefly in the exercise yard before being marched off to the courtroom. Schirach, because he received newspapers from American relatives, was always asked what was happening in the world outside. His news this morning threw a pall over the group. The Japanese "Tiger of Malaya," General Tomoyuki Yamashita, had just been executed for war crimes. Hans Frank mentioned the news to Göring to see how the "strongman" took it. Frank was annoyed that Göring still expected him to approach from behind and take his place at Göring's left, as though they were walking in the court of the Reich Chancellery rather than in a prison yard. "So what," Göring said of Yamashita's end. "You should brace yourself for a death with dignity. We will be martyrs. Even if it takes fifty years, the German people will recognize us as heroes. They'll put our bones in marble caskets in a great national shrine." Frank looked dubious. Still, Göring's bravado had its appeal to waverers like himself. Breast-beating, groveling before the victors, and self-flagellation were barely preferable to Göring's proud defiance. Often Göring made much sense, Frank thought, as when he reminded Keitel, Schacht, and Schirach that their wives, along with his Emmy, had been arrested. "You see," Göring lectured, "they are just as bad as the Gestapo. Don't let them pretend they're democratic. What do women and children have to do with all this?"

The case announced on the bulletin board that day made all uncomfortable but the Russians. They had insisted on charging the Germans with the Katyn massacre, the murder of thousands of Polish POWs in a forest near Smolensk in Russia. The Americans and British had hoped against hope that the Soviet Union would drop the charge. All Katyn did was to call attention to the ambiguous position of Russians sitting in judgment of others on charges of aggression and wartime atrocities. The Soviets had snatched almost half of Poland through their pact with Hitler. They had attacked Finland, annexed Estonia, Latvia, and Lithuania, and seized Bessarabia from Romania. No one denied that once they had gone to war the Russian armies and people had suffered monstrous atrocities at the hands of the Germans. There was so much evidence of this that the Western Allies believed it was both unnecessary and foolish to bring up the shaky Katyn charge.

Colonel Y. V. Pokrovsky, Rudenko's deputy, began introducing document USSR 34, the report of an Extraordinary Soviet State Commission claiming that the Nazis had murdered over eleven thousand Poles in the Katyn forest. Göring and Hess ostentatiously ripped off their earphones. Schirach chuckled in derision. The defendants' scorn had some justification, the Western lawyers knew. The prosecution had in hand strong evidence suggesting that the Russians, not the Nazis, had murdered the Poles. They appeared to be seizing a chance to palm off on the Nazis a war crime of their own. Robert Jackson was dismayed. The Russians were playing right into the defendants' hands. Doubts over Katyn could color the entire prosecution case.

On Saturday, Captain Gilbert was told to report to Colonel Andrus as soon as court adjourned. Gilbert made his way down to Andrus's first-floor office, glad to be wearing the colonel's new shoulder patch. On his arrival, Andrus handed him a new regulation growing out of Göring's disruptive behavior, particularly during the Paulus testimony.

He already knew what Gilbert was going to say, Andrus observed. This new rule would have a bad psychological effect on the defendants' morale. But Sir Geoffrey was on his back. Göring was a threat to the dignity of the proceedings. Gilbert finished reading the document, hard pressed to conceal his delight. This was essentially the isolation plan that Speer had urged on Gilbert and that he had recommended to the colonel weeks before. The colonel's proposal was necessary, Gilbert agreed. Good, Andrus said, because he expected the psychologist to work out the details and deliver the news.

Gilbert knew that Andrus's animus toward Göring bordered on an obsession. The colonel suspected Göring of being homosexual, though there was no proof. He told people that Göring wore rouge and lipstick and painted his toenails, basing the charge on the fact that Göring had brought to Nuremberg a leather case full of male toiletries. Gilbert found the colonel's easy aspersions unhelpful, and preferred to seek understanding of the Göring character in cell visits and in studying the man's dossier.

In the latter, he would find early clues to Göring's persona. Göring's father had been German consul general in Haiti at the time the mother came back to Germany to give birth to Hermann. Almost immediately, she returned to her husband, leaving the infant in the care of a friend. She did not see her son again for three years. According to the dossier, Göring's earliest memory was of his mother's return. She had opened her arms to embrace the child, who rushed at her and beat her in the face with his small fists. A person's first memory, Gilbert believed, was psychologically significant. In Göring's case, the memory revealed an ego, even at that tender age, offended at not being the center of his mother's universe. Gilbert also came across Frau Göring's early estimate of her son. "Hermann," she had said, "will either become a great man or a criminal." She was right, Gilbert thought; he had become both.

Upon leaving Andrus this Saturday, Gilbert returned to his office to begin what he considered an agreeable task—reducing the influence of the inmate Hermann Göring.

Andrus felt that his endurance had been tested to the limit. The wishes of Justice Lawrence—the reasonable requests of a civil man—did not upset him. But the memo he now held was from a deliberate tormentor. General Leroy Watson had continued to pull surprise inspections of the prison. In the latest—on Saturday, February 16—refuse had been found in the exercise yard, a guard was posted in the wrong place, a German civilian had a key to the ammo room. The report ended with Watson's customary officiousness: "You will report to my office Monday, February 18, with your explanation of these deficiencies."

What did they expect? Andrus complained. They sent him green kids. His personnel turnover had reached over 600 percent for enlisted men and 125 percent for officers. And the 21 defendants on cellblock C were not his only responsibility. He had 250 more prisoners in nine separate categories of confinement. Though he had been allotted four officers for his operations staff, he had only two. When replacements finally arrived, Watson had blithely informed Andrus that he was overstaffed and took the new men for himself.

Burton Andrus was a proud man, a professional. He knew that the one fatal reputation a soldier could acquire was to be labeled a whiner. For over twenty-seven years, he had taken his army assignments and carried them out without complaint. The Nuremberg job was a man-killer, the pressure unrelenting. He was on call virtually twenty-four hours a day, seven days a week. For reasons he could not fathom, he was being hounded by a man who wanted to break him and was coming close to succeeding. Andrus decided to do something he would never before have contemplated. He had a cousin, General Clint Andrus, at First Army headquarters, to whom he wrote a personal letter describing his treatment at the hands of Leroy Watson. He needed help, he said, before he was driven from his post and had an honorable career end in undeserved disgrace.

The defendants were taken to the prison basement for their weekly shower and strip search. In the meantime, their cells were searched and sprayed for vermin. Gus Gilbert decided to break the news on their return to the cellblock. He had the duty officer line them up in the corridor. The privilege of speaking to each other had been abused, he explained, particularly in recent outbursts in the courtroom. Henceforth, by order of Colonel Andrus, they were going to be assigned a new dining arrangement. Gilbert knew that the closest they came to normal socializing was in the lunchroom in the courthouse attic, time which they treasured. In the future, however, they would have lunch there in six separated dining spaces. Gilbert had designed the breakup to work to the prosecution's advantage. To what he called the "youth lunchroom" he assigned Speer, Fritzsche, Schirach, and Funk. His strategy was to have Speer and Fritzsche wean the other two from Göring's influence. Next, he set up an "elders' lunchroom," to include Papen, Neurath, Schacht, and Dönitz. The dynamic here was to have the others work on the admiral's loyalty to Hitler. To the next room, he assigned Frank, Seyss-Inquart, Keitel, and Sauckel. His hope was that Frank might crack the loyalty of his companions. Raeder, Streicher, Hess, and Ribbentrop were to dine together. Streicher's odious presence, Gilbert believed, would neutralize them. Jodl, Frick, Kaltenbrunner, and Rosenberg were put together because their lack of affinity might defuse any mischief. Hermann Göring was to dine alone. Göring cursed at the news.

That afternoon, Dr. Pfluecker visited the defendants to see who might be needing a sleeping pill that night. The doctor virtually clicked his heels as he entered each cell. In Pfluecker's mind, he was still in the presence of his superiors. He told Göring that the new lunch plan was shameful and added, "We Germans must stick together in good times and bad."

That evening, Lieutenant Tex Wheelis came on duty after having a few beers at the Snake Pit, one of the 27th Regiment's clubs. On learning of the new regulation, Wheelis stopped by Göring's cell. Tex Wheelis was controversial, a man whose brash camaraderie split people between admirers and detractors. He and Göring got along famously. Recently, Wheelis had had his picture taken with Göring, who inscribed it "To the great Texas hunter." One night at the bar of the Grand, Wheelis had shown a handsome silver watch to his friends. He turned it over and revealed the engraved signature of Hermann Göring. Göring had given it to him as a gift, he boasted.

This Saturday night, Wheelis told Göring how sorry he was about the unfair policy on the new lunch arrangement. But, the *Reichsmarschall* should be aware, he had a friend in Tex Wheelis.

On Sunday, February 17, Captain Gilbert visited Baldur von Schirach, a possible convert to repentance. He asked Schirach what had made him an anti-Semite. "Henry Ford," he answered. "In my youth, I moved in aristocratic circles and never came into contact with Jews." At age seventeen, he read Ford's book, *The International Jew*, and became an anti-Semite overnight. He thought he had discovered a great truth to guide his life. It was, he said, a form of perverted idealism, and had been his downfall. Nothing could have been more idealistic than his creation of the Hitler Youth, he had believed. Now he was regarded as the breeder of little Nazi monsters.

His wife's idealism, he told Gilbert, had even done him in with Hitler. He had married Henriette, the surprisingly refined daughter of the hustler photographer and Nazi court jester, Heinrich Hoffmann. As the wife of a prominent Nazi, Henriette had enjoyed freedom to travel abroad. In 1943, while in Lisbon, she picked up a copy of *Life* magazine and was horrified to read in it about Nazi atrocities. She went on to Amsterdam and watched from her hotel window as the Gestapo conducted a roundup of Dutch Jews. She saw them clubbed, kicked, and robbed of their valuables. She made up her mind. She must warn the Führer of this barbaric behavior.

The opportunity came that June when she and Baldur were invited to join Hitler at his retreat in Berchtesgaden. At what seemed an appropriate moment, Henriette gave Hitler an impassioned description of what she had read about in *Life* and witnessed with her own eyes in Amsterdam. "Pure sentimentality," Hitler said dismissively. He wished to hear no more of it. Thereafter, for the rest of the stay, Baldur von Schirach could do nothing right. When he began to describe his plans for refurbishing Vienna after the war, Hitler shrieked that Vienna must never be allowed to compete with Berlin. The couple left after two days and were never invited to Berchtesgaden again.

After the German surrender Schirach threw away his uniform, took the name Richard Falk, and disappeared into Austria. He could not believe his good fortune when he learned, over the BBC, that Baldur von Schirach was dead. He found a room in the Austrian town of Schwaz and began work on a mystery novel, *The Secrets of Myrna Loy*. But when he heard that Nazi leaders were being placed under arrest, he gave himself up to the Americans. He did so, he said, "in order to answer for my actions before an international court." At the same time, he volunteered to reeducate German youth in the ways of democracy.

Gilbert asked him if his turning over sixty thousand Viennese Jews to the SS had been another act of idealism. He had genuinely believed, Schirach said, that these people were being resettled in the East. That, Gilbert knew, was a lie. Schirach had been on the distribution list for Heydrich's and later Kaltenbrunner's weekly extermination reports.

This Sunday afternoon, Gilbert particularly wanted Schirach's reaction to the new segregation plan. He reminded Schirach that he was one of those who had been misbehaving in the dock, especially during the Katyn case. Instead of defending himself, Schirach collapsed in syrupy apology. That was precisely what worried Gilbert. The man seemed to surrender to the influence of the last person who talked to him. Schirach said he was pleased with the new dining arrangement. At least it placed him beyond Göring's reach.

Gilbert heard the same reaction in virtually all the cells. He had not realized how much they all feared Göring. Most relieved was Speer, who looked upon the separation as a personal victory, since he had originally planted the idea with Gilbert. As for Göring, Gilbert found him bewildered, like a prankish schoolboy surprised to find himself expelled. "Don't you see," he pleaded to Gilbert, "all this joking and horseplay is just comic relief. We've got to let off a little steam. If I didn't pep them up, some of them would simply collapse.

"Don't you think, in the loneliness of this cell, I reproach myself?" he went on. "Don't you think I wish my life had taken a different road instead of ending up like this?" Gilbert listened, surprised at the unaccustomed humility. As he prepared to leave, Göring begged him to change the arrangement at least so that he did not have to eat alone. He began to berate Andrus. "Just because I am the number-one Nazi in this group doesn't make me the most dangerous. The colonel ought to bear in mind that he is dealing with a historic figure. Right or wrong, we are historic personalities. And he is a nobody!"

Gilbert left the cell feeling that never had he been more right than in assigning Göring the solitary position.

52

ROMAN RUDENKO WAS NO FOOL, and when the Soviet prosecutor seemed to be one, it was usually because of actions—such as the raising of the Katyn issue—forced on him by Moscow. It pained Rudenko to realize that his people, who had suffered so incomparably at the hands of the Nazis, had failed thus far to win commensurate sympathy among the other Allies. Nikitchenko had tipped him off that the alternate American justice, Parker, even scoffed at "exaggerated Soviet claims" of atrocities. Rudenko vowed to reverse that perception in the days remaining to the Soviet prosecution.

The lack of understanding was explained in part by the Russians' poorly concealed conviction that they had won the war alone. At the press bar, *Pravda*'s man, Boris Polevoi, liked to toast "the Soviet people, who singlehandedly broke the backbone of the Nazi beast." To Robert Jackson, the Russians at Nuremberg failed to win sympathy because their heroism and suffering were so often demeaned by Communist claptrap. He winced as his Soviet counterparts claimed that "Nazism was the child of capitalism," implying that not only Nazism, but capitalism, was on trial in Nuremberg.

On Monday afternoon, February 18, Rudenko launched his effort to make known the truth of the Soviet ordeal. The opening salvo was to be a film entitled *Documentary Evidence of the German Fascist Invaders*. The film opened with the camera silently panning a snowy Russian landscape. It moved in on a huddled form, lying in the snow, a small boy. In his outstretched hand a live dove fluttered. The narrator explained that the child had been shot because he refused to give up the dove to an SS man. From this single death, the film cut to a city square filled with bodies stacked as evenly as Christmas trees. A close-up revealed bloody bandages on dead Soviet soldiers. The narrator read from a captured document the words of a German commander: "I once again inform you that hereafter each officer has the right to shoot prisoners of war." The scene lent meaning to a cold statistic: of 5.7 million Soviet POWs taken by the Germans, 3.7 million died in captivity.

Long shots of acres of bodies were interspersed with close-ups of weeping mothers gently patting the faces of their dead children. Captured German films showed naked women herded into a ditch, forced to lie down as German guards shot them and then smiled for the camera. Gus Gilbert studied the faces in the dock. All but Göring, who pretended to be reading a book, watched openmouthed.

The judges had heard testimony on Auschwitz; now they saw film. Thousands of neatly sorted pairs of shoes, hundreds of battered suitcases with names stenciled on the sides, mounds of human hair turned gray by the Zyklon B gas passed silently across the screen. The film lasted for forty-five minutes. Judge Parker, who had found the Russian claims exaggerated, asked to be excused. He was not feeling well.

Rudenko spent the next five days producing eyewitnesses and survivors. One man described the fate of the people of the village of Kholmetz. A German army officer had ordered the villagers to dig up mines in a road with farm tools. All were killed. Another Soviet prosecutor presented evidence, entitled "Crimes Against Culture and Scientific Treasures." In Kharkov, the Germans had gone into the city's library and used the books as bricks to firm up a muddy road for their armored vehicles. At Yasnaya Polyana, the estate of Leo Tolstoy, a German officer used the author's books as firewood. When told there was plenty of wood around, he replied that he preferred the light of Russian literature. The home of Tchaikovsky was used by the Germans as a motorcycle garage and heated by burning the composer's manuscripts. Using the Germans' own reports, the Russians proved that these were not isolated incidents, but the product of a deliberate policy to obliterate Russian culture.

The testimony, after six straight days, became repetitious. Points already proved were proved again and again. Still, a change had come over the court, as though the justices recognized that something more than law was at work here. The Russians needed this outpouring as a catharsis, the opportunity to say at last to the world, This was our sorrow. Instead of cutting witnesses short or, as so often, demanding to know the relevance of the testimony, Sir Geoffrey let them vent their pain uninterrupted.

For the Americans, with their nation spared, the reasons for Soviet bitterness and truculence became more understandable. As one American prosecutor put it, what the Germans had done in the Soviet Union was tantamount to rounding up all the Democratic or Republican leaders in Detroit and shooting them; or going into a school in

the Bronx and sending all the Jewish children to a death camp. It was
the equivalent of an enemy invader's embarking on a deliberate campaign to destroy every trace of American culture between New York
City and Chicago, and using the Lincoln Memorial as a latrine.

Back in the cellblock, Gilbert sought reactions to the film. The usually
glib Hans Fritzsche, face pale, cheek muscles twitching, said, "I am
drowning in filth, I am choking in it. . . . I cannot go on. This has
become a form of daily execution."

Gilbert reminded Göring of his blasé behavior in court. "Anybody can make an atrocity film," Göring answered. "You only have
to take the corpses out of the grave and show a tractor shoving them
back again. I am not a callous monster who has no use for human
life," he went on. "It's not that atrocities make no impression on me.
But I've seen so much already. Thousands of maimed and half-burned
bodies in the First World War. The starvation. I don't have to see a
film to be horrified." Göring turned the conversation to the new dining arrangement. How did the other defendants feel about his being
left alone? he wanted to know. Gilbert said that he had heard nothing
but satisfaction expressed so far.

53

THE INTERRUPTION ANNOYED Justice Jackson. He was already late to
the courthouse this morning. He hated all the fuss over security. Nevertheless, Moritz Fuchs, his bodyguard, told the driver he had better
stop. Up ahead was a roadblock and a jeep full of GIs armed with
tommy guns. Recognizing the passengers, the young lieutenant at the
roadblock saluted and waved them through.

The gateway to the Palace of Justice bristled with machine guns.
Sandbags and gun emplacements had been thrown up around the entrance. M-4 Sherman tanks frowned in front of the iron fence. The
Nuremberg military district was under a major alert. The cause of this
activity was a report from a German named Max Manlin, ex-Gestapo,
in the pay of General Watson's counterintelligence unit. Manlin provided a steady stream of intelligence of imminent uprisings, jailbreaks,
sightings of Martin Bormann, and rumors that Eva Braun was still

alive. This time, Manlin had persuaded General Watson to expect a breakout from Stalag D-13, followed by an attempt to rescue the defendants. D-13 was a POW camp, located north of Nuremberg, holding twenty thousand hardened SS veterans.

Boris Polevoi approached Colonel Andrus during the recess that morning and asked why the courthouse looked like a fortress under siege. Today's measures were purely psychological, to reassure people, particularly the women working in the palace who had heard the rumors of an SS breakout, Andrus explained. "Every possibility of escape from my prison has been eliminated," he said. How could the colonel be so confident? Polevoi wanted to know. Andrus began to tell him how the prison worked, from the twenty-four-hour watch on each cell to the rectal examinations. Polevoi was impressed.

54

HEINRICH HOFFMANN'S SUPERVISOR, Richard Heller, the young navy lieutenant who had toured Bavaria with the photographer, had gone home on points. But not before Hoffmann had landed, quite firmly, on his feet. He was driven daily from his lodgings at Countess Kalnoky's Witness House to the courthouse. He had amassed so many thousands of photographs to classify that his employment was guaranteed indefinitely. Did the prosecution require a shot of Hjalmar Schacht, preferably smiling, standing next to Hitler? Hoffmann would produce it. Did they need a photograph of Kaltenbrunner at Mauthausen? Hoffmann would find one. His room 158 on the second floor of the Palace of Justice witnessed a parade of GIs seeking photos of Hitler with Göring, with Eva Braun, or with his dog Blondi. Hoffmann would also sketch quick, deft likenesses of his visitors. In return, he acquired a store of whiskey, cigarettes, soap, gum, chocolates, and nylons. He managed to persuade the Americans that he needed an assistant, and was allowed to hire Helga, a buxom, blue-eyed nineteen-year-old with straw-blond hair who doted on "Herr Professor Hoffmann." The color returned to his cheeks and he started to grow a paunch.

Countess Kalnoky found herself, against her will, yielding to Hoffmann's cheapjack charm. The man was generous; he would return to the house with his pockets stuffed with precious soap for her and PX candy for her children. Hoffmann's presence in the house was not, however, without tense moments. The prosecutors occasionally boarded concentration camp witnesses there who were horrified to learn the identity of their fellow guest. Hoffmann seemed barely thrown off his stride by their accusing stares in the dining room. He would introduce himself and explain away his role in the regime with his pet rationalization: "The camera has no politics." He would spin amusing stories about life in the Nazi court, usually with Göring or Ribbentrop as the butt. Guests laughed in spite of themselves.

One afternoon, Hoffmann invited Kalnoky to his room. He had something he wanted to show her, he said. He took out some water-color landscapes. Did she know who had done them? he asked. The countess found them undistinguished and said she had no idea who the painter was. "My friend," Hoffmann said, "Adolf Hitler. You know," he went on, "they show the other side of his personality." What other side? she asked. "The calm, gentle side," Hoffmann answered.

55

On February 23, Katy Walch, the Defense Rebuttal researcher, was delighted to find herself at General Rudenko's party to celebrate Red Army Day. Walch's situation was typical of that of young British women at Nuremberg who had worked or studied in Germany before the war and spoke the language. Walch had first gone there during the mid-thirties as an au pair in the castle of a German count in the SS. That was how she had found herself one Sunday as the croquet partner of the count's guest, Reichsführer Heinrich Himmler. What she remembered most vividly about this trifling man was that he had cheated, sneaking his ball through the wicket with his foot. His hosts had merely turned a blind eye and gushed at what a wonderful player the *Reichsführer* was.

During the Russians' party, Walch found herself taken aside by Tania Giliarevskaya, Nikitchenko's interpreter. The two women had grown friendly. The beautiful Russian rarely visited the Defense Rebuttal office without wheedling copies of *Mademoiselle* from Katy. She confided to Walch that she was desperate. Why? Katy asked. Tania looked furtively around the room, and whispered. She had taken great risks in seeing Major Robert Stewart. She was afraid something terrible was about to happen.

56

On entering the courthouse on March 6, Boris Polevoi ran into young Oleg Troyanovsky, the interpreter, who had returned for the Russian prosecution. An alarmed Troyanovsky was carrying an armful of newspapers. "What's going on?" Polevoi asked. "Look at this," Troyanovsky said, holding up an English paper headlined SIR WINSTON CALLS FOR UNITED FRONT AGAINST SOVIET UNION. Troyanovsky next showed Polevoi the American GI newspaper, Stars and Stripes. UNITE TO STOP RUSSIANS, CHURCHILL WARNS, the headline read. The former British prime minister had made a speech the day before at a small college in Fulton, Missouri, claiming, "From Stettin in the Baltic to Trieste on the Adriatic, an iron curtain has descended across the continent." Churchill had pronounced the death of the wartime alliance and was calling for Western resistance to Communist expansion.

That day, with the completion of the Soviet presentation, the prosecution rested its case. While the moment should have sounded a chord of doom for the defendants, it was, by a quirk of fate, ending on a note of hope. True, the Allied prosecutors had achieved what they had set out to do. The four counts in the indictment had been proven indisputably and repeatedly, mostly through documentary evidence that the Germans had generated themselves. The charges had been lent flesh-and-blood believability by the testimony of thirty-three prosecution witnesses. Not the slightest doubt could remain that Nazi Germany had planned and waged aggressive war, that it had fought that conflict with flagrant disregard for the rules of warfare, and that, independent of any military necessity, it had committed mass murder on an inconceivable scale. Yet, that morning, an undercurrent of excitement coursed through the dock as the defense counsels held up their newspapers so that their clients could read the Churchill headlines. Knowing smiles flashed from defendant to defendant.

At the morning recess, it was as if a dam had broken. The defense lawyers rushed to their clients, and a cheerful babble ensued. Göring virtually did a jig in the dock. "What did I tell you?" he said. "Last summer I couldn't even hope to live till autumn. And now, I'll probably live through winter, summer, and spring and many times over. Mark my word. They'll be fighting among themselves before sentences can be pronounced on us." The washed-out, wrung-out Ribbentrop suddenly displayed his old hauteur. "I always expected it," he said. "Churchill is no fool. He knows we Germans are closer to him than the Reds." Hess dropped his catatonic stare and leaned over to Göring. "You will yet be the führer of Germany," he predicted.

That evening, Janet Flanner spotted a table of Russians in the press club bar and expressed her disappointment over Churchill's speech. She found them unperturbed. Boris Polevoi said with a shrug, "We've heard so many thousands of harsh capitalist words already. A few more from Churchill can't hurt us."

In cellblock C, Dr. Pfluecker made a happy observation on his final rounds. That night there were fewer requests for sleeping pills.

57

COLONEL LEON DOSTERT DEPARTED Nuremberg, leaving Alfred Steer, now promoted to full navy commander, as head of the Language Division. Steer was happy to see the man go. He had worked as deputy to the temperamental Dostert since the trial began. In Steer's eyes, Dostert was a manipulative opportunist, a peacock who used people below him while shamelessly ingratiating himself with those above. One of his pet boasts to Steer upon returning from meetings with the top brass was: "I have just seduced Justice so-and-so, or General so-and-so."

Steer, thirty-three, an energetic amalgam of man of action and scholar, with a Ph.D. from the University of Pennsylvania, had inherited a crushing responsibility. Though simultaneous interpretation was complex and just born at Nuremberg, it had quickly been taken for granted. Justice Birkett enjoyed exercising his talent for invective against the interpreters. A speech in the vigorous, masculine Russian of the prosecutor, Rudenko, had been rendered into English by an effete interpreter whom Birkett complained sounded like "a 'refayned' decaying cleric, a latecomer making an apology at the vicarage garden party rather than the prosecutor of major war crimes." Gruff German generals were interpreted by young women with chirpy little voices, diminishing the power of the witnesses' testimony. On one occasion, after the aristocratic Erwin Lahousen had been interpreted by a barely educated German-American, Birkett asked, "And what language was that?" "Brooklynese," Steer answered.

The interpreters also faced linguistic booby traps. Germans had a tendency to begin speaking with "*Ja.*" Interpreted literally, the utterance could amount to an admission of guilt. "Did you realize that what you were doing was criminal?" a prosecutor might ask. "*Ja,*" the witness would reply, meaning not "Yes," but a space-filler, more accurately translated as "Well . . ."

What his critics should know, Steer thought, was how many candidates he rejected. The Pentagon shipped him batches of new interpreters, mostly ill-prepared. When he heard clumsy, made-up cognates such as *judgify* or *tribunalize*, he knew he did not have a linguist. The rejects were consigned to an area called "Siberia," performing menial tasks until they could be shipped back to the States. And when all else ran smoothly, someone was always tripping over the cables that snaked through the courtroom, plunging the interpreting system into silence.

The defense was due to begin its case on March 8. Two days before, Hans Laternser, a lawyer defending Nazi organizations, stormed into Steer's office. "Don't you understand, we must be ready soon," Laternser complained, "and you have many documents you have not yet translated for us." Steer explained the demands on his operation, the shortage of personnel, the lack of funds. But, Laternser pointed out, they had the best interpreter in all Europe right here in Colonel Andrus's prison. Who was that? Steer asked. Paul Otto Schmidt, who was being held as a material witness, Laternser answered.

Schmidt had been Hitler's personal interpreter, present at every critical meeting Hitler had held with foreign leaders. When, in September of 1939, the British ambassador delivered his government's ultimatum to Germany—get out of Poland or face war—it was Paul Schmidt who had translated the message for Hitler. The beleagured Steer went to Colonel Andrus and explained the jewel he held. Andrus agreed that Steer could use Schmidt. But the prisoner would have to be placed in a secure area under armed guard.

The interpreters stood around the room like fellow violinists who had come to hear Heifetz. The center of attention was a tall, pale man needing a shave and wearing a shabby suit jacket over an undershirt. Steer had put together a team of stenographers to work in relays—the only way to keep up with Paul Schmidt's output. The man picked up a document in English from a stack, and, while pacing back and forth, sight-translated it into German, then into French. Most translators worked best in one direction. But with Schmidt, it made no difference. He went as easily from English to German as he did from German to English, and did the same with other languages. He stopped only long enough to go to the bathroom or to refuel with Cokes and sandwiches.

After virtual nonstop round-the-clock days, Schmidt was taken back to his cell, exhausted, clutching the packs of cigarettes with which Steer had rewarded him. He slumped onto his cot. He had tried to make Colonel Andrus understand. He had not become a party member until 1943, and then only because his lack of membership was becoming conspicuous in the circle around Hitler. This translating performance for the court, he hoped, would earn his way out of prison. Yet he was still being held as a common criminal.

CHAPTER III

THE DEFENSE

1

THE BACK OF WINTER had been broken. The days were turning longer and warmer, and weeds had begun to sprout in the ruins. Newly arrived GIs made what now amounted to a pilgrimage out to Zeppelin Field, where they posed before Brownie cameras, making mock Nazi salutes from the platform where Hitler had roused the multitudes.

On the evening of March 7, several defense attorneys gathered at the Gasthaus zum Stern to drink beer and discuss the opening of their case the next day. They spoke like athletes who had been trained in a strange new sport and who would be taking the field for the first time. The Anglo-Saxon forms of law still fitted them like a poorly tailored suit. Even the point of the trial still puzzled them. Was it an honest effort to elicit guilt or innocence? Or was it a victor's spectacle? Admittedly, Sir Geoffrey's fairness was beyond question. The Germans were given access to the same documents as their opponents. They were allowed virtually unlimited time to confer with their clients. They were well paid—by the Allies. But why? Why would victors go through this protracted and costly exercise? It fit nothing in the Germans' experience.

Something in the courtroom was different. The regulars sensed it instantly. The witness stand, which until now had stood midway between the bench and the dock, had been moved during the night. The Russian judges had been outraged to learn that the defendants would testify from the same box as their accusers. Sir Geoffrey had found a last-minute compromise. Instead of replacing the box, he suggested that they simply move it away from the bench and closer to the dock so that the Russians would not find the nearness of the defendants so offensive.

The visitors' gallery was filled to overflowing. Göring, dark star of Nazism, was expected to take the stand as the first defense witness.

Instead, the first person Otto Stahmer called was Luftwaffe General Karl B. Bodenschatz, an old flying pal from Göring's Richthofen squadron, and later the *Reichsmarschall*'s liaison to Hitler. Bodenschatz's testimony was intended to establish that after 1943 Göring had stood discredited before Hitler and no longer exercised any significant power. Field Marshal Erhard Milch, the former plane production chief, followed. A barely suppressed ripple of laughter ran through the prosecution table as one of the attorneys reminded the others, sotto voce, of the status Milch had held in Göring's estimation. Göring had described Milch as "a fart out of my asshole."

The trial recessed and resumed Monday morning, with Stahmer continuing to call witnesses. It was not until the afternoon of Wednesday, March 13, that Göring would take the stand.

Dr. Pfluecker came to see Göring the night before. He found his patient agitated, sitting at his table, a dog-eared sheet of paper in his hand, talking out loud. Hans Fritzsche, as a professional broadcaster, had analyzed the failings of previous German witnesses and had written out advice which he entitled "Suggestions for Speakers." The Germans were often mistranslated, Fritzsche noted, because they used long sentences with the verb at the end, and because they spoke too fast. They should speak slowly, use short sentences, and move the subject and verb as close together as possible. They should pause between thoughts to give the interpreter time to catch up. Göring was now memorizing Fritzsche's advice.

He greeted his visitor gratefully. Dr. Pfluecker's attentions always buoyed him. He asked if he might have a stronger sedative that night. He doubted that he would sleep a wink. Pfluecker reminded him of the difference between natural sleep and drugged sleep. He must be alert the next day, Pfluecker cautioned. Göring settled for his regular pill.

If Paul Schmidt was the best that the Nuremberg interpreters had ever witnessed, Wolfe Frank ran a close second. Peter Uiberall had not expected a linguist when the dashing figure in the beribboned uniform of a British army captain first came to be tested. Frank spoke English with an upper-class accent, and, like Schmidt, could move flawlessly back and forth between English and German. The son of a

Jewish BMW plant manager, Frank had escaped to England in the late thirties. He had passed up the safe language positions offered him, and had volunteered for the commandos. At Nuremberg, he had set for himself one objective: to be the sole interpreter for English and German, with no relief, when Hermann Göring took the stand. Commander Steer could find no reason to deny him.

At 2:30 p.m., Stahmer, in his lilac university robe, rose from the defense counsel table and called his witness. Göring began to make his way to the small door that opened from the dock onto the courtroom floor. His dove-gray uniform was freshly pressed, but hung poorly. He had lost seventy-six pounds in captivity. The little door opened, revealing Göring's polished yellow boots, the pants bloused over the top. Around his neck he wore a wine-red scarf, suggesting his days as an air ace. He moved with a determined stride toward the witness box, clutching a thick purple folder. His face was flushed as Justice Lawrence asked, "Will you repeat this oath after me: I swear to God almighty and omniscient that I will speak the pure truth and will withhold or add nothing." Göring raised his right hand, trembling visibly, and repeated the oath in a quavering voice.

Did Göring believe that the Nazi party had come to power legally? Stahmer asked. The pages of his opened notebook shook in his hand. The sound of his voice, uncertain at first, gradually reassured him. It became more sonorous, precise in articulation, with the *r*s rolled vigorously. Göring proceeded to give a well-organized history of the rise of Nazism, barely glancing at his notes. "Once we came to power," he said, "we were determined to hold on to it under all circumstances. . . . We did not want to leave this any longer to chance, to elections and parliamentary majorities. . . ." The words were ice water flung in the face of the court. No apology, no evasion, no softening marked his recital. Once in the saddle, he explained, the party had intended to eliminate the Reichstag, to dissolve the regional parliaments, to end individual rights. The answer had taken twenty minutes, an annoyed Jackson noted, and Lawrence had never interfered.

Stahmer cued Göring to explain where the idea had come from to combine the ceremonial head of state and the head of government in one person, Adolf Hitler. That was simple, Göring explained. They had taken their example from the similar dual roles of the president of the United States. Concentration camps? Stahmer asked. Göring described in detail why and how he had started them. How could the party rule until it had established order? And how could it maintain order with its deadly enemies, particularly the Communists, running free? "It was a question of removing danger," Göring said. "Only one course was available, protective custody." And as for the name *concentration camp*, it had originated not with the Nazis, but with the foreign press. The Nazis had just accepted it. He spoke for over two hours, moving from stage fright to confidence to obvious relish in his own performance.

Janet Flanner left the courthouse stunned. She sat in the press bus, silent, digesting the meaning of Göring's debut. On arriving at the Stein castle, she began writing her column for *The New Yorker*. She had witnessed, she wrote, "one of the best brains of the period of history when good brains are rare." Göring, she concluded, however, was "a brain without a conscience."

Howard Smith had gone from the courtroom down to the pressroom, pondering the afternoon's significance. Hermann Göring in the witness stand had far outperformed the dissolute *Reichsmarschall* whom Smith remembered from the early years. "When a clever man is facing death and has nothing to lose," Smith told his radio audience, "it concentrates his mind marvelously."

Gustav Gilbert accompanied the defendants on their walk back to the cellblock. Göring had to be restrained from bursting out ahead of the pack. The guards also had to stop the others from gripping his hand and treating him like an athlete who had just saved the game. Dönitz turned to Speer. "You could see, even the judges were impressed," he said. Speer had to agree. Gilbert later stopped by Göring's cell. The man was sitting on his bed, his supper untouched. He could not eat a thing, he told Gilbert. He was too excited. "It was a strain for me," Göring went on, "especially the first ten minutes when I couldn't make my hands stop shaking." He was, however, looking forward to tomorrow.

Sir Norman Birkett sat in the study of his villa, also reviewing the day. Sir Geoffrey Lawrence's behavior had shocked him. Hermann Göring's so-called testimony had been a farce. The man had simply been allowed uncontested ownership of the court for as long as he chose to speak. Birkett intended to urge Lawrence to put some decent limits on Göring's tongue before the next day's session.

Göring was back on the witness stand at ten the next morning. The Nazi regime, he said with Stahmer's light prodding, was being vilified for imposing rigid obedience on its followers. In the prosecution's argument, this pyramid of unthinking submission from the top downward ended in places like Auschwitz and Mauthausen. But the *Führerprinzip*—the leadership principle—was merely sound management, Göring asserted: "Authority from above downward and responsibility from the bottom upward." Was this concept adopted only by power-crazed Nazis? Göring asked. "I should like to mention some parallels," he said. "The *Führerprinzip* is the same principle on which the Catholic church and the government of the USSR are both based." He nodded in the direction of the Soviet prosecution.

So far, he had not equivocated. But when Stahmer put the next question to him, the audience braced for an evasion. "To what extent did you participate in issuing the Nuremberg Laws of 1935?" Stahmer asked. Göring barely paused. "In my capacity as president of the Reichstag, I promulgated those laws, here in Nuremberg, where the Reichstag was meeting at the time."

During the lunch break, a dismayed Gilbert passed from the "youth room" to the "elders' room" to the other rooms, feeling the buoyed morale. The only bright patch was Hans Frank's feisty outburst. As they filed back down to the courtroom, Frank looked to Göring and said, "Well done, *Herr Reichsmarschall*. It's too bad you weren't thrown into jail years ago."

Göring waited until the third and final day of his direct examination to rebut the prosecution charges against the Luftwaffe. The world had been horrified at the German bombing of Rotterdam *after* the Netherlands had surrendered. It was true, Göring said, he had sent a squadron to bomb Rotterdam. But when the Germans learned that surrender negotiations were under way, they fired red flares into the sky to ward off their bombers. The first group did not understand the signal and, unfortunately, struck the target. The two groups behind did understand and turned back. Rotterdam had not been an atrocity, Göring argued. It had been a tragic error.

Göring next dealt head-on with the issue of how he had acquired his art treasures. "I decided that after the war, or at some time when it seemed appropriate to me, I would found an art gallery, either through purchase, or gifts, or through inheritance, and present this art to the German people." For the first time since he had taken the stand, the snickering from the audience was audible.

It was late in the afternoon Friday, March 15. Göring had been testifying for five hours. After the first day, he had no longer bothered to bring the purple file folder. In the final question, Stahmer asked if Germany had behaved any differently than her Allies in observing the rules of civilized conflict. Instruments like the Geneva and Hague conventions, Göring said, had been overrun by modern warfare. "At this point, I should like to say the very words which one of our greatest, most important and strongest opponents, the British prime minister Winston Churchill, used: 'In the struggle for life and death, there is, in the end, no legality.'" Sir Geoffrey adjourned the court. Hermann Göring had spoken, virtually without interruption and largely without notes, for over two and a half days. His cross-examination would begin after the weekend.

The Göring testimony had been brilliant enough, without his flinging Churchill's words in their faces, Maxwell-Fyfe believed. A message was fired off to Whitehall to find out where or when Sir Winston might have said such a thing. The closest, the Foreign Office replied, was a speech Churchill made in 1940 while still first lord of the Admiralty. "There could be no justice, if in a mortal struggle, the aggressor tramples down every sentiment of humanity, and if those who resist remain entangled in the tatters of violated legal convention." Göring had the words wrong, but the sentiment was uncomfortably close.

2

WAR CRIMES CERTAINLY PRODUCED strange bedfellows, Drexel Sprecher thought, as he took another game, nineteen to twenty-one. He was in the hunting lodge of a rich German industrialist playing Ping-Pong with Paul Schmidt, Adolf Hitler's personal interpreter, while Rudolf Diels, who had once headed the Gestapo under Hermann Göring, awaited his turn. In the meantime, his host, Roland Faber-Castell, was seated in a deep leather chair chatting with Fritz Sauter, counsel for Funk and Schirach. Sprecher rarely missed a weekend at his cousin Nina's country retreat. He never knew who would be the Faber-Castells' guests, since they cut across the upper spectrum of German society. Paul Schmidt was personally indebted to Sprecher, who had managed to spring him from the Nuremberg jail in part because of Schmidt's translating services to the IMT.

Sprecher had been astonished to find Diels here, and curious to talk to him. Göring's performance was on everybody's mind, and Diels had known the man when the Nazi regime was young. But it was a custom at the Faber-Castells' not to discuss the trial—or, as the host put it, not to speak of rope in the house of a condemned man. In Diels's case, what once had seemed bad luck turned out to be his salvation. When Göring realized that the Gestapo had become an international scandal, he let the insatiable Himmler have it. Diels, more a political policeman than a political assassin, was soon shoved aside in favor of Himmler's own men. Diels then went into conventional police work as head of the Cologne constabulary. He was at Nuremberg waiting to be called as a witness.

Drexel Sprecher was a valued guest at the lodge. Having a well-situated American friend was virtually every German's desire. Besides, Sprecher, amiable and an excellent conversationalist, was good company. As a guest, he left his prosecutor's hat at the court. His presence here with former Nazis and a defense lawyer would likely have shocked his courthouse colleagues, so he chose to say nothing about the nature of his weekend escapes. When he went back to Nuremberg, he put on the prosecutor's hat and applied to convicting Nazis the same energy that he put into pleasure. He knew that when the present trial was over, he would not be going home. After the top defendants were tried, a new court was to be constituted for the lesser fry—hundreds of defendants such as Einsatzgruppe D commander Otto Ohlendorf. Telford Taylor had already been picked by Justice Jackson as the chief prosecutor for these "subsequent proceedings," and Drexel Sprecher was to be his leading deputy.

Sprecher's cousin Nina came in, her cheeks red from a walk around the grounds. She reminded Roland of how lovely it was outdoors and suggested that he and Drexel might want to take a walk. The gesture almost seemed scripted, and as the two men moved into the woods, Sprecher realized that the house rule was about to be broken. After pointing out how his bomb-shattered trees were being removed, Faber-Castell suddenly asked Sprecher if Nazi industrialists were likely to be tried at these subsequent proceedings. Yes, Sprecher answered. "That is wrong," the German said. "They were only businessmen, like me." "Yes, and they were only too willing to use slave labor in their businesses," Sprecher countered. "They confiscated foreign property. They helped put Hitler into power, my friend." This was a Sprecher that Faber-Castell had not heard before. "I'm not sure, under the circumstances, that anyone else would have behaved differently," the German observed. "Will you be prosecuting these cases?" He probably would, Sprecher answered.

That night after dinner Sprecher found himself enjoying a cigar with Fritz Sauter and Rudolf Diels. He respected Sauter. The lawyer admitted that he had been a party member for five years. When, however, Communists and anti-Nazis had asked him to defend them, what else could he do? He took their cases and, consequently, was thrown out of the party. He was delighted to have been fired as the exasperating Ribbentrop's lawyer before the IMT, he said, since he was already stretched thin with his two other clients.

Diels finally raised the unspoken subject on everyone's mind—the Göring testimony. Diels said that Heinrich Hoffmann, who like himself was staying at the Witness House, had stopped making Göring the butt of his jokes. The Allies' error, Diels went on, had been to equate Göring's hedonism with softness of intellect. Justice Jackson would have to be very good indeed to catch this corpulent fox, he concluded.

3

Sir Norman Birkett had written to a colleague back home, "The first really great dramatic moment of this trial will come when Göring is cross-examined by the American prosecutor, Jackson. It will be a duel to the death between the representative of all that is worthwhile in civilization and the last important surviving protagonist of all that was evil. In a sense, the whole result of the trial depends on that duel."

On Sunday evening, March 17, Robert Jackson, at home on Lindenstrasse, was making last-minute preparations for the duel. The conservatory was again quilted with piles of documents he expected to employ. He had gathered his son, Bill, Elsie Douglas, and Whitney Harris, the prosecutor who had unearthed Otto Ohlendorf, to review strategy. He knew, Jackson said, that Göring could not beat the charges. The evidence was too overwhelming. "But he's showman enough to make a farce of it or go over the heads of the tribunal to the German people," Jackson said. That he intended to stop. But what was the best approach? His staff had developed two possible lines of questioning. The first was a series of rifle shots, intended to hit Göring with specific charges—for instance, that he had forced the Jews to pay for Kristallnacht, that he had signed anti-Semitic legislation, and that he had played a role in the execution of downed airmen. The other strategy was to employ heavy artillery and bombard Göring with sweeping questions, forcing him to accept his leading role in destroying German democracy, in arming Germany for war, in planning Nazi aggressions. By the time the group broke up late that evening, Robert Jackson had still not decided which weapon would best sink Hermann Göring.

The courtroom was packed as it had not been since opening day. Most of the morning was consumed by the defense counsels, finishing up Göring's direct examination, asking questions of him designed to absolve their clients. Göring readily obliged, manfully assuming responsibility for virtually everything. Meanwhile, the visitors fussed impatiently like fight fans compelled to endure lightweights before the main bout.

Not until 12:10 p.m. did Justice Lawrence ask, "Do the chief prosecutors wish to cross-examine?" Jackson moved to the prosecution stand with confident pugnacity. Behind him, to one side, sat Whitney Harris with a file box of folders neatly tabbed for quick retrieval. Jackson unbuttoned his morning coat and shoved his hands into his back pockets. He studied Göring in the witness stand. Göring stared back like an air ace gauging the enemy before a dogfight. "You are perhaps aware that you are the only living man who can expound to us the true purposes of the Nazi party and the inner workings of its leadership," Jackson said. He had made his decision earlier that morning. He was going to hit Göring first with artillery rather than rifle fire. Maxwell-Fyfe, a legendary cross-examiner, heard Jackson's bland query with surprise. It was not how he would have begun—but Jackson, no doubt, had a hidden strategy.

"I am perfectly aware of that," Göring answered. Jackson next asked if it was not true that the Nazis had intended to overthrow the Weimar Republic. "That was my firm intention," Göring answered, unblinking. When Jackson asked him if it was also true that on taking power the Nazis abolished democratic government, Göring responded, "We found it no longer necessary."

Jackson asked Göring if it was not true that people were thrown into concentration camps without recourse to the courts. Göring began a lengthy answer, but Jackson interrupted, trying to limit him to yes or no. Göring shot back that he needed to explain. Jackson shut him off. Any such amplification, he said, could be brought out on redirect examination by Göring's counsel. He started asking Göring another question, when he saw Biddle lean over and whisper to Lawrence. Sir Geoffrey nodded, then stopped Jackson in mid-query. "Mr. Jackson," he said, "the tribunal thinks the witness ought to be allowed to make what explanation he thinks right in answer to this question." Jackson flushed angrily. This ruling was contrary to cross-examination custom, Jackson knew, and he was convinced that Biddle was pulling Lawrence's strings. The prosecutor impatiently tapped his pen on the stand as Göring was allowed virtually to lecture the court at will.

Jackson next asked, "Now, was the leadership principle supported and adopted by you in Germany because you believed that no people are capable of self-government, or that you believed that some may be, but not the German people: or for that matter whether some of us are capable of using our own system but it should not be used in Germany?" Not only Göring, but the judges looked baffled. He did not understand the question, the witness said, but he would attempt to answer it anyway. Sir David Maxwell-Fyfe became increasingly mystified. Ten minutes into the cross-examination, he could still discern no overarching strategy in Jackson's approach.

Göring appeared to be enjoying himself, a prizefighter who has yet to feel his opponent's glove. He was also shrewdly exploiting an advantage. Between Jackson's long-winded questions and Wolfe Frank's translations, Göring had ample time to frame his answers, especially since he understood the questions in English before they were translated. Jackson was deprived of the cross-examiner's classic tactic: he could not "crowd" the witness with quick, hard, successive questions.

As Sir Lawrence adjourned for lunch, a journalist in the press gallery gestured toward Jackson and whispered, "Saved by the bell." Jackson's deputy prosecutors, who had come to watch their champion, filed out of the courtroom eyeing each other uneasily.

When the court resumed after lunch, Jackson began questioning Göring about the Nazi invasion of the Soviet Union. The charge of "conspiracy to commit aggression" had been eagerly embraced by him as far back as the earliest Bernays proposal. The Soviet example, however, was poorly chosen, in Göring's case. The defendant was able to point out, persuasively, that he had opposed Hitler on the invasion of the Soviet Union. Jackson kept plodding on, like an animal in a maze chasing the uncatchable, giving Göring further opportunity to demonstrate that if there had been a conspiracy to invade Russia, he had not been a supporter of it.

Throughout the afternoon, Göring continued to respond adroitly, displaying a phenomenal memory and, thanks to the court's indulgence, having all the time in the world to exercise it. At the end of the day, Maxwell-Fyfe came over to Jackson, his hand outstretched, and said, "Well done. All our worries are over about the conspiracy count." It was a courteous gesture. What Maxwell-Fyfe could not say was that Jackson, after four years on the Supreme Court and years spent amid the legal bureaucracy of the Justice Department, had been too long out of the gladiatorial arena. The cross-examiner in him was rusty.

Airey Neave had dinner that night at Justice Birkett's villa. He enjoyed the association with this mercurial, proud, witty man; and Birkett wanted company with whom he could comfortably discuss the day's events. Neave, serious, intelligent, and discreet, would do nicely. Birkett feared, he said, that the great duel was being lost by the forces of right, and that once lost, the momentum might never be reversed. Göring's performance was bound to give the other defendants heart. Jackson had great rhetorical power, but he had not the slightest notion as to how the cross-examination game was played. His reading from documents left no time for the lightning questions that stunned and threw a witness off balance. Not once had Jackson employed the deadliest gambit at which all good cross-examiners excel—luring the witness toward a waiting pit, then forcing him into it with an answer that cannot be evaded.

Jackson, and no doubt all of them, had made a miscalculation, Airey Neave observed. They had allowed Göring's bluster and buffoonery to obscure a simple fact. Hermann Göring's brain was a formidable instrument. He had graduated from the military academy at Gross Lichterfelde, Germany's West Point or Sandhurst, summa cum laude. Another point, Neave added: Göring was a murderer and a bastard—but he was a brave bastard and that came through in court.

Granting all that, Birkett said, Jackson had operated under a severe handicap. Lawrence's ruling that Göring's answers would not be curtailed had been outrageous. The witness, not the prosecutor or even the bench, was in control of the court.

The private verdict became public that night. Hal Burson sat next to his announcer in the broadcast booth, listening to him read the script Burson had written for the Armed Forces Network: "As the day ended with the suspense of a Pulitzer prize–winning play's second act, the talk among correspondents at Nuremberg boiled down to a single comment: Göring, so far, has had his own way. Someone is going to have to stop him."

The duel did not resume immediately the next morning. Göring's lawyer, Stahmer, had won the court's permission to squeeze in a witness named Birger Dahlerus, a Swedish businessman called to testify that Göring had not wanted war with England. Not until midafternoon did the Göring-Jackson combat renew. At one point, Jackson quoted from a document designed to show that Göring had violated the Treaty of Versailles by planning "the liberation of the Rhineland." Göring possessed a copy of the same report. He pointed out that Jackson had mistranslated it. The document dealt not with the Rhineland, but with the Rhine River. And it spoke not of "liberation," but of "clearing" the river of impediments to navigation in case of mobilization. Göring, it turned out, was right.

Still, were these actions not intended as part of a plan to rearm the Rhineland? Jackson asked. All countries made contingency plans, Göring answered. But weren't these plans "kept entirely secret from foreign powers"? Jackson asked. Göring snapped back, "I do not think I can recall reading beforehand the publication of the mobilization preparations of the United States." Jackson looked to the bench. "I respectfully submit to the tribunal that this witness is not being responsive in his examination! . . . It is perfectly futile to spend our time if we cannot have responsive answers to our questions. . . . This witness, it seems to me, is adopting, in the witness box, and in the dock, an arrogant and contemptuous attitude toward the tribunal which is giving him the trial which he never gave a living soul, nor dead ones either." Sir Geoffrey looked to Biddle. He upheld the decision to let the witness have his say. Jackson appeared on the point of apoplexy. Biddle whispered to Lawrence that this was probably a good point to adjourn for the day.

Jackson saw no point in delaying further. The source of his torment had to be confronted. He did not bother to return to his office but went straight to Biddle's chambers. There he found both Biddle and Parker. Biddle greeted him calmly and offered a seat. He preferred to stand, Jackson said. He could come to no other conclusion, he began, than that Biddle was deliberately trying to thwart him. He had not left the U.S. Supreme Court to come here and be sabotaged by his own countrymen. "I'd better resign and go home," Jackson announced. No, Biddle said. He understood that Bob was under tremendous strain. He and Parker both knew it. They had enormous admiration for the difficult job he was doing. The decisions on Göring were not personal. They were designed only to give the man no alibis when the trial ended. And that goal would best serve them all, the judges and the prosecution. Jackson left, hardly mollified.

Biddle invited Colonel Harlan Amen to dinner that night. Jackson was surrounded by yes-men like the pliant Bob Storey, Amen charged, people who were not going to tell him he was making a mess of it. He doesn't prepare properly, doesn't master his material before he goes into court. Göring had proved it today, tripping Bob up on the Rhineland business. Biddle remained quietly discreet, as Amen went on inventorying his boss's failings.

That night, writing to his wife, Biddle held nothing back. "Jackson's cross-examination, on the whole, has been futile and weak," he wrote. "Göring listens to every question, takes his time, answers well. Bob doesn't listen to the answers, depends on his notes, always a sign of weakness. He hasn't *absorbed* his case." And Biddle could not suppress his role. To the world Sir Geoffrey Lawrence might seem the master of the courtroom. Biddle did not contest that public impression. But, he told Katherine, "I do really run this show and have won on every point."

Sir Norman Birkett had a visitor, the British chief prosecutor, Sir David Maxwell-Fyfe. The meeting brought together possibly the two ablest cross-examiners in Britain. The purpose of his visit, Sir David said, was to advise Birkett that Bob Jackson was in a terrible emotional state. The man might have his failings as a courtroom adversary; but with that eloquent opening address and his prominent position as chief American prosecutor of the Nazi leaders, Jackson was the moral heart of the trial. His departure, or his perceived failure, would be a disaster.

Jackson's plight was not entirely his own fault, Birkett pointed out. He and Maxwell-Fyfe would be hard-pressed to defeat a clever defendant in cross-examination who could say whatever he wanted for as long as he wished. And Birkett agreed that it was not simply Jackson's reputation at stake. If Göring was allowed to run riot, what had started as a trial would end as a circus. Worse still, people might start to believe his cunning rationalizations. Lawrence must make clear that no further irrelevancies in answering questions would be tolerated, Birkett said. He was going to draft a statement to that effect to be read by Sir Geoffrey in court tomorrow. That should get the cross-examination back on track. And it certainly ought to restore Jackson's confidence.

Birkett and Sir Geoffrey arrived in the Judges' Room before the others. The president of the court looked over Birkett's draft and agreed that it was a splendid idea. But when Biddle saw it, he asked Sir Geoffrey how it would look for the chief justice to shut off a man on trial for his life. Worse still, how would it look if he were seen as reversing his earlier decision? Lawrence glanced at his watch. It was time for them to repair to the courtroom. Birkett's proposal was forgotten.

Göring had ended the previous day's questioning with the riposte that he did not recall the United States publicizing its mobilization plans. Jackson resumed his questioning with a complaint about Göring's reply. If left unchallenged, Jackson said, Göring's gibe would mislead the world as to the openness of American society. Sir Norman Birkett listened in dismay. Another Birkett rule of cross-examination was that a witness's flip answers should be left to wither of neglect. Jackson instead launched into a drawn-out explanation of the alternatives facing him, either to allow Göring's impertinence to stand or to rebut it.

Biddle also listened in disbelief. Jackson was turning a molehill into a legal Mount Everest. Lawrence tried to move Jackson along by agreeing that Göring's remark had been irrelevant and that the court would so consider it. But that was not enough. The remark may be irrelevant, Jackson went on; but it was already in the record. Biddle whispered loudly to Parker, "How silly." Did Jackson want Göring's words stricken from the record? Lawrence asked.

That was not what he wanted, Jackson replied. He wanted the witness held to yes or no answers. Was the prosecution saying that a witness could make no explanation of any kind to his answer? Sir Geoffrey asked. "I think that is the rule of cross-examination under ordinary circumstances," Jackson said. Jackson was making far too much of Göring's glib retort, Lawrence advised: "Certainly it would be wiser to ignore a statement of that sort . . . the counsel for the prosecution does not have to answer every irrelevant observation made in cross-examination." The defendant, Lawrence ruled, "may make a short explanation" and is not confined simply to answering yes or no.

Jackson went on to the next issue. He took a sheaf of documents in hand. They were decrees, he said, signed by Göring in his various roles. Had he not issued a decree that a Jew could sell a business only with government permission? Göring said yes. Did Göring sign a decree that Jews might not own retail businesses, sell handicrafts, or form co-ops? Again Göring agreed. Jackson kept up the steady drumfire. Did Göring order Jews to surrender all their jewelry and gold to the government? Sequester Jewish property in Poland? Bar Jews from compensation for damage caused by German forces? At long last, Birkett thought, Jackson sounded like a cross-examiner.

Göring put one hand over the other to stop the trembling. Was it not true, Jackson pressed on, that on July 31, 1941, Göring signed the decree directing Reinhard Heydrich to plan a solution to the Jewish question? Göring protested that the document was in no way correctly translated. He then cleverly offered to read it himself. The word *Endlösung*, he said, had been rendered as "final solution" when it should have been "complete solution." He thereby robbed the document of the incriminating semantic power that "final solution" had already acquired. Actually, the phrase had been accurately translated in the first place. Jackson, a lawyer, not a linguist, did not pursue the matter.

The prosecutor moved the questioning to *Kristallnacht*, November 9, 1938, when storm troopers and Nazi hooligans looted and destroyed 815 Jewish shops and 76 synagogues and arrested twenty thousand Jews, of whom thirty-six died. *Kristallnacht* had allegedly been ignited by a report a few days before that a third secretary in the German Embassy in Paris, Ernst vom Rath, had been murdered by a seventeen-year-old German Jewish refugee, Herschel Grynszpan.

Jackson began reading into the record the grim inventory of destruction. His facts came from a report submitted to Göring the day after the rampage. Göring had then called a meeting at his air ministry, of Goebbels, Funk, Heydrich, and a man from the insurance industry, to discuss damage claims. Jackson read a verbatim exchange between Göring and the insurance representative. This man had pointed out that many goods in the burned-out Jewish shops had been there on consignment from non-Jewish suppliers. To which Göring said to Heydrich, "I wished you had killed two hundred Jews instead of destroying such valuables." Göring next announced that he was going to deny the Jews the right to insurance claims for their losses. That would save the insurance industry millions, he said. "All of a sudden an angel, in my somewhat corpulent shape, appears before you," he had told the insurance official. "I should like to go fifty-fifty with you."

Jackson threw at Göring the exact words he had used at the close of that meeting nearly eight years before: "I demand that German Jewry shall for their abominable crimes make a contribution of a billion marks. That will work. The pigs will not commit a second murder so quickly. I would not like to be a Jew in Germany." Was that a correct quote? Jackson asked. Göring answered gloomily that it was.

Jackson next nailed Göring with documentary proof of his art looting and his role in the wholesale pillaging of foodstuffs and resources from the Soviet Union. He finally had Göring reeling. A drumfire of hard, specific charges revealed the defendant as a coarse, venal, anti-Semitic co-architect of the worst evils of Nazism. Göring at last seemed to teeter on the edge of the pit.

And then Jackson let him get away. He began accusing Göring's Luftwaffe of destroying the house of the American ambassador during the bombing of Warsaw. The charge stood so dwarflike next to the horrors of mass murder, slave labor, and diabolical medical experiments heard in this courtroom, that it appeared as if Jackson were, willy-nilly, reading a list of pro forma questions prepared by some junior aide. To prove the bombing charge, Jackson introduced alleged Luftwaffe aerial photographs. Göring was allowed to examine them. The cocksureness returned. Before he became a World War I air ace, Göring had been an aerial photographer. He showed that, from the angle of the photographs, they were likely taken from a steeple, not an airplane. He turned them over. The backs of the photographs were blank—no date, no place, no identification, no authentication; unacceptable evidence in virtually any court of law.

Jackson moved on to questions about the execution of Allied fliers. But his queries were posed prosaically and with little follow-through, again as though he were merely reading down a list rather than stalking his quarry for the kill. The three days of Jackson versus Göring ended on a limp exchange over the authenticity of a signature on a minor order.

Francis Biddle wrote Katherine that Bob Jackson looked "beaten, full of a sense of failure. . . . I know he has it in for me. . . . I have repeatedly asked Bob to the house, but he never comes and I am afraid we are no longer friends." He believed Jackson's grievance stemmed from their reversed roles, he wrote. Now it was Jackson the courtroom supplicant and Biddle judging on high from the bench.

Whatever the ultimate verdict of the bench in room 600, the verdict at the Grand was clear. Göring had proved a brilliant villain, and Jackson a flawed hero. Barbara Pinion, an evidence researcher, echoed the grudging sentiments of the workaday staff. Göring at least knew what he believed. "The other defendants were always putting the blame on someone else. Not old Hermann," she observed.

4

TECH SERGEANT HAL BURSON'S REPORTS were broadcast daily from a powerful fifty-thousand-watt transmitter to over fifty outlets, in virtually every post in Germany where GIs were stationed. The Armed Forces Network had sent Burson to cover the trial to give American troops a sense of why they were in this country and, as a by-product, to expose the Germans to the truth of Nazism.

Burson sought occasionally to take the pulse of the man in the rubble by patronizing German bars. There he studied the face of defeat. German men had a hangdog, emasculated manner. Too many were dependent on their women, who worked for the victors or provided a service to which the men could only turn a blind eye. One story that Burson had not reported had occurred at Club 21 that spring. There, talk was not of legal fine points as in room 600, but of the going rate for a carton of cigarettes or a fräulein. That night, all eyes had turned to a pair of black GIs who suddenly appeared in the doorway. From a far corner, a voice in the accents of the South called out, "You boys better get out that door before it has time to hit your

black asses." The two blacks held their ground. A half dozen whites
sauntered belligerently toward them. The melee that followed spilled
into the street, where more blacks were waiting. Three jeeploads of
club-swinging MPs were required to break up the fracas.

Racial incidents had multiplied ever since a black unit had arrived in
Nuremberg. Gunther Sadel, General Watson's young counterintelligence agent, had quickly become caught up in America's exported
biases. Black soldiers wanted Sadel's coveted social passes for their
German girlfriends. Ordinarily, the passes were printed on pink paper,
but the printer had run out of pink stock. Sadel thus had the passes
printed on yellow paper. An immediate cry went up from the blacks,
with liberal journalists joining in. The army, obviously, had come up
with a scheme for identifying and discriminating against German
women who dated blacks. General Watson ordered Sadel to scour
Germany and come up with pink paper.

The racial clashes bothered Gustav Gilbert as he tried to piece together
his analysis of sanctioned mass murder. He had already concluded that,
beyond an obedient people, the next requirement for this kind of crime
was a belief in the inferiority of one's victims. He had had a discussion
on this point recently with Göring. Göring had asked him about the
black officers occasionally seen in the visitors' gallery. Could they
command troops in combat? Göring wanted to know. Could they ride
in the same buses as whites? Gilbert had just spent three days in court
watching Robert Jackson prosecute Göring for crimes against humanity, specifically for issuing anti-Semitic edicts. Jim Crow and the Nuremberg Laws—was it not just a difference of degree?

5

THE NEXT PROSECUTOR to cross-examine Göring would be Sir David
Maxwell-Fyfe. On the eve of his court appearance, Sir David stayed
up into the early-morning hours preparing himself, determined to
break through Göring's armor plating of ego and brains. The elements
of cross-examination were as natural to the Scot as breathing, beginning with rule one: Ask only questions to which the answer is known.

The Russians, unfamiliar with the technique, were likely to ask, "I show you document 819 PS. Is your impression positive or negative?" They made Sir David cringe. The objective was not to elicit information, but to get incriminating facts into the record. Rule two: Abandon a losing line of questioning. Jackson had ploddingly followed his script, at times clear off the track. Sir David accepted that he was going up against an adversary of cutting wit. Thus, rule three: Ignore the clever asides, the sallies and impertinences. Hang on to the essentials like a bulldog with his teeth buried in the enemy's throat. A trial, in the end, was a contest, theater, a debating match, a game—deadly enough, but a game all the same. Jackson had depended on moral outrage. Sir David intended to outplay his opponents.

He further intended to pick the right fight. By now, in room 600, the extermination of ten thousand Hungarian Gypsies was merely a statistic. Maxwell-Fyfe intended to lead off with an issue that the men on the bench could feel and grasp. He was convinced that he had found his opening in the fate of the RAF fliers who had escaped from Stalag Luft III. For the British chief judge and his alternate, these were not heaped, anonymous corpses bulldozed into a ditch—they were sons, neighbors, classmates, brothers.

At 4:50 p.m. on the afternoon of March 20, Maxwell-Fyfe took the prosecutor's stand, a time when people had begun looking at their watches, not a propitious moment for courtroom pyrotechnics. Still, he plunged in for the half hour remaining. He looked up from his papers into the broad face in the witness stand. Göring's set smile and hard eyes seemed to be saying, "I handled the American, and I shall do the same with you."

The Sagan affair had begun on March 14, 1944, when seventy-six RAF POWs managed to burrow their way out of Stalag Luft III, at Sagan in Silesia. Hitler, at his Berchtesgaden retreat, became furious on getting the news. The escape was the third from Sagan in two weeks, he yelled at Keitel, and the tenth recent POW breakout overall. "Dozens of officers have escaped," he went on. "They are an enormous source of danger. You, Keitel, don't realize that in view of six million foreigners who are prisoners and working in Germany, these officers are leaders who could organize an uprising." On their recapture, Hitler ordered, the Sagan escapees were to be turned over to Himmler's secret police for "special treatment."

Twenty of them had been retaken within two hours and returned to Sagan before Hitler's tirade. Three were never accounted for, and three eventually made it to Sweden. The remaining fifty were caught in various parts of Germany. They were loaded aboard trucks and told that they were being returned to Luft III. They were let out at remote places to urinate, at which time Gestapo agents shot them. Their bodies were cremated and their ashes displayed at Sagan as an example to other would-be heros. One of the murdered fliers was Roger Bushel, a criminal-law silk from the Old Bailey, a close friend of Khaki Roberts of the British prosecution staff.

Thursday morning, March 21, Maxwell-Fyfe resumed his cross-examination. Sagan had been a crime known to Göring's chief subordinates, Sir David noted. "I am suggesting to you that it is absolutely impossible that in these circumstances, you knew nothing about it."

"Field Marshal Milch was here as a witness," Göring answered, "and, regrettably, was not asked about these points."

Maxwell-Fyfe's memory was as good as Göring's. "Oh, yes he was," the prosecutor shot back. "Milch took the same line as you, that he knew nothing about it. . . . Both you and Milch are now trying to shift the responsibility onto the shoulders of your junior officers." The attack on his honor jarred Göring. "That is untrue," he shouted. "You did nothing to prevent these men from being shot," Sir David snapped back. "You cooperated in this foul series of murders."

Maxwell-Fyfe was "crowding" Göring, barely waiting for the answers to be translated before firing the next question. Göring's sneers and brittle asides were nowhere evident. Beads of sweat glistened on his brow. The simultaneous interpreters flashed their warning lights to indicate that they were barely able to keep pace with the prosecutor. Justice Lawrence tapped his pencil, signaling Maxwell-Fyfe to slow down. Sir David knew exactly what he was doing, and he was not going to relent. He was deliberately flustering the witness. "I did not hear about this incident until after it occurred," Göring insisted. In fact, he had been on leave at the time of the Sagan escape.

The prey had been led to the pit. Sir David tumbled him into it. True, the *Reichsmarschall* had been on leave until March 29, 1944, he said, reading from his personnel files. But the executions of the Sagan fifty had gone on until April 13.

Justice Lawrence adjourned for lunch. During the break, Airey Neave, twice escaped from German prison camps himself, approached Maxwell-Fyfe, smiling broadly. "You've got him," Neave said. "I know how that must feel to you," Sir David answered.

That afternoon, Göring returned to the witness stand palming a card in his hand. On one side he had written, "Speak slower. Pause," and on the other, "Stand firm." As Maxwell-Fyfe approached, the press gallery watched as if savoring a gifted stage performer. The reporters loved the prosecutor's Old Bailey locutions: a reasonably uttered, "Now, I want to be perfectly fair," followed by a bald accusation of murder. "Let me remind you of the affidavit of Hoettl of the RSHA," Maxwell-Fyfe began. "He says that approximately four million Jews have been killed in the concentration camps, while an additional two million met death in other ways. . . . Are you telling this tribunal that a minister with your power in the Reich could remain ignorant that this was going on?"

"These things were kept secret from me," Göring said. "I might add that, in my opinion, not even the Führer knew the extent of what was going on." The victim again stood on the edge of the pit. Was Hitler innocent? He was going to read, Sir David said, from the Führer's comments to the Hungarian leader, Admiral Horthy. "The Jews," Hitler had told Horthy, "have been treated as germs with which a healthy body had been infected." "What else could that mean?" Maxwell-Fyfe asked. Without waiting for an answer, he began quoting from a report made to Göring in 1942: "There are only a few Jews left alive. Tens of thousands have been disposed of," the report read. Göring insisted that he had only known of "a policy of emigration, not liquidation of the Jews." The answer rang so hollow that the old cross-examiner knew that this was the precise moment to stop. With a nod to the president of the court, Sir David resumed his seat. The Russian, Rudenko, took over, and the Frenchman, Champetier de Ribes, completed Göring's cross-examination the following day.

That Friday evening, as Captain Gilbert made his rounds, he found Göring in an edgy state. "I didn't cut a very pretty figure, did I?" he said. Gilbert was quick to agree. Göring packed his meerschaum pipe and puffed rapidly. "Don't forget," he continued, "I had the best legal brains of America, England, France, and Russia against me. And there I was, all alone. I bet even the prosecutors think I did well. Did you hear anything?" Gilbert did not respond. "Did you see Rudenko," Göring went on, "he was more nervous than I was. . . . I gave him a good dig when he asked me why I didn't refuse to obey Hitler's orders. I told him, if I did, I certainly would not have to worry about my health!" That, Göring explained, was the code in dictatorships for liquidation. He laughed with his old bravado. "Rudenko understood me, all right." The odd mixture of anxiety and egotism intrigued Gilbert. Which, in the days to come, he wondered, would take the upper hand in the soul of Hermann Göring?

Fellow prosecutors flocked to Maxwell-Fyfe's office, heaping praise on his performance. "Hermann Göring," Sir David said, "was the most formidable witness I ever examined."

6

RUDOLF HESS'S DEFENSE was scheduled to follow Göring's. The prosecutors were making bets as to whether this erratic figure would take the stand himself. It had been only four months since Hess had told the court that he had faked amnesia for tactical purposes and "henceforth my memory will again respond to the outside world." Captain Gilbert believed Hess's memory was genuinely faltering again.

Hess had acquired a new lawyer since firing Gunther von Rohrscheidt, whom he had accused of failing to defend him vigorously. His attorney now was Alfred Seidl, ex-Nazi, ex–army officer, and also Hans Frank's counsel. The guessing game about Hess's intentions finally appeared to be resolved when Seidl predicted to a reporter for the British Sunday *Express* that his client would take the stand. Seidl also took advantage of the interview to lay the foundation for an insanity defense. Hess was having difficulties, Seidl claimed. "He may be slow in answering questions . . . his mind is wandering and he may not be very lucid. . . . Anything can happen. I hope there will not be a scene."

Gustav Gilbert visited Hess on Sunday, March 23, the day before he was to testify. The deep-set eyes seemed to rove unanchored beneath the massive black brows. A permanent grimace cut above his blue-bearded chin like a thin scar. Hess's sudden, pointless bursts of laughter unnerved the psychologist. Just as suddenly, the laugh would stop and Hess would shoot a look of menace at his visitor. A few days before, Gilbert had brought Hess news of his old mentor, Professor Karl Haushofer, the man who had first influenced him to fly to Scotland. Professor Haushofer and his wife were dead, Gilbert had reported. They had recently gone into the garden of their home and drunk arsenic sweetened with a liqueur. When Frau Haushofer did not die immediately, she hanged herself. Gilbert reminded Hess that Haushofer was supposed to have been a witness for him. He vaguely remembered the name, Hess said. Then he added with a cackle, "I hope none of my other witnesses leave me in the lurch by preferring death." Hess mentioned another witness he wanted called—his brother, Alfred. Gilbert wondered, was this another Hess joke? Alfred Hess was insane. Gilbert had difficulty envisioning Hess as a power on any nation's stage. Yet, he was familiar enough with the man's history to know that this rattling husk had once been a serious figure. There was even a time when a self-conscious, socially insecure Adolf Hitler had used Hess as his liaison to Germany's aristocrats and wealthy industrialists.

Rudolf Hess had not lived in Germany until he was fourteen. His father had been a successful export-import merchant living in Egypt, where Rudolf was born. Hess still waxed rhapsodic over the land of his birth. "What a paradise it was," he wrote to his wife from prison. "I will never be completely free of the garden of Ibrahimieh, with its flowers and its scents and all the indecipherable, imponderable influences of the place."

The First World War had saved him from unwanted entry into his father's business. He wrote his mother, "Share my joy. I am in the infantry." Also in the List Regiment, in which Hess served, was a runner whom he never met, Corporal Adolf Hitler. Hess, however, left the infantry and finished the war as a pilot, infected with a love of flying that never deserted him. He first heard the former corporal of his old regiment speak in the backroom of the tiny Sternacher Tavern in Munich. Less than a dozen people had come to hear Hitler prophesy: "The banner of our movement shall one day wave over the Reichstag in Berlin, indeed, in every German home!" Hess had concluded that he was listening either to the country's savior or to a madman. He decided to enroll as the sixteenth member of the Nazi party on July 1, 1920.

When Hitler's 1923 putsch from the Munich Bürgerbraukeller failed to bring down the Bavarian government, Hess happily followed his Führer into Landsberg prison. The months in this comfortable minimum-security fortress, under house arrest really, became the making of Rudolf Hess. Later deprecators liked to say that Hess's chief service to Hitler had been to type *Mein Kampf*. Not true. The two men influenced each other, and it was Hess who brought into Hitler's orbit the geopoliticist Professor Karl Haushofer. Hess neither typed nor took dictation at Landsberg. He fed Hitler ideas, one of which was lebensraum, "living space," later used to justify Germany's attempts to absorb its neighbors.

On his release from prison, Hess became Hitler's secretary. When the Nazis took power, he was named deputy führer, and *Reichsminister* without portfolio. While a Goebbels or a Göring battled officials for positions bathed in public light, Hess worked tirelessly at unsung tasks. He became, in effect, the party's control over the German bureaucracy. No domestic public law, decree, or rule could be issued without first passing through Hess's hands. No act desired by the Nazis could be denied by the government. It was as if a Republican or Democratic national chairman were to take control over the Washington government apparatus.

As he rose in power, Hess could finally indulge the peculiar drives that pulsed beneath his conventional exterior. His marriage was already an odd, arid affair. As his wife, the former Ilse Proehl, described him, "Rudolf rarely smiled, did not smoke, despised alcohol and had no patience with young people enjoying dancing and social life. . . ." Their only child had been born ten years after a marriage that reportedly had been ordered by Hitler.

Hess took up vegetarianism and nature cures. He established a hospital for quack treatments rejected by the medical profession. He irritated Hitler by bringing his own health foods to dinner meetings. In the mid-thirties, Hess invited the Führer to his new home in Isartal, a fashionable Munich suburb. Party legend had it that this visit cost

Hess the position of successor to Hitler. The Führer was said to have found Hess's home in such unremitting bad taste that he decided no such person could ever lead Germany. That was the moment, allegedly, when Hitler turned to Göring as his successor. Thereafter, year by year, Hess had found himself outfoxed by craftier, tougher players. The flight to Scotland, his last desperate bid for influence, had followed.

Now he sat in a jail cell with a psychologist testing how many numbers he could remember. He gave up on four forward and three backward. Gilbert asked if he had made a decision about testifying in his own defense. No, he said, he would not testify. He did not want to be embarrassed by his bad memory. And he did not want to be questioned by people he disliked.

Alfred Seidl was relieved by his client's decision. But what was Seidl to do this Monday morning to defend Hess? A diversionary feint was the best strategy, he concluded. He came into the court with three copies of a "document book" which he shared with the bench and the prosecution. The book proved to be a paste-up of articles and newspaper stories criticizing the Treaty of Versailles. Seidl and the prosecution argued as to the admissibility of this material, until Lawrence could stand it no longer. However unjust the defense might find the treaty, Sir Geoffrey asked, was Seidl saying that it justified the war the Nazis started and the horrors that followed?

Seidl next sought to introduce the recently unearthed secret protocol from the German-Soviet nonaggression pact under which the two countries divided up Poland and allowed the Russians to seize the Baltics. His intent was to demonstrate the unfitness of the Soviets to sit in judgment on Rudolf Hess or any other German. Seidl eventually managed to get the treaty introduced, where it lay inert, neither supported nor rebutted. Two witnesses were called to prove that an overseas organization once under Hess's direction had not been a spy agency. With this limp performance, Hess's defense ended. Since the defendant had not taken the stand, he could not be cross-examined.

The shrewder lawyers recognized Hess's nonappearance as a remarkable instance of passive resistance, of being crazy like a fox. The eccentric in the rumpled tweed suit in the dock may have sat out the war, but he had been a charter Nazi, the planter of the aggressive seed of lebensraum. In his role in the issuance of the Nuremberg Laws for the Protection of Blood and Honor, Hess had been among those who had lit the fuse for the future Holocaust. His silence, however, spared him the cross-examination that Göring had gone through on the Jewish question or any other damning matters.

7

CAPTAIN GILBERT HAD BEEN UNEASY ever since Major Kelley had departed, particularly since Kelley had left no address where he could be reached. When in mid-March he received a letter from Kelley, Gilbert's apprehension was hardly relieved. The trial was evidently going to drag on much longer than any of them had expected, Kelley wrote. Consequently, he might go ahead with a Nuremberg book of his own—in addition, of course, to their joint project, in which his interest had revived. By the way, would Gus please forward to him transcripts of the trial as it progressed? Gilbert experienced the sinking sensation of a man whose partner was going in to collect the reward while he was still out chasing the desperadoes.

Kelley's letter also had the effect of sharpening Gilbert's sense of guilt. The trial's conclusion was indeed nowhere in sight. His wife, Matty, had watched her friends' husbands come home from the war and renew normal lives, yet she was still alone, making do on Gilbert's modest captain's pay. Lately, as the dreary, broken city pressed down on him, Gilbert thought increasingly of leaving and taking his wife and child to the warmth and sunshine of California. But the counterforce was still stronger. As he put it bluntly in a letter to Kelley, "I want to see them hang," a sentiment no one had ever heard this seemingly reserved professional utter aloud in Nuremberg.

Gilbert told Kelley that he, too, might write a book of his own, a Nuremberg diary. And he was sorry, but the administration had clamped down on trial transcripts. He was allowed only one copy, and consequently would not be able to oblige Kelley. He closed saying that he was delighted to know that Doug was still at work on their material.

He could not leave Nuremberg, not yet. Not when such possibilities beckoned as the one now open to him. He was going off to meet Göring's wife. No one Kelley could talk to in the United States could match that kind of raw material.

Emmy Sonnemann Göring was the *Reichsmarschall*'s second wife, a bosomy, warmhearted, generous woman who had never managed entirely to escape the shadow of the first wife. Göring's first marriage had been a fairy tale besmirched by scandal and tragedy. Among his desultory attempts to find employment after the Great War, Göring had worked for a time as an air taxi pilot in Sweden. On one job, he landed on the estate of a Swedish nobleman and there met Carin von Kantzow, a rich and beautiful baroness. Carin was married and the mother of an eight-year-old son, but love conquered discretion. She scandalized Swedish society by running off with Göring to Munich. There Hermann, now thirty, tried unsuccessfully to resume the life of a student. They were spared destitution only because Carin's husband, believing his wife was merely having a fling, supported her and her lover. The prudish Hitler, however, disapproved of the affair and put pressure on his disciple to get married, which Göring did in 1923, as soon as Carin's divorce came through.

On November 9 of that year, a cold and blustery day, Hitler and a band of two thousand Nazis, banners snapping, marched on Munich intent on toppling the Bavarian government. In the front rank, next to Hitler, strode Hermann Göring, his voice lifted in a Brownshirt marching song. As they reached the center of town, shots rang out from the police. Göring toppled to the ground, struck in the groin by a bullet ricocheting off the pavement. It was then that storm troopers carried him into the Jewish home where two sisters stopped the bleeding and saved Göring's life.

As soon as she could move him, Carin spirited Hermann to Austria, beyond the reach of German authorities. In a hospital, his wound suppurating, delirious with pain, Göring was given morphine twice daily. He soon became addicted. He and Carin drifted through Italy, then went back to Sweden, living on her money. Hermann was unable to hold a job. He became violent and had to be forcibly restrained from jumping out of an apartment window. He failed in a drug withdrawal clinic, and Carin was forced to commit him to an asylum.

There, in solitary confinement, he stormed about shrieking, "I am not insane. This is all part of a Jewish plot!" Hermann Göring had touched bottom.

Eventually, he was weaned from his addiction, and in 1926 returned to Germany with Carin to begin life anew. He begged Hitler to put him on the slate for the next elections of the Reichstag. Hitler saw in this desperate failure a salvageable wreck, and agreed. In June of 1928, Göring won one of twelve Nazi seats. His wily mind seized the possibilities. Göring asked for the party's transportation portfolio. He was soon taking fat bribes to steer government contracts to favored aircraft manufacturers. He went on the payrolls of the Heinkel and BMW companies as a "consultant." Lufthansa provided him an office and secretary. A steel magnate furnished his luxurious new apartment on Berlin's swank Badenschestrasse. The beautiful, aristocratic Carin became a leading Berlin socialite.

In October 1931, Göring's world again collapsed. Carin, always troubled by a weak heart, died. He tearfully confessed to her niece that all his boasting, his striving, his admitted megalomania, had had one root—his resolve to give Carin a life as good as the one she had abandoned for him.

Within nine months, he was consoling himself with Emmy Sonnemann, a pretty, good-natured, thirty-seven-year-old blond actress separated from her actor husband. Emmy was unsophisticated, undemanding, apolitical, and apparently had not a jealous bone in her body. Göring's first gift to her was a photograph of his late wife. After a nearly four-year affair, Göring married Emmy in 1935. He had in the meantime become the second-ranking figure in the state after Hitler. He lived like an Aryan pasha. He built a palatial estate northeast of Berlin on a bluff overlooking the city—his fifth home, including two castles. He built the estate with government funds and called it Carinhall. He also named his two yachts after his first wife. Emmy did not object.

Emmy had numerous Jewish friends in the theater, and as the anti-Semitic decrees of the thirties began to wreck their lives, she asked her husband to intervene. Her special pleading put Göring on the spot with his regime. Still, he helped occasionally, enriching himself along the way by taking a bribe to get a Jew out of a concentration camp or secure a passport. He did perform one act of common decency: he arranged for the two Jewish sisters who had saved his life after the failed putsch to get out of Germany with their money. When General Karl Bodenschatz had testified in Göring's defense before the IMT, Stahmer had made sure that Bodenschatz got that fact into the record.

In 1937, Göring suffered an excruciating toothache. Hitler sent him to his personal dentist, who prescribed a new drug, a morphine derivative called paracodeine. Göring was to take six of the little pills a day until the pain stopped. The pain did stop, but Göring continued to take the paracodeine. Within a few months, he was up to thirty pills a day.

In 1938, Emmy presented Göring with his first child, a daughter, Edda. There was something about his vanity, his figure swollen from too much rich living, that prompted endless gibes about Göring's potency. Fellow Nazis joked behind his back that a Göring aide had fathered the child and that Edda stood for *Es dankt der Adjutant*, "All thanks to the adjutant." Streicher had savored the rumors and had gone public in *Der Stürmer* with his claim that Göring's daughter was not conceived by him. Göring's best defense was the child. Edda had a debatable asset for a little girl: she looked just like Hermann Göring.

Emmy Göring's fortunes had followed a roller-coaster course since the war's end. Early in her husband's incarceration at Nuremberg, Ensign Bill Jackson had tracked her to one of her homes, a lodge near Rosenheim in Bavaria. Jackson was hunting for documentary evidence. The door was answered by an ample Nordic woman of middle age, cautiously cordial. Jackson informed Emmy that he was required to search the house. She made no objection. Jackson unearthed no useful documents, but in the cellar he uncovered magnums of champagne and cases of cognac and scotch. In the attic he discovered humidors filled with Havana cigars and a cache of Lucky Strike cigarettes in the green packages that Americans had not seen since before the war. He opened a steamer trunk and felt like a pirate discovering buried treasure. The trunk was crammed with silks, furs, jewels, and boxes of gold coins. Jackson left the contents undisturbed and bade good-bye to Frau Göring.

Weeks later, Emmy Göring was arrested and put into Straubing prison. Little Edda was sent to an orphanage. Emmy remained confined for five months, until February 1946. By then, Allied occupation officials feared that her plight might arouse sympathy for Göring. They released her. But Emmy could not return to any of her opulent residences. Instead, she, Edda, and a niece went to live in a shack in Sackdilling forest near Neuhaus, with no running water, electricity, or heat. It was here that Gus Gilbert was traveling to see her.

He arrived on March 23, armed with a sympathetic manner, cigarettes for the mother, and candy for the child. They sat in a primitive kitchen while Emmy tried to play the gracious hostess, and her niece served tea. As Edda happily scampered off with her candy, Emmy said, referring to Hitler, "Can you imagine that madman ordering that child shot?" It was the opening Gilbert had wanted. What he hoped to have by the time he left Sackdilling were weapons to break through Göring's emotional defenses and get him to acknowledge guilt and renounce Hitler. Emmy spoke bitterly of the days after Göring left the Führerbunker in Berlin, how he and his family were to be executed because Hermann had been "disloyal." Göring had gone wild with rage, she said, cursing Hitler so savagely that she feared their guards would shoot him on the spot.

It amazed him, Gilbert said, in view of the fact that the whole world now knew Hitler was a monster, that her husband persisted in remaining loyal to his memory. "The only reason I can imagine," Gilbert offered, "is that he does it just to spite a foreign court trying to judge him."

One had to understand Hermann's sense of honor, Emmy said. Today, Germany was full of hypocrites saying they had never supported Hitler and that they had been forced to join the party. "It's sickening," she said. "And Hermann wants to show that he, at least, is not backtracking like a coward." But wasn't her husband putting himself in a terrible light by this blind loyalty? Didn't it look as though he condoned Hitler's murderous policies? She took out a frayed handkerchief and wiped her eyes. "He is a fanatic on the subject of loyalty," she said. "That is the one thing on which we cannot agree. Loyalty to a man who would murder my child?

"Hitler must have been insane," she went on. Hermann had ad-

mitted as much to her. He told her it would have been far better had
Hitler been killed in 1938 in an auto accident. He would then have
died a great German.

On his return to Nuremberg on Sunday night, bearing a letter from
Emmy and a postcard from Edda, Gilbert went directly to Göring's
cell. Göring grabbed the letter and the postcard. He joked a bit about
Hess's phantom defense of the previous week. Gilbert then mentioned
his recent visit. Emmy was distressed, he said, by Göring's stubborn
fealty to a man "who ordered you arrested and shot at the end, and
little Edda too." Göring shrugged. He did not believe Hitler had ever
ordered him shot. "That was the work of that dirty swine Bormann,"
he said. Gilbert pressed on. His wife was desperate to see him, if only
for a few minutes. She wanted to talk him out of his misguided notion
of loyalty. "My wife can influence me in lots of things," he said, "but
as far as my basic code? Nothing can sway me." These matters were
in the realm of men, he declared. "It's not a woman's affair."

A tired Gilbert rose to leave. It had been a long weekend. He
bade Göring good night and went to the prison office, where he wrote:
"Göring's medieval egotistical sense of values is complete down to the
'chivalrous' attitude toward women, which conceals its narcissistic purpose behind a façade of condescending protective indulgence and al-
lows no womanly humanitarian values to interfere with that purpose."

Gilbert's visit had nevertheless unsettled Göring. The psychologist's
words had forced him to consider the posture he had taken. But the
alternative to defiance was the belly-crawling contrition of a Speer or
a Frank, and that was not for Hermann Göring. He was fidgeting on
the edge of his cot, glaring angrily at the ever-present face in the
square porthole. Colonel Andrus had recently added a new security
measure; all chairs were taken from the cells during the night.
PFC Vincent Traina was leaning on the little shelf-door that hung
outward from the port. Göring came up to the door and ordered, "Get
me my chair!" The guard, jolted from his reveries, seized the blackjack
off the wall, rapped Göring's hand, and told him to sit down. Göring
began cursing and shrieking, "I have rights!" The guard flung the door
open, went in, and again ordered Göring to sit. Göring continued a
torrent of abuse. Traina beat him on his shoulder and then on his

upraised hands with the blackjack. Fritzsche, from the opposite side of the corridor, shouted for help. The duty officer came running, and led Traina out of the cell. What was going on? the officer wanted to know. Göring claimed that instead of giving him the chair when he asked for it, Traina had sat in it and made fun of him. Fritzsche called from across the way that what Göring said was true.

The puzzled officer looked to Göring. "You know me, Lieutenant," Göring said to him with melting sincerity. "Sure you know him," Traina broke in. "He's a Nazi killer and I'm just a GI." The fracas was duly reported to Colonel Andrus. His sentinel, Andrus ruled after an investigation, had "acted quite properly."

Riling his keepers was not a policy Hermann Göring could afford. He needed not antagonists but friends, like Tex Wheelis. He had already given Wheelis a handsome watch. Within the next few days, he managed to have a gold cigarette case extracted from his luggage in the baggage room, and he gave it to the lieutenant.

8

JOACHIM VON RIBBENTROP, once foreign minister of the Third Reich, was scheduled to begin his defense Tuesday, March 26. The week before, Ribbentrop's new lawyer, Martin Horn, had cornered Captain Gilbert during a midmorning recess. Horn, a young man with slicked-back black hair and a superior air, asked Gilbert if he had noticed anything strange lately in his client. The doctor no doubt knew, Horn said, that Ribbentrop had sent a letter to the tribunal offering to have himself tortured to death in expiation for Nazi atrocities. Yes, Gilbert said, he was familiar with the letter. Clearly, Horn went on, the man was suffering a nervous breakdown. Gilbert smelled an insanity plea and excused himself.

Horn found Ribbentrop as exasperating as had his predecessor, Fritz Sauter. The defendant's attention could not be focused long enough to proceed from A to B, before he was shooting off to Z, Horn complained. Ribbentrop paced constantly in his cell, rifling through disordered papers for the one document that would save him, and which he could never find. Horn had tested the insanity ploy because his client seemed to him a plausible candidate.

The night before Ribbentrop was to begin his defense, Colonel Andrus visited the cellblock. He looked into Ribbentrop's cell, but did not tarry. The mess and the odor repelled this spit-and-polish soldier. He asked only how Ribbentrop was sleeping. Ribbentrop ceased his dithering long enough to say, "You Americans certainly have better drugs than we Germans." Andrus agreed and walked on. He had discussed Ribbentrop's insomnia with the POW doctor, Ludwig Pfluecker. Andrus was afraid that if Ribbentrop hoarded sleeping pills, he might kill himself. If he took them, they could make him lethargic in the courtroom. The colonel feared a headline, DRUGGED PRISONER DRAGGED TO NUREMBERG DOCK. Pfluecker had come up with the solution—placebos compacted of baking soda provided by the mess hall. Thereafter, Ribbentrop slept like a lamb.

That evening, Ribbentrop was led to the visitors' room for a final conference with Horn before his defense opened the next day. As they faced each other through the chicken wire, Horn handed a single sheet of paper to the guard to check before passing it through the slot to his client. Earlier, Ribbentrop had written a note to Göring asking that he testify in his behalf. Göring had attended Hitler's key foreign policy sessions, and the *Reichsmarshall* could attest that the foreign minister had always tried for peaceful diplomatic solutions, Ribbentrop believed. He snatched at the letter. Göring had drawn a line through Ribbentrop's request and had written at the bottom, "I am only aware that Ribbentrop advised in favor of war."

Drexel Sprecher, making his own last-minute preparations to rebut the Ribbentrop defense, was discussing strategy with Colonel Harlan Amen over dinner at the Grand. Amen had been drinking heavily, which had no visible effect on his mind or his pugnacity. Sprecher was surprised to find himself working with Amen. His usual immediate superior was Amen's rival, Colonel Robert Storey.

The night after Jackson's cross-examination of Hermann Göring, Sprecher had talked with the chief prosecutor about the upcoming Ribbentrop case. He had been at work for some time on the rebuttal, and assumed that he would be helping Jackson prepare to cross-examine Ribbentrop. He found Jackson miserable with a head cold, impatient and irritable. Colonel Amen would be handling the cross-examination of Ribbentrop, Jackson informed Sprecher. Sprecher started to express his disappointment, when Jackson cut him off. That was all there was to it, he said. Sprecher wondered why Jackson was leaving the ring. Had the Göring experience shaken him that badly?

Ribbentrop, breaking the rules, jumped out of his bed after lights-out. A radio in the prison office was blaring American pop tunes. The guards playing basketball in the gym next to the exercise yard never stopped shouting. Even the thump of the ball on the gym floor could be heard in the cellblock. Ribbentrop yelled at his guard. They must cease all this racket. Tomorrow, he was going on trial for his life. The guard ordered him to shut up and go back to bed.

For Ribbentrop, driven to distraction by "Deep in the Heart of Texas," classical music had always been his greatest consolation. Ribbentrop thought of his violin as "the comrade who never let me down." Its song had given him solace after his mother's early death. The violin had quelled his adolescent passions. And when the war news was at its worst, he had played. But the sweetest notes for him had sounded in the wilds of Canada, his paradise lost.

Ribbentrop had gone to Canada in his youth in pursuit of a girl. He had lost the girl but had fallen in love with the country. Of course, Canadians could be rough. He had learned his English in England, and the Canadians were always mocking his "la-de-da" accent. They played tricks on him. Every time he went to put on his British tweed jacket, he would find the pockets full of stones, until finally he had to throw away the shapeless garment. It was just their unsophisticated sense of humor, he had concluded. He had stayed on, holding several jobs along the way—bank clerk in Montreal, draftsman for a construction company, newspaper reporter in New York. In 1914, the war broke out. He was back in Canada by then, intending to make it his home. He had only one kidney and could easily have avoided military service. But the pull of the fatherland proved too strong. Ribbentrop returned to Germany and to war.

Boris Polevoi leaned over the shoulder of Russia's famed cartoonist, Boris Yesimov. Polevoi watched, impressed at how quickly the artist caught Ribbentrop—the frightened, searching eyes, the shabby clothes, the look of an unemployed salesman with no job prospects. "You made the suit too baggy," Polevoi observed. "Don't worry," said Yesimov with a smile. "It will straighten out when they hang him."

"He always reminded me of impending doom," Howard Smith remarked. "In the old days, he looked handsome, even strong. He'd come into the reception room saying things like, 'Meine Herren, our abundant patience is exhausted. An hour ago, the Wehrmacht crossed the Russian border.' We were actually afraid of Ribbentrop in those days."

Justice Lawrence called the court to order. Martin Horn's first witness, Baron Gustav Steengracht von Moyland, was bald, distinguished, wearing a dark gray suit with a bloused handkerchief in his breast pocket. The baron had run the Foreign Office while Ribbentrop was running after Hitler. In the witness box he performed a useful if humiliating function for his old chief. Ribbentrop had repeatedly told him, the witness testified, that Adolf Hitler needed no foreign minister. He, Ribbentrop, was merely the Führer's traveling secretary.

Fräulein Margarete Blank, Ribbentrop's personal secretary, followed next. Horn asked what her boss's attitude was toward Adolf Hitler? "Herr von Ribbentrop always showed the greatest admiration and veneration for the Führer," she said. "To enjoy Hitler's confidence was his chief aim in life. In carrying out the role set him by the Führer, Herr von Ribbentrop showed utter disregard for his own interests." The prosecutors could barely contain their laughter. Maxwell-Fyfe whispered to an associate, "Don't they ever rehearse a witness?" No prosecutor asked to cross-examine Fräulein Blank. What she had said could scarcely be improved upon.

On April 1, Ribbentrop took the stand. After direct examination by Horn, Colonel Harlan Amen went after the witness with his customary ankle-biting ferocity. But it was Sir David Maxwell-Fyfe whom the audience had crowded the visitors' gallery to watch. Ribbentrop, during Horn's direct examination, had protested his innocence of Hitler's aggressive intentions. He had in his hand, Sir David said, a document dated March 15, 1939, surrendering the remaining independent part of Czechoslovakia to Germany. "Will you agree that the document was obtained from Czechoslovakia's president by the most intolerable threats of aggression?" the prosecutor asked. "No," Ribbentrop answered. But what further pressure could you put on the head of a country, Sir David asked, than to threaten that you would march in, in overwhelming strength, and also bomb Prague? "War, for instance," Ribbentrop answered primly. "War!" Sir David said in a moan of disbelief. "What is that *but* war?" Hjalmar Schacht leaned over to Gilbert standing near the dock. "Ribbentrop should be hanged for stupidity," he whispered. "There is no greater crime."

Ribbentrop had tried to pass off his rank as a general in the SS as merely honorary and foisted on him by Hitler. Sir David read from an application demonstrating that Ribbentrop had asked to join the SS three years before Hitler appointed him to any office. Furthermore, the papers established that he had applied for admission to the "Totenkopf," the Death's-Head Division, which ran the concentration camps. "Are you saying that you did not know that concentration camps were being carried on in an enormous scale?" Sir David asked. "I knew nothing about that," Ribbentrop answered. Maxwell-Fyfe asked that a map of Germany furled behind the witness box be unveiled. He then proceeded to read off the list of Ribbentrop's several homes. "These red dots on the map are concentration camps," he pointed out. Did Ribbentrop see how close five of his homes were to the camps? Maxwell-Fyfe snapped his folder shut, concluding his cross-examination.

The next day, Ribbentrop faced the French and Russian cross-examiners. Was it possible that Herr von Ribbentrop knew nothing of the extermination of the Jews? French prosecutor Edgar Faure began. Faure then read a memorandum prepared by Paul Schmidt, Hitler's interpreter, reporting a meeting between the Führer, Ribbentrop, and Admiral Miklós Horthy, the regent of Hungary. Hitler was quoted as demanding that Horthy hand over all the Jews in his country. Faure read Ribbentrop's words from the Schmidt account: "The foreign minister declared that the Jews were either to be exterminated or sent to concentration camps. There was no other alternative." "Did you say that?" Faure asked. Ribbentrop pouted. "Not in those words," he replied.

During Rudenko's turn, the Russian asked Ribbentrop, "Do you consider the seizure of Czechoslovakia an act of aggression?" "No," Ribbentrop answered. "Poland?" "No." "Denmark?" "No." "Norway?" "No." "Greece?" "No." "The Soviet Union?" "No." Ribbentrop was dismissed and returned to the dock. "You were not even interesting," Göring muttered.

Young Bill Jackson was in the Palace of Justice coffee shop when a guard approached to tell him that a woman wanted to see him. She had said she was Frau von Ribbentrop. Jackson told the guard to bring her to his office.

She was tall, dignified, refined. Gertrud von Ribbentrop explained that she had come to Nuremberg to see her husband. She hoped Mr. Jackson would help her. No family visits were permitted, Jackson explained; but he asked if he might otherwise be useful. Yes, she said, she wanted someone to tell Joachim that he should make out his will.

9

EIGHTEEN-YEAR-OLD PFC BILL GLENNY entered the cellblock singing. "Someday my grandchildren will ask me, Grandpa, what did you do in the war? And whatever else can I tell them? I opened and closed the cell door!" The parody had been written by another guard to the tune of "If I Had the Wings of an Angel." Glenny wailed the closing lyric, "Oh, if I had the bars of a captain, or the leaves of a major in gold, I would fly from this Nuremberg prison, and forever be quit of this hole!" Glenny relieved his predecessor and began a two-hour stint of watching Wilhelm Keitel play solitaire.

It was likely the worst job in Nuremberg, bracketed on one side by stupefying boredom and on the other by Colonel Andrus's ceaseless pressures. Virtually every combat veteran was long since gone from the prison staff. Glenny typified the men Andrus was now getting, young postwar draftees. On reporting for duty, he had been lectured, along with a half dozen other newcomers, by the colonel personally. They had been sitting in a room, chairs tilted back, telling jokes, until an officer with a pencil mustache, a riding crop, and a shining helmet appeared. The lieutenant accompanying him barked "Ten-shun!" Chairs clattered as the men jumped to their feet and, with barely an amenity, Colonel Andrus began to speak in staccato bursts: "You will never take your eye off the prisoner for more than two seconds. You will never allow a prisoner in bed to turn his back on you. You will never allow the prisoner to speak to another prisoner." To Glenny, the rules sounded farfetched, and the performance struck him as overacted.

Colonel Andrus had long ago given up trying to make the ISD into an elite unit. As he wrote to a friend after the latest batch of replacements arrived, "Some of the draftees are rubbish. Some of the officers shouldn't even have been enlisted men." But at least he now understood why all his requests for more and better-qualified personnel were rejected, even though the ISD was twenty percent below strength. General Lucian Truscott, now commanding the Third Army, always skimmed off the best new troops. "I get the slops they don't want," Andrus wrote. The implication was clear to him: the Americans, as they stiffened toward the Russians, were softening toward the Germans. Weak replacements were no accident. The army's apparent policy was to get seasoned, possibly vengeful soldiers out of Germany and replace them with GIs who had not seen the war and would get along well with the German people. "General Truscott," Andrus ended his letter, "is not in sympathy with the trial and hopes it will fail." Burt Andrus had been an army observer in London during the blitz. He remembered talking with a chambermaid cleaning his hotel room. She had lost her husband and a son at Dunkirk, and her home in the bombing. He himself had seen Dachau. How could people forget it all so soon? he wondered.

Admittedly, he leaned hard on his men, but he was merely passing along the pressure he took from above. Andrus was still summarily called in by General Leroy Watson and blamed for every theft, rape, or brawl in Nuremberg remotely attributable to his men. The colonel's letter of complaint to his cousin, General Clint Andrus, had been bucked up to headquarters for U.S. forces in the European theater. The chief of staff had written back saying that if the colonel could not get along with General Watson, perhaps he should ask to be relieved. This, Andrus felt, would have been an ignominious end to his career.

10

IF COLONEL ANDRUS HAD a model prisoner, it was Field Marshal Keitel, the man who never complained. This stoicism, however, won Keitel little credit among his countrymen. Göring described him as "a sergeant's mind in a field marshal's body." When Captain Gilbert once suggested to Keitel that he write his memoirs, Keitel asked what profit there would be in facing up to his life. It seemed to him an unbroken chain of misery; his youngest daughter dead of tuberculosis in 1940; one son killed and two more missing in Russia; his home destroyed in an air raid; his wife a virtual widow surviving on the charity of friends. In the end, the man for whom all the sacrifices had been made, all the humiliations swallowed, had repaid him with scorn. Hitler had written in his final testament that Keitel and the High Command were responsible for Germany's defeat.

During the war, Keitel had occasionally tried to salvage scraps of honor. He knew that the Wehrmacht intelligence chief, Admiral Wilhelm Canaris, was a patriot. Yet, Canaris had been among the nearly five thousand Germans executed in the orgy of vengeance following the Twentieth of July plot. Keitel had quietly slipped money to the Canaris family. But that was hardly redemption.

Early in the trial, his lawyer, Otto Nelte, a fifty-nine-year-old pragmatist, had tried to convince Keitel to confess. Even if they found him guilty, a soul-baring admission could mitigate his sentence, Nelte had argued. Keitel had agreed to consider the idea. But first he needed to consult with Göring, which he did in the exercise yard. Out of the question, Göring had told him. They had to present a united front. After a sleepless night, Keitel had told Nelte no—that because Göring had objected, he could not confess. Even in Nuremberg, he still obeyed orders.

Lackey, parrot, bootlicker, patsy, fall guy, weakling, messenger boy—all these gibes he had endured. What respect could such a man hope to retrieve? Admittedly, Keitel still cut an imposing figure as he walked, shoulders squared, to the witness box to begin his defense on April 3. His outward bearing, however, seemed merely to mock the craven interior man his colleagues knew. Maxwell-Fyfe waited his turn to cross-examine Keitel\ like a lion resting between feedings.

Keitel's lawyer rose from the defense table. Nelte's intention was to follow the Göring example, to ask his client questions eliciting full, self-serving answers, since Sir Geoffrey appeared content to let the defendants have their say. Who had been responsible for the sins laid at the feet of the German armed forces? Nelte asked. Keitel paused, then spoke firmly. "As a German officer, I consider it my duty to answer for all I have done," he said. "It will not always be possible to separate guilt from the threads of destiny. . . . But the men in the front lines, their officers and noncommissioned officers at the front, cannot be charged with guilt while the highest leaders reject responsibility. That is wrong and unworthy." The defendants in the dock sat up. The judges leaned forward. This was a Keitel none of them had expected to hear.

Nelte pointed out that Keitel's name appeared on the most odious orders. "What," the lawyer asked, "can you say in your defense?" "I bear the responsibility for whatever resulted from those orders. Furthermore, I bear the moral as well as the legal responsibility." Nelte raised an issue that to British eyes was the soul of dishonor, Keitel's role in passing along Hitler's order to execute the escaped Sagan RAF fliers. He had initially tried to avoid reporting the escape to Hitler, Keitel said, because he knew the Führer would react vengefully. But Himmler had already informed Hitler. Keitel thereafter argued against the Führer's determination to have the escapees shot, which merely made him the target of Hitler's wrath. He did at least talk Hitler out of shooting the men who had already been returned to Stalag Luft III, he explained. But in the end, he admitted, he had caved in to Hitler's demand for death.

General Jodl, in the back row of the dock, watched his old comrade with a flicker of sympathy. He remembered the day perfectly. He had known that Keitel was not the man to stand up to Hitler on this matter. He also knew instantly that this atrocity could never be explained away. Jodl had, in fact, told Keitel when the British arrested them in May 1945, "It is the Stalag Luft III business."

Keitel's defense entered its fourth day. On Saturday, April 6, Roman Rudenko led off the cross-examination. Rudenko relished the moment. To the Soviet prosecutor, Keitel's sudden nobility was poor recompense for the suffering the man's orders had inflicted on the Soviet people. He read from document R-98, the Reprisal Order, issued by Keitel, under which fifty Soviet hostages had been shot for every German soldier killed by partisans. Rudenko quoted Keitel: "One must bear in mind that in the countries affected, human life has absolutely no value." Had he signed the order containing this statement? Rudenko asked. Keitel answered yes. Rudenko asked if he considered this a proper order. Sweat beaded Keitel's brow. He had originally called for shooting five to ten hostages, he explained, but Hitler had upped the figure to fifty. Rudenko read from the same document. "The troops are, therefore, authorized and ordered to take any measures without restriction, even against women and children." Did not "any kind of measures" include murder? "Yes," Keitel admitted, barely audible, "but not of women and children."

Sir David Maxwell-Fyfe rose to continue the cross-examination. He questioned Keitel about Robert Paul Evans, a British seaman, age twenty. Evans had ridden a torpedo into a Norwegian fjord in an attempt to destroy the German battleship *Tirpitz*. "You have told us," Maxwell-Fyfe said, "that you have been a soldier for forty-one years. What in the name of all military tradition had that boy done wrong by operating a torpedo to attack a battleship?" Was this not a remarkable act of courage? "There is nothing wrong," Keitel agreed. "I recognize that it is right, a perfectly permissible attack." All the same, Robert Paul Evans on his capture had not been treated as a brave adversary, Sir David noted. He had been shot under Keitel's Commando Order. "What I want to understand is this," he went on. "You were a field marshal, standing in the boots of Blücher, Gneisenau, and Moltke. How did you tolerate all these young men being murdered?" He had explained, if not justified, his failure to resist Hitler in previous testimony, Keitel said. He could not go back and change that. But, he concluded, "I know that these incidents occurred and I know the consequences." Much of what he had gone along with, he said, was "against the inner voice of my conscience."

Sir David seized on the phrase. "Can you tell the tribunal the three worst things you had to do which were against the inner voice of your conscience?" It was a wild stab, the kind of self-incriminating question that a defendant usually dodges. Keitel, instead, spoke calmly, looking straight ahead as though examining his face in an unseen mirror. First, he said, were "the orders given for the conduct of the war in the East, which were contrary to the accepted usages of warfare." He paused and cleared his throat. "The question of the fifty RAF fliers. And, worst of all, the *Nacht und Nebel* decree. . . . I personally thought that to deport individuals secretly was much crueler than a death sentence." Maxwell-Fyfe had no further questions. Keitel's expression suggested a man from whom a heavy burden had finally been lifted.

As Keitel made his way back to the dock, Göring leaned toward him and hissed, "Why didn't you say anything about how the Allies treated our saboteurs? You bungled it!" Keitel simply resumed his seat. Göring's was a minority opinion. The men in the dock, the judges on the bench, the prosecutors at their table, all had come to the same conclusion. The man who left the witness box was better than the man who had entered it.

11

TELFORD TAYLOR HAD BEEN in Washington since mid-February, acting virtually as a recruiting sergeant. After the prosecution had rested its case, a mass exodus of staff had taken place. Colonel Robert Storey, in his fifties, too long away from home, had left. Jackson had been hard put to hold on to his next in line, the colorful Tom Dodd. Dodd was, underneath the raconteur and party lover, a family man who wrote to his wife every day and also longed to go home. Jackson had to beg him to stay.

Telford Taylor himself had thought hard about his own future. He was a man of acknowledged brilliance, certainly the most intellectual figure on the American side. Bobbie Hardy, his researcher, found Taylor, at age thirty-eight, "too young to be so wise." He was, she believed, "the most incisive mind I ever dealt with. He could pierce to the heart of your argument before you could explain it." On March 29, Jackson formally appointed Colonel Taylor to succeed him as chief counsel for the subsequent trials of hundreds of concentration camp operators, Nazi "scientists," and assorted butchers to be tried after the main trial ended. For a former government lawyer whose military service had been confined largely to code work, Taylor's rank of full colonel was already impressive. Still, if he was going to stay on, with some civilian lawyers earning a handsome ten thousand dollars per annum in Nuremberg, he wanted more inducement. He wanted a star. Thus, Telford Taylor was promoted to general that spring, an occurrence that momentarily united Colonel Andrus and General Watson. Watson, a West Pointer, and Andrus, with nearly twenty-eight years in the army, resented that a uniformed civilian, in effect, had won the rank regular soldiers spent a lifetime pursuing.

Back in Washington, the newly minted general was having little luck signing up lawyers. It was now peacetime. The men had come home and were not eager to leave again. Taylor informed Jackson of the one recruitment incentive that would work; he could persuade lawyers to sign on if they could bring their families.

That spring, the army at long last lifted the ban on spouses. Francis Biddle immediately sent for Katherine, who arrived in April with Elzie Wechsler, wife of Biddle's chief aide, Herb Wechsler. Biddle left the quarters he had shared with Judge Parker and their aides on Hebelstrasse and took one of the handsomest houses still standing, the Villa Conradti, bumping Frau Conradti, who became his housekeeper.

Katherine Biddle found Nuremberg abounding in ironies. As she explored the city by day and comforted her emotionally starved Francis by night, she tried to capture their singular existence. She sat in the library overlooking a green field and began writing "Love Song in an Occupied Country."

> More alone than survivors on a storm wracked island,
> Everywhere surrounded by alien sounds and faces,
> Alien earth and bread,
> Heart looks into heart to find its recognition.
> Love thrusts out the broken city,
> The shapes at the gabled windows.
> What lies in the unmarked mound under the leaves?
> Turn to me where the pallet is thin
> And the feather quilt smells of foreign herbs,
> The linen is rough and cold.

No longer alien or lost,
Your breast is all that I ask of home,
And your need of it my arms hold.

The departure of the Biddles for the Villa Conradti sharpened the
loneliness of Major Robert Stewart, Judge Parker's aide. Back at their
shared house on Hebelstrasse, Biddle had been Stewart's understanding ally in his daring romance with Tania Giliarevskaya. Now, Tania
was gone. Overnight she had simply disappeared back into the maw
of Russia. The researcher who had befriended her, Katy Walch, had
approached a Soviet officer at the Grand Hotel and demanded to know
what had happened to her. "Tania?" he said. "What Tania? We have
many Tanias."

Robert Jackson virtually disappeared from the court once the defense
case began. His subordinates had, however, warned him that the bench
was allowing the defense to introduce a deluge of irrelevant documents, bogging down the trial interminably. And so Jackson returned
on April 9 to make a heated criticism of the court's permissiveness.
The great majority of these documents, he argued, were useless, a
waste of the court's and the translators' time. Jackson was becoming
increasingly bitter, convinced that he had been ill used by the bench.
Geoffrey Lawrence's vaunted "fair play," he told his staff, was letting
the court get out of hand. Maybe the man could run a trial, but he
seemed to have no grasp of what was happening historically in this
room. Lawrence was refereeing a great moral contest as if it were a
cricket match, even bending the rules to give the foreign team a break.
Jackson was merely disappointed with Lawrence, but furious over
Francis Biddle. Once the man had been his friend. Now, through the
lens of repeated rejections in court, he saw only a puffed-up ego—a
man who, when he wasn't flaunting his French, was aping an English
lord, chewing his mustache and saying things like " 'Shtirring times,
indeed. Shtirring times.' "

Francis Biddle returned to his chambers as soon as court adjourned,
eager to be whisked home where his wife waited for him. His secretary
advised him, however, that Justice Jackson was demanding to see him
and Parker immediately.

Sir Geoffrey Lawrence was always ruling against him, Jackson said testily, pacing, hands jammed into his pockets. Lawrence had just done so again on his request to limit the defense to relevant documents. He was fully aware that Biddle controlled Lawrence like a puppeteer. Did Biddle realize what he was doing? Jackson asked. He was demoralizing people who were working night and day to bring justice to a wounded world. Biddle sat behind his desk, fingertips pressed together, presenting the exterior coolness produced by five generations of good breeding. Parker sat, hands folded across his paunch, studying Jackson over the tops of his glasses, his round face pained. Jackson went on: He had said it before and he would say it again. If he and his people were to be continuously overruled, while the bench stood the law on its head to favor the defendants, then he might as well go home. With that, Jackson stormed out.

12

To CAPTAIN GILBERT, Ernst Kaltenbrunner was among the most detestable defendants. Kaltenbrunner's guilt was immediate and personal. Alone among them, he had set his hands directly on the levers of extermination. As chief of the RSHA, the Reich Central Security Office, serving directly under Himmler, Kaltenbrunner had been responsible for the SD and the Gestapo, which had dispatched people to the camps. Adolf Eichmann, now understood to be the engineer of extermination, and who had managed to slip through the Allied dragnet, was a Kaltenbrunner subordinate and friend. In cell visits to the others, Gilbert strove to maintain his posture of professionalism, and, with his little gifts of cigars or candy, even to appear sympathetic. But to be in Kaltenbrunner's presence was akin to sitting with the murderer of one's mother, one's wife, one's child. Still, Gilbert had an obligation to the court to monitor the mental state of every defendant. He also had at his disposal in Kaltenbrunner an executive of mass murder to dissect for his book. And so, early Thursday morning, April 11, the day Kaltenbrunner's defense was to begin, Gilbert stopped by cell 26.

The prisoner seemed in reasonably good emotional condition, except for a slight hesitation in his speech traceable to his stroke. Kaltenbrunner mouthed the same rationalizations that Gilbert had heard from him before. His relationship to the concentration camps existed only on organization charts. Others had run them at Himmler's direction. He had occupied himself solely with intelligence matters. He had never issued an order for anyone's death. He had never seen a death camp. He had not known they existed.

Kaltenbrunner's lawyer, Kurt Kauffmann, forty-four years old, spare, tall, had the hot eye of the fanatic. As soon as his client was sworn in, he plunged ahead. "You are aware that you are under extremely serious charges," he said. "The prosecution connects your name with the Gestapo terror and the atrocities of the concentration camps. I now ask you, do you assume responsibility for the counts as charged?" The lawyers at the prosecution table looked on with admiration. Few of the Germans seemed to have grasped the dynamics of the Anglo-Saxon adversarial system, the duel of wits between lawyers. Kauffmann appeared to have absorbed a defense fundamental: Get the worst out under direct examination on your own terms. Steal the cross-examiner's thunder. Kaltenbrunner answered that, technically, he accepted responsibility for actions carried out in his domain. "I know the hatred of the world is directed against me," he went on, now that Himmler, Gestapo chief Heinrich Müller, and Oswald Pohl, who ran the concentration camps, were all dead. But his liability was solely technical. These men had been the actual evildoers. Kauffmann asked about his client's signature on thousands of orders sending people to the camps and to their death. "Not once in my whole life did I ever see or sign a single protective custody order," Kaltenbrunner answered. The signatures Kauffmann was referring to were facsimiles, or had been typewritten. "You will admit this statement of yours is not very credible. It is a monstrosity," Kauffmann observed.

Kauffmann read into the record from a document indicating that Kaltenbrunner had ordered the execution of a team of OSS agents captured in uniform behind the lines. He asked his client to explain. "Completely out of the question," Kaltenbrunner answered. Such behavior would have been "a crime against the laws of warfare."

Kauffmann referred to earlier testimony by a prosecution witness, a camp guard, who had sworn that Kaltenbrunner watched while the gas chamber was demonstrated on Mauthausen inmates. "I never saw a gas chamber," Kaltenbrunner answered. "I did not know they existed at Mauthausen. . . . I never set foot in the detention camp at Mauthausen—that is, the concentration camp proper." Under Kauffmann's relentless pounding, Kaltenbrunner began shrieking his answers.

Kauffmann finished his direct examination and yielded to the prosecution. Sir David Maxwell-Fyfe and the other prosecutors recognized that they had overestimated their man. It was not that Kauffmann had picked up the subtleties of the adversarial system. He had learned only the prosecutorial side of it. Maxwell-Fyfe himself could not have done a better job of incriminating Ernst Kaltenbrunner.

During cross-examination, a voice reached from the grave to condemn Kaltenbrunner. The RSHA chief had heard earlier, to his relief, that the Mauthausen commandant, Fritz Ziereis, had died in a shootout at the end of the war. But John Harlan Amen produced a deathbed confession that Ziereis had made implicating Kaltenbrunner in the plan to suffocate surviving Mauthausen inmates in a sealed-off tunnel and in other atrocities.

The prosecution also questioned Kaltenbrunner about earlier testimony that placed him at Mauthausen, where, reportedly, he had witnessed demonstration executions by shooting, hanging, and gassing.

As the cross-examination ended and Kaltenbrunner returned to the dock, he passed Captain Gilbert. "I saw your people holding their sides with laughter," he said. "Please extend my congratulations to them for finding me such a stupid attorney."

13

GUNTHER SADEL, of General Watson's counterintelligence unit, enjoyed sitting in the visitors' gallery watching Kaltenbrunner laid bare. Such men had destroyed Sadel's family, parting his Jewish father and Gentile mother, and forcing Sadel to flee to America with his father seven years before. When he arrived at Nuremberg, he had had no idea if his mother was dead or alive.

On learning of this situation, Watson had told Sadel to cut himself a set of orders, take a jeep, go to Berlin, and look for her. Sadel had found Berlin no less devastated than Nuremberg, except that its state pained him more. Berlin had been home. He located the apartment house—scarred but still standing—where he had grown up. He walked to the third floor and there on the door was a tarnished plate with "Sadel" inscribed on it. His mother answered the bell.

Watson, on learning the news, had done the sort of thing that would inspire Sadel to walk through fire for him. The general had ordered Sadel's mother to Nuremberg as a "witness," entitling her to government transportation, rations, and living accommodations.

Sadel was summoned from the visitors' gallery during the Kaltenbrunner testimony to take on a new assignment for the general, one no odder than a dozen others the young PFC had already performed—setting up the social pass system, tracking down rumors of prison breaks, finding a pedigreed dog for an American reporter, and slipping a German into Andrus's jail as a "material witness" to spy for Watson. Sadel's latest task, the general told him, involved the daughter of the novelist Thomas Mann. Erika Mann, who was covering the trial, was rumored to be a lesbian and living with a Frenchwoman. Watson did not give a damn, he said, about the woman's love life. But she was well connected, and he was responsible for security. Watson suspected that another reporter was playing Peeping Tom on her apartment. Sadel was to stop it.

14

LIEUTENANT COMMANDER WHITNEY HARRIS COULD scarcely believe his good fortune. The British, he learned, had in custody Rudolf Franz Ferdinand Hoess, whose name was similar to that of the sometime amnesiac already in the dock, Rudolf Hess. Harris arranged to have Hoess transferred to Nuremberg, where he interrogated him for three days. What Hoess revealed was staggering, even by Nuremberg standards. But what to do with the information? Harris wondered. The prosecution case had already ended. Then, incredibly, Kaltenbrunner applied to have Hoess appear as a witness in his defense. Why he had done so was a mystery, unless he hoped to diminish his own guilt by comparison with someone whose deeds were even blacker. Rudolf Hoess had been the commandant of Auschwitz.

In the end, as in the case of Einsatzgruppe D commander Otto Ohlendorf, Whitney Harris was deprived of the full reward of his enterprise. If there was any cross-examining of Hoess to be done, John Harlan Amen would do it. That was how it worked in the big law firms, Harris suspected. Unsung young men did the plowing and the sowing; the older partners came along and reaped the harvest.

Rudolf Hoess's family, devout Catholics, had intended him for the priesthood. His father was stern, unapproachable, a godlike figure in young Rudolf's mind. The elder Hoess had made his son feel that his every misdeed wounded him personally. Rudolf had protected himself by gradually withdrawing from involvement with other people where he might run afoul of his father's strictures. He did not, however, become a priest. Instead, early in the Hitler regime, Hoess became a professional concentration camp administrator, starting at Dachau in 1934.

Whitney Harris watched from the sidelines, still struck by the ordinariness of this civil service cipher, as Hoess took the stand. Kurt Kauffmann, Kaltenbrunner's lawyer, invited Hoess to tell his story. In the summer of 1941, Hoess began, he was commandant at Auschwitz, a new concentration camp built on farmland in Poland. He was enlarging the camp to accommodate 100,000 prisoners, whom he expected to employ in agriculture. Instead, he explained, "I had to go to Himmler in Berlin where he imparted to me the following: 'The Führer has ordered the Final Solution, the *Endlösung*, of the Jewish question. We, the SS, have to execute it.'" Auschwitz had been picked because it was well situated for transportation and isolated enough for secrecy. Hoess still did not fully understand what he was supposed to do. Shortly afterward, Obersturmbannführer Adolf Eichmann came and explained Hoess's new duties in greater detail. He would get a better idea, Eichmann told him, by visiting a camp at Treblinka, near Warsaw.

In the course of Hoess's recital, only one point made was of any possible value to the defendant for whom he had been called. Kurt Kauffmann elicited that while Hoess was commandant of Auschwitz, Ernst Kaltenbrunner had never visited the camp. For the prosecution, this admission was a cheap price to pay for the coming right to cross-examine Hoess.

John Harlan Amen replaced Kauffmann at the stand and read aloud from the affidavit Whitney Harris had taken from Hoess describing his visit to Treblinka. In it, Hoess explained that he had been unimpressed by the Treblinka operation. It had taken the commandant there six months to eliminate eighty thousand Jews using monoxide gas. Hoess had a better idea. One of his Auschwitz guards had accidentally taken a whiff of Zyklon B, a chemical disinfectant used in the camp laundry. The man had passed out instantly. If a little of the chemical killed lice, enough should kill humans, Hoess and his staff reasoned. He tested the Zyklon B on Soviet prisoners of war locked in a room, and it worked. The substance was dropped from a hole in the ceiling, reacted instantly with oxygen in the air, and within three to fifteen minutes, the victims were dead.

Hoess outdid Treblinka tenfold. He built gas chambers to accommodate two thousand inmates at a time, compared to Treblinka's two hundred. He had two large crematoria built with four double ovens heated by coke. With these facilities, "It was possible to get rid of ten thousand people in twenty-four hours," Hoess affirmed. But that peak had been reached only once, in 1944, "when train delays caused five transports to arrive all in one day."

Hoess had overcome other deficiencies spotted at Treblinka. There, the prisoners realized what was happening to them, which created control problems. At Auschwitz, Hoess worked out a less stressful system. Freight cars would pull up to a railhead, where the passengers were unloaded. Upon delivery of their human cargo, train crews and guards were sent away, replaced by camp personnel sworn to secrecy; any revelation of what went on at Auschwitz was punishable by death. The new arrivals were then marched past SS doctors, who judged their fitness to work. The able-bodied, averaging twenty-five percent of a shipment, were taken into the camp and issued black-and-white-striped uniforms. Those unfit to work—the old, the sick, and those "of tender years," as Hoess described them—were taken directly to the gas chambers. They were ordered to undress and told not to forget where they had left their clothes, while they went in to take a shower. The chambers actually had showerheads, pipes, and drains. Usually the ruse worked. As Hoess wrote in a poem:

> In the spring of '42 many blossoming people walked under
> 　　the blossoming fruit trees of the old farmstead,
> To their death, without premonition.

These innovations enabled Hoess to dispose of some two and a half million people during his tenure at Auschwitz.

After reading the affidavit, Amen asked Hoess how many people it had taken to kill two thousand persons a day. Hoess explained that he had had a staff of approximately three thousand men. He also made clear that he had not tolerated gratuitous cruelty. His men were there to exterminate people, not to torment them. Any misconduct by guards was punished by detention, transfer, and, if serious enough, by whipping. No guards, however, were compelled to kill. If they protested, they would simply be assigned to other duties.

At the end of the day, Captain Gilbert went to Hoess's cell on the second tier of the prison. The man jumped to his feet, but otherwise his face retained the same expression of ennui that the courtroom spectators had seen. "I suppose you want to know if my thoughts and habits are normal," Hoess said. "What do you think?" Gilbert asked. "I am entirely normal," Hoess answered. "Even while doing this extermination work, I led a perfectly normal family life." Gilbert invited the man to go on. Hoess did admit to one peculiarity: "I always felt happiest alone. . . . I was always self-sufficient. I never had close relationships, even in my youth. I never had a friend." He could watch people enjoying themselves, he said, but he could never join in. He had enjoyed most the period after the war, when he was a fugitive hiding on a farm with horses as his sole companions. "No," he went on, "I never had any need for friends. I never had any real intimacy with my parents, with my sisters."

Gilbert asked Hoess whether the Jews he had murdered had deserved their fate. He had never in his life heard anything else, Hoess explained. His whole political and educational formation had taught him that the Jew was Germany's enemy. He had never considered that there might be another side to the question, because he had never heard another side. Even so, it did not matter. He was an SS man. "We were all so trained to obey orders without thinking that the thought of disobeying never occurred to anybody. . . . I never gave much thought to whether it was wrong. It just seemed a necessity."

For Gilbert, it had all fallen into place at last. The puzzle of "why" was complete. He sat in his half-lit office in the courthouse, eyes fixed on a wall papered with duty rosters and the colonel's regulations. Gilbert's knowledge of German history was sufficient to tell him that Hitler had not invented anti-Semitism or the cult of obedience. At the beginning of the nineteenth century, the philosopher Johann Gottlieb Fichte had preached from the University of Berlin that Latins and Jews were decadent. Later, Georg Wilhelm Friedrich Hegel, from the same professorial chair, had glorified the state and ridiculed the pursuit of individual human happiness. Periods of "happiness" were the fetid pools of history, Hegel taught. War and heroes, absolved of conventional considerations of morality, were like cleansing winds that swept a nation to greatness. Another early thinker, Heinrich von Treitschke, had taught young Germans, "It does not matter what you think, as long as you obey." Adolf Hitler had merely sown his seed in receptive earth.

Today, in room 600, Gilbert had seen it all converge in one insignificant human being. Talking to the condemned SS prisoners at Dachau, he had concluded that institutionalized slaughter demanded a culture that placed obedience above thinking. "The thought of disobeying an order would simply never occur to anybody," Hoess had said. In the earlier testimony of Otto Ohlendorf, as he coolly explained how his Einsatzgruppe D shot ninety thousand people, the second piece of the puzzle had slipped into place: You can do it when you are persuaded that you are killing not people but pernicious, subhuman creatures. The indoctrination film *The Eternal Jew*, shown to German troops, had depicted Jews as rats infesting and infecting the nation. "We took it for granted we had to protect Germany from the Jews," Hoess had told Gilbert.

But these two forces, blind obedience and race hatred, while sufficient to account for the assembly-line slaughterers, still did not explain the architects and engineers of the Final Solution, such educated, even sophisticated men as Ohlendorf and Hoess. The final piece had been provided to Gilbert by the latter, the man who "never had a friend," who preferred the company of horses to that of people. Gilbert began writing: Rudolf Hoess was "outwardly normal, but lacked something essential to normality, the quality of empathy, the capacity to feel with our fellow man." Hoess had described the millions at Auschwitz not as people, but as "shadows passing before me." Combine unthinking obedience, racism, and a disconnection from the kinship of mankind, and you could produce an Auschwitz commandant.

His arriving at a solution that satisfied the mind served only to depress Gilbert's spirits. Every society had its authority-ridden personalities. Bigots exist all over. And schizoids, dead to normal feeling, walk the streets every day. The latent ingredients could be found everywhere. The distinction in Nazi Germany had been that these people had not functioned on the margins of society. They had run it.

15

COLONEL ANDRUS STUDIED the invitation with mixed astonishment, curiosity, wariness, and not a little pleasure. The press corps was inviting him to a party to celebrate his birthday at the Faber-Castell castle in Stein. The colonel's relations with the press had scarcely improved over the months. The stories reporters wheedled out of his staff got him into hot water with the court. Recently, *Stars and Stripes* had carried what appeared to be an interview with Hermann Göring, for which Andrus had caught hell from Justice Lawrence. Actually, an enterprising reporter had managed to get Otto Stahmer to slip a list of questions to his client.

To Andrus, the best way to get one's hand bitten was to feed the press. For their part, the reporters regarded Andrus with frustration. As much as the cells, sentries, and walls of the prison, he stood between them and the stories they wanted most—direct interviews with the defendants. Their invitation, Andrus thought, might be part of a softening-up operation. On the other hand, he personally had enjoyed a good press. In most stories, he was portrayed as an American archetype, the broncobuster who could break the toughest Nazi, the nononsense jailer of Nuremberg. He decided to accept the invitation.

The date set was April 15, the day after Rudolf Hoess completed his testimony.

The colonel found the press bar crowded with faces he recognized from the courtroom. Boris Polevoi, an admirer, threw a welcoming arm around the colonel. A correspondent from Chicago joshed Andrus about an article reporting that he used profanity in dealing with his prisoners. Andrus had a theory about cussing that he would share with them, he said. Swearing fit two occasions: "When you can't get people to believe you unless you get mad, and when you deal with a select group of sophisticates, like you people, who find a well-placed 'son of a bitch' amusing." The crowd laughed, and the colonel beamed. He was off to a good start.

The talk turned to the Hoess testimony. An English reporter asked what the moral difference was if you gassed people on the ground or cooked them from the air. Look at the firestorms in Hamburg and Dresden. Some 600,000 Germans had died in air raids, twenty times more than in Britain. Arthur "Bomber" Harris, British author of the level-the-cities strategy, had as much blood on his hands as a Rudolf Hoess. The Americans had better not be so bloody high-minded either, the Englishman went on. Look at Hiroshima and Nagasaki.

Andrus said that he was a simple soldier and had no intention of getting enmeshed in ethical dilemmas. An American reporter offered an answer. He had not noticed any Allied bombs dropped on Germany since the war ended, the reporter said. But did anyone believe that the slaughter of the Jews would have stopped if Germany had won the war? Besides, how many SS men had died pushing helpless people into gas chambers? Over sixty thousand Allied airmen had lost their lives pounding Germany into surrender.

The reporters went virtually down the cellblock, asking the colonel about each defendant's quirks. Andrus avoided personal observations and confined himself to describing his rigid security measures. As the evening ended, he concluded that they were not such a bad lot. He had enjoyed his birthday party.

16

Hans Frank's DEFENSE represented something of a personal invest-
ment to Captain Gilbert. He did not want Frank or any of them
absolved. What he hoped for on the stand was admission of wrong,
remorse, repentance. To Frank's credit, he had been virtually the first
to stand up to Göring's bullyragging. His reborn Catholicism, with
its promises of an afterlife, seemed to have given him reason to die,
if not to live. But the man was subject to manic swings. In one recent
visit, Frank had told Gilbert, "Today is Palm Sunday and I swore by
the crucifix that I will tell the truth and expose the sin as my last act
on earth. Let the chips fall where they may." But the very next day,
after a recess in the Hoess testimony, Gilbert had overheard Frank
tell Rosenberg, "They are trying to pin the murder of two thousand
Jews a day in Auschwitz on Kaltenbrunner. What about the thirty
thousand people killed in the bombing of Hamburg in a few hours?
How about the eighty thousand deaths from the atomic bombing of
Japan? Is that justice?" Frank's spine, Gilbert feared, was malleable.

Two days before Frank's defense was to begin, Gilbert had found
the man in his cell close to tears. He had read in a newspaper of the
death at Auschwitz of a Dr. Jacoby. He realized that this victim had
been his father's dearest friend in Munich, "a fine, kindly, upright old
man." After listening to Hoess, it had sunk in; Jacoby had been one
of that nameless herd extinguished daily at Auschwitz. "And I had
done nothing to stop it," Frank cried. "No, I didn't kill him myself.
But the things I said, and the things Rosenberg said, made those horrors possible. I have decided I must expiate my guilt." Gilbert had left
the cell with no idea which side this unstable figure would come down
on when he took the stand.

Hans Frank was sworn in on the morning of April 18. His lawyer,
Alfred Seidl, small, fussy, unimpressive, had been dubbed "Mickey
Mouse" by Göring. "Did you," Seidl asked, "ever participate in the
annihilation of the Jews?" In truth, Frank could evade. He had run
no death camps. He had risked going back to Germany from Poland
to make speeches supporting the rule of law. He had hated Himmler.
Auschwitz had not been in the part of Poland under his control. And

he had a gift for rationalizing his behavior. "I say, yes," Frank responded, his voice tremulous. "And the reason I say yes," he continued, "is because having lived through the five months of this trial, and particularly after having heard the testimony of the witness Hoess, my conscience does not allow me to throw the responsibility solely on minor people. I myself have never installed an extermination camp for Jews . . . but we have fought against Jewry for years; and we have indulged in the most horrible utterances. My own diary bears witness against me. Therefore, it is my duty to answer your question with yes." He paused, then spoke with quiet force. "A thousand years will pass and still Germany's guilt will not have been erased."

Gus Gilbert heard the answer with something that fleetingly approached admiration.

Waiting for the elevator, Frank looked around at his countrymen. Who was with him? Who reviled him? Hans Fritzsche, the old radio propagandist, edged his way toward him. Fritzsche was a reasonable man, one of those most shamed by the revelations of atrocities. "According to your own diary," Fritzsche said, "you not only smelled what was going on, you knew what was going on. It would have been more honest if you said so, instead of trying to hide among the millions of our people, hanging them"—he mimicked Frank's witness-stand emotion—"with one thousand years of guilt!" Fritzsche spun away. Frank was stung. He had felt cleansed by his unburdening. But Fritzsche, whom he regarded as a friend, had turned on him. What were the others thinking?

17

JUSTICE JACKSON WAS DELIGHTED to get away from Nuremberg and spend a few days in the baroque splendor of Prague, to which the Czechoslovakian president, Edvard Beneš, had invited him. He had left in mid-April, and entrusted direction of the American cross-examination to John Harlan Amen. In Prague, Jackson attended the trial of Karl Hermann Frank, the "Butcher of Lidice," no relation to Hans Frank. This Frank, among other crimes, had presided over the razing of the Czech city and the execution of all its male inhabitants in retribution for the assassination of Reinhard Heydrich. The trial was over quickly. Frank's execution was set for May 22, less than five weeks after the trial's beginning.

The swiftness of Czech justice heightened Jackson's concern over the seemingly interminable character of the Nuremberg trial. He had believed at one time that the case would be wrapped up by Christmas. Four months later, the end was still nowhere in sight, thanks in part to the limitless latitude Lawrence was granting the defense. The longer the trial dragged on, Jackson feared, the less sharp would be the bite of its judgments. Moral outrage, even over the Nazis' enormities, could not be sustained at a befitting level indefinitely.

While in Prague, Jackson was treated royally by the Czech government, a welcome sensation after the pressures and irritations of Nuremberg. Lately, a new source of friction had added to his discontent. He was being sniped at by colleagues on the Supreme Court. Jackson was not surprised that his archfoe, Justice Hugo Black, had ridiculed the IMT, calling it a "serious failure" and blaming the chief prosecutor. But his Washington agent, Charlie Horsky, had recently reported more dismaying news. Good, gray, upright Chief Justice Harlan Fiske Stone was telling intimates that Bob had gotten himself into a nasty business. The Nuremberg trial, according to America's ranking jurist, was nothing but "a high-grade lynching." To Jackson, returning to the Palace of Justice held out scant appeal.

The court went into Easter recess on April 19, and was not to resume until Tuesday, April 23. Captain Gilbert by now moved like a blinkered workhorse, permitting himself virtually no life outside the cells and the courtroom. The day before the recess, Gilbert had spoken at length with Göring on the nature of war. "Of course, the people don't want war," Göring told him. "Why would some poor slob on a farm want to risk his life in a war when the best he can get out of it is to come back in one piece? The common people don't want war; not in Russia, not in England, not in America, not for that matter in Germany. It's the leaders who determine the policy . . . and the people can always be made to do the leaders' bidding. All you have to do is tell them they are being attacked and denounce the pacifists for lack of patriotism. It works the same way in any country." Gilbert wondered what was the point of discussing morality with a man who understood the world with such crystalline cynicism.

On April 22, Harlan Stone, the chief justice, while reading a dissenting opinion in the U.S. Supreme Court, collapsed and died. Jackson's friends were instantly on the transatlantic telephone with one message. If he wanted to succeed Stone as chief justice, he must come home at once. Jackson conferred with people he trusted—Elsie Douglas, his son, Bill, a few others. Bob Jackson was a romantic with a realistic streak. He wanted the chief judgeship desperately. It would make his return to the court a triumph instead of a chore. But how could he walk out on the unfinished business in Nuremberg to lobby for a job in Washington? It was unseemly. If he gave an interview to the press, if he went to visit the troops, Marble Room pundits already had it that he was laying pipe for a run for the presidency. The month before, James Farley, the manager of two of Franklin Roosevelt's presidential victories, had been among the VIPs who flocked to the visitors' gallery. According to the Nuremberg party circuit, Farley had obviously come to sound out Jackson about a White House bid.

    Columnist Drew Pearson broke a story claiming that Justices William O. Douglas and Hugo Black had threatened to quit the court if Truman named Jackson as chief justice. No denials were heard from either man. Jackson could not openly express his hunger for the job. He could only stay in Nuremberg and hope for Harry Truman's nod.

18

THE COUNTESS INGE KALNOKY OFTEN FELT herself playing the role of animal tamer, keeping congenital enemies apart. Under the roof of the Witness House she lodged camp survivors and former Gestapo agents, members of the anti-Hitler resistance and intimates of the Führer, such as Heinrich Hoffmann. The most unsympathetic of the guests turned out to be a huge-bodied, half-blind giant with thick glasses, Hans Bernd Gisevius, whose natural pose was arrogance and whose native language was sarcasm. Kalnoky, however, extended her considerable charm even to Gisevius. The effort was part of her desire to think better of her fellow Germans. She was sickened by the way they groveled before the Americans, denounced and spied on each other. Even Gisevius, so ready to demolish his intellectual inferiors, scraped before every American second lieutenant who stopped by the Witness House. And, Kalnoky was honest enough to admit, she did the same.

However dismissive of her other guests, Gisevius treated Kalnoky with rare chivalry. He revealed to her that he had been a member of the early Gestapo, was ousted in a power play, and wound up in the *Abwehr*—military intelligence. He was now feted by the Americans, he pointed out, because he had been a spy for the OSS during the war and part of the Twentieth of July plot. He had been called to Nuremberg as a defense witness for his former boss, onetime Nazi minister of the interior Wilhelm Frick. It struck Kalnoky as odd that this former Allied spy, this member of the anti-Hitler resistance, was to be a witness for a Nazi. Gisevius answered slyly that he did not know how useful he would be to Frick.

Among the defendants in the dock, Wilhelm Frick was the invisible man, his only distinguishing feature being the incongruous checkered sport jacket he wore every day. His lawyer, Otto Pannenbecker, had had to scramble desperately to find anyone who could help his client. Frick certainly could not help himself. The man was capable only of parroting stale Nazi dogma; thus Pannenbecker had no intention of putting him on the stand. Gisevius had been a long shot. Since he had worked for Frick, he might at least be able to establish that the man had exercised no real power, since he had lost it all to smarter, more ruthless Nazis.

Gisevius testified on April 24. Pannenbecker went through the direct examination and yielded to the American prosecutor. All eyes turned to Robert Jackson, who had grown tired of behind-the-back critics whispering that he had lost his taste for combat. By the end of Jackson's cross-examination, Gisevius had happily admitted that Hermann Göring had ordered a subordinate to murder Gregor Strasser, a rival to Hitler in the Nazi party; that Kaltenbrunner was more dangerous as chief of the RSHA than the dread Reinhard Heydrich; and that Field Marshal Keitel had been kept fully informed of the emergence of death factories in the East. Of the man he had supposedly come to defend, Gisevius said that the Twentieth of July plotters would certainly have had Frick on the list of Nazis to dispose of, had they succeeded. By the end of the testimony, Göring was on his feet cursing the perfidy and stupidity of Pannenbecker for calling Gisevius as a defense witness. The *Reichsmarschall* had to be dragged away and shoved into the elevator.

Hans Gisevius rose from the witness stand with ponderous importance. He had enjoyed himself enormously.

19

HANS FRANK HAD BEEN the keeper of a secret, and he was now writing about it in the memoir that occupied his hours in cell 15. It had all started in 1930, before the Nazis took power. Frank, then Hitler's youthful lawyer, had been summoned to the Führer's home. A distraught Hitler showed him a letter and spoke of a "disgusting blackmail plot." Frank was surprised to learn that Hitler had a half-nephew living in England. William Patrick Hitler, the son of Hitler's half-brother, Alois, had written to say that it would benefit Uncle Adolf if certain rumors circulating in the press were not confirmed. The rumors were that Adolf Hitler had Jewish blood. Hitler viewed William's letter as a veiled threat of exposure. The conversation left Frank with legs trembling, since he lived in fear of his own Jewish ancestry's being exposed. To Frank's astonishment, Hitler asked him to make a confidential investigation of his family tree.

What he discovered, Frank now revealed in his memoirs, was that Hitler's paternal grandmother, Maria Anna Schicklgruber, had worked in Graz, Austria, as a cook in the home of a Jewish family named Frankenberger. At age forty-two, still unmarried, Maria Anna gave birth to a son. No father was indicated on the baptismal record. She named the child Alois Schicklgruber, and this Alois grew up to become Adolf Hitler's father.

Maria Anna's employers had a son, Frank wrote, and "On behalf of this son, then about nineteen years old, Frankenberger paid a maintenance allowance for Alois Schicklgruber from the time of the child's birth until his fourteenth year." The implication seemed fairly straightforward. The son of the household, not for the first time in history, had impregnated the maid. During his investigation, Frank discovered correspondence between the Frankenbergers and Maria Anna "betraying on both sides the tacit acknowledgment that Schicklgruber's illegitimate child had been engendered under circumstances which made the Frankenbergers responsible for his maintenance."

When the child was five, Maria Anna married a mill worker named Johann Georg Hiedler. The Frankenbergers' support payments nevertheless continued. The new husband showed no interest in legitimizing his wife's child. Young Alois himself later changed his name from Schicklgruber to Hitler, the spelling of Hiedler having been mangled by a priest on an official record.

In his memoir, Frank described his fear of reporting his findings to Hitler. For if the Frankenberger youth had indeed fathered Alois, then Adolf Hitler was one-quarter Jewish. To Frank's amazement, Hitler did not tear off his head. He denied nothing, including the Frankenbergers' support payments for his father. He appeared to know all about this background and seemed to have dispatched Frank only to find out how much others knew. As for the putative Jewish grandfather, Hitler had an explanation. It was Johann Hiedler who had been having an illicit relationship with Maria Anna. When she became pregnant, she accused the Frankenberger son only in order to extract money from the family. According to Hitler, "The Jew paid without going to court probably because he could not face the publicity that a legal settlement might have entailed." Given the choice of being the heir of Jews or of a blackmailer, Hitler had chosen a blackmailer.

The lawyerly Frank had deduced the only possibilities: either the Frankenberger youth was indeed the father, making Hitler one-quarter Jewish; or Johann Hiedler was the father, making Hitler one hundred percent Gentile; or Maria Anna had been involved with both men and did not know herself who had fathered her child. At the close of the entry, Frank wrote: "The possibility cannot be dismissed . . . that Hitler was one-quarter Jewish."

To Frank, the irresistible question was how this uncertain ancestry might have shaped Hitler's murderous anti-Semitism. Streicher's ravings in *Der Stürmer* always had a rich old Jew seducing an innocent

German maiden. Oddly, in *Mein Kampf*, Hitler had a "black-haired Jewish youth" lurking in wait to corrupt her. And among the Nuremberg Laws, Hitler, at one point, had insisted on a peculiar clause: any Aryan female under the age of forty-five—three years older than his grandmother had been when she gave birth—was forbidden from working as a servant in a Jewish home.

Frank found other startling parallels in *Mein Kampf*. Mixed-race children, Hitler wrote, "beginning in the third generation . . . invariably reveal their mixed breeding by one infallible signal. In all critical moments in which the racially pure make correct, that is, clear decisions, the racially mixed person will become uncertain, that is, he will arrive at half measures." *Mein Kampf* repeatedly condemned "half measures" and "halfheartedness." Hitler's decisions, whether right or wrong, had been certain and unhesitating. He was deaf to anyone who sought to temper them with contradicting facts or pleas for moderation. The way to prove that he did not suffer from third-generational indecision that would expose him as racially mixed—part Jew—was to overcompensate, to be more decisive, more certain, and more anti-Semitic than anyone else.

Herb Wechsler, Jim Rowe, Adrian Fisher, and Bob Stewart acted as law clerks to the court, helping the judges determine, for each defendant, which charges had been proven and which disproved. With the prosecution and the defense of a half dozen defendants completed, this staff began preparing draft verdicts. The premier question, because it dealt with the most monstrous crime, was to determine who bore responsibility for the Final Solution. In the carloads of documents, the one piece of paper that forever eluded the prosecution was a direct written order from Hitler setting the machinery in motion. Hitler's managerial style did not help. He had been an intuitive leader, no respecter of organization charts, likely to issue oral orders to whoever sprang into his mind or his vision. Consequently, Nazi Germany was a clutter of competing, overlapping fiefdoms.

As nearly as the court could determine, the phrase "final solution" had first been used by Hitler himself in 1935. In a talk on the Nuremberg Laws, he had said that if the nation's statutes were inadequate to deal with the Jewish question, "the problem must be handed over to the National Socialist party for a final solution." In November of 1938 Hitler ordered Göring, as his deputy, to devise a solution for the "Jewish question." On January 24, 1939, Göring delegated the assignment to Reinhard Heydrich, then head of the RSHA. Himmler entered the picture with the testimony of Rudolf Hoess. Hoess had stated that in June of 1941, Himmler told him that the Führer had ordered the final solution of the Jewish question through extermination.

On July 31, 1941, Göring sent an order to Heydrich that read, "Complementing the task assigned to you on January 24, 1939, which dealt with carrying out by emigration and evacuation a solution of the Jewish problem, I hereby charge you with making all preparations . . . I request furthermore, that you send me an overall plan . . . for the desired final solution of the Jewish question." With exterminations already under way at Treblinka, Auschwitz, and other camps, Reinhard Heydrich, on January 20, 1942, called a meeting of fourteen party and government bureaucrats at the old Interpol headquarters in the Berlin suburb of Wannsee. Heydrich had one item on his agenda. Referring to Göring's order, he said that Europe was to be cleared of its eleven million Jews. They were to be sent to the East, where those able would work until decimated "by natural reduction." The rest would be subject to "special treatment." The witness Dieter Wisliceny had testified that in July or August of 1942, Eichmann showed him a written order from Himmler calling for the Final Solution.

The judges could conclude from this tangled skein the following: The original order for a final solution had been passed from Hitler to Göring to Heydrich. But Göring could argue that his orders mentioned only "emigration and evacuation." The actual killing order appeared to have been given orally from Hitler to Himmler, and was initially applicable to Polish Jews. Once this plan was in operation, Heydrich called together the bureaucratic apparatus to apply the final solution to the whole of Europe. Hitler, Himmler, and Heydrich were dead. Of the survivors, Göring and Kaltenbrunner, Heydrich's successor, could be tied directly to the solution of extermination.

As for guilty knowledge, Josef Goebbels had written in his diary, "Göring perfectly realizes what is in store for us if we show any weakness in this war. On the Jewish question especially, we have taken a position from which there is no escape." The passage made two points clear: the leading Nazis understood the incriminating nature of the Final Solution, and their determination to fight to the bitter end had little to do with ideological conviction and much to do with saving their own skins.

20

MONDAY MORNING, April 29, the courtroom was packed with secretaries, researchers, and others eager to satisfy their curiosity. What sort of a woman would marry Julius Streicher, a man who washed his face in the toilet bowl, who talked dirty to children, who told Colonel Andrus that Eisenhower was a Jew and that Jackson had changed his name from Jacobson, who claimed the destruction of the dirigible *Hindenburg* had been a Jewish plot, and who was treated even by his fellow defendants like spit on the sidewalk? Streicher's counsel, Hans Marx, had called Frau Streicher to testify in her husband's defense.

The previous Friday, Streicher had made a perfect ass of himself on the stand. He beamed foolishly, as if glorying in the attention. He interrupted Marx so often that the lawyer asked the court if he might be relieved of the case. The British cross-examiner, the aristocratic Mervyn Griffith-Jones, tore Streicher apart with a rapier tongue. At one point Griffith-Jones noted that Streicher, in *Der Stürmer*, had referred to the Jews as "a nation of bloodsuckers and extortionists," and asked, "Do you think that's preaching race hatred?" "No," Streicher answered. "It is not preaching hatred. It is just a statement of fact."

Adele Streicher turned out to be an attractive blonde in her late thirties, at least twenty years younger than her husband. She moved gracefully, spoke sensibly and with undeniable charm. Her devotion to Streicher was evident; and, in this moment with his life in the balance, she served him well. In January 1940, she had come to work as secretary to Julius Streicher at his dairy farm in Pleikershof near Nuremberg, she testified. By then, he was already out of power and, she made clear, he had spent virtually the entire war doing "peasant" work, breaking stones, cutting wood, feeding cattle. As she left the stand, carriage erect, General Jodl, not noted for his spontaneity, remarked, "Wondrous are the ways of love."

When Adele Streicher left the courthouse, she went directly to the Nuremberg home of Dr. Pfluecker. Pfluecker had managed to get word to his family to take her in after the Americans had turned over Streicher's Pleikershof farm to displaced Jews. She eventually managed to get herself arrested for her unrelenting and vocal anti-Semitism.

21

"IF WE CAN'T CONVICT Hjalmar Schacht, we can't convict anybody on the industrial side," Justice Jackson told General Telford Taylor. Taylor listened in dismay. Jackson was such a fine man, a gifted man. Yet, here in Nuremberg, his judgment seemed to be clouded by unremitting tensions. He was obviously still smarting from the early defeat when he had been prevented from bringing the arms maker Alfried Krupp to trial in place of Krupp's semi-senile father. What was so crucial about the industrialist case? Taylor wondered. The industrialists, Jackson believed, had conspired to put Hitler into power. They had conspired to rearm Germany, and for what purpose but to wage aggressive war? Condemnation and punishment of the industrialists was key if the conspiracy strategy was to hang together.

Taylor, possibly the ablest American legal mind at Nuremberg, was by now convinced that the conspiracy theory had become obsolete. What was the point of taking up the IMT's time to convict the defendants of conspiring to commit aggression when ample evidence existed to convict them of actually committing aggression? Taylor sometimes found Jackson's rigid judgments and righteous posture hard to take. Yet he knew there was little he could do to dissuade the man. Jackson, determined to claim Schacht's scalp, had decided to go into the pit again for the cross-examination. He had chosen, Taylor believed, an elusive target.

In all these months in court, Hjalmar Schacht had assumed a pose that suggested he was trying to avoid being contaminated by his colleagues in the dock. Back in the fall, Schacht had told an interrogator, Lieutenant Nicholas Doman, "Young man, do you know why I am here?" Of course, Doman had replied. Schacht, wagging a finger, had said, "No, you do not. I am here because Justice Jackson wants an innocent man among these defendants who can be acquitted to prove this is a fair trial." On April 30, Schacht sat in the witness box, not as one facing his accusers, but as one eager to share his brilliant insights with lesser mortals.

This turn-of-the-century man, his steel-gray hair parted in the middle, his collar stiff, his neck corded, cut an unlikely romantic figure. At the age of sixty-four, however, with a daughter from an earlier marriage already forty, Schacht had won the hand of Nanci Vogler, a beautiful woman thirty years his junior. He had fathered his last child at sixty-six. Now sixty-nine, he was, according to the test, the most intelligent man on trial.

It cannot have harmed Schacht that of all the defendants, he was the only one to testify in English. He had been born Horace Greeley Hjalmar Schacht, named after the crusading American journalist. Schacht's father had lived in America for several years, and had even become an American citizen before resettling in Germany. Schacht was considered the financial wizard chiefly responsible for bringing Germany's catastrophic inflation under control in the twenties. On coming to power, Hitler had shrewdly named Schacht president of the Reichsbank, and later, minister of the economy.

During cross-examination, Jackson intended to destroy Schacht's denials that he helped plan and carry out aggressive warfare. The prosecution had a 1934 decree signed by Hitler and naming Schacht secret plenipotentiary general for the war economy. Jackson further had proof that Schacht's schemes had indeed financed Germany's rearmament, that he had made speeches praising Hitler, that he had called people who patronized Jewish shops "traitors," and that he had contributed money to the Nazi party. Jackson introduced photos showing Schacht marching with leading Nazis, giving the Nazi salute, and sitting next to Hitler.

The Nazis, however, had inadvertently provided Schacht with a powerful defense against Jackson's onslaughts. Schacht had not been part of the Twentieth of July plot against Hitler. When approached by the conspirators, he had stalled, saying he would have to know more about their new government. Nevertheless, after the attempt, he had been arrested and ended up at Dachau. Trying to convict a man of war crimes who had been liberated by American troops after spending ten months in a concentration camp tested Jackson's prosecutorial gifts to the utmost.

22

WINTER HAD SUITED the trial. The leaden skies, gray rubble, and wan faces in the dock blended in melancholy harmony. Now, spring had come. In the old town, people emerged from their caves and pitched tents, or rigged shelters from charred timbers, corrugated sheets of tin, and empty U.S. Army crates. On the outskirts, farmers poured liquid manure from oxcarts onto thirsty fields. Anglers from the IMT, like Sir David Maxwell-Fyfe, fished a Pegnitz River teeming with trout. The windows of the courtroom were thrown open and the stagnant air gave way to the fragrance of hawthorn. Spring mocked the trial, made it seem out of step with a world being reborn.

On Saturday, May 4, a lovely night, the best boxes at the Nuremberg opera house were reserved for prominent members of the IMT, come to hear a newly arrived ensemble. The group had originally numbered thirty-five musicians and first played together in the ghetto of Kaunas, Lithuania, soon after the Nazi occupation. Their music had saved them, at least some of them. The Germans had them perform at labor roundups and executions. Later, they had toured concentration camps. Only the twelve playing tonight had survived the war.

The performance began lightly enough, with a standard romantic repertoire—Leoncavallo, Meyerbeer, and Rossini. Toward the close, the ensemble performed a song evoking a different world:

> Ghetto, I will never forget you,
> Dark and crooked streets,
> Death looms from every corner.
> No home. No parents, hungry, forgotten by God and man.
> Where is your wife, your child, your family?
> Where to? Why? What for?

For the staff of the IMT, more than the torrent of words and numbing statistics they heard day in, day out, the music plumbed a feeling not yet touched—the incomprehension of a doomed yet innocent people.

Tom Dodd was again the toast of the Marble Room. His performance in court the day before had made his staying on in Nuremberg worthwhile. With the support of the anonymous staffers who prepared his appearances, he had shattered the defense of Walther Funk. Round, soft, weeping, dark-jowled Funk might have seemed an unworthy adversary, a preposterous war criminal. His weak bladder had gotten Funk out of the German army during World War I. At Nuremberg, he often had to be led from the courtroom to the men's room. To the guards he was "the pisser." This unlikely figure, however, had been indicted on all four counts.

The winding trail that had led Funk to the Nuremberg dock had begun at what seemed a moment of success. Hitler had summoned him during a Berlin performance of *La Bohème* and said, almost as though he could not believe it himself, "I'll have to make you the minister of economy after all." Thus Funk had succeeded the old wizard Schacht. He was, in fact, bright and capable. But Funk was known best in party circles as a bon vivant who savored fine cigars, good scotch, risqué stories, and all-night revelry. Though he was married and liked to play the lecher, Funk discreetly chose his own sex for his most intimate companionship.

The worst thing he had done was to draft a law in the thirties barring Jews from operating retail businesses, a blow that had doomed tens of thousands to poverty or flight. What hovered over Funk at Nuremberg, however, was something more tangibly horrifying. After the conquest of Frankfurt, a U.S. army film unit had made a motion picture of unusual deposits in the vaults of the Reichsbank—heaps of diamonds, pearls, gold eyeglass frames, gold rings, gold earrings, gold watches, and gold teeth. The vault looked more like a hock shop than part of a bank. The prosecution had shown the film in court.

Earlier in Mondorf, in a fit of remorse, Funk had admitted to Colonel Andrus that he knew how the valuables, including the gold teeth, had found their way into his bank. Once the trial began, however, Funk had denied any knowledge of these deposits. In cross-examining him, Dodd read from an affidavit given by Emil Puhl, Funk's assistant at the Reichsbank. Puhl claimed that Heinrich Himmler had arranged with Funk to accept valuables collected by the SS in the East. When Puhl asked Funk the source of these valuables, Funk had told him to stop asking questions. Puhl further deposed that he and Funk had gone to the vaults from time to time to see the accumulation of this trove.

On the stand, Funk insisted that Puhl's affidavit was a lie. Why did they not produce the man himself? Funk protested. Puhl would clear his old chief. Dodd pressed the witness on his continued denial of the nature of the SS deposits. "Many people deposited valuables, although the bank was not required to look into them," Funk said petulantly. "Nobody," Dodd observed, "ever deposited his gold teeth in a bank."

Emil Puhl did, in fact, testify days later, only to incriminate Funk. There had been seventy-seven SS deposits of valuables, he told the court. Funk knew about them, and they were, he said, *Schweinerei*—they smelled bad from the start.

23

ON MAY 8, General Alfred Jodl watched from the dock, listening to Grand Admiral Karl Dönitz being sworn in. The date held a stinging memory for Jodl. Just over one year before, Dönitz had dispatched him to a French boys' school in Rheims with orders to employ every possible delaying tactic before signing Germany's surrender. Jodl's icy reception by the victors had opened his eyes to a bitter truth. The German military were not regarded as defeated yet honorable adversaries, but as pariahs.

During the lunch break, Captain Gilbert reminded Admiral Dönitz that this was the date celebrating the defeat of the Nazis. "Why do you think I'm sitting here?" Dönitz responded. Still, his truculence had waned in recent months. When Major Neave first delivered the indictments, Dönitz had scrawled on his, "Typical American humor!" Later, the revelations had begun to weigh on him. Gilbert had overheard Dönitz say in the elders' lunchroom, "I was furious with the idea of being dragged to the trial in the beginning, because I knew nothing about these atrocities. But, after all this evidence, the double-dealing, the dirty business in the East, I am satisfied there was good reason to get to the bottom of it." Get to the bottom of it, yes. But not necessarily at the cost of Karl Dönitz's neck. He still argued his own innocence.

Dönitz's lawyer, Flottenrichter Otto Kranzbuehler, was a familiar figure around the courthouse, as the only German permitted to wear his full uniform. Navy blue flattered Kranzbuehler, a good-looking man much admired by the women in court. As a career naval officer, he looked upon the Dönitz case as a defense not simply of the admiral, but of the German navy, to which the lawyer had given eleven years of his own life. To Kranzbuehler, the most dangerous piece of paper in the prosecution's hands was the *Laconia* Order, which his client had issued to the submarine fleet on September 17, 1942. The order—not to rescue survivors of sunken ships, and not to give them food or water—had applied to merchant vessels as well as warships. Subsequently, one German U-boat captain had spent five hours hunting down and machine-gunning the survivors of the Greek steamer *Peleos*. The *Laconia* Order had figured significantly in Dönitz's indictment for "crimes against persons and property on the high seas."

His task, Kranzbuehler knew, was to educate the judges as to what lay behind the admiral's seemingly heartless directive. The facts were that the *Laconia*, a well-armed British merchantman sailing the South Atlantic, had been sunk by submarine U-156. After the ship went down, the U-boat captain found the sea full of survivors. He wired Dönitz for instructions. Dönitz dispatched two more submarines to aid in a rescue operation. The three subs took survivors aboard until they were full, and towed the rest in lifeboats toward land. During this rescue operation, the U-156 flew a large Red Cross flag.

To the disbelief of the submariners, an American Liberator bomber arrived on the scene and began attacking the U-156. The submarine took a hit amidships. Crowded lifeboats were sunk. The attack was reported to Dönitz, who now ordered the U-156 to put all survivors back into lifeboats and break off the rescue. However, he ordered the other two vessels to continue to bring their survivors to port. Hitler was enraged by what he regarded as Dönitz's misguided compassion. He demanded that the safety of the U-boats must take priority over all else. Thus it was that Dönitz had subsequently issued the aid-no-survivors order.

Otto Kranzbuehler had read and reread the tu quoque prohibition of the London Charter. It said in effect that even though the Allies might have committed wrongs, this fact did not excuse the Germans. There had to be a way around this provision. If only he could get a high-ranking Allied officer to testify that the war on the high seas had been fought the same way on both sides, he might save Dönitz. Five weeks before, Kranzbuehler had petitioned the court to allow him to seek an affidavit from Admiral Chester Nimitz, commander of the U.S. Pacific fleet. "I in no way wish to prove or even maintain that the American admiralty in its U-boat warfare against Japan broke international law," Kranzbuehler argued. "On the contrary, I am of the opinion that it acted strictly in accordance with international law." He was not saying that we Germans did wrong, but so did you; rather, he was saying, you did right, and so did we.

The British, French, and Russian judges were ready to reject these legal acrobatics out of hand; but Francis Biddle was intrigued by Kranzbuehler's ingenuity. He used his accustomed influence over Lawrence to win approval for the lawyer's petition. At the time, the move had confirmed Dönitz's good judgment in enlisting not just a navy man, but a resourceful one, as his defense counsel. Nevertheless, Dönitz was getting discouraged. Weeks had passed. He would soon face cross-examination by Maxwell-Fyfe, and still no affidavit from Nimitz had arrived.

During these weeks, Kranzbuehler had not been idle. Sixty-seven German U-boat captains were still imprisoned in England in Camp 18 in Featherstone Park. Kranzbuehler had dispatched an assistant to the camp with a statement averring that Admiral Dönitz had never ordered his crews to kill survivors. They had been directed not to rescue them. All sixty-seven captains had signed the statement, and Kranzbuehler had managed to have it accepted into evidence.

Captain Heinz Eck had commanded the submarine that shot up survivors of the sunken Greek steamer Peleos. Nothing could have served Eck better during his own war-crimes trial than to have claimed that he had acted under Dönitz's orders. Kranzbuehler instead managed to obtain a deposition from Eck, just before his execution, in which the U-boat captain admitted that he had acted on his own.

On Thursday, May 9, the cross-examination began. Still Kranzbuehler had no word from Nimitz. Maxwell-Fyfe read from Dönitz's speeches, exposing him as a rabid anti-Semite. Sir David proved that Dönitz was well aware of the existence of concentration camps. Had he not requested twelve thousand inmates to work in his shipyards? And Dönitz was the man whom Adolf Hitler had found most worthy to succeed him, a successor who mouthed praises of the dead leader until Nazi Germany's last gasp.

During a recess on the last day of the prosecution's counterattack, Dönitz watched an unknown American naval officer leave the visitors' gallery and approach Kranzbuehler. He saw his lawyer nod and smile. Kranzbuehler immediately reported to Dönitz. They might soon have good news from America.

The day after Dönitz's defense ended, Admiral Nimitz had gone to his office at the Navy Department in Washington. It was a Saturday afternoon, and the crusty admiral was in sports clothes, an informality that did not ease the task of Commander Joseph Broderick of the judge advocate general's office. Broderick read from a list of questions provided by Kranzbuehler. "Did U.S. submarines in the Pacific attack merchantmen without warning?" Broderick asked. Yes, Nimitz said without hesitation, except for hospital ships. Under whose authority? the lawyer asked. By order of the highest naval authority, the chief of naval operations, dated December 7, 1941, Nimitz responded. Did American submarines rescue survivors? Broderick went on. U.S. submarines did not rescue survivors, Nimitz said, if such action would place the submarine at risk. The deposition was soon on its way to Kranzbuehler, who introduced it into evidence.

The night of Dönitz's appearance in court, Katherine Biddle had hosted a combination VE-day celebration and sixtieth-birthday party for her husband at a grand house reserved for VIP entertainment, the Villa Schickedanz. Jim Rowe, Biddle's clerk, had put aside his work on a draft of the Göring verdict to come to the party. Rowe was a man's man, a thirty-seven-year-old frontier intellectual out of Mon-

tana, a reformed two-fisted drinker. He had been Oliver Wendell
Holmes's law clerk, an insider at the FDR White House, a war hero
who had pulled strings to get into, not out of, combat. Rowe's respect
mattered to other men. Earlier in the day, Biddle had received a letter
from Rowe. "I confess to thinking many years ago," Rowe had written,
"that you were just a dilettante, a Philadelphia gentleman, a Grotonian, and a Harvard man who was amusing yourself by being a New
Deal liberal." But, Rowe went on, he had studied Biddle closely at
Nuremberg and concluded, "Well done, Francis. You have measured
up." Biddle, like any son of privilege, wondered in the privacy of his
soul how much he had earned and how much he had merely inherited.
Rowe's birthday message provided an answer he prized.

24

COLONEL BURTON ANDRUS LEFT the courthouse Friday night, May 10,
concerned about the appearance of the courtroom guards. Their uniforms were rumpled. Sharp, hard creases had vanished. His subordinate in charge of the guard detail had reminded the colonel that the
men stood for hours in a poorly ventilated room wearing olive drab
wool jackets and trousers, bathed in their own sweat. That afternoon
Andrus had Rose Korb type out an order: as of the following week,
the ISD would switch to summer khakis. He asked her to run off the
directive and circulate it before she left for the day.

That night, Andrus attended a dinner party at the residence of a
British prosecutor. By eleven p.m. he was home in bed. He was jarred
from his sleep at dawn by someone banging on his door. He answered
it to find a captain from the army's Criminal Investigation Division.
Rose Korb, the officer informed him, was being questioned about a
shooting.

Korb had looked forward to that Friday night. Two friends working
for *Stars and Stripes*, Sergeants William Timmons and Paul Skelton,
were in Nuremberg, eager to do the town. Korb had finished the
colonel's assignment and gone home to Girls' Town to dress for the
evening. At eight p.m., the two GIs picked her up in a jeep. They
drove to the enlisted men's favorite, the Stork Club, upstairs over the

Nuremberg Opera House. At 11:45 p.m., after a night of singing and jitterbugging, Korb was ready to go home. The colonel expected her in the office early on Saturday morning. By now, her party included another GI and two British women. The six piled into the jeep and headed for Girls' Town. They were proceeding down Morgenstrasse past a park, a favorite trysting place for GIs and their German girlfriends, when a blurred figure stepped out of the shadows. Three shots rang out. Timmons managed to bring the wobbling jeep to a halt and then toppled forward. In the back, Shelton was also slumped over. Both men died soon afterward of gunshot wounds to the chest.

Rose Korb was distraught and red-eyed by the time Colonel Andrus arrived at the Nuremberg headquarters of the Criminal Investigation Division. The CID men had been terrible, she said, asking her the most intimate questions, making it seem as if she had been involved in a sordid affair that had ended in murder. She was also being hounded by reporters eager for a sensational story during a slow news cycle.

The CID chief told Andrus that he had a dragnet out combing every building and ruin in a four-mile-square area of Nuremberg. It could have been an ambush by "werewolves," he thought. Nazi diehards. His men had already arrested six Germans, but he had no real evidence connecting them to the crime.

Colonel Andrus obtained Rose Korb's release and took the young woman back to her apartment building. He confined Korb to quarters to protect her from the relentless pursuit of the press. A few days later, she informed the colonel that she had had enough of international justice. She was going home.

The investigation went on, with fifty Nuremberg police joining one hundred American MPs. In the end, the investigators suspected that the killing had nothing to do with vengeful Germans. The sketchy but more promising lead was one the U.S. Army was uneager to confirm. The volatile relations between American blacks and whites appeared finally to have exploded. According to witnesses in the park, the killings had most likely been committed by an unidentified black GI for uncertain motives—possibly a dispute over a German girlfriend, possibly mistaken identity, possibly racial hatred. The crime was never solved.

25

REPORTERS HAD OBSERVED the odd relationship for months. Two former commanders of the German navy sitting side by side in the second
row of the dock, day after day, barely exchanging a glance. Seventy-
year-old Grand Admiral Erich Raeder had been a cart-before-the-
horse defendant. He had been indicted, along with the propagandist
Hans Fritzsche, at the insistence of the Russians because they too
wanted to produce war criminals, and these were the best they could
unearth. Thereafter, prosecution researchers had to scramble to find
evidence to match the charges. The case finally prepared alleged that
Raeder had violated the Treaty of Versailles by building up the
German navy, that he had been present at the Hossbach Conference,
where Hitler laid out his aggressive intentions, and that he had been
party to the plan to invade Norway. The most curious document in
the prosecution's possession was the "Moscow Statement," which
Raeder had made while in Russian captivity. Several defendants, the
prosecutors knew, would not enjoy having its contents revealed in
court.

The Moscow Statement surfaced on May 20, when deputy Soviet
prosecutor Colonel Y. V. Pokrovsky introduced it during cross-
examination. Pokrovsky got Raeder to agree that he had given the
statement freely, without coercion. The reason behind the coolness
between Dönitz and Raeder immediately became apparent. Pokrovsky,
quoting from the document, read Raeder's opinion of Dönitz: He was
"conceited," and "hardly qualified" to head the German navy. By calling for continued resistance after he succeeded Hitler, Dönitz had
"made a fool of himself." Dönitz reddened visibly as Pokrovsky read
from a speech Dönitz had once given to the Hitler Youth. After that
speech, Raeder had said in his statement, Dönitz "was ridiculed in all
circles and earned himself the title of 'Hitlerboy Dönitz.' "

Göring fared scarcely better. Raeder's statement said of the
Reichsmarschall, "Göring had a disastrous effect on the German Reich.
His main peculiarities were unimaginable vanity, and immeasurable
ambition . . . he was outstanding in his greed, wastefulness and soft,
unsoldierly manner." Field Marshal Keitel, in Raeder's words, was "a

man of unimaginable weakness . . . the Führer could treat him as badly as he wished and Keitel took it."

Raeder was unconcerned by the bridges he had burned with these exposures in court. When the day ended, he told Gilbert, "Naturally, I will be hanged or shot. I flatter myself to think I will be shot. I have no desire to serve a prison sentence at my age."

26

CAPTAIN GILBERT WAS APPREHENSIVE as Baldur von Schirach took the stand on the morning of May 23. If Gilbert had made one strategic contribution to this trial, he believed, it had been to split up the defendants, and to isolate Göring so that the others would be free of his intimidation. Gilbert had particularly wanted Schirach and Speer together during lunches at the "youth table," where Speer's strength and shrewdness might influence Schirach's naïveté and weakness. Schirach was capable of extraordinary self-delusion, Gilbert knew. The man saw himself, because of family ties and his command of English, almost as one of the Americans. He had once explained to the cell guard, Emilio DiPalma, "You see, our Hitler Youth was the same as your Boy Scouts." To which DiPalma, a combat veteran, replied, "I never saw a Boy Scout take apart an automatic rifle and reassemble it in one minute flat."

Göring had stayed in his cell this morning, complaining of sciatica. His absence should help buck up Schirach's resolve, Gilbert believed. Still, he was not sure what to expect from this educated patrician who admitted that his political philosophy could be shaped by the likes of Julius Streicher. Schirach went to the witness box, the wunderkind of the Hitler circle—and now, at thirty-nine, the youngest major war criminal.

While Schirach was testifying, Robert Jackson found himself facing another Russian enigma. Rudenko came to his office asking permission to remove a body from Nuremberg to Leipzig in the Soviet Zone. Who was it, and what had happened? Jackson asked. The dead man was General N. D. Zorya, the prosecutor who had introduced Field Marshal Paulus's testimony. Zorya had accidentally shot himself

while cleaning his gun, Rudenko explained. Jackson was relieved that
Rudenko was not reporting another American shooting of a Russian,
as had occurred outside the Grand Hotel in December. He decided
to bypass the army's Criminal Investigation Division, and sent two of
his people out to the Russian compound in suburban Erlenstegen to
check the story quietly. They subsequently informed Jackson that it
was highly unlikely that a Russian general would be cleaning his own
gun, particularly with the muzzle pointed between his eyes. But what
to do? Jackson had no idea why the Russians had not simply spirited
the general's body out of Nuremberg themselves. His principal objective here was to keep this trial moving, not to trigger an international
incident. The general's demise was strictly an internal Russian matter,
he decided, and gave Rudenko permission to move the body. The
alliance was indeed under stress, and Jackson had no desire to aggra-
vate it further.

Schirach's counsel began his second day of direct examination by deliberately raising his client's worst offenses. He drew an admission that
Schirach knew about the mass exterminations in the East. He referred
to the testimony of Rudolf Hoess and asked Schirach to comment.
Those millions of murders were not committed by Hoess, Schirach
said, in a firm voice: "Hoess was only the executioner. The murder
was ordered by Adolf Hitler." The defendants looked toward the witness box as if controlled by a single string. "It was my guilt, which I
will have to carry before God and the German nation, that I educated
the youth of our people . . . for a man who for many years I considered
impeccable as a leader and as a head of state. . . . I educated German
youth for a man who committed murders a millionfold." Gilbert, to
whom Schirach's repentance was something of a cause, felt agreeably
relieved.

Tom Dodd, in his cross-examination, however, did not spare
Schirach. He forced him to admit that he had recommended the spite
bombing of an English cultural town in reprisal for the Heydrich assassination, and that he had evacuated from Vienna sixty thousand
Jews who were later murdered. Yet, however briefly, Baldur von Schirach had displayed a spine that few had believed he possessed.

Back in the cellblock, Gilbert sought out Albert Speer's reaction.
Speer said that he was delighted to see Göring's united front collaps-

ing, as first Keitel, then Frank, and now Schirach had accepted personal guilt and condemned the regime. He and Schirach, Speer said, had become *Duzfreund:* they used the familiar *du* in addressing each other. Of more immediate concern to Speer than Schirach, however, was the testimony of the next defendant due on the stand, Fritz Sauckel.

27

ROBERT SERVATIUS HURRIED through the cavernous halls of the Palace of Justice to the visitors' room, where he was to have a last-minute meeting with his client. The fifty-two-year-old Servatius had won a reputation in court for being logical and reasonable, and for cutting to the marrow of an issue. A sophisticate who had lived and studied in England, Paris, and Moscow, he had never succumbed to the lure of the Nazi party. As one reporter saw him, Servatius was a first-rate lawyer with a third-rate client. Servatius had no particular affection for Sauckel either. But he had come out of six years in the German army as an overage officer, and Nuremberg offered him an opportunity once again to make his mark in his profession. Servatius wanted this final meeting because Fritz Sauckel, he had found, required close supervision. He sat down opposite Sauckel on the other side of the mesh screen and went directly to the point. He was going to throw the toughest possible questions at Sauckel concerning the forced labor program, he explained. Better he should do it than the prosecution. Did Sauckel understand? Sauckel nodded eagerly. And do not babble, Servatius warned. Speak slowly. Use short sentences. Give the interpreters a chance to keep pace.

On Tuesday, May 28, Fritz Sauckel approached the witness box, bouncing on the balls of his feet like a referee at a boxing match. Servatius began quoting Sauckel's words at a meeting of the Central Planning Board. Sauckel had boasted there that, when necessary, his agents resorted to shanghaiing foreign workers. Explain this statement, Servatius asked. Sauckel looked stunned, as though a parent had delivered an unexpected slap. His speech revealed a provincial, uneducated German. Servatius shook his head in despair. Sauckel was

pausing between every word, sounding like a zombie. Justice Lawrence
interrupted the witness. "I do not know the German language," he
said, "but it might make some sense for the defendant to pause at the
end of the sentence rather than on every syllable."

Servatius asked Sauckel what he meant when he had said that, if
the French failed to come up with enough workers, "we might have
to put a prefect up against a wall." This time, Sauckel spewed out the
answer so rapidly that Lawrence had to tell him to slow down. As the
day wore on, however, Servatius made some headway, getting into
the record evidence that his client had issued directives calling for
decent treatment of workers and that Sauckel himself controlled no
police or troops but depended on others to carry out his roundups.

The subject foremost on everyone's mind was broached the next
day. "What was the relationship of your office to Speer's?" Servatius
asked. At last, Sauckel spoke clearly and directly. "My office had to
meet the demands made by Speer."

A worse moment for Speer occurred two days later, when Servatius called as a witness Max Timm, a Sauckel deputy. The lawyer
asked the witness, "Could Speer give orders to Sauckel?" Timm gave
a rambling answer. Servatius pressed harder. "Could Albert Speer give
orders and instructions and did he give them?" "Yes," Timm answered.

Ironically, it was Sauckel's stunning ineptness that might present
the greatest danger to Speer. Sauckel had been a terrible witness, losing control of himself, screeching hysterically at times, missing every
opportunity his lawyer gave him to win the court's sympathy by ad-
mitting at least some guilt. Instead, he continued defending his behavior in outworn Nazi clichés. Often he simply missed the point of
a question. Speer's problem was that people might not believe that so
pathetic a creature could have been his equal, much less superior to
him in the forced labor program.

28

FEW NOTICED THE FLOWERS on the witness box the morning of June 3
until General Alfred Jodl took the stand. Underneath the small glass
vase of pink and white phlox, a note in a familiar hand read, "Calm,

calm, oh so calm, my dear. Do not lose your temper." Jodl smiled briefly at his wife, Luise, in the visitors' gallery, then resumed his customary mask. As secretary to her husband's lawyer, Franz Exner, Frau Jodl was occasionally able to get into court to see Alfred. She had arrived early this morning to boost his spirits.

In the beginning, Alfred Jodl had not figured on all the Allied war-criminal lists. But the Russians had insisted; they wanted him indicted for transmitting to German armies in Russia Hitler's orders for virtually unrestricted barbarism. The Americans had eventually settled on him to round out the list of defendants in keeping with the philosophy of collective guilt that Jackson favored: thus, Göring represented the Nazi leadership and the Luftwaffe, Schacht the industrialists, Keitel the general staff, Dönitz the navy, Kaltenbrunner the SS, and Jodl the army.

On the stand, Jodl's defense was that he tempered Hitler's worst impulses. "Among officers who dared look the Führer squarely in the face and speak in a tone and manner that made listeners hold their breath because they feared catastrophe," he testified, "among these few officers, I myself belonged." It was true. Unlike Keitel, who would be nodding before he knew what the Führer was saying, Jodl did speak out. He had been shunned by Hitler for months after his mission to the Caucasus, where he had defended the behavior of General List. He protested to Hitler when some eighty American POWs were murdered by SS troops near the Belgian village of Malmédy during the Battle of the Bulge.

Jodl had confessed to Gilbert, in a rare moment of self-revelation, that he often despised the Führer. "The things that made me hate Hitler," he said, "were his contempt for the middle class, with which I identified myself, his suspicion and contempt for the nobility, to which I was married, and his hatred of the general staff, of which I was a member." Jodl was the model officer, unafraid to undergo fire whether in the face of the enemy or a megalomaniac leader. But, as the prosecution was bent on proving, Jodl also displayed the other face of the German militarist—indiscriminate obedience once an order was given.

If Maxwell-Fyfe was the cross-examining scourge of the defendants, his countryman Geoffrey Dorling Roberts was close behind. "Khaki" Roberts was a huge man swathed in yards of double-breasted serge who had won his blue for rugby and played for England. He had a large mustache and large square teeth that he flashed at his prey in smiles of exuberant contempt. Some of his colleagues found Roberts bombastic; the defendants found him unnerving. Was it true that Hitler had wanted to drop Germany from the Geneva Convention, which governed the conduct of warfare, and that Jodl had resisted the move? Roberts asked. Jodl warily agreed. But what was Jodl's reason? Roberts shot back. Was it not as described in document D 606? He then proceeded to quote Jodl's words from the minutes of a meeting with Hitler: "Adherence to the accepted obligations [of the convention] does not in any way demand that we should have to impose on ourselves any limitations which will interfere with the conduct of the war." Jodl shifted uneasily as Roberts continued quoting him. "For instance, if the British sink a hospital ship, this must be used for propaganda purposes. That, of course, in no way prevents our sinking an English hospital ship at once as a reprisal and then expressing our regret that it was a mistake." Roberts asked Jodl to justify such hypocrisy. Jodl tried to explain that this was the only kind of reasoning that worked with Hitler. Legal or moral arguments for observing the Geneva Convention would only have inflamed him.

Wasn't Jodl's claim that he opposed brutal orders equally hypocritical? Roberts asked. He turned to a document signed by Jodl ordering troops in the East to punish guerrilla actions "not by legal prosecution of the guilty, but by such terror as to eradicate every inclination to resist," and by using "draconian methods." Barely pausing for Jodl's answer, Roberts attacked again. Were those not Jodl's words, uttered just before the Blitz? "Terror attacks against English centers of population . . . will paralyze the will of the people to resist." And after the plot against Hitler, didn't Jodl make a speech to staff officers in which he said, "The twentieth of July was the blackest day that Germany has yet seen and will remain so for all time"? "Why," Roberts asked, "was it such a black day for Germany when someone tried to assassinate a man who you now admit was a murderer?" Before Jodl could complete his response, Roberts shouted, "Do you still say that you are an honorable soldier, a truthful man?" Without waiting for a reply, Roberts turned his back on the witness and returned to the prosecution table.

29

On June 6, President Truman named Fred Vinson, his treasury secretary, as chief justice of the Supreme Court. Robert Jackson took the loss of the post he coveted without complaint—yet some of his associates thought they saw deep disappointment in the man.

30

Arthur Seyss-Inquart sat next to Albert Speer in the dock. While Speer drew attention, Seyss-Inquart, with rimless glasses, pale skin, mouse-brown hair, and a defeated air, went practically unseen. The man had a keen mind as measured on Gilbert's intelligence test, and was capable of perceptions rare in the Nazi mentality. After the Auschwitz commandant, Rudolf Hoess, had appeared in court, Dönitz and Göring made the point that Hoess was a southern German. A Prussian could never have done such things, they claimed. Gilbert had asked Seyss-Inquart's opinion. "The south German has the imagination and the emotionality to subscribe to a fanatic idea," Seyss-Inquart had explained. "But he is inhibited from excess by his natural humaneness. The Prussian, on the other hand, lacks the imagination to think in terms of abstract racial and political theories. But if he is told to do something, he does it." Hitler's genius, Seyss-Inquart concluded, was that he had "amalgamated emotionalism with authoritarianism." Hoess offered the perfect example.

On June 10, a limping Seyss-Inquart, crippled in a long-ago mountaineering accident, approached the stand. As his testimony unfolded, the contradictions amazed the court—the mild manner, the terrible deeds, the quiet speech, the horrific record. The subjects raised by his counsel on direct examination merely positioned the witness in the gunsights for his cross-examiner. Seyss-Inquart emerged as a man who had sold out Austria to Hitler's Reich, who apprenticed in Poland under Hans Frank, who brutalized his own fiefdom of occupied Holland. Under what Seyss-Inquart regarded as his firm but humane rule, 41,000 Dutch had been shot as hostages, 50,000 died of starvation, and fifty-six percent of Dutch Jews perished.

Seyss-Inquart had neither lied nor pleaded in his testimony, but had assumed a fatalist's resignation. When he rode down the elevator that day with Hans Fritzsche, Seyss-Inquart observed that it did not matter how he behaved: "Whatever I say, my rope is being woven from Dutch hemp."

Someone had described Franz von Papen as "an aristocrat who looked like an actor playing an aristocrat." Papen had managed to maintain that appearance through all these months in jail. On June 14, as he left the prison to begin his defense, his diplomat's aplomb and splendid appearance concealed his anxiety. He emerged from his cell, hair combed back in silver strands, face handsomely planed, blue pin-striped suit sharply creased. In the courthouse basement, he fluffed the snow-white handkerchief in his breast pocket and waited to board the elevator. "Think of it, excellency, if it weren't for you," Hermann Göring said, "none of us would be here." Papen recognized the truth in Göring's gibe. He had served briefly as chancellor of Germany in 1932, and then advised President von Hindenburg to replace him and make Hitler chancellor. Hitler had later remarked, "I shall never forget it, Herr von Papen." Papen had been indicted on counts one and two as part of the cabal that brought the Nazis to power. As he emerged from the elevator, his eyes went immediately to the defense counsel's table, where he was relieved to see one of the more admired lawyers, his son, also Franz von Papen, waiting to defend him.

31

TOM DODD HAD BEEN preparing himself for the Albert Speer cross-examination, when Speer asked if he might see the deputy prosecutor in the visitors' room. Speer told Dodd that Hermann Göring was his chief rival for the soul of the defendants. Göring stood for truculent defiance. Speer stood for admission of Nazi guilt. Göring had been cross-examined by Jackson, the chief Nuremberg prosecutor. But Speer was going to be questioned by a subordinate. With all due respect to Dodd, would not this difference be noticed by the other defendants? And would it not put Speer, in their eyes, in an inferior status to Göring, thus making it more difficult for Speer to win them to his side? Dodd was perplexed by Speer's peculiar measure of status. He nevertheless took up the matter with Jackson and recommended that the chief prosecutor take over Speer's cross-examination. If it made the man feel more important, if it made him a more cooperative and useful witness, why not? He had no ego stake in the assignment, Dodd said. Jackson agreed.

When word of the change got out, some of the prosecution staff became suspicious. Speer sat in court every day. He could not be unaware that Dodd was a tough, skilled, dangerous prosecutor. Jackson's performance in the adversarial arena was of another caliber, and Speer knew it.

Suspense mounted as the day approached for Speer to take the stand. The man presented an anomaly—an indicted war criminal who could easily have walked straight from the dock to dinner with the judges at the Grand. Speer tested the court's powers of objectivity. Could they discern the fine fault line of guilt between this brilliant, attractive figure and the lumpen Fritz Sauckel? Or, as one reporter put it, when babies born to women on forced labor transports had been thrown from the train, who was most responsible—Sauckel, who had conscripted the women, or Speer, who had demanded them as workers?

Speer had recently confided to Captain Gilbert that his lawyer, Hans Flächsner, tried to talk him out of confessing to war crimes that might incur the ultimate penalty. He was not going to hide the truth just to wangle a life sentence, Speer had told Gilbert, "and hate myself for the rest of my life." He had seen that Gilbert was favorably impressed.

On June 20, the eve of his defense, Speer mentally reviewed his assets one last time. What hard truths had he been telling Hitler when others pretended the war could still be won? What action had he taken when Hitler ordered Germany destroyed in a pointless Armageddon?

What heroic solution had he plotted while others still trembled in the Führer's presence? He and Flächsner had gone through it all, rehearsing the questions that would elicit the most beneficial answers.

At breakfast on June 21, Dr. Pfluecker brought Speer a tranquilizing pill in case he felt he needed it on the stand. Speer put the pill in the pocket of his newly pressed dark gray suit. He felt the smoothness of his freshly shaved chin, adjusted his tie, and stood waiting for the guard to unbolt the door.

Speer had instructed Flächsner to get the Sauckel business out of the way quickly. He must not carry his heaviest cross any longer than necessary. And he must not appear to be shifting blame for conscript labor. To seem to be ducking responsibility would tarnish himself worse than Sauckel. Thus, early in the direct examination, Flächsner asked Speer if he disapproved of Sauckel's recruitment of labor. On the contrary, Speer answered, "I was grateful to Sauckel for every worker he provided me with. Often when we failed to meet armament quotas because of a shortage of workers, I would blame Sauckel." He felt calm and controlled as he spoke. He had taken Dr. Pfluecker's pill.

Flächsner noted that Sauckel had claimed he worked for Speer. Would the witness please comment? It was the question at the heart of the matter. Speer hesitated as if contemplating icy water, then plunged in. "Of course, I expected Sauckel to meet, above all, the demands of war production," he said. But he did not control Sauckel, as proved by the fact that he did not get all the workers he requested.

Sauckel was jumping up and down, trying to signal his lawyer, Robert Servatius. He had told his interrogators months ago that Speer actually stockpiled workers, hoarding more than he could possibly use. Servatius whispered to Sauckel to be patient.

Flächsner asked Speer if Göring, as head of the Four Year Plan, had been included in manpower meetings. "I wouldn't have had any use for him," Speer said. "After all, we had practical work to do."

The morning session ended. Among those in the visitors' gallery that day was Lady Sylvia, the wife of Sir David Maxwell-Fyfe. During the lunch hour, she ran into the junior British prosecutor Mervyn Griffith-Jones in her husband's office. She was much impressed by

Herr Speer, Lady Sylvia said. Here was the sort of man Germany was going to need in the years ahead. Griffith-Jones went to a closet and brought out a ten-foot length of telephone wire. He showed her bloodstains on it. This was a whip used on conscript laborers at the Krupp arms works, he told her, a plant in Speer's munitions empire.

Speer had saved the afternoon session for his masterstroke. Since he held a "technical" ministry, Flächsner asked, "Do you wish to limit your responsibility to your sphere of work?" "No," Speer answered, "this war has brought an inconceivable catastrophe. Therefore, it is my unquestionable duty to assume my share of responsibility for the disaster of the German people. . . . I, as an important member of the leadership of the Reich, share in the total responsibility." The statement—so at odds with the whining, self-pitying, hand-wringing moral blindness of a Ribbentrop, a Kaltenbrunner, a Sauckel—clearly pleased the court.

Speer went on. By March of 1945, he said, "Hitler intended, deliberately, to destroy the means of life for his own people if the war were lost. I have no intention of using my actions during that phase of the war to help me in my personal defense." But he wanted those who sat in judgment on him to understand that period. Though Hitler was ordering German industry razed, Speer explained, he had made the perilous decision to thwart the Führer and to preserve a base on which a defeated people could rebuild their country. He made sure that the court understood the high price of such defiance. Hitler had had eight officers shot for failing to blow up the bridge over the Rhine at Remagen, Speer pointed out.

He chose to read himself, rather than have his lawyer read, a memorandum he sent to Hitler in March 1945. "Nobody has the right to destroy industrial plants, coal mines, electric plants, and other fa-cilities. . . . We have no right at this stage of the war to carry out destruction which might affect the life of the people." Other defen-dants had condemned Hitler—Frank with strident emotionalism, Schirach with abject apology—but Speer did so with manly com-posure.

Earlier in the trial, during Otto Ohlendorf's testimony back in January, Speer's lawyer had briefly mentioned his scheme to assassi-nate Hitler. Speer said that he now wanted to discuss that issue in some detail, not to cast himself in a heroic light, but only to show

how thoroughly he had become convinced of Adolf Hitler's insane destructiveness. "I am most unwilling to describe the details because there is always something repellent about such matters," he began. He would only do so, he went on, "if it was the tribunal's wish." Sir Geoffrey could barely conceal his eagerness. "The court would like to hear the details," he announced.

Speer explained that he knew of an air-intake shaft in the Reich Chancellery garden that ventilated the Führerbunker below. The shaft was covered by a grate at ground level, hidden behind shrubs. In February of 1945, he confided to the head of his munitions department, Dieter Stahl, that there was only one way to end the war. He asked Stahl to procure a poison gas which he intended to drop into the ventilating system. When Speer revisited the site in March, he found a twelve-foot chimney protecting the ventilator. From that point on, he banished all further thoughts of killing Adolf Hitler.

For his closing, Speer took the rhetorical high ground. "The sacrifices which were made on both sides after January 1945 were senseless," he said. "The dead of this period will be the accusers of the man responsible for the continuation of that struggle." That man was Adolf Hitler.

Captain Gilbert had been much moved this day by Albert Speer's contrition. He stopped by the man's cell that night and found him deathly pale, stretched out on his cot, holding his stomach. He was exhausted, Speer explained, and he was suffering painful cramps. "That was quite a strain," he said, "but I'm glad I got it out of my system. I spoke the truth and that's all there was to it."

On Friday afternoon, June 21, the courtroom filled as spectators gathered to watch Robert Jackson cross-examine Speer. Arkady Poltorak, a Russian documents specialist, wandered to the windows behind the bench. Poltorak pulled aside the heavy drapes and looked out on a sun-drenched street. He came back to the Russian prosecutors' table. "I'd like to tear those curtains down," he announced. "I want to throw those windows open and let sunbeams and street noises in here so that those criminal bastards can feel the pulse of life and know it's still going on in spite of all their efforts."

"Attention! All rise," the marshal called out. "The tribunal will now enter." Jackson took his place at the prosecutor's stand. "Will you tell me," he asked Speer, "whether you were a member of the SS?" "No," Speer answered, "I was not a member of the SS." Jackson went on: "You filled out an application at one time, or one was filled out for you and you never went through with it, I believe. Or something like that." Jackson trailed off, to the surprise of those at the prosecution table. They had documents that proved indisputably that Speer had been a member of the SS. Jackson, however, did not press the matter.

He asked Speer about German production of poison gas. Yes, Speer explained, three factories had been working on a gas of extraordinary lethality, but when he learned Hitler might actually use it, Speer claimed, he ordered production stopped. Jackson asked Speer about German experiments with the atom bomb. "We had not got as far as that," Speer answered, "because the finest minds we had in atomic research had emigrated to America." No one had to be told who most of these scientists were and why they had fled Germany.

"Is it not a fact," Jackson asked, "that in the circle around Hitler there was almost no one who would stand up and tell him that the war was lost, except yourself?" Jaws dropped among the British prosecutors. "That is correct to a certain extent," Speer answered modestly.

"Well, now I am going to give you some information about the Krupp labor camp and I am going to ask you some questions about it," Jackson said. "And I am not attempting to say that you were personally responsible for these conditions." He proceeded to read into the record from affidavits of Krupp conscript workers describing the horrors they had endured. The evidence seemed to dangle in the air without point, since the prosecutor had exonerated the witness of any responsibility in advance. Jackson then read from a document about steel whips used on workers at the Krupp works, the kind Maxwell-Fyfe's wife had just been shown. Speer mumbled something about there being no rubber truncheons available. "So the guards probably had something like this . . ." Jackson asked no further questions about steel whips. He moved instead to Hitler's scorched-earth policy. "You wanted to see Germany have a chance to restore her life.

Is that not a fact?" he asked. "Whereas Hitler took the position that if he couldn't survive, he didn't care whether Germany survived or not?" Speer found no reason to disagree.

The questioning turned to Speer's final visit to Hitler. Speer knew that Jackson was treading near a weak patch in the fabric of his defense. He had said earlier that he had planned to assassinate Hitler. Yet, after that, he had taken enormous risks to fly into doomed Berlin to see the Führer in the bunker. Why? Jackson asked. "I felt," said Speer, "that it was my duty not to run away like a coward, but to stand up to him again."

That was a new twist. Speer's visit had but one purpose, to bid a final farewell to his leader. At the time, he had been hurt by Hitler, who dismissed him with a weak handshake and no expression of gratitude or friendship.

Jackson accepted the present reply and went on to another area. "This policy of driving Germany to destruction after the war was lost had come to weigh on you to such a point that you were a party to several plots, were you not?" Speer had been a party to no plots, but again saw no reason to disagree with Jackson. The prosecutor reached his final question. "You as a member of the government and a leader in this period acknowledge a responsibility for its large policies but not for the details that occurred in their execution. Is that a fair statement of your position?" "Yes, indeed," Speer answered. He could not have phrased it more profitably himself.

A deputy Russian prosecutor, M. Y. Raginsky, was scorching in his cross-examination of Speer. But unremitting hostility and a hunger for vengeance were expected of the Soviets. As Speer's defense ended and he left the stand, his stomach pains ended as well.

Airey Neave left the courtroom much dismayed. He had expected the Sauckel-Speer controversy to turn on social class, the mailed fist for one defendant and the velvet glove for the other. His fears, he believed, had been borne out. Speer had performed brilliantly. The man was not being charged with destroying or saving Germany's industrial base. He was not being accused of trying or failing to assassinate Hitler. Yet he had managed to make these issues the keystones of his defense. As for the assassination story, how far had it gone? Speer had talked to numerous Allied interrogators before being taken to Nuremberg, always putting himself in the best possible light. Yet he had never uttered a word about a plan to kill Hitler to any of them.

Yet Neave was enough of a lawyer to detach his personal doubts from the positive impact of Speer's performance before the court. Speer had accepted his share of responsibility for slave labor; he had declared Hitler guilty of the senseless deaths of thousands on both sides for his insane continuation of a lost war. Indeed, Speer held Hitler responsible for starting the war, yet asserted that he too must bear a quota of personal guilt for this "disaster." And he had tried to thwart Hitler's scorched-earth orders and claimed to have planned to assassinate the man.

The admirable side of Speer's character appeared to have touched Jackson. The American prosecutor had made no attempt to question Speer about his awareness of the extermination of the Jews, which Himmler had described at a conference that Speer attended. Nor had he dealt with Speer's presence at the Mauthausen concentration camp. Speer had been allowed to talk of the production miracles he had performed, testimony that virtually cried out for cross-examination on the role slave labor played in these feats. He had not been asked.

Neave, then, was hardly surprised at the account that appeared in the *Daily Telegraph* after Speer's defense. The London paper's stance reflected the majority opinion reported out of Nuremberg. Speer had delivered "a tremendous indictment which might well stand for the German people and posterity as the most important and dramatic event of the trial."

32

By the end of June, reporters could easily get a room in the dormitories at the Stein Castle. The Nuremberg story had slipped to the back pages. The names of the only two defendants left to testify struck no fearsome images. Konstantin von Neurath and Hans Fritzsche sat next to each other in the far corner of the dock, rarely among those pointed out to curious spectators. Neurath, at seventy-three the oldest defendant, was exhibiting incipient senility. He had been Ribbentrop's predecessor as foreign minister and, like Papen and Schacht, had lent a patina of respectability to the Hitler regime.

Neurath's sin, as Maxwell-Fyfe put it in his cross-examination, was to have been foreign minister while Germany was "breaking only one treaty at a time." In 1939, Hitler named him Protector of Bohemia and Moravia in Czechoslovakia, nominally above the SS and Gestapo. But these organizations carried out their grim work ignoring this gentleman of the old school. A handful of reporters in the press gallery suffered hours of Neurath's rambling rationalizations, and then his defense ended.

Hans Fritzsche was the second defendant provided by the Russians. As with Raeder, the prosecution had been put in the position of working backward, of having the man first and then having to rustle up evidence to convict him. Fritzsche had headed the radio division in the Nazi Propaganda Ministry, and had been a popular commentator himself. Drexel Sprecher had applied his notable energy over several months trying to prove that Fritzsche used his broadcasts "to advocate, encourage, and incite" war crimes, particularly offenses against the Jews. But in a confidential memorandum, Sprecher admitted that the evidence was "utterly inadequate . . . to establish that Fritzsche had any intimate connection with the claims mentioned in counts three and four."

On the 166th day of the trial, Fritzsche left the stand. The last man in the dock had completed his defense.

It was Sir Geoffrey Lawrence's pleasure to take an evening stroll with his wife through the park near his home. This evening was particularly agreeable, with poppies and peonies somehow prospering in neglected beds. The Soviet documents man, Arkady Poltorak, and Lev Shenin, an assistant prosecutor, had also chosen the park for a walk. On seeing the justice and his wife approach, Poltorak mentioned to his companion that this might be a good chance to ask Sir Geoffrey if he intended to reopen the issue of the Katyn massacre. Shenin looked horrified. Didn't Poltorak know one of the cardinal rules of the IMT? One must never talk shop to Sir Geoffrey outside the court. Then what did one talk to him about? Poltorak asked. His horses, of course, Shenin replied, his dogs, his cows.

The Western judges had thought it foolish of the Soviet government to insist on introducing the Katyn massacre during the prosecution phase. Now, at the close of the defense phase, they had no choice but to allow the Germans to rebut the charge. The basic facts were clear enough. Sometime after the defeat of Poland, approximately 11,000 of her soldiers, including 8,300 officers, had disappeared. In February 1943, a German communications regiment stumbled onto the unmarked graves of 4,800 of these men in the Katyn forest near Smolensk. At issue was the question of which side, the Russians or the Germans, had killed these men.

For two days, July 1 and 2, forensic experts battled in room 600. Guilt turned on fixing the date when the Poles had died. The Russians claimed the deaths occurred in the autumn of 1941, after the Soviet Union had been invaded and while the Germans occupied the Katyn forest. The Germans claimed the Poles had died earlier, in 1940, when the Russians still held this territory.

In the end, the Germans had the better of it. Among their most persuasive evidence was the fact that all letters from the Poles had ceased after April 1940, at which time the Russians controlled the forest. The judges, except for Nikitchenko, were dismayed that the issue had ever arisen. To conclude that the Russians themselves had shot thousands of Poles would dilute the horror of the crimes of the Nazis. What was the court to do with this moral morass? Their responsibility, they decided, was not to place blame on one of the countries, but to determine if a certain charge against German war criminals was proved. They simply took the position that the Russian accusation against the Germans lacked sufficient evidence, and let the Katyn issue drop.

33

As HE HEADED for the Judges' Room this July morning, Justice Jackson felt better than he had in months. The next time he spoke in the courtroom, it would be in the realm where he was master, delivering the American prosecution's closing speech. The night before, he had withdrawn alone to his room with pen and legal pad to start forming his thoughts. For now, however, he had to resolve a debate over the time the defense attorneys would be allotted for their summations. He was painfully familiar with the stupefying lengths to which they could go, and the Germans were asking for unlimited time. If the trial did not end soon, he feared, its moral force would seep away. Jackson had polled his fellow prosecutors, and they agreed that three days was ample time for the defense to sum up its case. He was bringing this recommendation to the judges this morning.

Francis Biddle was coolly aloof, Sir Geoffrey seemed impatient, and the French judges' expressions revealed nothing. Only the two Russians were openly sympathetic to Jackson. Finally, Sir Geoffrey ruled. He had given the defendants not the slightest reason to attack the fairness of this trial thus far. He was not about to give them that opportunity now by gagging them. Biddle nodded. Otto Stahmer, Sir Geoffrey said, as spokesman for the defense, had asked for one day per defendant. If that meant a summation lasting three weeks, so be it.

Jackson forced himself to attend court on July 4, the day the defense summations began; his worst fears were confirmed. The defense lawyers had flooded the Language Division with documents to translate —many of them of dubious relevance—on a scale unknown since the opening of the trial. This morning, a few glassy-eyed reporters studied the floor and ceiling as Otto Stahmer explained why Hermann Göring was innocent. "When by the advent of the Renaissance and the Reformation," Stahmer droned on, "the spiritual basis of the medieval order was broken, this development into a universal world peace was reversed. Life, formerly tending toward stagnation and tranquillity . . ." Jackson could take no more and left. Stahmer was beginning his client's defense in the sixteenth century.

The posters had long since become faded and tattered—some 200,000 of them, bearing the photograph of Martin Bormann, plastered on walls, trees, telephone poles, and boxcars all over Germany. Bormann was a wanted man. As the Führer's secretary, he had exercised only borrowed power, but he had wielded it with ingenious malice. He had been particularly energetic in transmitting orders to shoot captured Allied fliers. His proximity to Hitler and his rabid hatred of Jews and

Slavs meant that he had full knowledge of the regime's foulest crimes. The problem with the Bormann case was that the man had disappeared in the last days of the war. The prosecution, nevertheless, wanted Bormann indicted, and the court had agreed. On July 6, the defense summations were interrupted so that the court could try Bormann in absentia.

Göring had made something of a cottage industry out of locating Bormann. He told Theodore Fenstermacher, a prosecutor who grilled him in the visitors' room, that Bormann was "a left-wing Nazi and had fled to the Soviet Union." "Mark my words," Göring had said, "he'll show up as the head of a Soviet-dominated puppet government." Navy lieutenant Thomas F. Lambert, Jr., who had had the semisurreal task of prosecuting Bormann, also interrogated Göring on the missing defendant's whereabouts. Bormann, Göring said with breezy assurance, was in Argentina, protected by President Juan Perón. Questioned later still, Göring confided to Fenstermacher that Bormann was in Spain with Generalissimo Franco. Fenstermacher described these conflicting accounts to Colonel Andrus. "Don't you know the man will do anything to get out of his cell?" Andrus explained.

Hans Fritzsche claimed to have been with Bormann on May 1, 1945, the day of his disappearance, when both men fled the Führerbunker. They were moving behind a tank with other fleeing Nazis when it exploded, probably from a shell hit. Fritzsche believed Bormann had been killed outright, but had not seen his body.

In January, during the prosecution phase, Lieutenant Lambert had submitted evidence displaying the heights and depths of Bormann's malice. He signed or issued orders that expelled millions of European Jews from their homes, forbade prosecution of German civilians who lynched downed Allied fliers, and barred the use of coffins to bury Soviet war prisoners. On July 6, Friedrich Bergold, the German lawyer given the task of defending Bormann, took virtually the only course left him—he declared his client dead.

After the Bormann hiatus, the defense summations resumed before a virtually empty courtroom, save for the captive audience of judges and defendants. Only during the remarks of Schacht's attorney,

Rudolf Dix, did the court come to life. Dix gestured toward Kalten-brunner, former head of the RSHA, and then toward Schacht, once a prisoner in Dachau. "It is surely a rare and grotesque picture to see a jailer and a prisoner sharing a bench in the dock," Dix noted. The court had seen for itself the shocking behavior of Judge Roland Freis-ler in the film shown of the People's Court. During the Nazi era, Dix defended Schacht as an enemy of the regime before Freisler, he ex-plained. And now he was defending Schacht before the Allies as a war criminal. Need he say anything else in his client's defense? Schacht's situation summoned up the story of Seneca, Dix said, who had been put on trial by Nero for treason—and who then, when Nero died, had been placed on trial "for complicity in Nero's misgoverning and cruelties."

Colonel Andrus took advantage of the dog days to get his newly ar-rived wife, Katharine, and his daughter Kitty settled in Nuremberg. Kitty, the youngest of the colonel's four children, fresh from an Amer-ican high school, soon received a practical European education. She became friendly with Hedda, the Andruses' maid, who was eager to improve her English. They were the same age, and Kitty Andrus lis-tened agog at the living Hedda had done. The German girl had served as a nurse in the amputation ward of a military hospital. Her pilot fiancé had been killed on his first mission. She had watched from a hospital window as her city turned to ashes during the heaviest RAF raid of the war. The only time the maid's English faltered was when Kitty asked if Hedda had attended the Zeppelin Field rallies during Party Days. She did not understand, Hedda said, and returned to her work.

Two voluble men sat drinking in the Marble Room. Lieutenant Tex Wheelis was telling Captain John Vonetes, the American housing of-ficer, how well he got along with the defendants. Hermann Göring was a friend of his, Wheelis claimed. The *Reichsmarschall* had given him this watch with his facsimile signature, the lieutenant noted, flash-ing it before Vonetes. He also had Göring's Mont Blanc pen with the name engraved on the cap, and photographs of the *Reichsmarschall* with personal inscriptions. There was only one thing wrong with prison duty in Nuremberg, Wheelis confided. What was that? Vonetes wanted to know. "It's the guy I have to work for," Wheelis answered. Vonetes knew Colonel Andrus, he said, but made no other comment.

Robert Jackson worked with the fervor of a man doing what he had been put on earth to do. In the waning days of July, he spared himself the agony of hearing the lawyers for Kaltenbrunner, Sauckel, Frick, Funk, the lot of them, excusing and explaining their clients' crimes. Instead, he stayed home in his study and worked on his closing speech. In the rough draft, so far, he hit Göring on virtually every page. He denounced the industrialists, thus preparing the ground for Telford Taylor's subsequent prosecutions of them after his own departure. Above all, he wanted the speech to proclaim to the world that the Nazi conspiracy to conquer, exploit, and exterminate had been proved.

These passages formed the muscle and sinew of his text. But he enjoyed just as well playing with language, trying out and testing aloud, in his rich baritone, the lyrics of condemnation: "Ribbentrop, that salesman of deception"; "Rosenberg, Nazism's intellectual high priest"; "Kaltenbrunner, the grand inquisitor"; "fanatical Frank" and "Streicher, the venomous vulgarian"; "Schirach, poisoner of youth"; "Sauckel, cruelest slaver since the pharaohs"; and "Funk, banker of gold teeth, the most ghoulish collateral in history." He asked Elsie Douglas to find a volume of Shakespeare. He wanted those lines between Gloucester and Lady Anne from *Richard III*, perfect for his peroration.

The defense summations ground on for a full three weeks, an arid stretch epitomized by Flottenrichter Kranzbuehler's dropping a 105-page "Closing Defense for the Defendant Dönitz" on the translations unit. The last summation was delivered by Alfred Seidl for Rudolf Hess, on July 25. Next, the prosecution would have its final word.

34

THE MORNING OF JULY 26, the defendants left their cells to hear the prosecution summation. Men in straits similar to their own, they knew, were faring badly. They had just learned the fate of Karl Hermann Frank, whose trial Justice Jackson had witnessed in Prague. Frank, who had erased Lidice and slaughtered its men, had gone to the gallows. Of seventy-seven Waffen SS troops convicted for murdering American POWs near Malmédy, forty-three had been sentenced to death.

Robert Jackson took advantage of the drive to the courthouse to make last-minute revisions to his speech. His fellow passengers included his ever-present bodyguard, Sergeant Moritz Fuchs. Young Fuchs had recently confided his post-trial hopes to Jackson. Before the war, the sergeant had been an engineering student at Purdue. But after the revelations heard day after day in room 600, and after meeting the German Catholic stigmatic Teresa Neumann, Fuchs found the prospect of a life spent at a drafting table unappealing. He had told Jackson that he intended to enter the priesthood. Jackson found the young soldier's decision moving, an affirmation of the moral awakening that he hoped the trial would prompt well beyond room 600.

The car slowed to a halt. Elsie Douglas checked Jackson's appearance one last time as the party entered the courthouse.

The American prosecutor conferred briefly with his son, Bill, who was posted behind him holding relevant documents, as Sir Geoffrey called the court to order. Robert Jackson was to speak first. Sir Hartley Shawcross, supplanting Maxwell-Fyfe on this key occasion, would succeed Jackson, followed by Auguste Champetier for France and, finally, Roman Rudenko for the Soviet Union. The visitors' gallery and the press area were once again thronged. The ex post facto issue had to be dealt with early, Jackson began, not necessarily to persuade the court, but to satisfy world opinion. Naturally, the defendants' "dislike for the law which condemns them is not original," he noted. "It has been remarked before, 'No thief e'er felt the halter draw with good opinion of the law.'" He had staked his prosecution on the conspiracy theory, and he pronounced it proven beyond a doubt in the written and uttered words of the conspirators themselves.

He pointed to Schacht, sitting in his customary pose, legs crossed, arms folded, head turned away, the picture of a man much put-upon. The absence of German industrialists in the dock still displeased Jackson; but Schacht would do. "Twenty days after the seizure of power, Schacht was host to Hitler, Göring, and some twenty leading industrialists," Jackson noted. He described the financier as "a Brahmin among the untouchables. . . . He could not bear to mingle with the Nazis socially, but never could he afford to separate from them politically. . . . Schacht always fought for his position in a regime he now affects to despise."

Only Göring came in for more killing fire. The *Reichsmarschall*, with perverse pride, stopped counting after Jackson's references to him surpassed forty. Jackson indicted the other defendants in turn: "the zealot Hess," "Keitel, the willing tool," and "Dönitz, the legatee of defeat." He accused the stolid philosopher Rosenberg of adding "boredom to the list of Nazi atrocities."

Albert Speer listened with a surface calm. Jackson's cross-examination of him the month before had been solicitous, even gentle, and, so far, the prosecutor had omitted Speer from his catalogue of villains. Suddenly, Jackson was quoting Speer. As Speer himself had said on the stand, Jackson noted, "the sacrifices which were made on both sides after January 1945 were without sense." And Speer had made clear that the monster responsible for these squandered lives was Adolf Hitler. Yes, Jackson had used Speer's words, but not against him. Was it possible to dream of acquittal?

Elsie Douglas had located the passage from Shakespeare that Bob wanted and listened intently as he approached his peroration. "These defendants now ask the tribunal to say that they are not guilty of planning, executing, or conspiring to commit this long list of crimes and wrongs," he began. "They stand before the record of this trial as blood-stained Gloucester stood by the body of his slain king. He begged of the widow, as they beg of you: 'Say I slew them not.' And the queen replied, 'Then say they are not slain. But dead they are . . .' If you were to say of these men that they are not guilty, it would be as true to say that there has been no war, there are no slain, there has been no crime."

The hush in the courtroom was complete. Jackson gathered up his papers and returned to the prosecution table. Neave and Justice

Birkett exchanged nods. Jackson might have his superiors in the thrust and parry of the game. But in finding the words that captured the majesty of justice, they had just witnessed the master.

In the "elders' " lunchroom, Franz von Papen grumbled to Gilbert that Jackson had ignored their defenses. The old diplomat, usually the soul of reserve, complained, "Why have we been sitting here for eight months? The prosecution still insisted on calling us liars and murderers."

Julius Streicher approached Gilbert. He was now ready to join the Jews in their fight for a homeland, he wanted the psychologist to know. He had read of recent rioting in Palestine. "Anybody who can fight and resist and stick together, and stick to their guns, for such people I can only have the greatest respect," he said. "Even if Hitler was living now, he too would admit they are a scrappy race. I'm ready to join and help them in their fight. I am not joking! The Jews will dominate the world. And I would be happy to help lead them to victory. I have studied them so long that I suppose I have adopted their characteristics. I'll make a proposition. Let me address a gathering at Madison Square Garden in New York. It will be a sensation!" Jodl and Rosenberg, overhearing Streicher, burst out into laughter.

Streicher's little speech suggested the ironies in the life of this coarse anti-Semite. Whenever a synagogue in Franconia had been desecrated or a rabbi turned out of his home, Streicher, as *Gauleiter*, had all books and manuscripts slated for destruction brought to him first. From them he selected the rarest, most valuable items for the library of *Der Stürmer*. Thus, with the war ended and with so much Jewish scholarship in ashes, the premier Jew-baiter had rescued a priceless collection of Judaica from the flames.

The lawyer in Hans Frank had picked up on something in Jackson's summation that the rest of his lunch partners had missed. He pointed out that, no matter how unrelenting the prosecutor's condemnation, he had not called for the death penalty.

In the afternoon session, Justice Lawrence called on the patrician Labourite Sir Hartley Shawcross. In a summation approaching Jackson's in eloquence, Sir Hartley called not simply for the defendants' conviction but for the death of them all. The French and Russian prosecutors also closed by demanding capital punishment.

Only the defense of the Nazi organizations and brief final statements by the defendants remained. Colonel John Harlan Amen's interrogations unit, its work done, had disbanded. Robert Jackson felt sufficiently comfortable to turn the direction of the prosecution temporarily over to Tom Dodd while he went home to remind the U.S. Supreme Court that he was still a member. In the courthouse, the climate of argument began to yield to a climate of judgment.

35

EMMY GÖRING HAD WRITTEN to Sir Geoffrey begging to be allowed to visit her husband. Lawrence had bucked the letter to Burt Andrus with a note saying, "The tribunal has no objection." Her request was a matter of prison security and thus entirely up to the colonel. Her appeal seemed a simple enough human cry. Why not let her come? But what if something went wrong? If, somehow, in spite of all his precautions, she brought Göring a plan for a breakout, or slipped him a concealed weapon, or poison? If he lost the court's prize catch, whose fault would it be? Certainly not that of the august British jurist; it would be Burt Andrus's neck. He had already been reprimanded by General Watson because of Frau Göring. A few days before, Watson's counterintelligence people had tailed the chaplain, Major Gerecke, on an errand of mercy to her cabin, and Andrus, as the minister's superior, had taken the rap. Even more baffling to Andrus, Robert Kempner, a Jew fired by Göring from the Prussian police and driven from Germany by the Nuremberg Laws, was known to be visiting Emmy laden with PX luxuries. What was Kempner trying to prove by showing kindness to his persecutor's wife? he wondered. Burt Andrus was not trying to prove anything. He knew his duty, and he knew the price if he failed. His mind was made up. He was going to deny Emmy Göring's request.

The colonel loved one part of the job. The stream of famous names drawn to Nuremberg was beginning to pick up again as the trial approached judgment day. They all wanted front-row seats in the gallery and visits to the prison. Lord Maugham, the leading British jurist and brother of the novelist Somerset Maugham, came to Nuremberg. Virgil Thomson and Charles Munch, figures from the world of music, came. So did former mayor of New York Fiorello LaGuardia, as well as actresses Rita Hayworth and Marlene Dietrich. *Pravda*'s Boris Polevoi flirted with Dietrich in the visitors' gallery, not knowing who she was. And Andrus noticed that somehow the itineraries of congressmen and government officials who visited Nuremberg always ended up at resorts in Garmisch-Partenkirchen.

The justices made an exception to their overall prohibition and allowed Andrus to take a few select journalists through cellblock C. Helmet gleaming, his riding crop tucked into place, he led them through the barrier of locks and sentries into the jail. Among the reporters was Andy Logan, age twenty-four, who had literally stepped from college onto the staff of *The New Yorker* and had managed a Nuremberg assignment to be with her prosecutor husband. Logan found most of the cells' inhabitants taciturn and Göring determinedly mute. But Albert Speer charmed the press people, behaving as though he were their delighted host, asking which papers they represented, answering their questions volubly. Logan also cast a journalist's eye over the colonel. Here was a man in his element, interspersing explanations of security measures with the history of each prisoner as the visitors passed by the cells. Forgotten for the moment were the pressures, collisions, and rivalries that plagued him daily. Colonel Andrus, the Nuremberg jailer, cut quite a figure.

36

On July 30, the defense of seven indicted Nazi organizations—the Nazi party leadership, the Reich cabinet, the SS, the Gestapo, the SD, the SA, and the High Command—began. As in December, when the prosecution made its case against them, the Palace of Justice mail room was again inundated. The court had ordered notices placed throughout Germany describing how affected parties could apply to testify; over 313,000 people responded. From these, 603 members of the indicted groups were brought to Nuremberg and screened as potential witnesses. In the end, the tribunal took affidavits from ninety of them. Over and over, they expressed the same words or sentiments: "As a member of the SS, I was never expected to perform a dishonorable act. Never was I commanded to commit a crime."

Justice Francis Biddle heard the organization cases with scarcely concealed impatience. He recognized the neat logic of the prosecution: individuals conspire to evil intent; they create organizations to achieve their ends; therefore, both the individuals and the organizations are criminal. Appealing symmetry, Biddle thought, but poor law. Conviction of the Nazi party leadership alone would automatically brand over 600,000 Germans as war criminals. Yet the culpability of a *Reichsleiter* like Rosenberg and that of a block leader who had done little more than collect dues were hardly comparable. To Biddle, the prosecution of the organization cases was a result of Bob Jackson's righteous streak.

The organizations' defense continued uneventfully until August 20, when the courtroom suddenly crackled with anticipation. The press and visitors' galleries were again packed. Hermann Göring was returning to the witness stand.

During the SS case, the prosecution had cross-examined a witness named Wolfram Sievers, head of the German Ancestral Heritage Society. Sievers had described an arrangement he had made with the SS, under which the latter would kill "Jewish-Bolshevik" commissars and send him their skulls for scientific study. In the course of his testimony, Sievers implicated Göring as president of the Reich Research Council. Göring's lawyer, Otto Stahmer, persuaded his client that he had to disprove his complicity. Thus, Göring testified again. Had he ever given an order for medical experiments on humans? Stahmer asked the *Reichsmarschall*. Did he know Dr. Rascher, who performed the research on human guinea pigs at Dachau for the Luftwaffe? Did Göring order freezing experiments to be conducted on inmates? As president of the Reich Research Council, had he ordered studies carried out on germ warfare? Göring denied it all.

On arriving in the dock this morning, the *Reichsmarshall* had noticed that Justice Jackson was absent—which likely boded cross-examination by Maxwell-Fyfe. Sir David indeed rose, as Stahmer yielded the witness. He led the questioning to experiments on cold-weather clothing worn by fliers. "You have been a practical airman yourself, with a very gallant record of service in the air in the last war," he began. Given this personal interest, was it possible "you don't remember about experiments on these concentration camp detainees for testing air clothing?" He wore so many hats, Göring said. Tens of thousands of orders had been issued in his name. Even though Mr. Jackson, in his summation, had accused him of having his "fat fingers in every pie," he could not possibly have known of all medical experiments carried out in the Third Reich.

Maxwell-Fyfe produced a document containing correspondence between Heinrich Himmler and Field Marshal Erhard Milch, Göring's deputy. In one letter, Milch thanked Himmler for Dr. Rascher's work on problems confronted in flying at high altitudes. One test involved putting a Jewish inmate at a simulated height of 29,000 feet without oxygen. The subject had expired after thirteen minutes. Was it possible that a high-ranking, close associate like Milch could have knowledge of these deadly experiments, while Göring had not? Sir David asked. Göring explained that matters under his control had been classified as "very important," "important," and "routine." Experiments reviewed by the Luftwaffe Medical Inspectorate fell into the lowest category and were not brought to his attention. Sir David found the answer sufficiently incriminating and let it stand.

Russian prosecutor Major General Alexandrov followed Maxwell-Fyfe. Alexandrov called upon Walter Schreiber, a fifty-three-year-old German army doctor, and asked him to describe a medical conference the German had attended near Berlin in 1943. At this meeting, Schreiber said, a Dr. Kramer discussed experiments carried out for the Luftwaffe at Dachau, particularly tests on the warmth retention of various items of flying gear. The tests were performed by dropping inmates into freezing water. "Please tell the court what the defendant Göring had to do with such experiments," Alexandrov asked. Dr. Kramer had explained to them, Schreiber said, "that Göring had ordered these experiments, and that Reichsführer Himmler had kindly made available the subjects for the experiments." As he left the dock, Göring muttered at his lawyer. Stahmer had urged the gamble, but Göring had lost.

On August 30, the court heard final testimony on the indicted organizations, the last evidence to be presented before the IMT. The next day, each individual defendant would have fifteen minutes for a final statement. The judges would then retire to deliberate their fates.

37

JIM ROWE CAME into Francis Biddle's office and asked if he might speak privately with the American justice. Biddle admired the Montanan as a first-rate legal mind and a get-it-done administrator. During the war, Rowe's carrier, the *Sewanee,* had been among the first hit by Japanese kamikazes. With most of the firefighting crew killed outright, Rowe had grabbed a hose and braved the flames to save his men. He had won eight battle stars in the Pacific. Rowe's opinions carried weight with Biddle.

They had a security problem, Rowe said. Somebody was rifling Biddle's office at night. It could be thieves, an aggressive journalist, someone acting for the defense. The courthouse was a sieve. Just this morning, Rowe had found, lying around in the Language Division, the French translation of a secret session of the justices. He calculated that, between secretaries, translators, interpreters, typists, proofreaders, mimeograph operators, and other technical staff, fourteen people saw classified documents intended only for the eyes of the justices and their immediate aides. "If you're interested in hearing what the verdicts are going to be," Rowe said, "just sit in the lobby of the Grand Hotel." The leaks had to be stopped. Once the innermost deliberations of the judges fell into the hands of the press, the work of the court would be seriously compromised.

What did Rowe suggest? Biddle asked. First, Rowe answered, kick all the interpreters out of the judges' private meetings, except for one Russian. Biddle himself could handle the French. In the meantime, Rowe would devise a system to keep the judges' private sessions secure.

For two months, the justices' aides had been evaluating the evidence and preparing preliminary verdicts. Birkett, the great pen on the bench, had completed an early draft of the final judgment. The justices had met to review Birkett's fifty-thousand-word effort while the last defendant, Hans Fritzsche, was still on the stand. They had immediately grasped a nettle in the case: the conspiracy theory. The prosecution was relying on the Hossbach conference of November 1937 and other evidence to prove that several of the defendants conspired to launch an aggressive war. The French judge, Donnedieu de Vabres, who never asked a question in court and rarely uttered a word in their private sessions, finally spoke out. A conspiracy, Donnedieu de Vabres said, connotes participation among more-or-less-equal parties. The defendants themselves would be the first to laugh at the notion of Streicher, Funk, Frick, Sauckel, and Ribbentrop as Hitler's conspiratorial peers. It was ridiculous, the Frenchman said. By pursuing this mad idea of conspiracy, going back to events taking place in a sovereign country over the course of twenty years, they were feeding the critics who decried ex post facto justice. Judge these men by what they have done, Donnedieu de Vabres cautioned, not by what they allegedly planned to do. Drop the conspiracy charge.

But, Sir Geoffrey countered, Article 6 of the charter specifically included the crime of conspiracy. And they were bound by the charter.

Biddle spoke to the chief judge like a professor confronting an obtuse pupil. Because a statute described a crime, must they say the crime was committed? Could they not say of the conspiracy charge, "not proved," and save a lot of grief? The guilty would be convicted anyway, for the *commission* of crimes. There was little point in attempting to establish that a conspiracy to conquer the world had already been in place in some Munich beer hall in 1919. They should limit the conspiracy charge to events occurring after 1937, Biddle urged. Donnedieu de Vabres objected. If they accepted that the *Führerprinzip* meant ironbound obedience to the leader, then the idea of true conspirators made no sense either before or after 1937. He wanted conspiracy dropped.

Sir Norman Birkett paced agitatedly. He too had originally disliked the conspiracy charge, he said. But, as the trial unfolded, he had come to see Jackson's larger objective. If individuals were convicted only for individual acts, the trial would never rise above the level of an ordinary criminal prosecution. What they wanted to present to the world was the condemnation of a regime deliberately embarked on war. To drop conspiracy was to lose the trial's moral grandeur.

38

WHAT GÖRING AND COMPANY TALK ABOUT IN THEIR CELLS, the headline promised in the Sunday, August 25, London *Express*. "Hitler's Stomach Cause of All the Trouble," "When Ribbentrop Wanted a Medal," "Why Hitler Delayed Marriage," the subheads read. The *Express*'s source was Dr. Douglas Kelley, described as "Chief Psychiatrist at the Nuremberg Trials." The article included quotations from Göring, Hess, and Ribbentrop, divulging heretofore unrevealed secrets from inside the Reich and the Nuremberg prison. Colonel Andrus held the clipping like a contaminated object. The man he so admired, Sir Geoffrey Lawrence, had sent it to him with a note reading, "We shouldn't want any more of this, Colonel."

Andrus tossed the clipping at Gustav Gilbert and asked what he knew about it. Gilbert answered that he knew nothing about the origins of the Kelley story. Did Gilbert know that his psychiatrist friend was on the lecture circuit back in the States, criticizing the trial? the colonel asked. He intended to investigate this business, and he expected Gilbert's cooperation.

To Gilbert, even more alarming news had come earlier. Since Kelley appeared to have struck off on his own, Gilbert had started to shape his cell-visit notes, which he had taken as the prison psychologist, into his own book, tentatively entitled *Nuremberg Diary*. He had engaged a literary agent, who had negotiated a contract with the publisher Farrar, Straus. The agent had recently cabled Gilbert to tell him that Kelley was negotiating with Simon and Schuster. It had become a race, with Kelley holding the better post position. He was already in the States. He had completed whatever research he intended to use, while Gilbert was still making cell visits over 3,500 miles away. Farrar, Straus had informed Gilbert that they could not get his book out before March 1947. The best card that Gilbert held was a half-finished manuscript. He gave it to a friend returning to the States and asked him to take it to his agent. His hope was to demonstrate that he was well ahead of his rival and that it would be a mistake for Simon and Schuster to try to beat Gus Gilbert.

Colonel Andrus sent a report to Sir Geoffrey explaining that Major Kelley had left Nuremberg on February 7, "under a cloud, as the impression had been gained that he was subordinating all his professional duties to an effort to gather information to publish for personal gain." In pursuit of this objective, "He has gone so far as to misappropriate in part official files of the tribunal."

Of course, the colonel had never been entirely comfortable with Gustav Gilbert either. The army recently had assigned Lieutenant Colonel W. H. Dunn as prison psychiatrist, and Andrus sent Justice Jackson a note saying that Gilbert was therefore of no further use to the ISD. He would keep the man, but only if Jackson insisted.

39

ON AUGUST 31, a Saturday session, the defendants were to make their final statements before the verdicts were handed down. Most spent the night before honing their thoughts with their lawyers in the visitors' room. Hess remained in his cell writing to his wife. "You most certainly heard over the radio," he wrote, "that there has been another 'miracle' and I have completely recovered my mind. Or they may tell you that I have lost my reason or suffer from an 'idée fixe.' I hope you will see the humorous side of all this. Karl [Haushofer] once wrote that for the sake of a great cause one must be able to suffer the strain of seeming to one's own people, for a time, to be a traitor. To that I would add, or seem to be crazy. . . . I will face fate with . . . the same imperturbability with which I shall receive the verdict."

At the end of the block, in cell 17, Albert Speer concluded that honesty had proved to be the best defense after all. The more he admitted to himself the truth of his seduction by Hitler and the perversion of his talents in the service of Nazism, the easier it became to accept guilt and abandon denials. Not only did the truth relieve him of the baggage of self-deception, but it freed his mind to see beyond his own small fate. The same grasp of technology that he had once applied to pumping more tanks out of factories, he now applied to predicting the human condition in the atomic age. That was what he would devote his fifteen minutes to—not to saving the hide of Albert Speer, but to suggesting a path of hope for mankind into this new world.

After a brief chat, Jodl gave his lawyer, Franz Exner, a letter for his wife. Since he could occasionally see Luise in court, Jodl was judged one of the luckier defendants. But having her witness his humiliation also sharpened his pain. Underneath the indecipherable countenance, he was a confused man. Alfred Jodl genuinely did not understand why he was on trial. "I cannot rid myself of the conviction that I have not merited this fate," he wrote his wife. Still, if the worst came to pass, "Death will find here no broken, penitent victim, but a proud man who can look him coldly in the eye. . . . Yet, in my heart of hearts, I do not believe that this will be my sentence." He watched Exner disappear with the letter, hoping, however painful it would be, that Luise would appear in court when he spoke the next day.

The town was aswarm with journalism's luminous names—Joseph Alsop, Walter Lippmann, Harold Nicolson, and Rebecca West among them. Francis Biddle was delighted to have West back in town. During her July Nuremberg stint, he had set his sights on the writer and succeeded. They had gone off together for four days in Prague. Now, with West back to cover the trial's denouement, she became his houseguest at the Villa Conradti. On the eve of the defendants' final speeches, Biddle threw a cocktail party in West's honor. The guests were surprised to find this woman, who wrote so poetically at times and so scathingly at others, a small, dowdy figure. Still, they gathered like bees around the queen to hear her facile sketches of the men in the dock: She called Julius Streicher "a man a sane Germany would have sent to an asylum long ago." Of Göring: "When he's in a good humor he resembles the madam of a brothel." She loved Sir Geoffrey Lawrence, with that "voice of a silvery querulousness that flays without drawing a drop of blood."

After she retired to the Biddle guest room, West jotted down notes on the world of her Nuremberg hosts. The Britishers reminded her of life in some Kiplingesque "colonial hill station," where people insisted on traditional conduct and dress out of fear of going native.

As for the Americans, she wrote: "It is as if all the employees of the New York Telephone Company were transported to such a town as Toledo, Ohio, which by some melancholy visitation had been deprived of its amenities, and were forced to live there for ten months, during which they all had particular reasons for wanting to do something else, under an ordinance which forbade them any intercourse with the native Toledans. . . ."

The defendants were to make their final statements in the order in which they had been indicted. As Göring moved to the middle of the dock, a guard dangled before him a microphone suspended from a pole. He did not fail those who had grudgingly come to admire his belligerent consistency. This had been a poor excuse for a trial, Göring began: "The statements of defendants were accepted as true when they supported the prosecution. They were treated as perjury when they refuted the indictment." Why was he in the dock being treated as a common criminal? Let his judges have no illusions. "Since the three greatest powers on earth, together with other nations, fought against us, we finally were conquered by tremendous enemy superiority." Justice had nothing to do with this trial.

Hess was next. He asked the chief judge if he might remain seated, "because of the state of my health." He spoke in a reedy voice of his days in England: "The people around me during my imprisonment acted toward me in a way which led me to conclude that these people somehow were acting in an abnormal state of mind. . . . Some of the new ones who came to me in place of those who had been changed had strange eyes. They were glassy like eyes in a dream." The judges exchanged uneasy glances. Hess's lawyer, Seidl, looked as though he wanted to disappear. Hess went on. "In the spring of 1942, I had a visitor. . . . This visitor also had these strange eyes." Hess switched suddenly to the Moscow show trials of 1938. "One got the impression that these defendants, through a means unknown up until now, had been transported into an abnormal state of mind. . . ." Göring jammed Hess with his elbow and told him to stop. "Shut up," Hess shot back. Sir Geoffrey reminded the defendant that he had exceeded his fifteen minutes. "It was my pleasure that many years of my life were spent in working under the greatest son which my people produced in its thousand-year history," Hess concluded, folding his arms and sitting back, chin uplifted.

Major Airey Neave watched from the visitors' gallery. He had measured these men since the day he had delivered their indictments. Some had grown. Some had not. Ribbentrop, the next defendant, was among the latter. What Germany had attempted, the former foreign minister said, was what Great Britain had done in sweeping a fifth of the globe under her wing of empire, what America had done in occupying the New World, what Russia had done in spreading her dominion from Europe to Asia. A trace of the old hauteur appeared as Ribbentrop finished his statement and sat down.

As a soldier himself, Neave had been appalled at Keitel's prostitution of the warrior's code of honor. But Keitel was one who had grown, Neave believed. He detected a serenity in the man today. His tragedy, Keitel told the court, was that "the best I had to give as a soldier, obedience and loyalty, was exploited for purposes which could not be recognized at the time . . . and that I did not see that there is a limit set even for a soldier's performance of his duty. That is my fate."

Frank had moved the court during his earlier testimony with his fervent indictment of Nazism. Today he began, "On this witness stand, I said that a thousand years would not suffice to erase the guilt brought upon our people because of Hitler's conduct of this war." That debt "has already been completely wiped out." It was canceled by the mass crimes "which have been and still are being committed against Germans by Russians, Poles, and Czechs." Frank had recanted. At the last minute, a man who might have helped Germany shed the destructive myths of its past had instead chosen to poison the future.

Walther Funk wept and passed himself off as little more than a bank teller. Sauckel described having spent Christmas with the conscript workers he was accused of exploiting. Jodl justified German reprisals against "partisans who used every means which they considered expedient." Seyss-Inquart devoted his time to inventorying the health, insurance, and infant welfare programs he had introduced into Holland. Justice Biddle wrote in the margin of a document, "I am always struck by the apparently sincere and passionate idealism of so many of these defendants. But what ideals!"

Speer's steady, confident voice compelled silence in the courtroom. What would be Hitler's place in history? he asked. "After this trial the German people will condemn him as the originator of their misery and despise him." Dictatorship? "The German people will learn from these happenings not only to hate dictatorship . . . but to fear it." How could so advanced, so cultured, so sophisticated a nation as Germany have fallen under Hitler's demonic sway? The explanation was modern communications, Speer explained—the radio, the telephone, the teleprinter. No longer did a leader have to delegate authority afar to subordinates exercising independent judgment. Given modern communications, a Hitler could rule directly and personally through puppets. "Thus, the more technical the world becomes, the more individual freedom and the self-rule of mankind becomes essential."

Neave had long meditated on the relative guilt of Speer versus Sauckel. There was, in his mind, no possible confusion as to who had been superior and who subordinate in Hitler's court. Sauckel had been pathetic in his final plea today, as at every other point in the trial. Yet, Neave wondered, on what basis would the court judge their respective guilt, on substance or style, on class prejudice or hard evidence?

"This war has ended on the note of radio-controlled rockets, aircraft approaching the speed of sound, submarines and torpedoes which can find their own targets, atom bombs and the horrible prospect of chemical warfare," Speer went on. "In five to ten years, this kind of warfare will offer the possibility of firing rockets from continent to continent with uncanny precision. Through the smashing of the atom, it will be possible to destroy a million people in New York City in a matter of seconds with a rocket serviced by perhaps ten men. . . . A new large-scale war will end with the destruction of human culture and civilization. That is why this trial must contribute to the prevention of such wars in the future . . . a nation believing in its future will never perish. May God protect Germany and the culture of the West."

In the hush that followed, Neave sensed that the spectators had listened to Speer not as a man pleading for his life, but as one who had something valuable to tell them, someone with a vision born of redemption, after immersion in evil. They had heard what they wanted and even more: Hitler would be despised by posterity. Democracy must prevail over despotism. Life on earth had become infinitely more perilous. And heeding the lessons of this historic tribunal could save mankind from suicidal aggressions in an atomic age. After today, the world would likely remember Albert Speer more for his sensibilities as a human being than for his crimes as a Nazi. In truth, Neave noted, Speer had said not a word about himself or his guilt.

Hans Fritzsche concluded the statements of the defendants. Sir Geoffrey adjourned the court. The last of ninety-four witnesses had been heard, the last of over four thousand documents entered into evidence. The next time the defendants filed into room 600, it would be to learn their fates.

CHAPTER IV

JUDGMENT DAY

1

Everyone at the courthouse had a story about the Germans. Ted Fenstermacher, the prosecutor who had questioned Göring about Bormann, struck up a conversation with an ex-soldier in an Afrika Korps cap, one of thousands of jobless men haunting the streets. The veteran waved his arm across the panorama of ruin and remarked what a shame it was—the bombing had been so unnecessary, so near the war's end and against a city of no military importance. Fenstermacher asked how long it would take to rebuild Nuremberg. "Oh, ten, maybe twenty years," the soldier had answered. "But with a man like the Führer, we could do it in five."

2

On Monday, September 2, the justices met to begin final debate on the verdicts. Jim Rowe briefed them on security measures he had devised. The phones would be disconnected while they deliberated. Any waste paper, unwanted notes, or unused copies of documents were to be placed in special bags to be burned. To protect the judges during this tense period, General Watson's office was arranging bulletproof cars for them. When Rowe had finished, Sir Geoffrey reminded his colleagues of their ultimate responsibility, and read aloud from Article 27 of the charter: "to impose upon a defendant, on conviction, death or such other punishment as shall be determined to be just."

They were still haunted by the fragility of this instrument, this International Military Tribunal. Was their jurisdiction rooted in any principle higher than the notion that might makes right? What authority did an American have to pass judgment on a German for a crime committed in Poland? If the issue was crimes committed during the war, why were only Germans on trial? What about war criminals among the Germans' allies, the Italians? Or, for that matter, crimes committed by their enemies, now their judges? And still more troublesome, what of the argument that the laws had been invented after the fact to fit the acts? Even now, after all these months, the judges hungered for assurances of legitimacy.

Rowe and his colleague Adrian "Butch" Fisher had ransacked the archives to put the justices' consciences at ease on the ex post facto issue. Biddle read to his colleagues a brief his aides had prepared. Going back to the adoption of the first of the Hague Conventions in 1899, they had pointed out, military courts had tried and punished individuals for violating the rules of warfare. Yet, these agreements did not define these violations as "crimes," or provide for enforcement or a court to try offenders or specify punishments. Still, no one questioned the legitimacy of such trials. Just since they had been sitting, military courts had meted out punishment to the German general Anton Dostler in Italy, to six German civilians who had murdered downed American fliers, to SS guards at Dachau, and to the killers of American GIs at Malmédy. What was the IMT but the extension of this precedent to the highest level?

John Parker raised the question of the alternates' role in determining the verdicts. Were they again to be the IMT's fifth wheel? Sir Geoffrey had already consulted with the other principal judges and decided that, on test votes, all eight judges would vote. On final votes, only the four principals would take part. Nikitchenko again proposed that two out of four votes be sufficient to convict. He was overruled. Three of four votes would be required for a finding of guilty.

If Burton Andrus had learned anything in twenty-eight years in the military, it was that idle troops are trouble-prone troops. One diversion he had authorized was use of the gym next to the exercise yard for the Twenty-seventh Infantry Regiment basketball league. Andrus had also picked up enough from the Kelleys and Gilberts of his acquaintance to know that he had to find something to occupy the anxious men on cellblock C, since Sir Geoffrey had informed him that deciding the verdicts could take a month. He thereupon devised the social hour. Unoccupied cell 32 was converted into a club room, stocked with playing cards, chess sets, and other games. Each defendant was allowed to host two parties there to which he could invite three other defendants. That meant forty-two chances for the Germans to get out and enjoy rare, normal companionship. The social hour became an instant success. Even Streicher, Kaltenbrunner, and the dull Frick received invitations. But, Andrus noted, the games were never touched. The defendants talked. They never stopped talking.

Early in the judges' deliberations, Henri Donnedieu de Vabres raised a question. If the judgment was death, might they not consider the firing squad for the military defendants? Nikitchenko objected. The bullet was the fate of honorable adversaries, not of butchers. For once, the Russian prevailed. Death sentences, the court decided, must be carried out by hanging. With the last of the ground rules set, they began to vote on the verdicts.

Biddle's secretary, Dorothy Owens, spent more time typing the judgment on Göring than it took for the court to reach it. Hess, however, was a more complex case. Was he a healthy, normal personality? Obviously not. Yet Hess understood the difference between right and wrong and the consequences of his acts, the medical experts had concluded. The judges also had to confront another anomaly. Hess had clearly been a leading Nazi, one who helped Hitler shape his warped philosophy. He was at least a co-inventor of the concept of lebensraum, Hitler's rationale for aggressions intended to increase Germany's living space. Hess had a role in the issuance of the Nuremberg Laws. He had been third in line, after Göring, in the Nazi dynasty. Yet Hess had launched a peace mission, however quixotic, and had spent most of the war in British prisons. The key question, according to Biddle, was why Hess had gone to Scotland. If it was a sincere bid for peace, that fact should be mitigating. If it was a cunning tactic to get Britain out of the war and facilitate the defeat of the Soviet Union, then he had played another role in the conspiracy of aggression.

Sir Geoffrey looked to Nikitchenko. The Russian had made his government's position clear. The Soviet Union wanted Rudolf Hess's head. The man's Scottish adventure had obviously been intended to isolate the Soviets for the kill. Lawrence therefore assumed that Nikitchenko would favor a guilty verdict on all counts, and the death penalty for Hess. Yet when it came to the vote, Nikitchenko hesitated. In the preliminary deliberations, he indeed favored death. But with a deadlock looming, he feared the others might seek to compromise on too lenient a level. He had reexamined this defendant, he said, and would not vote for Hess's death, but could support a life sentence. His decision stunned his colleagues. Biddle had grown fond of Nikitchenko as an amusing and appealing friend. But this stand, flying in the face of Moscow's demands, showed courage of a high order. They went to a vote.

How were they to judge the crimes of Ribbentrop, the spineless messenger boy for Hitler's foreign policies? The law clerks' memorandum summarized the worst of his behavior. He had ordered his ambassadors serving in the capitals of Germany's allies, Italy and Romania, to speed up the deportation of Jews to the East, knowing the fate awaiting them. He had urged that downed Allied fliers be turned over to lynch mobs. The only sympathy shown to Ribbentrop was a recognition of his fecklessness. As they went to a vote, Sir Norman Birkett remarked, "The mainspring of this man's life has been broken."

During the first week of deliberations, the halls of the Palace of Justice rang with an incongruous sound, the peal of children's laughter. Colonel Andrus had finally decided it was safe to allow the defendants family visits. The justices agreed, and asked the army to provide travel permits, transportation, and meals in a special canteen in the courthouse for the visitors.

Emma Schwabenland, an American civilian employee who managed the visitors' center, moved briskly, matching defendants with wives and children. She admired the colonel for allowing the visits, but was disappointed that he had insisted on keeping up the mesh wire. He had been adamant. No touching, no kissing, no hand-holding. That was how weapons and means of suicide were delivered.

The little girl with the thin legs and her father's broad face stood on a chair reciting poems and singing songs her mother had taught her for the occasion. Nearly a year and a half had passed since Hermann Göring had seen his wife and his daughter, Edda. Emmy, so vivacious in the past, looked as faded as the old print dress she wore. Her eyes darted nervously at the guards posted around the visitors' room. She continually twisted her handkerchief while little Edda burbled. "Daddy," she asked, "when you come home, will you wear all your medals in the bathtub like everybody says you do? I want to see them all covered with soapsuds."

Hans Frank awaited his family with a divided heart. Brigitte had written to him of their hand-to-mouth existence, of their children begging on the streets. When she told them that they would be able to visit their father, the eldest girl, Siegried, responded, "Oh, they haven't shot him yet?" Frank's wife, his onetime queen of Poland, had been plump and fashionable during the war, troubled only by his liaison with Lilli Gau. The woman coming to him now was thin, hard-faced, and shabby. His children approached uneasily.

Hjalmar Schacht sat as he did in the dock, erect, aloof, but with the satisfied smile of an old man who knows he has surprised his audience. His wife, an art expert thirty years his junior, was undeniably striking. Smiling at him were his two scrubbed, blond daughters, four and five years old.

Rosenberg's wife spoke to him, while his daughter waited in the hallway. Chaplain Henry Gerecke tried to talk to her there. The girl was thirteen and precociously pretty. Would she like to pray with him? Gerecke asked. "Don't give me that prayer crap," the girl answered. A startled Gerecke asked if there was anything else he might do for her. "Yes," she said, "how about a cigarette?"

With the visits over, a weeping Emmy Göring approached Emma Schwabenland. "Do you think the court will send my husband to an island, like Elba?" she asked. "Maybe I could join him there."

Back in the cellblock, the unvisited defendants waited. The Russians claimed they had been unable to find Frau Raeder, who lived in the Soviet Zone of Berlin. Hess refused to see visitors. "I am being held illegally," he had told Colonel Andrus, "and I do not wish my family to see me in this state of indignity." Keitel said he had disgraced himself and therefore could not face his wife.

As the justices considered the conspiracy charge against Wilhelm Keitel, Birkett pointed out that they were facing a paradox. Could a military robot like Keitel be considered a conspirator, one who schemed with Hitler to invent aggressions? Keitel's defense was a soldier's duty to obey. He virtually admitted that he did no thinking. Biddle thumbed through his copy of the charter. Here it was: Article 8. Following superior orders was not a permitted defense, "but may be considered in mitigation of punishment." They went to a vote on Keitel.

Guessing had become an obsessive game at the Stein Castle. The reporters gathered around the bar tended to agree on the "orders are orders" defense: It was not going to work for the staff chief of the German military; however much a lackey, Keitel would be convicted. Jodl, the thoroughgoing soldier, however, would not, they believed.

The justices polished off Kaltenbrunner quickly. The only argument centered on count one—whether he was significant enough to have conspired with Hitler to launch a war.

Alfred Rosenberg presented a trickier case. Up to his final statement, Rosenberg continued to embrace the National Socialist philosophy he had midwifed. He had also burglarized the art of a continent for Hitler's and Göring's personal enrichment, but not for his own. His defense counsel had proved that Rosenberg condemned the atrocities in the East, where he governed in name only. Rosenberg had, in effect, argued that he had tried to do the devil's work humanely. The judges' challenge was to determine how much he had succeeded in that inherent contradiction. Rosenberg was a fool and a bore, Biddle believed, but should that cost a man his life? On September 10, the vote for Rosenberg's conviction and execution stood at two to one. Biddle held the deciding vote and told the others he would have to sleep on it.

They found Hans Frank oddly tragic. Cultured, brilliant, he had struck a Faustian bargain—his conscience for riches and power—and lost all. His remorse seemed genuine. The Cracow opportunist had become the Nuremberg penitent, almost ecstatic in his sackcloth and ashes, even if his final statement could have been more contrite. When the emerging liberal force on the bench, Donnedieu de Vabres, suggested sparing Frank's life, Biddle was receptive. Nikitchenko insisted on hanging. Given his influence with Lawrence, Biddle again found a man's survival could depend on his nod.

Tex Wheelis leaned into the porthole, chatting with Hermann Göring while the cell guard stood aside. Göring congratulated Wheelis on his recent promotion to first lieutenant. Göring had two large suitcases, a small valise, and a hatbox in the baggage room. As the duty officer in the cellblock this day, Wheelis had the key. From this luggage, Göring's third gift to Wheelis had been retrieved, a pair of fine gray gloves.

PFC Bill Glenny watched the easy camaraderie, puzzled. The first Sunday that Glenny had escorted Göring to church service, he had blithely sat down next to him in the front row. The *Reichsmarschall* glared at him with such malevolence that Glenny fled to the back of the chapel. Thereafter, every time he was in Göring's presence, he felt the man's unnerving stare. Glenny, ordinarily a cocky soldier, was annoyed that he let this prisoner intimidate him. He was particularly upset that he lacked only Göring's signature for a full set of defendant autographs. Hess did not count. Hess gave autographs to no one. As the trial drew to its finale, the value of these signatures kept rising like a commodity in a seller's market. A complete set might fetch two hundred dollars. Most of the defendants would comply for a couple of cigarettes, and Streicher for a pack of gum.

One morning, Glenny worked up his courage. He had a sheet of paper and a pen ready. He thrust them through the square porthole. "Hermann," he said, "I want your autograph." Again, Göring gave him a chilling look, but seized the pen and scrawled his name. He flung the paper back at Glenny and said, "In fifty years, that will be priceless." Young Glenny had never found anything of the clown or buffoon in Hermann Göring.

A conspiracy is a chain. That was what the Anglo-Saxons had taught him, Nikitchenko said. Therefore, Julius Streicher should be found guilty of count one, conspiracy to commit aggression, and count four, crimes against humanity. Streicher had marched alongside Hitler from the beginning. Streicher's mouthpiece of race venom, *Der Stürmer*, taught millions of Germans that it was not simply right but necessary to hate the Jew and kill him. Streicher provided the motive for ordinary Germans to carry out mass murder the way other nations produced alarm clocks. *Der Stürmer*, the Russian argued, had paved the way to Auschwitz. Chief Justice Lawrence was receptive to Nikitchenko's rationale. Biddle listened until he could take no more. "It's preposterous to convict a little Jew-baiter like Streicher," he said,

"simply because he was a friend of Hitler, or a *Gauleiter* or a Nazi."
They were here to decide points of law, not to convict a man because
to do so fit an exaggerated notion of conspiracy. Lawrence called for
a vote.

Walther Funk was disposed of quickly, and the deliberations
moved on to Hjalmar Schacht. Biddle took this opportunity to prove
that his disagreements with Jackson were not personal. He knew Jackson was eager for a conviction of Schacht as a representative of the
industrialist-financier class that had helped put Hitler into power.
Biddle aligned himself with Nikitchenko, favoring conviction of
Schacht on count one. Donnedieu de Vabres, however, wanted to acquit Schacht, as did Lawrence. John Parker did not have a counting
vote, but suggested a way to break the stalemate. The justices, he said,
should take into account Schacht's profession: "Herr Schacht was a
banker and therefore a man of character."

Jim Rowe had worked out a system with the chief of the Language
Division, Commander Alfred Steer, to keep the verdicts secret until
judgment day. They took over a former German army barracks in
nearby Furth. Steer recruited translators, typists, and others willing to
be sequestered. A separate mess hall and dormitories were set up for
the volunteers. No phones were permitted. Pages were handed to typists in random order, and the defendants' sentences were left blank
until the last minute. A company of U.S. infantry posted guards outside the barracks around the clock.

Arthur Seyss-Inquart's best defense was faceless anonymity. Still,
Seyss-Inquart filled a place in the mosaic of conspiracy, both as an
Austrian who schemed to hand over his country to Germany, and as
an occupation czar who brought untold suffering to Holland. The vote
went quickly.

In naval matters, Francis Biddle was disposed to defer to Jim
Rowe's firsthand experience over his own theorizing, and Rowe recommended acquittal for Grand Admiral Karl Dönitz. The man was
unsympathetic—a rigid Nazi, a rabid anti-Semite, and Hitler's hand-
picked heir to boot—but he had to be judged for his acts, not his
personality or politics. Admittedly, the order not to pick up defenseless survivors of sunken ships sounded brutal; but Kranzbuehler had

been more right than he knew. Not only had the American navy fought no differently than the German fleet had, Rowe explained, but the Americans he served with fought the sea war more ruthlessly than the Germans. If the admiral was convicted, everything that Göring had been saying would be confirmed. "We'd be punishing Dönitz not for starting a war, but for losing one." These arguments were fresh in Biddle's mind as the court debated Dönitz's case.

What about the *Laconia* Order, and those helpless survivors clinging to lifeboats while German submariners cold-bloodedly machine-gunned them? Judge Parker asked. The perpetrator of that crime, Lieutenant Eck, had already been executed, Biddle pointed out. And Dönitz had never ordered survivors shot; he ordered that they not be rescued. But what about Dönitz's willingness to use twelve thousand of Himmler's concentration camp slaves to build ships? And his passing along the Commando Order? Nikitchenko asked. Now they were on firm ground, were they not? Sir Geoffrey brought them to a vote, with two quickly for condemnation. Once again, Biddle found that he could tip the scales.

Forget about the Hitler Youth business, Nikitchenko urged, as they took up the case of Baldur von Schirach. Let them concentrate on Schirach the *Gauleiter* of Vienna. Could there be any other punishment than his own death for a man who turned over sixty thousand Viennese Jews to certain slaughter? And, Sir Geoffrey added, Schirach was a villain who, to avenge the assassination of Reinhard Heydrich, wanted to bomb a center of English culture. Lawrence, too, favored the death penalty. Far too excessive, Donnedieu de Vabres protested. Twenty years would do. Biddle agreed. Sir Geoffrey decided that they would reconsider the case and vote again later.

Nikitchenko led the assault against Grand Admiral Raeder, the Russians' prize catch. Since the other Soviet contribution, Hans Fritzsche, was embarrassingly low-level and a possible candidate for acquittal, Nikitchenko wanted death for the admiral. Would not life imprisonment be harsh enough for a man over seventy? Sir Geoffrey asked. "Twenty years," Donnedieu de Vabres said. No, Nikitchenko insisted. Raeder had been present at the Hossbach Conference when Hitler unveiled his decision to launch the war, yet he had stayed on as chief of the German navy. Raeder spoke of honor, yet applied the infamous Commando Order to brave men captured in uniform, who were then executed. Either General Nikitchenko would have to come down, or Justice Donnedieu de Vabres would have to come up, Sir Geoffrey observed, or they were deadlocked.

The intelligence report from Third Army headquarters had alarmed Colonel Andrus. He directed his deputy, Major Teich, to muster the entire ISD in the exercise yard at 0900 hours on Friday, September 13.

Somehow the idea had circulated that they were past the worst of it, the colonel began. That was dead wrong. They were entering the most sensitive stage of their mission, from this moment until the sentences were carried out. He read from the Third Army report: "A very definite effort has been made on the part of certain persons to organize some means of either the liberation of some of the defendants now before the tribunal or for some other way of insuring that they escape the consequences of their acts." Men died in jailbreaks, he warned, and not just prisoners. Until the defendants walked out of this prison or were carried out, the ISD was not slackening its efforts.

Jodl's case again raised the question in Donnedieu de Vabres's mind. Could soldiers initiate a war or only fight it, question orders or only follow them? And again, if they found Jodl guilty and handed down the maximum sentence, should it be the firing squad or the rope? That had already been decided, Sir Geoffrey pointed out. They must deal with Keitel and Jodl identically, and if the judgment was death, the method was hanging.

During the deliberations over Sauckel, Sir Norman Birkett observed that of course the man was a boor; but should one hang for lack of breeding? Speer's fate sparked a more fierce debate. Francis Biddle was deeply troubled by Speer. He read from an analysis that Butch Fisher had prepared: "Sauckel had never had responsibility for any major policy decisions, but was always used to execute policies which had been decided on by more powerful men such as Göring and Speer." Furthermore, Speer acted with "complete ruthlessness and unfeeling efficiency in the application of a program which took

five million into slave labor and countless numbers to their death."
Speer always got his way over Sauckel, Fisher's analysis went on. "The
violence used in recruiting was largely in response to Speer's high
labor demands." Biddle set the paper aside. There was no doubt in
his mind. Speer's penalty must be death. Nikitchenko immediately
concurred. Only one more vote was needed.

Sir Geoffrey was troubled. What of the evidence that this man
had stood up to Hitler's scorched-earth madness, even considered as-
sassinating the tyrant? What about the man's obvious remorse and the
character and wisdom displayed in his final plea? These were not the
points at issue, Nikitchenko argued; they must consider only Speer's
commission of crimes as described in his indictment. Donnedieu de
Vabres argued that Speer deserved fifteen years. Another impasse.
They would vote again tomorrow, Sir Geoffrey ruled.

The principals let the alternates decide Hans Fritzsche's fate.
Propaganda had been a principal Nazi weapon, Lieutenant Colonel
Volchkov argued, and Fritzsche had wielded it over German radio
with deadly results. His "racial spittle," his contempt for Russians
and Slavs as subhumans, had sanctioned the deaths of Soviet POWs
and civilians in the millions. Judge Parker observed that Volchkov's
rhetoric was fine, but his law was weak. "Adolf Hitler wouldn't
have wasted five minutes with Hans Fritzsche," Parker noted. "The
man's here because Josef Goebbels is dead." Biddle concurred. Volchkov reddened angrily. What was the difference between the despised
Streicher and Fritzsche, he asked, except for a bit of polish in the
latter? Both championed racial hatred. They went to a vote on
Fritzsche.

Francis Biddle could not sleep. He had gladly exercised his intellectual
authority over his colleagues these past months. But now, particularly
in the verdicts of Frank, Speer, and Rosenberg, his persuasiveness
could determine who lived and who died. Speer's case continued to
trouble Biddle. The man's prostitution of his talent and intelligence
was appalling. If Biddle chose to, he could probably work on Lawrence
for the decisive death vote. Should he? The struggle in Biddle's soul
raged all night, until, at dawn, he made up his mind and at last fell
asleep.

The last votes—on the deferred cases—were taken on Thursday, September 26. The verdicts would be handed down within days.

On Friday, four unfamiliar officers checked into the Grand Hotel: Brigadier General Roy V. Rickard, U.S. Army, Brigadier Edmund Paton Walsh of Great Britain, Major General Georgi Malkov of the Soviet Union, and Brigadier General Pierre Morel of France. They formed the Quadripartite Commission for the Detention of War Criminals. They had come to Nuremberg to plan and supervise executions.

3

ROBERT JACKSON HAD RETURNED to Nuremberg on September 18, accompanied by Colonel Robert Storey, who wanted to watch the final curtain drop, and by his Washington liaison man, Charles Horsky. The chief U.S. prosecutor stepped into a backlog of administrative headaches. Reporters complained that only a pool would be allowed to cover executions. The recently arrived Quadripartite Commission wanted seats not in the visitors' gallery but on the courtroom floor when the verdicts were delivered. That struck Jackson as having the hangman sit in court holding a noose. The commission would occupy the gallery with the other visitors, he decided.

Sir Geoffrey summoned Colonel Andrus to review the special precautions the colonel was taking for judgment day. Andrus explained that final family visits would take place on September 28. Thereafter, relatives were to leave Nuremberg. On September 30, when the verdicts were to be handed down, Andrus would have a doctor in the basement, in addition to two guards who would be standing by in the elevator with a stretcher and a straitjacket in case any defendant went berserk. Another doctor and a nurse would be stationed in the visitors' gallery. After the men returned to the cellblock, he intended to implement new cell assignments: third tier, term sentences; second tier, life sentences; first tier, death sentences.

Justice Lawrence did not want the defendants passing through

the usual gauntlet of gawkers on their way to lunch on judgment day.
Andrus understood. He would send the prisoners back down by the
elevator to eat in the basement. And Lawrence wanted no cameras in
the courtroom when the men were sentenced. This was to be a civilized occasion, he warned.

Reporters at the press bar continued making bets on the verdicts. The
latest tally showed four journalists predicting death for Schacht, eleven
for Speer, thirty-two for Kaltenbrunner. The odds on Jodl's survival
had risen over the past hours.

4

Monday, September 30, broke sunny and clear. Bullet-proof cars arrived at the courthouse, sirens wailing, led by jeeps spiked with machine guns. The eight justices exited between protective files of armed
infantry; a thousand troops circled the building, and sharpshooters
stood silhouetted on surrounding rooftops.

In the Judges' Room, the two Frenchmen donned their gowns
and placed ruffled jabots around their necks. Nikitchenko's and Volchkov's chocolate-brown uniforms displayed razor-edge creases. Biddle
had abandoned natty waistcoats and bow ties in favor of a dark gray
suit and robe. His mood was equally somber. He dreaded entering the
courtroom this morning and facing the men in the dock. Lawrence
appeared unruffled, his voice cool as he went over their final instructions. He would lead off, reading the passages of the judgment describing Nazism's rise to power. Donnedieu de Vabres and his
alternate, Falco, would trace Germany's aggressions, country by country. Lawrence deliberately chose Biddle to handle the conspiracy
charge. Biddle had been its harshest critic, and Lawrence wanted the
court to present a united front. He selected mild John Parker to recite
the most horrifying passages of the judgment, the crimes against humanity. The court's findings would echo more credibly from this
placid American than from the implacable Russians. The Soviets
would deliver the judgment on slave labor and Nazi organizations.

Lawrence picked up a thick black notebook. The others fell in behind him as he headed for the small door that opened onto the bench in room 600.

The visitors shifted restlessly as the voices of the judges droned on hour after hour, in effect recapping the history of an age. Not until four p.m. did Lieutenant Colonel Volchkov announce the verdicts on the indicted organizations: the Nazi party leadership, "Criminal"; the SS, "Criminal." The Gestapo and the SD, "Criminal." That league of Brownshirt bullies, the SA, was acquitted for having lost significance after the thirties, as was the Reich cabinet. The High Command was not judged criminal since, as Justice Lawrence explained, so few officers were involved that individual trials were preferable to a blanket judgment.

The court's guilty verdicts meant that anyone who was a member of the convicted organizations after 1939 was, automatically, a war criminal. Biddle, however, had successfully lobbied for exemptions for anyone drafted into membership or who had no knowledge of the organization's criminal purposes. While the trial was under way, however, U.S. occupation authorities had set up German-run denazification courts to review the status of over 3.5 million organization members. These bodies and subsequent war-crimes courts took into account a former Nazi's membership in a convicted organization in determining guilt or in barring that person from certain posts and rights of citizenship. Similar machinery was employed in other occupation zones. No member of a convicted organization, however, was punished solely on the strength of the IMT verdicts. To Biddle and other critics, the organization cases had largely been a pointless exercise.

The following morning, October 1, Colonel Andrus addressed the defendants gathered in the corridor of the cellblock. He spoke firmly but not unkindly. "You men have a duty to yourselves, to the German people, and to posterity, to face this day with dignity and manliness," he said. "I expect you to go into that courtroom, stand at attention, listen to your sentence, and then retire. You may be assured that there will be people to assist you after you have moved out of the sight of the general public."

The verdicts would be delivered first, the chief judge announced, followed by sentencing. The twenty-one men in the dock were to remain seated while they heard the judgments on the four counts applicable to them—conspiracy to commit aggression, the commission of aggression, crimes in the conduct of warfare, and crimes against humanity. Lawyers, researchers, and off-duty translators sat packed shoulder to shoulder at the prosecution tables. Movie cameras whirred and still cameras clicked in fluorescent lighting that gave the defendants a corpse's pallor.

"The defendant, Hermann Göring, was the moving force for aggressive war, second only to Adolf Hitler," Sir Geoffrey began. Göring created the Gestapo and concentration camps, before releasing them to Himmler. He signed the harshest anti-Semitic decrees. "He directed Himmler and Heydrich to 'bring about a complete solution of the Jewish question in the German sphere of influence in Europe.'" And, Sir Geoffrey added, he was a thief.

Göring, his uniform immaculate but drooping around the neck, his hair neatly combed, ground a fist into his jowl as Lawrence spoke. There was nothing to be said in mitigation, Lawrence concluded. The tribunal found Hermann Göring guilty on all four counts of the indictment.

Rudolf Hess refused to put on his earphones and rocked back and forth as Lawrence began to read his verdict. It was true, the justice said, that this man acted abnormally and suffered from lapses of memory. "But there is nothing to show that he does not realize the nature of the charges against him or is incapable of defending himself." Nevertheless, he had not participated in the physical abominations of the Reich, and therefore the tribunal found him, on the charge of crimes against humanity, not guilty. Hess, however, had been part of the original Nazi collusion, outranked only by Hitler and Göring. He had signed decrees dismembering Czechoslovakia and Poland. Hess was guilty on counts one and two: conspiracy to commit and the commission of aggression.

In the press gallery, *Newsweek*'s correspondent, James P. O'Donnell, jotted down impressions of the next defendant. "Ribbentrop . . . in worst shape of any man on dock . . . looks as if noose already around neck . . . sweating." The tribunal found the former foreign minister guilty on all four counts.

Field Marshal Keitel sat up like a cadet as his name was called. "Superior orders, even to a soldier, cannot be considered in mitigation where crimes so shocking and extensive have been committed," the justice read. "Guilty on all four counts."

Kaltenbrunner wore his customary hangman's scowl. Witnesses had placed him at Mauthausen, the judge read, and "testified that he had seen prisoners killed by the various methods of execution, hanging, shooting, gassing . . ." Guilty on counts three and four.

Nikitchenko read the judgment on Rosenberg: "21,903 art objects seized in the West," "stripping Eastern Territories of raw materials," "cleansing the occupied territories of Jews." Guilty on all four counts.

Hans Frank listened to Biddle read his verdict with the curiosity of a lawyer following an interesting case. It began well enough. "Most of the criminal program charged against Frank was put into effect through the police. Frank had jurisdictional difficulties with Himmler. . . . Hitler resolved many of these disputes in favor of Himmler. . . . It may also be true that some of the criminal policies did not originate with Frank." Did he dare hope? Biddle read on, "But, on taking over as governor-general of occupied Poland, Frank had said, 'The Poles will become the slaves of the Greater German World Empire.' " The defendant had cooperated in every brutal policy, Biddle continued. When he took over the government-general, there were two and a half million Polish Jews. When he left there were 100,000. Guilty on counts three and four.

The torpid Frick, onetime minister of the interior, the man who arranged Hitler's German citizenship, was found guilty of three of four counts.

Streicher nibbled on K-rations as Sir Geoffrey resumed reading the judgment, citing passages from *Der Stürmer*. "Streicher's incitement to murder and extermination," the justice said, ". . . clearly constitutes persecution on political and racial grounds . . . and constitutes a crime against humanity." Guilty on count four.

Walther Funk sank almost below the dock as Nikitchenko revived images of steel boxes full of gold teeth in the Reichsbank vaults. But "Funk was never a dominant figure in the various programs in which he participated." The judge's words hinted at mitigation of sentence, though Funk was found guilty on three counts.

Robert Jackson believed the next defendant was the linchpin required to hold the conspiracy case together. He had told his staff this morning that he regarded Hjalmar Schacht as the most contemptible individual on trial. "Schacht had freedom of choice. He could have gone with or against the Nazis. He did more to bring them to power than any other single individual." He was not alone in this sentiment. William L. Shirer, in the press gallery for CBS, had observed Nazi Germany longer than any of them. Shirer was convinced that the regime could not have risen without Schacht's misapplied genius.

Francis Biddle read the verdict. Hjalmar Schacht was acquitted on all counts. Jackson might well believe that it was Biddle, out to thwart him again on the conspiracy case. In fact, Schacht had escaped only through a two-to-two voting deadlock. Biddle had voted with Nikitchenko for conviction.

The courtroom was abuzz at an acquittal. After ten guilty verdicts in a row, it had begun to seem that the trial was indeed an elaborate exercise in vengeance. Schacht, from the outset, had cockily predicted his exoneration. He accepted it now as his due, without a trace of emotion.

Admiral Dönitz's prospects also looked brighter as Donnedieu de Vabres began: "The tribunal is not prepared to hold Dönitz guilty for his conduct of submarine warfare against armed British merchantmen. Nor was he guilty of ordering the killing of survivors." The tribunal accepted the position taken in the affidavit of Admiral Nimitz: the German navy had acted no differently from the American navy. Göring turned and smiled at the admiral. But Donnedieu de Vabres was not finished: Dönitz, however, had set up zones in which his U-boats could sink anything in sight, a clear violation of the Treaty of London on naval warfare. Dönitz's anger was visible. He had made part of the Atlantic a sinking zone; but the Americans had made the whole Pacific a sinking zone. The French judge continued. Dönitz had also passed along the Commando Order and sought to use concentration camp labor in shipbuilding. He was guilty of counts two and three, commission of aggression and military atrocities. His predecessor as chief of the navy, Grand Admiral Raeder, was judged guilty of counts one, two, and three.

Just days before, Biddle had received a letter from Baldur von Schirach's wife, Henrietta. "Our children love America," she had written in English. "It is their grandparents' country. They have a merry imagination of the ice cream and Walt Disney movies. The flags, the history, are as familiar to them as their own. Do I have to tell my children now that this America let your father die the most disgraceful death a man can find?" Biddle, reading the verdict, could well ask how many children among the sixty thousand Jews Schirach had shipped to the East had dreamed of ice cream and the movies of Walt Disney. The man, however, was too trifling to be convicted as a major conspirator. The court found him guilty on count four, crimes against humanity.

"Sauckel argues that he is not responsible for the excesses in the administration of the slave labor program," Biddle read. "He says that the total number of workers to be obtained was set by demands from agriculture and industry. . . . He testifies that insofar as he had any authority, he was constantly urging humane treatment. . . . There is no doubt, however," the judge went on, "that Sauckel had overall responsibility for the slave labor program, which he had carried out under terrible conditions of cruelty and suffering." Guilty on counts three and four.

The final odds on Jodl at the press bar the night before had been three to one for acquittal. He sat in defiant dignity as the court, with Donnedieu de Vabres reading, recounted his guilt in drafting plans for aggressive warfare and in passing along the Commando and Commissar orders. "He cannot now shield himself behind the myth of soldierly obedience at all costs," the judge concluded. Jodl was guilty on all four counts.

Suave Konstantin von Neurath, a gleaming white handkerchief in place, Ribbentrop's predecessor as foreign minister, had helped bring the Nazis to power and supinely signed death orders put in front of him by the SS in Czechoslovakia, the court concluded. Guilty on all four counts. Seyss-Inquart, professorial Reich commissar of the Netherlands, who sent 65,000 Dutch Jews to die, was declared guilty on three of four counts.

Robert Jackson watched Speer, usually so cool, looking tortured, his face a mass of blotches. If he could acquit one defendant, Jackson had concluded, it would be this man. "Speer's activities do not amount to . . . preparing wars of aggression," Biddle declared. Not guilty of counts one and two. As for atrocities against soldiers and civilians—counts three and four—"Speer knew when he made demands on Sauckel that they would be supplied by foreign laborers serving under compulsion . . . he used concentration camp labor in the industries under his control." He used Russian POWs in arms industries in likely violation of the Geneva Convention.

To Airey Neave, it seemed that the court had found Speer's guilt equal to Sauckel's, until the judge read, "Speer himself had no direct administrative responsibility for the program . . . he did not obtain administrative control over Sauckel . . . he was not directly concerned with the cruelty in the administration of the slave labor program. . . . He carried out his opposition to Hitler's scorched-earth program . . . at considerable personal risk." Speer was guilty on counts three and four. The chief burden for enslaving five million foreign workers had, however, been placed on the narrow shoulders of Fritz Sauckel. If any sentences less than death were to be handed down, Speer had reason to hope.

Two more acquittals followed. Franz von Papen, the former chancellor who had made the deal whereby Hitler succeeded to the post, was found innocent. Hans Fritzsche, third-rung radio propagandist, was also acquitted. Göring whispered to Hess that this insignificant fellow had no business in the dock with them anyway. Martin Bormann was convicted in absentia.

Sir Geoffrey adjourned the court at 1:45 p.m. They would reconvene for sentencing after lunch.

5

DURING THE BREAK, Robert Jackson took General Lucius Clay, General Eisenhower's deputy, and Ambassador Robert Murphy to lunch in the VIP dining room. He was furious at Schacht's acquittal, Jackson said. Not only did it wreck his conspiracy case; Schacht's release proved what the Russians had been saying all along—that the Western powers would never convict a capitalist. But didn't the acquittals establish the court as a legitimate bar of justice? his companions suggested. In Schacht's case, Jackson observed, it had taken a subversion of justice to achieve the appearance of it. As he left the dining room, reporters ambushed him, pressing for his reaction. As far as he was concerned, Jackson said, the unfortunate escape of Schacht, Papen, and the German High Command had been facilitated by the American judge. However, it would not be helpful to relations among the Allies to attribute this criticism to him. Those remarks, he said, were off the record.

The freed men stood in the pressroom, hemmed in by shouting reporters who urged cigarettes, candy, and drinks on them. Tom Dodd presented Schacht with a box of Havana cigars. Rebecca West watched with disgust. In Schacht and Papen she saw two sly old foxes who had gotten away with something approaching murder. A German policeman elbowed his way to the ex-defendants to announce that Dr. Wilhelm Hoegner, minister president of Bavaria, had issued a warrant for their arrest. They were still to be tried by a German court for the commission of war crimes. He also warned that an ugly mob was outside waiting for them. Schacht asked Colonel Andrus if he would allow them to stay in prison a few more days, until it was safe to leave. Andrus agreed.

An American reporter asked Karl Haensel, a defense lawyer, why Germans should be so unhappy that three of their own had escaped punishment. It was more than seeing people who had prospered during the regime going free, Haensel explained. Guilty verdicts, by fixing guilt on individuals, in effect absolved the German people. The more personal guilt, the less collective guilt.

A British reporter buttonholed the star interpreter, Wolfe Frank. Would Frank be handling the afternoon session? the reporter asked. "Yes," Frank answered. "I've been practicing my '*Tod durch den Strang* [death by the rope]' for days."

At 2:50 p.m. the justices' door opened, and Sir Geoffrey Lawrence emerged. At his nod, the others took their seats. Simultaneously, Hermann Göring, flanked by two white-helmeted guards, entered from the sliding door behind the dock. Göring's face looked deathly pale, even powdered. Sir Geoffrey began to read: "Defendant Hermann Göring, on the counts of the indictment on which you have been convicted, the International Military Tribunal sentences you—" Göring was waving his arms for Lawrence to stop. His earphones were dead, he said. Two GI technicians rushed to the dock. Lawrence looked on in despair: with effort, one achieved a frame of mind to condemn men, only to have the decorum shattered by an errant piece of wire. Göring indicated that all was well. Lawrence began again: "The International Military Tribunal sentences you to death by hanging." Göring, expressionless, dropped the headset, turned on his heels, and disappeared into the elevator.

Rudolf Hess swayed aimlessly, his eyes fixed on the ceiling, again refusing to put on earphones. "The tribunal sentences you to imprisonment for life," Sir Geoffrey announced. Nikitchenko fingered a ten-thousand-word dissent he intended to issue to the press as soon as the court adjourned. In it, he disowned Hess's life sentence, though he had voted for it. It would be difficult to make his overlords in Moscow understand the bargains struck in the Judges' Room—but the voting had been in secret, and the vehemence of his dissenting opinion might save his neck back home. His dissent also reviled the acquittals, especially of Schacht. The capitalists had underwritten the war of aggression, his dissent argued, and Schacht was the quintessential capitalist.

When Lawrence sentenced Joachim von Ribbentrop to hang, the man slumped, as if taking a body blow. Wilhelm Keitel heard his death sentence and nodded curtly, a subordinate who has just received an order.

"*Tod durch den Strang,*" death by the rope, Kaltenbrunner heard through his earphones. The same fate befell Alfred Rosenberg. When Biddle had gone to bed on the night of September 10, the fate of Rosenberg had lain in his hands. The next morning, he cast the vote that condemned him.

Hans Frank moved like a sleepwalker, banging into the dock chairs as he came forward. He heard his death sentence and held out his hands in wordless supplication. Wilhelm Frick heard the same sentence with impassivity. Julius Streicher virtually trotted forward, spread his legs wide, and stuck out his chin. "*Tod durch den Strang*," Wolfe Frank translated over the interpreters' circuit.

The roll of death was finally broken. Walther Funk and Admiral Raeder received life sentences, and Admiral Dönitz ten years.

Henrietta von Schirach and Heinrich Hoffmann huddled by the radio in the Witness House to hear the broadcast of the trial. She held her father's hand as her husband's fate was announced. "The tribunal sentences you to twenty years' imprisonment," Justice Lawrence said. "He's going to live," Henrietta cried, jumping up and embracing her father. "Anything as long as he does not have to die!"

The remaining defendants stood in the basement, watching the men already sentenced exit from the elevator in handcuffs, some silent, some denouncing their verdicts. The acquittals of Schacht and Papen, men of his station, had heartened Albert Speer. He watched Fritz Sauckel enter the elevator; the man was back in barely a minute, bearing the expression of a terrified animal. "Death," Speer heard a guard say of Sauckel's sentence. Three more defendants and it would be Speer's turn.

General Jodl heard his death penalty, tore off the earphones, and stalked out. Konstantin von Neurath received fifteen years; Arthur Seyss-Inquart, death.

Speer entered the elevator. On seeing him emerge, Francis Biddle felt his gloom lift. Speer's fate had also been in his hands that sleepless night. The vote for Speer's death had been deadlocked at two to two, with Biddle and Nikitchenko in favor. Albert Speer, Biddle had finally concluded, was impressionable, idealistic, and prone to hero worship. The next morning, he changed his vote. "The tribunal sentences you," Sir Geoffrey announced, "to twenty years' imprisonment."

As the elevator descended, Speer felt as if he had been snatched from the edge of an abyss. But as the cold metal of the handcuffs encased his wrists and he was marched back to the cellblock, his mood began to shift. Yes, truth and contrition had succeeded in defeating the hangman. But twenty years? He would be an old man before he was free. Schacht and Papen had been acquitted. Lies, smoke screens, and dissembling might have worked better after all.

In the courtroom, the missing Martin Bormann was sentenced to death in absentia. After 315 days, the work of the tribunal was complete. The war-crimes trial had ended.

The press gallery erupted in pandemonium, with correspondents pushing and spilling over each other in a race for the telephones and telegraph office. The floor of the courtroom became a curious amalgam of handshaking, backslapping, and smiling faces in one quarter, and grim expressions and listless retreats elsewhere. Before well-wishers could descend on him, Robert Jackson slumped down in his seat, wondering what they had achieved. Had they merely routed a pack of villains? Or had they contributed to the march of civilization? Had they placed future aggressors on notice? Or would a bellicose mankind learn nothing? That jury was still out.

6

UNCERTAINTY COMPOUNDED the anxiety of the condemned eleven. The Allied Control Council, which governed Germany, had ruled that the executions were to be carried out fifteen days after sentencing. But did the ACC mean exactly fifteen days later, or at some point after fifteen days had elapsed? The defense lawyers were consequently unable to tell their clients exactly when they could expect to die.

Jodl had warned his wife in his last letter not to do anything "to fill my stupid old heart with hopes. Let it quietly swing itself away." Nevertheless, as soon as she learned Alfred's fate, Luise sent a telegram to the now-out-of-power Winston Churchill. "You have always been proud of being a soldier," it read. "You were the mast, when, in deadly peril, England kept the flag flying. May I, as the daughter of a British-born mother, appeal to you as a soldier, to give your voice of support for the life of my husband, Colonel General Jodl, who, like yourself, did nothing but fight for his country to the last." She dispatched similar pleas to General Eisenhower and Field Marshal Montgomery, asking how an officer who honorably signed Germany's surrender at Rheims could possibly "be treated like a common criminal."

Marguerite Higgins filed the story to the New York *Herald Tribune* from the courthouse telegraph room. Colonel Andrus, she reported, had switched all cell assignments to deprive the prisoners of access to old hiding places. Her story was not entirely accurate. The colonel had dispatched the men given jail terms to the upper tiers. But the condemned men were still in their same cells on what the guards now called Death Row.

Higgins returned to the press bar to find a new debate under way. Who was dying for what? Keitel for the general staff? Jodl for the German army? Kaltenbrunner for Himmler? As for the convictions of crazy Hess and Admiral Raeder, weren't they a sop to the Russians? Who was Sauckel dying for? a correspondent for the left-wing American paper *PM* asked: "the working stiffs of the world"? How could anyone lay the case against Sauckel alongside the case against Speer, and give one man death and the other twenty years? Wasn't it Speer who had cried at Adolf Hitler's death? Wasn't Speer at Mauthausen? Didn't he probably hear that grisly speech in which Himmler described the slaughter of the Jews? What about that pathetic sod, Streicher, what was he dying for? a British reporter asked. For incitement to murder, a companion answered. But that was the same thing Fritzsche had been accused of, and he went free.

A United Press reporter tracked down General Eisenhower at a castle in Ayrshire, Scotland. On the whole, he was pleased with the verdicts, Ike said, although "I was a little astonished that they found it so easy to convict military men."

"If the war had gone the other way, General," the reporter asked, "do you think they would have hanged you?"

"Such thoughts you have, young man," Ike answered.

The corridors of the Palace of Justice were eerily silent, as the staff fled as from a sinking ship. By noon of the day after the verdicts, the British delegation, luggage in hand, had assembled at Y28 for the flight back to England. Sir Geoffrey deflected reporters' questions about the verdicts and shifted the conversation to his pleasure at returning to Hill Farm in Wiltshire. His conversion over the past months from an anonymous entity to a figure of near-universal admiration did not interest him. It had never occurred to him that it could be otherwise.

Surely honors of some kind, even a peerage, must flow from this service, Sir Norman Birkett believed. But what kind and for whom? Was it possible that his behind-the-scenes contributions could somehow shine through the official role of Sir Geoffrey Lawrence?

By the time Robert Jackson's plane reached the mid-Atlantic, he was experiencing profound contentment. He looked around at the others who had helped him survive the ordeal—Bill, Elsie Douglas, his colleagues—and assessed the past year. Whatever the failures, the enemies, the aggravations and defeats, the balance was clear. He had been told that his opening speech would live in the annals of courtroom eloquence, and he tended to believe it. As he later reported in a letter to Whitney Harris, "The hard months at Nuremberg were well spent in the most important, enduring work of my life."

As he dismantled his office, Francis Biddle confessed to Jim Rowe a sense that the great adventures of his life were over, and that all that remained was the commentary.

The French and the Russians soon left too. The government of the latter took the position that the Western Allies had been too lenient on the Nazi gangsters who escaped death. But the Russians who had carried on the day-to-day courtroom battle left with satisfaction that they had set before the world the depths of their people's wartime agony. Nikitchenko, Rudenko, and a handful of others also had earned the respect, even the affection, of their Western colleagues. The Russians' departure, however, had an eye-for-an-eye quality, avenging the Germans' conduct in the Soviet Union. When the U.S. Army went to reclaim the houses where the Soviets had lived, they found them stripped of everything movable—furniture, light fixtures, bathtubs and toilet bowls, and every spoon, dish, cup, and saucer. It was all loaded aboard trucks, headed for the Soviet Zone.

7

On October 1, Lieutenant Tex Wheelis was appointed property officer in charge of the defendants' baggage room. Four days later, Hermann Göring requested a meeting with his defense counsel, Otto

Stahmer. Göring brought with him into room 57 a blue briefcase. It was a gift for his lawyer, Göring told the guard. The guard immediately summoned Major Teich, who recognized the briefcase from the baggage room. He examined it, found it empty, and allowed Stahmer to keep it. Teich, however, did not remember anyone's obtaining the required written permission for Göring to enter the baggage room to get Stahmer's gift. Someone else must have retrieved it for him.

Soon afterward, Stahmer got word to Emmy Göring in her cabin in Sackdilling that he had been able to arrange one last visit with Hermann. She was logged into the visitors' room at 2:45 p.m. Minutes later, Göring appeared in handcuffs. His first questions were about Edda. Did she know of the sentence? Did she understand what it meant? Yes, Emmy answered, Edda knew that her father was going to die. There was something worse than dying, Göring told her. It was the form of death these foreigners had imposed on him. "They can murder me," he told her, "but they have no right to judge me. That I deny them." Surely they would not hang him, Emmy said, as the visit ended. They could not hang Hermann Göring. They would take him away and intern him on an island, like Napoleon, she believed. He doubted that, Göring said. But of one thing she could be sure: "They will not hang me."

Gustav Gilbert wanted out. After the sentencing on October 1, he had waited in cellblock C to get the condemned men's reactions. It was the logical end of his work, the circle completed. After that, he could not get home soon enough. By sending his partial manuscript to New York, he had managed to kill off Douglas Kelley's bid to Simon and Schuster. But Kelley would no doubt find another publisher, and Gilbert was determined to beat him into print. He had submitted a request for his release to Colonel Andrus, who had forwarded it to Jackson before the latter's departure. Jackson had refused Gilbert, telling the puzzled psychologist that he wanted him to stay on as one of his "representatives." From that point, Gilbert found it impossible to continue wearing his mask of cool professionalism. He told a United Press reporter, "Hermann Göring's front of bravery is all baloney. They're all cowards, every one of them, including Göring. They're all trembling in their cells right now. The front they put up in court was all bravado. They don't find death as easy to take as it was to dish it out."

The heaviest emotional burden they now bore, he knew, was not knowing when they would die. In the meantime, sixteen of the defendants had appealed to the Allied Control Council, their last hope for clemency. The London Charter granted the ACC power to reduce, even to commute, sentences. Robert Servatius, Sauckel's lawyer, appealed to the ACC to consider the illogic of his client's death sentence. "Sauckel had nothing to do with concentration camp labor," Servatius petitioned; "that was an enterprise between Speer and Himmler. . . . Sauckel remained an outsider among the Nazi elite. Speer was a close friend of Hitler." Keitel had petitioned the ACC that he be shot. Göring, Frank, and Streicher did not want appeals, but their lawyers filed anyway. On October 9, the ACC met in closed session for three and a half hours. The four members, one from each of the occupying powers, weighed the appeals on two scales: Was there any political advantage to the Allies in reducing a sentence? Had the defendant rendered useful service to the prosecution? They made their decisions but chose not to inform the prisoners immediately.

On October 10, Colonel Andrus returned from a short trip to Belgium. The stream of what he called "tourists" waiting to visit his "zoo" had not abated. As time grew short, the famous and curious were eager to come to cellblock C. And the press continued to hound him. Was it true that Rosenberg had managed to commit suicide, that Hess had drafted a scheme for the Fourth Reich? The Quadripartite Commission, in charge of planning the executions, questioned him about his arrangements for a hangman. He explained that Master Sergeant John C. Woods was coming down from Landsberg. A thoroughgoing professional, Woods had "dropped" 347 men in a fifteen-year army career, most recently the Dachau SS murderers whom Captain Gilbert had interviewed over Christmas.

The colonel obtained fresh briefings on the prisoners' mental health from Lieutenant Colonel William Dunn, his current prison psychiatrist, and on their physical condition from Dr. Pfluecker and an army physician, First Lieutenant Charles J. Roska. Several of the condemned men, they reported, were taking cold morning showers, and most were joining in the exercise period permitted in the cellblock corridor—except for Göring, who never left his cell. You could not force hygiene and health on a man about to die, the colonel observed.

Hans Frank remained Father Sixtus O'Connor's prize convert. Frank might have partially reneged on his renunciation of the Nazi regime, but he had held faithful to his return to the church. In her last letter, his wife, Brigitte, had informed Frank that she and the children were living in a cold-water flat and that all their possessions had been confiscated. His present circumstances were such a mockery of the respectability and prestige he had sought all his life that he had no quarrel with his death sentence. An end to thinking and feeling was, he told the priest, a gift. In the time left him, Frank worked desperately to finish his memoirs. He had completed 1,090 pencil-written pages. Father O'Connor promised that he would smuggle the manuscript out to Frank's wife, if he had to carry it himself.

The army censor scanned the letter from Rudolf Hess to his wife, the first written since his sentencing. "I am greatly surprised," he wrote, "for I had reckoned with the death sentence." He reiterated his reasons for not seeing her "through a wire net with guards on both sides . . . it is beneath our dignity. Nevertheless," he told her, "I find myself in a state of most perfect calm, disturbed only by the thought that I cannot transfer my state to comrades who cannot feel the same way." He closed by saying, "In accordance with my refusal on principle to recognize the court, I paid no attention—ostentatiously—when the judgment in my case was announced. . . . As a matter of fact, it was quite long before I discovered, accidentally, what the sentence had been." The letter was one of dozens from Hess that the censor had cleared. And like all the others, this one struck him as a model of rationality.

Keitel pleaded with Dr. Pfluecker to use his influence to stop the mournful music. Every night the SS organist played "*Schlafe, mein Kindchen, schlaf ein*"—"Sleep My Little One, Sleep." Keitel, too, after initial resistance, had also begun an autobiography and felt himself drowning in melancholy memory. The song recalled his lost sons, dead or missing in the invasion of the Soviet Union which their father had helped launch. How fortunate it would have been, Keitel noted in his memoir, if he had been permitted a hero's death that steaming twentieth of July when the bomb intended for Hitler went off in the Wolf's Lair in Rastenburg. Later, after the war, he had been left unguarded for hours on end by his captors. How easy suicide would have been then, how preferable to this "Via Dolorosa to Nuremberg," he wrote.

How much more fortunate Erwin Rommel had been. In October 1944, Hitler learned that Germany's noblest soldier had supposedly supported the Twentieth of July plotters. Hitler told Keitel that they had only two options. The first was to arrest Rommel and court-martial him. That would be a terrible blow to the German people, who revered Rommel, Keitel said. The only other course, Hitler said, was to inform Rommel of what lay in store for him, should he fail to do "the right thing."

Keitel sent two generals, Wilhelm Burgdorf and Ernst Maisel, to Rommel's home near Ulm, where the field marshal was recuperating from a skull fracture suffered when his staff car had been strafed. They carried with them a vial of poison. They explained Rommel's choices to him, and promised protection for his family and a state funeral if he did what was expected.

On October 15, 1944, Keitel wrote his wife, "Rommel has died after all from the multiple skull injuries he received in a car accident. It is a heavy blow and a loss of a commander well favored by the gods." In an official announcement to the German people, Keitel told the same lie.

Pfluecker promised that he would speak to Colonel Andrus about the organist. Alone in his cell, Keitel understood fully, at last, the old proverb "Hell is truth seen too late." He had served evil with the same soldierly devotion with which he would have served good. His crime was that he had made no distinction.

8

COLONEL ANDRUS DELIVERED the news to the prisoners after morning church services on Sunday, October 13. The ACC had rejected all appeals for clemency. Before leaving Nuremberg, Justice Jackson had notified the commission that none of the defendants had provided service to the prosecution meriting mitigation. And clemency offered no political dividends, the ACC itself had concluded.

After seeing the prisoners, Andrus left for the airport, accompanied by his daughter Kitty. It was hardly an ideal time to be leaving Nuremberg. The hour of execution had to be imminent. Still, the Grand Duchy of Luxembourg had invited the colonel to receive the Order of the Oak Wreath Crown for his earlier direction of the prison at Mondorf. Kitty was to be presented to the grand duchess at a reception honoring her father. He had known little enough reward in this job, his wife had said, and he must not miss this trip. In any case, Andrus would be back the next day.

The day before, he had checked the latest psychiatric reports on his wards. Lieutenant Colonel Dunn had warned of potential difficulty with Sauckel and Ribbentrop; he described the latter as "a house that was not built of very good material originally and was now in the process of disintegration." As for Göring, Dunn reported, "He will face his sentence bolstered by his egocentricity, bravado, and showmanship. Göring will seize any opportunity to go out fighting."

Alfred Jodl received the word of the ACC decision with customary stoicism, outwardly at least. He knew of Luise's efforts, another dream to be dashed. Winston Churchill had replied that he had received her communication "and passed it to Attlee, the prime minister." Montgomery had reacted similarly. Her telegram to Eisenhower had been returned with a note, "Addressee has left town. No forwarding address given."

Jodl welcomed the arrival of the prison barber. As the POW trusty shaved him, he asked Jodl about a faded photograph on the table, a young woman holding an infant. That was him with his mother, Jodl answered. "It's too bad I didn't die then. Look how much grief I would have been spared. Frankly I don't know why I lived anyway."

On Sunday evening, Gilbert made a last visit to the prison, asking the condemned men how they felt about the denial of their appeals. Sauckel displayed the most palpable fear of dying. He had always done what he was told to the best of his ability, he told the psychologist.

How could he now be a condemned criminal? Yet, as Gilbert discussed the collapse of Sauckel's appeal, a ray of reality appeared to penetrate that modest intelligence. "We have an old saying, Doctor," Sauckel said. "The dogs will always catch the slowest one."

Julius Streicher spoke again of his mounting admiration for the Jews. Of course, Gilbert must know about his people's celebration of Purim, he said. Imagine the irony of that event; Haman, the cruel minister of Xerxes, and his ten sons, marched to the same gallows where the Persian had intended to hang the Jews. Streicher continued to astonish Gilbert with his biblical erudition.

Göring lay stretched on his cot, apathetic yet curiously alert about certain matters. He questioned Gilbert closely on one point. Was there absolutely no possibility that he would be allowed to face a firing squad? None, Gilbert answered. It was just as well, Göring said. He had heard the Americans were poor shots. His rounds completed, Gustav Gilbert left cellblock C for the last time.

Monday, October 14, the cellblock bustled with the customary morning routine for all but Göring, who still had his cell cleaned by a POW trusty. He lingered in the corridor, talking to Tex Wheelis, while the others mopped their cells. The guards liked having Lieutenant Wheelis on duty. His supervision was marked by an amiable laxity. Göring next spoke quietly and intently to Dr. Pfluecker until the guards locked him up again.

In his cell, Göring could slip his hand into the cavity where the flush pipe entered his toilet bowl. There he would find the cold, hard, reassuring tip of the cartridge. Inside was a glass vial of cyanide. How the cartridge had traveled from the baggage room to its present hiding place was known only to him and a probably unwitting accomplice. It was most likely Tex Wheelis who had retrieved from that room the gifts Göring had given the soldier and possibly other items, including the blue briefcase that Göring had presented to Stahmer.

9

COLONEL ANDRUS returned from Luxembourg Monday afternoon to find Master Sergeant John C. Woods, the Third Army executioner, waiting in his office. The sergeant had come by his trade while serving as a witness at a hanging. When the executioner had asked for a volunteer, Woods came forward and discovered his calling. The pot-bellied, ruby-faced forty-three-year-old commanded a certain awe wherever he served; this had engendered in the man a coarse confidence that grated on Andrus. Woods said that he had been told he would do the job on Wednesday, the sixteenth. True, Andrus said. The Quadripartite Commission was meeting at this moment to determine the exact hour and the disposition of bodies and personal effects.

Andrus reminded Woods that secrecy was vital. They did not want to trigger any fuss by the Germans—demonstrations, escape attempts, or uprisings. Woods explained that he had managed to get his team and equipment into town unobserved, traveling from Landsberg by back roads during the night, avoiding the reporters who had virtually staked out the city. His crew was now waiting at the Nuremberg military district headquarters. He had two boys in his five-man team, Woods said, who had never dropped anybody before; but he had been training them hard for three weeks.

Andrus slid open a desk drawer and handed Woods a sheet of paper, a list of the height and weight of the eleven condemned men. Woods had heard that Göring was enormous; but, he noticed, the prisoner who had weighed 262 pounds on his capture was down to 186. A basketball game would be under way tonight in the makeshift gym next to the exercise yard, Andrus said. That was the best time to slip into the yard. The noise of the game would help cover Woods's arrival.

That evening near eight p.m., the prisoners heard a commotion at the far end of the block. Word passed quickly that Colonel Andrus had ordered a surprise inspection. He wanted the cells turned inside out. Göring had to remove the capsule from the toilet. There was only one other place to conceal it temporarily during the inspection: in his rectum. Arriving at cell 5, First Lieutenant John W. West went through Göring's box of personal belongings, checked the underside of the table, the window ledge, and the toilet bowl. He looked under the bed, lifted the mattress, took it out into the corridor, shook it vigorously, inspected it, found no tears, and placed it back on the cot.

Göring waited until lights out. Once in bed, he could remove the cartridge, manage to work a tear in the mattress, and slip the cartridge into it.

The gym was dirty, the air foul, and the ceiling too low for set shots. "You boys go on, finish your game," an unfamiliar master sergeant drawled as he stood, arms folded, watching from the doorway. Woods estimated the dimensions of the gym at about eighty by thirty feet, plenty of room for his needs. He turned and left. Minutes later, the GIs heard vehicles pull up alongside the gym. They continued playing, the ball beating a thumping cadence against the wooden floor, counterpointed by their shouting. Woods and his assistants remained by their trucks, smoking, until the players headed for the showers in the prison basement. When the last of them was out of sight, Woods gave a signal and his men dropped the tailgates.

Willi Krug, on the third tier, was awakened after midnight by hammering and the sound of voices, but soon fell back asleep. Dr. Pfluecker heard the noise too, as did Albert Speer, whose speculations sent a chill down his spine.

While his men assembled the portable equipment, Sergeant Woods ran his hands over the ropes, waxed and flexed them until he was satisfied that he had achieved the right elasticity. He should have tested them with weights first, but could find none in the prison. He began weaving the nooses. By the time he finished, the hammering was stilled.

He observed his crew's handiwork with satisfaction. Three gallows stood in the middle of the gym, painted black, eight feet high, each approached by thirteen wooden steps. The front three sides below the landing were of wood; a black drape covered the back end. Woods mounted the first gallows and shifted his weight, testing its stability. A metal hook hung from the crossbar. Woods attached a noose to the hook. A lever jutted from the floor. Woods yanked it. The trapdoor opened with a metallic screech. He gave the lever a drop of oil. He repeated the ritual at each of the scaffolds.

One more task remained. His men strung a black curtain at one end of the gym, and behind it placed coffins and stretchers taken from

the trucks. By the time they finished, dawn was washing away the dark
of night. They piled into their vehicles and drove out of the prison
yard. The whining motors awakened Willi Krug again. This time he
decided to get up.

10

THE DAY BEGAN like any other in the fixed round of their lives. Krug
collected the washbasins; the prisoners cleaned their cells and break-
fasted on oatmeal and coffee. Rosenberg wanted a complaint brought
to the colonel's attention. The nights were getting cold again, and he
simply could not sleep with his hands outside the blankets. For all the
surface calm, they kept asking Krug, was this the day?

The POW barber came to Hermann Göring's cell first, as usual.
The escort guard handed him a blade, which the barber inserted into
Göring's razor. The escort and the cell guard chatted animatedly
about baseball. Something important in the sport was happening that
night, Göring gathered. As the barber was leaving, Göring asked him,
could this be the day?

The cell doors were thrown open for morning exercise—several
brisk turns around the corridor, guard and prisoner shackled together.
Once the men were locked up again, the librarian, Otto Streng, performed his other role, jailhouse mailman. Streicher received one letter,
Ribbentrop five, Jodl seven, and Frank nine. Sauckel received none.
Frank asked, with childlike eagerness, if he was the winner this morning. Several asked Streng if this was the day.

On days when the evidence in court had been horrifying, a smell
of shame clung to the cellblock. On a day brightened by a hopeful
decision from the bench, a whiff of the old arrogance permeated the
corridor. Today, cellblock C was electric.

Ribbentrop complained of insomnia to the army physician, First
Lieutenant Roska. Roska reminded him that Dr. Pfluecker would
bring the usual sedatives that evening. The former foreign minister
wanted to read to the doctor a letter he had just written to his wife:
"Millions have fallen. The Reich is destroyed and our people lie pros-
trate. Is it not right that I too should fall? I am perfectly composed
and will hold my head high, whatever happens. I will see you in an-

other world." What did the doctor think of that? Ribbentrop wanted to know. Roska was impressed that this "disintegrating personality," whom he had been told especially to watch, had revealed unexpected dignity. It was a fine letter, the doctor said.

Roska interrupted Keitel in the midst of work on his memoirs. He was struck by the sparkling cleanliness the field marshal had somehow achieved in a jail cell. Keitel was downcast but told the doctor he felt fine and went back to his writing. Tomorrow would be October 16. Five years ago, to the day, he had drafted the Reprisal Order. "A human life in unsettled countries frequently counts for nothing," he had written, and then he had gone on to order the execution of fifty hostages for the death of a single German soldier. That and similar orders had led him to this cell, where his own life now counted for nothing.

Chaplain Gerecke and Father O'Connor sat in the prison office keeping their minds occupied by discussing the World Series game to be played that night. Gerecke was ready to put ten dollars on his hometown St. Louis Cardinals. O'Connor, ordinarily a Dodger fan, settled for the Boston Red Sox. Dr. Pfluecker listened, understanding nothing. A guard arrived and informed the chaplains and Pfluecker that the colonel wanted to see them in his office.

Andrus was subdued. He had just received word from the Quadripartite Commission. The condemned men were to be awakened at 11:45 this evening. They would receive their last meal and then be taken to the gym, where the executions would begin after midnight. Could they be told now? Pfluecker asked. No, Andrus said. Until they were awakened tonight, all was to proceed normally, even to distributing sleeping pills for those who used them. Not a word he had uttered in this room, he warned, was to be repeated. Though Pfluecker was a German and still technically a POW, Andrus's trust in him was total.

That afternoon, Father O'Connor visited the cells of Frank, Kaltenbrunner, and Seyss-Inquart to ask if they would like to make their confessions and take Communion. He read the alarm in their eyes, and to their inevitable questions, pretended that he had no information.

Dr. Pfluecker asked the corporal of the guard, Sergeant Denzil

Edie, to accompany him to Göring's cell. He wanted to give Göring
a light sedative, he said. Edie accompanied the doctor to cell 5 and
watched Pfluecker take Göring's pulse and give him a small white pill.
Göring prodded the doctor for the latest word. The colonel's warning
rang fresh in Pfluecker's ears. Still, Pfluecker thought, he must do
something to help. All he dared say was, "This night might prove to
be very short." He did not want to do anything to draw attention to
himself by varying his usual routine, Göring said. But he had to remain
alert. How could he, if he took his usual sleeping pills? Pfluecker
promised to find a way. Immediately upon Pfluecker's departure, Göring called to Otto Streng for some stationery. On the librarian's return, Göring seated himself at the flimsy table and began writing, in
a bold, vigorous hand:

> To the Allied Control Council:
> I would have had no objection to being shot. However, I
> will not facilitate execution of Germany's *Reichsmarschall* by
> hanging! For the sake of Germany, I cannot permit this.
> Moreover, I feel no moral obligation to submit to my ene-
> mies' punishment. For this reason, I have chosen to die like
> the great Hannibal.

He signed his name with a flourish.

Hermann Göring saw himself as a man of honor. Certain people
in this prison had shown him kindness at some risk to themselves,
especially Wheelis and Dr. Pfluecker. He owed them something. He
took another sheet of paper and began:

"To the Commandant: I have had the poison capsule with me
ever since the beginning of my imprisonment." He went on to explain
that he had brought three capsules into Mondorf, the first deliberately
left to be found in his clothes, another hidden in a container of skin
cream still in his toiletry case in the baggage room. The third capsule,
he said, he had hidden "here in the cell so well that in spite of repeated
and thorough searches, it could not be found." While he was in the
courtroom, he said, he had hidden the capsule in his boots. "None of
those responsible for the searches is to be blamed," he ended, "for it
was practically impossible to find the capsule. It would have been pure
coincidence." He signed the letter, then decided to add another line.
There was one person he did not have to protect. "Dr. Gilbert," he

wrote, was the one who "told me that the control council had refused my petition to change the method of execution to shooting."

The next letter was to his wife.

> My one and only sweetheart, after serious consideration and sincere prayer to the Lord, I have decided to take my own life, lest I be executed in so terrible a fashion by my enemies. . . . My life came to an end when I bade you farewell for the last time. Ever since then, I have felt wonderfully at peace with myself and consider my death a deliverance. I take it as a sign from God that throughout all the months of my imprisonment, I was left with the means which now set me free of my temporal existence and that they were never found. . . . All my thoughts are with you and Edda and my dearest ones. My last heartbeats are for our great and eternal love.

He penned a quick note to Chaplain Gerecke asking his forgiveness, but saying, "for political reasons, I had to act this way."

He placed the four letters in an envelope and put them under his blanket. For reasons known only to himself, he had dated them October 11, 1946—clearly incorrect, since Gilbert had not talked to him about the ACC decision until October 13.

Kingsbury Smith, correspondent for the International News Service, recognized that he had been deeded a title to history. Smith was one of eight pool reporters chosen by lot to witness the executions. His instructions were to present himself at eight p.m. at the visitors' room, where, over the past eleven months, the defendants had met with their lawyers and more recently bade good-bye to their families. When Smith arrived, he found correspondents for Tass and *Pravda* chatting with Colonel Andrus. The other pool correspondents, representing French and British papers, arrived soon afterward. The colonel announced that the pool was to be given a tour of cellblock C. After that, the journalists would be held incommunicado until the hour of the executions. They were to take no photographs in the gym. The Third Army had sent down its own man from the Signal Corps in Frankfurt to serve as official photographer. They were fortunate to be allowed to cover the story at all. Justices Lawrence and Birkett, Andrus pointed out, had vigorously opposed any press presence at this "grue-some spectacle." But American officials feared creating future Bor-manns by allowing rumors to spread that Göring or Ribbentrop or Kaltenbrunner was still alive. The Americans wanted the press to con-firm the deaths to the world.

Dr. Pfluecker went to the prison dentist, Dr. Hoch, another POW trusty. Pfluecker had a problem. Every night, the guards watched him give Göring two sleeping pills, Seconal in a red capsule, which acted quickly but did not last long, and Amytal in a blue capsule, which produced deep sleep. He must not let Göring slip into a stupor this night. He asked Hoch to empty the blue capsule and fill it with sodium bicarbonate.

That evening, official word that the executions were imminent was passed to the press at the Faber-Castell castle. The reporters piled into buses for the trip to the Palace of Justice, where they were briefed by an army public information officer. They could expect no further news until after the hangings, he warned, which were scheduled to take place at an undisclosed hour on the sixteenth. They would get eyewitness accounts from the pool reporters. The correspondents be-gan crowding the windows, which offered a view of the lights burning in cellblock C. The officer warned them not to try to open the win-dows and lean out. Sentries had orders to shoot on sight.

In nearby buildings and bombed-out shells, journalists comman-deered vantage points. Dana, the German news service, had a three-man team, equipped with binoculars, posted in a roofless attic offering a view of the prison yard and gymnasium only two hundred yards away.

Göring impatiently surveyed the fleshy, kindly face of Chaplain Ge-recke. He had written a special devotional just for him, Gerecke said. Göring told him to leave it on his table. He would read it later. When would the executions take place? Göring asked. Gerecke ignored the question. Would Göring join him in prayer? No, Göring replied, he would watch the chaplain pray from his cot. "You'll never see your daughter, Edda, in heaven if you refuse the Lord's way of salvation," Gerecke warned, dropping to his knees. When the chaplain finished,

Göring asked again about the execution. He had a Christian duty not to let these men suffer the cruelty of not knowing, Göring said. Look at poor Sauckel; he was practically gibbering. Gerecke felt Göring's powerful will working on him. He insisted that he did not know and quickly left.

Göring heard the heavy door of the cellblock open and recognized the voice of Colonel Andrus above the hum of several others. The eight correspondents became silent at a signal from the colonel. They looked down a long, grayish corridor, the gloom broken only by eleven bare lights over eleven cell doors. Eleven cell guards leaned on the outer shelves peering in, frozen as if in a tableau. The press party started to follow Andrus, past the prison office, the baggage room, and the cells. In them they glimpsed men reading, pacing, smoking. Andrus then took the reporters to a tier in the prison where they were to remain until they were escorted to the gym after midnight.

As soon as Göring heard Andrus's party leave, he got up and retrieved his letters from beneath the blanket. He found the letter to the Allied Control Council and added a page. "I consider it in extremely bad taste," he wrote, "to present our deaths as a spectacle to the sensationalist press. . . . This finale is certainly in keeping with the baseness which the prosecution as well as the court have demonstrated. The whole thing is merely a show trial, a bad comedy. Personally, I shall die without this sensationalism and without an audience."

At 9:30 p.m., Dr. Pfluecker, in the company of the duty officer, Lieutenant Arthur McLinden, made his sleeping-pill rounds. They found Göring in his blue silk pajamas already in bed. Pfluecker gave Göring the blue and red capsules, which McLinden watched him take. McLinden noted the warm parting handshake of the two men. It had the quality of a farewell.

11

THE DANA NEWS CREW huddled in its attic perch, shivering in a wind-driven rain. Below them, Nurembergers hurried by, coats clutched to their throats, and a policeman stood beneath a feeble streetlamp, stamping his feet. The crew could make out people emerging from army staff cars in front of the courthouse. Dignitaries, the Germans guessed. The man with the binoculars swung them in a slow arc across the prison wall. Lights out, he reported, and checked his watch. The time was 9:35 p.m.

Among the passengers deposited at the Palace of Justice was Dr. Wilhelm Hoegner, minister president of Bavaria, chosen by the American occupation authorities as a German witness for the executions. Inside the courthouse, Hoegner was directed to a remote vaulted room, where the Quadripartite Commission had done its work, and where the witnesses were gathering. In addition to the eight pool reporters and four Quadripartite Commission members, thirty others would witness the final act of the trial, including doctors, chaplains, and German civil officials such as Hoegner. A stenographer from the Language Division had been assigned to capture the prisoners' last words. Colonel Andrus asked for the group's attention and began reading seating assignments in the gym.

The colonel had imposed a communications cutoff between the prison and the outside world. The only exception he had agreed to was one phone call to the prison office after each inning to give the score of the World Series. The Red Sox had tied up the game and Chaplain Gerecke, Father O'Connor, and a handful of guards impatiently awaited the next ring of the phone. The cellblock was otherwise still, the prisoners in bed, some already asleep.

Suddenly, shouts of "Corporal of the guard!" and heavy footsteps echoed down the empty corridor. Staff Sergeant Gregory Tymchyshyn came bursting into the prison office. "Chaplain, chaplain, there's something wrong with Göring!" Tymchyshyn shouted. Gerecke followed the sergeant to cell 5, where Göring was lying on his back, his right hand dangling over the side of the bed, his face a sickly green. Froth bubbled in one corner of his mouth as he breathed loudly and unnaturally. One eye was shut, the other open. Gerecke took his pulse. "Good Lord," he said, "this man is dying." Gerecke ordered a guard to fetch Dr. Pfluecker. The chaplain asked PFC Harold Johnson, the cell guard, what had happened. Johnson had seen Göring bring his arm to his face, fist clenched, as though shielding his eyes. Göring had then let his hand fall back. That was at exactly 10:44 p.m., the GI said. About three minutes later, Göring had started making choking noises. That was when he had shouted for the corporal of the guard.

Dr. Pfluecker arrived as Göring exhaled for the last time. The doctor took his pulse. There was nothing to be done, Pfluecker said. He had no experience with poisons. The army doctor, Lieutenant Roska, must be summoned. Pfluecker pulled back the blanket, revealing two envelopes resting on Göring's stomach. Captain Robert Starnes, the chief prison officer, arrived as Pfluecker was putting his head to Göring's chest to listen for the heartbeat. "Yes, he's dead," Pfluecker said, handing Starnes the two envelopes. Starnes felt something heavy in one, and extracted a cartridge, two and a half inches long, with a removable cap. In the other he found Göring's letters.

Dr. Roska arrived and made his way through the crowd outside Göring's cell. He was immediately struck by the odor of bitter almonds. He ran his finger around inside Göring's mouth and brought out tiny shards of glass. "Cyanide," Roska said.

Colonel Andrus was giving the witnesses the order of the executions when the call came. The colonel had better get over to the cellblock right away, Captain Starnes urged. Andrus ran all the way. Starnes met him and explained what had happened as they hurried to Göring's cell. The knot of people parted to let Andrus through. He stared at the face, now a concrete gray. With the one eye closed, Göring appeared to be winking at the colonel. Andrus glanced at his watch. It was 11:09 p.m. He told Starnes to have the guards wake up the other prisoners. He left the cell to phone the Quadripartite Commission. Starnes handed him the two envelopes and asked if the prisoners were still to be given their last meal. Andrus nodded and headed down the cellblock to the prison office. An incredulous General Rickard answered his call. The colonel heard a hurried conversation at the other end. Rickard came back on the line; the commission members were coming right over, he said.

The four officers arrived within minutes and cleared the cell of all but the two doctors. The Russian representative, General Georgi

Malkov, gave Göring a hard slap across the face. What was that for?
Brigadier Paton Walsh asked. "You can't fake death," the Russian said.
"The eyes always move. He's dead."

Andrus handed the envelopes with the cartridge and letters to
General Rickard. The colonel had not read them, even the one addressed to him; he feared that doing so might incriminate him. He
asked to be excused. It was his responsibility to inform the prisoners
that their sentence was about to be carried out. General Rickard
shouted after him that, as of now, he wanted them handcuffed.

The commission members pressed the doctors for details. Cyanide acted swiftly, Roska explained. It blocked the body's cells from
taking oxygen. Death could occur in three to five minutes. The four
men excused the doctors and began debating their alternatives. They
considered having Göring brought to the gym on a stretcher, telling
the witnesses that he had fainted, and then hanging the body. The
idea was dismissed. Too many people already knew what had happened. The story would inevitably leak out and damage the credibility
of the court. The sensible thing, they concluded, was to appoint a
board to begin an immediate investigation, and to proceed with the
executions.

General Rickard came out of the cell, looking for Colonel Andrus. He saw the prisoners, each handcuffed to a guard, sitting on
their cots in their cells, the doors open. A last meal of sausage, potato
salad, and fruit salad rested on their laps. Few touched the food. Rickard located Andrus. The two men found it difficult to look at each
other; Andrus was mortified, and Rickard wanted to conceal his
disbelief. Rickard told the colonel that he needed two senior officers
from the ISD to serve on an investigating board. Andrus recommended Lieutenant Colonel W. H. Tweedy and Major Stanley Ro-
senthal. Rickard said that he himself would provide the board
president, Colonel B. F. Hurless. One more thing. Andrus would have
to tell the eight reporters in the pool what had happened.

The colonel returned to the tier where he had sequestered the
reporters. He wore the shellacked green helmet and carried the riding
crop. Only his tie was askew. "Göring is dead," he began. "He committed suicide by poisoning himself." They peppered him with questions. "The Quadripartite Commission is investigating," the colonel
responded. "I have no further details." They made a reflexive bolt for

the door, and then realized they were locked in. The executions would proceed on schedule, Andrus said. They would be taken to the gym at the appropriate time.

12

"THEY'RE COMING," the Dana man with the binoculars announced. He could make out a man between four guards and several unidentifiable officers following behind, coming from the jail. He stopped to wipe the lens of the binoculars. The rain had turned into a drizzle, still driven by a wind that whistled eerily through the ruins.

Colonel Andrus walked behind Joachim von Ribbentrop the thirty-five yards from the cellblock across the exercise yard to the gym. At the entrance, he removed his helmet and bowed stiffly. The German, his sparse gray hair whipped by the wind, returned the bow. To Andrus's relief, Ribbentrop had walked steadily, head held high, hands handcuffed behind him. The colonel remained outside the gym. He had been with these men too long to want to watch them die.

The time was 1:11 a.m. as Ribbentrop went through the door. He blinked in the harsh, unforgiving light. Two men from Master Sergeant Woods's detail removed his handcuffs and retied Ribbentrop's hands with a leather strap. Most witnesses sat at the tables; a few others stood against the wall. Ribbentrop was led to the gallows on the left. Woods's plan was to use two gallows and hold the third in reserve. An American army colonel stood at the foot of the steps and asked the prisoner to state his name. Ribbentrop did so in a firm voice, then mounted the stairs. Waiting for him at the top were Chaplain Gerecke and a stenographer, poised to record his last utterance. Another of Woods's men bound Ribbentrop's legs at the ankles with an army web belt. Ribbentrop was asked if he had anything to say. "My last wish," he said, "is that Germany realize its destiny and that an understanding be reached between East and West. I wish peace to the world." Woods slipped the noose over Ribbentrop's neck and a black hood over his head. He stepped back, and yanked the lever. The trapdoor opened with a crash and the body disappeared as down a mineshaft.

Two minutes later, Field Marshal Keitel stepped briskly up the stairs of the middle gallows as if he were mounting a reviewing stand. As he turned around to face the witnesses, he could see the rope in the gallows to his right twisting slowly. "More than two million soldiers went to their death for the fatherland before me," he said. "I now join my sons. *Deutschland über Alles!*"

After the trap was sprung on Keitel, the colonel in charge asked General Rickard if the witnesses might smoke while they waited for the doctors to pronounce the prisoners dead. Roska and a Russian physician disappeared behind the black curtain at the rear of Ribbentrop's scaffold, one carrying a flashlight, the other a stethoscope. The gym was quickly filled with smoke and the hum of subdued conversation. Kingsbury Smith, gesturing toward Keitel's gallows, said to a British reporter, "We've just witnessed history, probably the first professional soldier who wasn't able to hide behind his orders."

Fifteen minutes passed. The witnesses began to eye each other uneasily. They talked in hushed tones about the broken neck that was supposed to produce merciful, almost instant death. The doctors finally emerged. Ribbentrop was dead, Roska announced. Woods went behind the curtain and cut the rope with a large commando knife. Two GIs brought the body out on a stretcher and set it on top of a coffin behind the black curtain. The American colonel announced, "Cigarettes out, please, gentlemen," and gave the signal to bring in Kaltenbrunner, who was hanged while Father O'Connor, wearing a Franciscan habit, prayed next to him.

The doctors went under the middle gallows and pronounced Keitel dead. The British reporter leaned toward Kingsbury Smith and whispered, "That took forever."

Rosenberg died wordless. Frank faced his executioners with the beatific smile of a man happy to throw off the burden of life. Frick stumbled on the top step and had to be caught.

A commotion broke out at the entrance to the gym. Two GIs propelled a resistant Julius Streicher through the gym door. Back in his cell, the guards had had to force Streicher into his clothes. At the foot of the gallows, he refused to give the American colonel his name, screeching instead, "Heil Hitler!" "For the love of God, Julius," Father O'Connor pleaded, "tell them your name and get it over with." Streicher shouted, "*Purim Fest*, 1946," and then, turning to Sergeant

Woods, said, "Someday, the Bolsheviks will hang you!" After Streicher disappeared through the trapdoor, an eerie moan persisted.
Woods descended the steps and vanished behind the curtain. Soon the
moaning stopped.

Albert Speer, from his cell on the second tier, could hear the
guards call out the names, one by one. This time it was "Sauckel."
He heard the familiar thud of the prison door slamming shut.

Standing on the gallows, eyes darting wildly, Fritz Sauckel cried
out, "I am dying an innocent man!" Jodl arrived with the collar of his
tunic sticking up in the back. He licked his lips nervously as Woods
slipped the hood over his head. The last to die was Arthur Seyss-
Inquart, at 2:45 a.m.

Four GIs came into the gym bearing a stretcher covered by an
army blanket. They set the stretcher down between the first two gallows. The American colonel asked the witnesses to come forward. As
they did, he pulled off the blanket and revealed the corpse of Hermann
Göring. Hoegner, the minister president of Bavaria, muttered, "The
scoundrel. He should be hanged anyway." The British reporter whispered to Smith, "Only Germans can hate so, and then only one another."

Lieutenant Maurice McLaughlin, the Third Army photographer,
stepped behind the curtain. No one was to doubt that these men were
dead, the Quadripartite Commission had told him. McLaughlin inserted the first flashbulb and began shooting Göring, one frontal, one
left side, one right side, one naked. As he worked, he noticed bloody
bruises about the mouths and noses of several of the bodies.

The reporters in the pressroom had been waiting throughout the
night. Now, as dawn approached, the place was a shambles of paper
cups half full of cold coffee, the remains of sandwiches, cigarette butts,
and sleeping bodies coiled in corners or stretched out on tables. The
last desultory card game had broken up long before. In the first few
hours, the room had been a babel of speculation, interrupted by phone
calls from bureau chiefs demanding to know why their reporters had
not yet filed. When word raced through the pressroom that Dana, the
German agency, had broken a story that all the war criminals had
been executed, the pressure became unbearable. The correspondent
of the London *News Chronicle* began pounding out a gripping eyewit-

ness account of Hermann Göring mounting the gallows. One by one, others submitted their stories. The piece by the New York *Herald Tribune*'s correspondent produced an early-edition headline: 11 NAZI CHIEFS HANGED IN NUREMBERG PRISON: GOERING AND HENCHMEN PAY FOR WAR CRIMES. The AP's Thomas Reedy held out against repeated howling from his chief in New York that everybody was scooping him. Reedy resisted. As the hours passed, the pressroom had gradually died down. Suddenly, someone shouted, "Andrus is coming!" and the room shook itself back to life.

The colonel had spent the night with the investigating board trying to piece together Göring's last movements. He then had gone to his office to draft a statement. Finally, he braced himself for the inevitable confrontation with the press corps. He had been awake for nearly twenty-four hours. His skin was pale and mottled, his eyes red-rimmed. He had a prepared statement, he announced. "Göring was not hanged," he began. "He committed suicide last night by taking cyanide of potassium. He was discovered at once by the sentinel who watched him make an odd noise and twitch. The sentinel called the doctor and chaplain. There were pieces of glass in his mouth and an odor of cyanide of potassium." Groans and shouts went up from several reporters who bolted for the phones and telegraph office to correct their stories. The rest continued pelting Andrus with questions. How good had the colonel's security been? Hadn't he said the prisoners couldn't breathe without his knowing it? Wasn't Göring the third prisoner he had lost? Andrus refused to answer questions.

Back in his office, he slumped into his chair. His conviction was that the suicide demonstrated Göring's cowardice, the man's inability to face his fate. But others, he knew, would simply conclude that the Nuremberg jailer had been outfoxed. He pulled himself together and began moving slowly down the corridor to go home and confront his own self-flagellating demons.

Later, Robert Jackson would issue a public statement praising Colonel Andrus as "a fine officer in a difficult task" who had been "diligent and intelligent and in all respects faithful to his trust." The colonel treasured the words.

It was still dark when two army six-by-six trucks pulled alongside the gym. The eleven coffins were quickly loaded. The trucks pulled away escorted by two unmarked cars bearing armed guards. By seven a.m., the small caravan had arrived at a forbidding gray stone building in East Munich's Ostfriedhof Cemetery. The German attendants had been alerted that the bodies of several American soldiers, killed during the war, would be arriving for cremation. Each coffin bore a label. The one marked "George Munger" held the body of Hermann Göring.

When the cremations were completed, including nooses and hoods, the ashes were taken to a white stucco villa in the Munich suburb of Solln. The house, which had once belonged to a wealthy merchant, was now the U.S. Army's European Theater Mortuary Number One. Shortly afterward, a group of army officers stood on the bank of the Contwentzbach, a stream running behind the house. They watched the mortuary staff bring down eleven aluminum cylinders. One by one the ashes were emptied into the water. The cylinders were chopped with axes and smashed flat with boot heels. The Contwentzbach carried the ashes into the Isar River, which conducted them to the Danube, which emptied them into the sea. The Quadripartite Commission had fulfilled its aim, to obliterate any corporeal trace of these men and any relic around which a shrine to Nazism might rise.

Master Sergeant John Woods was enjoying the glow of celebrity. Woods had been brought back to the Stein Castle to hold his first press conference. The coarse red face beamed. "I hanged those ten Nazis and I'm proud of it," he said. "I did a good job of it too. Everything clicked. I hanged 347 people and I never saw one go off better. I wasn't nervous. I haven't got any nerves. A fellow can't afford to have nerves in this business." What had he done immediately after the executions? a reporter asked. "Had me and my boys a stiff drink." He smiled. "We earned it."

Cecil Catling, veteran crime reporter for the London Star, asked Woods about reports that an unconscionable amount of time had elapsed before some of the men were pronounced dead—seventeen minutes for Ribbentrop, eighteen minutes for Jodl, a startling twenty-eight minutes for Keitel. He further had it on good authority, Catling said, that some of the men's faces were smashed. Woods looked briefly uncomfortable. Any noises heard from hanged men were reflex reactions, as any doctor could confirm, he said. And the blood? "Perfectly natural. That happens when the condemned man bites his tongue at the moment of the drop." Someone tossed the sergeant a noose and asked him to pose for photographs. He held the rope in powerful hands and smiled into the flashing lights.

What did Catling think of Woods's performance? his colleagues asked later. Rubbish, Catling said. The men had not been properly tied, nor had they been dropped from a sufficient height. He had witnessed enough hangings to know that they had not experienced the instant unconsciousness of a broken neck, but death by strangulation. Catling likely had it right. The army never used Master Sergeant Woods as a hangman again.

While the remaining prisoners awaited transfer to their new home, Spandau prison, a medieval fortress in Berlin, they were dispatched to clean up the recently vacated first-tier cells. Mess trays bearing the remains of the last meal still rested on cots and tables. Papers and bedding lay scattered about. Only Keitel's and Jodl's cells were immaculate, blankets neatly folded at the foot of each bed. Speer noticed that Seyss-Inquart had marked October 16 on his wall calendar with a penciled cross.

Speer, Schirach, and Hess were sent to mop the gym. Sunlight flooded through windows that had been blacked out during the executions. The light fell mercilessly on the wooden floor where the gallows had stood. They came upon a brown-red stain. Blood, Speer thought. He had difficulty maintaining his composure. Hess stood on the spot, clicked his heels, and raised his arm in the Nazi salute. Was it an act of mockery, madness, or sincerity? Speer wondered. With Hess, one never knew.

13

IN AMERICA AND EUROPE, those who had conducted the trial, the prosecutors and judges, watched their monumental effort disfigured at the last moment by a Nazi's cunning. The wrong headline had come out of Nuremberg—not JUSTICE TRIUMPHS, but GÖRING CHEATS HANGMAN. The trial had been intended to convict and punish the guilty, and, more loftily, to deter future aggressors. But it had had another objective: to force the German people to recognize the horrendous fruits of Hitler and Nazism. The day after the executions, John Stanton, *Time* magazine's Nuremberg correspondent, had gone into the streets to sample reactions. He found the Germans "suddenly straightened up. Men with eyes glistening stopped for excited talks with one another. . . . Germans who had avoided the eyes of Americans the night before, now looked at them frankly, with derisive smiles." Suddenly Göring was "our Hermann," the one who had "put one over" on Germany's conquerors. "Goering's dramatic gesture in death appeared to have helped these Germans forget his crimes," *The New York Times* editorialized. "The weapon that was to have been a weapon in the hands of democracy suddenly became one in the hands of unrepentant German nationalists."

A favorite Göring theme throughout the trial had been that the Soviet alliance with the West was a wartime shotgun marriage, doomed to failure. In death, he contributed to the breakup. Russian officials began speculating aloud that the Americans had connived to help Göring salvage his reputation and honor from ignominy.

Ten days after the executions, on October 26, the Quadripartite Commission released its public report on the suicide, a terse one-page statement. The commission fully endorsed the findings of its three-man investigating board. The members accepted Göring's claim that the cyanide capsule had always been in his possession. The commission accepted the investigating board's opinion that at various times Göring had secreted the capsule inside the toilet bowl, in his alimentary tract, and in the cavity of his umbilicus. The commission exonerated the cell guard on duty and all other prison personnel of negligence. "The security measures taken were proper in the peculiar conditions of the trial and were satisfactorily carried out," the commission's statement concluded.

The commission chose not to release the detailed top secret report of the investigators' findings. Nor did it reveal the existence of Göring's suicide notes. In their unpublished report, the investigators had described Göring as "clever and unrepentant . . . a subtle individual who outwitted his guards by clever maneuvering." The implication was that a round-the-clock detachment of approximately 120 men guarding one cellblock, carrying out strict regulations including constant surveillance and frequent searches, was no match for one crafty man locked in a cell.

As for the vaunted security, cell assignments had not been changed for a year. No rectal examinations had been made for six months. Göring had said in his note to the colonel that he had another cartridge concealed in a jar of face cream in his toiletry case. The investigating board found it, demonstrating that the defendants' baggage had never been thoroughly searched. PFC Bill Glenny later confided that many guards, like himself, had found the regulations—shining lights in sleeping men's faces, poking them if they slept facing the wall, forcing them to keep hands above the blankets, prohibiting conversation—to be "unrealistic," and had not uniformly enforced them.

Army laboratory tests confirmed that, at some point, the cartridge containing the fatal capsule had been secreted in Göring's rectum, since traces of fecal matter were found on it. The investigating board further determined that the cartridge could be temporarily hidden in the flush pipe of the toilet. And rips were found in Göring's mattress after the suicide which had not been there before.

The investigating board interrogated only five persons: Andrus; his deputy, Major Teich; Dr. Pfluecker; Dr. Roska; and Robert Starnes, the chief prison officer. Sworn statements were taken from thirty-four more prison personnel. Tex Wheelis's statement read: "I have had in my possession the key to the baggage room of the prison during the period 10 October 1946 to 15 October 1946 and can state positively that Göring received nothing from, nor had access to the baggage room during this period." It was a form statement identical to one signed by ten other officers who also had access to the baggage room. Neither Wheelis nor the other nine were questioned personally. The fact that two of three officers on the board were members of Andrus's staff left the impression that the ISD had investigated itself.

Those familiar with the ways of bureaucracies recognized what the army had done. Of course, an investigation had to be conducted; but the objective had not necessarily been to reveal the truth and punish the derelict. That, by extension, would be to rebuke the American army. British and French members of the Quadripartite Commission had no wish to embarrass brother officers. The only member likely to dispute the findings was the Soviet general, Malkov. And the commission's report was issued while he was conveniently away on business in Berlin.

Göring had made it easy for the commission. In his note to Andrus, he had explained how he had done it. Hence, a more penetrating inquiry was unnecessary. What would it have said about the U.S. Army had it been found that a POW trusty, or infinitely worse, a member of the American prison staff, had helped Hermann Göring commit suicide? Göring had neatly foreclosed that conclusion by exonerating everybody in advance. His access to the poison, he claimed, was the result of his own ingenuity. And the army accepted his explanation.

In Washington, Robert Jackson pondered the effect of Göring's dramatic exit on the work of the IMT. Undeniably, the suicide occupied center stage for the moment. But in time to come? The court had delivered its verdict on the accused with some dispatch, in less than a year. History would take far longer, he knew, to deliver its verdict on the IMT. The court's mission had been unprecedented—too novel, too far-reaching for contemporary judgment. Only time and its perspective could unveil the enduring meaning, if any, of those eleven months in room 600.

THE VERDICT
OF TIME

DID IT MATTER? Viewed through the lens of almost half a century, what was the significance of the events of Nuremberg 1945–1946? Did the trial, at the time, fairly judge the men brought before it? Did its grander objective of deterring aggression succeed? Did subsequent warmakers fear the measured fury of the law? Did Nuremberg bequeath permanent legal machinery for dealing with future war criminals?

The answers are not inspiring. The validity of the court is still debated. Criticisms that the IMT lacked jurisdiction, that it was imposing ex post facto law, and that it tried only the losers all contain seeds of truth. An editorial in *Fortune* magazine, written at the time, raised the point that, given the destructive power of the atomic bomb, it was futile to argue that there were "legal and proper as against illegal and improper" ways to kill hundreds of thousands of innocent people. The point is not easily gainsaid. Yet Nuremberg's defenders counter that the atomic bomb, however devastating, was used to end a war. The death factories operated by Nazi Germany exterminated people from nations already defeated. A war ending in German victory would certainly not have meant an end to mass murder, but its unfettered continuation.

The dilemma the victors faced at the time was simply to determine what to do after the Nazis had caused the deliberate deaths of some six million Jews and millions of others in killings divorced from any military necessity. Could the Allies merely walk away from murder so vast and so calculated? Critics, including Winston Churchill, continued to maintain, even after the trial, that the Nazi leaders should have been shot outright. That solution had a certain rough appeal. Yet, if it was wrong to punish people because the trial machinery was less than perfect, how could it be right to punish them with no trial at all? Senator Robert Taft, a conservative American leader of that

era, and the British political scientist Harold Laski debated Nuremberg at Kenyon College in Ohio just days after the verdicts were
handed down. Taft believed that "the trial of the vanquished by the
victors cannot be impartial no matter how it is hedged about with the
forms of law." He branded the death sentences "a miscarriage of justice that the American people will live to regret." A student in the
audience asked, "What would you have done with these criminals?"
Taft answered, "Life imprisonment, the same as Napoleon." "If it is
proper to send a man to life in prison in an ex post facto proceeding,"
Laski retorted, "it is no more improper to hang him."

The IMT's legitimacy can be attacked on purist legal grounds.
But once it was created, how fair a trial did the defendants receive?
Germany was scoured to provide them with any German lawyer they
wanted, including Nazis. The defense attorneys were paid and granted
special privileges by the court. They were provided with secretarial,
stenographic, and translation services, and with office space, at no cost.
They enjoyed virtually unlimited time with their clients. They had
access to all the documents in the hands of the prosecution. As Herbert Wechsler, Francis Biddle's aide, put it, "I just wish the average
impecunious defendant in an American court could count on assistance
as extensive in the preparation of his defense as those men enjoyed."

The wisdom of the individual verdicts can be debated endlessly.
The indictment of Hans Fritzsche, a propagandist not even on the
outer rim of the inner circle, was a pure concession to the Soviet
Union. And Fritzsche was right; had Goebbels lived, Fritzsche would
never have been tried. But Fritzsche was acquitted. More troublesome
is the execution of Julius Streicher. Today, we are still debating
whether violence in films and television induces violent behavior in
audiences, and we do not have an answer. Was there a path that led
from the rabid anti-Semitism of Streicher's *Der Stürmer* to the gas
chambers at Auschwitz? Streicher and his works were loathsome. But
one can ask, with Francis Biddle, is loathsomeness a capital offense?

Alfred Rosenberg's situation parallels Streicher's, to a point. Then
they part. Streicher preached raw anti-Semitism. Rosenberg concocted
a pseudosophisticated anti-Semitic philosophy. But Rosenberg was
also the minister of the brutally subjugated Occupied Eastern Territories, where the lethal racial policies he had helped author were put

into practice. Rosenberg did not disavow these policies, only their barbaric implementation.

Clearly, the most unfair verdict involved the treatment of Sauckel relative to that of Speer. Given the death and suffering inflicted by the forced labor system, few would argue that Sauckel should have been punished less severely, but rather that Speer should have been punished equally. Between slave trader and slave master, one discerns scant moral superiority. In sending Sauckel to die and allowing Speer to live, the court, consciously or unconsciously, made a class judgment.

Hjalmar Schacht may have felt unlucky when the Nazis clapped him into Dachau. The experience, however, saved him. Absent this badge of honor, and given Jackson's will to convict him, it is difficult to imagine that a lesser minister of economics, such as Walther Funk, would get life, while the man whose financial prowess enabled Hitler to come to power and rearm Germany would go free.

Many at Nuremberg believed Rudolf Hess insane and unfit for trial. Yet one cannot read the literally hundreds of letters that this man wrote, from the time of his internment in England in 1941, throughout the trial, and during the Spandau years, without concluding that here was a clear mind at work. If there was anything mad about Rudolf Hess it was his decision to act mad for nearly half a century. As for his guilt on the merits, if the conspiracy count had any validity, Hess, a founding Nazi, was certainly guilty.

But did the conspiracy count have validity? It was the charge least appreciated by the judges themselves; it required a tremendous stretch of the evidence to prove; and it risked ridicule because the defendants obviously had not been independent partners but henchmen in Hitler's thrall. And, viewed practically, the conspiracy charge was unnecessary. Had the Nazis conspired but never made war, obviously no trial would have ensued. As it turned out, not one defendant was charged only with conspiracy, and none was convicted solely of conspiracy. It was committing aggression, not scheming to commit it, that doomed them.

And the enormous effort invested in trying the organizations? When Murray Bernays first hatched the idea, its purpose was to provide a legal weapon against the thousands of rank-and-file who had knowingly and willingly done Hitler's dirtiest work. It is difficult to imagine an injured world simply turning away from an organization like the Gestapo, or from the assembly-line foremen who ran the death camps. At the time that Bernays's idea was accepted, however, no denazification machinery for reviewing low-level cases had yet been envisioned. The best that can be said is that, as it turned out, the trial of the organizations was not vital.

The military verdicts discomfited professional soldiers in nations other than Germany who could imagine themselves in Keitel's, Jodl's, Dönitz's, or Raeder's boots. Keitel was foredoomed by his position as chief of staff of the armed forces. But Jodl, had he managed to escape the major war criminals list, would likely not have paid with his life in the subsequent trials. In a later High Command case, six officers of equal or superior rank, though none so close to Hitler as Jodl, were convicted of the same offenses that had doomed him. Their sentences ranged from three years to life; and as the Allies began to commute sentences wholesale in the fifties, none of these men came close to serving a full life term.

It is difficult to reconcile Admiral Raeder's life sentence with one of ten years for Admiral Dönitz, except that Raeder had been Dönitz's superior until January 1943, and was thus responsible for his subordinate's acts as well as his own. Raeder had also been among the handful of top leaders to hear Hitler declare his aggressive intentions at the Hossbach Conference; and Raeder had stayed on after hearing it. In the end, the aging admiral served nine years of his life sentence.

The trial, in the final analysis, raises the distinction between law and justice. No saint or statesman lost his life or his freedom at Nuremberg. All the men who went to prison or mounted the gallows were willing, knowing, and energetic accomplices in a vast and malignant enterprise. They were all there for valid moral, if not technically perfect legal, reasons; but then, the murderer who gets off on a technicality has experienced law, not justice. The execution of a professional hate-monger like Julius Streicher, if legally debatable, does not begin to compare with the injustice done to a five-year-old sent to a gas chamber, an end encouraged by Streicher's race preachments. It can be argued that evil unpunished deprives us of a sense of moral symmetry in life, and that to punish evil has a healthy cathartic effect, confirming our belief in the ultimate triumph of good over evil. Nuremberg may have been flawed law, but it was satisfying justice.

But what of the long-term residue? Did the trial have any lasting impact beyond deciding the fate of twenty-one individuals? If so, were those effects salutary? The Nuremberg legacy is mixed. The one indisputable good to come out of the trial is that, to any sentient person, it documented beyond question Nazi Germany's crimes. To those old enough to remember personally the first horrifying film images of piles of pallid corpses being bulldozed into mass graves, it is hard to believe that this evidence of our eyes would ever be challenged. However, two generations have had time to grow up with no personal knowledge of World War II. Polls have shown that as many as twenty-two percent of all Americans doubt the Holocaust as historic fact. These people are prey to the revisionists—crackpots at best, masked racists at worst—who argue that the Holocaust is a Jewish-inspired hoax, that if people did die in concentration camps, they were few, not millions, and the causes were disease and wartime food shortages. One cannot know of the forty-two-volume transcript of the Nuremberg trial, the hundreds of official German documents, the Mauthausen "death books," the boastful reports of improved productivity in gas chambers and crematoria, the signed extermination orders, the films taken by German cameramen, the testimony of German witnesses like Ohlendorf and Hoess, in short the whole crushing weight of *German* evidence and not believe that it all happened, just as the Nazis themselves recorded it. Not a single defendant at Nuremberg ever denied that the mass killing had taken place, only that he had lacked personal knowledge and responsibility.

Another reward of Nuremberg was to destroy any Nazi dreams of martyrdom. Hermann Göring's predictions of grand statues in public squares and statuettes in every home never materialized. After World War II, no cries were heard about brave German soldiers stabbed in the back by homefront politicians, as were heard after World War I. The Third Reich was a foul creation, and the revelations at Nuremberg made that fact palpable.

Did Nuremberg contribute to a democratic Germany? Arguably yes, despite the disturbing emergence of neo-Nazis on the desperate edge of German political life today. Since World War II, no avowed Nazis have won significant public office in Germany. It cannot be assumed that the same flowering of democracy would have occurred had the Nazi leaders been shot out of hand, and had the revelations of the trial thus never become so public. Willy Brandt, who covered the trial as a journalist, managed to become West Germany's chancellor—a man who had turned his back not only on Nazism but on Germany itself in the Nazi era, and who had taken Norwegian citizenship. It is unlikely that Brandt could have come home and risen so high in a Germany spared the truths confirmed by the trial. He more likely would have been condemned as a traitor, not elected as leader.

But what of the brightest hope of the trial? Did it ever deter a single would-be aggressor? Did it lead to a permanent international tribunal where crimes against peace and crimes against humanity would be tried? Between 1945 and 1992, the world experienced twenty-four wars between nations, costing 6,623,000 civilian and military lives. Ninety-three civil wars, wars of independence, and in-surgencies have cost 15,513,000 additional lives. Until 1993, no inter-national instrument had been convened to try any aggressor or any perpetrator of war crimes in any of these 117 conflicts. Virtually all war-crimes trials that have occurred since Nuremberg were for of-fenses committed in World War II; and these trials have been con-ducted by individual nations, not international bodies. They have in-cluded the prosecution of Adolf Eichmann and John Demjanjuk in Israel and Klaus Barbie in France. In one of the few non–World War II trials, a U.S. military tribunal sentenced Lieutenant William Calley to life imprisonment for his role in the Vietnam My Lai massacre. But Calley's sentence was soon commuted.

Sites of savage depredations against the innocent can be found almost by sticking a pin in a map: in Algeria in the sixties; in Cambodia and Uganda in the seventies; in El Salvador, Nicaragua, and Beirut in the eighties; in the former Yugoslavia in the nineties. The two million to four million Cambodians exterminated by the Pol Pot regime be-tween 1979 and 1981 proportionately exceeded the victims of the Holocaust in Europe. As for crimes against peace, the likelihood of anyone's being prosecuted for committing aggression has been even more remote than for committing atrocities. Aggression appears to be in the eye of the definer. The old Soviet Union crushed liberation movements in East Germany, Hungary, Czechoslovakia, and Poland, and invaded Afghanistan. America's critics would find elements of aggression in the U.S. interventions in Lebanon, the Dominican Republic, Cuba, Grenada, Panama, Libya, and Vietnam.

Less than a month after the executions at Nuremberg, the UN General Assembly unanimously adopted Resolution 95(I), affirming "the principles of International Law recognized by the Charter of the Nuremberg Tribunal and the judgment of the Tribunal." Until virtually yesterday, they remained no more than principles. They were never applied to any nation or individual. Then, in 1992, the ghost of Nuremberg began to stir. On October 6, the UN Security Council voted unanimously to establish a commission to collect evidence of war crimes in the former Yugoslavia. The actions, initially of Serbia and her irredentists, of annihilation, deportation, incarceration, and rape of the Muslims in Bosnia, under the chillingly familiar cry of "ethnic cleansing" (Hitler's call had been "to cleanse the world of Jewish poison"), outraged world opinion. On February 22, 1993, the UN Security Council again voted unanimously, this time to create an international war-crimes tribunal to prosecute atrocities perpetrated in the same region. Prosecution of aggression, however—the larger issue on which the legal pioneers of Nuremberg pinned their hopes —is left untouched by these actions.

Still, until this moment, the example of Nuremberg had remained what a philosopher called "a beautiful idea murdered by a gang of ugly facts." The recent UN initiatives raise cautious hopes that reports of this murder may have been exaggerated. By its very occurrence in the past, Nuremberg increases the prospects for effective war-crimes trials in our time. The denunciations that plagued that tribunal—that it was an ex post facto proceeding, that it lacked jurisdiction, that it amounted to victor's vengeance—need not be heard again. The world now has a legal precedent, set in the Palace of Justice almost half a century ago. Law that supersedes nations, and justice that penetrates frontiers may yet be achieved. But, history teaches us, not easily.

APPENDIX

The Göring Suicide: An Unclosed File

THE PRECISE DETAILS of Hermann Göring's suicide can no more be known than those of the perennially debated Kennedy and Lincoln assassinations. In all these cases, certain facts have vanished in the mist of history or have been lost to the grave. The reconstruction of Göring's suicide described here likely comes as close as the knowable evidence permits. My information has been drawn largely from files provided by the Berlin Documents Center, a key repository of material on the Nazi era. These files include the top secret report of the investigating board, which was not released at the time of the suicide, the testimony of witnesses on the scene, medical reports, and the original Göring suicide notes (all four of which were made available to the author). Ben E. Swearingen's *The Mystery of Hermann Goering's Suicide* is the most thorough study of the question to date, an admirable work of historical detection invaluable to anyone writing on this subject.

That the cyanide capsule initially entered the prison with Göring's luggage appears beyond dispute. It is not credible that he kept it in his cell throughout his captivity. It would have been foolhardy to do so, except during the very last hours. The baggage room, we know, had not been thoroughly searched, because the investigators did find another cyanide capsule there in Göring's belongings after his suicide. Cells and clothing had been searched, and fairly often, according to this author's interviews with guards and an examination of prison records. First Lieutenant John West carried out just such a search of Göring's cell and his personal possessions on October 14, 1946, the day before the man's death.

Though the prison logs do not show that Göring ever asked permission to visit the baggage room, we know that possessions of his were removed from time to time, as evidenced by the gifts he gave Lieutenant Wheelis and the blue briefcase he gave to his lawyer, Otto

Stahmer. These were obtained either by a prison officer who, like Wheelis, possessed the baggage-room key, or by Göring, who might have been admitted to the room without the visit's being logged as required.

Subsequent statements by Emmy Göring as to how her husband obtained the capsule are not helpful or convincing. On her last visit to her husband, on October 7, 1946, she asked if he had the capsule yet, to which Göring answered no. She never saw or spoke to him again. Immediately after the suicide she speculated to a reporter that "it must have been an American friend who did it." But twenty-eight years later she told Robert Kempner, the German-American prosecution staff member, that an unspecified friend *definitely* passed her husband the poison. Thus, her memory appeared to have improved over time. Later still, her daughter, Edda, hinted that someone had helped her father. A hearsay 1991 report has it that Klaus Riegele, a Göring nephew, admitted that it was Lieutenant Wheelis who gave his uncle the poison. This is possible, but not provable. Neither Göring's daughter, who was eight years old at the time of his death, nor his nephew could be any more certain of what had happened than their likely source, Emmy Göring, had been. Prison mates who might have known and lived to tell—Speer, Fritzsche, Pfluecker—all later wrote about their Nuremberg experiences, and it is unlikely that they would have omitted this book-selling bombshell from their accounts, had they known of it.

This author's conclusion is that Göring had conditioned a member of the prison staff, most likely Wheelis, to take items or pieces of luggage from the baggage room for him. And in the last such retrieval, Göring withdrew a hidden capsule. Alternatively, he himself could have been allowed into the baggage room, again most likely by Wheelis, and have been left there to his own devices. It is harder to believe that any American with access to the baggage room, including Wheelis, would knowingly have retrieved the capsule and have given it to Göring, thus enabling the major surviving war criminal of World War II to thwart justice. To have done so would have been a criminal act risking serious punishment. The character of Wheelis appears capable of foolishness, but not of criminality.

Why Göring dated his suicide notes October 11, 1946, remains a mystery. The date cannot be correct. It would have been reckless for Göring to have kept in his possession for five days letters revealing that he planned suicide. In two of the letters he makes reference to the decision on his appeal to the Allied Control Council, which he did not learn of until October 13. A further puzzle is why he felt the need to write the letter to Andrus saying that he had always had the capsule, unless it was to clear friends and to crow over outwitting his chief antagonist.

The years have produced a stream of explanations of the Göring suicide: the poison was hidden in his clay pipe, which he broke open on execution night; he hid it in his navel (which Dr. Roska declared physically impossible); he swallowed it (which the investigating board believed); and more bizarre solutions. Obviously, all hope of incontrovertible truth is lost when the only man in possession of it not only takes his secret to the grave, but releases a cloud of misinformation in his wake.

At least eleven prison personnel were in reasonably close contact with Göring the day he died. On other days, that number could reach as high as twenty-six. The possibilities are infinite. But the number is quickly thinned by probability. What actually happened may differ from the reconstruction offered here, but only in details that do not change the essential thrust—that the capsule was in the baggage room, and Göring managed to take it out or have it brought to him. The author, of course, assumes sole responsibility for the validity of this explanation.

AFTERMATH

What is known of the subsequent lives of principal figures in the trial:

Burton C. ANDRUS: Retired from the army; became a professor of geography and business administration at the University of Puget Sound in Tacoma, Washington; died in 1977, at the age of eighty-five. (In his final hours, he cried out, "Göring's just committed suicide. I must inform the Council.")

Roger BARRETT: Returned to practice law in Chicago.

Francis BIDDLE: Retired; wrote his autobiography, *In Brief Authority*; died in 1968 at age eighty-two.

Norman BIRKETT: Entered the House of Lords in 1947; died in 1962 at age seventy-nine.

Martin BORMANN: Remains were tentatively identified in Berlin in 1972; declared legally dead in 1973 by a West German court.

Walter BRUDNO: Returned to practice law in Texas.

Harold BURSON: Founded Burson Marsteller, a public-relations firm in New York.

Ray D'ADDARIO: Returned to Holyoke, Massachusetts; built a business in camera and gift shops.

Thomas DODD: Served as Connecticut Democratic member of the House of Representatives, 1953–1957; U.S. senator, 1959–1971; died, 1971.

Karl DÖNITZ: Served his ten-year sentence at Spandau prison; died in 1981 at the age of eighty-nine.

Leon DOSTERT: Returned to the language department of Georgetown University; reportedly developed the simultaneous-translation system for the United Nations.

Edgar FAURE: Became premier of France.

Theodore FENSTERMACHER: Returned to practice law in Cortland, N.Y.

Hans FRITZSCHE: After his acquittal at Nuremberg, was convicted by a German court; freed in 1950; died in 1953 at age fifty-three.

Moritz FUCHS: Ordained a Catholic priest in 1955.

Walther FUNK: After serving eleven years of a life sentence, released from Spandau in 1957 for reasons of poor health; died two years later at age sixty-nine.

Gustav GILBERT: Completed his book, *Nuremberg Diary*, which came out shortly after Douglas Kelley's book (see below); pursued a teaching and writing career in psychology; died in 1977 at age sixty-five.

Whitney HARRIS: Returned to practice law in St. Louis; wrote *Tyranny on Trial* on the Nuremberg trial.

Richard HELLER: Returned to practice law in New York City.

Rudolf HESS: Spent the rest of his life in Spandau prison; supposedly died by his own hand in 1987 at age ninety-three. (Hess's son believed he was murdered to prevent his divulging information on his flight to Scotland.)

Rudolf HOESS: Hanged by Polish authorities at Auschwitz in 1947.

Charles HORSKY: Continued to practice law in Washington, D.C.

Robert JACKSON: Returned to the U.S. Supreme Court; served until his death in 1954 at age sixty-two.

William E. JACKSON: Returned to practice law in New York City.

Ingeborg KALNOKY: Rejoined by her husband and emigrated to the United States.

Douglas KELLEY: His book, *22 Cells at Nuremberg*, was published shortly before Gustav Gilbert's book; he committed suicide on New Year's Day in 1957, reportedly with a cyanide capsule brought back from Nuremberg.

Robert KEMPNER: Returned to live in Germany; reportedly established a practice representing Jewish clients in Nazi restitution cases.

Daniel KILEY: Returned to become an award-winning architect, including the rebuilding of Pennsylvania Avenue in Washington, D.C.

Otto KRANZBUEHLER: Defended German industrialists in subsequent war-crimes trials; later developed a corporate law practice.

Thomas LAMBERT, Jr.: Became head of the American Trial Lawyers Association; taught law.

Geoffrey LAWRENCE: Elevated to the peerage for his work at Nuremberg, becoming Baron Oaksey; died in 1971.

Daniel MARGOLIES: Joined the U.S. State Department; worked on the German peace treaty.

David MAXWELL-FYFE: Elevated to the peerage, becoming Earl Kilmuir.

Airey NEAVE: Became a conservative member of Parliament; campaigned for the release of Rudolf Hess; became a key advisor to Prime Minister Margaret Thatcher; killed by an IRA car bomb in 1980.

Konstantin von NEURATH: Served seven years of a fifteen-year sentence; released for reasons of poor health in 1954; died two years later at age eighty-three.

Ion Timofeevich NIKITCHENKO: Nothing known beyond a Soviet report of his death several years after the trial.

Otto OHLENDORF: Convicted at a subsequent trial in Nuremberg; hanged with three other *Einsatzgruppen* commanders in 1951.

Friedrich PAULUS: Returned to the Soviet Union; went to live in East Germany in 1953; died in 1957.

Erich RAEDER: Served nine years of a life sentence; released in 1955 at age eighty; died in 1960 at age eighty-four.

James ROWE: Returned to practice law with fellow New Dealer Thomas Corcoran; participated in Democratic political campaigns; died in 1984.

Roman RUDENKO: Became chief prosecutor of the Soviet Union; prosecuted the American U-2 pilot, Gary Powers, shot down over the Soviet Union in 1960.

Gunther SADEL: Settled in Washington, D.C., and developed an insurance business.

Hjalmar SCHACHT: After his acquittal at Nuremberg, was sentenced to eight years by a German court; was cleared on appeal in 1950; died in 1970 at age ninety-three.

Baldur von SCHIRACH: Served his twenty-year sentence; released from Spandau prison in 1966; died in 1974 at age sixty-seven.

Robert SERVATIUS: Returned to private practice; defended Adolf Eichmann at the latter's war-crimes trial in Israel in 1961.

Sir Hartley SHAWCROSS: Left his career in Labour party politics; became a successful corporate lawyer.

Albert SPEER: Served his twenty-year sentence; released from Spandau prison in 1966; wrote two books on his life; died in 1981 at age seventy-six.

Drexel SPRECHER: Stayed on in Nuremberg to become, eventually, chief prosecutor at the subsequent trials; returned to the United

States in 1952 as a government lawyer; served as deputy chairman of the Democratic party.

Alfred STEER: Taught languages at Columbia University and the University of Georgia; authored several books on Goethe.

Robert STOREY: Became dean of the Southern Methodist Law Center and president of the American Bar Association.

Telford TAYLOR: After serving as chief prosecutor at subsequent Nuremberg proceedings, returned to the United States to practice law, teach, and write; in 1992, published his account of the major Nuremberg trial.

Peter UIBERALL: Served as a career officer in the U.S. Army.

Marie Claude VAILLANT-COUTURIER: Became a member of the French Senate.

Herbert WECHSLER: Returned to the Columbia University law faculty; taught and wrote.

Jack G. "Tex" WHEELIS: Served with the army in Korea and later as an ROTC instructor; died of a heart attack in 1954 at the age of forty-one.

John WOODS: Killed serving with the U.S. Army during the Korean War, reportedly in an accident involving a high-tension wire.

ACKNOWLEDGMENTS

EARLY IN WRITING the story of Nuremberg, I was fortunate enough to find, through the Nuremberg alumni directory, Drexel Sprecher, a prosecutor at the main trial and at the subsequent trials, and a scholar of those events ever since. Drex Sprecher was the soul of generosity in the time he granted me for extensive interviews, leads to other interviewees, and loans from his comprehensive personal Nuremberg library. He became not only a mainstay, but a good friend. Another indispensable contributor has been Colonel Burton Andrus, Jr. (USAF Ret.), son of the Nuremberg prison commandant, who for over forty-five years has maintained his father's personal files, an invaluable source. I owe Burt Andrus an unpayable debt of gratitude for opening those files to me. In them I was able to locate much material never before used. I am also grateful to Burt for introducing me to Duane J. Reed, chief of the special collections branch at the U.S. Air Force Academy library, who managed to locate Nuremberg-related photographs for me.

I owe a special debt to the distinguished broadcast journalist Howard K. Smith and his wife, Benedicte. Mr. Smith was generous in sharing his memories as one of the first newsmen on the scene at Nuremberg. Mrs. Smith obligingly ransacked their personal papers to produce her husband's broadcasts and letters from Nuremberg, a priceless trove. Harold Burson, who covered the trial for the Armed Forces Network, generously provided me with all his broadcasts for that period.

The Nuremberg lode at the National Archives in Washington amounts to thousands upon thousands of files. For helping me thread my way through that wealth of material and for pursuing my special requests, I am grateful for the cooperation of Robert Wolfe, Robin E. Cookson, and William Cunliffe of the archives' Captured German Records staff.

At the Library of Congress I again benefited from the wise guidance of my friend Margrit Krewson, of the German branch. As with my other books, Mrs. Krewson was again relentless in unearthing hard-to-locate materials for me.

My research took me to several other libraries and archives where people were unstinting of their time and expertise. These include Carolyn Davis and Karin D'Agostino at the Syracuse University Archives, where I worked with the papers of Francis Biddle, American justice on the Nuremberg tribunal; David Marwell, director of the Berlin Document Center, who provided me with heretofore unpublished Nuremberg material; Elizabeth Denier of the Franklin Delano Roosevelt Library, where the papers of James Rowe, a key Nuremberg figure, are held; Richard J. Sommers and his staff at the Military History Institute in Carlisle, Pennsylvania; Bernard Cavalcante of the Naval Historical Center, who helped me track missing persons; Father Julian Davies of the Franciscans, at Siena College, Albany, New York; the staff of the Columbia University Oral History Project; and Gunter Bischoff of the Eisenhower Center at the University of New Orleans.

Jean Hargrave of the New York State Library in Albany made available, under the most convenient conditions, the entire transcript of the trial. My college classmate Joan Barron, of the Guilderland, New York, Library, helped me track obscure but essential facts. Richard Waugh was similarly helpful at the Albany Public Library.

I owe special thanks to Ray D'Addario, a U.S. Army photographer at Nuremberg, who not only has amassed a valuable collection of trial photographs and films, but has an excellent private archive as well. Mr. D'Addario made all this material available to me. Dr. Charles Gilbert, son of the Nuremberg prison psychologist, Gustav Gilbert, took the trouble to locate his father's personal papers and gave me access to them, for which I am in his debt.

On a note of serendipity, my winter neighbor and friend in San Miguel de Allende, Mexico, Katherine Walch, turned out to have been a member of the Nuremberg prosecutor's staff and had gathered an impressive library over the years, including mimeographed transcripts used during the course of the trial. My deepest thanks go to her for the loan of this material and for her shared memories of Nuremberg. Also in San Miguel de Allende, Gloria Grant of the local *biblioteca* helped me with reference queries.

Father Moritz Fuchs, who served on the personal staff of chief Nuremberg prosecutor Justice Robert Jackson, spoke to me at length and risked lending me his irreplaceable collection of Nuremberg photographs. Ben E. Swearingen, author of the splendid book on Hermann Göring cited elsewhere, was also generous in answering my questions. In Germany, Dr. Klaus Kastner, vice president of the Nuremberg-Furth Court, proved invaluable, both by taking me through the courthouse where the trial took place and by sharing his boyhood memories of Nuremberg at the time of the trial.

My friends Richard Rosenbaum and Rena Button helped me in my requests for material from the archives of Yad Vashem in Jerusalem.

Dr. Guenter Bischof of the Eisenhower Center in New Orleans helped me to understand the postwar conditions in Germany; Captain John P. Bracken (USMC Ret.) provided useful material explaining the naval case at Nuremberg; and I much appreciate the curious sidelights about the defendants passed along to me by Angus Mclean Theurmer. Genya Markon of the Holocaust Museum in Washington kindly helped me to locate key photographs. I thank Dave Dynan of the Eighth Air Force Association, who led me to John "Marty" Shea, a World War II flier who proved a gold mine of information on the air raids that destroyed Nuremberg. Thomas and Renate Barker skillfully translated key documents for me.

I am grateful to Nan Graham, my editor at Viking Penguin, for sharing my enthusiasm for the project early on and for her sensitive and skillful editing of the manuscript, and my thanks to her assistant, Courtney Hodell. As ever, my friend and agent Clyde Taylor displayed his customary skill, concern, and judgment in representing me. Finally, my wholly inadequate gratitude goes to my wife, Sylvia, who not only struggled with the manuscript, but made valuable suggestions and original contributions to it.

Those persons who were good enough to grant me interviews are Margaret Allen, Burton C. Andrus, Jr., William Baldwin, Roger Barrett, Ruth Holden Bateman, Raymond Belanger, Barbara Pinion Bitter, Thomas Brown, Walter Brudno, Harold Burson, Albert Callan, Raymond D'Addario, Emilio DiPalma, Nicholas Doman, Arthur Donovan, Theodore Fenstermacher, Moritz Fuchs, Charles Gilbert, Matilda Gilbert, Robert Gilbert, William Glenny, Charles Gordon, Bobbie Hardy, Whitney Harris, Richard Heller, Charles Horsky, William Jackson, Klaus Kastner, Robert Keeler, Daniel Kiley, Thomas Lambert, Andy Logan, Daniel Margolies, David Marwell, Hans Nathan, David Pitcher, Dorothy Owens Reilly, Walter Rockler, Gunther Sadel, Peter Samulevich, John Martin Shea, Benedicte Smith, Howard K. Smith, Drexel Sprecher, Alfred Steer, Telford Taylor, Peter Uiberall, John Vonetes, Katherine Walch, Rolf Wartenberg, Herbert Wechsler, Katharine Williams, and Rose Korb Williams.

BIBLIOGRAPHY

BOOKS

ALEXANDER, Charles W., and Anne KEESHAN. *Justice at Nuremberg: A Pictorial Record of the Trial of Nazi War Criminals by the International Military Tribunal at Nuremberg, Germany, 1945–1946.* Marvel Press, 1946.

AMBROSE, Stephen E., and Guenter BISCHOF, eds. *Eisenhower and the German POWs: Facts Against Falsehood.* New Orleans: LSU Press, 1992.

ANDRUS, Burton C. *I Was the Nuremberg Jailer.* New York: Coward-McCann, 1969.

BACQUE, JAMES. *Other Losses: An Investigation into the Mass Deaths of German Prisoners at the Hands of the French and Americans after World War II.* Toronto: Stoddard, 1989.

BIDDLE, Francis. *In Brief Authority.* Garden City, N.Y.: Doubleday, 1962.

BROWN, Anthony Cave. *The Last Hero: Wild Bill Donovan.* New York: Times Books, 1982.

BULLOCK, Alan. *The Ribbentrop Memoirs.* London: Weidenfeld & Nicolson, 1953.

BYTWERK, Randall L. *Julius Streicher: The Man Who Persuaded a Nation to Hate Jews.* New York: Dorset Press, 1983.

CONOT, Robert E. *Justice at Nuremberg.* New York: Harper and Row, 1983.

COOPER, Robert W. *The Nuremberg Trial.* New York: Penguin Books, 1947.

COSTELLO, John. *Ten Days to Destiny.* New York: William Morrow, 1991.

CUMOLETTI, Henry V. *Crimes Against Humanity.* Gouverneur, N.Y.: MRS, 1989.

DASTRUP, Boyd L. *Crusade in Nuremberg: Military Occupation, 1945–49.* Westport, Conn.: Greenwood Press, 1985.

DAVIDSON, Eugene. *The Trial of the Germans.* London: Macmillan, 1966.

DÖNITZ, Karl. *Memoirs: Ten Years and Twenty Days.* Trans. R. H. Stevens. Annapolis, Md.: Naval Institute Press, 1959.

DREYFUSS, Allan. *These 21.* Stars and Stripes, 1946.

ELWYN-JONES, Lord. *In My Time: An Autobiography.* London: Weidenfeld & Nicolson, 1983.

FRITZSCHE, Hans. *The Sword in the Scales*, as told to Hildegard Springer. Trans. Diane Pike and Heinrich Fraenkel. London: Alan Wingate, 1953.

GASKIN, Hilary. *Eyewitness at Nuremberg*. London: Arms and Armour, 1990.

GERHART, EUGENE C. *America's Advocate: Robert H. Jackson*. New York: Bobbs-Merrill, 1958.

GILBERT, Gustav M., Ph.D. *Nuremberg Diary*. New York: Farrar, Straus, 1947.

———. *The Psychology of Dictatorship*. New York: The Ronald Press, 1950.

GLENDINNING, Victoria. *Rebecca West: A Life*. New York: Alfred A. Knopf, 1987.

HARRIS, Whitney R. *Tyranny on Trial*. Dallas: Southern Methodist University Press, 1954.

HECHT, Ingeborg. *Invisible Walls: A German Family Under the Nuremberg Laws*. Trans. J. Maxwell Brownjohn. New York: Harcourt Brace Jovanovich, 1984.

HIGHAM, Charles. *The Duchess of Windsor: The Secret Life*. New York: McGraw-Hill, 1988.

HYDE, H. Montgomery. *Lord Justice: The Life and Times of Lord Birkett of Ulverston*. New York: Random House, 1965.

IRVING, David. *Goering*. New York: William Morrow, 1989.

JACKSON, Robert H., and Eugene C. GERHARD. *America's Advocate*. Indianapolis and New York: Bobbs-Merrill, 1958.

KALNOKY, Ingeborg, with Ilona HERISKO. *The Witness House*. London: New English Library, 1975.

KEITEL, Wilhelm. *The Memoirs of Field Marshal Keitel*. Walter Gorlitz, ed. Trans. David Irving. New York: Stein & Day, 1966.

KELLEY, Douglas M., M.D. *22 Cells in Nuremberg*. New York: Greenberg, 1947.

KILMUIR (David MAXWELL-FYFE). *Political Adventure: The Memoirs of the Earl of Kilmuir*. London: Weidenfeld & Nicolson, 1964.

MANVELL, Roger, and Heinrich FRAENKEL. *Hess*. New York: Drake Publishers, 1973.

MASER, Werner. *Nuremberg: A Nation on Trial*. Trans. Richard Barry. New York: Charles Scribner's Sons, 1979.

MOSLEY, Leonard. *The Reich Marshal: A Biography of Hermann Goering*. Garden City, N.Y.: Doubleday, 1974.

NEAVE, Airey. *On Trial at Nuremberg*. Foreword by Rebecca West. Boston: Little, Brown, 1979.

POLEVOI, Boris. *The Final Reckoning: Nuremberg Diaries*. Moscow: Progress Publishers, 1978.

POLTORAK, Arkady. *The Nuremberg Epilogue*. Trans. David Skvirsky. Moscow: Progress Publishers, 1971.

Posner, Gerald L. *Hitler's Children*. New York: Random House, 1991.

Rosenbaum, Ron. *Travels with Dr. Death and Other Unusual Investigations*. New York: Penguin Books, 1991.

Shirer, William L. *End of a Berlin Diary*. New York: Alfred A. Knopf, 1947.

Smith, Bradley F. *Reaching Judgment at Nuremberg*. New York: Basic Books, 1977.

Speer, Albert. *Inside the Third Reich*. New York: Avon, 1971.

———. *Spandau: The Secret Diaries*. New York: Pocket Books, 1977.

Storey, Robert G. *The Final Judgment: From Pearl Harbor to Nuremberg*. San Antonio: Naylor, 1968.

Swearingen, Ben E. *The Mystery of Hermann Goering's Suicide*. New York: Dell, 1985.

Taylor, Telford. *The Anatomy of the Nuremberg Trials: A Personal Memoir*. New York: Alfred A. Knopf, 1992.

Tusa, Ann, and John Tusa. *The Nuremberg Trial*. New York: Atheneum, 1984.

Wechsler, Herbert. *Principles, Politics, and Fundamental Law*. Cambridge, Mass.: Harvard University Press, 1961.

Williams, Joseph H. *Captor-Captive*. Jacksonville, Fla.: Girtman Press, 1986.

Yahil, Leni. *The Holocaust: The Fate of European Jewry 1932–45*. New York: Oxford University Press, 1991.

PERIODICALS

Daniel, Raymond. " 'So What,' Say the Germans of Nuremberg." *New York Times Magazine*, December 3, 1945.

Gerecke, Henry F. "I Walked to the Gallows with the Nazi Chiefs." *Saturday Evening Post*, September 1, 1951.

Harris, Martyn. "House Party." *The Spectator*, October 24, 1992.

Kempner, Robert M. W. "Impact of War on the German Mind." *New York Times Magazine*, October 6, 1946.

Low, David. "Portrait of the Master Race in the Dock." *New York Times Magazine*, December 23, 1945.

Persico, Joseph E. "The Last Days of the Third Reich." *American Heritage*, April–May 1985.

Prendergast, Mark. "Trial and Error." Interview with Dan Kiley. *North by Northeast* (Vermont Public Radio Magazine), July 1988.

Taylor, Telford. "The Nuremberg Trials." *Columbia Law Review*, vol. 55, April 1955.

Wolfe, Robert. "Putative Threat to National Security as a Nuremberg Defense for Genocide." *Annals of the American Academy of Political and Social Science*, July 1980.

ARCHIVAL AND LIBRARY SOURCES

BIDDLE, Francis. Papers. Syracuse University Library, Syracuse, N.Y.

FRANKLIN, Robert, Sr. Oral History, October 25, 1982. U.S. Army Military History Institute, Carlisle Barracks, Pa.

JACKSON, Justice Robert H. Interview by Harlan Phillips, February 1955. Oral History, Butler Library, Columbia University.

ROWE, James. Papers. Franklin Delano Roosevelt Library, Hyde Park, N.Y.

DOCUMENTS

Nuremberg: A History of U.S. Military Government. Issued by U.S. Forces European Theater, 1946.

Office of U.S. Chief of Counsel for Prosecution of Axis Criminality. *Nazi Conspiracy and Aggression*, vols. 1–8 and supplements A and B. U.S. Government Printing Office, Washington, D.C.

Report of Board of Proceedings in the Case of Hermann Goering Suicide, October 1946. Berlin Documents Center.

TOMASZEWSKA, Halina. Notes on interview with Lilli Gau, mistress of Hans Frank, September 6, 1945. Trans. from Polish. National Archives, Washington, D.C.

Trial of Major War Criminals Before the International Military Tribunal. 42 vols. U.S. Government Printing Office, Washington, D.C.

WALKER, Kenneth. "The Enemy Side of the Hill." *World War II German Military Studies*, vol. 1, July 30, 1949. U.S. Army Historical Division. National Archives, Washington, D.C.

FILMS

The following films were reviewed by the author: British Paramount News Reels, Nuremberg, 1945–1946; *Hitler's Final Solution: The Wannsee Conference*, screenplay by Paul Mommortz, directed by Heinz Schirk; *The Memory of Justice*, a documentary produced and directed by Marcel Ophuls, Stuyvesant Films, 1976.

SOURCE NOTES

Source notes are keyed to the page number and a phrase occurring on that page. Citations from books, periodicals, and other attributed sources begin with the author's name, followed by page numbers. The source is fully identified in the bibliography. Where more than one work by the same author is cited, a distinguishing word from the appropriate title appears after the author's name. Sources not listed in the bibliography are identified in the note. The full names of interviewees cited can be found in the acknowledgments. Frequent sources cited are abbreviated as follows:

AFN   Armed Forces Network
BAP   Papers of Colonel Burton Andrus
BDC   Berlin Document Center
BIDP   Papers of Francis Biddle, Syracuse University
GGP   Papers of Gustav Gilbert
IMT   Trial of Major War Criminals before the International Military Tribunal, 42 volumes
JXO   Robert Jackson Oral History, Columbia University
RG 238 National Archives Collection, World War II War Crimes Records
ROWP   Papers of James Rowe, Franklin D. Roosevelt Library

Chapter I: Prelude to Judgment

3 *He had made this dawn descent every day:* Prison routine, BAP directives to staff August 13, 1945–October 15, 1946; interviews William Glenny, Emilio DiPalma.

4 *drag out the surrender:* German forces flee west, Persico, "The Last Days of the Third Reich," *American Heritage* April–May 1985, 66–73.

4 *died by the thousands:* Conditions in Allied POW camps, Ambrose and Bischof, draft manuscript, introduction 1–25. In 1989, a Canadian novelist, James Bacque, in a book entitled *Other Losses,* surprised World War II historians with claims that up to one million German prisoners of war died of mistreatment in American and other POW camps. Subsequent scholars have convincingly refuted Bacque's charges, which appear to have been based on misinterpretation of data and careless methodology. Ambrose and Bischof do suggest that the American victors were not wholly free of vindictiveness. General Lucius Clay is quoted as saying in 1945, "I feel that the Germans should suffer from hunger and from cold, as I believe such suffering is necessary to make them realize the consequences of a war which they caused." And between 56,000 and 78,000 German POWs did die in captivity, according to U.S. and German sources. However deplorable these deaths, they amounted to about one percent of German prisoners, roughly the same as the number of American POWs who died in German captivity.

6 *followed his lead:* Göring in World War I, Mosley 29–43; Irving 32. Prior to becoming an ace fighter pilot, Göring served a year as an aerial photographer.

8 *shooting the Nazi leaders:* Roosevelt position on war criminals, B. Smith 314. Secretary of War Henry Stimson also reports being told early in the war that President Roosevelt was "definitely in favor of execution without trial."

8 *Bob Jackson to prosecute:* Rosenman presents Truman's offer, JXO 1159.

9 *certificate of completion:* Jackson's legal training, Gerhart 32. Jackson read law in a Jamestown, N.Y., firm for a year, completed two years in one at Albany Law School, and received not a degree but a certificate of completion because he was still under twenty-one.

10 *"admire your intentions":* Jackson recruited for the New Deal, Gerhart 59–66.

10 *vice-presidential running mate:* Jackson political ambitions, Gerhart 122, 169, 199. Before the 1940 vice-presidential feeler, Jackson in 1937 did some speaking around New York State to test his prospects for a gubernatorial bid. He did not catch fire.

11 *when Stone left:* Jackson's hopes for the chief judgeship, Gerhart 231.

11 *study at Hickory Hill:* Jackson's home at Hickory Hill in northern Virginia, interview W. Jackson. This home later became the residence of Robert F. Kennedy and his family.

11 *He confided to Barkley:* Jackson's skepticism over war crimes, JXO 1181; IMT vol. 2, 130.

11 *laughably light sentences:* War-crimes history, Davidson 2, 3; Shirer 291; Tusa 19.

12 *"home before Christmas":* Jackson's acceptance of the post, Gerhart 32, 242, 253, 336; JXO 1163, 1577, 1656; interview W. Jackson.

12 *Axis war criminals:* Jackson appointed, White House Executive Order 9547 May 2, 1945; interview C. Horsky.

14 *rounding up war criminals:* Göring leaves Hitler; surrenders, Mosley 274, 310–11, 313, 317, 319–21; Irving 17, 19; Conot 32; interview R. Wartenberg.

15 *copy of Morgenthau's plan:* Stimson's reaction to the plan, Tusa 51, 54; B. Smith 23, 26; Conot 10.

17 *a criminal conspiracy, a gigantic plot:* Bernays proposal for conducting trials, B. Smith 27, 28; Tusa 54–55; Conot 12. Bernays wanted to consider the conspiracy as having begun well before the outbreak of war so that the Allies might try as criminal offenses the depredations against the Jews in Germany beginning with the Nazi accession to power in 1933.

17 *aggressive war a crime:* A new crime added to Bernays approach, Taylor 37.

18 *plan was full of holes:* Wechsler denigrates the Bernays proposal, Tusa 57; interview H. Wechsler. "Criminal conspiracy," such as Bernays proposed for war criminals and which Wechsler questioned, is defined in *Black's Law Dictionary*, 1933, as "a combination or agreement between two or more persons for accomplishing an unlawful end by unlawful means."

19 *to hire Murray Bernays:* Jackson meets Bernays, Taylor 48.

19 *"The Jew butcher of Cracow":* Capture of Frank, *New York Times* May 6, 1945; RG 238 Frank interrogation June 25, 1945; Maser 47.

19 *the motive force:* Frank's early life and relationship to Lilli Gau, RG 238 Frank interrogation June 25, 1945, Halina Tomaszewska transcript of interview of Lilli Gau, September 6, 1945; Davidson 427–28; Gilbert *Psychology* 138; Kelley 175; Posner 13–14.

22 *Frank began to rule:* Frank's early rule from Wawel Castle, RG 238 Frank interrogation June 26, 1945, September 6, 1945; IMT vol. 5, 78; Conot 214; Posner 19–20.

22 *Frank had a dark secret:* Frank background, Gilbert *Psychology* 37; Frank revealed in a July 7, 1945, interrogation by his American captors that his father was part Jewish and that his family name may have been Frankfurter.

24 *accepted Himmler's conditions:* Frank's conflicts with Himmler; his wife's corruption; son's visit, Posner 21–22; IMT vol. 10, 582, vol. 12, 132; RG 238 Tomaszewska transcript.

24 *he had been reborn:* Frank's resumption of the Lilli Gau affair; hopes for divorce; rule-of-law speeches, RG 238 Tomaszewska transcript, Frank interrogation September 10, 1945; IMT vol. 12, 153; Posner 24–25, 27–28, 30, 37.

25 *"We are on Mr. Roosevelt's list":* Frank and others cited as war criminals, Davidson 439.

25 *among other art treasures:* Frank flees Poland, RG 238 Frank interrogations September 10, 1945, October 8, 1945. The Da Vinci, *Lady with an Ermine,* which Frank stole, has long since made its way back from Germany to Cracow, where it now hangs in the Czartoryski Museum.

26 *face trial for war crimes:* Frank's capture by the Americans; suicide attempts, RG 238 Frank interrogations June 26, 1945, October 3, 1945; Conot 37; Maser 47.

28 *"I'll think about it":* Jackson hopes to recruit Donovan, JXO 1202, 1213; interview W. Jackson.

29 *After the surrender:* Jodl negotiates the German surrender, Persico, *American Heritage* April–May 1985, 66–73.

29 *Potemkin village government:* Dönitz succeeds Hitler, Persico *American Heritage* April–May 1985, 66–73; RG 238 Dönitz interrogation September 18, 1945.

29 *"the Rommel of the Seas":* Dönitz naval strategy, *London Times* May 2, 1945. While Dönitz's wolfpack strategy produced heavy Allied shipping losses, the price became exorbitant. With Allied intelligence and strategy breakthroughs the German submarine service suffered such heavy losses that the wolfpack strategy was essentially abandoned by February 1944.

30 *to mask his shock and outrage:* Dönitz and others arrested as war criminals, Associated Press May 23, 1945. Dönitz's surprise at his arrest is understandable considering the fact that shortly before his arrest he had been writing a long memorandum to Eisenhower describing his plans for rebuilding postwar Germany.

31 *Jackson began questioning Storey:* Storey's recruitment by Jackson; flight to London; Storey's description of Soviet war-crimes trials, B. Smith 322; Gerhart 115; JXO 1203, 1220, 1234, 1491.

32 *"Swarthy and ugly":* Jackson works with Maxwell-Fyfe, JXO 1240; Kilmuir 9.

32 *Nikitchenko, fifty years old:* Participants in the London meetings, Tusa 74–79; Poltorak 15, 153–54; Neave 235.

34 *"in every civilized code":* Jackson on the ex post facto problem, Tusa 81; Shirer 292.

34 *an alien court system:* Differences in Anglo-Saxon and Continental law, JXO 1564. With only two military men on the court (the two Russians, who were military legal officers) and only five military men among the defendants, why was the court called the International *Military* Tribunal? It was customary for breaches of the rules of warfare to be tried by military courts. But beyond custom, President Roosevelt had expressed a preference for a military court as one less likely to become entangled in legal technicalities and thus swifter in its justice (Tusa 61). And Jackson believed that the decisions of a military court would not create precedents that might subsequently be applied to American civilian courts (IMT vol. 3, 543). The rules of evidence eventually adopted by the IMT were, in fact, far less constrictive than those of an Anglo-Saxon court. Only two tests had to be met: Is the evidence relevant? Does it have probative (evidentiary) value? (IMT vol. 3, 543).

36 *tu quoque was inadmissible:* Jackson, Maxwell-Fyfe discussions on the *Führerprinzip;* ex post facto; tu quoque; superior orders defense; organization of the IMT, B. Smith 58; Conot 325; Tusa 132.

36 *After his denunciation:* Kaltenbrunner's capture; his reactions, RG 238 Kaltenbrunner dossier; Conot 95; Gilbert 255.

37 *to look for a trial site:* Jackson inspection of possible sites, B. Smith 134.

38 *treasure chest of his kingdom:* Descriptions of prewar Nuremberg, *Nuremberg: A History of U.S. Military Government* 1946; Poltorak 16; H. Smith broadcast December 18, 1945; Janet Flanner *The New Yorker* December 15, 1945; Neave 42.

38 *at the words of Adolf Hitler:* Nazi preferment of Nuremberg; rallies; issuance of anti-Semitic decrees, Poltorak 19; Davidson 310; *Nürnberg 1933–1945,* Staat Presse, Nuremberg 1990.

39 *"among the dead cities":* Destruction of Nuremberg, *History, 388th Bombardment Group (H)* U.S. Air Force History Office; interview J. Shea; Neave 44; *U.S. Strategic Bombing Survey* October 26, 1945; Dastrup 22–23; *Nuremberg: A History of U.S. Occupation* 6; Storey 87; Wechsler 139; Gerhart 1. Peter Uiberall, an army translations officer, recalled being so stunned at the totality of Nuremberg's destruction that he visited an air force intelligence unit housed in the Palace of Justice to ask what bombing strategy had been employed. He was shown a dotted map marking military targets and felt some relief that the destruction had not been deliberately indiscriminate. The result, however, was little different from carpet bombing.

39 *The Jackson party landed:* Jackson's inspection of Nuremberg and the courthouse, interviews W. Jackson, J. Vonetes; B. Smith 352; Conot 131; JXO 1300; Gerhart 334–35; *Life* September 3, 1945, 36; Neave 46.

41 *a knack for spotting significant documents:* Graebe's affidavit; organization of the documents operation, interview R. Barrett; IMT vol. 4, 253–57, vol. 2, 151–56; Storey 81–85.

42 *an urgent phone call:* Acquisition Rosenberg's papers, Davidson 126; *Washington Post* May 6, 1945; Conot 25; interview W. Baldwin.

42 *485 tons of diplomatic papers:* New caches of documents, Tusa 97.

43 *"my last will and testament":* General Hossbach's notes found, B. Smith 333; IMT vol. 2, 262–63, 269.

43   *a Frankfurt symposium:* Speer's early experiences upon capture, Conot 101–2, 253.

43   *the wunderkind:* Speer's arms-production achievements, Tusa 395; Davidson 484, 502; IMT vol. 16, 448.

44   *saving their skins through knowledge:* Speer's friendly interrogations, Neave 313; RG 238 *U.S. Strategic Bombing Survey Special Document* May 22–23, 1945.

45   *a major war criminal:* Speer's arrest, Conot 253.

46   *relieved to have Maxwell-Fyfe along:* Jackson's second visit to Nuremberg, Kilmuir 85. While the Labour party won the British parliamentary elections by a two-hundred-seat majority in the summer of 1945, the Conservative Sir David Maxwell-Fyfe managed to hold on to his seat in West Derby by 3,428 votes.

47   *trial of the Nazi war criminals should be held here:* Selection of Nuremberg, interviews J. Vonetes, D. Kiley; JXO 1303; "Backstage Battle at Nuremberg," *Saturday Evening Post*, January 19, 1946; Tusa 84.

47   *ready to sign an agreement:* London negotiations completed, RG 238 The London Agreement, August 8, 1945.

47   *who was to be tried:* Deciding the defendants, Poltorak 224–25; B. Smith 6, 30; Tusa 92–93.

48   *"I'm only a dreamer":* Departure of Murray Bernays, Conot 25; B. Smith 335; interview R. Barrett.

49   *He recognized Hermann Göring:* Flying the accused from Bad Mondorf to Nuremberg, BAP account by pilot, Lieutenant Robert G. Denson (undated); *Life* September 3, 1946; Andrus 62.

49   *had first gone under hostile fire:* Andrus's background, Neave 61; interview B. Andrus, Jr.; Andrus 15–16; BAP chief prosecutor's office personnel file of B. Andrus, Andrus letter to William Stebbins August 27, 1945.

50   *"I hate these Krauts":* Andrus's attitudes toward Germans, BAP Andrus letter to Marjorie D. Peck (undated).

50   *"lack of judgment":* Opinions of Andrus, Walker, 23; interview A. Steer.

51   *he intended to whip into line:* Andrus relations with Göring, Andrus 29–31, 34; Conot 31.

51   *left a cyanide capsule in his clothes:* Göring deceptions at Bad Mondorf, Andrus 32.

51   *"You are no longer soldiers":* Keitel and Jodl stripped of insignia, Davidson 353.

51 *something he had to get off his chest:* Funk and removal of gold teeth, Andrus 55.

51 *Anne Frank, who died:* Seyss-Inquart in Holland, Neave 168; Davidson 466.

52 *Andrus's total confidence:* Dr. Pfluecker's relations with Andrus, Fritzsche 51; Swearingen 100; BAP memorandum to staff September 2, 1945.

52 *"my name is Meir":* Göring boasts of air superiority, Swearingen 46.

53 *an office in the Pentagon:* Horsky as Jackson's Washington liaison, interview C. Horsky.

53 *The language problem:* testing and adapting the IBM simultaneous interpreting system, interviews C. Horsky, W. Jackson; Gaskin 43; Biddle 398; JXO 1318.

55 *Kiley arrived at the Palace of Justice:* Restoring the courthouse, interview D. Kiley; JXO 1298. Kiley tried to persuade Jackson to hold the trial in the Nuremberg opera house, arguing: "We could stage it in a dramatic, thrilling way, a sort of world stage, the defense on the stage and the judges around them." Jackson turned down the idea after one of his staff remarked, "Yes, the IMT presents Jackson's Follies."

56 *"I have been here before":* The prisoners are assigned cells, Kelley 11; Speer *Inside* 645; Neave 64; Maser 61; *Stars and Stripes* August 13, 1945; Andrus 84, 143; Conot 35; BAP memorandum to staff September 2, 1945; interview W. Glenny.

57 *on a field of azure:* The IMT symbol, BAP memorandum to Justice Jackson September 28, 1945; interviews R. D'Addario, R. Korb Williams.

57 *His visitor was Major Douglas Kelley:* Arrival of the prison psychiatrist, Andrus 35; BAP General Eisenhower message to Eastern Military District October 23, 1945, Andrus draft ms. 101.

58 *going to be a proud outfit:* The guards' responsibilities, interviews E. DiPalma, W. Glenny; Tusa 126; BAP Andrus orders September 2, September 11, November 10, 1945, Andrus letter to S. Schneider September 19, 1945.

60 *Göring had raged:* Göring's exemption from chores, Maser 91; Swearingen 69.

60 *What rank did he want:* Jackson meeting with Truman, JXO 1246.

61 *happily name Parker:* Parker as alternate judge, Biddle 372–73; *New York Times* October 16, 1991.

61 *a call from Francis Biddle:* Biddle-Jackson meeting, Gerhart 256; JXO 1322, 1324, 1326; Biddle 128, 364, 372; Conot 62; Tusa 229; Taylor 95.

63 *"Exercise is important"*: Exercise yard rules, Kelley 166; Tusa 126; Maser 60; BAP Andrus order September 11, 1945.

64 *return to the cellblock*: First day in the exercise yard, Tusa 127; Fritzsche 20; AFN broadcast November 22, 1945.

65 *They entered Dambach*: Jackson's living quarters, JXO 1304, 1334, 1339; Storey 99; interviews W. Jackson, M. Fuchs, J. Vonetes; Taylor 216.

65 *People without a roof*: German opinions of the trial, JXO 1031.

65 *"The Tom Dewey of Brooklyn"*: Background, John Harlan Amen, interviews W. Baldwin, W. Jackson, J. Vonetes; AFN broadcast March 27, 1946; Conot 38.

66 *Albert Göring was an engineer*: Göring's brother questioned, RG 238 A. Göring interrogation September 25, 1945.

66 *brother Hermann's attitudes*: Göring and the Jews, RG 238 A. Göring interrogation September 25, 1945; Mosley 230. Göring had an important Jewish figure in his growing-up. Hermann von Epenstein, a wealthy Jewish physician, owned Veldenstein Castle in Franconia, where the Göring family lived during Hermann's childhood. Epenstein was godfather to the Göring children and their mother's lover. Göring ultimately inherited the castle.

68 *Ribbentrop was ready to take responsibility*: Jackson questions Ribbentrop, RG 238 Ribbentrop interrogation October 5, 1945; interview T. Lambert; Neave 230, 239; Kelley 112. Ribbentrop's disconnection from reality is suggested in this passage from a letter he wrote to Winston Churchill at the end of the war (whom he addressed as "Vincent" Churchill): "I do not know, if the old and noble English custom of fair play is also applicable for a defeated foe. I also do not know if you wish to hear the political testament of a deceased man [Hitler]. But I could imagine that its contents might be adapted to heal wounds . . . [and] in this perilous epoch of our world be able to help bring about a better future for all people."

70 *Andrus had lost his first prisoner*: Conti suicide, Andrus 87; Neave 76.

70 *workmen ripped the bars out*: Tightened security after Conti's suicide, Swearingen 98; Andrus 25, 29; Tusa 133; interview W. Glenny; Speer *Spandau* 5.

71 *one of the most sensational flights*: Hess's flight to Scotland, Manvell 32, 80, 82, 88–89, 92, 102; Conot 46; Kelley 24.

74 *"a victim of hallucinations"*: Hitler on the Hess flight, Manvell 107, 111, 112, 214.

74 *a disturbed mind*: Hess's internment in Britain, Gilbert, *Psychology* 124; Manvell 107, 109, 113–17, 119, 124–25, 128.

75 *the Russians insisted*: Why Hess was tried, Tusa 92; B. Smith 178.

75 *His best strategy:* Hess feigning amnesia, Manvell 135, 149. In June 1991, reports appeared that Hess had been lured to fly to Scotland by British intelligence. The claim was based on recently revealed KGB files which supposedly established that Hess had been in correspondence with the duke of Hamilton and that his letters had been intercepted by MI5. Thereafter, MI5 reportedly faked correspondence from Hamilton to Hess, without the duke's knowledge, that lured Hess to fly to Scotland for peace discussions. The matter is discussed in John Costello's *Ten Days to Destiny*, and the story appeared in the June 9, 1991, *New York Times*. While it is possible that the KGB had such information, its accuracy is questionable. Albrecht Haushofer's letter to the duke was indeed intercepted by British censors on November 2, 1940. And British intelligence apparently did hatch a plan—but a plan to put the duke and Haushofer (not Hess) together in Lisbon. As for Hess's being lured to England, he, by his own admission, had already made two attempts to fly to Scotland before the intelligence scheme was devised. Further, he never mentioned any correspondence between them on his meeting Hamilton or at any time during his captivity. Indeed, one of his early problems on parachuting into Scotland was to prove his identity, hardly necessary for a major Nazi presumably stepping into a British trap. In 1992, a year after the opening of the KGB files, the British released intelligence files that "contained nothing to support assertions, buttressed by KGB files . . . that British intelligence knew in advance that Hess was coming."

76 *Birkett was trapped:* Background and selection of Birkett for the IMT, Hyde 1–2, 472, 494; Neave 232–33; Conot 63–64; Biddle 380.

77 *His father had been lord chief justice:* Background and selection of Lawrence, B. Smith 4; Neave 231; Biddle 379; Tusa 112.

77 *product of two blue-blooded lines:* Biddle background, Biddle preface 4; Tusa 209; Neave 233; Conot 63–64.

78 *no intention of losing:* Biddle on the IMT's legitimacy, B. Smith 74; BIDP box 1 journal entry October 3, 1945.

78 *Lawrence to accept:* Lawrence over Biddle for the presidency of the court, B. Smith 3–4, 77; Kilmuir 90; BIDP box 1 journal entry October 10, 1945; JXD box 95. Biddle had already had experience with Nazi defendants. He was attorney general when eight German saboteurs were captured in the U.S. While the men might have been tried in a federal court (and likely would have received light sentences, since they were caught before they did anything beyond conspiring), President Roosevelt wanted them condemned to death and pressured the Justice Department to create a military tribunal. Biddle, ever eager to please Roosevelt, volunteered to prosecute. Six of the men were executed.

80 *"He's crazy":* Hess interrogated before Göring over his amnesia claim, Manvell 138; RG 238 Göring interrogation October 9, 1945; Davidson 301; Manvell 236.

81 *Hess was a fake:* Kelley 23, 26; Andrus 73; BAP Andrus memorandum "Suggestions to Major Kelley Concerning Interrogation of Hess" October 15, 1945.

81 *Sprecher had no business here:* The documents-versus-witnesses controversy, interview D. Sprecher.

82 *Biddle informed Neave:* Delivery of the indictments, Neave 64–226; Gilbert *Diary* 5; Speer *Inside* 642; Kilmuir 60.

86 *most of them were to keep talking:* Defendants' right to refuse interrogation after indictment, RG 238 interrogations Sauckel October 18, 1945, Frank October 19, 1945.

86 *"Man hat uns belogen und betrogen":* Gilbert volunteers for Nuremberg, GGP Gilbert speech draft (undated) "The men and women of defeated Germany," Gilbert letter to Kelley December 28, 1946; Conot 69; Gilbert *Diary* 3.

87 *Keitel had been interrogated:* Keitel signing and issuance of the Commando Order, RG 238 Keitel interrogation (date illegible); Davidson 381–83; IMT vol. 8, 547, vol. 9, 220, vol. 15, 321; Conot 307. The futility of trying to conduct modern warfare in civilized fashion is perhaps demonstrated in this excerpt from the *Handbook of Irregular Warfare* issued to British commandos and which Hitler used, in part, to justify the Commando Order:

> In the past we as a nation have not looked upon gangsters and their methods with favour; the time has now come when we are compelled to adopt some of their methods. . . . Remember you are not a wrestler trying to render your enemy helpless, you have to kill. And remember you are out to kill, not to hold him down until the referee has finished counting. . . . In finishing off an opponent use him as a weapon as it were, beating his head on the curb or any convenient stone. Do not forget that good weapons are often lying about ready at hand. A bottle with the bottom smashed off is more effective than a naked hand in gouging an opponent's face. . . . The vulnerable parts of the enemy are the heart, spine and privates. Kick him or knee him as hard as you can in the fork. While he is doubled up in pain get him on the ground and stamp his head in.

88 *"neither Bolshevism nor Czarism":* Issuance of the Reprisal and Commissar orders, IMT vol. 4, 438–39; Gilbert *Diary* 112; Maser 295.

89 *"I could never get away with this":* Keitel's unlikely rise, IMT vol. 10, 473; Gilbert *Psychology* 213; Gilbert *Diary* 25; RG 238 Keitel memoirs 147, 188, 231; Davidson 331, 333; Tusa 307; Cooper 124–25.

89 *"No enemy can be killed":* Keitel's blind obedience, IMT vol. 4, 473.

89 *"Thank God you're alive":* Keitel's loyalty to Hitler, RG 238 Keitel interrogation October 10, 1945.

90 *the psychiatrists' interpreter:* Andrus reaction to Gilbert, BAP draft Andrus ms. (no page shown).

90 *"if you have one German":* Kelley and Gilbert visit Göring, Kelley viii, 35–36, 71–73, 75.

91 *a study of the Nazis:* Kelley and Gilbert's book collaboration, GGP Gilbert letter to Kelley December 28, 1946.

91 *to choose the first witness:* Jackson and Donovan differ on strategy, interviews R. Barrett, H. Smith; Conot 150–51; JXO 1384–85.

92 *far less daunting:* Jackson's preference for documents, interview T. Taylor.

93 *the Judges' Room:* Who may defend the defendants, Gaskin 87; Neave 228, 237; Hyde 497, 498; Tusa 228.

94 *throw the Noak woman out:* Stahmer's anti-Semitism, RG 238 Frau Noak letter to U.S. occupation authorities October 1945; Otto Stahmer letter to Frau Utermoehlen January 14, 1945.

94 *Nazi defense lawyers:* Former Nazis may represent defendants, Neave 120–21, 228, 230.

94 *Allied war crimes:* Jodl raises tu quoque, B. Smith 210.

95 *Luise Jodl had been married:* Frau Jodl comes to Nuremberg; the Jodl marriage, interview H. Wechsler; Maser 192; Davidson 354; Kelley 122; Conot 94.

96 *"scornful laughter of God":* Frank rediscovers his faith; background of Father O'Connor, Gilbert *Diary* 20–21; Fritzsche 55; Tusa 235; Gerecke *Saturday Evening Post* September 1, 1951; interview R. Holden Bateman; Andrus 110.

98 *"Stand us against a wall":* Background Robert Ley, Gilbert *Diary* 7–8, 13, 33; Maser 47; Poltorak 32; Polevoi 118; Kelley 170; RG 238 Ley interrogation October 18, 1945.

99 *"I needed that":* Background Streicher; his troubles with Göring, Bytwerk 34, 40–43; Fritzsche 130; Conot 383–84; Maser 50; Neave 96.

100 *"He is sane":* Psychiatric examination of Streicher, Gilbert *Diary* 9–10; BAP Kelley report to Andrus January 4, 1946.

101 *"Ley has killed himself":* The Ley suicide, Andrus 88–89; BAP Lieutenant Paul H. Graven letter to Major Teich October 29, 1945; Gaskin 30; Kelley 73. Ley left a suicide note that read:

> Farewell. I can't stand this shame any longer. Physically, nothing is lacking. The food is good. It is warm in my cell. The Americans are correct and partially friendly. Spiritually, I have reading matter and write what-

ever I want. I receive paper and pencil. They do more for my health than necessary and I may smoke and receive tobacco and coffee. I may walk at least 20 minutes every day. Up to this point, everything is in order but the fact that I should be a criminal—this is what I can't stand.

101 *His jail . . . was now suicide-proof:* Tightened security, Swearingen 65; Polevoi 120.

102 *"six hundred people just to hang twenty-one":* Jackson-Biddle administrative quarrels, BIDP box 1 journal entry October 21, 1945; JXO 1364, 1368.

103 *staying on in Nuremberg:* Gilbert background, interviews R. Gilbert, C. Gilbert.

104 *to be a spy:* Gilbert's covert intelligence for Andrus, BAP Andrus letter to his wife January 24, 1946; GGP Kelley letter to Gilbert December 24, 1946.

105 *"only you showed independence":* Göring conversation with Dewitt C. Poole covering foreign policy, Soviet Union invasion, Göring's rise to power, RG 238 Göring interrogation November 6, 1945, Göring dossier; Irving 21–22, 44, 105, 408; Mosley 178, 204, 239, 275; IMT vol. 1, 35.

107 *burning of the Reichstag:* Göring's explanation, Irving 115–17; RG 238 Göring interrogation October 13, 1945.

107 *the world press began descending:* Press facilities, interviews H. Smith, A. Logan; Flanner *The New Yorker* October 26, 1946, 92; Polevoi 69–70, 81. Boris Polevoi, the *Pravda* correspondent at Nuremberg, complained that Soviet correspondents were not billeted in the castle, but in "the Russian Palace," cramped rooms previously occupied by workers from the pencil factory.

108 *a curtain had descended on civilization:* Day-to-day life in Nuremberg, interviews H. Smith, R. D'Addario, R. Keeler, C. Gordon, P. Uiberall, A. Donovan, B. Hardy; Cumoletti 89, 99–100; H. Smith broadcasts November 25, 1945, January 31, 1946.

109 *he wanted an equivalent vote:* Role of alternate justices, Conot 85; BIDP box 2 Biddle memorandum for the record November 14, 1945.

110 *"not a football match":* Jackson wants Krupp indicted, Hyde 496; IMT vol. 2, 1; Biddle 401; B. Smith 80; interview H. Wechsler.

111 *Speed was the acid test:* Setting up the simultaneous-interpretation system, interviews A. Steer, D. Kiley, P. Uiberall, T. Brown; Gaskin 38–39; Gerhart 358. In addition to the courtroom interpreters, court reporters took down the proceedings of the trial in shorthand, which was later transcribed. The U.S. Army Signal Corps recorded the trial on disks, magnetic tape, or wire recorders.

113 *organized bedlam:* Operation of the documents room, interviews R. Barrett, B. Pinion Bitter, T. Taylor, W. Brudno, R. Holden Bateman; Tusa 99, 215; Gaskin 51, 53.

115 *"Melancholy grandeur":* Jackson prepares for his opening address, Gerhart 304–305, 441; JXO 1389–96; interviews W. Jackson, H. Wechsler, D. Sprecher; IMT vol. 2, 130.

116 *"You are not here to convert anybody":* Chaplain Gerecke arrives, BAP Andrus draft ms. (undated); Tusa 235; Fritzsche 55; Gerecke *Saturday Evening Post* September 1, 1951.

116 *Gilbert was recording the answers:* The defendants take intelligence tests, Gilbert *Psychology* 107, 127, 143; Gilbert *Diary* 15, 30; Tusa 129–30. A score of 100 was considered average. University graduates would be expected to score in the 120–140 range. Gilbert recorded the following results for the defendants: Schacht 143; Seyss-Inquart 141; Göring 138; Dönitz 138; Papen 134; Raeder 134; Frank 130; Fritzsche 130; Schirach 130; Ribbentrop 129; Keitel 129; Speer 128; Jodl 127; Rosenberg 127; Neurath 125; Funk 124; Frick 124; Hess 120; Sauckel 118; Kaltenbrunner 113; Streicher 106.

118 *burned the Soviet files:* Rudenko background; complaints of destroyed Soviet documents, Conot 61; JXO 1539, 1550.

119 *"an officer of high standing":* Schacht courts Donovan; Jackson objects, Conot 151–52; interviews R. Holden Bateman, J. Vonetes; B. Smith 270–71; Swearingen 131–32.

120 *"I have the responsibility":* Jackson fires Donovan over trial strategy, Storey 98; Conot 150–51, 154–55; Brown 744; Harris xxxvi; JXO 1386–87; Gerhart 115; interviews T. Taylor, D. Sprecher.

121 *"I am in possession of certain information":* Speer tries to cut a deal, B. Smith 221; RG 238 Speer interrogation November 2, 1945.

123 *"a toast to the defendants":* Vyshinsky at a banquet; a Russo-American romance, Martyn Harris, "House Party," *The Spectator* October 24, 1992, 54; Kilmuir 107, 109; BIDP box 1 Biddle letter to son, Randolph, October 17, 1945; Biddle 376–77, 428.

124 *a national inferiority complex:* Jackson on Russian psychology, JXO 1558.

125 *Fear and stress:* Problems in the prison; Kaltenbrunner's illness, Davidson 531–33; B. Smith 292; Andrus 141; Kelley 134.

126 *"they think it's all propaganda":* Eve of the trial, Shirer 306, 313.

126 *He had come down with malaria:* Soviets seek to stall the trial opening, JXO 1375–83; Gerhart 509; Storey 111.

Chapter II: The Prosecution Case

132 *this dishrag in the dock:* Opening day, H. Smith broadcast November 20, 1945; J. Flanner *The New Yorker* January 5, 1946; IMT vol. 2, 30; Neave 243.

133 *"steak the day before they hang us":* The defendants during the first day, Fritzsche 73; Gilbert *Diary* 35–36.

134 *Donovan would be flying home:* The general's departure, JXO 1366–67.

134 *"This is history":* The gavel is stolen, interview R. D'Addario.

135 *"find myself a courthouse":* Jackson prepares to deliver opening speech, Shirer 301; Gerhart 353; Tusa 151.

135 *"not to make a speech":* The defendants enter pleas, Shirer 305; Tusa 150; Neave 245; IMT vol. 2, 98. The prepared statement that Göring twice attempted to deliver read:

> As *Reichsmarschall* of the Greater German Reich, I accept the political responsibility for all my own acts or for acts carried out on my orders. These acts were exclusively carried out for the welfare of the German people and because of my oath to the Führer. Although I am responsible for these acts only to the German people and can be tried only before a German court, I am at the same time prepared to give all the necessary information demanded of me by this court and to tell the whole truth without recognizing the jurisdiction of this court. I must, however, most strongly reject the accusation that my acts for which I accept full responsibility should be described as criminal. I must also reject the acceptance by me of responsibility for acts of other persons which were not known to me, of which, had I known them, I would have disapproved and which could not have been prevented by me anyway.

135 *"the first trial in history":* Jackson's opening address, IMT vol. 2, 98–102, 120, 154–55; Gerhart 363; *Life* December 10, 1945; JXO 1397–98.

138 *what must be their own fate:* Other executions and death sentences for war crimes, *New York Times* November 18, 22, 1945.

138 *"Murder hasn't been made a crime yet":* Shawcross and Rudenko opening speeches, Gilbert *Diary* 425–26; Tusa 179; Ophuls *Memory of Justice.*

139 *call him Tex:* Second Lieutenant Jack Wheelis is promoted, BAP Wheelis's transfer orders to Nuremberg September 26, 1945; personnel file, Jack Wheelis 0-1330498 November 22, 1945.

140 *Wheelis was a friend:* Göring courts Wheelis and other GIs, H. Smith broadcast November 27, 1945; Swearingen 198; Gilbert *Diary* 87; Gaskins 86.

141 *Smith finished his broadcast:* An evaluation of the trial, H. Smith broadcast November 27, 1945.

142 "Guten Morgen, Herr Reichsmarschall": Kempner prewar relations with Göring and Frick, Mosley 151, 324; *New York Times* October 6, 1946; Dreyfuss 26.

142 *directing the takeover by telephone:* Göring and the annexation of Austria, IMT vol. 2, 418.

143 *"I refer to document number 2430 PS":* Film, Nazi concentration camps, shown, IMT vol 2, 432–33; Neave 246; JXO 1407–8.

144 *no rank, no title:* Göring's cell marked, Polevoi 120.

145 *"These facts are the most fearful heritage":* Defendants' reactions to the concentration camp film, Gilbert *Diary* 43, 46–47; Maser 107.

146 *She seized the opportunity:* Operation of the Witness House, Kalnoky 1–10, 155–56.

146 *Lahousen marched to the witness stand:* Lahousen at the Witness House; subsequent testimony, Kalnoky 78–80; IMT vol. 2, 435, 449–50, vol. 3, 10, vol. 5, 33.

147 *"The order to liquidate":* Keitel orders execution of French generals, IMT vol. 2, 463–64, 474; Gilbert *Psychology* 228–29.

148 *amnesia would "interfere with his ability":* Hess's sanity hearing, BAP Report of Psychiatric Board to the IMT December 12, 1945; IMT vol. 1, 157, vol. 2, 493; Kelley 31, 35.

148 *"You probably won't be coming to court":* Gilbert warns Hess if he is found unfit for trial, Gilbert *Diary* 11, 51; Gilbert *Psychology* 129; Conot 159.

149 *"my memory will again respond":* Hess recants on amnesia, Shirer 319; Polevoi 89; IMT vol. 2, 478–79, 496; Gilbert *Diary* 51; Poltorak 50.

149 *"I decided to stop playing the game":* Doctors ponder authenticity of Hess's recovered memory, Kelley 52–53; Gilbert *Diary* 54.

150 *distinguish between right and wrong:* The court finds Hess can stand trial, IMT vol. 3, 1; BAP Report of Three Man Panel to IMT December 5, 1945. While the ten-doctor panel had concluded that Hess's condition would interfere with "his ability to conduct his defense," the court appears to have been influenced by an earlier report by a three-doctor panel which found:

> To the psychiatrist, the word insanity means the existence of unsoundness of mind of such a nature and degree as to prevent him from distinguishing between right and wrong and from adhering to the right . . . our examination revealed that Hess has no disorder of consciousness, understands perfectly everything that is said to him and therefore understands the nature of the proceedings against him.

150 *a bloodcurdling scream:* The noose trick, Fritzsche 44; Oral History, Colonel Robert Franklin, Sr., October 25, 1982, U.S. Army Military History Institute.

151 *"You are hereby informed":* Andrus wearies of complaints, BAP Andrus memorandum to "Persons concerned" December 3, 1945.

152 *"I wonder what facilities the Germans would provide":* Storey shows Birkett the defense counsels' resources, Storey 64, 101.

153 *"The nastiest person present":* David Low sketches, *New York Times Magazine* December 23, 1945.

155 *nor one so stupid:* Kaltenbrunner background; recovery from illness, RG 238 Kaltenbrunner dossier; IMT vol. 11, 233; Davidson 318, 321–22; Poltorak 80; Polevoi 265.

156 *"There goes the alliance":* East-West tensions mount, interview A. Callan.

157 *"I can't be held responsible":* Andrus's conflicts with Watson, Andrus 76; BAP Andrus message to Second Army HQ November 13, 1945.

158 *implementing the pass system:* Sadel establishes the social pass, interview G. Sadel.

158 *film from captured German newsreels:* The Nazi Plan screened in court, IMT vol. 3, 400–403, Conot 197; Poltorak 142; Gilbert *Diary* 66.

159 *"you filthy rogue":* Film of the People's Court, Ophuls *Memory of Justice;* H. Smith broadcast December 11, 1945; Cooper 30. In order to contrast Nazi-style justice with what Nazi defendants were receiving from the IMT, Robert Kempner arranged to have German government officials, politicians, teachers, clergymen, and judges visit the Nuremberg courtroom. Afterward, they were taken to a projection room where the Freisler People's Court film was shown.

160 *"if Hitler were to walk into this room":* Defendants' reaction to the film *The Nazi Plan,* Kelley 112–13; Gilbert *Psychology* 195.

160 *Dodd cut an impressive figure:* Dodd's first appearance in court, interviews T. Taylor, D. Margolies, W. Baldwin, W. Harris; IMT vol. 3, 403.

161 *"I had found a man":* Sauckel background, RG 238 Sauckel interrogations September 11, 12, 13, October 14, 1945.

162 *"We've taken heavy manpower losses":* Hitler makes Sauckel the labor czar, IMT vol. 19, 189, 196, vol. 14, 610, 622; Conot 142; RG 238 Sauckel interrogation September 12, 13, 19, 20, 21, 1945.

163 *"They fell on their knees":* Roundups of conscript workers, Conot 245–46.

166 *"I am really not responsible"*: Sauckel puts blame on Speer, Gilbert *Diary* 75.

167 *merriment of the Marble Room:* After-hours atmosphere, Neave 43, 53–54; Tusa 227–28; interviews J. Vonetes, G. Sadel, D. Owens Reilly, K. Walch.

168 *no reason to keep him locked up:* Hoffmann background; photography expedition, Poltorak 140; Polevoi 106; Conot 93; interview R. Heller.

169 *a man untouched by shame:* Hoffmann at the Witness House, Kalnoky 42–43.

170 *"six feet under"*: Andrus complains of press revelations, Reuters dispatch December 12, 1945; *London Daily Express* December 13, 1945; AFN broadcast November 23, 1945; interview H. Burson.

171 *"the money that bastard made"*: Göring on Hoffmann, Bullock 174.

171 *chief cause of Germany's defeat:* Göring and Ribbentrop mutual opinions, RG 238 Göring dossier; Gilbert *Diary* 13, 67; Tusa 241.

172 *a courtroom barometer:* Göring's dominance of the dock, H. Smith broadcast December 9, 1945.

172 *whisked the sheet from USA exhibit 254:* Dodd enters exhibits, IMT vol. 3, 516–17; interview R. Barrett.

173 *"among the clubs and kicks"*: Ghetto atrocity film shown, J. Flanner, *The New Yorker* January 5, 1946, 44.

175 *"Hitler got us into this"*: Defendants' reaction to ghetto atrocity film, IMT vol. 3, 536–37, 542, vol. 5, 200; Gilbert *Diary* 70–71.

176 *"my knees knocking"*: Frictions among Allied staffs, Gaskin 143; Neave 254; Kilmuir 101; Tusa 136. Wide discrepancies existed in pay scales. The American judge Biddle was paid at an annual rate of $15,000 and an American civilian staff lawyer about $7,000. Sir Geoffrey Lawrence's annual salary was closer to $2,000.

176 *"privatize, finalize, visualize"*: Birkett's disdain for the American staff, Hyde 515.

177 *"I accept Christ"*: Religious life in the cellblock, Fritzsche 125; Gerecke *Saturday Evening Post* September 1, 1951; Andrus 137.

178 *you could call him Meir:* Göring humiliated by Hitler, Mosley 289, 299; IMT vol. 15, 590.

178 *crush these "leftist" Nazis:* Göring and the Roehm purge, Gilbert *Diary* 79; Mosley 190–95. Göring at one point gave out the figure for deaths during the purge as seventy-two; but Himmler reportedly used the occasion to wipe out more than a hundred more of his enemies. After the slaughter, President Hindenburg sent Göring a telegram: "Accept my approval and gratitude for your successful action in suppressing the high treason."

181 *"those who merely did their bidding":* German people react to indictment of Nazi organizations, AFN broadcast January 10, 1946; Davidson 556; RG 238 Kempner memorandum to Jackson January 23, 1946.

181 *went into convulsions and died:* Medical experiments, Gerhart 115, 371; Polevoi 147–49.

184 *"Hitler appears on the screen":* Frank reflects on his relations with Hitler, Gilbert *Diary* 22, 82–83.

184 *"I decide the fate of criminals":* Frank and the Roehm purge, Davidson 441; Gilbert *Psychology* 149; Posner 15.

187 *"They disappeared into the night and fog":* Keitel issues the *Nacht und Nebel* decree, Davidson 338; Gilbert *Psychology* 228–32.

187 *"if we had disobeyed":* Jodl defends obedience of orders, IMT vol. 19, 23, 26, 32; Gilbert *Diary* 28.

189 *"We didn't dare oppose the orders":* Gilbert goes to Dachau; ponders impulses of mass murderers, interview R. Barrett; RG 238 Kaltenbrunner dossier; GGP Gilbert speech notes (undated); BAP Gilbert report to Andrus on Dachau visit January 3, 1946.

190 *His most vivid childhood memory:* Speer's early background, Speer *Inside* xiii, 32, 40; Conot 239.

191 *he won a commission:* Speer as Hitler's architect, Speer *Inside* 46, 52, 69, 71, 93–94, 137, 164, 166, 440; IMT vol. 16, 430.

192 *Dr. Todt had been killed:* Speer becomes armaments chief, Speer *Inside* 263–64; Conot 438; IMT vol. 16, 437.

193 *"These people must disappear":* Speer's knowledge of slave labor conditions, concentration camps, and extermination, Conot 256, 437, 441; Speer *Inside* 474–75; IMT vol. 16, 444, 480.

194 *"The best have fallen":* Speer resists Hitler's scorched-earth policy, Speer *Inside* 557, 592; Davidson 486; RG 238 U.S. Strategic Bombing Survey Special Report of Interrogation of Speer May 23, 1945.

195 *"So you're leaving. Good":* Speer's farewell to Hitler; activities prior to capture, U.S. Strategic Bombing Survey Special Report May 23, 1945; Speer *Inside* 612, 615–17.

195 *Speer to the visitors' room:* Speer discusses strategy with his lawyer, BAP visitors' room log December 27, 1945.

196 *Ribbentrop pestered the old physician:* Ribbentrop behavior, Conot 53; IMT vol. 2, 254–55.

197 *He might have become a Canadian:* Early Ribbentrop background, Bullock 18, 109; Davidson 148; RG 238 Ribbentrop dossier.

197 *he persuaded Hitler:* Ribbentrop's rise to foreign minister, Conot 152; Higham 141; Davidson 151.

199 *failed to wish him a happy New Year:* Ribbentrop fires his lawyer, Neave 224.

199 *"the ninth crime":* Evidence against Kaltenbrunner, interview W. Harris; IMT vol 4, 306–7.

200 *"How many people did you kill":* W. Harris interrogates Ohlendorf, interview W. Harris; Wolfe, *Annals of the American Academy of Political Science* July 1980.

201 *"ninety thousand people liquidated":* Ohlendorf testimony, IMT vol. 4, 311, 319–23, 332.

201 *an attempt on Hitler's life:* Lawyer gives preview of Speer defense, IMT vol. 4, 343.

202 *"But did you have no scruples":* Ohlendorf's cross-examination, IMT vol. 4, 353–54.

203 *the Final Solution:* Witness Wisliceny sees a written order, IMT vol. 4, 357–60.

203 *"five million people on his conscience":* Emergence of Eichmann through Wisliceny's testimony, IMT vol. 4, 308, 355, 357–60, 371; B. Smith 115; Poltorak 344. Wisliceny testified that "the chief of the Security Police and the SD and the Inspector of Concentration Camps were entrusted with carrying out this so-called final solution. All Jewish men and women who were able to work were to be temporarily exempted from the so-called final solution and used for work in the concentration camps. The letter was signed by Himmler himself. I could not possibly be mistaken since Himmler's signature was well known to me."

203 *"this is serious business":* Dwindling press coverage, interview H. Burson; Andrus 173.

204 *taking on the German High Command:* Taylor for the prosecution; Taylor background, interviews T. Taylor, W. Rockler; IMT vol. 4, 390; Gaskin 133.

206 *"the Jews are not even human":* Testimony of Bach-Zelewski incriminates the Wehrmacht; interests Gilbert, Gilbert *Diary* 109, 114; IMT vol. 4, 451; Poltorak 126; GGP Gilbert speech notes (undated).

209 *"I was the pupil"*: Keitel's relationship to Hitler and rise to chief of staff, IMT vol. 9, 371, vol. 10, 600; Gilbert *Psychology* 208, 210; Davidson 341; Speer *Inside* 323; RG 238 Keitel interrogation October 1, 1945.

211 *"he would renounce the church"*: Rosenberg's *The Myth of the Twentieth Century*, Kelley 39, 47–48. Rosenberg's book appears to be one of the great unread German works of that era. In 1934, its year of publication, the book sold 250,000 copies. By the war's outbreak it had sold 1 million copies and, according to Rosenberg, was in the home of "every decent party member."

211 *"We don't want to hear about it"*: Brudno prosecution of Rosenberg, IMT vol. 5, 41; interview W. Brudno.

212 *she did not appear before the court:* Women at Nuremberg, H. Smith broadcast January 25, 1946.

213 *"cold-bloodedly and without pity"*: Baldwin begins Frank prosecution, interview W. Baldwin; IMT vol. 5, 82–83.

214 *spirited from their homes:* Dr. Blaha's testimony incriminates defendants, IMT vol. 5, 176–77, 181; interview D. Margolies.

216 *Kaltenbrunner knew what had really happened:* Speer's connection to the Twentieth of July plot, Speer *Inside* 501.

217 *"Göring keeps whipping them into line"*: Speer proposes splitting the defendants at lunchtime, Gilbert *Diary* 122.

218 *three-quarters American:* Sprecher prosecutes Schirach, Shirach background, interview Drexel Sprecher; Conot 421; IMT vol. 14, 363; Davidson 285. While membership in Schirach's Hitler Youth was technically voluntary, the pressures to join were formidable. An apprentice who was a member got a job more easily. Only members could win school prizes. In some districts, youths who did not want to be members had to sign a form, which singled them out as unpatriotic. In other areas, pressure was applied by setting a deadline beyond which the young person could never join.

219 *"The Revenge of Heydrich"*: Schirach proposes vengeance bombing; ships Jews from Vienna, Conot 423; IMT vol. 14, 491.

223 *"An insane clique of generals"*: Dönitz attacks the Twentieth of July plotters, RG 238 BBC intercept, Dönitz broadcast July 21, 1944; Posner 150.

224 *He was mortified:* Kranzbuehler contemplates his behavior during the Nazi era, Ophuls *Memory of Justice.*

225 *to make Adolf Hitler a German:* Frick's role in Hitler's citizenship, Davidson 264–65.

226 *Their German identity was effaced:* Frick's role in anti-Semitic decrees, Davidson 264, 267–68; IMT vol. 3, 523–25; Hecht 57, 63.

227 *"they haven't had a classical education"*: British judged better prosecutors, Neave 253; H. Smith broadcast January 17, 1946; J. Flanner *The New Yorker* January 5, 1946; interviews R. Barrett, D. Owens Reilly, K. Walch, H. Burson.

227 *his staff was melting away:* High American turnover, JXO 1402; Conot 283.

228 *"the most amazing stroke of genius"*: Gilbert visits Streicher; Streicher background, Gilbert *Diary* 117, 125; Davidson 47; Neave 94; Bytwerk 2, 5–6.

229 *"as a gift"*: Streicher's rise and fall, IMT vol. 12, 308; Bytwerk 8–15; RG 238 Streicher interrogation November 6, 1945.

232 *a deterioration in Hess's mental condition:* Gilbert believes amnesia has returned, Gilbert *Diary* 121, 130.

232 *What Kelley left unsaid:* Andrus wants to dismiss Gilbert, GGP Kelley letter to Gilbert December 24, 1946.

232 *he would defend himself:* Hess fires his lawyer, interview T. Fenstermacher; Neave 251.

233 *"I draw the attention"*: Hess complains about his lawyer, Neave 252; Hess's letter of January 30, 1946, to the court hardly suggests an addled mind:

> In the *New York Herald Tribune*, dated 27th January 1946, there is a report of an interview given by my former defending counsel, Dr. von Rohrscheidt. This contains a passage in which strictly confidential instructions given by me to Dr. von Rohrscheidt in respect of my defence, are given publicity, while at the same time it is emphasized that these were my instructions. This constitutes a breach of confidence and an offence against the secrecy to which an advocate is pledged; it is a grave professional offence, which in normal times would lead to denunciation before the governing Chamber of Lawyers. I therefore hereby place on record that I no longer have any confidence whatever in my former advocate. At the same time I draw the attention of the Court to the fact that I have now been a whole week without a defending counsel, while I have not been permitted to take advantage of the right to which the statute entitles me of pleading my own case. In consequence of this state of things, I was prevented from questioning even a single witness of all those who came forward during this period, although again I was entitled by the statute to do this.

234 *"He would enter a room"*: Ribbentrop, a problem client; his subservience to Hitler, Kelley 98; Poltorak 224; IMT vol. 10, 110; Gilbert *Diary* 130.

235 *"He bought his name"*: Schirach on Ribbentrop, Gilbert *Diary* 141; Tusa 299.

235 *he never said anything:* Description of Donnedieu de Vabres, Polevoi 294; J. Flanner *The New Yorker* March 30, 1946; Neave 234–35.

236 *goods stolen from France:* Opening of the French case; Göring's reaction, IMT vol. 5, 308–309, vol. 6, 184; Ophuls *Memory of Justice.*

236 *In 1942, she was arrested:* Testimony of Marie Claude Vaillant-Couturier on Auschwitz; Kranzbuehler's reaction, IMT vol. 6, 203–206, 215; Ophuls *Memory of Justice;* Poltorak 135.

238 *"I recognized Speer":* Boix's and other testimony damages Speer, IMT vol. 3, 440, 463–64, 492, vol. 6, 264, 269; H. Smith broadcast January 8, 1946.

240 Stars and Stripes *had broken the hushed-up story:* Conti suicide exposed, Swearingen 226–27.

240 *he was going home:* Kelley departs under conditions that Andrus questions, BAP Andrus memorandum February 7, 1946; GGP Gilbert letter to Kelley December 28, 1946, Gilbert letter to Dr. Lewis March 10, 1946.

240 *"I'm saving all that for a book":* Polevoi learns of the Gilbert-Kelley book project, Polevoi 185–86.

241 *"I intend to plunder in France":* Göring, Rosenberg, and prosecution of the art-looting operation, J. Flanner *The New Yorker* March 9, 1946; Mosley 253; Davidson 127; RG 238 Rosenberg dossier; IMT vol. 4, 90–91, vol. 9, 328.

242 *"My orders are final":* Rosenberg empties Jewish homes; Göring berates Bunjes, Davidson 138; RG 238 Bunjes letter to Dr. Turner February 5, 1941. Included in the art of the Old Masters that Göring amassed were works of Hals, Van Dyck, Goya, Velázquez, Rubens, Titian, Raphael, and Fragonard.

245 *Paulus stirred bitter memories:* Introduction of Paulus's affidavit, interview T. Taylor; Taylor 309; Tusa 195.

245 *a lone figure appeared:* Russians produce Paulus as a surprise witness, Polevoi 194, 196, 198–99; interview P. Uiberall; Poltorak 102–3; Fritzsche 116, 121; IMT vol. 7, 254–55, 261.

248 *"cross between a monastery and a concentration camp":* Jodl's background and troubled relationship with Hitler, Davidson 328, 343, 347–48; Tusa 498. Hitler's total conquest of Jodl in the early days is suggested in the general's diary entry for August 10, 1938:

> It is tragic that the Führer should have the whole nation behind him with the single exception of the Army generals. In my opinion it is only by action that they can now atone for their faults of lack of character and discipline. It is the same problem as in 1914. There is only one

undisciplined element in the Army—the generals, and in the last analysis this comes from the fact that they are arrogant. They have neither confidence nor discipline because they cannot recognize the Führer's genius.

248 *"This is not an able crowd"*: Biddle criticizes his colleagues and Jackson, BIDP Biddle letter to his wife, Katherine, February 13, 1946.

250 *"they are just as bad"*: Death of Yamashita; Göring criticizes arrest of Nazi wives, Poltorak 169; Gilbert *Diary* 55; GGP Gilbert memorandum to Andrus January 9, 1946.

250 *Doubts over Katyn could color the entire prosecution case:* The Russian prosecution presents the Katyn massacre, Conot 23; Tusa 113; Maser 109; IMT vol. 9, 3.

251 *The colonel suspected Göring:* Andrus's animus against Göring; wants to split defendants, Kelley 57–59, 61.

251 *"a great man or a criminal"*: childhood influences on Göring, Gilbert *Psychology* 84, 88.

252 *"your explanation of these deficiencies"*: Andrus-Watson clash, BAP Watson memorandum to Andrus February 14, 1946, Andrus memorandum for the record February 18, 1946, Andrus letter to General Clint Andrus February 20, 1946.

253 *Göring cursed at the news:* Gilbert announces new seating divisions for lunch, Gilbert *Diary* 158–59.

253 *"To the great Texas hunter"*: Wheelis befriends Göring, Swearingen 204; Mosley 204.

254 *Schirach could do nothing right:* Schirach becomes a Nazi anti-Semite; loses favor with Hitler over his wife's comments, IMT vol. 14, 308, 427–29; Gilbert *Diary* 23.

255 *"just comic relief"*: Defendants' reaction to separation; Göring complains, Gilbert *Diary* 155–56, 162; Kilmuir 69.

256 *"broke the backbone of the Nazi beast"*: Soviet boasts irk other Allies, Poltorak 5; Polevoi 175; Kilmuir 7.

256 *"the right to shoot prisoners of war"*: Soviet film, *Documentary Evidence of the German Fascist Invaders;* Nazi human and cultural atrocities in Russia, Polevoi 180; Tusa 198–99; IMT vol. 1, 48, vol. 8, 53, 75.

258 *"I've seen so much already"*: Göring and others react to Soviet atrocity film, Gilbert *Diary* 164, 171.

261 *"Unite to Stop Russians"*: Soviet correspondents learn of Iron Curtain speech, Polevoi 209–210. The *Stars and Stripes* enjoyed a great vogue in Nuremberg and elsewhere in Germany. The U.S. Military Government also sponsored a good, factual paper, *Die Neue Zeitung*, but the Germans had become so suspicious of any "official" news source that they far preferred the GIs' paper, assuming it to be an insider source.

262 *"Churchill is no fool":* Reaction of the defendants to the Iron Curtain speech, Polevoi 211; J. Flanner *The New Yorker* March 9, 1946.

263 *"And what language was that":* Simultaneous-interpretation problems, interviews A. Steer, P. Uiberall, T. Brown, D. Margolies; Hyde 521; Gaskins 47. On the witness stand and counsel's lectern were lights which would flash, yellow signaling the speaker to slow down, and red signaling the speaker to stop until the interpreter could catch up.

Chapter III: The Defense

268 *the first person Otto Stahmer called:* Göring's defense begins with Bodenschatz, IMT vol. 1, 1–4, 8–9.

269 *"Once we came to power":* Göring takes the stand, IMT vol. 9, 235, 250, 252–58.

270 *"one of the best brains":* Göring's performance wins grudging admiration, J. Flanner *The New Yorker* March 23, 1946; interview H. Smith; Gilbert *Diary* 194; Neave 257.

271 *"I promulgated those laws":* Göring defends the *Führerprinzip;* takes responsibility for the Nuremberg Laws, IMT vol. 1, 31, vol. 9, 263, 276; Gilbert *Diary* 197.

272 *Göring had been testifying for five hours:* Göring explains Rotterdam bombing, art thefts, cites Churchill, IMT vol. 9, 327, 340, 364; Gerhart 513.

274 *"They helped put Hitler into power":* Sprecher discusses Göring's defense and the case against the industrialists, interview D. Sprecher.

275 *"a duel to the death":* Birkett stresses the importance of Jackson's cross-examination of Göring, J. Flanner *The New Yorker* March 30, 1946; Hyde 509.

276 *"the witness ought to be allowed":* Jackson and the court clash over Göring's answers, JXO 1429, 1434; IMT vol. 9, 418–19.

278 *"Someone is going to have to stop him":* First round of cross-examination goes to Göring, Hyde 509–11; Neave 246, 248; AFN broadcast March 18, 1946.

279 *"an arrogant and contemptuous attitude":* Göring disputes translation of a document; angers Jackson, Tusa 281; IMT vol. 9, 507–508.

279 *"I'd better resign and go home":* Jackson confronts Biddle, Biddle 410; BIDP box 19 Biddle letter to his wife, Katherine, March 19, 1946.

281 *get the cross-examination back on track:* Birkett wants Göring reined in, Tusa 282; Hyde 512; Neave 255, 260. Maxwell-Fyfe, writing years later, said:

> I have been interested to see Birkett's comment that if the Tribunal had insisted on Goering answering the questions put to him without branching off into monologues "he would certainly have been much more under control, and the lost confidence of Mr. Justice Jackson would have been restored for the ultimate benefit of all concerned in the trial." Looking back, I am sure that Birkett's judgment was, for once, seriously at fault. If Goering—who, after all, was on trial for his life—could run rings round prosecuting counsel, that was a matter for counsel to put right without assistance from the Tribunal. Public opinion would not have tolerated—either at the time or subsequently—the constant interference of the judges on behalf of the prosecution.

281 *"it would be wiser to ignore a statement of that sort":* Jackson protests Göring gibe against the U.S., IMT vol. 9, 509–12.

282 *to plan a solution:* Jackson questions Göring on the Final Solution, IMT vol. 9, 517–19. Göring's shrewdness is demonstrated in an exchange between him and the prosecutor. On page 519, Jackson is questioning Göring over a decree in which Göring orders Heydrich to plan a *"Gesamtlösung"* and, later in the same document, an *"Endlösung."* The former translates as "complete solution" and the latter as "final solution." But Göring gives an answer making it appear that the translation of *both* words is "complete solution."

283 *"I would not like to be a Jew in Germany":* Jackson questions Göring on Kristallnacht, IMT vol. 9, 521, 532–33, 544.

284 *Jackson versus Göring ended:* Göring challenges the authenticity of photographs, IMT vol. 9, 565, 571.

284 *a brilliant villain:* Judgments on the Göring-Jackson confrontation, Tusa 290; Gerhart 399; interviews, T. Taylor, P. Uiberall, D. Margolies, B. Pinion Bitter, H. Smith.

284 *"You boys better get out":* GIs off duty; American race relations in Nuremberg, interviews H. Burson, R. Keeler, G. Sadel; Gilbert *Diary* 57. At the time of the trial, the U.S. military was still segregated by race. Not until 1948 did President Truman issue Executive Order 9981 integrating the armed forces.

286 *Sir David intended to outplay his opponents:* Maxwell-Fyfe prepares to cross-examine Göring, Ophuls *Memory of Justice;* JXO 1543; Biddle 410.

286 *"Dozens of officers have escaped":* Background, the Sagan case, Conot 309; Cooper 203; Elwyn-Jones 102; Neave 262.

287 *"You cooperated in this foul series of murders":* Maxwell-Fyfe questions Göring on the Sagan escape, IMT vol. 9, 579, 594–95, 614.

288 *"These things were kept secret from me"*: Maxwell-Fyfe questions Göring on extermination of the Jews, Gaskins 94; IMT vol. 9, 611, 619.

289 *"the most formidable witness I ever examined"*: Gilbert discusses the cross-examination with Göring, Gilbert *Diary* 208.

289 *"He may be slow in answering questions"*: Hess defense approaches; Hess's background, Conot 347; Manvell 17, 20, 27–28, 39; Posner 42; *Foreign Affairs* vol. 20, 1941.

291 *"Rudolf rarely smiled"*: Hess as third-ranking Nazi, Manvell 22, 37, 46–49, 52, 63; Posner 45; Kelley 21; Davidson 111. A typical example of the kind of errand Hess could perform through his connections on behalf of the socially insecure Hitler: the Nazis had purchased the Brown House in Munich as party headquarters and were having trouble paying for it. Hess went to see the powerful banker Fritz Thyssen about a loan. The Nazis kept the house; but the loan was never repaid.

292 *a remarkable instance of passive resistance:* Hess does not testify, Tusa 295, 299.

293 *"I want to see them hang"*: Gilbert's true feelings toward the defendants; his competition with Kelley, GGP Gilbert letters to Kelley March 13, April 5, April 13, 1946.

294 *a fairy tale besmirched:* Göring's fall and rise; marriage to Carin; addiction, Irving 39–40, 42, 46, 54–55, 63–64.

295 *"I am not insane"*: Göring is committed; recovers; elected to Reichstag, Irving 86–89, 90–95.

295 *He lived like an Aryan pasha:* Göring remarries, becomes addicted again, Irving 102, 104, 136–37; RG 238 Göring dossier; Mosley 213–14, 257.

297 *a shack in Sackdilling forest:* Emmy Göring's postwar odyssey; visit by Gilbert, interview W. Jackson; W. Jackson letter to author December 30, 1991; Posner 197; Davidson 101.

297 *"He is a fanatic on the subject of loyalty"*: Gilbert discusses with Emmy the Göring-Hitler relationship, Gilbert *Diary* 212–13.

298 *"It's not a woman's affair"*: Göring will not renounce Hitler, Gilbert *Diary* 213–14.

299 *"He's a Nazi killer"*: Göring's clash with a guard, Fritzsche 45; BAP statement of PFC Vincent Traina March 26, 1946.

299 *He needed not antagonists but friends:* Göring's gifts to Wheelis, Swearingen 146.

300 *"Ribbentrop advised in favor of war"*: Ribbentrop prepares for his defense, J. Flanner *The New Yorker* March 9, 1946; Gilbert *Diary* 195; Andrus 165; Davidson 87.

301 *Amen would be handling the cross-examination:* Jackson will not question Ribbentrop, interview D. Sprecher.

301 *intending to make it his home:* Ribbentrop in Canada, Bullock 5, 7, 9; Conot 51.

302 *"We were actually afraid of Ribbentrop":* Ribbentrop takes the stand, Poltorak 51; H. Smith broadcast November 24, 1945; IMT vol. 10, 347, 367, 386–87.

304 *"You were not even interesting":* French and Russian cross-examination of Ribbentrop, IMT vol. 10, 409, 426–28.

304 *he should make out his will:* Frau von Ribbentrop speaks with William Jackson, interview W. Jackson.

305 *"I get the slops they don't want":* Prison routine and Andrus's dissatisfaction with his personnel, interview W. Glenny; BAP Andrus draft manuscript 87. Andrus was in fact considerably short-handed. His table of organization called for 142 officers and men. At any given point, he averaged about 117, almost eighteen percent below strength.

306 *"a sergeant's mind":* Background Keitel; he rejects confession, Hyde 215; Kelley 123; Conot 259; Tusa 259.

307 *"I bear the responsibility":* Keitel admits blame on direct examination, IMT vol. 10, 470–71, 565, 628; Conot 310–11.

308 *"even against women and children":* Rudenko cross-examines Keitel on the Reprisal Order; Maxwell-Fyfe on the Commando Order, IMT vol. 10, 617, 623–25. During his testimony, Keitel gave an interesting inside observation on Hitler's leadership style: "[Hitler] made his accusations, objections and criticisms as a rule at people who were not present. I took the part of the absent person as a matter of principle because he could not defend himself. The result was that the accusations and criticisms were then aimed at me."

309 *"too young to be so wise":* Jackson losing staff; Taylor to succeed him in subsequent trials, JXO 1493; interviews E. Hardy, T. Taylor.

310 *"More alone than survivors":* Katherine Biddle writes on Nuremberg, BIDP box 19. General Joseph T. McNarney, commander of U.S. Forces European Theater, lifted the ban on civilian and military spouses coming into the U.S. occupation zone in mid-March 1946. The first spouses departed the United States on April 16.

312 *he might as well go home:* Jackson again threatens to leave, Neave 260; B. Smith 109; Conot 363.

313 *"this statement of yours is not very credible":* Defense lawyer Kauffmann questions Kaltenbrunner on concentration camps and atrocities, IMT vol. 11, 232, 243, 248–49, 324, 330–31, 532; Gilbert *Diary* 407. The prosecution, on cross-examination, introduced an affidavit made by two surviving Mauthausen inmates, "corpse carriers" who carried to the crematorium the bodies of fifteen people killed before Kaltenbrunner to demonstrate various extermination techniques.

316 *"The Führer has ordered the Final Solution"*: Interrogation and background of Hoess, interview W. Harris; Gilbert *Psychology* 241.

318 *"To their death without premonition"*: Hoess relates the history of Auschwitz on cross-examination, IMT vol. 10, 648, vol. 11, 398, 401, 404, 416–17. In his affidavit to Whitney Harris, Hoess described the effect of the gas used: "It was Zyklon [Cyclone] B, crystalline prussic acid which volatilized immediately upon contact with oxygen. The people became stunned with the first breath of it, and the killing took three to 15 minutes according to the weather and the number of those locked in."

319 *"I never gave much thought to whether it was wrong"*: Gilbert visits Hoess, draws final conclusions on mass murderers, Gilbert *Diary* 258–59; GGP Gilbert speech notes (undated).

321 *He had enjoyed his birthday party:* Andrus meets the press socially at the Faber-Castell castle, BAP logbook entry April 15, 1946; Conot 20; B. Smith 299.

323 *"A thousand years will pass"*: Frank's defense, Gilbert *Diary* 265, 280; IMT vol. 12, 2, 13, 19, 156; Fritzsche 199; Polevoi 301.

324 *"a high-grade lynching"*: Jackson witnesses a Prague trial; is criticized by Supreme Court colleagues, Tusa 481; Gerhart 257, 259, 399–402, 436; Neave 246.

325 *and hope for Harry Truman's nod:* Death of Supreme Court Chief Justice Stone; Jackson's prospects to succeed him, IMT vol. 12, 97; Gerhart 258, 403; interview W. Jackson.

327 *He had enjoyed himself enormously:* Gisevius testimony damages Keitel and Göring, IMT vol. 12, 156, 169–70, 269; Kalnoky 178.

327 *a "disgusting blackmail plot"*: Possibility of Hitler's Jewish ancestry, Rosenbaum 450–89; Davidson 429.

329 *who bore responsibility:* Tracing the Final Solution, Conot 259, 261; Davidson 75; B. Smith 176; IMT vol. 11, 50–51, 398; Film, *Hitler's Final Solution: The Wannsee Conference*; Maser 231; Wolfe *Annals of the American Academy of Political Science* July 1980; Swearingen 48. According to Ohlendorf, orders to the *Einsatzgruppen* to execute Jews reportedly went orally from Hitler to Himmler to Heydrich. Upon receiving this order, Bruno Stechenbach, then personnel chief of the RSHA, issued it in writing to *Einsatzgruppen* leaders in June of 1941, shortly before the attack on the Soviet Union.

332 *"Wondrous are the ways of love"*: Frau Streicher testifies in her husband's defense, Tusa 333; Davidson 45, 101; IMT vol. 12, 305, 307, 348, 388.

332 *"If we can't convict Hjalmar Schacht"*: Jackson's eagerness to convict the financier, interview T. Taylor.

333 *"do you know why I am here"*: Schacht background and defense testimony, interview N. Doman; Kelley 187; Posner 95, 100; IMT vol. 12, 417, 578, 584–85; H. Smith broadcast December 1, 1945. Schacht's imperturbable confidence is demonstrated by the fact that during his defense, he asked Speer to start designing a house for him to be built after the trial.

335 *"I'll have to make you the minister of economy"*: Funk background and rise, IMT vol. 13, 78, vol. 5, 160; Conot 402; Davidson 247–51.

336 *"Nobody . . . ever deposited his gold teeth in a bank"*: Funk on the stand, IMT vol. 13, 166, 169, 170–71; Conot 403; Davidson 250.

336 *"Why do you think I'm sitting here"*: Dönitz as Hitler's surrogate, Gilbert *Diary* 176, 299, 325.

337 *the most dangerous piece of paper*: Kranzbuehler seeks to defend the *Laconia* Order; prohibition of tu quoque, Davidson 403–405; B. Smith 249–50; IMT vol. 8, 625.

339 *the man whom Adolf Hitler had found most worthy*: Maxwell-Fyfe cross-examination hits Dönitz on anti-Semitism, concentration camps, and the Hitler succession, IMT vol. 13, 342, 392.

339 *questions provided by Kranzbuehler*: Nimitz affidavit aids Dönitz, IMT vol. 17, 377–80. Had Dönitz not been a rabid anti-Semite, not requested concentration camp labor for shipyards, and not passed along the Commando Order, it is unlikely he would have come to trial for his naval activities alone. A U.S. Navy captain, John P. Bracken, who advised on naval matters had made a report to Jackson on August 24, 1945, saying, in part: "Unless additional information implicating Doenitz in political as distinguished from military acts has been uncovered . . . it is believed there is insufficient evidence to convict him or to warrant his being tried."

341 *Both men died:* A potentially racially related double murder, interview R. Korb Williams; BAP logbook entries May 10, 13, 1946; BIDP box 19 Biddle letter to his wife, Katherine, May 17, 1946; *New York Times* May 12, 13, 14, 1946.

342 *The most curious document:* Introduction of Raeder's Moscow Statement damages Dönitz, Göring, and Keitel, Gilbert *Diary* 342, 346; Davidson 368–69.

344 *"murders a millionfold"*: Schirach takes the stand, IMT vol. 14, 361; Gilbert *Diary* 348–50. Schirach was fortunate that the prosecution failed to present evidence that he, along with Speer, had attended the 1943 meeting in Posen where Himmler spoke and left no doubt about what the Final Solution meant.

346 *"What was the relationship of your office to Speer's"*: Sauckel's defense; responsibility for slave labor, IMT vol. 14, 618, 620, 622, 626, vol. 15, 3, 6, 9, 55, 233.

347 *"The things that made me hate Hitler"*: Jodl almost escaped prosecution; his disillusionment with Hitler, Neave 314; Conot 27; Gilbert *Diary* 361.

348 *"an honorable soldier"*: Roberts's cross-examination hits Jodl on Geneva Convention, the Reprisal Order, terrorism against England, and loyalty to Hitler, IMT vol. 15, 506, 508–11; Davidson 350. While he was generally loyal, Jodl's occasional outspokenness toward Hitler could be breathtaking. After the Twentieth of July plot, Jodl spoke of a general he admired, named Bonin, who had been arrested by Hitler in 1934 on flimsy evidence. "You cannot be surprised, my Führer," Jodl said, "if you throw a man like Bonin into jail without any proof being found, and apparently only on the basis of rumor, that the spirit of July 20 dominates the General Staff."

349 *Truman named Fred Vinson:* Jackson misses out on chief judgeship, Conot 442; Biddle 411.

350 *"my rope is being woven from Dutch hemp"*: Seyss-Inquart analyzes the Germans; takes the stand, Gilbert *Diary* 286–87; Conot 446.

351 *Speer was going to be questioned by a subordinate:* Speer prefers Jackson to cross-examine, JXO 1448–49; Speer *Inside* 651.

352 *"I was grateful to Sauckel for every worker"*: Speer's lawyer tackles Speer-Sauckel controversy, IMT vol. 16, 429, 447, 456, 479.

353 *"We have no right at this stage of the war to carry out destruction"*: Speer describes actions to thwart Hitler's scorched-earth policy, IMT vol. 16, 489–90, 496, 499. Speer described the false reasons that the staff had to use to persuade Hitler to do what was right. As he testified: "I made him decide between the two situations: Firstly, if these industrial areas were lost, my armament potential would sink if they were not recaptured; and secondly, if they were recaptured, they would be of value to us only if we had not destroyed them."

354 *He asked Stahl to procure a poison gas:* Speer's plan to assassinate Hitler, IMT vol. 16, 494–95, 504.

355 *Jackson took his place at the prosecutor's stand:* Cross-examination of Speer, IMT vol. 16, 482, 514–15, 527, 563.

357 *"a tremendous indictment"*: Speer wins public acclaim, London *Daily Telegraph* June 20, 1946.

358 *Fritzsche left the stand:* Neurath and Fritzsche, the last defense cases, Conot 450; Davidson 168, 171, 175; Tusa 403–406.

359 *forensic experts battled in room 600:* Responsibility for Katyn massacre, IMT vol. 17, 337, 350; Biddle 416.

360 *ample time for the defense to sum up:* The court gives unlimited time for defense summations, interview D. Sprecher; JXO 1574; IMT vol. 17, 500.

360 *Bormann was a wanted man:* Göring "reveals" Bormann's whereabouts; Bormann tried in absentia, interviews T. Fenstermacher, T. Lambert; IMT vol. 2, 26, vol. 5, 304, vol. 19, 111; Neave 239; Taylor 465.

363 *"It's the guy I have to work for":* Wheelis's dislike of Andrus, interview J. Vonetes.

364 *he pronounced it proven beyond a doubt:* Jackson begins his summation; the conspiracy charge; the guilt of Schacht, IMT vol. 19, 392, 398, 400, 407, 415–17, 419, 428–29.

365 *"But dead they are":* Jackson ends his summation, IMT vol. 19, 432.

367 *for the death of them all:* Summations of other nations' prosecutors, Tusa 421, 423–24; Davidson 357; Neave 300; IMT vol. 19, 433, vol. 20, 1–14. Rudenko closed saying, "I appeal to the Tribunal to sentence all the defendants without exception to the supreme penalty, death. Such a verdict will be greeted with satisfaction by all progressive mankind."

367 *He was going to deny Emmy Göring's request:* Andrus initially opposes visits, Andrus 161; Mosley 347; BAP logbook entry August 3, 1946.

368 *take a few select journalists through:* Andrus escorts reporters through cellblock C, interview A. Logan.

369 *Biddle heard the organization cases:* Defense of the organizations begins; Biddle is skeptical, Neave 151. North of Nuremberg was Stalag D-13, a POW camp containing some 20,000 SS veterans, many of whom had submitted requests to be heard in defense of the organizations. Jackson dispatched Drexel Sprecher and three others to talk to these men. The POWs maintained, Sprecher reported back, that the SS was highly compartmentalized; most men were not assigned to concentration camps and they denied knowledge of the camp's operations. They had been, the POWs claimed, almost all infantrymen and artillerymen fighting with purely military units.

369 *Sievers implicated Göring:* Göring returns to testify in the organization case; Maxwell-Fyfe cross-examines, IMT vol. 21, 302–17; 524–25; 547.

372 *this mad idea of conspiracy:* The judges debate the conspiracy count, Biddle 465; BIDP box 1 Biddle letter to Wechsler July 10, 1946, box 14 minutes of judges' meeting August 14, 1946, box 19 memorandum Rowe to Biddle July 11, 1946; Neave 123–24, 128, 133; interview H. Wechsler.

374 *"see the humorous side of all this":* Hess, Speer, et al. prepare their final statements, Manvell 172.

375 *"I do not believe that this will be my sentence":* Jodl writes to his wife, Maser 237–38.

375 *they gathered like bees around the queen:* Rebecca West and Biddle, Taylor 548; Glendinning 193; Biddle 425; R. West, *The New Yorker* September 7, October 26, 1946.

376 *"conquered by tremendous enemy superiority":* The defendants make final statements, IMT vol. 22, 365–410. Lawrence's scrupulous impartiality was again demonstrated when, in connection with threats the defense counsels had received, he announced:

> The Tribunal have been informed that the defendants' counsel have been receiving letters from Germans improperly criticizing their conduct as counsel in these proceedings. The Tribunal will protect counsel insofar as it is necessary so long as the Tribunal is in session, and it has no doubt that the Control Council will protect them thereafter against such attacks. In the opinion of the Tribunal, Defense Counsel have performed an important public duty in accordance with the high tradition of the legal profession, and the Tribunal thanks them for their assistance.

Chapter IV: Judgment Day

383 *still haunted by the fragility of this instrument:* The judges begin deliberating verdicts; confront the ex post facto criticism; ROWP box 44 Rowe memorandum to Biddle July 11, 1946; Taylor 10. Though forty-three death sentences were handed down against SS troops judged guilty of the murders of eighty-one American POWs near Malmédy, none was ever carried out. As a result of subsequent reviews and the desire to win German support during the Cold War, American officials substantially reduced most Malmédy sentences.

385 *they began to vote on the verdicts:* Göring, Hess, and Ribbentrop cases decided, B. Smith 177, 182, 184; Neave 316; IMT vol. 1, 282, vol. 5, 14–15, vol. 22, 532–33; ROWP box 44 Rowe notes on Hess deliberation (undated).

386 *safe to allow the defendants family visits:* Andrus approves, BIDP box 14 Andrus request to the tribunal September 2, 1946; Posner 12, 198; Conot 481; Andrus 182; Gerecke *Saturday Evening Post* September 1, 1951.

388 *he had struck a Faustian bargain:* Verdicts on Keitel, Kaltenbrunner, Frank, and Rosenberg, IMT vol. 1, 292; B. Smith 189, 193, 196. Donnedieu de Vabres was inclined to grant condemned military defendants death by the firing squad. Biddle was initially receptive. Nikitchenko argued vociferously for the rope, the position that, in the end, prevailed.

389   *Glenny watched the easy camaraderie:* The Göring-Wheelis relationship, Swearingen 146; interview W. Glenny.

389   *"a little Jew-baiter":* Verdicts on Streicher, Funk, and Schacht, IMT vol. 5, 118; B. Smith 173, 200, 206, 279; Neave 176; BIDP box 14 Biddle notes on court's meeting September 6, 1946.

390   *The vote went quickly:* verdicts on Seyss-Inquart, Dönitz, Schirach, Raeder, B. Smith 213, 238, 247, 254, 261–63; Davidson 382, 422.

392   *the ISD was not slackening its efforts:* Andrus alerts his men to a possible jailbreak, Andrus 157.

392   *should one hang for lack of breeding:* Verdicts on Frick, Jodl, Sauckel, Speer, Neurath, Papen, et al., B. Smith 207, 209, 211, 219, 222, 294–95; Neave 134, 199, 312.

393   *Biddle could not sleep:* Biddle ponders verdicts on Frank, Speer, and Rosenberg, B. Smith 222.

395   *Bullet-proof cars arrived at the courthouse:* Judgment day, Conot 492; Tusa 11; Poltorak 459.

396   *a pointless exercise:* Verdicts on the organizations, IMT vol. 22, 505–23. The entire Nazi party leadership was not found guilty. The cutoff point was *Ortsgruppenleiter. Amtsleiter* and below were exempt.

396   *"You men have a duty to yourselves":* Andrus addresses the defendants before judgment, Andrus 175.

397   *"second only to Adolf Hitler":* Individual verdicts handed down, IMT vol. 22, 526–80. In convicting Streicher of count four, crimes against humanity, the tribunal made a daring leap to connect words to acts. The judgment on him read: "In his speeches and articles, week after week, month after month, he infected the German mind with the virus of anti-Semitism and incited the German people to active persecution."

The tribunal was curiously dismissive of some of the most odious evidence against Speer. Acknowledging that Speer had used slave labor "in the industries under his control," the IMT concluded that he "attempted to use as few concentration camp workers as possible." The "few" numbered 30,000, thousands of whom were worked and starved to death. While the use of POWs in armaments production violated the Geneva Convention, Speer did employ Soviet prisoners, defending his actions with a technical argument—the Soviet Union was not a signatory to the Convention.

401   *He was furious at Schacht's acquittal:* Jackson insinuates that Biddle undermined the prosecution, JXO 1619. While not mentioning Biddle specifically, Jackson issued a public statement saying, "Our arguments for their conviction [Schacht and Papen] which seemed so convincing to all of us prosecutors seems not to have made a similar impression on the Tribunal."

402 *The more personal guilt, the less collective guilt:* Germans object to acquittals, B. Smith 300; Davidson 177; Cooper 271.

403 *"death by hanging":* Sentences handed down, Neave 311; Biddle 443, 476; IMT vol. 22, 588–90; Polevoi 315–16; Fritzsche 325; Speer *Spandau* 3. In his dissenting opinion, Nikitchenko also opposed the acquittals of Papen, Fritzsche, and particularly Schacht.

405 *Uncertainty compounded the anxiety:* An unclear execution date, BDC Board of Investigation Report 3. Some sources say that the executions were to be carried out fifteen days after sentencing. However, the Board of Investigation noted that "the charter which was furnished the accused prisoners provided that should execution be the sentence of the court, it will be carried into effect after the elapse of 15 days after the sentence was announced, *excluding Sundays.*" By this definition the executions could not have taken place before October 18, instead of October 16, when, in fact, they occurred.

405 *"treated like a common criminal":* Luise Jodl's appeals for clemency, Cooper 249; Maser 249.

405 *Higgins filed the story:* Cell transfers, *New York Herald Tribune* October 3, 1946.

406 *"so easy to convict military men":* Eisenhower on the verdicts, *New York Herald Tribune* October 3, 1946.

407 *"the most important, enduring work of my life":* Jackson reflects on the trial, Harris, introduction.

408 *"They will not hang me":* Stahmer given Göring's briefcase; Emmy visits Göring, BAP Andrus order on the prisoners' property November 23, 1945; BDC Report of Board of Proceedings October 1946; Mosley 352; Swearingen 25–26, 183.

408 *"They're all cowards":* Gilbert speaks out, *New York Times* October 3, 1946; BAP Andrus memorandum to General Rickard October 12, 1946.

409 *their last hope for clemency:* Appeals to the Allied Control Council, B. Smith 299; Conot 500–501; Maser 248–49; BIDP box 14 Biddle notes October 4, 1946.

410 *"I had reckoned with the death sentence":* Frank, Hess correspondence with spouses, Posner 37; Rosenbaum 460; Manvell 173, 176, 247.

411 *"the right thing":* Keitel's memoirs; his role in Rommel's death, BDC Report of Board of Proceedings October 1946; Maser 15–16, 53, 245; RG 238 Keitel interrogation September 28, 1945; Davidson 572. The repeated refrain of Keitel and the other military men was that they had no choice but to obey Hitler. Germany's Military Law Book, however, seems to allow for disobeying orders known to be unlawful. It reads:

1) If carrying out an order in the course of duty should violate a law, only the superior who gives the order is responsible. However, the subordinate who obeys it is punishable as a participant a) if he goes beyond the given order; or b) when he knows that the superior's order would have the purpose of leading to a military or other crime."

411 *Andrus delivered the news:* Clemency rejected; Göring defiant, Neave 299–300; Conot 503; BDC File 6a; BAP Lieutenant Colonel William Dunn report to Andrus August 28, 1946.

413 *Gilbert left cellblock C:* Gilbert's last visits; no firing squad for Göring, Maser 249; Swearingen 88; BDC Report of Board of Proceedings October 1946.

413 *a glass vial of cyanide:* Göring preparations for suicide; baggage room controls, interview W. Glenny; Swearingen 95, 211, 233; BDC Report of Board of Proceedings October 1946.

414 *His crew was now waiting:* Andrus meets the hangman; background Woods, *Buffalo* (New York) *Courier Express* October 19, 1946; Williams 66–70; BAP Andrus letter to G. Aitken March 15, 1968; BDC Report of Board of Proceedings October 1946; Andrus 187, 193, 198; interview R. Keeler.

414 *Word passed quickly:* The last cell inspection, BDC Report of Board of Proceedings statement of First Lieutenant West, statement of Lieutenant Roska October 16, 1946; Swearingen 249.

415 *Woods ran his hands over the ropes:* Preparation of the gallows, BAP Andrus draft ms. 71; Andrus 187, 193; Williams 64; Speer *Spandau* 9; Tusa 482; Kingsbury Smith, "The Execution of Nazi War Criminals, 16 October 1946"; *It Happened in 1946–1947*, edited by Clark Kinnard and Kingsbury Smith 641–48.

416 *The day began like any other:* The last day, *New York Times* October 16, 1946; Andrus 184, 187; Swearingen 253, 269; BDC Report of the Board of Proceedings October 1946; Bullock 200; Gilbert *Diary* 112.

417 *Father O'Connor visited the cells:* The priest offers to hear confessions; Dr. Pfluecker visits Göring, *New York Times* October 16, 1946; J. Powers *New York Sunday News* April 20, 1947.

418 *"This night might prove to be very short":* Dr. Pfluecker tips off Göring, Maser 250; Swearingen 153.

419 *He placed the four letters in an envelope:* Göring's suicide notes, Swearingen 220; BDC collection of last letters of the defendants. While some works on the trial refer to three Göring suicide notes, the Berlin Documents Center has four, all of which the author was permitted to see.

420 *He must not let Göring slip into a stupor:* Dr. Pfluecker arranges phony sleeping pills for Göring, Maser 250; BDC Report of Board of Proceedings October 1946 Exhibit AC.

420 *The reporters piled into buses:* The press prepares to cover the executions, Tusa 482; *New York Times* October 16, 1946; *Washington Post* October 15, 1946.

421 *eleven bare lights over eleven cell doors:* The press pool visits the jail; Göring adds to a letter, Taylor 608; Poltorak 467–69; Polevoi 317–21. The Göring letter to the Allied Control Council has a Roman I at the top. A loose page among the four suicide letters has a Roman II at the top. This latter page, in which Göring protests, "I consider it in extremely bad taste to present our death as a spectacle to the sensationalist press," strongly suggests that he added it to the letter to the ACC in response to Andrus's taking the press pool through the cellblock shortly before the executions.

422 *Lights out:* Activities outside the prison, Andrus 193; BDC Report of Board of Proceedings October 1946; interview R. Keeler.

422 *"there's something wrong with Göring":* Göring's suicide, J. Powers, *New York Sunday News* April 20, 1947; Swearingen 269, 283; Andrus 193; BDC Report of Board of Proceedings October 1946 statements of G. Tymchyshyn, H. Gerecke, H. Johnson, J. Carver, L. Pfluecker, C. Roska, R. Starnes. Pfluecker's behavior upon being called to Göring's cell strongly supports the conclusion that he knew Göring's intentions. Upon entering the cell, he said that Göring was dying and nothing could be done, because "I didn't have any experience with dying from poisoning." At this point no one had yet mentioned poisoning, though Pfluecker may have smelled cyanide, or he may have recognized poison symptoms, which contradict his claim of ignorance. In any case, he made no effort to revive Göring, though, at the time of Ley's suicide, he made vigorous efforts to revive that prisoner, including injections of Cardiozol and Lubulin, and he attempted artificial respiration.

423 *people parted to let Andrus through:* Andrus is notified of Göring's suicide; the Quadripartite Commission arrives, *Time* October 28, 1946; Andrus 191; Swearingen 79, 95; Gerecke *Saturday Evening Post* September 1, 1951.

424 *appoint a board:* The Quadripartite Commission examines alternatives; appoints a board, Andrus 192; Swearingen 93; interview K. Andrus Williams, BDC Report of Board of Proceedings Appointment of Board of Investigation October 15, 1946.

425 *The executions would proceed:* Andrus informs the prisoners; orders the last meal; tells the press pool of Göring's suicide, Tusa 484; *Life* October 28, 1946; Maser 250; Gerecke *Saturday Evening Post* September 1, 1951.

425 *Ribbentrop was led to the gallows:* The executions begin, *New York Herald Tribune* October 16, 1946; Andrus 194–96; BAP Andrus draft ms. 74; *It Happened in 1946–1947* Kinnard and Smith 641–48; *New York Times* October 16,

1946; *Life* October 28, 1946; Maser 252–53; Speer *Spandau* 9. Bureaucratic squabbles carried over even into the executions. Jackson had refused as unseemly a request by the Quadripartite Commission to be allowed to sit among the officers of the court on judgment day; he relegated the members to the visitors' gallery. When Whitney Harris arrived at the courthouse to witness the executions as Jackson's representative, he was refused entry by the Quadripartite Commission.

428 *"Göring was not hanged":* Andrus faces the full press corps, Swearingen 82–84; Tusa 484; Andrus 192; Interview K. Andrus Williams.

430 *raised his arm in the Nazi salute:* Speer and others clean the death house, Speer *Spandau* 10–11. The cremation and disposition of the condemned men's ashes were not fully revealed until the United Press broke the story on March 20, 1947. Even then, the editors included felt obliged to include an explanation:

> UP carries the following story, not to afford future German nationalists locations for shrines to late leading Nazis, but because the facts are increasingly generally known in Munich and it is understood that photographs of the disposal of the Nazi ashes are being offered for sale in the U.S. Thus the once-quadripartite secret is a secret no longer.

430 *The wrong headline:* Public reaction to the Göring suicide, *Time* October 28, 1946; Swearingen 123–24.

431 *The members accepted Göring's claim:* The public and secret reports of the Quadripartite Commission's investigation, BDC Report of Board of Proceedings "Findings" October 26, 1946, Report of Investigating Board to the Quadripartite Commission October 24, 1946 1–7, statement of J. West; Andrus 184; Swearingen 95, 107, 109, 214–15, 241. While Colonel Andrus fell under the blanket exoneration of the Quadripartite Commission (that "no individual or individuals be held responsible for the death by suicide of Hermann Goering"), he received personal vindication three months later. The War Department issued a statement saying:

> In response to queries from the press concerning the return to the United States of Colonel B. C. Andrus, formerly Commandant of the Nuremberg jail, the War Department stated today that Colonel Andrus's relief from duty at Nuremberg was in no way connected with the suicide of Hermann Goering. Colonel Andrus has had 31 months of overseas service and was eligible for return to the United States under the provisions of War Department policy for the rotation of personnel.

Epilogue

437 *The validity of the court is still debated:* The controversy, Gerhart 506; *Fortune* December 1945; *New York Times* October 6, 1946.

442   *the world experienced twenty-four wars:* Conflict and aggression continue, *World Military and Social Expenditures 1991* 22–25; World Priorities, Washington D.C., 1991; Conot 521; Maser 266; Tusa 488.

443   *never applied to any nation:* War crimes inaction through 1992, Taylor 637, 640.

INDEX

FOR THE BEST IN PAPERBACKS, LOOK FOR THE

In every corner of the world, on every subject under the sun, Penguin represents quality and variety—the very best in publishing today.

For complete information about books available from Penguin—including Puffins, Penguin Classics, and Arkana—and how to order them, write to us at the appropriate address below. Please note that for copyright reasons the selection of books varies from country to country.

In the United Kingdom: Please write to *Dept. JC, Penguin Books Ltd, FREEPOST, West Drayton, Middlesex UB7 0BR.*

If you have any difficulty in obtaining a title, please send your order with the correct money, plus ten percent for postage and packaging, to *P.O. Box No. 11, West Drayton, Middlesex UB7 0BR*

In the United States: Please write to *Consumer Sales, Penguin USA, P.O. Box 999, Dept. 17109, Bergenfield, New Jersey 07621-0120.* VISA and MasterCard holders call 1-800-253-6476 to order all Penguin titles

In Canada: Please write to *Penguin Books Canada Ltd, 10 Alcorn Avenue, Suite 300, Toronto, Ontario M4V 3B2*

In Australia: Please write to *Penguin Books Australia Ltd, P.O. Box 257, Ringwood, Victoria 3134*

In New Zealand: Please write to *Penguin Books (NZ) Ltd, Private Bag 102902, North Shore Mail Centre, Auckland 10*

In India: Please write to *Penguin Books India Pvt Ltd, 706 Eros Apartments, 56 Nehru Place, New Delhi 110 019*

In the Netherlands: Please write to *Penguin Books Netherlands bv, Postbus 3507, NL-1001 AH Amsterdam*

In Germany: Please write to *Penguin Books Deutschland GmbH, Metzlerstrasse 26, 60594 Frankfurt am Main*

In Spain: Please write to *Penguin Books S. A., Bravo Murillo 19, 1° B, 28015 Madrid*

In Italy: Please write to *Penguin Italia s.r.l., Via Felice Casati 20, I-20124 Milano*

In France: Please write to *Penguin France S. A., 17 rue Lejeune, F–31000 Toulouse*

In Japan: Please write to *Penguin Books Japan, Ishikiribashi Building, 2–5–4, Suido, Bunkyo-ku, Tokyo 112*

In Greece: Please write to *Penguin Hellas Ltd, Dimocritou 3, GR–106 71 Athens*

In South Africa: Please write to *Longman Penguin Southern Africa (Pty) Ltd, Private Bag X08, Bertsham 2013*